Biographical Dictionary
of American Educators

Biographical Dictionary of American Educators

edited by JOHN F. OHLES

Volume 1

GREENWOOD PRESS

WESTPORT, CONNECTICUT
LONDON, ENGLAND

Library of Congress Cataloging in Publication Data

Main entry under title:

Biographical dictionary of American educators.

Includes index.
1. Educators—United States—Biography. I.   Ohles, John F.
LA2311.B54   370'.973 [B]   77-84750
ISBN 0-8371-9893-3

Library of Congress Catalog Card Number: 77-84750
ISBN: 0-8371-9893-3 (set)
     0-8371-9894-1 (vol. 1)

First published in 1978

Greenwood Press, Inc.
51 Riverside Avenue, Westport, Connecticut 06880

Printed in the United States of America

10 9 8 7 6 5 4 3 2

To
Frederik, Janet, Margaret and Judith

_____CONTENTS _____

_____CONTRIBUTORS_____

Dr. Charles M. Achilles, Professor of Educational Administration
  University of Tennessee
  Knoxville, Tennessee
Dr. Ralph E. Ackerman, Chairperson
  Division of Behavioral Sciences
  Edinboro State College
  Edinboro, Pennsylvania
Joe Adams, Instructor
  University of Toledo
  Toledo, Ohio
Dr. Walter F. C. Ade, Emeritus Professor
  Department of Modern Languages and Education
  Purdue University, Calumet Campus
  Hammond, Indiana
Dr. C. Len Ainsworth, Associate Vice-President for Academic Affairs
  Texas Tech University
  Lubbock, Texas
Dr. Jerry L. Ainsworth, Chairman
  Health Department
  Southern Connecticut State College
  New Haven, Connecticut
Dr. Abdul A. Al-Rubaiy, Assistant Professor of Education
  University of Akron
  Akron, Ohio
Dr. Leo J. Alilunas, Professor of Education
  State University of New York College
  Fredonia, New York
Dr. J. Stewart Allen, Dean
  College of Humanities
  Sam Houston State University
  Huntsville, Texas
Dr. Clinton B. Allison, Associate Professor of Education
  University of Tennessee
  Knoxville, Tennessee
Dr. Vernon E. Anderson, Emeritus Professor
  University of Maryland
  College Park, Maryland

Dr. A. Rolando Andrade, Director
  Chicano Studies Program
  University of Oklahoma
  Norman, Oklahoma
Dr. Phyllis Appelbaum, Associate Professor of Education
  C. W. Post College
  Greenvale, Long Island, New York
Dr. Mary H. Appleberry, Associate Professor of Elementary Education
  Stephen F. Austin State University
  Nacogdoches, Texas
Dr. Jerry B. Ayers, Assistant Dean
  College of Education
  Tennessee Technological University
  Cookeville, Tennessee
Dr. Christine W. Ayoub, Professor
  Department of Mathematics
  Pennsylvania State University
  University Park, Pennsylvania
Peter J. Bachman, Instructor in Education
  Pennsylvania State University
  Delaware County Campus
  Media, Pennsylvania
R. Samuel Baker, Assistant Director
  Illinois Board of Regents
  Springfield, Illinois
Dr. Michael A. Balasa
  Department of Education
  Washington State University
  Pullman, Washington
Dr. K. J. Balthaser, Director
  Learning Resources Center
  Indiana University-Purdue University at Fort Wayne
  Fort Wayne, Indiana
Dr. Richard Bancroft, Associate Professor
  Department of Music
  Westminster College
  New Wilmington, Pennsylvania
Dr. Joseph E. Barbeau, Professor of Educational Administration
  Northeastern University
  Boston, Massachusetts
Gary D. Barber, Associate Librarian
  Reed Library
  State University of New York College
  Fredonia, New York

Dr. Gary C. Barlow, Coordinator of Art Education
  Wright State University
  Dayton, Ohio
Dr. Thomas A. Barlow, Associate Dean
  School of Education
  University of Colorado at Denver
  Denver, Colorado
Dr. LeRoy Barney, Professor of Education
  Northern Illinois University
  De Kalb, Illinois
Dr. Bonnie B. Barr, Associate Professor of Elementary Education
  Slippery Rock State College
  Slippery Rock, Pennsylvania
Dr. Saul Barron, Professor of Chemistry
  State University of New York College
  Buffalo, New York
Dr. J. W. Batten, Professor of Secondary Education
  East Carolina University
  Greenville, North Carolina
Professor Norman J. Bauer
  Division of Educational Studies
  State University of New York College
  Geneseo, New York
Dr. M. Dale Baughman, Professor of Education
  Indiana State University
  Terre Haute, Indiana
Dr. Ernest E. Bayles, Emeritus Professor of Education
  University of Kansas
  Lawrence, Kansas
Ted Beach, Graduate Student
  University of Tennessee
  Knoxville, Tennessee
Doree Dumas Bedwell, Graduate Assistant
  Indiana State University
  Terre Haute, Indiana
Dr. Claude A. Bell, Associate Professor of Industrial Technology
  Illinois State University
  Normal, Illinois
Dr. Ishmael C. Benton, Vice-President
  National River Academy
  Helena, Arkansas
Dr. Thomas L. Bernard, Director
  Division of Community Education
  Springfield College
  Springfield, Massachusetts

Dr. George R. Berrian
   Manhattan College
   Bronx, New York
Iris Hiller Berwitt, Teacher
   East Clark School
   Cleveland, Ohio
Dr. Leonidas Betts, Associate Professor
   Departments of English and Curriculum and Instruction
   North Carolina State University
   Raleigh, North Carolina
Dr. Jane M. Bingham, Associate Professor of Children's Literature
   Oakland University
   Rochester, Michigan
Dr. Robert W. Blake, Professor of English Education
   State University of New York College
   Brockport, New York
Teri Bland, Graduate Student
   University of South Florida
   Tampa, Florida
Dr. Abraham Blinderman, Professor of English
   State University of New York at Farmingdale
   Farmingdale, New York
Dr. Paul A. Bloland, Chairman
   Department of Counselor Education
   University of Southern California
   Los Angeles, California
Dr. Harry P. Bluhm, Associate Professor of Educational Psychology
   University of Utah
   Salt Lake City, Utah
Dr. Winifred Wandersee Bolin, Instructor
   St. Cloud State University
   St. Cloud, Minnesota
Dr. Daniel J. Booth, Director
   Daniel J. Booth Associates
   Boulder, Colorado
Dr. D. Richard Bowles, Associate Professor (retired)
   School of Education
   Southwest Texas State University
   San Marcos, Texas
Dr. Anita Bozardt, Assistant Professor
   School of Education
   Oakland University
   Rochester, Michigan

Professor Nicholas A. Branca
  Department of Mathematical Sciences
  San Diego State University
  San Diego, California
Dr. Barbara Braverman, Research Associate
  National Technical Institute for the Deaf
  Rochester, New York
Dr. Nancy Bredemeier, Associate Professor
  College of Education
  Kent State University
  Kent, Ohio
Dr. William W. Brickman, Professor of Educational History
  and Comparative Education
  University of Pennsylvania
  Philadelphia, Pennsylvania
Dr. S. S. Britt, Jr., Associate Director
  Division of Continuing Education
  Louisiana State University and Agricultural and Mechanical College
  Baton Rouge, Louisiana
Dr. Joseph C. Bronars, Jr., Assistant Professor of Elementary
  and Early Childhood Education
  Queens College of the City University of New York
  Flushing, New York
Dr. Leon W. Brownlee
  Memphis State University
  Memphis, Tennessee
Dr. Carey W. Brush, Vice-President for Academic Affairs
  State University of New York College
  Oneonta, New York
Dr. John P. Burgess, Associate Professor of Education
  West Virginia Wesleyan College
  Buckhannon, West Virginia
Dr. Kenneth L. Burrett, Assistant Professor
  Russell Sage College
  Troy, New York
Norman H. Calaway, Teaching Assistant
  College of Education
  University of Oklahoma
  Norman, Oklahoma
Dr. Stratton F. Caldwell, Professor
  Physical Education Department
  California State University
  Northridge, California
Dr. Jack K. Campbell, Associate Professor

Educational Curriculum and Instruction
Texas A&M University
College Station, Texas
Ann Candler, Research Assistant
College of Education
University of Houston
Houston, Texas
Dr. Joseph P. Cangemi, Associate Professor of Psychology
Western Kentucky University
Bowling Green, Kentucky
Dr. Ralph M. Carter, Assistant Professor
College of Education
Texas Tech University
Lubbock, Texas
Nicholas Celso III, Graduate Student
Rutgers University
New Brunswick, New Jersey
Jean Challman, Chief Librarian
Metropolitan Community College
Minneapolis, Minnesota
Dr. Fredrick Chambers, Associate Professor
College of Education
Kent State University
Kent, Ohio
Dr. Charles C. Chandler, Chairman
Department of Secondary Education
Kent State University
Kent, Ohio
Dr. Francine C. Childs, Assistant Professor
Center for Afro-American Studies
Ohio University
Athens, Ohio
Dr. Alfred J. Ciani, Assistant Professor of Education
University of Cincinnati
Cincinnati, Ohio
Michael R. Cioffi, Assistant Principal
Public School 91 Bronx
New York, New York
Dr. Stephen J. Clarke, Associate Professor
Department of Education
Salem State College
Salem, Massachusetts
Dr. Ronnie W. Clayton, Chairman
Division of Social Sciences

Meridian Junior College
Meridian, Mississippi
Linda Cogar, Graduate Student
University of South Florida
Tampa, Florida
Dr. Richard M. Coger, Assistant Director
Regional Medical Education Center
Veterans Administration Hospitals
St. Louis, Missouri
Jaclyn S. Cohen, Graduate Student
University of South Florida
Tampa, Florida
Dr. Ronald D. Cohen, Associate Professor
Department of History
Indiana University Northwest
Gary, Indiana
Dr. Adelaide M. Cole, Director of Graduate Studies and Research
School of Physical Education and Athletics
Ball State University
Muncie, Indiana
Dr. June M. Collins
Department of Anthropology
State University of New York College
Buffalo, New York
Anne M. Condon, Student
State University of New York College
Geneseo, New York
Dr. E. C. Condon, Director
Institute of Intercultural Relations and Ethical Studies
Rutgers University
New Brunswick, New Jersey
Robert E. Conner, Graduate Student
Delta State University
Cleveland, Mississippi
Dr. Phil Constans, Jr., Associate Professor of Educational Foundations
Western Kentucky University
Bowling Green, Kentucky
Dr. Fannie R. Cooley, Professor
Guidance and Counseling
Tuskegee Institute
Tuskegee Institute, Alabama
Dr. Francesco Cordasco, Professor of Education
Montclair State College
Upper Montclair, New Jersey

Dr. Rafael L. Cortada, President
  Metropolitan Community College
  Minneapolis, Minnesota
Richard J. Cox, Curator of Manuscripts
  Maryland Historical Society
  Baltimore, Maryland
Dr. Doris Cruger Dale, Associate Professor
  Department of Curriculum and Media
  Southern Illinois University
  Carbondale, Illinois
Dr. Walter C. Daniel, Vice-Chancellor
  University of Missouri-Columbia
  Columbia, Missouri
Dr. Harris L. Dante, Professor of History and Secondary Education
  Kent State University
  Kent, Ohio
Dr. Charles E. Davis, District Superintendent
  Board of Cooperative Educational Services
  Stamford, New York
Dr. Michael L. Davis
  Office of Academic Planning and Faculty Development
  University of the Pacific
  Stockton, California
Dr. George G. Dawson, Acting Dean
  Empire State College
  Old Westbury, New York
Dr. David Delahanty, Associate Professor
  Education Department
  Manhattan College
  Bronx, New York
Professor Daniel J. Delaney
  Psychiatry and Behavioral Sciences
  Eastern Virginia Medical School
  Norfolk, Virginia
Norman E. Delisle, Director of Public Relations
  Connecticut Education Association
  Hartford, Connecticut
Dr. Marie Della Bella, Assistant Professor
  Teacher Education
  Coe College
  Cedar Rapids, Iowa
Dr. Paul W. DeVore, Professor
  Technology Education
  West Virginia University

Morgantown, West Virginia
Donald O. Dewey, Dean
School of Letters and Science
California State University
Los Angeles, California
Dr. Thomas E. Dinero, Assistant Professor
College of Education
Kent State University
Kent, Ohio
Dr. M. Ann Dirkes, Assistant Professor of Education
Indiana University-Purdue University at Fort Wayne
Fort Wayne, Indiana
Dr. Ralph Dirksen, Assistant Professor of Industrial Education
Western Illinois University
Macomb, Illinois
Dr. Billy G. Dixon, Professor
Curriculum, Instruction and Media
Southern Illinois University
Carbondale, Illinois
Dr. Robert L. Doan, Associate Professor of Elementary Education
Indiana University-Purdue University at Fort Wayne
Fort Wayne, Indiana
Dr. Larry Donahue, Assistant Professor
Continuing Medical Education
University of Arkansas for Medical Sciences
Little Rock, Arkansas
M. Jane Dowd, Teacher
Manheim Township Middle School
Neffsville, Pennsylvania
Dr. Morgan D. Dowd, Dean
Graduate Studies and Research
State University of New York College
Fredonia, New York
Mary Doyle, Graduate Student
North Texas State University
Denton, Texas
Dr. Walter Doyle, Associate Professor
Department of Education
North Texas State University
Denton, Texas
Dr. Lionel S. Duncan, Director
Communications Media
Morgan State University
Baltimore, Maryland

Dr. John C. Durance, Associate Professor
   College of Education
   Kent State University
   Kent, Ohio
Dr. Edward J. Durnall, Director
   Division of Continuing Education
   University of New Hampshire
   Durham, New Hampshire
Dr. Richard G. Durnin, Associate Professor
   School of Education
   City College of the City University of New York
   New York, New York
Dr. Victor R. Durrance, Director of Student Teaching
   Texas Women's University
   Denton, Texas
Dr. Charles M. Dye, Assistant Professor
   College of Education
   University of Akron
   Akron, Ohio
Dr. J. Lee Dye, Professor of Business Education
   and Office Administration
   Ball State University
   Muncie, Indiana
Dr. Patricia L. Earls
   Miami Shores, Florida
Dr. Glen I. Earthman, Director of Field Services
   College of Education
   Virginia Polytechnic Institute and State University
   Blacksburg, Virginia
Dr. Dennis East II, Archivist
   Archives of Labor and Urban Affairs
   Walter P. Reuther Library
   Wayne State University
   Detroit, Michigan
Dr. Jean L. Easterly, Assistant Professor
   School of Education
   Oakland University
   Rochester, Michigan
Dr. William E. Eaton, Assistant Professor
   Educational Leadership
   Southern Illinois University
   Carbondale, Illinois
Dr. Alan H. Eder, Assistant Professor of Education

Northern Arizona University
Flagstaff, Arizona
Daniel D. Edgar, Graduate Assistant
University of Akron
Akron, Ohio
Dr. Judy Egelston-Dodd, Curriculum Development Specialist
National Institute for the Deaf
Rochester, New York
Dr. William G. Ellis, Vice-President
Thomas College
Waterville, Maine
Dr. Dana T. Elmore, Associate Professor of Education
San Jose State University
San Jose, California
Dr. Robert Emans, Associate Dean
School of Education
College of William and Mary
Williamsburg, Virginia
Joseph Engle, Director of Professional Development
Pima Community College
Tucson, Arizona
Dr. William Engelbrecht, Assistant Professor
Department of Anthropology
State University of New York College
Buffalo, New York
Dr. Gary C. Ensign, Staff Associate
Division of Continuing Education
University of New Hampshire
Durham, New Hampshire
Dr. Samuel A. Farmerie, Associate Professor
Westminster College
New Wilmington, Pennsylvania
Dr. Richard D. Featheringham, Professor of Business Education
Central Michigan University
Mount Pleasant, Michigan
Harvey Feldstein, Graduate Student
State University of New York College
Geneseo, New York
Dr. H. Thompson Fillmer, Professor of Education
University of Florida
Gainesville, Florida
Darlene E. Fisher
Evanston, Illinois

Evelyn Patricia Flowers, Graduate Student
  University of South Florida
  Tampa, Florida
John L. Flynn, Graduate Student
  University of South Florida
  Tampa, Florida
Dr. Patrick J. Foley, Associate Professor of Education
  Southeastern Massachusetts University
  North Dartmouth, Massachusetts
Dr. Richard J. Frankie, Professor of Higher Education
  George Washington University
  Washington, D.C.
Dr. Kenneth J. Frasure, Dean of Education
  University of Tennessee
  Nashville, Tennessee
Dr. Mark Fravel, Jr., Chairman
  Curriculum and Instruction
  Old Dominion University
  Norfolk, Virginia
Larry Froehlich, Director
  Vocational Curriculum Laboratory
  Cedar Lakes Conference
  Ripley, West Virginia
Ruth Ledbetter Galaz, Teaching Associate
  College of Education
  University of Oklahoma
  Norman, Oklahoma
Dr. Ricardo L. Garcia, Assistant Professor
  College of Education
  University of Oklahoma
  Norman, Oklahoma
Dr. David C. Gardner, Chairperson
  Department of Business and Career Education
  Boston University
  Boston, Massachusetts
Dr. Linda C. Gardner
  Hendersonville, North Carolina
Dr. Richard W. Gates, Dean
  School of Education
  Saint Bonaventure University
  Saint Bonaventure, New York
Dr. Anne R. Gayles, Chairperson
  Area of Secondary Education
  Florida A&M University

Tallahassee, Florida
Dr. T. S. Geraty, Chairman
   Department of Education
   Andrews University
   Berrien Springs, Michigan
Dr. Marvin Gerber, Professor of Secondary Education
   San Francisco State University
   San Francisco, California
Vincent Giardina, Graduate Student
   University of Miami
   Coral Gables, Florida
Dr. David Alan Gilman, Professor of Education
   Indiana State University
   Terre Haute, Indiana
Charlotte G. Glashagel, Teaching Assistant
   University of Akron
   Akron, Ohio
Dr. Ralph E. Glauert, Assistant Professor of Education
   University of Missouri-Columbia
   Columbia, Missouri
Dr. Edward B. Goellner, Assistant Professor of Education
   University of Southwestern Louisiana
   Lafayette, Louisiana
Professor Erwin H. Goldenstein, Coordinator
   Doctoral Studies in Education
   University of Nebraska-Lincoln
   Lincoln, Nebraska
Dr. Orin B. Graff, Distinguished Science Professor Emeritus
   University of Tennessee
   Knoxville, Tennessee
Dr. James M. Green, Assistant Professor of Education
   Marquette University
   Milwaukee, Wisconsin
Dr. Joe L. Green, Assistant Professor of Education
   University of Southwestern Louisiana
   Lafayette, Louisiana
Jordan Greer, Senior Engineering Instructor
   Litton Industries, Inc.
   Woodland Hills, California
Dr. Carl H. Gross, Chairman
   Department of Secondary Education and Curriculum
   Michigan State University
   East Lansing, Michigan
Karen L. Hadley, Student

Dickinson College
Carlisle, Pennsylvania
Dr. Nelson L. Haggerson, Professor of Education
Arizona State University
Tempe, Arizona
Dr. Alda A. Harper, Associate Professor of Education
Georgia College at Milledgeville
Milledgeville, Georgia
Dr. Betty S. Harper, Administrative Assistant
Office of the Graduate Dean
Middle Tennessee State University
Murfreesboro, Tennessee
Dr. Mary Harshbarger, Associate Professor
Reading Center
Ball State University
Muncie, Indiana
Dr. Richard L. Hart, Associate Dean
College of Education
Kent State University
Kent, Ohio
Dr. Robert Hassenger, Associate Dean
Empire State College
State University of New York
Buffalo, New York
Karen Ann Hayward
Southern Connecticut State College
New Haven, Connecticut
Steven H. Heath
Southern Utah State College
Cedar City, Utah
Dr. Robert A. Henderson, Professor of Special Education
University of Illinois
Urbana, Illinois
Dr. Robert D. Heslep, Professor of Philosophy and Education
University of Georgia
Athens, Georgia
Dr. Robert L. Hillerich, Associate Professor
Bowling Green State University
Bowling Green, Ohio
Barbara Hinderscheid
University News Service
Kent State University
Kent, Ohio

Professor N. Ray Hiner
  Department of History
  University of Kansas
  Lawrence, Kansas
Dr. Katharine W. Hodgin, Associate Professor
  Department of Mathematics
  East Carolina University
  Greenville, North Carolina
Dr. Robert H. Hoexter, Associate Professor of Curriculum and Instruction
  Eastern Michigan University
  Ypsilanti, Michigan
Dr. John C. Hogan
  Rand Corporation
  Santa Monica, California
Jill Holland, Graduate Student
  University of South Florida
  Tampa, Florida
Dr. Jerrold D. Hopfengardner, Supervision of Teacher Education
  Division of Teacher Education and Certification
  Ohio Department of Education
  Columbus, Ohio
Dr. Thomas R. Hopkins, Chief
  Division of Evaluation and Research
  U.S. Bureau of Indian Affairs
  Albuquerque, New Mexico
Dr. Robert House, Director
  Academic Planning
  San Francisco State University
  San Francisco, California
Gary Howieson, Student
  Kent State University
  Kent, Ohio
Dr. Maxine Huffman, Assistant Professor of Education
  Indiana University—Purdue University at Fort Wayne
  Fort Wayne, Indiana
Erika Hugo, Senior Editor
  Harper & Row, Publishers
  Evanston, Illinois
Dr. Jack W. Humphries, Vice-President for University Affairs
  Sam Houston State University
  Huntsville, Texas
Dr. J. Franklin Hunt, Chairman
  Department of Education

Hamilton College
Clinton, New York
Ronald Iannarone, Graduate Assistant
University of South Florida
Tampa, Florida
Dr. Freeman R. Irvine, Jr.
Florida A&M University
Tallahassee, Florida
Dr. Dan L. Isaacs, Director
Instructional Media Center
Florida State University
Tallahassee, Florida
Dr. John M. Ivanoff, Professor of Educational Psychology
Marquette University
Milwaukee, Wisconsin
Dr. Ellis Ivey II, Chairman
Education Department
West Virginia Wesleyan College
Buckhannon, West Virginia
Dr. J. Marc Jantzen, Professor and Dean Emeritus
School of Education
University of the Pacific
Stockton, California
John W. Jenkins, Program Assistant
Office of the Dean
College of Education
University of Wisconsin-Madison
Madison, Wisconsin
Dr. Glenn Jensen, Head
Department of Adult Education and Instructional Services
University of Wyoming
Laramie, Wyoming
Dr. E. V. Johanningmeier, Director
Foundations of Education
University of South Florida
Tampa, Florida
Dr. Jerry L. Johns
Reading Clinic
Northern Illinois University
De Kalb, Illinois
Gary C. Johnsen, Student
State University of New York College
Geneseo, New York

Dr. David L. Jolliff, Assistant Professor
  Indiana University-Purdue University at Fort Wayne
  Fort Wayne, Indiana
Dr. Donald Corwin Jones, Educational Consultant
  Gaston, Oregon
Dr. Franklin Ross Jones, Program Leader
  Historical Foundations
  School of Education
  Old Dominion University
  Norfolk, Virginia
Dr. Roger H. Jones, Associate Professor of Art
  Morehead State University
  Morehead, Kentucky
Nancy Baldrige Julian, Graduate Student
  New Mexico State University
  Las Cruces, New Mexico
Dr. T. J. Kallsen, Dean
  School of Liberal Arts
  Stephen F. Austin State University
  Nacogdoches, Texas
Professor David E. Kapel, Associate Dean of Instruction and Research
  University of Nebraska at Omaha
  Omaha, Nebraska
Jo Ann Kaufman, Assistant Librarian: Education
  Reed Library
  State University of New York College
  Fredonia, New York
Dr. Phyllis F. Kavett, Chairperson, Professor,
  Educational Arts and Systems
  Kean College of New Jersey
  Union, New Jersey
Dr. Peter W. Keelin, Assistant Professor of Guidance and Counseling
  School of Education
  Oakland University
  Rochester, Michigan
Dr. Hubert J. Keenan (deceased)
  3900 Bailey Avenue
  Bronx, New York
Dr. Earl E. Keese, Director
  Public Service
  Middle Tennessee State University
  Murfreesboro, Tennessee
Sister Karen Kennelly, Academic Dean

College of St. Catherine
St. Paul, Minnesota
Dr. Harry A. Kersey, Jr., Professor of Education
Florida Atlantic University
Boca Raton, Florida
Dr. Thomas E. Kesler, Computer Analyst and Social Statistician
Indiana University
Bloomington, Indiana
Dr. Reese Danley Kilgo, Associate Professor of Education and Sociology
University of Alabama in Huntsville
Huntsville, Alabama
Dr. Joan Duff Kise, Assistant Professor
College of Education
Kent State University
Kent, Ohio
Dr. Octavia B. Knight, Director of Special Education
North Carolina Central University
Durham, North Carolina
Dr. Sylvester Kohut, Jr., Coordinator of Teacher Education
Dickinson College
Carlisle, Pennsylvania
Dr. David E. Koontz, Associate Professor
Marshall University
Huntington, West Virginia
Dr. William Kornegay, Professor of Education
University of Massachusetts
Amherst, Massachusetts
Dr. Robert V. Krejci, Associate Professor
University of Minnesota-Duluth
Duluth, Minnesota
Dr. Marcella L. Kysilka, Associate Professor of Education
Florida Technological University
Orlando, Florida
Dr. E. Robert LaCrosse, President
Pacific Oaks College
Pasadena, California
Dr. James R. LaForest, Dean
Community Services
Orange County Community College
Westtown, New York
Dr. Elaine L. La Monica, Associate Professor
Department of Nursing Education

Teachers College, Columbia University
New York, New York
Dr. Ming H. Land, Assistant Professor
Industrial Education Department
Miami University
Oxford, Ohio
Dr. Frank T. Lane, Associate Provost for Undergraduate Education
State University of New York-Central Administration
Albany, New York
Gertrude Langsam, Instructor
Education Department
Adelphi University
Garden City, Long Island, New York
Dr. Everett D. Lantz, Professor of Education
University of Wyoming
Laramie, Wyoming
Dr. Arved M. Larsen, Chairman
Music Department
Southern Connecticut State College
New Haven, Connecticut
Robert C. Laserte, Supervisor of Pupil Personnel Services
Leominster Public Schools
Leominster, Massachusetts
Dr. James R. Layton, Associate Professor
Department of Teacher Education
Southwest Missouri State University
Springfield, Missouri
Dr. Jerome E. Leavitt, Professor of Education
California State University
Fresno, California
Stanley A. Leftwich, Assistant Commissioner of Education
Colorado Department of Education
Denver, Colorado
Roger Lehecka, Assistant Dean
Columbia College
Columbia University
New York, New York
Dr. Harold D. Lehman, Professor of Secondary Education
Madison College
Harrisonburg, Virginia
Dr. Robert L. Leight, Director
Secondary Education

Lehigh University
Bethlehem, Pennsylvania
Professor Jay L. Lemke, Assistant Professor
    School of Education
    Brooklyn College
    City University of New York
    Brooklyn, New York
Dr. Leo D. Leonard, Professor of Educational Theory and Sociology
    University of Toledo
    Toledo, Ohio
Betty Leslein, Teacher
    Henderson High School
    Chamblee, Georgia
Dr. Adeline L. Levin, Professor of Health Science
    Mankato State University
    Mankato, Minnesota
Dr. Arnold Lien, Professor of Education
    University of Wisconsin-Whitewater
    Whitewater, Wisconsin
Kathryn D. Lizzul, Teacher-Counselor
    Newtown High School
    Queens, New York
Dr. Don C. Locke, Assistant Professor
    Guidance and Personnel Services
    North Carolina State University
    Raleigh, North Carolina
Dr. Carroll A. Londoner, Associate Professor of Education
    Virginia Commonwealth University
    Richmond, Virginia
Professor Wilma S. Longstreet
    University of Michigan-Flint
    Flint, Michigan
Dr. Jerome E. Lord, Chief
    Open Learning Branch
    National Institute of Education
    Washington, D.C.
Wendy M. Losey, Student
    Dickinson College
    Carlisle, Pennsylvania
Dr. George Lucht, Assistant Dean
    College of Education
    Kent State University
    Kent, Ohio

Dr. David E. Luellen
 Chelsea, Alabama
Dr. Donovan Lumpkin, Director
 The Reading Center
 Ball State University
 Muncie, Indiana
Joanne B. Lyon, Graduate Assistant
 University of Missouri at St. Louis
 St. Louis, Missouri
Morton Patrick Mabry, Jr., Graduate Student
 Texas A & M University
 College Station, Texas
Dr. Joseph M. McCarthy, Division Director
 Foundations of Education
 Suffolk University
 Boston, Massachusetts
Professor B. Edward McClellan
 School of Education
 Indiana University
 Bloomington, Indiana
Dr. Robert D. MacCurdy, Professor of Education
 Bridgewater State College
 Bridgewater, Massachusetts
Dr. Harold G. MacDermot, Research Scientist
 Wisconsin Research and Development Center for Cognitive Learning
 University of Wisconsin-Madison
 Madison, Wisconsin
Joyce McDonnold, Teaching Associate
 College of Education
 University of Oklahoma
 Norman, Oklahoma
Dr. Jerry C. McGee, Dean
 Continuing Education
 Middle Tennessee State University
 Murfreesboro, Tennessee
Dr. Robert McGinty, Associate Professor
 Mathematics Department
 Northern Michigan University
 Marquette, Michigan
Patricia Kern McIntyre, Education Program Specialist
 Division of International Education
 U.S. Office of Education
 Washington, D.C.

Dr. Harold J. McKenna, Assistant Professor of Science Education
Environmental Studies Program
The City College of the City University of New York
New York, New York
Professor Louise W. MacKenzie
College of Home Economics
University of Rhode Island
Kingston, Rhode Island
Dr. Jonathan C. McLendon, Retired Professor of Social Science Education
(deceased)
University of Georgia
Athens, Georgia
Elaine F. McNally, Assistant Professor of Education
Iowa State University
Ames, Iowa
Dr. George H. Maginnis, Director
The Reading Center
Western Carolina University
Cullowhee, North Carolina
Dr. Joel H. Magisos, Associate Director
Center for Vocational Education
Ohio State University
Columbus, Ohio
Dr. John Mahoney, Vice-President for Academic Affairs
William Paterson College
Wayne, New Jersey
Dr. Wayne Mahood, Associate Professor
Division of Educational Studies
State University of New York College
Geneseo, New York
Dr. Marlis Mann, Director of Early Childhood Education
University of San Francisco
San Francisco, California
Dr. Edythe Margolin, Associate Professor
Early Childhood Education
Florida International University
Miami, Florida
Dr. Edward T. Marquardt, Associate Professor
Department of Early Childhood and Elementary Education
Central Michigan University
Mount Pleasant, Michigan

Dr. William F. Marquardt, Retired Professor (deceased)
Fort Hays Kansas State College
Hays, Kansas

Jeffrey Martin, Graduate Student
Delta State University
Cleveland, Mississippi

Dr. S. V. Martorana, Professor of Higher Education
and Research Associate
Pennsylvania State University
University Park, Pennsylvania

Pamela G. Massey, Assistant Librarian
State University of New York College
Fredonia, New York

Dr. Lawrence S. Master, Consultant-Social Studies and Reading
Area Education Agency 1 (State of Iowa)
Dubuque, Iowa

Dr. Bruce D. Mattson, Professor of Education
Area of Special Education
Texas Tech University
Lubbock, Texas

Charles L. Maynard, Graduate Student
Michigan State University
East Lansing, Michigan

Professor Jerome F. Megna
School of Education
Brooklyn College of the City University of New York
Brooklyn, New York

Dr. Thomas Meighan, Associate Professor-Learning Disabilities
Western Illinois University
Macomb, Illinois

Marilyn Meiss, Instructor
Department of Secondary Education
State University of New York College
Oswego, New York

Connie S. Menges, Graduate Student
University of South Florida
Tampa, Florida

Dr. D. Eugene Meyer, Associate Professor of Education
Northern Illinois University
De Kalb, Illinois

Dr. Genevieve R. Meyer, Associate Professor
Department of Counselor Education
California State University at Los Angeles
Los Angeles, California

Dr. John C. Meyer, Professor of Secondary Education
  Student Teaching Center
  Central Michigan University
  Oscoda, Michigan
Dolores Michalski, Supervisor
  Social Studies Department
  Oakland University
  Rochester, Michigan
Dr. George J. Michel, Assistant Professor
  School of Education
  Catholic University of America
  Washington, D.C.
Dr. Gary M. Miller, Associate Professor
  College of Education
  University of South Carolina
  Columbia, South Carolina
Dr. Gorman L. Miller, Assistant Professor of Education
  Bloomsburg State College
  Bloomsburg, Pennsylvania
Dr. Larry E. Miller
  Agricultural Education Program
  Virginia Polytechnic Institute and State University
  Blacksburg, Virginia
Dr. Bruce G. Milne, Director
  Educational Research and Service
  University of South Dakota
  Vermillion, South Dakota
Professor Raymond A. Mohl
  Department of History
  Florida Atlantic University
  Boca Raton, Florida
Dr. Richard B. Morland, Professor of Educational Philosophy
  Stetson, University
  De Land, Florida
Amelia Lubrano Morrill, Graduate Student
  University of South Florida
  Tampa, Florida
Robert C. Morris, Assistant Professor of Education
  Auburn University
  Auburn, Alabama
Peter Moses, Student
  Dickinson College
  Carlisle, Pennsylvania

Professor Marjorie Muntz, Assistant Director
  Continuing Education
  University of Cincinnati
  Cincinnati, Ohio

Dr. C. Kenneth Murray, Coordinator
  Economic Education Programs
  West Virginia University
  Morgantown, West Virginia

Dr. Thomas D. Myers, Vice-President for Student Affairs
  Eastern Kentucky University
  Richmond, Kentucky

Dr. Grace Napier, Professor of Special Education
  University of Northern Colorado
  Greeley, Colorado

Dr. Natalie A. Naylor, Assistant Professor
  Foundations of Education Department
  Hofstra University
  Hempstead, New York

Dr. Frederick C. Neff, Professor
  College of Education
  Wayne State University
  Detroit, Michigan

Dr. Robert D. Neill, Professor of Education
  Management Information Systems
  University of Louisville
  Louisville, Kentucky

Professor Frances H. Nelson
  School of Education
  College of William and Mary
  Williamsburg, Virginia

Dr. Jack L. Nelson, Professor
  Graduate School of Education
  Rutgers University
  New Brunswick, New Jersey

Dr. Murry R. Nelson, Assistant Professor
  College of Education
  Pennsylvania State University
  University Park, Pennsylvania

Dr. Arthur J. Newman, Professor of Education
  Glassboro State College
  Glassboro, New Jersey

Dr. Richard J. Nichols, Professor of Education
Kean College of New Jersey
Union, New Jersey

Dr. Robert H. Niederkorn, Principal
Peterson Elementary School
Kalispell, Montana

Dr. Albert Nissman, Professor of Education
Rider College
Trenton, New Jersey

Dr. Edward J. Nussel, Associate Dean
College of Education
University of Toledo
Toledo, Ohio

Dr. Russell C. Oakes, Professor of Education
State University of New York College
Geneseo, New York

Dr. William S. O'Bruba, Associate Professor
Department of Elementary Education
Bloomsburg State College
Bloomsburg, Pennsylvania

Dr. James J. O'Connor, Director
Liberal Studies and Social Science Education
Oregon State University
Corvallis, Oregon

Dr. John R. O'Donnell, Professor of Education
University of Dayton
Dayton, Ohio

Dr. Elizabeth S. Oelrich, Instructor
Belleville Area College
Belleville, Illinois

Dr. Richard S. Offenberg, Assistant Vice-Chancellor
Massachusetts Board of Higher Education
Boston, Massachusetts

James Ogan, Student
Kent State University
Kent, Ohio

Dr. Ronald E. Ohl, Acting Chairman
Relations Division
Fairleigh Dickinson University
Rutherford, New Jersey

Frederik F. Ohles, Graduate Student
Brandeis University
Waltham, Massachusetts

Dr. John F. Ohles, Professor
  College of Education
  Kent State University
  Kent, Ohio
Shirley M. Ohles
  Kent, Ohio
Dr. Bill W. Oldham, Associate Professor of Mathematics
  Harding College
  Searcy, Arkansas
Dr. Delmar W. Olson, Executive Director
  Epsilon Pi Tau, Inc.
  Casper, Wyoming
Carol O'Meara, Teaching Assistant
  State University of New York College
  Brockport, New York
Marion Nolan O'Quinn, Visiting Instructor
  North Carolina State University
  Raleigh, North Carolina
Olga Padron, Graduate Student
  University of South Florida
  Tampa, Florida
Dr. Stuart B. Palonsky, Assistant Professor
  Department of Education
  Rutgers University
  New Brunswick, New Jersey
Dr. William J. Parente, Dean of the College
  University of Scranton
  Scranton, Pennsylvania
Dr. Barbara M. Parramore, Head
  Department of Curriculum and Instruction
  North Carolina State University
  Raleigh, North Carolina
Charles V. Partridge, Librarian
  Professional Library
  Detroit Board of Education
  Detroit, Michigan
Dr. Anthony V. Patti, Associate Professor
  Department of Secondary and Continuing Education
  Herbert H. Lehman College of the City University of New York
  Bronx, New York
Dr. Daniel L. Paul, Associate Professor of Education
  Hope College
  Holland, Michigan
Dr. Prodeep K. Paul, Project Director

1202 Commission
West Virginia Postsecondary Education Commission
Charleston, West Virginia
Dr. Barbara Ruth Peltzman
Laurelton, Queens, New York
John E. Phillips, Student
East Stroudsburg State College
East Stroudsburg, Pennsylvania
Mary Paula Phillips, Graduate Assistant
Southwest Missouri State University
Springfield, Missouri
Dr. Paul C. Pickett, Professor Emeritus
Upper Iowa University
Fayette, Iowa
Dr. Gerald A. Ponder, Assistant Professor of Education
North Texas State University
Denton, Texas
Audrey Potter, Teaching Assistant
Marquette University
Milwaukee, Wisconsin
C. Michael Powell, Director
Clinical Management Services
Community Mental Health and Psychiatric Institute
Norfolk, Virginia
Dr. H. J. Prince, Assistant Professor
Lake Superior State College
Sault Ste. Marie, Michigan
Dr. Wilma J. Pyle, Chairperson
Elementary and Early Childhood Education Department
State University of New York College
Fredonia, New York
Dr. Raymond Quist, Associate Professor
Department of Special Education
Indiana State University
Terre Haute, Indiana
Dr. Alan N. Rabe, School Health Coordinator
Central Michigan University
Mt. Pleasant, Michigan
Gina L. Randolph, Graduate Student
University of South Florida
Tampa, Florida
Professor Paul G. Randolph
Department of History

Morehead State University
Morehead, Kentucky

Dr. Roger Rasmussen, Associate Professor of Education
Bemidji State University
Bemidji, Minnesota

Dr. Anne Raymond-Savage, Associate Professor
Department of Curriculum and Instruction
Old Dominion University
Norfolk, Virginia

Dr. Charles A. Reavis, Associate Professor of Supervision and
Administration
Old Dominion University
Norfolk, Virginia

Dr. Richard T. Rees, Assistant Professor of Education
Wilkes College
Wilkes-Barre, Pennsylvania

Professor Thomas F. Reidy, Assistant Professor of Educational
Administration
Villanova University
Villanova, Pennsylvania

Gail Pasciuta Reigel, Graduate Student
University of South Florida
Tampa, Florida

Charlene Gail Revels, Graduate Student
University of South Florida
Tampa, Florida

Dr. Agnes Fenster Ridley, Dean
School of Home Economics
Mississippi University for Women
Columbus, Mississippi

Dr. Ernest D. Riggsby, Professor of Science Education
Columbus College
Columbus, Georgia

Dr. Dennis Rittenmeyer, Assistant Dean
School of Education
Old Dominion University
Norfolk, Virginia

Renaldo E. Rivera, Graduate Assistant
University of Akron
Akron, Ohio

Dr. Haig A. Rushdoony, Professor of Education
California State College, Stanislaus
Turlock, California

Dr. S. E. Russell, Chairman
  Vocational and Technical Education
  University of North Florida
  Jacksonville, Florida
Dr. Charles W. Ryan, Professor of Education
  University of Maine
  Orono, Maine
Dr. Margaret W. Ryan, Associate Professor
  University of South Mississippi
  Hattiesburg, Mississippi
Dr. Exyie C. Ryder, Associate Professor of Education
  Southern University
  Baton Rouge, Louisiana
Dr. C. Roy Rylander, Professor
  Division of Physical Education and Athletics
  University of Delaware
  Newark, Delaware
Abdul Samad, Teaching Assistant
  Department of Educational Leadership
  Southern Illinois University
  Carbondale, Illinois
Dr. Walter J. Sanders, Associate Professor of Elementary
  Education
  Indiana State University
  Terre Haute, Indiana
Dr. James V. Sandrin, Associate Professor of Education
  Missouri Southern State College
  Joplin, Missouri
Dr. Rita S. Saslaw, Associate Professor
  Department of Educational Foundations
  University of Akron
  Akron, Ohio
Dr. Paul J. Schafer, Director of Teacher Education
  Saint Bonaventure University
  Saint Bonaventure, New York
Dr. Anne E. Scheerer, Dean
  Summer Session and Lifelong Education
  Creighton University
  Omaha, Nebraska
Professor Jerome D. Schein, Director
  Deafness Research and Training Center
  New York University
  New York, New York

Dr. John W. Schifani, Coordinator of Undergraduate Studies
   Department of Special Education and Rehabilitation
   Memphis State University
   Memphis, Tennessee
Dr. Ned V. Schimizzi, Associate Professor
   Curriculum and Instruction
   State University of New York College
   Buffalo, New York
Professor Roy V. Schoenborn, Associate Professor of Art and Education
   Southeastern Missouri State University
   Cape Girardeau, Missouri
Dr. E. A. Scholer, Director
   Center for Leisure and Recreation
   University of New Mexico
   Albuquerque, New Mexico
Joanne L. Schweik, Technical Assistant
   Reed Library
   State University of New York College
   Fredonia, New York
Dr. Diana Scott, Assistant Professor
   Florida State University
   Tallahassee, Florida
Dr. Kim Sebaly, Assistant Professor
   College of Education
   Kent State University
   Kent, Ohio
Sister M. Theodine Sebold, Professor Emeritus
   Viterbo College
   La Crosse, Wisconsin
Dr. Marie M. Seedor, Associate Professor
   Teachers College, Columbia University
   New York, New York
Dr. Martin W. Sharp, Jr., Assistant Professor
   Delaware County Campus
   Pennsylvania State University
   Media, Pennsylvania
Dr. Vernon Lee Sheeley, Associate Professor of Education
   Western Kentucky University
   Bowling Green, Kentucky
Dr. Robert R. Sherman, Chairman
   Foundations of Education
   University of Florida
   Gainesville, Florida

Dr. Robert V. Shuff, Chairman
  Department of Educational Administration
  Eastern Illinois University
  Charleston, Illinois
Dr. B. Richard Siebring, Professor of Chemistry
  University of Wisconsin at Milwaukee
  Milwaukee, Wisconsin
Dr. Dorothy J. Sievers, Associate Professor
  Yeshiva University
  New York, New York
Dr. John R. Silvestro, Assistant Professor
  Department of Secondary Education and Educational
  Foundations
  State University of New York College
  Fredonia, New York
Dr. Robert J. Simpson, Professor of Education
  University of Miami
  Coral Gables, Florida
Dr. Kenneth Sipser, Professor of Education
  State University of New York College
  Oswego, New York
Sister Stephanie Sloyan, Professor
  Georgian Court College
  Lakewood, New Jersey
Dr. Lee H. Smalley, Professor
  Industrial Teacher Education
  University of Wisconsin-Stout
  Menomonie, Wisconsin
Dr. Lawrence Byron Smelser, Professor
  Department of Library and Audiovisual Education
  St. Cloud State University
  St. Cloud, Minnesota
Professor Robert F. Smith, Assistant Professor
  School of Education
  Brooklyn College of the City University of New York
  Brooklyn, New York
Susan Margot Smith, Teaching Associate
  American Studies
  University of Minnesota
  Minneapolis, Minnesota
Dr. Arthur E. Soderlind, Social Studies and Independent
  School Consultant
  Bureau of Elementary and Secondary Education

State Department of Education
Hartford, Connecticut
Dr. Isadore L. Sonnier, Associate Professor of Science Education
University of Southern Mississippi
Hattiesburg, Mississippi
Roberta Sorenson, Graduate Assistant
University of South Florida
Tampa, Florida
Dr. Marjorie E. Souers, Assistant Professor of Education
Indiana University-Purdue University at Fort Wayne
Fort Wayne, Indiana
Dr. Rebecca L. Sparks, Associate Professor of Education
Southwest Texas State University
San Marcos, Texas
Dr. Fred L. Splittgerber, Associate Professor of Education
University of South Carolina
Columbia, South Carolina
Dr. Henry J. Sredl, Director
Career and Vocational-Technical Education
Alleghany Intermediate Unit
Pittsburgh, Pennsylvania
Dr. Frank H. Stallings, Professor of Education Emeritus
University of Louisville
Louisville, Kentucky
Sister Ann Stankiewicz, Assistant Professor of Philosophy
Mount Saint Mary College
Newburgh, New York
Deborah Staton
Elkins Park, Pennsylvania
Dr. John Steinert-Earls, Psychologist
Miami, Florida
Dr. W. Richard Stephens, Vice-President for Academic Affairs
Greenville College
Greenville, Illinois
Donald C. Stephenson, Chairman
Social Studies Department
Rockdale County High School
Conyers, Georgia
Marie V. Stephenson, Teacher
Honey Creek School
Conyers, Georgia
Dr. Curtis C. Stone, Associate Professor
College of Education

Kent State University
Kent, Ohio
Dr. Donald B. Stone, Associate Professor of Health Education
University of Illinois
Urbana, Illinois
Professor H. Keith Stumpff, Head
Mathematics Department
Central Missouri State University
Warrensburg, Missouri
Dr. William J. Sullivan, Assistant Director
Division of Graduate Study
Springfield College
Springfield, Massachusetts
Dr. Harry L. Summerfield, Resident Scholar
Wright Institute
Berkeley, California
Dr. William Summerscales, Director of Development
Teachers College, Columbia University
New York, New York
Dr. Jacob L. Susskind, Assistant Professor
Capitol Campus
Pennsylvania State University
Middletown, Pennsylvania
Dr. Jeffrey Sussman, Instructor
Empire State College
Old Westbury, New York
Ronald D. Szoke, Research Consultant
Educational Policy Studies
University of Illinois
Urbana, Illinois
Dr. Gerald G. Szymanski, Assistant Professor of Education
Indiana University-Purdue University at Fort Wayne
Fort Wayne, Indiana
Dr. Fred W. Tanner, Professor of Education
North Texas State University
Denton, Texas
Professor Virginia Taylor, Assistant Professor
Mathematics Department
University of Lowell
Lowell, Massachusetts
Dr. Sue C. Tenorio, Assistant Professor of Special Education
Oakland University
Rochester, Michigan

Steven A. Thiel, Graduate Student
  Kent State University
  Kent, Ohio
Dr. Earl W. Thomas, Associate Professor of Education
  Radford College
  Radford, Virginia
Janet Durand Thomas
  Jenkintown, Pennsylvania
Joan W. Thompson, Lecturer
  University of Arizona
  Tucson, Arizona
Larry C. Thompson, Instructor
  General Studies
  Pima Community College
  Tucson, Arizona
Allen Lee Thornell, Graduate Assistant
  Arkansas State University
  Jonesboro, Arkansas
Dr. Sara Throop, Assistant Professor of Elementary Education
  Youngstown State University
  Youngstown, Ohio
Marjorie Tillotson
  Juneau, Alaska
Dr. Audrey N. Tomera, Assistant Professor
  Department of Curriculum, Instruction and Media
  Southern Illinois University
  Carbondale, Illinois
Dr. Gloria Tribble
  Elementary Education Department
  Youngstown State University
  Youngstown, Ohio
Dr. Robert H. Truman, Assistant Professor
  College of Education
  Kent State University
  Kent, Ohio
Dr. Mary J. Tull, Assistant Professor
  Southern Connecticut State College
  New Haven, Connecticut
Dr. Paul Unger, Professor of Education
  College of William and Mary
  Williamsburg, Virginia
Dr. James J. Van Patten, Professor
  Graduate School of Education

University of Arkansas at Fayetteville
Fayetteville, Arkansas
Dr. Carl F. Vaupel, Jr., Associate Professor of Education
Arkansas State University
State University, Arkansas
Dr. Eli Velder, Professor of Education
Goucher College
Towson, Maryland
Dr. James M. Vosper
Centralia, Washington
Dr. Jennings L. Wagoner, Jr., Director
Center for Higher Education
University of Virginia
Charlottesville, Virginia
Dr. Benjamin F. Walker, Professor
Secondary Education
Indiana State University
Terre Haute, Indiana
Professor Robert A. Waller, Associate Professor of History
University of Illinois
Urbana, Illinois
Dr. J. K. Ward, Assistant Professor of Educational Technology
Gallaudet College
Washington, D.C.
Dr. Paul L. Ward, Associate Professor of Education
Eastern Illinois University
Charleston, Illinois
Dr. Donald R. Warren, Associate Professor
College of Education
University of Illinois at Chicago Circle
Chicago, Illinois
Dr. James F. Warwick, Associate Professor of Education
Queens College of the City University of New York
Flushing, New York.
Donna H. Wernz, Counselor
Clinton High School
Clinton, Indiana
Dr. Sally H. Wertheim, Associate Professor
Department of Education
John Carroll University
Cleveland, Ohio
Karen Wertz
Albuquerque, New Mexico

Dr. William W. West, Professor of Education
University of South Florida
Tampa, Florida
Karen H. Westerman, Graduate Fellow
Indiana State University
Terre Haute, Indiana
Albert S. Weston
New York, New York
Professor Louise H. Wheeler
Department of Vocational Education
Kent State University
Kent, Ohio
Dr. Foster F. Wilkinson, Chairman
Elementary Education Division
Delta State University
Cleveland, Mississippi
Dr. Joan Williams, Professor of Elementary Education
Ball State University
Muncie, Indiana
Thomas L. Wilton, Research Associate
Boston University
Boston, Massachusetts
Dennis M. Wint, Graduate Assistant
Case Western Reserve University
Cleveland, Ohio
Dr. Lew E. Wise, Assistant Professor of Education
Indiana University-Purdue University at Fort Wayne
Fort Wayne, Indiana
Dr. Dennis G. Wiseman, Assistant Professor of Education
Coastal Carolina College of the University of South Carolina
Conway, South Carolina
Dr. William D. Wolansky, Head
Industrial Education
Iowa State University
Ames, Iowa
Dr. Paul Woodworth, Instructional Development Specialist
University of Arkansas Medical Center
Little Rock, Arkansas
Dr. Dee Wyckoff, Assistant Professor
Oakland University
Rochester, Michigan
Robert Wyly, Graduate Student
University of Arkansas

Fayetteville, Arkansas
Dr. Daniel S. Yates, Curriculum Specialist
    Mathematics and Science Center
    Glen Allen, Virginia
Farouk Zalatimo, Teaching Assistant
    Southern Illinois University
    Carbondale, Illinois
Dr. Harold C. Zimmerman, Professor of Education
    California State College at Bakersfield
    Bakersfield, California
Lorraine M. Zinn, Teaching Assistant
    Department of Adult Education
    Florida State University
    Tallahassee, Florida

PREFACE

The *Biographical Dictionary of American Educators* was initiated in early 1974 to provide a ready source of biographical information about those people who have shaped American education from colonial times to the American bicentennial of 1976. Because education in the United States developed on the state level, leaders in education in the states have been included, as well as national figures and those who have been leaders in subject matter fields. Basic criteria for selection were persons who had been engaged in education, were eminent, and had reached the age of sixty, had retired, or had died by January 1, 1975.

A letter was sent on February 1, 1974, to state departments of education, historical societies, and educational associations and to one or two major colleges or universities in every state requesting nominations of eminent educators. A similar request was sent to the major national professional education associations.

In addition to the responses from most states and professional associations, the editor consulted educational histories, encyclopedias, and standard biographical references, including the *Dictionary of American Biography, Notable American Women,* and *National Cyclopedia of American Biography*. Many nominations were received and were screened through the above references and *Who's Who, Who Was Who, Who's Who in American Education, Appleton's Cyclopedia of American Biography, The Twentieth Century Biographical Dictionary of Notable Americans, Current Biography,* and *Leaders in Education*.

The most useful means of recruiting contributors of biographies was by extending invitations to people listed in volume 5 of *Leaders in Education*, (1974), to participate in the project. Additional contributors were recruited from the faculties of the college of education of Kent (Ohio) State University and the State University of New York College at Fredonia and the membership of the Society of Professors of Education. Notices were published in the newsletter of Phi Delta Kappa, *News, Notes, and Quotes; The Social Studies Professional* of the National Council for the Social Studies; the History of Education Society *Newsletter*; and *NCTM Bulletin for Leaders* of the National Council of Teachers of Mathematics. A notice was also published in the Santa Clara (California) Mathematics Association *Newsletter*. A total of 465 people from across the country contributed biographical sketches, including the editor, who contributed 224 sketches.

[xlvii]

Significant assistance was accorded to contributors and the editor by librarians and others in resolving questions of accuracy in references used or to provide information that had not previously been generally available. A case in point is William N. Bartholomew, the pioneer art educator in the Boston public schools. Identified in standard references as William "Newton" Bartholomew, a copy of an obituary published at his death received through the courtesy of the Newton (Massachusetts) Public Library identified him as William Nelson Bartholomew, which was in accordance with listings in the Library of Congress *Union Catalogue*. Similar corrections have been made in other sketches. Materials used in the compilation will be deposited in the archives of the Reed Library, State University of New York College at Fredonia.

Many people must be credited with assistance in completion of the compilation. In addition to the contributors, acknowledgment of essential assistance is extended to many librarians, staff members of educational associations and state departments of education, historical societies, colleges, universities, and school systems, as well as acquaintances and relatives of the biographees and, in certain cases, the biographees themselves. Appreciation for their assistance is directed to Donald W. Robinson, editor of *News, Notes, and Quotes*; Judith Gaykowski, editor of *The Social Studies Professional*; Murray S. Shereshewsky, editor of the History of Education Society *Newsletter*; and Joseph R. Caravella, director of professional services for the National Council of Teachers of Mathematics.

In particular, the editor is indebted for encouragement and assistance from Kent State University colleagues, including Dr. Richard L. Hart, Dr. Charles C. Chandler, Dr. Robert H. Truman, and Dr. Joan Duff Kise, and to Dr. Leo J. Alilunas and Dr. Dallas K. Beal of the State University of New York at Fredonia. The Kent State University librarians were particularly helpful. Dr. Benjamin F. Walker of Indiana State University, Dr. William W. West of the University of South Florida, and Dr. Paul W. F. Witt of Michigan State University were among the many who assisted in recruiting participants for the compilation. Finally, the successful completion of the project is due to the help of my wife Shirley M. Ohles, who served as associate editor and typist. My son Frederik Ohles provided valuable reference and research assistance, and my daughters Janet Ohles and Margaret Ohles helped with important typing duties and Judy Ohles performed necessary clerical tasks.

____INTRODUCTION____

The *Biographical Dictionary of American Educators* represents the combined efforts of several hundred American educators to identify and report on 1,665 educators, who have been major figures in the development of American education. The final responsibility for the selection of biographees and for the content of the biographical sketches rests with the editor of course. With any selection of a representative group of people, there may be disagreement among professionals about those to be included. However, it is expected that there is general agreement about those who have been the major figures in American education; disagreement increases as less influential figures are included or excluded from the list.

The content of each biographical sketch is basically a short description of the subject's education, employment, contributions to education, and participation in professional activities. References for further information are provided at the end of each entry, followed by the name of the contributor of the sketch. All sketches are written in the past tense; those of living educators are intended to include activities up to the compilation of the sketch and not those in progress.

The length of a sketch does not necessarily represent the importance of the contributions of the biographee but may be related to the number of educational institutions attended, positions held, books published, and associations in which the person was active. Biographical sketches of educators from the early history of the United States are generally shorter in length and more subjective in content because the size of the country, the limited number of scholarly organizations, and the few demands for expertise by government or private agencies limited the opportunities for these people to contribute. To keep sketches to a reasonable length, all publications, activities, or awards are not listed for every individual.

A special effort was made to include women and minority groups in the compilation. It is with particular reference to groups previously underrepresented that new information is available in this work.

Each entry contains a heading in which certain basic information is contained. The information includes *(B)*: date and place of birth and names of parents; *(M)*: date of marriage and name of spouse; *(Ch)*: the total number of children from all marriages and names of eminent children; and *(D)*: date and place of death. Information that has not been available is noted *n.a.*; approximate dates are noted *c*. The least reliable information is the number of children; the information is frequently not included in biographical references and is further complicated by the high incidence of infant and child mortality up to the recent past. Those named in sketches whose biographies are also included in the compilation are noted *q.v.*

Following the biographical sketches are lists of references. Frequently used references are abbreviated (see the list on page xliii). References that are arranged in alphabetical order, such as *Dictionary of American Biography*, do not include page numbers; references that are not arranged in alphabetical order, including *National Cyclopedia of American Biography*, contain page numbers. The *National Cyclopedia of American Biography* references use arabic numerals, even though some volumes are published with Roman numerals. Supplementary volumes of the *National Cyclopedia of American Biography* are identified as lettered volumes (A, B, C, etc.), and the numbered supplements of the *Dictionary of American Biography* are indicated as, for example, supp. (supplement) 1. Some common references, such as *Dictionary of American Biography, Encyclopaedia Britannica, Dictionary of Scientific Biography,* and *Notable American Women,* include lists of additional references that are not duplicated in this *Dictionary*.

Appendixes are provided that identify states (or countries) of birth of biographees, the states of their major service to education, major field of specialization, chronological listing of birth dates of biographees, and the important dates of the history of American education. Appendixes of place of birth and chronology of birth years include all biographees; a few biographees do not conform to the categories established in other appendixes. All biographees are listed in the index.

____Abbreviations____

Biographical Dictionary
of American Educators

A

ABBOT, Benjamin. B. September 17, 1762, Andover, Massachusetts, to John Abbot and n.a. M. 1791 to Hannah Tracy Emery. M. 1798 to Mary Peck Perkins. Ch. three. D. October 25, 1849, Exeter, New Hampshire.

Benjamin Abbot entered Phillips Academy in Andover, Massachusetts, at the age of twenty-one. He and classmates John T. Kirkland (*q.v.*) and Josiah Quincy (*q.v.*), both of whom became president of Harvard, were taught by Jeremiah Smith, later a prominent New Hampshire jurist. Abbot continued his education at Harvard College. Graduating with the B.A. degree in 1788, he delivered the salutatory oration. On October 8, 1788, he was appointed principal of Phillips Academy in Exeter, New Hampshire, a position he held for fifty years.

Abbot submitted his resignation after forty-four years as principal, but the trustees encouraged him to remain six more years. His retirement on August 28, 1838, was celebrated by a day known as the Abbot Festival, at which nearly four hundred of his past students gathered to honor him. Among his more distinguished students were Lewis Cass, Edward Everett, Jared Sparks (*q.v.*), Francis Bowen, and Daniel Webster, who presided over the event.

Abbot has been credited with establishing the character of the school as a famous center for scholarship and graduates who distinguished themselves in the service of church and state. In 1811 he received the LL.D. degree from Dartmouth College.

REFERENCES: *DAB; NCAB* (10:104); *WWW* (H); Laurence M. Crosbie, *The Phillips Exeter Academy: A History* (Exeter, N.H.: the Academy, 1923); Myron R. Williams, *The Story of Phillips Exeter* (Exeter, N.H.: The Academy, 1957).   *Larry Froehlich*

ABBOTT, Gorham Dummer. B. September 3, 1807, Brunswick, Maine, to Jacob and Betsey (Abbot) Abbot. M. to Rebecca S. Leach. Ch. one. D. August 3, 1874, South Natick, Massachusetts.

Gorham Dummer Abbott, educator, clergyman, and author, and his brothers Jacob (*q.v.*) and Charles, changed the spelling of the family name. He was graduated from Bowdoin College in Brunswick, Maine, in 1826 and from the Andover (Massachusetts) Theological Seminary in 1831. He was ordained in the Congregational church (1831). He traveled through the South to restore his health and developed strong ideas about the needs of public education. In Boston he joined his brother Jacob in the Mount

Vernon School for Young Ladies. He served as pastor of the Presbyterian Church at New Rochelle, New York (1837–41). In 1836 he organized the Society for the Diffusion of Useful Knowledge, which selected books that were published as a school library of fifty volumes and also sponsored the writing of textbooks. The society sought to increase and improve educational materials available to schools.

With his brothers Jacob and Charles, he founded in 1843 the New Seminary for Young Ladies in New York City. By 1848 he established the Spingler Institute, one of the finest educational institutions for women in America, which enrolled pupils from wealthy homes across the country. It featured a broad academic program and recruited a distinguished faculty.

Abbott established a college in 1861 and acquired the Townsend mansion at Fifth Avenue and Thirty-fourth Street in New York City. The Abbott Collegiate Institution existed for five years before the financial difficulties associated with the Civil War and the failing health of the Abbotts led to its termination.

Abbott was author of *Mexico and the United States: Their Mutual Relations and Common Interests* (1869) and several articles in weekly religious papers.

His counsel was sought by the founders of Vassar and Wellesley colleges, who incorporated some of his ideas for the education of women into their courses of instruction.

REFERENCES: *AC; DAB; NCAB* (10:355); *TC; WWW* (H); *NYT*, August 6, 1874, p. 4.   *Michael R. Cioffi*

ABBOTT, Jacob. B. November 14, 1803, Hallowell, Maine, to Jacob and Betsey (Abbot) Abbot. M. May 18, 1828, to Harriet Vaughan. M. November 1852 to Mary Dana Woodbury. Ch. six. D. October 31, 1879, Farmington, Maine.

Jacob Abbott attended Hallowell (Maine) Academy as preparation for college. At the age of fourteen he entered Bowdoin College in Brunswick, Maine (where he added the extra "t" to his name), receiving the A.B. (1820) and A.M. (1823) degrees. He studied for the ministry at Andover (Massachusetts) Theological Seminary and was ordained in the Congregational church.

Abbott taught school in Portland, Maine, and Beverly, Massachusetts (1820–24). In 1824 he was appointed tutor and later a professor of mathematics at Amherst (Massachusetts) College, where he served until 1829. He founded the Mount Vernon School for Young Ladies in Boston, one of the first schools in the United States offering a curriculum equivalent in excellence to that at male institutions. Mount Vernon was noted for its many educational innovations, including principles of self-government for students. Abbott turned to preaching and writing and was the organizer and first pastor of the Eliot Church in Roxbury, Massachusetts (1833–37). He cofounded with his brothers Gorham Dummer (*q.v.*) and Charles the Abbott Institute in New York City (1843), where he worked until 1851.

Abbott was the author of 180 and coauthor or editor of 31 books. He is most noted for the Rollo series (28 volumes), which contained many practical hints on human relations. He also wrote Lucy books (six volumes), Jonas books (six volumes), Franconia stories (ten volumes), Marco Paul series (six volumes), Gay Family (twelve volumes), Juno books (six volumes), and Rainbow series (five volumes). In 1832 he published his first important work, *The Young Christian,* a widely read and famous book. Another important early work, *The Teacher* (1833), was used as a textbook in early teacher-training programs. Among many other books were *The Little Philosopher* (1833), *New England and Her Institutions* (1835), *Franklin, the Apprentice Boy* (1855), *The Little Learner* (1856), and *Science for the Young* (1871–72).

REFERENCES: *AC; DAB; EB; NCAB* (6:136); *TC; WWW* (H); *NYT,* November 1, 1879, p. 2.   *David C. Gardner*

ABERCROMBIE, John William. B. May 17, 1866, Kelly's Creek, Alabama, to Henry M. and Sarah (Kendrick) Abercrombie. M. January 1, 1891, to Rose Merrill. Ch. four. D. July 2, 1940, Montgomery, Alabama.

John William Abercrombie spent most of his life in Alabama. He attended the public schools of St. Clair County and received the A.B. degree (1886) from Oxford College. He was principal and teacher in Ashland (1886–87) and then entered the University of Alabama Law School where he received the LL.B. degree and was admitted to the bar in 1888.

For the next two years, he was principal of the Cleburne Institute, handled a few law cases, and owned and edited a weekly newspaper in Edwardsville, where he also was the mayor. In 1890 he served as president of Bowdon College (Georgia). He returned to Alabama as superintendent of the city schools of Anniston (1891–97) and president of the Southern Female Seminary (later, Anniston College for Young Ladies). He was state superintendent of education (1898–1902).

He resigned as superintendent in 1902 to accept the presidency of the University of Alabama. In 1911 he resigned as president, in part over a dispute over athletics. He felt that athletes should observe the same academic requirements as other students. Abercrombie was credited with establishing a summer school at the University of Alabama (1904) and the school of education (1909) as a means of improving the competency of public school teachers.

Abercrombie served as a member of the state legislature (1896–99) and was elected United States congressman-at-large (1913–17). President Woodrow Wilson (*q.v.*) appointed him solicitor and acting secretary of the

United States Labor Department (1918–20).

He was again Alabama state superintendent of education between 1920 and 1927. Ineligible for reelection by state law, he served as assistant superintendent of education (1927–35) and supervisor of the division of certification in the state department of education (1935–40).

He was a member of numerous state and national organizations and consulting author for the Library of Southern Literature and advisory editor of the *History of Alabama and Her People* (1927). He favored the expansion of studies in the high school with the inclusion of vocational subjects.

REFERENCES: *NCAB* (12:297); *WWW* (I); *NYT,* July 3, 1940, p. 17; Jesse M. Richardson, *The Contributions of John William Abercrombie to Public Education* (Nashville, Tenn.: George Peabody College for Teachers, Bureau of Publications, 1949).   *S. S. Britt, Jr.*

ADAMS, Charles Kendall. B. January 24, 1835, Derby, Vermont, to Charles and Maria (Shadd) Adams. M. August 13, 1883, to Abigail Disbrow Midge. M. to Mary Mathews Barnes. Ch. none. D. July 26, 1902, Redlands, California.

Charles Kendall Adams attended the district school in the township of Derby, Vermont, where his father was a farmer. He returned to the school as a teacher until the family moved to Denmark, Iowa, in 1856. He studied at the Denmark Academy to prepare for college.

In 1857 he entered the University of Michigan and was graduated in 1861. During his student days, he showed a special interest and aptitude in the study of history. Andrew D. White (*q.v.*), professor of history at Michigan, showed great interest in him and became a major influence on his studies and career. Through White's influence, Adams was appointed assistant professor of history and, later, professor when White resigned in 1867.

Adams studied for a year in Germany and observed methods of instruction in history at leading universities. Returning to the University of Michigan, he introduced the seminar method of instruction in 1869.

Andrew D. White, president of Cornell University, invited Adams to give a series of lectures (1881–85), and when White resigned, he nominated Adams for the presidency. Adams served as president of Cornell (1885–92), where he established new schools and recruited outstanding scholars for the faculty.

In 1892 he accepted the presidency of the University of Wisconsin, where he was particularly successful in working with the legislature to appropriate funds, and he became known as a building president. Ill health forced him to resign in 1901.

Adams earned a reputation as a scholar and editor; his important publications include *Democracy and Monarchy in France* (1874), *A Manual of*

Historical Literature (1882), and *Christopher Columbus: His Life and Work* (1895). He was editor of the three-volume *Representative British Orations* (1884) and editor-in-chief of the *Universal Cyclopedia and Atlas* (1901), *Johnson's Cyclopedia* (1893–97), and *A History of the United States* (with William P. Trent, *q.v.,* 1903).

REFERENCES: *AC; DAB; EB; NCAB* (4:477); TC; WWW (I); *NYT,* July 27, 1902, p. 7; Charles Foster Smith, *Charles Kendall Adams, A Life Sketch* (Madison: University of Wisconsin, 1924). *John C. Durance*

ADAMS, Daniel. B September 29, 1773, Townsend, Massachusetts, to Daniel and Lydia (Taylor) Adams. M. August 17, 1800, to Nancy Mulliken. Ch. none. D. June 8, 1864, Keene, New Hampshire.

Daniel Adams was graduated from Dartmouth College in 1797 and received the Bachelor of Medicine (1799) and Doctor of Medicine (1822) degrees from the Dartmouth Medical School. He began the practice of medicine in Leominster, Massachusetts, where he delivered the eulogy at the memorial service for George Washington on February 22, 1800.

Concerned with the lack of adequate textbooks in the schools, he wrote *The Scholar's Arithmetic* (1801), followed by *The Thorough Scholar or the Nature of Language* (1802), *The Understanding Reader or Knowledge Before Oratory* (1803), *Geography, or a Description of the World* (1814), *The Agricultural Reader* (1824), *Adams' New Arithmetic* (1827), *The Monitorial Reader* (1839), *Primary Arithmetic* (1848), and *Bookkeeping* (1849). Adams's arithmetic texts were the most popular of those available in the first quarter of the 1800s.

In 1806 Adams moved to Boston where he opened a private school and edited a monthly periodical, the *Medical and Agricultural Register.* In 1813 he moved to Mount Vernon, New Hampshire, where he resumed the practice of medicine. He became a prominent consulting physician and was active in school and civic affairs, serving as a member of the New Hampshire State Senate (1839–40). He was president of the State Bible Society and, briefly, of the State Medical Society. In 1846 Adams moved to Keene, New Hampshire, where he spent the rest of his life.

REFERENCES: *AC; DAB; NCAB* (20:438); *WWW* (H). *John F. Ohles*

ADAMS, Ebenezer. B. October 22, 1765, New Ipswich, New Hampshire, to Ephraim and Rebecca (Locke) Adams. M. July 9, 1795, to Alice Frink. M. May 17, 1807, to Beulah Minot. Ch. seven. D. August 15, 1841, Hanover, New Hampshire.

Ebenezer Adams, one of nineteen children of a farmer of moderate means, was nearly of age when he began preparing for college at the local academy under John Hubbard, principal and, later, his predecessor in the language department at Dartmouth College. At twenty-two, he entered

Dartmouth and was graduated with honors in 1791.

From 1792 to 1806 Adams was preceptor of the Leicester (Massachusetts) Academy, while also serving as justice of the peace and the first village postmaster. He taught in an academy in Portland, Maine (1806–08), and was the first professor of mathematics and natural philosophy at Phillips Academy in Exeter, New Hampshire. He left Phillips Exeter after one year to accept the chair of languages in Dartmouth College in 1809 on the death of John Hubbard.

Adams was professor of mathematics and natural philosophy from 1810 to his retirement in 1833. He served as acting president of Dartmouth during the illness and after the death of Francis Brown (1818–20). While at Dartmouth in 1816, Adams was at the center of the celebrated dispute between the state and the college that was resolved in the United States Supreme Court decision in the *Dartmouth College* case, which established the validity of charters to private colleges and universities.

Adams was trustee and treasurer of Kimball Union Academy in Meriden, New Hampshire, and president of the New Hampshire Bible Society; he was active in the Colonization Society and temperance and foreign mission groups; and he was a member of many literary and scientific societies.

REFERENCES: *DAB; NCAB* (9:91); *WWW* (H).   *Joseph P. Cangemi*
Thomas E. Kesler

ADAMS, Henry Brooks. B. February 16, 1838, Boston, Massachusetts, to Charles Francis and Abigail Brown (Brooks) Adams. M. June 27, 1872, to Marian Hooper. Ch. none. D. March 27, 1918, Washington, D.C.

Henry Adams was born into the famous Adams family of Massachusetts and received his early education in the Boston Latin School. He entered Harvard University in 1855; from Harvard he went to Berlin intending to study law. He withdrew from legal studies after hearing one lecture and spending three months attempting to master German. He then toured parts of the Continent and returned to Boston in 1860. In 1861 he accompanied his father as personal secretary when Abraham Lincoln appointed Charles Francis Adams to be ambassador to the Court of St. James.

Adams returned to the United States in 1869 after two articles, "Pocahantas" and "British Finance," were accepted for publication. He became editor of the *North American Review* in 1870. In the same year, he also accepted an appointment as professor of medieval history at Harvard. He introduced the seminar approach to the American university system. He was the first to utilize modern historical research techniques, and students like Ernest Young, Lawrence Laughlin, and Henry Cabot Lodge became eminent scholars as a result of his influence.

Adams left Harvard after seven years and became involved in a distinguished writing career. His first major work was *Essays in Anglo-Saxon*

Law (1876), followed by *Documents Relating to New England Federalism* (1877), *The Life of Albert Gallatin* (three volumes, 1879), a novel entitled *Democracy* (1879) written under a pseudonym, *The Life of John Randolph* (1882), and a second novel *Esther* (1884).

After his wife's death in 1885, he settled in Washington, D.C. In 1886 a series of short articles previously written by Adams and his father were collected into a book entitled *Chapters of Erie*. In 1889 the first two volumes of *History of the United States* appeared, followed by four more volumes in 1890 and the last three in 1891. Adams achieved universal recognition with the publication of *Mont St. Michel and Chartres* (1904) and his autobiography, *The Education of Henry Adams*, written in 1905 but not published until 1918. His last major work, *The Degradation of the Democratic Dogma* (1919), was published posthumously by Brooks Adams; it contained Adams's famous *Letter to American Teachers of History*, which had originally been published in 1910.

REFERENCES: *DAB; EB; NCAB* (11:475); *NYT*, March 28, 1918, p. 11; *TC; WWW* (I); John C. Cairns, "The Successful Quest of Henry Adams," *South Atlantic Quarterly* 57 (Spring 1958):168–93; Herbert Edwards, "Henry Adams: Politician and Statesman," *New England Quarterly* 22 (March 1949):49–60; Marian D. Irish, "Henry Adams: The Modern American Scholar," *The American Scholar* 1 (March 1932):223–29.

James J. O'Conner

ADAMS, Herbert Baxter. B. April 16, 1850, Shutesbury, Massachusetts, to Nathaniel Dickinson and Harriet (Hastings) Adams. M. no. D. July 30, 1901, Amherst, Massachusetts.

Herbert Baxter Adams attended Phillips Academy in Exeter, New Hampshire, and Amherst (Massachusetts) College, from which he was graduated at the head of his class in 1872. He traveled in Europe and studied in Germany at the universities of Göttingen, Berlin, and Heidelberg, which awarded him the Ph.D. degree with highest honors in 1876. Returning to the United States, he joined the faculty of Johns Hopkins University where he remained until shortly before his death in 1901.

Adams attracted outstanding graduate students to the study of history and continued to encourage and influence them in their scholarly activities in their postgraduate careers. Among these students were Woodrow Wilson (*q.v.*), Charles M. Andrews (*q.v.*), Charles H. Haskins, Frederick Jackson Turner, and others. Adams pioneered in use of the seminar in his classes, a method that had found favor in Germany.

Adams founded the Johns Hopkins University Studies in Historical and Political Science (1882) and served as its editor until 1898, when he resigned and the series was terminated. From 1887 he edited numerous special studies and monographs on American educational history and practice for the United States Bureau of Education.

Among Adams's writings, mostly monographs, are *Maryland's Influence in Founding a National Commonwealth* (1877), *The Germanic Origin of New England Towns* (1881), *Methods of Historical Study* (1884), *Thomas Jefferson and the University of Virginia* (1888), *The State and Higher Education* (1889), and the two-volume *Life and Writings of Jared Sparks* (1893).

In 1894 Adams, Andrew D. White (*q.v.*), Moses Coit Tyler (*q.v.*), and others founded the American Historical Association; Adams served as secretary until 1900.

REFERENCES: *EB; DAB; NCAB* (8:270); *WWW* (I); *Herbert B. Adams: Tributes of Friends* (Baltimore: The Johns Hopkins Press, 1902).

Paul G. Randolph

ADAMS, Romanzo. B. March 22, 1868, Bloomingdale, Wisconsin, to Mighill Dustin and Catherine (Wolf) Adams. M. September 16, 1902, to Nellie Cronk. Ch. one. D. September 10, 1942, Honolulu, Hawaii.

Romanzo Adams was graduated from Iowa State Teachers College (later, University of Northern Iowa) in Cedar Falls, Iowa, in 1892 and received the Ph.B. (1897) and Ph.M. (1898) degrees from the University of Michigan and the Ph.D. degree (1904) from the University of Chicago.

Adams was a public-school principal at Ireton, Iowa (1892–94), and professor of economics and sociology at Western College in Toledo, Iowa (1898–1900). He was dean of the normal school (1902–06) and professor of education and sociology (1902–11) at the University of Nevada. He was professor and head of the department of economics and sociology (1911–20) there. Adams was involved in educational problems in the state, producing monographs on state taxation and on the impact of federal land policy in Nevada.

Adams moved to Hawaii in 1920 where he joined the faculty of the University of Hawaii and introduced instruction in anthropology and sociology. He became interested in the study of race and racial problems in the Hawaiian Islands. He retired from the University of Hawaii in 1935.

Adams was the author of *Taxation in Nevada* (1918), *Statistical Studies of the Japanese in Hawaii* (1923), *Interracial Marriage in Hawaii* (1937), and several monographs on racial relations and education.

He was active in professional associations, serving as president of the Nevada State Teachers Association (1905–10), director of the National Education Association (1908), and secretary of the Nevada Committee on Economy and Taxation (1912–13). In 1935 the Social Research Laboratory at the University of Hawaii was named in his honor.

REFERENCES: *WWW* (II); Arthur L. Dean, "A Memorial: Dr. Romanzo Adams," *Social Process in Hawaii* 8 (1943): 82–83; Samuel Bradford Doten, *An Illustrated History of the University of Nevada* (Reno: University of Nevada, 1924), pp. 121–22; James W. Hulse, *The University of*

Nevada: A Centennial History (Reno: University of Nevada Press, 1974), pp. 114–15.   *John F. Ohles*

ADERHOLD, Omer Clyde. B. November 7, 1899, Lavonia, Georgia, to Joseph Peter and Mary Catherine (Farmer) Aderhold. M. June 30, 1926, to Bessie Parr. Ch. two. D. July 4, 1969, Athens, Georgia.

Omer Clyde Aderhold received his public school education in his home town of Lavonia, Georgia, and received the B.S.A. (1923) and M.S. (1930) degrees from the University of Georgia. He received the Ph.D. degree (1938) from Ohio State University.

Aderhold began his career in education at the Martin Institute in Jefferson, Georgia, where he served as principal (1923–26) and superintendent of the Jefferson public schools (1926–29). He joined the faculty of the University of Georgia as an associate professor of education (1929), was named dean of the college of education (1946), and served as president of the university from 1950 until his retirement in 1967.

During his tenure as president of the University of Georgia, Aderhold originated the Minimum Foundation Program in Georgia. Administered by the state department of education, it reorganized the state's public education system and provided a more adequate educational program. Under Aderhold's administration, the University of Georgia moved ahead rapidly in instruction, research and service.

Aderhold was coauthor of *Farm Crops and Soils* (with others, 1940) and *School Leaders Manual* (with others, 1946). He was the author of several bulletins published by the University of Georgia, including *The Needs for Vocational Education in Agriculture in Georgia* (1939), and several surveys of education in selected counties in Georgia (1948–50). He was editor of *National Magazine for Teachers* (1939–40), published many bulletins in the field of vocational education, and contributed articles to a number of professional journals.

Aderhold was director of the educational panel of Georgia's Agricultural and Industrial Development Board (1942–44) and was director of a statewide survey of public education in Georgia and consultant to a similar study in North Carolina. He was president of the Georgia Education Association (1949–50), the Georgia Association of Colleges, the Southeastern Conference (1954–56), and the Southern Association of Land Grant Colleges and State Universities (1954–55). He was also a member of the executive committee of the American Association of Land Grant Colleges and State Universities, the National Association of State Universities, the Southern Regional Education Board, the National Commission on Accrediting, and the American Council on Education. He was a member of the commission on instruction and evaluation of the American Council on Education (1952–56), the Southern Regional Conference on Education for Graduate Study, and the Georgia Nuclear Advisory Committee, and he was vice-chairman of the Veterans Education Council of Georgia. He received an honorary degree from Mercer University in Macon, Georgia.

REFERENCES: *LE* (III); *NCAB* (I:129); *WWAE* (XVI); *WWW* (V); *Who's Who in the South and Southwest,* 11th ed. (Chicago: Marquis, 1969).

Dennis G. Wiseman

ADLER, Cyrus. B. September 13, 1863, Van Buren, Arkansas, to Samuel and Sarah (Sulzberger) Adler. M. September 1905 to Racie Friedenwald. Ch. one. D. April 7, 1940, Philadelphia, Pennsylvania.

Cyrus Adler was an outstanding Jewish scholar, educational administrator, and leader in Jewish communal, religious, and international affairs. Taken to Philadelphia at the age of four after his father's death, he attended a Jewish day school run under the auspices of the Hebrew Education Society. After two years in a dual program of religious and secular studies, he attended a public elementary school, and studied Hebrew and other Jewish learning with private instructors. He continued his education at Central High School (1874–79) and the University of Pennsylvania where he received the B.A. (1883) and M.A. (1886) degrees. He engaged in private study of the Jewish religion and Semitic languages. From 1883 to 1887 he studied Semitic and other linguistics, pedagogy, and psychology at the Johns Hopkins University, earning the first American Ph.D. degree in Semitics (Assyriology) in 1887.

The outstanding characteristic of Adler's career and life was his ability to carry on two and even more significant tasks simultaneously and successfully. At Johns Hopkins (1887–93) he taught courses in Hebrew, Assyrian, Ethiopic, Arabic, biblical archaeology, and history of the ancient Near East. In 1888 he also began his association with the Smithsonian Institution as director of the museum's ancient Near East department (1888–1909), librarian (1892–1905), and assistant secretary (1905–08). He was associated with the Jewish Theological Seminary in New York City as lecturer in biblical archaeology (1887–89), president of the board of trustees (1902–05), acting president (1915–23), and president (1924–40). He served as president of Dropsie College in Philadelphia from 1908 to 1940.

Adler contributed to the religious, social, intellectual, and philanthropic growth and development of American and world Jewry. He was founder of the American Jewish Historical Society in 1892 (president, 1898–1921), Gratz College in Philadelphia in 1893, the American Jewish Committee in 1906 (president, 1929), and the United Synagogue of America in 1913 (president, 1914). He was president of the Philadelphia Jewish Community (1911–15), a member of the Philadelphia Board of Education (1921–25), president of the board of trustees of the Free Library of Philadelphia (1925), and vice-president of the American Philosophical Society (1938).

Adler was editor of the *American Jewish Yearbook* (1899–1905) and coeditor (1901–16) and editor (1916–40) of the *Jewish Quarterly Review*. He was an editor of the *Jewish Encyclopedia* (twelve volumes, 1901–06) and chairman of the board of editors (1908–15) of the English translation of the scriptures. He participated in the founding of the National Jewish Welfare Board (1917) and was a non-Zionist cochairman of the International Jewish Agency for Palestine.

He wrote more than six hundred articles, reports, notes, catalogs, bibliographies, translations, and book reviews. His books include *Told in the Coffee House* (with Allen Ramsey, 1898), *International Catalogue of Scientific Literature* (1905), *Jews in the Diplomatic Correspondence of the United States* (1906), *Jacob H. Shiff: His Life and Letters* (1928), and the autobiographical *I Have Considered the Days* (1941).

Adler received honorary degrees from Hebrew Union College (1925) and the University of Pennsylvania (1930).

REFERENCES: *CB* (May 1940); *DAB* (supp. 2); *EB; NCAB* (41:16); *WWW* (I); Cyrus Adler, *I Have Considered the Days* (Philadelphia: Jewish Publication Society of America, 1941); *Encyclopedia Judaica* (New York: Macmillan, 1971); Abraham A. Neuman, *Cyrus Adler: A Biographical Sketch* (New York: American Jewish Committee, 1942); *NYT,* April 8, 1940, p. 1.   *William W. Brickman*

ADLER, Felix. B. August 13, 1851, Alzey, Germany, to Samuel and Henrietta (Frankfurter) Adler. M. May 24, 1880, to Helen Goldmark. Ch. five. D. April 24, 1933, New York, New York.

Felix Adler came to New York City in 1857 when his father became rabbi at the Temple Emanu-El. He was graduated from Columbia University in 1870 and left for Germany to study for the rabbinate. There his interests shifted, and he gave up theology for the study of philosophy. He received the Ph.D. degree from the University of Heidelberg in 1873.

Upon his return from Europe, he taught Hebrew and Oriental literature at Cornell University (1874–76). In 1876 he went to New York City where he founded the New York Society for Ethical Culture. The society attracted many who were disenchanted with traditional sectarian creeds, and the movement spread to other cities in America and Europe. In 1889 the American societies federated as the American Ethical Union, and in Europe the International Union of Ethical Culture Societies was established in Zurich, Switzerland, in 1896.

The New York Society for Ethical Culture was especially active in educational reform. Under Adler's leadership it created a variety of innovative educational institutions, including the city's first free kindergarten, a workingman's school that emphasized manual training in the early grades, an advanced high school, a teacher-training school, and a summer camp that combined recreation with manual training. All of these institutions operated under the auspices of the Ethical Culture School, an agency created in 1878 to direct and coordinate the society's educational activities. The schools were coeducational and nondiscriminatory. All offered scholarship aid to the poor, and some were meant to serve the needs of working-class children specifically.

The principles that guided Adler are put forth in *Creed and Deed* (1877), *The Ethics of the Political Situation* (1884), *The Moral Instruction of Children* (1892), *Essentials of Spirituality* (1905), *Religion of Duty* (1905), *What the Ethical Culture School Stands For* (1910), *Life and Destiny* (1913), *Marriage and Divorce* (1915), *The World Crisis and Its Meaning* (1915), *An Ethical Philosophy of Life* (1921), *Reconstruction of the Spiritual Ideal* (1922), and *Incompatibility in Marriage and other Addresses* (1930).

In 1888 Adler helped organize a society for the scientific study of children, a group that became the Child Study Association in 1907. He served as chairman of the National Child Labor Committee (1904–21). His major academic post was at Columbia University where he held a chair in social and political ethics created especially for him. He held the post at Columbia from 1902 until his death in 1933.

REFERENCES: *DAB* (supp. 1); *EB; NCAB* (23:98); *WWW* (I); *NYT,* April 26, 1933, p. 15; Adolph Klein, "Felix Adler's Contribution to Experimental Education" (diss., New York University, 1935).   *B. Edward McClellan*

AGASSIZ, Elizabeth Cabot Cary. B. December 5, 1822, Boston, Massachusetts, to Thomas Graves and Mary (Perkins) Cary. M. April 25, 1850, to Louis Agassiz. Ch. none. D. June 27, 1901, Arlington Heights, Massachusetts.

Elizabeth Cabot Cary Agassiz was not sent to school because of her health; she was trained by a governess and received a classical education in study at home in a well-to-do section of Boston. Through her sister, the wife of a Harvard professor of Greek, she met and married the Swiss naturalist Louis Agassiz (*q.v.*), whose first wife had recently died of tuberculosis.

Although fifteen years Louis Agassiz's junior, Elizabeth Agassiz proved to be a stabilizing partner in the marriage. She cared for the three children of Agassiz's first marriage, guarded his health, took over management of his correspondence and debt-ridden finances, and attended nearly all of his lectures, taking notes that served as the backbone for many of his publications.

She founded a select school for girls in their large home (1854). Her husband was a teacher in the school, which continued until 1863. Agassiz served as recorder for her husband's expedition to Brazil in 1865, around

Cape Horn in 1871, and for the Hassler expedition through the Strait of Magellan (1871–72). She assisted Louis Agassiz in planning and managing the Anderson School of Natural History on Penikese Island, Buzzard's Bay, Massachusetts (1873).

After Louis Agassiz's death on December 14, 1873, she became active in the establishment of the Harvard Annex. The Annex opened in 1879, was incorporated as The Society for the Collegiate Institution of Women in 1882, with Elizabeth Agassiz as president, and was named Radcliffe College in 1894. Agassiz became honorary president in 1899.

Elizabeth Agassiz was the author of *A First Lesson in Natural History* (1859), coauthor of *A Journey to Brazil* (with Louis Agassiz, 1868), and *Seaside Studies in Natural History* (with Alexander Agassiz, 1865). She edited the *Life and Correspondence of Louis Agassiz* (two volumes, 1885).

REFERENCES: *AC; DAB; NAW; NCAB* (12:46); *WWW* (I); Lucy Allen Paton, *Elizabeth Cary Agassiz* (Boston: Houghton Mifflin, 1919).

Nancy Bredemeier

AGASSIZ, Jean Louis Rodolphe. B. May 28, 1807, Motier, Switzerland, to Rodolphe and Rose (Mayor) Agassiz. M. to Cecilé Braun. M. April 25, 1850, to Elizabeth Cabot Cary. Ch. three, including Alexander Emmanuel Rodolphe Agassiz, a naturalist. D. December 14, 1873, Cambridge, Massachusetts.

Louis Agassiz decided to become a naturalist at the age of fifteen. Recognized as gifted by his teachers, he attended the academy at Lausanne and universities at Zurich, Heidelberg, and Munich instead of being apprenticed in commerce. In May 1829 he earned a doctorate in natural history at Munich, publishing in the same month an outstanding monograph, *Brazilian Fishes*. In this work, he described collections made by Johann Baptist von Spix during an Amazon expedition between 1817 and 1820. A year later, in 1830, Agassiz took a medical degree at Munich to please his family.

Already considered a remarkable icthyologist and paleontologist, Agassiz determined to write a definitive work on European fossil fishes. Traveling to Paris, he became a protégé of Georges Cuvier and Alexander Humboldt, the leading naturalists of the time. Agassiz took a position as a professor of natural history in a new school established in Neuchâtel, Switzerland, home of his parents. He made field studies the focus of his teaching. He directed a museum that had been constructed to house his specimens and started one of Europe's finest lithographic shops to print his many works, including the *Poissons fossiles* volumes that brought him fame as one of Europe's outstanding naturalists while he was still in his thirties.

With a grant from the king of Prussia, obtained through the offices of

Humboldt, Agassiz traveled to the United States in September 1846. His Lowell Institute lectures in the winter of 1846–47 set the pattern for a decade of lectures that brought the wealth with which to pay off debts accumulated at Neuchâtel and to continue his work. Settling in Boston, he accepted an appointment at Harvard University with the establishment of the Lawrence Scientific School in 1847. He was founder and first curator of the Harvard Museum of Comparative Zoology. He revolutionized the teaching of natural science in the United States.

In 1855 his second wife, Elizabeth Cabot Cary Agassiz (*q.v.*), and the two daughters of his first wife established a school for young ladies in their home. Agassiz taught natural history in this school, which for eight years generated the income he needed for his work.

Agassiz helped to establish both the American Association for the Advancement of Science (1847) and the National Academy of Sciences (1863), serving as president of the AAAS (1851-52). He lectured before these groups and in cities throughout the East, South, and Midwest and studied fish, ecology, and glacial remains throughout this area. He published *Principles of Zoology* (with Auguste A. Gould, 1848), *Lake Superior* (1850), a scientific report of an expedition he led in the summer of 1848, and *Contributions to the Natural History of the United States* (1857-62) in three volumes and a fourth unfinished, as well as popular articles about later expeditions to South America in the *Atlantic Monthly*. Agassiz was accorded the highest scientific honors by England, France, Brazil, and the United States.

REFERENCES: *AC; DAB; EB; NCAB* (2:360); *NYT,* December 15, 1873, p. 1; *TC; WWW* (H); Elizabeth Cary Agassiz, ed., *Louis Agassiz, His Life and Correspondence,* 2 vols. (Boston: Houghton Mifflin, 1885); Edward Lurie, *Louis Agassiz, A Life in Science* (Chicago: University of Chicago Press, 1960); Jules Marcou, *Life, Letters and Works of Louis Agassiz,* 2 vols. (New York: Macmillan, 1895); Lane Cooper, *Louis Agassiz as a Teacher* (Ithaca, N.Y.: Comstock, 1917, rev. ed., 1945).

Russell C. Oakes

AGNEW, David Hayes. B. November 24, 1818, Lancaster County, Pennsylvania, to Robert and n.a. (Henderson) Agnew. M. November 21, 1841, to Margaret Irwin. Ch. none. D. March 22, 1892, Philadelphia, Pennsylvania.

D. Hayes Agnew was educated at Moscow College, Pennsylvania, and Jefferson College at Canonsburg, Pennsylvania, finishing with a year at Delaware College (later, University of Delaware) in Newark, Delaware. After studying with his father, Agnew was graduated from the medical department of the University of Pennsylvania (1838).

Agnew practiced medicine at Noblesville, Pennsylvania (1838–43), and joined his brother-in-law in operating an iron foundry (1843). The business failed in 1846, and Agnew returned to practice in Lancaster and Chester counties.

Determined to pursue his interest in anatomy and surgery, he moved to Philadelphia, where he bought and reestablished the Philadelphia School of Anatomy (1852–62). For as many as eighteen hours a day, he lectured and demonstrated at times to more than two hundred and fifty students from the University of Pennsylvania, Jefferson Medical College, and from out of the state. He acquired a reputation for his teaching and organized the Philadelphia School of Operative Surgery (1863). He was elected a surgeon to the Philadelphia Hospital (1854), the Wills Eye Hospital (1863), and the Orthopedic Hospital (1867) and taught clinical surgery at Philadelphia Hospital. He taught at the University of Pennsylvania (1864–89) and was professor of surgery from 1871.

During the Civil War, Agnew was affiliated with army hospitals as surgeon-in-charge of Hestonville Hospital and consulting surgeon for Mower General Hospital, the largest in the country. He was the chief consultant in the case of President James A. Garfield when he was shot in 1881. He was president of the Philadelphia College of Physicians (1889).

Agnew's sixty-six published titles include *Practical Anatomy: A New Arrangement of the London Dissector* (1856), *Anatomy in Its Relations to Medicine and Surgery* (1859–64), *Clinical Reports* (1859–71), and his great work, *Treatise on the Principles and Practice of Surgery* (three volumes, 1878, 1881, and 1883).

REFERENCES: *AC; DAB; NCAB* (8:203); *TC; WWW* (H).

M. Jane Dowd

AHERN, Mary Eileen. B. October 1, 1860, Marion County, Indiana, to William and Mary (O'Neill) Ahern. M. no. D. May 22, 1938, near Atlanta, Georgia.

In 1870 her Irish immigrant parents left the farm for Spencer, Indiana, where Mary Eileen Ahern finished high school in 1878. After graduation from Central Normal College in Danville, Indiana (1881), she taught in Bloomfield, Spencer, and Peru, Indiana.

Ahern became assistant state librarian of Indiana in 1889. After she cataloged the state library virtually unassisted, the legislature appointed her state librarian in 1893. Ruling out her own reelection, Ahern waged a successful campaign to have her position removed from politics and placed under the state board of education. She organized the Indiana Library Association in 1891.

Ahern left the state library to enter Armour Institute of Technology (later, Illinois Institute of Technology) in Chicago, Illinois, in 1895. On graduation in 1896, she became editor of *Public Libraries* (later *Libraries*), continuing until her sight failed and publication was discontinued in December 1931 when the publishers announced, "It is our opinion that

Libraries without its present editor is impossible.'' Thirty-six volumes of *Libraries* were edited by Ahern. Using the periodical as a teaching instrument, she disseminated advice, information, and technical instruction, encouraged young librarians, and emphasized the importance of business-like administration. She was a major force in the development of standards for library training.

A life member of the American Library Association, she served as publicity agent with the United States military in France from January to July 1919. In 1927 she returned to France and England to study their library structures and administrations. Ahern was an organizer and secretary of the library department of the National Educational Association (1896–1907) and was influential in developing cooperation between schools and libraries. She was a fellow of the American Library Institute.

REFERENCES: *NAW; NCAB* (A:538); *WWW* (I); *NYT*, May 25, 1938, p. 23; *Library Journal* 63 (June 1, 1938):455.   *M. Jane Dowd*

AINSWORTH, Dorothy Sears. B. March 8, 1894, Moline, Illinois, to Harry and Stella (Davidson) Ainsworth. M. no. D. December 2, 1976, Moline, Illinois.

Dorothy Sears Ainsworth received her early instruction in the public schools of Moline, Illinois, earned the A.B. degree from Smith College in Northampton, Massachusetts (1916), and A.M. (1925) and Ph.D. (1930) degrees from Columbia University. She also studied at the Neils Bush School of Gymnastics in Denmark, the Bode School in Germany, and the Duncan School of Dance in Austria.

Ainsworth began teaching physical education at Moline High School (1916–18); she instructed in the hygiene and physical education department at Smith College (1921–23) and at Skidmore College (1925–26). In the fall of 1926 she became associate professor and director of physical education at Smith. In 1937 she became full professor and held both positions until her retirement in 1960 as professor emeritus.

Devoting herself to physical education, Ainsworth devised a number of approaches at Smith that were later used in schools. She liberated physical education from the narrow concept of gymnastic instruction to a selection of many offerings. An advocate of intramural programs, she established tournaments geared to all levels of ability, developed a dance program within the framework of the physical education department, and systematized student participation in coaching and teaching duties.

She lectured throughout the United States and traveled as both a delegate to conferences and consultant in Europe, Asia, Central and South America, Australia, and New Zealand. She chaired the United States Joint Council on International Affairs in Health, Physical Education and Recreation from 1951 to 1958. Ainsworth was a consultant in international affairs for the American Association for Health, Physical Education and Recreation.

Ainsworth wrote *The History of Physical Education in Twelve Colleges For Women* (1930) and *Basic Rhythms* (with Ruth Evans, 1955). She served as editor of *Individual Sports for Women* (with others, 1955). She received numerous awards for her contributions to education in the United States and abroad: the Gold Medal of the Ling Society, Sweden (1949), the Gold Medal of Honor from the ministry of education of the French Republic (1953), the Gulick Award (1960), the Cross of Honor of Finland (1961), the Hetherington Award of the American Academy of Physical Education (1962), the Women of Conscience Award of the National Council of Women (1968), and, for her efforts in behalf of the physical education of the women of Japan, the Fourth Class of the Order of the Precious Crown (1970).

REFERENCES: *LE* (III); *NCAB* (L:300); *NYT,* December 4, 1976, p. 28; *WW* (XXXVIII). *Kathryn D. Lizzul*

ALBERTY, Harold Bernard. B. October 6, 1890, Lockport, New York, to Willard and Carrie L. (Post) Alberty. M. August 24, 1916, to Anna Hower. M. December 11, 1954, to Elsie June Stalzer. Ch. two. D. February 2, 1971, Columbus, Ohio.

After graduating from Baldwin University (later, Baldwin-Wallace College) in Berea, Ohio, with the Ph.B. degree (1912), Harold Bernard Alberty entered Cleveland Law School and was awarded the LL.B. degree (1913). After a year of teaching experience, he became deeply interested in education and for the next sixteen years served as teacher, principal, and superintendent in the public schools of Medina and Cuyahoga counties, and Berea, Ohio. He received A.M. (1924) and Ph.D. (1926) degrees from Ohio State University.

After completing his doctorate, Alberty was appointed an assistant professor at Ohio State in 1927 and was promoted to professor in 1932. Although accepting many special assignments during his career, he remained at Ohio State until his retirement on September 1, 1959, when he was named professor emeritus.

Alberty published widely; a bibliography of his writing contains more than a hundred titles. His first book, *Supervision in the Secondary School* (with V. T. Thayer, 1931), denied the prevailing mode of scientism in supervision in favor of a democratic supervision for teacher growth and student guidance. This book set the stage for the modern concept of supervision, directed to teacher growth in service. Alberty was an enthusiastic advocate of the core curriculum.

Alberty served as coeditor with Boyd H. Bode (*q.v.*) and contributor to the second yearbook of the John Dewey Society, *Educational Freedom and Democracy* (1938). He was particularly well known for his classic *Reorganizing the High-School Curriculum* (1947). This book followed years of teaching and writing in the field of secondary curriculum, together with a wealth of practical experience in curriculum experimentation involving all schools of the Eight-Year Study (1932–40). On December 18, 1970, he received the Ohio State University Centennial Achievement Award and in 1971 the John Dewey Society Award for distinguished service to education.

REFERENCES: *LE* (III); *WWAE* (XXII); *WWW* (V); "Resolution in Memoriam," Board of Trustees, The Ohio State University, March 5, 1971.   *Orin B. Graff*

ALCOTT, Amos Bronson. B. November 29, 1799, near Wolcott, Connecticut, to Joseph Chatfield and Anna (Bronson) Alcox. M. May 23, 1830, to Abigail May. Ch. three, including Louisa May Alcott, author. D. March 4, 1888, Concord, Massachusetts.

Amos Bronson Alcott attended a local school near his Wolcott, Connecticut, home until 1813, when he moved in with an uncle in Cheshire, Connecticut. He served as an errand boy and attended the district school. From 1818 to 1823, he toured the South as a peddler.

Returning to New England, he taught school in Connecticut in Bristol, Wolcott, and Cheshire (1823–28) and in Boston, Massachusetts (1828–30), and Germantown, Pennsylvania (1831–33). Alcott's schools were unusual for the times because he discarded textbooks in favor of instruction by conversations with his pupils. He introduced play, gymnastics, and libraries in his schools. He used the honor system and limited use of corporal punishment; discipline matters were referred to the class.

In 1834 Alcott opened a school in Boston in the Masonic Temple, assisted by Elizabeth Palmer Peabody (*q.v.*) and Margaret Fuller. Even more radical than previous schools, the Boston school emphasized education in morals, instructed through the conversational technique. His educational practices were publicized in *The Record of a School, Exemplifying the General Principles of Spiritual Culture* (1835) edited by Elizabeth Peabody and *Conversations with Children on the Gospels* (volume one, 1836, and volume two, 1837). Reaction to the books and enrollment of a black girl in the school aroused criticism by the press and the withdrawal of youngsters from the school by parents. The school closed in 1839.

Alcott moved to Concord, Massachusetts, in 1840. In 1842 he was in England, where he became interested in mysticism and the collective ideas of Henry Wright and Charles Lane, with whom he established the Fruitlands community near Harvard, Massachusetts (1844–45). Until the writings of his daughter Louisa May Alcott realized financial returns in 1868, the Alcotts lived off his lecture income and the sewing and teaching of his wife and daughters.

Alcott served as appointed superintendent of schools for Concord from 1859. He introduced singing, calisthenics, and physiology into the Concord schools and organized a parent-teacher association. He organized the Concord Summer School of Philosophy and Literature in 1879 and conducted it in his home until illness forced his retirement in 1882.

Alcott was the author of several books, including *Observations on the Principles of Infant Instruction* (1830), *The House I Live In* (1834), called the first physiology text for children, *The Doctrine and Discipline of Human Culture* (1836), *Tablets* (1868), *Concord Days* (1872), *Table Talk* (1877), *New Connecticut* (1881), *Sonnets and Canyonets* (1882), and *Ralph Waldo Emerson* (1882).

REFERENCES: *AC; DAB; NCAB* (2:218); *TC; WWW* (H); *NYT,* March 5, 1888, p. 5; Dorothy McCuskey, *Bronson Alcott, Teacher* (New York: Macmillan, 1940). *Thomas L. Bernard*

ALCOTT, William Andrus. B. August 6, 1798, Wolcott, Connecticut, to Obed and Anna (Andrus) Alcox. M. 1836 to Phebe Bronson. Ch. two. D. March 29, 1859, Auburndale, Massachusetts.

William Andrus (Alcox) Alcott, also known as William Alexander Alcott, was brought up on his father's farm and attended the district school with his cousin A. Bronson Alcott *(q.v.),* who later joined him in changing the spelling of the family name. He taught school in Connecticut for four years; at the age of twenty-two he left with his cousin to teach school in the Carolinas. Unsuccessful in their attempts to find employment, they returned home the following year. At this point in his life, his serious devotion to education began to manifest itself. When not in the classroom, he spent most of his time instructing children and their parents in their own homes.

In 1824–25 Alcott was head of the Central School in Bristol, Connecticut, and also studied medicine to gain an understanding of physiology and the laws of healthful living to improve his effectiveness as a teacher in the classroom. He received his diploma to practice medicine and surgery from Yale Medical School in 1826. Later he joined W. C. Woodbridge *(q.v.)* in establishing a Fellenberg school near Hartford and eventually went to Boston to assist Woodbridge in editing the *Annals of Education* and the *Juvenile Rambles,* the first weekly periodical for children published in the United States.

An advocate of school reform, he replaced crude school benches with seats and inaugurated a system of ventilation in the classroom. His enthusiasm for teaching is exemplified in his book *Confessions of a Schoolmaster* (1839). He was an editor of *Parley's Magazine* and a voluminous writer on medical, health education and other educational topics and published more than a hundred books and pamphlets. He was the first author to write a health book that was suitable for use by children. Among the most noteworthy of his publications were *Essay on the Construction of Schoolhouses* (1832), *Lectures for the Fireside* (1852), *The Home Book of Life and Health* (1856), and *Forty Years in the Wilderness of Pills and Powders* (1859).

Due to his foresight and concern with the health of children, Alcott has been called the Father of Health Education. His contributions were influential when school health education was emerging as a course of study. His writings and lectures aided in the progress of educational reform throughout the country.

REFERENCES: *AC; DAB; NCAB* (12:59); *TC; WWW* (H); S. Kunitz and H. Haycraft, eds., *American Authors: 1600–1900* (New York: The H. W. Wilson Co., 1938); R. Means, *A History of Health Education in the United States* (Philadelphia: Lea & Febiger, 1962), *NYT,* March 31, 1859, p. 4.

Donald B. Stone

ALDEN, Joseph. B. January 4, 1807, Cairo, New York, to Eliab and Mary (Hathaway) Alden. M. 1834 to Isabella Livingston. M. June 30, 1882, to Amelia Daly. Ch. one. D. August 30, 1885, New York, New York.

Joseph Alden gained recognition as teacher, administrator, and author. Alden's teaching career started as a fourteen-year-old district school-teacher; he rapidly advanced and became a professor at Williams College in Williamstown, Massachusetts, at the age of twenty-eight. After graduating from Union College in Schenectady, New York (1829), he was a student at Princeton Theological Seminary for two years. He was ordained as pastor of the Congregational church in Williamstown, Massachusetts (1834), but resigned to accept a professorship at Williams in 1835, where he remained for seventeen years, first as professor of Latin and then of English language and literature, political economy, and history. In 1852 he accepted the chair of mental and moral philosophy at Lafayette College in Easton, Pennsylvania.

From Lafayette Alden moved in 1857 to his first administrative position as president of Jefferson College in Canonsburg, Pennsylvania. In 1867 he became principal of the state normal school in Albany, New York, closing his career with this position.

Alden wrote more than seventy volumes, including works on philosophy, religion, government, and language. Among his writings were: *The Jewish Washington, or Lessons in Patriotism and Piety Suggested by the History of Nehemiah* (1846), *Anecdotes of the Puritans* (1849), *Christian Ethics* (1866), *Elements of Intellectual Philosophy* (1866), *Science of Government* (1866), *Introduction to the Use of the English Language* (1875), *First Principles of Political Economy* (1879), *Self-Education: What to Do and How to Do It* (1880). A frequent contributor to periodical literature, he served as editor of the *New York Observer* and the Philadelphia *Christian Library*.

REFERENCES: *AC; DAB; NCAB* (5:406); *TC; WWW* (H).

Ruth Ledbetter Galaz

ALDERMAN, Edwin Anderson. B. May 15, 1861, Wilmington, North Carolina, to James and Susan Jane (Corbett) Alderman. M. December 29, 1885, to Emma Graves. M. February 10, 1904, to Bessie Green Hearn. Ch. four. D. April 29, 1931, Connellsville, Pennsylvania.

Edwin Anderson Alderman attended private schools in Wilmington, North Carolina, and spent two years at Bethel Military Academy in Bethel Academy, Virginia, before enrolling at the University of North Carolina in 1878. At North Carolina he won the prestigious Mangum Medal for oratory and received the Ph. B. degree with honors in English and Latin (1882).

Following graduation, Alderman began teaching in the graded schools of Goldsboro, North Carolina, and three years later became superintendent of schools. In 1889 he joined forces with a college classmate, Charles D. McIver (*q.v.*), and the two began conducting teachers' institutes throughout North Carolina as agents of the state board of education. For more than three years they stumped the state instructing teachers in improved pedagogical methods and fostering citizen support of public education. The campaign Alderman and McIver launched prepared the way for the educational revival that bore fruit a decade later under the administration of another classmate, Governor Charles B. Aycock (*q.v.*).

In 1891 Alderman and McIver played a leading role in drafting the law that led to the creation of the Normal and Industrial School for Women (later, University of North Carolina at Greensboro) in Greensboro. In 1892, with McIver as president and Alderman as the "leading professor," the institute opened with two hundred students.

In 1893 Alderman assumed the post of professor of the history and philosophy of education at the University of North Carolina and in 1896 was elected president. During his administration existing departments were strengthened, new departments of pharmacy and education were created, and an extension school was inaugurated. Alderman served as the president of Tulane University from 1900 until 1904.

In 1904 he was elected first president of the University of Virginia; since its founding Virginia had been administered by the faculty via a rotating chairmanship under the direction of the board of visitors. Until his death in 1931, Alderman labored successfully to further the university's academic standing while at the same time making it more responsive to the needs of the commonwealth. Alderman sought to unify the state's system of public education and to make the university the capstone of the educational system and an institution designed to serve society.

Alderman received numerous honors, including honorary doctorates from many universities. He was a member of several scholarly societies as well as a member of the General Education Board, trustee of the Woodrow

Wilson Foundation, and director of the Thomas Jefferson Memorial Foundation. In addition to many articles and speeches, Alderman was editor-in-chief of the *Library of Southern Literature* (1907) and coauthor with Armistead Churchill Gordon of *J. L. M. Curry; A Biography* (1911). Praised as an orator and acknowledged as a leading educational statesman, Alderman is best remembered for his pioneering role as an advocate of the expansion of educational opportunity in the South.

REFERENCES: *DAB* (supp. 1); *NCAB* (23:38); *TC; WWW* (I); Philip Alexander Bruce, *History of the University of Virginia, 1819–1919* (New York: Macmillan, 1922), vol. 5; Dumas Malone, *Edwin A. Alderman: A Biography* (New York: Doubleday, 1940); *NYT,* April 19, 1929, p. 24, April 30, 1931, p. 26.   *Jennings L. Wagoner, Jr.*

ALEXANDER, Hartley Burr. B. April 9, 1873, Lincoln, Nebraska, to George Sherman and Abigail Gifford (Smith) Alexander. M. July 15, 1908, to Nell King Griggs. Ch. two. D. July 27, 1939, Claremont, California.

Hartley Burr Alexander was graduated with the A.B. degree (1897) from the University of Nebraska and served there for a year as instructor in English. He received a Harrison Fellowship and studied at the University of Pennsylvania (1898–1900) and at Columbia University, where he received the Ph.D. degree (1901).

Alexander moved to Boston, unsuccessfully sought a career as a writer, and served as office editor and contributor to the *New International Encyclopedia* (1903) and editor and contributor to Webster's dictionaries in Springfield, Massachusetts.

He was invited to the University of Nebraska, where he was professor of philosophy (1908–27). He became a well-known lecturer and wrote poetry and wrote and produced pageants and a light opera. He was a contributor to scholarly publications in philosophy and became an expert in the life, mythology, and arts of the American Indian. He moved to Claremont, California, as professor of philosophy and head of the department at Scripps College. He served there to his death in 1939, also lecturing at the University of Southern California in Los Angeles. He was influential at Scripps in curricular reform and setting standards of scholarship.

Alexander was author of many books, including *The Problem of Metaphysics* (1902), *Pilgrim Alden* (published anonymously, 1903), *Poetry and the Individual* (1906), *Mid-Earth Life* (1907), *Odes on the Generation of Man* (1910), *The Religious Spirit of the American Indian* (1910), *The Mystery of Life* (1913), *Liberty and Democracy* (1918), *Letters to Teachers* (1919), *Odes and Lyrics* (1922), *Nature and Human Nature* (1923), *Manito Masks* (1925), *God's Drum* (1927), *Truth and the Faith* (1929), *Pueblo Indian Painting* (1931), and volume 10, *North American* (1916), and volume 11, *Latin American* (1920), of *Mythology of All Races*. He designed

the decorative scheme for the Nebraska capitol building and other buildings across the country.

Alexander was an honorary member of the American Institute of Archi-
tects and a member of many organizations, including president of the
American Philosophical Association (1919), Western Philosophical Asso-
ciation (1917), and first president of the Southwestern Archaeological
Federation (1928–29). He was awarded the Butler Medal by Columbia
University (1917).

REFERENCES: *DAB* (supp. 2); *NCAB* (46:538, A: 174); *WWW* (I); *NYT,*
July 28, 1939, p. 17.   *John F. Ohles*

ALISON, Francis. B. 1705, County Donegal, Ireland, to n.a.. M. to Hannah
Armitage. Ch. six. D. November 28, 1779, Philadelphia, Pennsylvania.

Francis Alison was educated in Ireland and at the University of Glasgow,
Scotland. He came to America in 1735, settling first in Talbot County,
Maryland, and then at New London, Pennsylvania.

Alison was a tutor in the home of Samuel Dickinson while he was in
Maryland. In 1737 he was ordained by the New Castle presbytery and for
fifteen years was pastor of a church in New London. Recognizing the need
for educational facilities in the area, he opened the New London Academy
in 1743, which was officially recognized and subsidized by the Synod of
Philadelphia a year later. When his school moved to Newark, Delaware, it
became the Newark Academy, which later became the foundation of the
University of Delaware.

Alison's fame as an educator spread, and in 1752 he accepted the position
of headmaster of the Philadelphia (Pennsylvania) Academy. The granting
of degrees to qualified students was approved, and on March 7, 1755,
Alison was chosen vice-provost of this new college in Philadelphia. While
vice-provost of the college and teacher of logic, metaphysics, geography,
and other arts and sciences, he continued to serve as assistant pastor of the
First Presbyterian Church of Philadelphia. Yale and Princeton colleges
granted him the A.M. degree in 1755 and the University of Glasgow the
D.D. degree (1758).

Alison was one of the best classical scholars of his day in this country,
especially in Greek, and he had an unusual fund of learning and knowledge
of history, ethics, and general literature.

REFERENCES: *DAB; NCAB* (1:346); *WWW (H).*   *C. Roy Rylander*

ALLEN, Arch Turner. B. January 10, 1875, Hiddenite, North Carolina, to
George James and Mary (Campbell) Allen. M. June 19, 1909, to Claribel
McDowell. Ch. two. D. October 20, 1934, Raleigh, North Carolina.

Arch Turner Allen was a student at Morganton (North Carolina) Academy (1892) and Voshti Academy (1893). He was graduated from the Uni-

versity of North Carolina with the Ph.B. degree (1897). He studied at the University of North Carolina, the University of Tennessee, and Columbia University.

Allen served North Carolina public schools as a principal in Statesville (1897–1904), Washington (1904–05), and Dilworth (1905–07). He was superintendent of schools in Graham (1907–10) and Salisbury (1910–17).

He became associated with the North Carolina State Department of Education (1917) and was secretary of the state board of examiners (1919–21) and director of teacher training (1921–23). He was appointed superintendent of public instruction for the state of North Carolina in 1923, serving to his death in 1934. During his administration great progress was made in improving public education in the state. The school year was lengthened to eight months; increased state contributions from indirect sources of revenue took the place of local support.

He served as president of the North Carolina City Superintendents' Association (1915) and the North Carolina Teachers' Assembly (1917 and secretary, 1919–22). He was a member of a number of honorary and professional organizations and coauthored *State Centralization in North Caroline* (1932). He was awarded honorary degrees by Elon College (1924) and the University of North Carolina (1927).

REFERENCES: *LE* (I); *NCAB* (26:294); *WWAE* (I); *WWW* (I).

S. S. Britt, Jr.

ALLEN, Charles Ricketson. B. August 6, 1862, New Bedford, Massachusetts, to John and Abbie (Chaddock) Allen. M. June 28, 1889, to Lissa H. Hall. Ch. none. D. July 6, 1938, San Antonio, Texas.

Charles Ricketson Allen received the B.S. degree from Massachusetts Institute of Technology in 1885. He studied at Johns Hopkins University (1893) and at Harvard University, where he received the M.A. degree in 1903.

He taught high school and was in charge of vocational education for New Bedford, Massachusetts (1906–09). He was agent for industrial training under the state board of education in Massachusetts (1911–17). He helped develop a plan for vocational education in connection with the public schools that served as a model for study and for action by other states.

Allen worked with the Emergency Fleet Corporation (1917–18). During World War I he served as a member of the training staff of the United States Shipping Board and planned a course of instructor training that was highly acclaimed by vocational educators.

Allen was director of training for the Niagara Falls, New York, Chamber of Commerce (1920–21) and director of training services at Dunwoody Institute in Minneapolis, Minnesota (1922–24). He was a staff member of the Federal Board for Vocational Education in Washington, D.C., from

1918 to 1919 and from 1924 until his retirement, where he served as an editor and educational consultant for vocational education. After retirement, he was active at St. Mary's University in San Antonio, Texas (1937–38).

Allen was the author of *Laboratory Manual of Physics* (1890), *The Instructor, the Man, and the Job* (1919), *The Foreman and His Job* (1921), *The Supervision of Vocational Education* (with J. C. Wright, *q.v.*, 1926), *The Administration of Vocational Education* (1927), *Efficiency in Education* (1928), *Efficiency in Vocational Education* (1929), *Vocational Education in a Democracy* (with C. A. Prosser, *q.v.*, 1929), and *Managing Minds* (1932).

He was a member of professional associations. Allen received an honorary degree from Stout Institute, Menomonie, Wisconsin, in 1927.

REFERENCES: *LE* (I); *WWW* (II); Charles A. Bennett (*q.v.*), *History of Manual and Industrial Education, 1870–1917* (Peoria, Ill.: Manual Arts Press, 1936); Melvin L. Barlow, *History of Industrial Education in the United States* (Peoria, Ill.: Charles A. Bennett Co., 1967); *Industrial Arts and Vocational Education* 27 (September 1938):314; *Occupations* 17 (October 1938):70; *School Life* 24 (October 1938):2.   *Ralph Dirksen*
J. K. Ward

ALLEN, Edward Ellis. B. August 1, 1861, West Newton, Massachusetts, to James Theodore and Caroline Augusta (Kittredge) Allen. M. July 9, 1891, to Katharine Francena Gibbs. Ch. three. D. April 14, 1950, Plainfield, New Jersey.

Edward Ellis Allen received his schooling at the English and classical school run by his uncle, Nathaniel T. Allen *(q.v.)* in West Newton, Massachusetts, and in German schools in Leipzig, Germany, and in Zurich, Switzerland. He was graduated from Harvard College in 1884 and entered Harvard Medical School but discontinued his studies after one year.

Allen taught at the Royal Normal College for the Blind (London, England) from 1885 to 1888 under Francis J. Campbell, a blind American who had taught at the Perkins Institution for the Blind in South Boston. Allen returned to America as head teacher at the Perkins Institution (1880–90) and then accepted the position of principal of the Pennsylvania Institution for the Instruction of the Blind in Philadelphia. He remained at that post until 1907 when he returned as director of the Perkins Institution and Massachusetts School for the Blind, relocating it in Watertown, Massachusetts. Allen was credited with rebuilding both the Philadelphia and Perkins institutions.

He conducted a survey in 1909 of European institutions for the blind and persuaded the Boston School Committee in 1913 to include a class for the semisighted in its public schools, a plan followed by other American and

Canadian cities. He pioneered in employing a resident psychologist and a vocational guide and home visitor at Perkins and by introducing field sports and athletics for the blind. He was an early supporter of the use of braille. At his suggestion, Harvard University gave the first college extension course of lectures on the education of the blind (1920–21). The course was given regular standing at the Harvard Graduate School of Education in 1924, with Allen as the lecturer. He sponsored scientific research into the psychology of blindness and attempted to raise the teaching of the blind to a professional level.

Allen wrote many papers and was a member of many professional organizations, holding offices in several of them. He served three terms on the Massachusetts Commission for the Blind. In 1931 he was forced to retire as director of the institute. He continued to write and engage in professional activities until his death.

REFERENCES: *DAB* (supp. 4); *LE* (I); *NCAB* (A:129); *WWAE* (VIII); *WWW* (III); *NYT,* April 15, 1950, p. 15.   *John W. Schifani*

ALLEN, James Edward, Jr. B. April 25, 1911, Elkins, West Virginia, to James Edward and Susan (Garrott) Allen. M. April 23, 1938, to Florence Pell Miller. Ch. two. D. October 17, 1971, Peach Springs, Arizona.

Allen was the son of James E. Allen, president of Davis and Elkins College in Elkins, West Virginia. He was educated in the public schools of Elkins and was graduated from Davis and Elkins in 1932. His father advised him not to go into education "because there is no future in it." He was a salesman for a brief time but the economic conditions of the times made a career in education more attractive. He became a member of the professional staff of the West Virginia State Department of Education, specializing in research and finance, a job he held until 1939.

He began graduate study in economics and public finance at Princeton University in 1939 and moved to Harvard University for further graduate study in education, earning M.A. (1942) and D.Ed. (1945) degrees.

Allen's professional career was marked by a steady rise to positions of ever greater scope and influence. During World War II he was an operations analyst for the United States Army Air Corps (1944–45). He returned from service to teach at Syracuse University (1945–47). He became executive assistant to the New York commissioner of education in 1947, deputy commissioner in 1950, and commissioner in 1955, a post he held for seventeen years.

Allen's tenure in New York was marked by the rapid growth in size of the educational system. He was offered the job of United States Commissioner of Education by President John F. Kennedy but refused it; he was appointed to the position in 1969 by President Richard M. Nixon.

Allen initiated the Right to Read program, was a strong advocate of vocational and technical education, and favored a large financial role for the federal government in public education. His most controversial stand was on the issue of school desegregation. He differed with Nixon on this issue, believing that the federal government must exercise strong leadership to see that all forms of segregation are ended. He was asked to resign from his post when he criticized the Cambodian invasion of May 1970.

Allen became visiting lecturer at the Woodrow Wilson School of Public and International Affairs at Princeton. He and his wife were killed in a plane crash in Arizona while sightseeing in the vicinity of the Grand Canyon. He was awarded seventeen honorary degrees from colleges and universities in the United States.

REFERENCES: *CB* (June 1969 and December 1971); *LE* (III); *WWW* (V); Matthew F. Doherty, "Dr. Allen: A Study in Greatness," *New York State Education* 56 (March 1969): 14–15; "An Interview with James E. Allen," *Harvard Educational Review* 40 (November 1970): 533–46; "An Interview with James E. Allen, Jr.," *Phi Delta Kappan* 50 (April 1969): 468–73; *NYT,* September 16, 1968, p. 52, October 18, 1971, pp. 1, 40; "The Tragic Deaths of Dr. and Mrs. James E. Allen, Jr.," *School and Society* 100 (February 1972): 80. *David E. Koontz*

ALLEN, Nathaniel Topliffe. B. September 29, 1823, Medfield, Massachusetts, to Ellis and Lucy (Lane) Allen. M. March 30, 1853, to Caroline Swift Bassett. Ch. four. D. August 1, 1903, Linekin, Maine.

Nathaniel Topliffe Allen was educated in the local district schools while he worked on the family farm. He went to Northboro, Massachusetts, to attend a private school conducted by an uncle, Joseph Allen. He attended an academy at Northfield, the normal school at Bridgewater, Massachusetts, and the Rensselaer Polytechnic School in Troy, New York.

He taught school in Mansfield, Massachusetts, in 1842 and had also taught at the Cedar Swamp School at Northboro. In 1848 he was in charge of the model school at the West Newton (Massachusetts) Normal School. When the normal school moved to Framingham in 1853, Allen bought the West Newton property and established the West Newton English and Classical School, which became an outstanding private college preparatory school.

In West Newton Allen had been associated with Horace Mann *(q.v.)* and Cyrus Peirce *(q.v.)* who encouraged him in establishing the school. Allen is credited with starting in his school one of the first kindergartens in the United States and one of the first gymnasiums at a private school.

From 1869 to 1871, he traveled in Europe as an agent of the United States Commissioner of Education and studied European school systems, making a report to the Bureau of Education. Allen was active in the anti-slavery movement and maintained a station in the underground railroad in his home. He was a vice-president of the Massachusetts Peace Society.

REFERENCES: *NCAB* (20:212); Joseph Allen, *Geneological Sketches of the Allen Family of Medfield* (Boston: Nichols and Noyes, 1869).

John F. Ohles

ALLPORT, Gordon Willard. B. November 11, 1897, Montezuma, Indiana, to John Edwards and Nellie Edith (Wise) Allport. M. June 30, 1925, to Ada Lufkin Gould. Ch. one. D. October 9, 1967, Cambridge, Massachusetts.

Gordon W. Allport, pioneer in personality theory and prejudice, was educated in the public schools of Cleveland, Ohio. He was graduated with the A.B. (1919), A.M. (1921), and Ph.D. (1922) degrees from Harvard University. He studied at the universities of Berlin and Hamburg, Germany (1922–23), and at Cambridge (England) University (1923–24) on a Sheldon Traveling Fellowship.

Allport returned to Harvard as an instructor of social ethics (1924–26) and was a teacher of psychology at Dartmouth College in Hanover, New Hampshire (1926–30). He returned to Harvard in 1930 and served as chairman of the department of psychology (1937–46).

Allport was the author of several important books in psychology; the most significant was *The Nature of Prejudice* (1954). His other books include *Studies in Expressive Movement* (with Philip E. Vernon, 1933), *The Psychology of Radio* (with Hadley Cantril, 1935), *Personality—A Psychological Interpretation* (1937), *The Use of Personal Documents in Psychological Science* (1942), *The Psychology of Rumor* (with Leo J. Postman, 1947), *The Individual and His Religion* (1950), *The Nature of Personality* (1950), *Becoming* (1955), *Personality and Social Encounter* (1960), *Pattern and Growth of Personality* (1961), and *Letters from Jenny* (1965). He was editor of the *Journal of Abnormal and Social Psychology* (1937–49).

Allport was a member of American and foreign professional and scientific organizations and was president of the American Psychological Association (1937), the Eastern Psychological Association (1943), and the Society for the Psychological Study of Social Issues (1944). He was a member of the emergency committee on psychology of the National Research Council during World War II, on the advisory committee of the Massachusetts Commission Against Discrimination, a founding member and secretary of the Ella Lyman Cabot Trust, and a member of the national commission for UNESCO. He received the Gold Medal Award from the American Psychological Foundation (1963) and was the recipient of three honorary degrees from American colleges and universities and from Durham University in England.

REFERENCES: *CA* (1–4); *CB* (September 1960); *EB; NCAB* (J:417); *WWW* (V); *NYT,* October 10, 1967, p. 47.   *John F. Ohles*

ALLYN, Harriet May. B. May 4, 1883, New London, Connecticut, to Charles and Helen Louisa (Starr) Allyn. M. no. D. July 7, 1957, Los Angeles, California.

Harriet May Allyn was graduated from Mount Holyoke College in South Hadley, Massachusetts, with the A.B. degree (1905). She received the M.S. (1910) and Ph.D. (1912) degrees from the University of Chicago.

She taught zoology at Lake Erie College in Painesville, Ohio (1908–09), and Vassar College in Poughkeepsie, New York (1912–13 and 1924–29). She was on the faculty of Hackett Medical College in Canton, China (1913–23), serving as dean from 1915 to 1923. She was at Monticello Seminary in Godfrey, Illinois (1923–24). Allyn returned to Mount Holyoke in 1929 where she was academic dean and professor of anthropology until her retirement in 1948.

Allyn contributed articles to scientific and professional journals. She was president of the National Association of Deans of Women and the Council of Guidance and Personnel Associations and held offices in a number of regional educational organizations. She participated in archeological expeditions in the field under the auspices of Yale University, the British School of Archeology, the Czechoslovakian Archeological Survey, and the Budapest Museum. In 1936 Allyn received a United States State Department appointment as a delegate to the Oslo, Norway, meeting of the International Congress of Prehistoric and Protohistoric Sciences.

REFERENCES: *LE* (III); *WWW* (III); *Directory of American Scholars*, 2d ed. (New York: R. R. Bowker, 1951); *NYT*, July 9, 1957, p. 27.

Genevieve R. Meyer

ALLYN, Robert. B. January 25, 1817, Ledyard, Connecticut, to Charles and Lois (Gallup) Allyn. M. November 18, 1841, to Emeline Denison. M. June 22, 1845, to Mary Budington. Ch. five. D. January 7, 1894, Carbondale, Illinois.

Robert Allyn was educated in the local district schools before entering Wesleyan University in Middletown, Connecticut, in 1837 where he was an outstanding student of mathematics and languages. Upon graduation (1841), he taught at the Wesleyan Academy of Wilbraham, Massachusetts.

Allyn entered the Methodist ministry in 1842 and accepted his first ministerial station at Colchester, Connecticut, in 1843. The remainder of his life was devoted to school and church. In 1846 Allyn was elected principal of the Wesleyan Academy, and in 1848 he became principal of the Providence Conference Seminary at East Greenwich, Rhode Island. While in Rhode Island, he was twice elected to the state legislature as a prohibition and abolition candidate. He was state commissioner of education (1854–57). During this time he founded and edited the *Rhode Island*

Schoolmaster, which continued after his service until 1875 when it merged into the *New England Journal of Education.*

In 1857 Allyn became a professor of ancient languages at Ohio University at Athens. In 1859 he became principal of the Wesleyan Female Academy at Cincinnati where he was also a member of the city board of education. He was president of McKendree College at Lebanon, Illinois (1863–74). While at McKendree, he was active in Illinois educational affairs and campaigned for a teachers' college for the southern part of the state. When the Southern Illinois State Normal University was built at Carbondale, Illinois, he accepted its first presidency (1874) and continued as president until 1892.

REFERENCES: *DAB; WWW* (H); Newton Bateman *(q.v.)* and Paul Selby, eds., *Historical Encyclopedia of Illinois* (Chicago: Munsell Publishing Co., 1917), pp. 15–16; John Williston Cook *(q.v.), Educational History of Illinois* (Chicago: Henry O. Shepard Co., 1912), pp. 235–37; Eli G. Lentz, *Seventy-Five Years in Retrospect: Southern Illinois University, 1874– 1949* (Carbondale, Ill.: Southern Illinois University, 1955).

William E. Eaton

ALMACK, John Conrad. B. October 15, 1883, Texas County, Missouri, to John Cullison and Amanda (Purcell) Almack. M. November 25, 1905, to Alice Ethel Jaeger. M. October 14, 1937, to Evelyn Miriam Foster. Ch. two. D. October 5, 1953, Palo Alto, California.

John Conrad Almack taught in the Rockford, Washington, public schools (1905–15) and was mayor of Rockford (1909–10). He was the editor of a weekly newspaper, *The Commoner,* of Colfax, Washington, from 1915 to 1916. Almack received B.A. (1918) and M.A. (1921) degrees from the University of Oregon. While a student at Oregon, he worked as an English instructor and as acting director of the university's extension division. In 1923 Stanford University conferred on him the Ph.D. degree.

From 1922 to 1949 Almack was a professor of education at Stanford University. He became a respected authority on school administration, hygiene, and teacher education. He wrote or coauthored many books, including *History of Oregon Normal Schools* (1918), *Education for Citizenship* (1924), *The Beginning Teacher* (1928), *History of the United States* (with E. D. Adams, 1930), *Modern School Administration* (1933), *A Clear Case Against Narcotics* (1939), *Social Living* (with Evelyn M. Almack, 1941), and *American Health Series* (with C. W. Wilson et al., 1942).

After retiring from Stanford, he was active in Republican politics.
REFERENCES: *LE* (III); *NCAB* (42:346); *WWW* (III).

Nancy Baldrige Julian

ALVORD, Henry Elijah. B. March 11, 1844, Greenfield, Massachusetts, to Daniel Wells and Caroline (Clapp) Alvord. M. September 6, 1866, to Martha Scott Swink. Ch. none. D. October 1, 1904, St. Louis, Missouri.

Henry Elijah Alvord was a student at Norwich (Vermont) University, where he received the B.S. degree (1863). During the Civil War, he enlisted in his junior year and served as a volunteer cavalryman in Massachusetts and Rhode Island until the end of the war. He continued in the army for six years, during which he became interested in the cattle industry. Alvord became the first army officer to be detailed as a military instructor at a land-grant college, Massachusetts Agricultural College (later, University of Massachusetts) (1869–71). In 1871 he moved to his wife's family estate in Virginia, known as Spring Hill Farm, where he engaged in dairying and raising Jersey cows.

Beginning with experimental work in New York (1880–86), Alvord performed a succession of educational services to agriculture, including professor of agriculture, Massachusetts Agricultural College (1886–87), president, Maryland Agricultural College (later, University of Maryland) (1887–93), president, Oklahoma Agricultural and Mechanical College (later, Oklahoma State University) (1894), and professor of agriculture, New Hampshire Agricultural College (later, University of New Hampshire). In recognition of his services to agricultural colleges, Alvord was elected president of the American Association of Agricultural Colleges and Experiment Stations (1894–95). When a dairy division was created within the Bureau of Animal Industry of the United States Department of Agriculture in 1895, Alvord was appointed its chief and held that position until his death.

Alvord gained a reputation as an authority on animal husbandry and dairying through his writing and public addresses. In 1881 he authored the American chapters published in Sheldon's *Dairy Farming*. Included among his other publications are *The Dairy Herd: Its Formation and Management* (1884), *Dairy Developments in the United States* (1899), *Dairying at Home and Abroad* (1902), and *The Milk Supply of Two Hundred Cities and Towns* (with R. A. Pearson, 1903).

REFERENCES:*AC; DAB; NCAB* (22:184); *TC; WWW* (I).

Larry E. Miller

AMES, James Barr. B. June 22, 1846; Boston, Massachusetts, to Samuel Tarbell and Mary Hartwell (Barr) Ames. M. June 29, 1880, to Sarah Russell. Ch. two. D. January 8, 1910, Wilton, New Hampshire.

James Barr Ames was educated in Boston, Massachusetts, at the Brimmer School and Boston Latin School; he entered Harvard College in 1863. Ill health in his sophomore year delayed his graduation until 1868. He received the LL.B. degree (1872) from Harvard Law School.

He taught for a year in the private school of E. S. Didwell in Boston (1868–69) and spent a year traveling in Europe (1869–70). On his return to Boston, he was a tutor in French and German in Harvard College (1871–72). He received an appointment to teach law in 1873 and was appointed Bussey Professor (1879) and became Dane Professor of Law (1903). For many years he assisted C. C. Langdell *(q.v.)* and in 1895 succeeded him as dean of the Harvard Law School, serving until a few months before his death in 1910.

Introduced to the case method of studying law by Langdell, Ames adopted the idea, and it became accepted as the most scientific method of instruction. His primary influence was as a teacher and a legal scholar. He compiled collections of various kinds of cases that were published as law textbooks for Harvard Law School. He founded the *Harvard Law Review* in 1887.

He was active in professional groups and served as chairman of the section of legal education of the American Bar Association (1904); he was an influential member of the National Commission of Uniformity of Legislation. Ames received honorary degrees from a number of American colleges and universities.

REFERENCES: *DAB; NCAB* (18:141); *TC; WWW* (I); *NYT,* January 9, 1910, p. 9.   *Joseph P. Cangemi*
                                                Thomas E. Kesler

ANAGNOS, Michael. B. November 7, 1837, Papingo, Epirus, Greece, to Demetrios and Kallina Anagnostopoulos. M. December 1870 to Julia Romana Howe. Ch. none. D. June 29, 1906, Near East, on a trip.

Born in a Greek province under Turkish control, Michael Anagnos (born Michael Anagnostopoulos) spent four years studying the classics and philosophy at the University of Athens. After graduation, he studied law four years before beginning a career in journalism. As a newspaper editor, he fought for human rights and liberty. His opposition to King Otho's government resulted in his imprisonment. After Otho's overthrow, King George came to power, and Anagnostopoulos again took an active part in political journalism.

In 1867 he first encountered Samuel G. Howe *(q.v.)* of Boston, Massachusetts; their relationship developed into a lifelong friendship. Howe was instrumental in bringing Anagnos (as he came to be known in the United States) to Massachusetts to assume a position as Howe's chief assistant at the Perkins Institution and Massachusetts School for the Blind. Upon Howe's death, Anagnos became director of the institute. He established a permanent printing fund for supplying the blind with raised-print books, a massive collection of teaching aids for the school, a library about blindness, and kindergarten programs for the blind.

Anagnos compiled annual reports that were significant contributions to the field of education because they discussed self-help skills, vocational training, and other important issues on the education of the blind. He authored *Education of the Blind* (1882), *Through Education to Independence* (1900) and several books for youth in raised print.

Despite his commitment to the blind, he never forgot his dedication to his homeland. He served as president of an American organization of Greeks and was responsible for the establishment and continued financial support of schools in the mountain village where he was born and reared.

REFERENCES: *DAB; NCAB* (13:257); *NYT,* July 6, 1906, p. 7.

Ann Candler

ANDERSON, Archibald Watson. B. September 21, 1905, Hammond, New Jersey, to Archibald Watson and Annie Mary (Meyers) Anderson. M. September 2, 1931, to Grace M. Bigler. Ch. one. D. July 1, 1965, Champaign, Illinois.

Archibald Watson Anderson attended public schools in Hammond, New Jersey, and Easton, Pennsylvania, and was graduated from Columbia University with the B.S. (1932) and A.M. (1933) degrees; he received the Ph.D. degree (1938) from the Ohio State University.

He taught in a rural school in Northampton, Pennsylvania (1927–28), and was an elementary school principal in Bangor, Pennsylvania (1928–30). He taught in a Madison, New Jersey, high school (1931–34). He was a graduate assistant at Ohio State University (1934–36) and assistant director of the school units project in the United States Office of Education (1936–38). He returned to Ohio State as an instructor and assistant professor of education (1938–40). In 1940 Anderson went to the University of Illinois, where he stayed to his death in 1965.

Anderson was the author of *Local School Units Organization* (with others, 1938), *Adventures in Reconstruction of Education* (with others, 1941), *Social Aspects of Education* (with others, 1948), *The Theoretical Foundations of Education* (with others, 1951), *The American Elementary School* (with others, 1953), *The Social Foundations of Education* (1956), and *The Education of the Negro in American Democracy* (1959). He was editor of *Readings in the Social Aspects of Education* (with others, 1951) and *Educational Freedom in an Age of Anxiety* (with H. G. Hullfish, *q.v.,* 1953). He edited the yearbook series of the John Dewey Society and was founder and first editor of *Educational Theory* (1951–65), associate editor (1947–50) and editor (1950–54) of *Progressive Education,* associate editor of *History of Education Journal* (1949–61), and associate editor (1947–53) and editor (1953–57) of *Educational Administration and Supervision.*

A member of many professional associations, Anderson was the recipient of a distinguished service award from the John Dewey Society in 1965.

REFERENCES: *LE* (III); *NCAB* (51:151); *WWW* (IV). *John F. Ohles*

ANDERSON, John Jacob. B. September 30, 1821, New York, New York, to n.a. M. August 3, 1848, to Elizabeth B. Baldwin. Ch. n.a. D. March 14, 1906, Brooklyn, New York.

John Jacob Anderson received his education at New York City public schools and at Rutgers College in New Brunswick, New Jersey. In 1845 he was appointed principal of one of the large public schools of New York City, a position he held for more than twenty years. He was also in charge of the evening schools in the city. He was a frequent lecturer to educational groups.

Anderson wrote a series of school histories. His first volume, *Introductory School History of the United States,* was not written for publication but was copied by one pupil after another in his class. In this book, he pioneered in associating narrative history with geography. He was the first to insert in his books sectional maps covering every part of the story and to recommend that these be reproduced on blackboards, slates, and paper by the pupils.

His publications include *A Practical System of Modern Geography* (1851), *Exercises in the Fundamental Rules of Arithmetic* (1854), *A School History of the United States* (1860), *New Manual of General History* (1861), *A Pictorial School History of the United States* (1864), *An Introductory School History of the United States* (1865), *A Common School History of the United States Arranged on the Catechetical Plan* (1868), *A Grammar School History of the United States* (1868), *A Manual of General History* (1869), *A School History of England* (1870), *The Historical Reader* (1871), *The United States Reader* (1872), *A Junior Class History of the United States* (1874), *A School History of France* (1878), *A Popular School History of the United States* (1879), *A Short Course of English History* (1879), *A Complete Course in History* (1881), *History: How to Teach It* (1884), *New Grammar School History of the United States* (1887), and *A Short History of the State of New York* (1901).

Anderson was awarded a medal for his books exhibited at the International Exposition in Paris in 1875, the only award for school histories conferred by the exhibition. The University of the City of New York granted him the Ph.D. degree in 1876.

REFERENCES: *AC; TC; WWW* (I); *Who's Who in American History,* vol. 1 (Chicago: Marquis, 1968).   *Michael R. Cioffi*

ANDERSON, Martin Brewer. B. February 12, 1815, Brunswick, Maine, to Martin and Jane (Brewer) Anderson. M. January 1848 to Elizabeth M. Gilbert. Ch. none. D. February 22, 1890, Lake Helen, Florida.

Martin Brewer Anderson was educated in Maine at Waterville (later, Colby) College. In 1840 he entered Newton Theological Institute in Massachusetts. After a year he returned to Waterville as an instructor in Greek, Latin, and mathematics, and, later, he was professor of rhetoric. He left this position in 1850 to become editor of *The New York Recorder,* a denominational weekly that debated the issues of the day.

Anderson was appointed the first president of the University of Rochester (New York) in 1853, where he proved his new idea of a practical education to be a success. He was one of the first men to advocate a practical, liberal college education with topics ranging from art to transportation and to the relations of ethics to jurisprudence. He favored use of both the scientific and historical methods of investigation in education.

Because of loyalty to Rochester, Anderson rejected opportunities for presidencies of Brown University, Union College, and other institutions. Until he retired in 1888, Anderson was active in the New York State Board of Charities, and the American Baptist Missionary Union (president), and he was an associate editor of *Johnson's Cyclopedia.* Among honors he received were honorary doctor of laws degrees from Waterville College and the Regents of the University of the State of New York.

REFERENCES: *AC; DAB; NCAB* (12:243); *WWW* (H); *NYT,* February 27, 1890, p. 4; *The University of Rochester: The First Hundred Years 1850–1950* (Rochester, N.Y.: Rochester Centennial Committee, 1950). *Anne M. Condon*

ANDERSON, William Gilbert. B. September 9, 1860, St. Joseph, Michigan, to Edward and Harriet (Shumway) Anderson. M. March 16, 1881, to Grace Lee Phillips. M. September 15, 1927, to Effie Adelaide Hammond. M. July 2, 1930, to Alice Wheeler Hawley. Ch. one. D. July 7, 1947, New Haven, Connecticut.

William Anderson, in his later years known as the Grand Old Man of Physical Education, learned the value of regular physical exercise from his father. He studied at Amherst (Massachusetts) College and the University of Wisconsin, leaving Wisconsin after his sophomore year to teach in Clayton, Illinois. In 1881, he was appointed superintendent of the Young Men's Christian Association in Cleveland, Ohio, and began part-time study at Cleveland Medical College. He received the M.D. degree in 1883 and immediately went into practice in Columbus, Ohio.

By 1884 his interest had turned toward physical education as a profession, and he accepted the position as director of the gymnasium at Adelphi Academy in Brooklyn, New York. While there, in 1885, he called the meeting to organize the American Association for the Advancement of Physical Education (later, the American Association for Health, Physical Education, and Recreation). In 1886 he established the Brooklyn (New York) Normal School for Physical Education.

He accepted the position of associate director of the Yale University gymnasium in 1892, becoming the director in 1894, and moved his normal school to New Haven, Connecticut, where it was renamed the Anderson Normal School of Gymnastics. This school subsequently became Arnold College and a part of the University of Bridgeport, Connecticut.

Anderson was the director of physical education at Yale from 1894 to 1930. While there he organized the College Physical Education Association (1897) and served as one of its first presidents.

Anderson made many contributions to the field of physical education. The acceptance of physical education as a legitimate academic discipline in U.S. colleges and universities was partially the result of his efforts. He made important contributions in counseling, teacher education, experimentation and research, and the administration of physical education.

He was granted several awards and honorary degrees; in 1949 the AAHPER established the William G. Anderson Award given to individuals outside the association who have contributed significantly to the fields of health, physical education and recreation. He authored numerous articles and books; among them *Light Gymnastics* (1889), *Methods of Teaching Gymnastics* (1896), *The Making of a Perfect Man* (1901), and *Manual of Physical Training* (1914).

REFERENCES: *LE* (II); *NCAB* (36:325); *WWW* (II); Ellen W. Gerber, *Innovators and Institutions in Physical Education* (Philadelphia: Lea & Febiger, 1971); *NYT,* July 10, 1947, p. 21; Harold Lloyd Ray, "The Life and Professional Contributions of William Gilbert Anderson, M.D." (Ph.D. diss. The Ohio State University, 1959); M. C. Brown and J. Beiderhase, "William G. Anderson," *Journal of Health, Physical Education, and Recreation* 31 (April 1960): 34.   *William J. Sullivan*

ANDREWS, Charles McLean. B. February 22, 1863, Wethersfield, Connecticut, to William Watson and Elizabeth Byrne (Williams) Andrews. M. June 19, 1895, to Evangeline Holcombe. Ch. two. D. September 9, 1943, New Haven, Connecticut.

Charles McLean Andrews received his early education in the high school in Hartford, Connecticut, and at Trinity College, where he was graduated with A.B. (1884) and A.M. (1890) degrees. He was principal of the high school at West Hartford, Connecticut (1884–86). Entering Johns Hopkins University, he was a scholar in history and fellow in history. He received the Ph.D. degree in 1889.

Andrews was an associate professor and later a full professor of history at Bryn Mawr (Pennsylvania) College (1889–1907). He was a professor of history at Johns Hopkins (1907–10) and Farnam Professor of History at Yale University (1910–31). From 1931 to 1933, he was director of historical publications at Yale and, after 1933, professor emeritus.

Andrews is best remembered for his 1935 Pulitzer Prize–winning *Colonial Period of American History,* the first of four volumes. He was a leader in colonial historiography, placing the emphasis on the American colonies as dependent parts of the British system so that the center of the colonial story belonged in Great Britain, an interpretation that influenced his widely accepted books and those of historians he trained. His other popular works were *Colonial Self-Government, 1625–1689,* volume 5 of *The American Nation: A History* (1904), and *The Colonial Period* (1912).

Other historical publications include *The River Towns of Connecticut* (1889), *The Old English Manor* (1892), *The Historical Development of Modern Europe* (two volumes, 1896), *Contemporary Europe, Asia and Africa, 1897–1901* (1902); *A History of England* (1903), *A Short History of England* (1912), *The Boston Merchants and the Non-Importation Movement* (1917), *Fathers of New England, and Colonial Folkways* (1919), and *The Colonial Background of the American Revolution* (1924).

Andrews served as editor of the Yale Historical Publications (1912–33). He was an associate fellow at Davenport College, Yale, lecturer at the University of Helsingfors, Finland, in October 1911, and visiting faculty member at several American institutions. He was a member of the American Historical Association and chairman of several committees, member of the executive council (1905–08), acting president (1924), and president (1925). He was also a member of many other historical and scholarly societies.

REFERENCES: *DAB* (supp. 3); *EB*; *LE* (II); *NCAB* (13:160); *WWAE* (XI); *WWW* (II); *NYT,* September 11, 1943, p. 13.   *Lawrence S. Master*

ANDREWS, Elisha Benjamin. B. January 10, 1844, Hinsdale, New Hampshire, to Erastus and Almira (Bartlett) Andrews. M. November 25, 1870, to Ella Anna Allen. Ch. two. D. October 30, 1917, Interlachen, Florida.

E. Benjamin Andrews attended a small school near Sunderland, Massachusetts. He enrolled in Connecticut Literary Institute in September 1860, only to leave the following May when he enlisted in the Union Army. He served in the Civil War and was discharged with the rank of second lieutenant. He was wounded in the siege of Petersburg, Virginia, and lost the sight of one eye.

After studying at Power's Institute and the Wesleyan Academy upon his discharge, he entered Brown University in Providence, Rhode Island, from which he received a baccalaureate degree in 1870. He was principal of the Connecticut Literary Institute in Suffield (1870–72). He attended the Newton (Massachusetts) Theological Seminary (1872–74) and completed the A.M. degree at Brown (1873). Upon his ordination, he served for one year as pastor of the First Baptist Church of Beverly, Massachusetts.

Andrews accepted the presidency of Denison University in Granville,

Ohio, in 1875. Four years later he returned to Newton to serve for three years as a professor of homiletics. He became a professor of political economy and history at Brown in 1882 but spent the first year of his appointment in Germany studying at the universities of Berlin and Munich. In 1888 he left Brown to serve one year as professor of political economy and public finance at Cornell University in Ithaca, New York, but returned the following year to serve as Brown's president until 1898. He became superintendent of the Chicago public schools (1898–1900) and was chancellor of the University of Nebraska from 1900 to 1908, when he retired because of ill health. Under Andrews's leadership both Brown and Nebraska universities grew in enrollment and faculty and improved in program quality.

Among Andrews's publications were *Institutes of Our Constitutional History* (1884), *Institutes of Economics, Wealth and Moral Law* (1894), *History of the United States* (two volumes, 1894, 1902), *An Honest Dollar: a Plea for Bimetallism* (1894), and *History of the United States during the Last Quarter Century* (two volumes, 1896).

Andrews was active in educational organizations. He served as president of the Nebraska State Teachers Association (1907–08) and was a member of the Rhode Island Historical Society. He was awarded honorary degrees by several universities.

REFERENCES: *DAB; NCAB* (8:26); *TC; WWW* (I); James E. Hansen II, "Gallant, Stalwart Bennie: Elisha Benjamin Andrews (1844-1917), An Educator's Odyssey" (Ph.D. diss., University of Denver, 1969); *NYT,* October 31, 1917, p. 13.   *Erwin H. Goldenstein*

ANDREWS, Eliza Frances. B. August 10, 1840, Haywood, Georgia, to Garnett and Annulet (Ball) Andrews. M. no. D. January 21, 1931, Rome, Georgia.

Eliza Frances "Fanny" Andrews was the daughter of a lawyer and judge who helped his children learn to love books and learning. The Andrews family resided on an imposing estate in Haywood (near Washington), Georgia.

She attended the Female Seminary for Girls and LaGrange (Georgia) Female College, from which she received the A.B. degree in 1857. Later she was awarded an honorary A.M. degree from Wesleyan College in Macon, Georgia (1882). From 1885 to 1897 she was a professor at Wesleyan.

During the Civil War, Fanny Andrews and her younger sister were sent to a plantation near Albany, Georgia, for added safety. Their active and gay social life turned to bitterness when the Confederacy lost the war. Andrews was said to have vowed to remain single and seek a career to ease the misery of disappointment. When her father died in 1873, poor investments brought about the loss of the Haywood estate, adding to her bitterness.

Andrews taught in the public schools of Washington, Georgia, and Yazoo City, Mississippi. She engaged in a writing career, using the pseudonym Elzey Hay. Among her books were *A Family Secret* (1876), *A Mere Adventure* (1878), *Prince Hal or the Romance of a Rich Man* (1882), and her most famous work, *The Wartime Journal of a Georgia Girl* (1908). She wrote serials for some newspapers: "How He Was Tempted" *(Boston Free Press)* and "The Story of an Ugly Girl; The Mistake of His Life" *(Chautauquan)*. Her lectures "The Novel as a Work of Art," "Jack and Jill," and "The Ugly Girl" attracted wide attention.

She was interested in botany and wrote two books that gained wide attention: *Botany All the Year Around* (1903) and *A Practical Course in Botany* (1911), which was translated into French and used in schools in France. In 1926 her work in botany was recognized by the International Academy of Science in Italy; Andrews was invited to Naples to address the academy, but she was eighty-six and declined the invitation.

Andrews bequeathed the royalties from her botany textbooks to the city of Rome, Georgia, to provide a public woodland where children could learn about the environment.

REFERENCES: *NCAB* (6:504); *NAW; WWW* (I); Eliza Francis Andrews, *Wartime Journal of a Georgia Girl: 1864–65* (New York: Appleton and Co., 1908); Spencer King, Jr., *Georgia Voices: A Documentary History to 1872* (Athens, Georgia: University of Georgia Press, 1966), pp. 295-97.

Ernest D. Riggsby

ANDREWS, Ethan Allen. B. April 7, 1797, New Britain, Connecticut, to n.a. M. 1815 to Lucy Cowles. Ch. ten. D. March 4, 1858, New Britain, Connecticut.

Ethan Allen Andrews attended Yale College, where he was graduated in 1810. He studied law, was admitted to the bar, and engaged in the practice of law for several years.

In 1822 Andrews went to the University of North Carolina where he was professor of ancient languages until 1828. He taught ancient languages at an academy in New Haven, Connecticut (1828), and founded an academy for girls there (1829). He went to Boston in 1833 to become principal of the Mount Vernon School for Girls and returned to New Britain, Connecticut, to engage in writing in 1839.

Andrews was best known as the author of Latin textbooks, which went through many editions. Among them were *Grammar of the Latin Language* (1836), *First Lessons in Latin* (1837), *Latin Exercises* (1837), *A First Latin Book* (1846), *A Copious and Critical English-Latin Lexicon* (1850), *A Synopsis of Latin Grammar* (1851), *Exercises in Latin Etymology* (1855), *Manual of Latin Grammar* (1859), and *Harper's Latin Dictionary,* based upon the *Wörterbuch der Lateinischen Sprache* by Wilhelm Freund and first published in 1871 after his death. While in Boston he edited the *Religious Magazine.*

Andrews was a probate court judge in Connecticut for several years and served in the Connecticut state legislature (1851).

REFERENCES: *A C; NCAB* (13:416).   *Frederik F. Ohles*

ANDREWS, Jane. B. December 1, 1833, Newburyport, Massachusetts, to John and Mary Demmon (Rand) Andrews. M. no. D. July 15, 1887, Newburyport, Massachusetts.

Jane Andrews received her preparatory training at Putnam Free School at Newburyport, Massachusetts, where she also participated in a small writing group directed by Thomas Wentworth Higginson, author and pastor of the Unitarian church. Her teaching career began in the winter of 1850–51, when she instructed cotton mill workers at an evening school organized by Higginson.

In the spring of 1851 Andrews entered the State Normal School (later, Framingham State College) at West Newton, Massachusetts, from which she was graduated as valedictorian two years later. There she was influenced by Lucretia Crocker *(q.v.)* with whom she lived. She frequently visited the Peabody home where she met Elizabeth's brother-in-law, Horace Mann *(q.v.),* who encouraged her to continue her education at Antioch College (Yellow Springs, Ohio) when he became its first president. A neurological disorder forced her to discontinue her studies within the year to return to Newburyport where she remained an invalid for six years.

By 1860 Andrews's health had improved sufficiently for her to begin a small primary school in her home. Instruction was based on direct experiences available to the children who learned about nature through firsthand observation, political events by studying local institutions, and geography by searching out information about the sources of imports at Newburyport harbor. Experiments, plays, games, and stories complemented this emphasis on active student involvement in learning. In 1885 recurrence of health problems forced her to close the school.

A major writer of children's literature, Andrews's books included *Seven Little Sisters Who Live on the Round Ball that Floats in the Air* (1861), a collection of seven stories of seven little girls who live in seven unusual places. A later book, *Ten Boys Who Lived on the Road from Long Ago to Now* (1866), followed the same approach in exploring historical periods. Other publications included *Each and All* (1887), *Geographical Plays for Young Folks at Home and School* (1888), and *The Child's Health Primer* (1885). Her writings were collected and published under three titles: *Only a Year and What It Brought* (1888), *The Stories Mother Nature Told Her Children* (1889), and *The Stories of My Son's Friends* (1900). Andrews's books continued to be popular a century after her death; *Seven Little Sisters* alone sold nearly five hundred thousand copies and was translated into German, Japanese, and Chinese.

REFERENCES: *NAW;* M. F. Altstetter, "Jane Andrews: Pioneer in Internationalism," *Elementary English Review* 13 (May 1936):165–166.

Joanne B. Lyon

ANDREWS, Lorin. B. April 1, 1819, Ashland, Ohio, to Alanson and Sally (Needham) Andrews. M. October 30, 1843, to Sarah Gates. Ch. three. D. September 18, 1861, Gambier, Ohio.

Recognized as a promising orator in an Independence Day speech at the age of seventeen, Lorin Andrews's short life of forty-two years included two school principalships, admission to the bar, participation in the founding of a state teachers' association, a college presidency, and service in the Civil War.

In 1841 Andrews became principal of the Ashland (Ohio) Academy. Six years later he helped found the Ohio State Teachers' Association and was appointed chairman of its executive committee. Concurrently he was admitted to the bar and championed the cause for free public education for all. In 1848 he became superintendent of the Massillon (Ohio) schools. Three years later he resigned his position to work toward securing the adoption of the School Law of 1853, which called for the election of a state school commissioner.

Andrews was elected president of Kenyon College in Gambier, Ohio, in 1854. The first layman of the Episcopal church to become a college president, he boosted the enrollment at Kenyon from thirty to two hundred students and solicited increased endowments for the college. The years of his presidency also included an active oratorical campaign to secure funds to purchase Mount Vernon as a national shrine. He was awarded an honorary degree by Princeton University.

In 1861 Andrews answered Abraham Lincoln's call for volunteers. Enlisting as a colonel, he formed a company. In the summer of 1861, he was stricken with camp fever; he was returned to his home in Gambier, Ohio, where he died. He was buried at Kenyon College.

REFERENCES: *DAB; NCAB* (7:6); 1938 scrapbook compiled at Lorin Andrews Junior High School, Massillon, Ohio.   *Elaine F. McNally*

ANDREWS, Lorrin. B. April 29, 1795, East Windsor, Connecticut, to Samuel and Triphena (Loomis) Andrews. M. August 16, 1827, to Mary Wilson. Ch. seven. D. September 29, 1868, Honolulu, Hawaii.

Lorrin Andrews received the B.A. degree from Jefferson College in Canonsburg, Pennsylvania, and entered Princeton (New Jersey) Theological Seminary where he completed the course for theological studies in 1825. On November 3, 1827, Andrews and his wife were among sixteen missionaries who sailed from Boston on the *Parthian* for the Hawaiian Islands. They reached the port of Honolulu on March 30, 1828, and Andrews was assigned to the station at Lahaina on the western shore of Maui.

Andrews's work as an educational pioneer for Hawaii began in 1831 when he accepted the principalship of the new school opened at Lahaina. The school, a combination of a seminary and a teachers' college, prepared native Hawaiians for teaching and the ministry. This modest educational beginning, which opened with an enrollment of twenty-five native students, became the University of Hawaii. In a short time Andrews introduced technical training courses, such as printing, to the school and in 1834 published Hawaii's first newspaper. He translated the Bible into the Hawaiian language. In 1837 he became the teacher and interpreter for Hawaiian chiefs.

In 1841 Andrews resigned his commission from the mission board in protest of the board's acceptance of contributions from slaveholders. He served for a time as seaman's chaplain but in 1845 moved to Honolulu where he accepted an appointment as judge in the government court. In 1846 he served as secretary for the Privy Council. He was appointed a member of the superior court of law in 1848. Resigning from the supreme court in 1855, Andrews became a probate and divorce court judge with jurisdiction throughout the Hawaiian Islands.

Retiring in 1859 on a government pension, Andrews devoted his remaining years to his research of the language and culture of the Hawaiian people. In 1865 he published a Hawaiian dictionary of seventeen thousand words. He also authored a Hawaiian grammar and studies of Hawaiian songs.

REFERENCES: *AC; DAB; NCAB* (9:209); *WWW* (H). *Thomas Meighan*

ANGELL, James Burrill. B. January 7, 1829, Scituate, Rhode Island, to Andrew Aldrich and Amy (Aldrich) Angell. M. November 26, 1855, to Sarah Swope Caswell. Ch. three, including James Rowland Angell *(q.v.)*, president of Yale University. D. April 1, 1916, Ann Arbor, Michigan.

James Burrill Angell graduated at the top of his class from Brown University in Providence, Rhode Island (1849). After working at Brown for a year as an assistant librarian, he traveled in the South forming firsthand opinions on the evils of slavery, opinions he reiterated later while editor of the *Providence Journal* (1860–66). He studied in Europe (1850–53) and returned to Brown as professor of modern languages and literature from 1853 to 1860.

He served as president of the University of Vermont (1866–71) and assumed the presidency of the University of Michigan in 1871. A strong advocate for public education, he built an expanded political and financial base for Michigan's state university. During his thirty-eight-year tenure, the University of Michigan was the intellectual center of the Midwest.

Angell served as American minister to China (1880–81) and negotiated agreements regulating emigration of Chinese to the United States. He served on the Anglo-American International Commission on Canadian Fisheries (1887) and as chairman of the Canadian-American Commission on Deep Waterways from Lake to Sea (1896).

Angell was author of *Progress in International Law* (1875), *The Higher Education* (1897), *Reminiscences of James B. Angell* (1912), and *Selected Addresses* (1912).

REFERENCES: *AC; DAB; EB; NCAB* (1:251); *NYT,* April 2, 1916, p. 19; *TC; WWW* (I); James B. Angell, *Reminiscences* (New York: Longmans, Green & Co., 1912); Shirley W. Smith, *James Burrill Angell: An American Influence* (Ann Arbor, Mich.: University of Michigan Press, 1954).

Robert H. Hoexter

ANGELL, James Rowland. B. May 8, 1869, Burlington, Vermont, to James Burrill *(q.v.)* and Sara Swope (Caswell) Angell. M. December 18, 1894, to Marion Isabel Watrous. M. August 2, 1932, to Katharine Cramer Woodman. Ch. two. D. March 4, 1949, Hamden, Connecticut.

James Rowland Angell's grandfather had been president of Brown University and his father president of the universities of Vermont and Michigan. Angell earned the baccalaureate degree in 1890 at the University of Michigan where he studied under John Dewey *(q.v.)*. In 1891 he earned a master's degree in psychology at Harvard University under William James *(q.v.)* and Josiah Royce and also earned a second master's degree while he was there. He studied in Germany at the universities of Berlin and Halle; although he pursued additional study and travel in Vienna, Austria, Paris, France, and Leipzig, Germany, he never completed the doctorate. Returning to the United States in 1893, he became an instructor in philosophy at the University of Minnesota.

In 1894 Angell joined Dewey at the University of Chicago as an assistant professor of psychology and director of the psychological laboratory and became the first head of the department of psychology in 1905. He was senior dean in 1908, dean of faculties in 1911, and acting president of the university from 1918 to 1919.

Angell became president of Yale University in 1921, the first nongraduate of Yale to be invited to that position in the institution's modern history. His administration embraced a significant transitional period for Yale: the concept of residential colleges was instituted, a school of nursing and an institute of human relations were established, and the schools of medicine, law, and fine arts enjoyed a major rebirth. After retirement in 1937, he was appointed educational director and consultant for public service broadcasting at the National Broadcasting Company.

Angell's first major published work was *Psychology* (1904), the first psychology textbook after William James's *(q.v.)* to be used extensively in American colleges. He was the author of *Chapters from Modern Psychology* (1912), *Introduction to Psychology* (1913), and *American Education* (1937), a collection of articles and speeches on higher education. *War Propaganda and the Radio* was published in 1940. From 1912 to 1922 he served as editor of *Psychological Monographs,* a series of research publications.

Angell was a member of a number of professional and special interest groups, including the American Psychological Association (first president, 1908) and the English-Speaking Union (president). He was the recipient of many honorary degrees and other awards from American and foreign institutions and societies.

REFERENCES: *CB* (1940 and 1949); *DAB* (supp. 4); *EB; LE* (III); *NCAB* (E:5); *WWAE* (VIII); *WWW* (II); *NYT,* March 5, 1959, p. 17.

Robert A. Waller

ANTHON, Charles. B. November 19, 1797, New York, New York, to George Christian and Genevieve (Jadot) Anthon. M. no. D. July 29, 1867, New York, New York.

Charles Anthon was the son of a German physician, who was a surgeon of the British Army stationed at Detroit, Michigan. In 1786 the family moved to New York City, where the elder Anthon's medical practice was successful, and he was elected a trustee of Columbia College (later, University).

Anthon entered Columbia College at the age of fourteen; twice awarded the gold medal for scholarship, he was excluded from further competition for honors. After graduating in 1815, he studied law in the office of his brother John and was admitted to the bar of the Supreme Court of New York in 1819. He never practiced law because he discovered that his real interest was teaching classical literature. He was appointed adjunct professor of Greek and Latin at Columbia in 1820. In 1830 he was chosen headmaster of the grammar school of Columbia College, a position he held until his retirement in 1864. He was also named Jay Professor of Greek Language and Literature at the College.

Anthon's series of classical publications did much to make the research work of European scholars available in the United States. As the first to introduce an exegetical and critical edition of an ancient author, he probably influenced the study of classics in the United States more than any other scholar. Among his publications, acclaimed both in the United States and Europe, were an American edition of *Lamprier's Classical Dictionary* (1822), *Horatii Poemata,* accompanied by exhaustive English notes and commentary (1830), *A System of Ancient and Medieval Geography for the*

Use of Schools and Colleges (1850), and a number of textbooks and dictionaries, each of which was published in several editions.

His retirement as headmaster of the grammar school did not end Anthon's career as he continued teaching classes at Columbia College and revising his books until illness intervened. He received the honorary degree of LL.D. from Columbia in 1831.

REFERENCES: *AC: DAB; NCAB* (6:345); *TC; WWW* (H).

J. Franklin Hunt

APGAR, Ellis A. B. March 20, 1836, Peapack, New Jersey, to David and Hannah (Whitehead) Apgar. M. December 25, 1867, to Camilla Swayze. Ch. n.a. D. August 28, 1905, East Orange, New Jersey.

Ellis Apgar attended the district schools of Somerset County, New Jersey, and the State Normal School (later, Trenton State College) at Trenton, New Jersey (1854–57). He taught in the district school at Townsbury and was appointed professor of mathematics at the normal school, a position he held while he attended Rutgers College (later, University) from which he was graduated in 1866. He received a master's degree from Rutgers in 1868.

On March 28, 1866, he was elected state superintendent of public instruction in New Jersey. Under his leadership as the state's chief education officer, a law was passed providing for county superintendents and school examiners. In 1871 he promoted the landmark act for the United States that levied taxes to support free public schools in New Jersey nine months each year.

New Jersey educational progress was highlighted at the centennial exhibition of 1876 in Philadelphia where Apgar served as superintendent of the department of education in the permanent international exhibition. Apgar was credited with a system of map drawing and a set of geographical wall maps. He was the author of *Apgar's Plant Analysis* (1874) and *A Brief History of New Jersey, for School Use* (with Josiah R. Sypher, 1870).

In 1878 Apgar was nominated by Governor George B. McClellan and appointed by President Rutherford B. Hayes as United States Commissioner to the Paris Exposition. After retirement in 1885 from the state superintendency, Apgar was employed by the Westinghouse, Church, Kerr Company to introduce arc lighting to American cities. In 1890 he was appointed superintendent of schools at New Brunswick for one year.

Apgar has been called the Father of Public Schools in New Jersey.

REFERENCES: *The Biographical Encyclopedia of New Jersey of the Nineteenth Century* (Philadelphia: Galaxy Publishing Co., 1877), p. 291; William A. Shine, "Ellis Apgar: Educational Leadership in New Jersey in an Era of Social Change" (Ed. D. diss., Rutgers University, 1964).

Albert Nissman

APPLE, Thomas Gilmore. B. November 14, 1829, Easton, Pennsylvania, to Andrew and Elizabeth (Gilmore) Apple. M. August 27, 1851, to Emma Matilda Miller. Ch. eleven. D. September 17, 1898, Washington, D.C.

Thomas Gilmore Apple (sometimes Appel) was graduated from Marshall College in Mercersburg, Pennsylvania, in 1850. He studied theology and was ordained as a minister in the German Reformed church in 1852.

Apple served churches from 1852 to 1865, when he became president of Mercersburg College, occupying the physical plant of Marshall College, which had moved to Lancaster, Pennsylvania, and merged with Franklin College in 1853 as Franklin and Marshall College. He was professor of church history and New Testament exegesis in the theological seminary in Lancaster, Pennsylvania (1871–89), and in 1877 served also as professor of philosophy and president of Franklin and Marshall College.

Active in church affairs, Apple was a delegate to every meeting but one of the general synod of the German Reformed church from 1863. He served on several important church committees and was editor of the *Mercersburg Review* (later, *Reformed Church Quarterly Review*) from 1868 to his death in 1898. He was the recipient of honorary degrees from Lafayette College (1866) and Franklin and Marshall College (1868).

REFERENCES: *AC; DAB; NCAB* (12:444); *WWW* (H).   *John F. Ohles*

ARBUTHNOT, May Hill. B. August 27, 1884, Mason City, Iowa, to Frank and Mary E. (Seville) Hill. M. December 17, 1932, to Charles C. Arbuthnot. Ch. none. D. October 2, 1969, Cleveland, Ohio.

Before receiving the Bachelor of Philosophy degree from the University of Chicago in 1922, May Hill Arbuthnot taught for five years at Superior (Wisconsin) State College and for four years at the Ethical Culture School in New York City. After graduation from Chicago, she went to Cleveland, Ohio, where she became a pioneer in organizing nursery schools. She was principal and director of the Cleveland Kindergarten-Primary Teaching School, which merged with Western Reserve University in 1927. In 1924 she earned the M.A. degree from Columbia University and served for twenty years as associate professor of education in the Flora Stone Mather College at Western Reserve (later, Case Western Reserve) University.

In 1930 Arbuthnot was a member of the White House Conference on Education, the first White House conference to recognize the importance of books and reading in the lives of young children. She retired from Western Reserve in 1947, the same year her widely acclaimed children's literature college textbook, *Children and Books,* was published. After retirement she spent her time reviewing children's trade books for the Association of Childhood Education and the National Council of Teachers of English and kept her booklist, *Children's Books Too Good to Miss,* up to date.

Among her other books were *Children's Reading in the Home* (1968) and several outstanding anthologies of children's literature: *Time for Fairy Tales* (1952, revised as *Time for Old Magic,* 1970), *Time for True Tales* (1953, revised as *Time for New Magic,* 1971), *Time for Stories* (1968), *Time for Biography* (1969), and *Time for Discovery* (1971).

In 1959 she received two awards in recognition of her work as critic, teacher, and writer in the field of children's literature: the Bookwomen of America Award and the Constance Lindsay Skinner Medal, given to provide recognition and commendation to women who have made imaginative and outstanding contributions to the world of books. In 1964 the Catholic Library Association presented her with the Regina Medal in recognition of a lifetime dedicated to children's literature. The May Hill Arbuthnot Honor Lecture was established in 1969 by Scott, Foresman publishers, providing for a yearly lecture to be given by a person deemed a significant and inspiring contributor to the field of children's literature. The lectureship is administered by the Children's Services Division of the American Library Association.

REFERENCES: *LE* (III); *WWW* (V); Anne Commire, *Something About the Author* (Detroit: Gale Research, 1971). *Jane M. Bingham*

ARCHER, Gleason Leonard. B. October 29, 1880, Great Pond, Maine, to John S. and Frances M. (Williams) Archer. M. October 6, 1906, to Elizabeth G. Snyder. M. May 11, 1963, to Pauline Clark. Ch. four. D. June 28, 1966, Quincy, Massachusetts.

Gleason Leonard Archer was educated in the public schools of Great Pond, Maine, and the Sabbatus (Maine) high school, graduating in 1902. He attended Boston University (1902–04), left because of eye problems, and returned to earn the LL.B. degree in 1906.

Archer founded the Suffolk Law School in Boston in 1906, receiving a charter from the state in 1914 after a long legislative struggle. Archer served as president of the school to his retirement in 1948. Under his leadership the school established an innovative program of evening instruction in law. In 1934 the college of liberal arts was established, and the name was changed in 1937 to Suffolk University.

Archer wrote law textbooks, including *Law Office and Court Procedure* (1910), *Ethical Obligation of the Lawyer* (1910), *Law of Contracts* (1911), *Law of Agency* (1915), *Law of Torts* (1916), *Equity and Trusts* (1918), *The Law of Evidence* (1919), *Criminal Law* (1923), *Law of Private Corporations* (1928), and *History of the Law* (1928). He also wrote *The Educational Octopus* (1915), *Building a School* (1919), *History of Radio* (1938), *Big Business and Radio* (1939), *On the Cuff* (1944), and other books.

Archer was arbitrator for the state of Massachusetts in a labor dispute in 1914 and special assistant to the Massachusetts Commissioners on Uniform Laws (1926–28). He received honorary degrees from Atlantic Law School and John Marshall Law School of Chicago.

REFERENCES: *LE* (III); *NCAB* (16:289); *WWW* (IV); *Boston Advertiser,* June 4, 1961; *Boston Sunday Post,* January 4, 1953.

Joseph M. McCarthy

ARMSTRONG, Richard. B. April 13, 1805, McEwensville, Pennsylvania, to n.a. M. September 25, 1831, to Clarissa Chapman. Ch. ten, including Samuel Chapman Armstrong *(q.v.),* founder of Hampton Institute. D. September 23, 1860, Honolulu, Hawaii.

Richard Armstrong was graduated from Dickinson College in Carlisle, Pennsylvania (1827), and Princeton (New Jersey) Theological Seminary (1831).

Armstrong was a teacher and surveyor in Pennsylvania and was an ordained minister. With his bride, he arrived in the Hawaiian Islands with the fifth mission party in 1832. He was sent to the Marquesas Islands as a missionary (1833–34) and returned to Hawaii where he was assigned to Haiku (1834), Wailuku (1835), and the Kawaiahoa Church in Honolulu (1840–48).

On the death of William Richards, who had held the position of first Hawaiian minister of public instruction for less than two years, King Kamehameha III offered the post to Armstrong. He served as minister from 1848 to his death in 1860. The Father of American Education in Hawaii, Armstrong organized the Hawaiian schools and provided leadership in the enactment of laws (1848–55) providing for local organization of schools, school taxes, and establishment of land grants for use of the schools. Armstrong supervised the training of teachers and preparation of instructional materials. He promoted education of girls and provided for instruction in home economics. He authorized instruction in elementary agriculture for boys. In an effort to improve the schools, Armstrong visited the United States in 1857. His conversations with Horace Mann *(q.v.)* were said to have been reflected in the school reform acts of 1859.

Armstrong was instrumental in providing translations into Hawaiian of books for use in the schools. From 1838 to 1841, he translated Francis Wayland's *(q.v.) Moral Philosophy, Tract on Popery,* and the newspaper *Nonanona.* He assisted others in translating a mathematics textbook and worked on translations of the *Book of Joshua* and *Book of Daniel.*

REFERENCES: *Missionary Album: Portraits and Biographical Sketches of the American Protestant Missionaries to the Hawaiian Islands* (Honolulu: Hawaiian Mission Children's Society, 1969); Benjamin O. Wist *(q.v.), A Century of Public Education in Hawaii* (Honolulu: The Hawaii Educational Review, 1940).   *John F. Ohles*

ARMSTRONG, Samuel Chapman. B. January 30, 1839, Island of Maui, Hawaiian Islands, to Richard *(q.v.)* and Clarissa (Chapman) Armstrong. M. October 10, 1869, to Emma Dean Walker. M. September 10, 1890, to Mary Alice Ford. Ch. four. D. May 11, 1893, Hampton Virginia.

Samuel Chapman Armstrong, the son of a missionary family, was raised in Hawaii. After his graduation from Williams College in Williamstown, Massachusetts (1860), he served as an officer in the Civil War, attaining the rank of brigadier general. Armstrong was appointed superintendent of the Ninth District of Virginia under the Freedman's Bureau; he administered a camp of several thousand emancipated slaves at Hampton and was responsible for finding employment for them.

About this time Benjamin F. Butler established a school in Hampton for black children. Armstrong conceived the idea of replacing this school with an institution designed to provide industrial education for freedmen; he was interested in training black men and women to be teachers and leaders of their people. With the financial support of the American Missionary Association and other donated funds, Armstrong purchased a 159-acre estate in Hampton and erected several buildings for the school.

By 1868 the Hampton Normal and Agricultural Institute was formally opened under Armstrong's leadership. Terminating his work with the Freedman's Bureau in 1872, he remained principal of the institute until his death in 1893. The school operated farms and workshops where students worked in return for their tuition. Indians were admitted to the school in 1878. By the time of Armstrong's death the student enrollment had grown to a thousand, and the institute had become a source of leaders and inspiration for other schools.

Armstrong received honorary degrees from Williams College and Harvard University. He served as a trustee of Tuskegee Normal and Industrial Institute.

REFERENCES: *DAB; NCAB* (38:427); *WWW* (H); Edith (Armstrong) Talbot, *Samuel Chapman Armstrong: A Biographical Study* (New York: Doubleday, Page & Co., 1904); Suzanne C. Carson, "Samuel Chapman Armstrong: Missionary to the South" (diss., Johns Hopkins University, 1952). *Harold D. Lehman*

ARMSTRONG, Wesley Earl. B. March 18, 1899, Fulton County, Arkansas, to William Alexander and Susan Victoria (Sears) Armstrong. M. May 24, 1924, to Oleta Berniece Sawyer. Ch. two.

Wesley Earl Armstrong was an influential educator with broad and varied experiences as a public school teacher, school administrator, college professor, education dean, government official, and chief of an accrediting agency.

Armstrong earned the A.B. degree (1927) from East Central State College in Ada, Oklahoma, the M.S. degree (1931) from Oklahoma Agricultural and Mechanical College (later, State University) in Stillwater, and the Ed.D. degree (1938) from Stanford (California) University.

He was a junior high school teacher (1921–23), principal of a high school in Wilson, Oklahoma (1927–29), state high school supervisor (1930–31), principal of the Muskogee (Oklahoma) High School (1931–34), and a high school supervisor in Salt Lake City, Utah (1934–37). He was chairman of the division of teacher education at Mills College in Oakland, California (1937–40). A field coordinator for the Committee on Teacher Education of the American Council on Education (1938–43), he served as dean at Ohio Wesleyan University in Delaware, Ohio (1943–45) and at the school of education of the University of Delaware (1945–49). He was chief for teacher education of the United States Office of Education (1949–54) and director of the National Council for Accreditation of Teacher Education (1954–64).

Among his writings were *The College and Teacher Education* (with Ernest V. Hollis and Helen E. Davis, 1944) and *Manual on Certification of School Personnel in U.S.* (annually from 1951).

He was a member of several professional associations and served on various committees concerned with curriculum development, school reorganization, and teacher education.

REFERENCES: *LE* (III); *WW* (XXXIV); *Higher Education* 1 (April 1949):179. *Albert Nissman*

ARNY, Clara Maude Brown. B. June 19, 1888, Grand Island, Nebraska, to Alfred F. and Mary A. (Richardson) Brown. M. October 12, 1946, to Albert C. Arny. Ch. none. D. January 26, 1966, St. Paul, Minnesota.

Clara Brown Arny received the A.B. degree (1913) from the University of Minnesota and the A.M. degree (1922) from Columbia University. After teaching in the public schools from 1906 until 1915, she became an instructor of home economics education at the University of Minnesota, where she remained until her retirement in 1953.

She first gained recognition through two books she coauthored, *The Teaching of Home Economics* (with Alice H. Haley, 1928) and *Clothing Construction* (with five collaborators, 1927). Later, she centered her interest in the field of evaluation and published the widely used text *Evaluation and Investigation in Home Economics* (1941), which was rewritten in 1953 under the title *Evaluation in Home Economics*.

With a keen interest in evaluation and research, Arny was typically involved in studies for the improvement of educational practices. As a result of these studies she was author of *A Study of Prerequisite Sciences and Certain Sequent Courses at the University of Minnesota* (1941), *Home Economics in Liberal Arts Colleges* (1945), and *The Effectiveness of the High School Program in Home Economics* (1952). She also coauthored

Employment Opportunities for Women with Limited Home Economics Training (with Ruth V. Arneson, 1941) and *Minnesota Tests for Household Skills* (with Dorothy T. Dyer and Margaret P. Proshek, 1952).

In 1937 she was named home economics consultant to President Franklin D. Roosevelt's advisory committee on education and in 1940 was asked to serve with the United States Office of Education as consultant. From 1945 to 1952 she served as chairman of the American Home Economics Association's Committee on Evaluation.

REFERENCES: *LE* (III); *WWAE* (XI); *Journal of Home Economics* 58 (March 1966): 242; *Who's Who of American Women* (Chicago: Marquis, 1958–59). *Louise MacKenzie*

ASHLEY, Samuel Stanford. B. May 12, 1819, Cumberland, Rhode Island, to Samuel and Lydia (Olney) Ashley. M. May 5, 1842, to Mary Elizabeth Eells. Ch. two. D. October 5, 1887, Northboro, Massachusetts.

Samuel Stanford Ashley was graduated from the Theological Seminary of Oberlin (Ohio) College in 1849 and was ordained as a minister at Wakeman, Ohio, on August 1, 1849. He served as acting pastor at Grove Village in Riverton, Rhode Island, from 1849 to 1852. In 1852 he was installed as pastor of a church in Northboro, Massachusetts, where he remained for twelve years.

Motivated by his concern for the intense suffering and neglect of blacks behind Union lines in the South, Ashley asked to be dismissed from his pastorate at Northboro in 1864 to go south as a missionary to the freedmen. He moved to eastern North Carolina where he assumed the duties of assistant superintendent of Negro affairs for the Freedmen's Bureau and superintendent of education for the Southern District of North Carolina. Ashley was also asked to serve as superintendent of the American Missionary Association schools in the Wilmington district.

Ashley became involved in organizing the Republican party in the state and was selected to serve as a delegate to the state constitutional convention in January 1868; he was appointed chairman of the education committee. He directed the study and writing of Article 9 of the state constitution, which provided the basis for reestablishing a system of public schools in North Carolina.

Ashley resigned his position with the Freedmen's Bureau and the American Missionary Association to run for the office of state superintendent of public instruction. After his election in April 1868, he wrote the bill implementing the constitution's education article. State superintendent from 1868 to 1871, he oversaw the establishment of a comprehensive system of public schools for the state.

In the fall of 1871, Ashley became acting president of Straight University in New Orleans, Louisiana. In 1873 he left New Orleans to become the minister of a Congregational church in Atlanta, Georgia, and returned to Northboro, Massachusetts, in 1875.

REFERENCES: "Biographical Sketch of Samuel Stanford Ashley," Oberlin College Archives, Oberlin College, Ohio, June 3, 1875; *Wilmington Weekly Post,* May 3, 1868; Marion N. O'Quinn, "Carpetbagger Samuel S. Ashley and His Role in North Carolina Education, 1865–1871" (Master's thesis, North Carolina State University, 1975). *Marion Nolan O'Quinn*

ASWELL, James Benjamin. B. December 23, 1869, Jackson Parish, Louisiana, to Benjamin and Elizabeth (Lyles) Aswell. M. 1896 to Cora Lee Wright. M. 1901 to Ella V. Foster. Ch. two. D. March 16, 1931, Washington, D.C.

James Benjamin Aswell enrolled in an academy called the Arcadia (Louisiana) Male and Female College in 1886. A year later he accepted his first teaching position at Flat Creek School near Eros, Louisiana. In 1890 he was awarded a two-year scholarship to study at Peabody Normal School (later, George Peabody College for Teachers) at Nashville, Tennessee. Two years later he was granted the licentiate of instruction diploma (1892). He received the B.A. degree (1893) from the University of Nashville.

Aswell returned to Louisiana where he served as principal-teacher at Indian Village and Calhoun schools in Ouachita Parish for four years. During this period he distinguished himself as an educator and was appointed state institute conductor in 1897. In this position he taught pedagogical classes at the Louisiana State Normal College (later, Northwestern State University) at Natchitoches and organized and conducted intensive short-term institutes for teachers throughout the state.

In 1900 Aswell was appointed president of Louisiana Industrial Institute at Ruston, an institution that later became Louisiana Tech University. Following four productive years in this position, Aswell was elected state superintendent of public education. As superintendent, he was instrumental in the progress made in Louisiana establishing public education on a broad scale, particularly at the secondary level. Immediately following reelection as state superintendent in 1908, Aswell resigned the position to serve as president of the Louisiana Normal College (1908–11). In 1911 he lost the race for governor but was elected to the United States Congress in 1913 and served until his death in 1931.

REFERENCES: *NYT,* March 17, 1931, p. 29; *WWW* (I); Monnie T. Cheves, "The Educational and Political Career of James Benjamin Aswell" (Master's thesis, Louisiana State University, 1937); Rodney Cline, *Builders of Louisiana Education* (Baton Rouge: Louisiana State University, College of Education, Bureau of Educational Materials and Research, 1963); Rodney Cline, *Pioneer Leaders and Early Institutions in Louisiana Education* (Baton Rouge: Claitor's Publishing Division, 1969);

T. H. Harris, *The Memoirs of T. H. Harris* (Baton Rouge: Louisiana State University, College of Education, Bureau of Educational Materials and Research, 1963); Sandra Kate Stringer, "James Benjamin Aswell: Louisiana Educator and Politician" (Master's thesis, Louisiana State University, 1970).   *Joe L. Green*

ATHERTON, George Washington. B. June 20, 1837, Boxford, Massachusetts, to Hiram and Almira (Gardner) Atherton. M. December 25, 1863, to Frances D. W. Washburn. Ch. eight. D. July 24, 1906, University Park, Pennsylvania.

George Washington Atherton was fatherless at the age of twelve and helped to support his mother and two sisters. He worked his way through Phillips (Exeter, New Hampshire) Academy and Yale College. He left Yale for Civil War service as a first lieutenant with the Tenth Connecticut Volunteers. In 1863 he resumed his work at Yale and was graduated with the class of 1863.

Atherton taught for four years at the Albany (New York) Boy's Academy and then went to Annapolis, Maryland, in 1866 to be a professor of Latin and acting principal of St. John's College. In 1868 he helped open the University of Illinois as one of its first three faculty members. The following year, he accepted an appointment as professor of history, political economy, and constitutional law at Rutgers College (later, University) in New Brunswick, New Jersey, where he spent fourteen years. While at Rutgers, he was admitted to the bar, practiced law, was a member of the board of visitors to the United States Naval Academy (1873), and served as New Jersey state tax commissioner (1879).

A strong supporter of the land-grant college movement, Atherton became the seventh president of Pennsylvania State College (later, University) in 1882 and spent the remainder of his life building the institution. A near failure when he assumed control with two buildings and thirty-three students, the college encompassed five schools, thirty buildings, and twelve hundred students by 1906.

Atherton served as chairman of a committee that was responsible for details of the Hatch Act (1887), which established experimental agricultural stations and he was instrumental in designing the second Morrill Act (1890). He was the first president of the Association of American Agricultural Colleges and Experimental Stations, which changed its name to the Association of Land-Grant Colleges and Universities in 1926.

REFERENCES: *DAB; NCAB* (20:486); *WWW* (I); Wayland F. Dunaway, *History of The Pennsylvania State College* (State College, Pa.: The Pennsylvania State College, 1946); Erwin W. Runkle, "The Pennsylvania State College, 1853–1932, Interpretation and Record" (unpublished manuscript); *NYT,* July 25, 1906, p. 7.   *Martin W. Sharp, Jr.*

ATKINSON, Alfred. B. October 6, 1879, Seaforth, Ontario, Canada, to Joseph and Isabella (Burns) Atkinson. M. June 13, 1906, to Barbara Miller. Ch. none. D. May 16, 1958, Tucson, Arizona.

Alfred Atkinson attended the Ontario Agricultural College (1899–1902) and received the B.S. degree (1904) in agriculture from Iowa State College (later, Iowa State University) in Ames and the M.S. degree (1912) from Cornell University in Ithaca, New York.

Atkinson was an assistant agronomist for the experiment station at Iowa State College. He taught agronomy at Montana State College (later, University) in Bozeman (1904–19) and was president (1919–37). He conducted agricultural studies that led to new farming methods in Montana and developed new varieties of grain, including Montana 36.

From 1937 to his retirement in 1947, Atkinson was president of the University of Arizona in Tucson. After his retirement, he served as adviser to the university board of regents and the State Colleges of Arizona (1947–55). While Atkinson was at Arizona, the student body doubled, and the faculty and physical plant were enlarged.

Active in professional associations, Atkinson was president of the Association of Land Grant Colleges and Universities (1936–37). He was president of the Northern Pure Seed Company of Forsyth, Montana (1906–13), and was a consultant on farm crops in Montana and Utah to the Anaconda Copper Mining Company. He was the Montana member of the Northwest Planning Board and served on the Arizona Interstate Water Commission (1948–55). He was food administrator for Montana during World War I. He received an honorary degree from Iowa State College (1920).

REFERENCES: *LE* (III); *NCAB* (48:302); *WWAE* (XI); *WW* (XXVIII).   *John F. Ohles*

ATKINSON, George Henry. B. May 10, 1819, Newburyport, Massachusetts, to William and Anna (Little) Atkinson. M. October 8, 1846, to Nancy Bates. Ch. seven. D. February 25, 1889, Portland Oregon.

George H. Atkinson, a Congregational minister, was sent to Oregon as a missionary by the American Home Missionary Society, a Congregationalist organization. He arrived at Astoria, Oregon, June 12, 1848, after the voyage around Cape Horn. Atkinson settled at Oregon City on the Willamette River, which was then the capital of Oregon.

A missionary and religious leader, Atkinson was interested in promoting the organization of private and public schools, reflecting the Congregational interest in education. He brought with him from the East several hundred textbooks, which he sold at cost through a bookstore in Oregon City. These were the first textbooks available in the Oregon Territory and helped stimulate organization of the first schools in the territory.

The American Home Missionary Society had charged Atkinson to aid in the work of education whenever possible. His first opportunity came in 1849 when Governor Joseph Lane, first territorial governor, asked him to write the portion of the inaugural address about educational policy for the new government. Unable to get financial support for a common school in Oregon City in 1849, Atkinson organized a private school, Clackamus County Female Seminary. It was staffed by teachers sent from the East by the missionary society. He continued to work to establish common schools; after 1860, public schools were organized in the territory.

Atkinson was the first superintendent of schools of Clackamus County (1861–62). He was the first principal and the major force in securing graded schools for Oregon City. He served as superintendent of schools for Multnomah County (Portland) for two terms.

In 1880 a major attack was launched against the Portland public school system; critics were especially opposed to the high school. The school board appointed a commission to make a complete evaluation of the school system with Atkinson as chairman. The report of the commission helped to support public schools in Oregon.

Atkinson helped organize Pacific University at Forest Grove and served as secretary of the first board of trustees (1854) and a trustee of Whitman College. He helped Whitman gain recognition as a college by the Washington legislature and made successful efforts to raise funds for the college. He was a trustee of Fidalgo Academy of Northeastern Washington (1880–89) and founded Sheilacom Academy (Washington). He assisted in establishing the Indian Industrial Training School at Forest Grove, Oregon.

REFERENCES: *DAB; NCAB* (6:496); *WWW* (H); Nancy Bates Atkinson, comp., *Biography of Rev. G. H. Atkinson, D.D.* (Portland, Ore.: F. W. Baltes & Co., Printers, 1893); Charles H. Carey, *A General History of Oregon* (Portland, Ore.: Metropolitan Press, 1936), vol. 2; H. K. Hines, *An Illustrated History of the State of Oregon* (Chicago: Lewis Publishing Co., 1893). *Donald Corwin Jones*

ATWATER, Lyman Hotchkiss. B. February 20, 1813, New Haven, Connecticut, to Lyman and Clarissa (Hotchkiss) Atwater. M. October 7, 1835, to Susan Howell Sanford. Ch. five. D. February 17, 1883, Princeton, New Jersey.

In 1825, at the age of twelve, Lyman Atwater began the study of Latin. He attended Yale College from 1827 to 1831, graduating at the age of eighteen, standing second scholastically in his class. He attended the Yale Divinity School (1832–34).

Atwater's varied career included many educational and theological posts. He was head of the classical department of Mount Hope Institute in Baltimore, Maryland (1831–32). He was tutor of mathematics at Yale

(1833–35). In 1834 he was licensed to preach, and in 1835 accepted the call to the First Church of Fairfield, Connecticut, a post he kept until 1854. From 1854 to 1883, he held many posts at the College of New Jersey (later, Princeton University), including professor of logic, moral and political science and mental and moral philosophy, and he taught economics, politics, metaphysics, ethics, religion, and philosophy. He was vice-president of the board of trustees of the Princeton Theological Seminary (1876–83).

Atwater was a contributor to the *Literary and Theological Review,* the *New Englander,* the *Biblical Depository,* and the *Princeton Review,* which he edited from 1869 to 1873. He wrote more than a hundred articles on many subjects, but his chief interests were philosophy and theology. He wrote the *Manual of Logic* (1867).

Atwater believed in stability of society via civil government, family, and tenure of property. He characterized the women's rights movement of his day as a "mad enterprise." He did not like reforms in higher education and was generally a sharp critic of the mid-nineteenth century rebellions.

REFERENCES: *DAB; NCAB* (12:429); *WWW* (H); James Mark Baldwin *(q.v.), Dictionary of Philosophy and Psychology* (New York: Macmillan, 1901), vol. 1; *NYT,* February 18, 1883, p. 7.   *Albert Nissman*

ATWATER, Wilbur Olin. B. May 3, 1844, Johnsburg, New York, to William Warren and Eliza J. (Barnes) Atwater. M. August 26, 1874, to Marcia Woodard. Ch. two. D. September 22, 1907, Middletown, Connecticut.

Wilbur O. Atwater was graduated from Yale College with a Ph.D. in agricultural chemistry in 1869 after completing studies at the University of Vermont and Wesleyan University in Middletown, Connecticut (1865). He engaged in further study at the universities of Berlin and Leipzig, Germany, and became acquainted with the European experiment station movement. After his return to the United States in 1871, he became professor of chemistry at East Tennessee University and two years later accepted a chair at Maine State College (later, University of Maine). Late in 1873 he was called to Wesleyan University as professor of chemistry, a position he occupied for the remainder of his life.

In 1875 the first agricultural experiment station in America was established at Middletown, Connecticut, with Atwater as director. The interest in agricultural experiment stations grew, and in 1887 the Hatch Act was passed by Congress establishing in every state and territory at least one experiment station. In 1888 Atwater founded the Office of Experimental Stations at the United States Department of Agriculture and was its director until 1891.

Atwater planned and supervised nutrition investigations in twenty states, the results of which were published in about a hundred technical and popular publications issued by the Department of Agriculture. In 1895 he authored *Methods and Results of Investigations on the Chemistry and Economy of Food*. He was a member of the National Academy of Science, the Swedish Royal Academy of Agriculture, and the Russian Imperial Academy of Medicine.

REFERENCES: *AC; DAB; NCAB* (6:262); *TC; WWW* (I); *NYT*, September 23, 1907, p. 9. *John W. Schifani*

ATWOOD, Wallace Walter. B. October 1, 1872, Chicago, Illinois, to Thomas Greene and Adelaide (Richards) Atwood. M. September 22, 1900, to Harriet Towle Bradley. Ch. four. D. July 24, 1949, Annisquam, Massachusetts.

Wallace Walter Atwood attended school in Chicago, Illinois, and enrolled in the University of Chicago where he was awarded the B.S. (1897) and Ph.D. (1903) degrees. He remained at the University of Chicago as a professor of physiography and geology (1903–13). From 1913 to 1920 he was a professor of physiography at Harvard University.

In 1920 Atwood became the president of Clark University in Worcester, Massachusetts; in addition to the administrative responsibility of that position, he developed a graduate school of geography. Many of his graduate students filled vital posts with the government during World War I. The school drew students from all over the world. Field research and firsthand observation were stressed over textbooks and encyclopedias. He established a women's college and divisions of nursing education and international affairs at Clark.

Atwood was credited with helping to popularize geography through his writing and public speaking. He was the author of a popular series of elementary and high school geographies, many of them written with Helen Goss Thomas. His courses of studies were used by over thirty thousand American schools.

Among his many books were *Interpretations of Topographic Maps* (1908), *Geology and Mineral Resources of the Alaskan Peninsula* (1911), *New Geography Book Two* (1920), *Home Life in Far Away Lands* (1928), *The World at Work* (1931), *The Growth of Nations* (1940), *The Protection of Nature in the Americas* (1941), *The United States in the Western World* (1944), and *Our Economic World* (1948).

Atwood contributed much research to the geographic field both in the United States and many foreign countries. He represented the United States in many international geography conferences. He was the founder and editor of *Economic Geography* (1925–46). A member of a number of professional associations, Atwood was president of the National Parks Association (1929–33), the Association of American Geographers, and the Pan-American Institute of Geography and History (1932–35).

One of the incorporators of Utopia College in Eureka, Kansas, he was chairman of the board of trustees until his death. Atwood was awarded several honorary degrees and awards, including the Distinguished Service Award of the National Council of Geography Teachers in 1941.

REFERENCES: *DAB* (supp. 4); *LE* (III); *NCAB* (37:46); *WWW* (II); *NYT*, July 26, 1949, p. 27.   *Daniel L. Paul*

AVERY, Elroy McKendree. B. July 14, 1844, Erie, Michigan, to Caspar Hugh and Dorothy (Putnam) Avery. M. July 2, 1870, to Catherine Hitchcock Tilden. M. June 15, 1916, to Ella Alice Wilson. Ch. none. D. December 1, 1935, New Port Richey, Florida.

Elroy McKendree Avery served in the Civil War, attaining the rank of sergeant major. He received the Ph.B. degree (1871) from the University of Michigan and the Ph.M. (1874) and Ph.D. (1881) degrees from Hillsdale (Michigan) College. Avery began his professional career as a high school principal in 1869 in Battle Creek, Michigan, and was superintendent and high school principal in East Cleveland and normal school principal in Cleveland, Ohio (1871–79). He became a member of the Cleveland City Council and later of the Ohio Senate (1893–97).

Following an early role as a correspondent for the *Detroit Daily Tribune,* Avery was a prolific textbook writer on the subjects of physics, chemistry, philosophy, United States history, language, and Cleveland history. Among these publications were *Elementary Physics* (1876), *Elements of Natural Philosophy* (1878), *Physical Technics* (1879), *Teachers Handbook of Natural Philosophy* (1879), *Elements of Chemistry* (1881), *Teachers Handbook of Chemistry* (1883), *First Principles of Natural Philosophy* (1884), *Words Correctly Spoken* (1887), *School Physics* (1895), *School Chemistry* (1904), *The Town Meeting* (1904), *History of the United States and Its People* (twelve volumes, 1913), and *Cleveland and Its Environs* (1918).

He was president of the Ohio conference of charities and corrections (1892) and managing director of the Children's Fresh Air Camp and Hospital of Cleveland (president, 1895–1907). He moved to New Port Richey, Florida, where he served as the first mayor of the town (1921–25). Avery was a fellow of the American Association for the Advancement of Science and a founding life member of the Western Reserve Historical Society. He served as president of the Sons of the American Revolution (1892).

REFERENCES: *NCAB* (26:57); *TC; WWW* (I).   *Sally H. Wertheim*

AXLINE, George Andrew. B. September 22, 1871, Fairfield, Iowa, to Andrew and Almira (Stever) Axline. M. October 20, 1898, to Mabel Estelle Rea. Ch. three. D. October 11, 1919, Long Beach, California.

George Andrew Axline was graduated from Parsons College in Fairfield, Iowa, with the A.B. (1892) and A.M. (1895) degrees. He studied at the Chicago Normal School (later, Chicago State University) in 1899.

Axline was principal of the high school at Cawker City, Kansas (1892–95), supervising principal of the Kirwin (Kansas) schools (1895–96), and superintendent of the Humeston (Iowa) public schools (1896–1903) and Corning (Iowa) public schools (1903–04).

In 1904 Axline became president of the Idaho State Normal School at Albion, where he developed the school into a major teacher-training institution in the region. He conducted teachers' institutes and was instrumental in providing leadership in education in the state. He also engaged in ranching.

Axline was active in professional organizations, serving as president of the Idaho State Teachers' Association (1907) and Inland Empire Teachers' Association (1909) and director of the National Education Association (1912–13). He was a veteran of the Spanish-American War and was a member of the Idaho State Council of National Defense during World War I. He received an honorary degree from Parsons College (1917).

REFERENCES: *NCAB* (19:214); *WW* (X). *John F. Ohles*

AXTELLE, George Edward. B. November 28, 1893, Crandale, Texas, to James Monroe and Marie Edith (Haney) Axtelle. M. May 28, 1916, to Jeanne B. Hauser. M. March 31, 1926, to Margaret Brown. Ch. one. D. August 1, 1974, Orange, California.

George E. Axtelle, educational philosopher, studied at Reed College in Portland, Oregon (1912–15), and received the B.S. degree (1923) from the University of Washington, the M.A. degree (1928) from the University of Hawaii, and the Ed.D. degree (1935) from the University of California.

Axtelle was a school administrator in Hood River County, Oregon (1920–24), in the Hawaii public schools (1924–30), and in Oakland, California, where he was a junior high school principal (1930–35). He taught at Northwestern University (1935–42). During and after World War II, he was a labor relations expert for shipbuilding with the War Production Board (1942–45) and director of employee relations for the Office of Price Administration (1945–46). He was a professor of education at New York University (1946–59). On his retirement, he was in charge of the Center for Dewey Studies at Southern Illinois University in Carbondale (1959–68) and professor of philosophy at the United States International University in San Diego, California, from 1968 to his death in 1974.

Axtelle was one of the foremost interpreters of John Dewey, (*q.v.*), demonstrating through his writings and by his actions that the politics of freedom are inseparable from the politics of education. A vigorous advocate of civil liberties, Axtelle was instrumental in founding the American Federation of Teachers. Throughout his career he championed the humanistic and pragmatic philosophy of life as the most effective means for achieving the potentials of democracy.

Axtelle wrote *The Improvement of Practical Intelligence* (with others, 1940). He was author of more than fifty published essays that reflected the scope of his professional interests and influence of John Dewey and Alfred North Whitehead on his thinking. His sustained interest in Dewey was reflected in *Teachers for Democracy,* the fourth yearbook of the John Dewey Society (1940), which he edited and to which contributed the final two essays, and in his essay in the *Guide to the Works of John Dewey,* edited by Jo Ann Boydston and published by the Southern Illinois University Press in 1970.

Axtelle was a Fulbright lecturer in Egypt (1952–53), trustee of the William Heard Kilpatrick Educational Foundation, and president of the Philosophy of Education Society (1950), the American Humanist Association (1959), and the John Dewey Society (1961–63). He was vice-chairman of the New York Committee to Abolish Capital Punishment and the New York Liberal party. He was a member of the American Federation of Teachers (vice-president) and member of the executive committee (1937–42).

REFERENCES: *LE* (III); *WWW* (VI); John A. Broyer, "Professor George Axtelle: A Critical Eulogy," prepared for the 1974 Conference of the International Foundations of Education Society; Phil Dennis, "Obituary for George E. Axtelle," United States International University, 1974; *Directory of American Scholars-Philosophy,* 4th ed. (New York: R. R. Bowker, 1963).   *Richard B. Morland*

AYCOCK, Charles Brantley. B. November 1, 1859, Wayne County, North Carolina, to Benjamin and Serena (Hooks) Aycock. M. May 25, 1881, to Varina Woodard. M. 1891 to Cora Lily Woodard. Ch. ten. D. April 4, 1912, Raleigh, North Carolina.

Charles Brantley Aycock began his formal schooling at Nahunta Academy in 1867. He attended Wilson (North Carolina) Collegiate Institute (1872–75) and the University of North Carolina, graduating in 1880. In 1881, he engaged in the practice of law.

Aycock showed an unusual interest in education and served as county superintendent and chairman of the board of trustees of the Goldsboro, North Carolina, graded schools. He was United States attorney for the eastern district of North Carolina (1893–97) and was a successful candidate for governor of North Carolina in 1900. As governor (1901–05), he led campaigns for improved education throughout the state.

The legislature of 1901 revised the general school law to improve supervision, raise teaching standards, set standards for school buildings, and encourage local school taxes. The supplementary appropriation for the public schools was raised from $100,000 to $200,000. The school year was extended from fewer than four months per year, and teachers' salaries were increased.

In the election of 1900, Aycock had campaigned for a state constitutional amendment that limited the franchise to those who met minimal educational standards. He was a white supremacist, believing in the separation of the races and the absolute right to rule for whites. Yet when some members of the legislature were in favor of improving the white schools without improving the black schools, Aycock threatened to resign. Educational services and standards were to be raised for all citizens. In addition to his concern for education, Aycock worked for legislation on behalf of child labor, reformatories with education, and good roads.

Aycock lived seven years after leaving the governorship; he planned to run for Senate, but died before the election.

REFERENCES: *DAB; NCAB* (13:356); *WWW* (I); Howard W. Odum *(q.v.), Southern Pioneers in Social Interpretation* (Chapel Hill, N.C.: University of North Carolina Press, 1925); Oliver H. Orr, Jr., *Charles Brantley Aycock* (Chapel Hill, N.C.: University of North Carolina Press, 1961); *NYT,* April 5, 1912, p. 13. *Linda C. Gardner*

AYDELOTTE, Frank. B. October 16, 1880, Sullivan, Indiana, to William E. and Matilda (Brunger) Aydelotte. M. June 22, 1907, to Marie Jeannette Osgood. Ch. one. D. December 17, 1956, Princeton, New Jersey.

Frank Aydelotte was born and raised in Sullivan, Indiana. Awarded the A.B. degree (1900) from Indiana University, he spent several years following his graduation as a teacher at Southwestern State Normal School (later, California State College) at California, Pennsylvania (1900–01), Indiana University (1901–02), and Louisville (Kentucky) Boys' High School (1903–05). After earning the master's degree at Harvard University (1903), Aydelotte became one of the early Rhodes scholars at Oxford (England) University (1905–07), an experience that had a profound impact upon his career.

After his return to the United States, Aydelotte taught English at Indiana University (1908–15) and Massachusetts Institute of Technology (1915–21). He wrote articles extolling the English university system. He founded and edited the *American Oxonian,* the quarterly of the Association of American Rhodes Scholars and was president of the association until his death. Aydelotte served as American secretary and chief administrative officer of the Rhodes Scholar Trust for thirty-five years. During his tenure changes were made to improve the operation of the program in America.

Aydelotte's interest in the Oxford system influenced him after he was appointed president of Swarthmore (Pennsylvania) College in 1921. During his nineteen years as president, he inspired program changes that enhanced Swarthmore's academic reputation. The most notable change was the implementation of an honors program, dubbed the Swarthmore plan, which was copied by many other American institutions of higher education.

He wrote many articles and several books, including *Elizabethian Rogues and Vagabonds* (1913), *College English* (1913), *The Oxford Stamp* (1917), and *Breaking the Academic Lockstep* (1944). Aydelotte was active in many professional groups. He was a trustee or adviser to the Carnegie Foundation for the Advancement of Teaching, the John Guggenheim Memorial Foundation, the World Peace Foundation, the Institute for International Education, and the Teacher's Insurance and Annuity Association of America. During his early postretirement years he was director of the Institute for Advanced Study at Princeton, New Jersey. He was a recipient of many honorary degrees and an Honorary Knight Commander of the Order of the British Empire (1953).

REFERENCES: *CB* (April 1952); *LE* (III); *NCAB* (F:354, 43:44); *WWW* (III); Frances Blanshard, *Frank Aydelotte of Swarthmore* (Middletown, Conn.: Wesleyan University Press, 1970); Faculty of Swarthmore College, *An Adventure in Education* (New York: Macmillan and Co., 1941); *NYT,* December 18, 1956, p. 31.   *Samuel A. Farmerie*

AYRES, Leonard Porter. B. September 15, 1879, Niantic, Connecticut, to Milan Church and Georgiana (Gall) Ayres. M. no. D. October 29, 1946, Cleveland, Ohio.

Leonard Porter Ayres was graduated from Boston University with the Ph.B. (1902), A.M. (1909), and Ph.D. (1910) degrees. He went to Puerto Rico after receiving the bachelor's degree where he was a teacher (1902), superintendent of schools for the district of Caguas (1903–04), San Juan city school superintendent (1904–06), and general superintendent of schools and chief of the division of statistics for Puerto Rico (1906–08).

He conducted a study of retardation for the Russell Sage Foundation in United States public schools, which led to a system of scientific measurement of public school procedures and results designed to standardize grade and age of pupils. In 1908 Ayres was appointed director of the Department of Education and Statistics of the Russell Sage Foundation for which he conducted studies in 250 cities.

When the United States entered World War I, Ayres became chief of the Division of Statistics of the Council of National Defense. He was appointed director of the Division of Statistics of the War Industries Board and chief statistical officer of the Priorities Committee and the Allies Purchasing Commission and, later, chief statistical officer of the American Commission to Negotiate Peace. After the war, he resumed work at the Russell Sage Foundation until 1920, when he became vice-president of the Cleveland (Ohio) Trust Company. In October 1940 he returned to active duty in the United States Army. After his discharge in 1942 for health reasons, he organized a statistical service for the War Manpower Commission that he administered until the end of the war.

Among his published writings are *Medical Inspection of Schools* (with Luther Gulick, *q.v.*, 1908), *Laggards in Our Schools* (1909), *Open Air Schools* (1910), *The Measurement of Spelling Ability* (1915), *School Buildings and Equipment* (1915), *Health Work in the Public Schools* (1915), and *Child Accounting in the Public Schools* (1915). He also wrote *Turning Points in Business Cycles* (1939) and many other books concerning business economics and statistics.

REFERENCES: *CB* (May 1940); *DAB* (supp. 4); *LE* (I); *NCAB* (45:347); *WWW* (II); *NYT*, October 30, 1946, p. 27.   *Alan N. Rabe*

AZARIAS, Brother. See **MULLANY, Patrick Francis.**

B

BABBITT, Irving. B. August 2, 1865, Dayton, Ohio, to Edwin Dwight and Augusta (Darling) Babbitt. M. June 12, 1900, to Dora May Drew. Ch. two. D. July 15, 1933, Cambridge, Massachusetts.

Irving Babbitt was graduated from Harvard University in 1889 and began his teaching career at Montana College. In 1891 and 1892 he studied in France. After receiving the A.M. degree (1893) from Harvard, he taught Roman languages at Williams College in Williamstown, Massachusetts (1893–94). He returned to Harvard in 1894 to teach French literature.

Babbitt's contributions did not become generally known until 1929–1930 when a public controversy arose between Babbitt, Paul Elmer More, and others over concepts of humanism. He published his position in several papers, "President Eliot and American Education," "Rousseau and Religion," and "On Being Creative, and Other Essays" (1932), and in a chapter "Humanism: An Essay at Definition" in Norman Foerster's *Humanism and America* (1930).

Masters of Modern French Criticism (1912) is Babbitt's chief contribution to the study of French literature. In *Literature and the American College: Essays in Defence of the Humanities* (1908), he contended that college training should ideally promote wisdom and character by the processes of assimilation and reflection rather than training for power and service. *The New Laokoön* (1910) and *Democracy and Leadership* (1924) represented a substantial contribution to the literature of the humanistic movement of his time and established his position as a spokesman for the movement.

Babbitt was a member of a number of professional organizations. He received an honorary degree from Bowdoin College in 1932.

REFERENCES: *DAB* (supp. 1); *LE* (I); *NCAB* (C:76, 23:19); *WWW* (I); *NYT,* July 16, 1933, p. 20.   *Charlene Gail Revels*

BACHE, Alexander Dallas. B. July 19, 1806, Philadelphia, Pennsylvania, to Richard and Sophia Burret (Dallas) Bache. M. c. 1828 to Nancy Clarke Fowler. Ch. none. D. February 17, 1867, Newport, Rhode Island.

Alexander Dallas Bache, great-grandson of Benjamin Franklin (*q.v.*), was graduated from the United States Military Academy in 1825 and entered a dual career as educator and scientist. He remained at the academy as assistant professor of engineering for one year, was appointed professor of natural philosophy and chemistry at the University of Pennsylvania (1828), and became the first president of Girard College in Philadelphia (1836). He became involved in other activities and did not serve in the Girard presidency when the college was actually opened in 1848.

Bache went to Europe in 1837 to study educational systems. On his return in 1839, he wrote *Education in Europe,* a voluminous report of his findings. He became superintendent of Philadelphia public schools and remained in that office until 1842, reorganizing the system into a widely emulated model.

As superintendent of the United States Coast Survey (1843–67), Bache achieved international recognition as a scientist. He was one of the incorporators of the Smithsonian Institution (1846), as well as of the National Academy of Sciences, for which he served as first president and to which he bequeathed his property (some $42,000) for physical research. His published papers were extensive and treated topics in physics, chemistry, and engineering. While serving as president of Girard College in its organizational stage, Bache established the first American magnetic observatory in 1840. He published *Observations at the Magnetic and Meteorological Observatory at the Girard College . . . (1840–47).*

He served as president of the American Philosophical Society and the American Association for the Advancement of Science. The Royal Society of London, the Institute of France, the Royal Academy of Turin, the Imperial Geographical Society of Virginia, and numerous other associations awarded him honorary memberships. He received several honorary degrees.

REFERENCES: *AC; DAB; DSB; NCAB* (3:348); Prof. Joseph Henry, "Eulogy on Professor Alexander Dallas Bache," *Annual Report of the Board of Regents of the Smithsonian Institution for the Year 1870* (Washington, D.C.: U.S. Government Printing Office, 1872), pp. 91–116; *NYT,* February 20, 1867, p. 2.   *Ruth Ledbetter Galaz*

BAGLEY, William Chandler. B. March 15, 1874, Detroit, Michigan, to William Chase and Ruth (Walker) Bagley. M. August 14, 1901, to Florence McLean Winger. Ch. four. D. July 1, 1946, New York, New York.

William C. Bagley attended elementary school in Worcester, Massachusetts, and high school in Detroit, Michigan. He obtained the B.S. degree (1895) from Michigan Agricultural College (later, Michigan State University), the M.S. degree (1898) from the University of Wisconsin, and the Ph.D. degree in psychology, neurology, and education (1900) from Cornell University. From 1895 to 1897, he taught in a one-teacher village school in Garth, Delta County, Michigan.

After serving as an elementary school principal in St. Louis, Missouri (1901–02), Bagley moved to Dillon, Montana, where he served as professor of psychology and pedagogy and vice-president at the State Normal School and superintendent of the Dillon public schools (1902–06). The following two years he was superintendent and professor of methods at the State Normal and Training School (later, State University of New York College) in Oswego, New York. He first gained national attention as professor of education and director of the school of education at the University of Illinois (1908–17). He served as professor of education at Teachers College, Columbia University (1917–40).

A professor, thinker, author, editor, and evaluator, Bagley contributed to educational psychology and theory, teacher education, instructional methodology, and education by radio. His books include *The Educative Process* (1905), *Classroom Management* (1907), *Craftsmanship in Teaching* (1911), *Educational Values* (1911), *School Discipline* (1915), *The Nation and the Schools* (with John A. H. Keith, 1920), *An Introduction to Teaching* (with John A. H. Keith, 1924), *Determinism in Education* (1925), *Education, Crime, and Social Progress* (1931), *Education and Emergent Man* (1934), *A Century of the Universal School* (1937), and *The Teacher of the Social Studies* (with Thomas Alexander, 1937), as well as a series of textbooks on American history in collaboration with Charles A. Beard *(q.v.)*. Among his other publications were contributions to reports of evaluative surveys of education in various parts of the United States. He served as editor of *Intermountain Education* (1905–06), *School and Home Education* (1912–21), *Journal of the National Education Association* (1921–24), and *School and Society* (1939–46), and as coeditor of *Journal of Educational Psychology* (1910–17) and *Educational Administration and Supervision* (1917–46).

As a theorist, Bagley stressed the equality of educational opportunity for all, regardless of race, religion, or other external consideration. He was a militant opponent of the racist theory of Nordic superiority, especially as it labeled blacks as inferior to whites in intelligence and ability to learn. He was a founder and exponent of the essentialist movement and a consistent critic of the extremist tendencies in progressive education.

REFERENCES: *DAB* (supp. 4); *LE* (II); *NCAB* (35:227, A:322); *WWAE* (XI); *WWW* (II); W. W. Brickman *(q.v.)*, "William Chandler Bagley (1874–1946), Exemplary Educator," *Intellect* 102 (March 1974): 354–55; Edell M. Hearn, "William Chandler Bagley: 'Teacher of Teachers,' " *Kappa Delta Pi Record* 4 (October 1967): 19–23; I. L. Kandel *(q.v.)*, *William Chandler Bagley* (New York: Teachers College, Columbia University, 1961); *NYT,* July 2, 1946, p. 25.   *William W. Brickman*

BAILEY, Ebenezer. B. June 25, 1795, West Newbury, Massachusetts, to Paul and Emma (Carr) Bailey. M. 1825 to Adeline Dodge. Ch. none. D. August 5, 1839, Lynn, Massachusetts.

After graduating from Yale College with honors in 1817, Ebenezer Bailey entered the education field. He held several tutorial positions at private schools in Connecticut and Virginia and then returned to Massachusetts where he founded a short-lived private school for girls in Newburyport (1819–23).

The first public high school for girls in the United States opened in Boston in 1825 with Bailey as its principal. The demand for secondary education was so great that the school was forced to close because of its inability to meet the surge of high school aspirants. The school was re-opened when the curriculum of the lower schools was broadened to provide a more comprehensive education for girls and thus relieved the pressure for admission to the high school. From 1827 to 1837 Bailey directed the private Young Ladies High School. Initially a success, it was forced to close during the depression of 1837. He opened a boys' school in Roxbury (1838) and moved it to Lynn (1839).

Bailey was one of the founders of the American Institute of Instruction (1830), president of the Boston Lyceum, director of the Boston Mechanics Institute, and a member of the Boston City Council.

He was the author of *Review of the Mayor's Report upon the High School for Girls* (1828) and a number of poems, several of which were read at Harvard University. He also wrote and edited *The Young Ladies Class Book* (1831), *Philosophical Conversations* (1833), and *First Lessons in Algebra* (1837).

REFERENCES: *AC; DAB; NCAB* (4:345); *WWW* (H).   *Patrick J. Foley*

BAILEY, Henry Turner. B. December 9, 1864, Scituate, Massachusetts, to Charles Edward and Eudora (Turner) Bailey. M. September 5, 1889, to Josephine Litchfield. Ch. five. D. November 26, 1931, Chicago, Illinois.

Henry Turner Bailey was graduated from Scituate (Massachusetts) High School in 1882 as class valedictorian. He continued his education at the Massachusetts State Normal Art School in Boston, graduating in 1887. He continued studies throughout his life taking courses in art at Harvard

University and studying abroad in Europe, Asia, and Africa eight times, beginning in 1898.

He began his career as an art educator while still a student at the Massachusetts State Normal Art School (later, Massachusetts College of Art). He served as a teacher of drawing in the Boston night school (1884–85) and was supervisor of drawing in the Lowell (Massachusetts) public schools (1886–87). He was an agent of the Massachusetts Board of Education with responsibility for promotion of industrial drawing in the state's public schools (1887–1902). In 1902 he resigned from the state board to serve as editor of *The School Arts Magazine* (also called *The School Arts Book*) in Boston to 1917. He was director of nonresident courses of the New York School of Fine and Applied Arts (1914).

Bailey moved to Cleveland, Ohio, as dean of the Cleveland School of Art and adviser in educational work for the Cleveland Museum of Art (1917). He was director of the School of Occupational Therapy in Cleveland (1917–19) under the auspices of the United States Surgeon General. He was director of both the Cleveland School of Art and the John Huntington Polytechnic Institute in Cleveland (1919), holding these positions until his resignation in 1930, when he left to devote the remainder of his life to writing and lecturing.

Bailey was author of *A First Year in Drawing* (1894), *The Blackboard in Sunday School* (1899), *School Sanitation and Decoration* (with Severance Burrage, 1899), *The Great Painters' Gospel* (1900), *Sketch of the History of Public Art Instruction in Massachusetts* (1900), *The City of Refuge* (1902), *Instruction in the Fine and Manual Arts* (1909), *Nature Drawing* (1910), *The Flush of Dawn* (1910), *Booklet Making* (1912), *Twelve Masterpieces of Painting* (1913), *Art Education* (1914), *Photography and Fine Art* (1919), *Symbolism for Artists* (with Ethel Pool, 1923), *The Tree Folk* (1925), *The Magic Realm of the Arts* (1928), and *Yankee Notions* (1929). He was editor of *Something-to-Do* (1916–17).

Bailey became nationally recognized as an art educator. He served as an official delegate to the International Congress of Public Art in Brussels, Belgium (1898), the Third International Congress on Art Teaching in London, England (1908), and the International Congress on Public Art in Dresden, Germany (1912) and was a member of the International Jury of Awards at the Panama-Pacific Exposition in San Francisco, California (1915). Bailey was a member of the Society of American Authors and the Twentieth Century Club of Boston. He served as moderator of the annual town meetings in Boston (1899–1915) and was park commissioner for Scituate, Massachusetts (1913–17). He exhibited works in major American cities.

While in Cleveland, Bailey was a delegate to the International Congress on Public Art in Prague, Czechoslovakia (1928). A popular lecturer on nature subjects and art, Bailey was a recognized authority on birds of the northeastern Ohio area. He received honorary degrees from Denison University in Ohio and Beloit (Wisconsin) College.

REFERENCES: *NCAB* (C:101, 23:306); *WWW* (I); P. J. Lemos, "Henry Turner Bailey, 1865–1931," *School Arts Magazine* 31 (February 1932): supp. xiii–xvi; *Industrial Arts and Vocational Education* 21 (January 1932): 38.   *Charles M. Dye*

BAILEY, Liberty Hyde. B. March 15, 1858, South Haven, Michigan, to Liberty Hyde and Sarah (Harrison) Bailey. M. June 6, 1883, to Annette Smith. Ch. two. D. December 25, 1954, Ithaca, New York.

Liberty Hyde Bailey was educated at public schools in Michigan and received the B.S. (1882) and M.S. (1886) degrees from Michigan Agricultural College (later, Michigan State University). He served as an assistant to Asa Gray (*q.v.*) at Harvard University. He was professor of horticulture at Michigan State College (later, University) from 1884 to 1888 and at Cornell University in Ithaca, New York (1888–1903), and first dean of the newly organized New York State College of Agriculture at Cornell (1903–13).

As a botanist, Bailey was an authority on the classification of the genera *carex, rubus, brassica,* and tropical American members of the palm family. He founded and was director of the Bailey Hortorium, the world's first botanical institution devoted to studies on the classification and identification of cultivated plants. He preached and practiced a new horticulture, holding that it must be an applied science based on pure biology. Early in his career, Bailey was influenced by the British naturalist Alfred Russel Wallace. This association led to later researches in taxonomic studies of the genera of bramble-fruits, cucurbits, and grapes.

In his middle years, Bailey was active in an effort to bring the science of botany to students at the secondary school level. From 1898 to 1909, he wrote six botany textbooks that were a direct contribution to education, meeting a lack of acceptable botanical texts for secondary courses. He changed the approach and emphasis in teaching, rejecting the formal parades and visits to the university farm, substituting indoor and outdoor laboratories and mixing with his students or demonstrating a principle to them.

Bailey struggled for years to convince state officials that agricultural courses taught in high schools throughout urban and rural New York State should be accepted by the board of regents and given equal academic recognition with other high school subjects. Nature study as a subject in grammar schools received great impetus from his efforts.

Bailey exercised much influence through his articles and books, including *The Horticulturist's Rule-Book* (1889), *Lessons with Plants* (1897),

The Principles of Agriculture (1898), *Botany* (1900), *The Nature-Study Idea* (1903), *First Course in Biology* (with Walter M. Coleman, 1908), *The Training of Farmers* (1909), *Beginner's Botany* (1909), *The Country-Life Movement in the United States* (1911), *The Amateur's Practical Garden-Book* (with C. E. Hunn, 1913), *Botany for Secondary Schools* (1913), and *The Holy Earth* (1915). He edited *Cyclopedia of American Horticulture* (four volumes, 1900–02), *Cyclopedia of American Agriculture* (four volumes, 1907–09), *The Standard Cyclopedia of Horticulture* (six volumes, 1914–17), and *The Cultivated Evergreens* (1923). He founded the periodical *Gentes Herbaum* and served as editor of several other journals. He also wrote two volumes of poetry and nine books in the fields of rural sociology, religion, and philosophy.

Bailey was chairman of Theodore Roosevelt's Commission on Country Life (1907–08) and the recipient of a number of honorary degrees, medals, and awards. He was a fellow of the American Academy of Arts and Sciences and was a member of many organizations, including the American Association for the Advancement of Science (president, 1926), the Botanical Society of America (president, 1926), and the American Society for Horticultural Science (first president).

REFERENCES: *DSB; EB; LE* (III); *NCAB* (43:514); *WWW* (III); Philip Dorf, *Liberty Hyde Bailey: An Informal Biography* (Ithaca, N.Y.: Cornell University Press, 1956); George Hill Mathewson Lawrence, "Liberty Hyde Bailey (1858–1954); An Appreciation," *Baileya* 3 (1954): 26–40; *NYT,* December 27, 1954, p. 17; Andrew Denny Rodgers, *Liberty Hyde Bailey: A Story of American Plant Sciences* (Princeton, N.J.: Princeton University Press, 1949).   *Ralph M. Carter*

BAILEY, Rufus William. B. April 13, 1793, North Yarmouth, Maine, to Lebbeus and Sarah (Myrick) Bailey. M. 1820 to Lucy Hatch. M. to Mariette (Perry) Lloyd. Ch. none. D. April 25, 1863, Sherman, Texas.

Rufus William Bailey was graduated from Dartmouth College (1813) and taught in academies at Blue Hill, Maine, and Salisbury, New Hampshire. After a year studying law with Daniel Webster, he enrolled at the Andover (Massachusetts) Theological Seminary. Bailey finished his theological studies with Francis Brown, president of Dartmouth College.

After a year as a tutor at Dartmouth (1817–18), Bailey was ordained and served as pastor of the Congregational church at Norwich, Vermont, where he also taught moral philosophy at the local military school. He was pastor at Pittsfield, Massachusetts (1824–28). He moved south for health reasons and spent a long and active career teaching and preaching in North Carolina, South Carolina, and Virginia. He became professor of languages (1854) and president (1858) of Austin College in Sherman, Texas, where he remained to his death in 1863.

Bailey was a prolific writer. In 1841 he became editor of the *Patriarch,* to which he made numerous contributions. He wrote many letters on the subject of slavery to newspapers, which were later collected and published as *The Issue* (1837). Many of his sermons were published as *The Family Preacher* (1837). He was best known for his textbooks in spelling and grammar, which were used throughout the South. By 1830 his revised edition of Henry Butter's *Scholar's Companion* had sold over one-half million copies. He was author of *Domestic Duties* (n.d.), *English Grammar* (1853), *Primary English Grammar* (1854), and *Daughters at School Instructed in a Series of Letters* (1857).

REFERENCES: *AC; DAB; TC; WWW* (H).   *Victor R. Durrance*

BAILEY, Thomas David. B. October 31, 1897, Lugoff, South Carolina, to Samuel David and Mary Julia (Campbell) Bailey. M. August 25, 1921, to Burness McConnell. Ch. two. D. August 12, 1974, Waynesville, North Carolina.

Thomas David Bailey received the A.B. degree (1919) from Wofford College in Spartanburg, South Carolina, and the M.A.E. degree (1939) from the University of Florida.

He served as principal of South Carolina high schools at Gowan (1919–20) and Georgetown (1924–28), as president of the Thomas Industrial Institute in De Funiak Springs, Florida (1920–24), and as supervising principal in Florida at De Funiak Springs (1928–39), Ocala (1939–43), and Tampa (1943–47). He was secretary for public relations for the Florida Education Association (1947–48).

Bailey served for sixteen years as Florida state superintendent of public schools from 1948 until 1965. In that capacity he was a member of the state cabinet. A leader of one of the nation's poorest school systems, he implemented a minimum foundation act that increased spending proportionately for rural schools. He guided the state into desegregation of public elementary and secondary schools and expansion of the state's community college system.

Bailey assumed professional responsibilities as a member of the state textbook rating committee, the state course of study committee (1943–47), the Florida Education Association (president, 1938–39, director, 1935–38), the National Association of Secondary School Principals (chairman, 1947), the National Education Association (state director, 1955–58), the National Council of Chief State School Officers (president, 1954–55), and he was organizer and director (1939–42) of the Florida state chapter of the Future Teachers of America. He was author of the autobiographical *An Odyssey in Education* (1974).

REFERENCES: *LE* (III); *WW* (XXXI); *WWAE* (XVI); *Miami Herald,* August 12, 1974.   *Vincent Giardina*

BAKER, Benjamin Franklin. B. July 10, 1811, Wenham, Massachusetts, to John and Sally Baker. M. November 21, 1841, to Sabra L. Heywood. Ch. none. D. March 11, 1889, Boston, Massachusetts.

Benjamin Franklin Baker began studying music at the age of fourteen when his family moved to Salem, Massachusetts. He continued his studies in Boston and sang at concerts and church services. From 1837 he studied with John Paddon. He was Lowell Mason's (*q.v.*) successor as Boston public school music instructor (1841–50). He was musical conductor for churches in Boston from 1839 to 1863.

In 1847 Baker began to organize a school of music that he hoped would be superior to all other American music schools. The Boston Music School opened in 1857 and flourished until Baker retired and closed the school in 1868.

Editor of the *Boston Musical Journal* in the 1870s, Baker wrote many musical compositions and was author and compiler of thirty books, including *A Book of Songs and Hymns* (with Isaac B. Woodbury, 1838), *Boston Musical Education Society's Collections* (with I. B. Woodbury, 1842), *Baker's American School Music Book* (1844), *The Choral* (with I. B. Woodbury, 1845), *Baker's Theory of Harmony* (1847), *Elementary Music Book* (1850), *Haydn Collection of Church Music* (with L. H. Southard, 1850), *Melodia Sacra* (with A. N. Johnson and Josiah Osgood, 1852), *Union Glee Book* (1852), *Baker's Church Music* (1855), and *Baker's Theoretical and Practical Harmony* (1870).

Baker was president of the Boston Musical Education Society for seven years and vice-president of the Handel and Haydn Society for six years.

REFERENCES: *AC; DAB; NCAB* (7:429); *TC; WWW* (H).

Barbara Ruth Peltzman

BAKER, Edna Dean. B. August 27, 1883, Normal, Illinois, to Joshua Edmund and Olive Elmira (Clark) Baker. M. no. D. March 20, 1956, Riverside, California.

Edna Dean Baker attended the public schools of Bellingham, Washington. She received the B.E. degree (1913) from the National Kindergarten College and the A.B. (1920) and M.A. (1921) degrees from Northwestern University in Evanston, Illinois, and did postgraduate work at Columbia University (1914 and 1916). Baker was appointed director of the Evanston Elementary School; under her leadership it evolved into an experiment in creative living designed to develop the whole child.

Baker became assistant to the president of the National College of Education (formerly the National Kindergarten College) in 1915 and served as president from 1920 to 1949. In 1926 the college moved from Chicago to Evanston, Illinois, and the curriculum was revised to include leadership in child education and in fields related to child development, guidance, teaching, clinical study, special education, music and art education, and physical education. A school for children was organized. In 1930 a four-year B.Ed. degree program was initiated, and in 1932 the college became fully accredited by the state of Illinois. The college was accredited by the American Association of Teachers Colleges (1942) and the North Central Association of Colleges and Secondary Schools (1947). In 1925 Baker and Jane Addams founded the Mary Crane Nursery School through which the college secured aid for underprivileged children.

Baker was the author of *Parenthood and Child Nature* (1922), *Kindergarten Methods in Church Schools* (1925), *The Worship of the Little Child* (1927), *A Child Is Born* (1932), *Adventures in Higher Education* (1956), and coauthor with Clara B. Baker of *Bobbs-Merrill Readers* (1923–39), *True Story Readers* (1928, 1938), and *Curriculum Readers* (1934–38).

Baker was a member of the board of the Kobe (Japan) College Corporation and the preschool committee of President Herbert Hoover's White House Conference on Child Health (1932), chairperson of the Illinois teacher certification committee (1942), and a participant in inter-American education discussions led by the United States Office of Education during World War II.

Baker received several honorary degrees and was a member of professional associations, including the Association for Childhood Education International (president, 1933–36).

REFERENCES: *LE* (III); *NCAB* (43:520); *WWAE* (XI); *WWW* (III); *Independent Woman* 16 (March 1937): 79.   *Barbara Ruth Peltzman*

BAKER, George Pierce. B. April 4, 1866, Providence, Rhode Island, to George Pierce and Lucy Daily (Cady) Baker. M. August 16, 1893, to Christina Hopkinson. Ch. four. D. January 6, 1935, New York, New York.

George Pierce Baker was graduated from Harvard University in 1887 and the following year became an instructor in English there. For the next few years he taught and coached debate and produced a series of books on the subject: *Specimens of Argumentation* (1893), *Principles of Argumentation* (1895), and *Forms of Public Address* (1904).

With his appointment as full professor in 1905, he turned his attention to drama, an early and enduring interest. He successfully experimented with a course in practical playwriting at Radcliffe College in 1905, which he brought to Harvard as English 47 in 1906. The course gained early publicity and acceptance when one of his first students, Edward Sheldon, sold a play he had written for class. English 47A was added to the original course and became known as the 47 Workshop, in which students produced experimental dramas with the aid of volunteers, outsiders, and audiences, who supplied written critiques. An enormous success, the workshop attracted such writers as Eugene O'Neill, S. N. Behrman, John Mason Brown, and Thomas Wolfe (who immortalized Baker as Professor Hatcher in *Of Time and the River*).

Baker was the author of a number of books, most notably *The Development of Shakespeare as a Dramatist* (1907), *Plays of the 47 Workshop* (four volumes, 1918–25), and *Dramatic Technique* (1919), which became the standard text for playwrights.

Harvard's persistent refusal to provide adequate theatrical facilities for the 47 Workshop led Baker to move to Yale University in 1925. He taught playwriting and theater history and directed the university theater, an excellent facility donated by Edward Harkness. By the time of his retirement in 1933, Baker's ideas had influenced university training for playwrights and the entire American theater, both amateur and professional.

REFERENCES: *DAB* (supp. 1); *LE* (I); *NCAB* (B:11, 25:28); *WWW* (I); John Mason Brown et al., *George Pierce Baker: A Memorial* (New York: Dramatists Play Service, 1939); *NYT*, January 7, 1935, p. 17; Eugene O'Neill, "Tribute to G. P. Baker," *NYT,* January 13, 1951, sec. 9, p. 1.   *Joseph M. McCarthy*

BAKER, James Hutchins. B. October 13, 1848, Harmony, Maine, to Wesley and Lucy (Hutchins) Baker. M. June 20, 1882, to Jennie V. Hilton. Ch. two. D. September 10, 1925, Boulder, Colorado.

After James Hutchins Baker was graduated from Bates College in Lewiston, Maine, with the B.A. degree (1873), he became a local schoolmaster and high school principal. After two years, he was advised by his physician to move west. In 1874 he was appointed principal of East Denver (Colorado) High School and continued there for seventeen years (1875–92). In 1892 he became the third president of the University of Colorado in Boulder, an institution fifteen years old with sixty-six students. When he retired as president emeritus in 1914, he had established a graduate department, a law school, and a college of engineering, and the student body numbered over a thousand. He secured legislation locating a medical, dental, and pharmaceutical school in Denver.

Baker authored seven books: *Elementary Psychology* (1890), *Education and Life* (1900), *American Problems* (1907), *Educational Aims and Civic Needs* (1913), *University Reform and College Progress Relative to School and Society* (1916), *After the War What?* (1918), and an autobiography, *Of Himself and Other Things* (1922).

Called the Eliot of the West, after Charles Eliot (*q.v.*) of Harvard University, Baker was recognized for advancing the cause of education in the West. He was active in interstate committees on general educational conditions and relations between public schools and colleges. He was a member of the National Educational Association Committee of Ten and headed the Committee of Economy of Time in Education (1907), which recommended establishing junior high schools and junior colleges. He was a fellow of the American Association for the Advancement of Science and president of the Colorado State Teachers' Association (1880), the State Educational Council, the National Council of Education (1892), the National Association of State Universities (1907), and a member of the Committee on University Standards. Bates College awarded him an honorary degree.

REFERENCES: *DAB; NCAB* (6:493); *WWW* (I).

Barbara Hinderscheid

BAKER, Samuel Aaron. B. November 7, 1874, Patterson, Missouri, to Samuel Aaron and Mary Amanda (McGhee) Baker. M. June 1, 1904, to Nell R. Tuckley. Ch. one. D. September 16, 1933, Jefferson City, Missouri.

Sam A. Baker was Missouri's only state superintendent of public instruction to be elected governor. The son of a country physician, he completed his early schooling in Mill Springs, Missouri. To finance further education he worked as a section hand on the Iron Mountain Railroad and in local mills. He was graduated from Cape Girardeau (Missouri) State Teachers College (later, Southeast Missouri State College) in 1897. He also studied as a special student at the University of Missouri.

Baker took his first of many educational positions in Missouri by teaching in Bethel (1895–96). Prior to completing his college degree, he became principal of Mill Springs School (1896). He served as superintendent in Piedmont (1897–99), high school principal in Jefferson City (1899–1905), high school principal at Joplin (1905–10), superintendent of schools at Richmond (1910–13), and superintendent of city schools at Jefferson City (1913–19). While at Jefferson City, Baker provided leadership for the passage of a school bond issue and supplied students with free textbooks. He also instituted commerce and manual training courses in the high schools.

In 1918 Baker ran successfully for state superintendent of public instruction. In four years training facilities for teachers were expanded, and teachers' salaries had doubled. He instituted vocational and rehabilitation programs and strengthened rural education throughout the state.

Baker was defeated for reelection in 1922 but was successful in his bid as governor in 1925. While he was in that office, Baker sought to set up a permanent school fund in which public schools and institutions of higher learning would share equally in the monies guaranteed by the state constitution. He proposed to set up the fund from taxes on inheritances, admission to recreational events, tobacco, and cigarettes. His proposal failed. In 1929 poor health forced Baker to retire as governor.

Baker held membership in professional associations and was president of the Wayne County Teacher's Association, the Missouri State Association of School Superintendents, and the Southwest Pedagogical Society. He received an honorary degree from Missouri Valley College (1922).

REFERENCES: *NCAB* (B:216); *WWW* (I); Floyd C. Shoemaker, *Missouri and Missourians* (Chicago: The Lewis Publishing Co., 1943), vol. 2, pp. 318–31.   *James R. Layton*

BALDWIN, James. B. December 15, 1841, Hamilton County, Indiana, to Isaac and Sarah (Clayton) Baldwin. M. 1864 to Mary S. Taylor. Ch. none. D. August 30, 1925, South Orange, New Jersey.

James Baldwin was educated at home and in a small school run by the Society of Friends. He spent most of his time reading and, although he received no formal instruction in composition, decided to become a writer. His first story, "Two Soldiers," was published in *Forrester's Boys and Girls Magazine* when he was eleven years old.

From 1865 to 1869 Baldwin taught in the Hamilton County, Indiana, district schools and organized Indiana's first graded public school system at Noblesville. In 1873 he established a larger public school system and a public library at Huntington. In 1882 Baldwin's *English Literature* was published; it used his method of teaching literature and illustrative criticism from many sources. This work won him recognition, and in 1884 he received an honorary doctorate from DePauw University.

In 1887 Harper and Brothers Publishing Company offered him a position in the education department; in 1890 he became assistant editor of Harper periodicals. Baldwin prepared *Harper Readers* (a five-volume series, 1887–1890) and *Harper's School Speakers* (a three-volume series, 1891). In 1894 he became an editor with the American Book Company, a position he held until 1924. He wrote and assisted in the publication of perhaps half of all the school readers used in American schools and won recognition as an authority on children's books and reading. The author of more than fifty volumes on a variety of subjects, Baldwin aimed to develop good literary taste. His work received praise for its high interest level and response to the needs of children at various ages.

Baldwin's writing included *The Story of Siegfried* (1882), *The Story of Roland* (1883), *The Book Lover* (1884), *A Story of the Golden Age* (1886), *Six Centuries of English Poetry* (1892), *The Book of Elegies* (1892), *The Famous Allegories* (1893), *Choice English Lyrics* (1893), *Fairy Stories and Fables* (1895), *Old Greek Stories* (1895), *Fifty Famous Stories Retold* (1895), *Old Stories from the East* (1895), *Guide to the Systematic Reading of the Encyclopedia Britannica* (1895), *Four Great Americans* (1896), *Baldwin's Readers* (eight volumes, 1897), *The Discovery of the Old Northwest* (1901), *The Conquest of the Old Northwest* (1901), *Barnes' Elementary History of the United States* (1903), *Hero Tales Told in School* (1904), *Abraham Lincoln, A True Life* (1904), *The Fairy Reader* (1905), *Thirty Famous Stories* (1905), *The Golden Fleece* (1906), *An American Book of Golden Deeds* (1907), *Stories of the King* (1909), *The Expressive*

Readers (eight volumes, 1911), *Fifty Famous People* (1912), *John Bunyan's Dream Story* (1913), *Fifty Famous Rides and Riders* (1915), and *The Story of Liberty* (1919).

REFERENCES: *NCAB* (14:134); *WWW* (I); *NYT,* September 3, 1925, p. 25.   *Barbara Ruth Peltzman*

BALDWIN, James Mark. B. January 12, 1861, Columbia, South Carolina, to Cyrus Hull and Lydia Eunice (Ford) Baldwin. M. November 22, 1888, to Helen Hayes Green. Ch. two. D. November 8, 1934, Paris, France.

James Mark Baldwin received the A.B. (1884) and Ph.D. (1889) degrees from Princeton University. He also studied philosophy at Berlin and Leipzig, Germany. He held one-year teaching appointments at Princeton and Lake Forest (Illinois) University.

After five years at the University of Toronto (1888–93), Baldwin returned to Princeton (1893–1903) where he wrote a number of important books, established a laboratory of experimental psychology, and made scientific excursions to Europe. He joined the faculty at Johns Hopkins University as professor of philosophy and psychology (1903) and became involved in the controversies about evolution and social psychology. In his later years, he was critical of the experimental method because it had produced such meager results in his area of special interest, genetics. He turned to the study of mental origins, development, and evolution and developed several theories.

Baldwin assisted during 1909 to 1913 in the establishment of the National University of Mexico. He moved to Paris in 1912 where he gained eminence in intellectual circles.

Baldwin was cofounder (1894) with James Cattell (*q.v.*) and editor (1894–1903) of the *Psychological Review.* His books included *Mental Development in the Child and the Race* (1895), *Social and Ethical Interpretations in Mental Development* (1897), *The Story of the Mind* (1898), *Handbook of Psychology* (two volumes, 1889–91), *History of Psychology* (two volumes, 1913), *France and the War* (1915), *American Neutrality* (1916), *The Super-State* (1916), and *Between Two Wars–Memoirs and Opinions* (two volumes, 1926).

His works on genetics had an influence on psychological thought, but he was best known for his collaboration, with sixty other scientists, in an attempt to standardize terminology for psychology. The result was *Dictionary of Psychology and Philosophy* (1901–06).

Baldwin was the recipient of several honorary awards and degrees, including the first to be awarded by Oxford (England) University in the field of science. He was active in national and international organizations, including the International Congress of Psychology (president, 1909–13) and the American Psychological Association (president, 1897–98), and he was a member or honorary member of several foreign associations.

REFERENCES: *DAB* (supp. 1); *LE* (I); *NCAB* (25:89); *WWW* (I); James Mark Baldwin, *Between Two Wars, 1861–1921* (Boston: The Stratford Co., 1926); *NYT*, November 9, 1934, p. 21.   John M. Ivanoff

BALDWIN, Joseph. B. October 31, 1827, New Castle, Pennsylvania, to Joseph and Isabella Henry (Cairns) Baldwin. M. 1852 to Ellen Sophronia Fluhart. Ch. nine. D. January 13, 1899, Austin, Texas.

Credited with founding normal school systems in three states, Joseph Baldwin was a leader in state and national education associations and an effective writer and speaker for the improvement of public education.

Baldwin attended local public schools and Bartlett Academy in New Castle, Pennsylvania. He received the B.A. degree (1852) from Bethany (Virginia; now West Virginia) College and attended Lancaster Normal School (later, Millersville State College) in Millersville, Pennsylvania, for a short time in 1857. He considered entering the Disciples of Christ ministry and was an active layman throughout his life.

A significant influence was said to have been Baldwin's contact with Horace Mann (*q.v.*) for a week in 1855 at an institute in St. Louis, Missouri.

After graduation from Bethany College, Baldwin taught at the Male and Female Academy, Platte City, Missouri. In 1854 he opened Savannah (Missouri) Collegiate Institute, and was its principal until 1857, when he conducted the Lawrence County Normal School in New Castle, Pennsylvania. Baldwin organized the private Indiana Normal School at Burnettsville, Indiana, in 1858, moving it to Kokomo in 1859. He served in the Union Army (1863–64). He was elected principal of Logansport (Indiana) Seminary in 1864.

Returning to Missouri in 1867, Baldwin founded the North Missouri Normal School (later, Northeast Missouri State University) at Kirksville. It became the First District State Normal School in 1870, one of the first two public normals in the state, with Baldwin as its president. In 1881 Baldwin accepted an appointment to be principal of the two-year-old Sam Houston Normal Institute (later, State University) at Huntsville, Texas, serving there until he was appointed the first professor of pedagogy at the University of Texas at Austin (1891). Uncertain about the role of the university in teacher education, the regents discontinued but then reactivated the school of pedagogy in 1896. Elected president of the Texas State Teachers Association (TSTA), Baldwin was granted a one-year leave; he retired a year later. His last two years were spent writing and lecturing as professor emeritus.

Among Baldwin's publications were *The Art of School Management* (1881), *Elementary Psychology and Education* (1887), *Psychology Applied to the Art of Teaching* (1892), and *School Management and School Methods* (1897). He was editor of *The Normal* (Kokomo, Indiana) and *The Normal American Journal of Education* (Kirksville, Missouri) and was one of the publishers of *The Texas School Journal* (Huntsville).

Besides serving as president of TSTA, Baldwin helped found and served as vice-president (1856) and president (1871) of the Missouri State Teachers Association and vice-president of the Indiana State Teachers Association (1861 and 1865). Baldwin was active in the National Teachers' Association as director (1870), vice-president of the Department of Normal Schools (1883), and chairman of the Committee on Moral Education (1892).

Baldwin was a pioneer in conducting and lecturing at local and county-wide teacher institutes in California and many other states, often sponsored by the Peabody Fund. He received an honorary degree from Bethany College.

REFERENCES: *DAB;* "Dr. Joseph Baldwin," *The University Record* 1 (April 1899): 179–182; Frederick Eby (*q.v.*) *The Development of Education in Texas* (New York: Macmillan, 1925); Claude V. Hall, "A Sketch of the Life and Work of Joseph Baldwin," *Texas School Journal* 27 (October 1909): 6–11; "Joseph Baldwin," *Texas School Journal* 17 (February 1899): 445–446; James Carl Matthews, "The Contributions of Joseph Baldwin to Public Education" (Ph.D. diss., George Peabody College for Teachers, 1932); "Professor Baldwin Dies," *Austin Daily Statesman* 28 (January 14, 1899).   *D. Richard Bowles*

BALDWIN, Maria Louise. B. September 13, 1856, Cambridge, Massachusetts, to Peter L. and Mary E. (Blake) Baldwin. M. no. D. January 9, 1922, Boston, Massachusetts.

Maria Louise Baldwin was a member of a family that encouraged her development and that of her sister and brother. Her father was a Haitian seaman who settled in Boston and became a postal clerk; his three children went on to become a principal, a high school teacher, and a lawyer.

Baldwin received her formal education in the schools of Cambridge, Massachusetts; in 1875 she completed a year in the teacher training school there. Unable to find work in Massachusetts, she became a teacher in Chestertown, Maryland. She returned to Cambridge in 1882 to teach at the Agassiz Grammar School and remained there for forty years. She was appointed principal in 1889, the first black principal in Massachusetts. In 1916 she became master, the only black and one of only two women in this position. The school had a faculty of twelve white teachers and five hundred students, nearly all of whom were white.

Baldwin continued her education during her forty-year career, taking courses at Harvard University. She moved freely and had many friends in the white community of greater Boston, and her contributions to the black community were numerous. She was associated with several scholarly black groups, including the Women's Era Club, the Banneker Club, and the Omar Circle. She conducted a weekly reading class for black students at Harvard. She also taught summer courses for teachers at Hampton Institute in Virginia and at the Institute for Colored Youth in Cheyney, Pennsylvania. She spoke often on behalf of her fellow blacks and against racial isolation.

REFERENCES: Benjamin Brawley *(q.v.), Negro Builders and Heroes* (Chapel Hill: University of North Carolina Press, 1937), pp. 277–79). *NAW;* Hallie Q. Brown (*q.v.*), *Homespun Heroines* (Xenia, Ohio: Aldine, 1937); *Boston Transcript,* January 10, 1922.

Rita S. Saslaw

BALDWIN, Theron. B. July 21, 1801, Goshen, Connecticut, to Elisha and Clarissa (Judd) Baldwin. M. June 1831 to Caroline Wilder. Ch. none. D. April 10, 1870, Orange, New Jersey.

Theron Baldwin, pioneer, western missionary, and educator, was graduated from Yale College in 1827 with high honors. He entered the theological department where he played a leading role among a small group of students who planned to go to the Midwest to promote education and religion. He was ordained in the ministry in 1829 and went to Jacksonville, Illinois, under the auspices of the American Home Missionary Society. He settled in Vandalia, the capital of Illinois at the time, as a home missionary, where he became influential in the public education movement. He was instrumental in securing a charter in 1835 from the legislature that established three colleges: Illinois, Shurtleff, and McKendree.

In 1838 Baldwin was appointed first principal of the Monticello Seminary, a new girls' school. Before the school opened, Baldwin undertook an extensive tour of the East, visiting the leading seminaries in New England and New York. He observed teaching methods and subject matter content and hired some teachers for the Illinois school. He was an advocate of education for women on an equal basis with men.

Baldwin was principal of Monticello Seminary until 1843, when he became the executive head of the Society for the Promotion of Collegiate and Theological Education in the West (better known as the College and Education Society). As secretary of the society (1843–70) he wrote annual reports and included addresses delivered by eminent educators and clergymen; these publications represent a valuable contribution to the history of higher education.

REFERENCES: *DAB; NCAB* (6:39); *TC; WWW* (H); Julian Monson Sturtevant *(q.v.) Sketch of Theron Baldwin* (Boston: A. Mudge & Son, 1875). *Abdul Samad*

BALLIET, Thomas Minard. B. March 1, 1852, New Mahoning, Pennsylvania, to Nathan and Sarah (Minard) Balliet. M. August 2, 1898, to Elizabeth Sterns. Ch. one. D. February 18, 1942, New York, New York.

Thomas M. Balliet attended Lehighton (Pennsylvania) Academy. He received the A.B. with highest honors (1876), A.M. (1879), and Ph.D.

(1887) degrees from Franklin and Marshall College in Lancaster, Pennsylvania, and attended Yale Divinity School (1877–78). For ten years he served in Pennsylvania as principal of a high school in Bellefonte, teacher of Latin and Greek in the normal school at Kutztown, and superintendent of schools in Carbondale. After a year as lecturer at the normal school of Francis Wayland Parker *(q.v.)* in Chicago, Illinois, Balliet became superintendent of schools in Reading, Pennsylvania.

He served as superintendent of schools in Springfield, Massachusetts (1887–1904), and was credited with making the Springfield schools into one of the most efficient and progressive systems in the country. He stressed individualized instruction, and instituted manual training. The first American public trade school was established while he was superintendent. He organized a technical high school and a four-year commercial course at Central High School in Springfield (later it became the High School of Commerce), which he equipped with laboratories for biology, chemistry, and physics. Balliet instituted major changes in the teaching of the common branches of instruction, including arithmetic and reading. Kindergartens were introduced, and music appreciation and domestic science classes were started in the schools. Balliet favored employing more male teachers in the public schools and educating the mentally and physically handicapped.

Balliet accepted the post of dean of the school of pedagogy of New York University (1904); he retired as dean emeritus in 1919. At New York University he established the first chair of experimental pedagogy in the United States. He provided lecturers for teachers of art, civic education, school hygiene, mental hygiene, physical education, and manual training. He taught classes in philosophy of education, methods of teaching, and school supervision and wrote articles on sex education and other professional topics.

Balliet served as a trustee of Springfield (Massachusetts) College. He was awarded an honorary degree by Franklin and Marshall College (1927).

REFERENCES: *LE* (II); *NCAB* (31:177); *WWW* (II); *NYT*, February 19, 1942, p. 19.   *Anthony V. Patti*

BANCROFT, Cecil Franklin Patch. B. November 25, 1839, New Ipswich, New Hampshire, to James and Sarah (Williams) Bancroft. M. May 6, 1867, to Frances Adelia Kittredge. Ch. five. D. October 4, 1901, Andover, Massachusetts.

Cecil Franklin Patch Bancroft attended the public schools in Ashby, New Hampshire, and the Appleton Academy in Ipswich before entering Dartmouth College at the age of sixteen. In 1860, after graduating from Dartmouth, he became principal of Appleton Academy in Mount Vernon, New Hampshire, and remained there until 1864 when he entered the Union Theological Seminary in New York. He transferred to the Andover

(Massachusetts) Theological Seminary in 1865 and was ordained a Congregational minister in 1867. Bancroft was director of an institution at Lookout Mountain, Tennessee, from 1867 until the school closed in 1872. He studied at the University of Halle, Germany, and returned to the United States in 1873 as principal of Phillips Academy in Andover, Massachusetts.

When Bancroft became principal, Phillips Academy was in financial straits, had a declining reputation for scholarship, and was decreasing in enrollment. He used the school's centenary celebration in 1878 to arouse alumni and public financial support and began a period of expansion. He liberalized the school program and revised the curriculum, introducing mathematics, science, and other subjects. During his twenty-eight years of administration, the school became one of the best-known preparatory schools in the United States.

Bancroft was a trustee of Dartmouth College, and president of the Dartmouth Alumni Association, the Headmasters Association of the United States, and the New England Association of Colleges and Preparatory Schools. He received several honorary degrees.

REFERENCES: *DAB; NCAB* (24:311); *WWW* (I); *The Boston Transcript,* October 5, 1901; Claude Moore Fuess, *An Old New England School: A History of Phillips Academy, Andover* (Boston: Houghton Mifflin, 1917). *Thomas Meighan*

BANCROFT, Jessie Hubbell. B. December 20, 1867, Winona, Minnesota, to Edward Hall and Susan Maria (Hubbell) Bancroft. M. no. D. November 13, 1952, New York, New York.

Jessie Bancroft obtained her original professional education from the State Normal School (later, Winona State College) in Winona, Minnesota, and studied at the Minneapolis School of Education. She also attended the Iowa Medical College and the Harvard Summer School of Physical Education.

Bancroft began her professional career in 1889 as a teacher at the Ida Institute in Davenport, Iowa. A year later, she moved to New York City to teach in private schools and at the Normal (later, Hunter) College. She was director of physical training in the public schools of Brooklyn, New York (1893–1903), the first woman to direct the physical education program of a large city school system. In 1904 she became assistant director of physical training in the public schools of New York City, a position she held until her retirement in 1928.

Bancroft introduced a graded system of physical education taught by classroom teachers. She developed the triple posture test and made anthropometric measurements, which were used in the manufacture of school desks, clothing, shoes, and subway seats.

Bancroft was the first woman to publish a considerable body of professional literature in physical education. Her best-known book was *Games for the Playground, Home, School and Gymnasium* (1909). Others were *School Gymnastics; Free Hand* (1896), *School Gymnastics with Light Apparatus* (1900), and *Handbook of Athletic Games for Players, Instructors, and Spectators* (with William Dean Pulvermacher, 1916).

One of the founders of the American Physical Education Association (APEA), she served as its executive secretary. Bancroft was the first woman to become a member of the American Academy of Physical Education and to receive the Gulick Award for distinguished service to the profession. She was a fellow of the American Association for the Advancement of Science and of the APEA (1931).

REFERENCES: *WW* (XII); Jessie H. Bancroft, "Pioneering in Physical Training—An Autobiography," *Research Quarterly* 12 (October 1941): 666–78; Ruth Evans, "Jessie H. Bancroft," *Journal of Health, Physical Education and Recreation* 31 (April 1960): 50; Ellen W. Gerber, *Innovators and Institutions in Physical Education* (Philadelphia: Lea and Febiger, 1971); "Jessie Hubbell Bancroft," *School and Society* 76 (November 22, 1952): 332; "Presentation of Fellowship Awards," *Journal of Health and Physical Education* 2 (June 1931); *NYT,* November 14, 1952, p. 23.   *Adelaide M. Cole*

BANISTER, Zilpah Polly Grant. B. May 30, 1794, Norfolk, Connecticut, to Joel and Zilpah (Cowles) Grant. M. September 8, 1841, to William Bostwick Banister. Ch. none. D. December 3, 1874, Newburyport, Massachusetts.

Zilpah Polly Grant Banister received her early education in the local district school. At the age of fifteen, she began her teaching career. With twelve years of teaching experience and a savings of fifty dollars, Banister entered the Byfield Female Academy conducted by Reverend Joseph Emerson *(q.v.),* a champion of women's education. Here she met Mary Lyon *(q.v.),* who became a friend and for many years her closest collaborator.

In 1824 Banister accepted the leadership of the Adams Female Academy in Londonderry, New Hampshire, but disagreements with the trustees led to her departure in 1828. She accepted an invitation to establish a seminary at Ipswich, Massachusetts. The Ipswich Female Academy began with Grant as the principal and Mary Lyon as a teacher and assistant principal. In 1834 Lyon left Ipswich to become the founder of Mount Holyoke Seminary.

At the schools Banister conducted, the curriculum stressed English, science, and biblical study. Teachers were expected to acquaint themselves with the health, habits, and intellectual and moral development of all girls in their sections. Grades were not stressed, and there were no academic prizes or honors. Students were taught to love the pursuit of knowledge. They received a formal and systematic preparation for careers as teachers. Interested in the needs of the West, she entered into a loan program designed to prepare Ipswich students to serve as missionary teachers.

During most of her teaching years, she suffered from recurring illnesses. In 1839 she left Ipswich and teaching and in 1841 married William B. Banister, a former Massachusetts state senator.

REFERENCES: *DAB; NAW; WWW* (H); Eliza Paul Capen, "Zilpah Grant and the Art of Teaching," *New England Quarterly* 20 (September 1947): 347–64; John Cowles, "Zilpah Grant Banister," *American Journal of Education* 30 (1880). *Ann Stankiewicz*

BAPST, John. B. December 12, 1815, LaRoche, Fribourg, Switzerland, to n.a. M. no. D. November 2, 1887, Baltimore, Maryland.

John Bapst was educated at Saint Michael's College, Fribourg, Switzerland. He entered the Society of Jesus in 1835 and taught at Saint Michael's (1840–43). He was ordained in 1846 and finished his formal theological studies in France. Much to his surprise and dismay, he was assigned to the American missions in 1848.

Knowing little English and no Indian languages, he was sent to minister to the Abnaki Indians in Old Town, Maine. To support himself, he moved from Old Town to Eastport, Maine, in 1850 and, over the next few years, with the help of several companions, began to serve Catholics in a wide area that included thirty-three towns and nine thousand people.

Two years later he moved his headquarters to Ellsworth, Maine, where he came into conflict with his Protestant neighbors. For the next few years, he worked tirelessly to have anti-Catholic prayers removed from the public schools. He found himself in constant and increasingly bitter confrontations with members of the Know-Nothing party who controlled the local government. In 1854 on the return from one of many trips to serve his far-flung parishioners, he was taken by an Ellsworth mob and tarred and feathered. His tormentors reportedly made an unsuccessful attempt to burn him to death. Responsible townspeople were horrified by these happenings and, soon after his recovery, honored him publicly. Following the incident he moved to Bangor where he stayed until the Jesuits withdrew from Maine in 1859.

In 1860 he was appointed superior of scholastics in Boston and in the autumn of that year was named first rector of the newly built Boston College (1860–67) and established a sound foundation for the college. He stayed in Boston until 1867 when he was made superior of all Jesuits in New York and Canada. He returned to Boston College as religious superior (1873–77) and moved to Providence, Rhode Island, as pastor of Saint Joseph's Church, where he founded a parish school. He spent his last years in Jesuit houses in Maryland.

REFERENCES: *DAB; New Catholic Encyclopedia,* (New York: McGraw Hill, 1967). *Anne E. Scheerer*

BARD, Samuel. B. April, 1742, Burlington, New Jersey, to John and Susanna (Valleau) Bard. M. 1770 to Mary Bard. Ch. ten. D. May 24, 1821, Hyde Park, New York.

Samuel Bard moved to New York City in 1746. After acquiring his grammar school education, he entered King's College at the age of fourteen. Immediately after graduating in 1760, he sailed for Europe to study medicine. The ship on which he sailed was captured by a French privateer, and he was held in confinement at Bayonne for six months. Upon his release, he studied first in London, England, and became an assistant at St. Thomas' Hospital; he then studied at Edinburgh, Scotland, receiving his medical degree in 1765.

On returning to New York City, Bard began practicing medicine with his father. Determined to establish a medical school in New York, his ambition became a reality in 1768 when the second medical school in North America was organized as the Medical School of King's College. At the age of twenty-six Bard became professor of the theory and practice of physic. He was instrumental in establishing the New York Hospital in 1791 where he became a visiting physician.

The medical school was closed during the American Revolution, and Bard was forced to leave New York City because of his unpopular political opinions; he went to Shrewsbury, New Jersey. When the American government was established, King's College was renamed Columbia College, and the medical school was reopened in 1792 with Bard as professor and, later, dean of the faculty. He was affiliated with the school for forty years.

Bard assisted in the establishment of the New York City Library and the New York Dispensary. Active in the management of the yellow-fever epidemic, he contracted the disease and was forced into retirement.

He was elected president of the original College of Physicians and Surgeons in 1811. Bard wrote several papers and books. His most famous writing was a textbook, *A Compendium of the Theory and Practice of Midwifery* (1807).

REFERENCES: *DAB; NCAB* (8:209); *WWW* (H). *Richard M. Coger*

BARDEEN, Charles William. B. August 28, 1847, Groton, Massachusetts, to William and Mary Ann (Farnsworth) Bardeen. M. July 15, 1868, to Ellen Dickerman. Ch. one. D. August 19, 1924, Syracuse, New York.

During the Civil War young Charles Bardeen left school and home to join the First Massachusetts Volunteers as a drummer boy. The diary he kept during this period was later published under the title of *A Little Fifer's War Diary* (1910). On his return from the war, he completed high school and then attended Yale College.

After graduation from Yale with the A.B. degree (1869), he worked as principal of Western Boarding School (1869), vice-principal of Connecticut State Normal School (later, Central Connecticut State College) in 1870, English teacher at Kalamazoo (Michigan) College (1871), superintendent of schools in Whitehill, New York (1872), and New York State agent for Clark and Maynard Educational Publications.

In 1874 he became managing editor of *School Bulletin,* a position he held for almost fifty years, and brought the journal to national prominence. He managed the publishing department of Davis Bardeen and Company from 1874 to 1880, when he bought the firm and continued it under his own name until he sold it in 1922.

Bardeen was the author of many books; some of the more important were *Common School Law* (1875), which had several editions, *History of Educational Journalism in New York* (1893), *Teaching as a Business* (1897), *A Dictionary of Educational Biography* (1901), *A Manual of Civics* (1902), *A System of Rhetoric* (1911), and *The Allibone Arithmetics* (1918). Bardeen also wrote many novels with schools and teaching as the setting, such as *Fables for Teachers* (1909), *Tom, Tom Tit and Other Stories About Schools* (1911), and *The Teacher's Wife* (1918).

Bardeen was a member of the Author's Club of London and the Royal Societies of London, president of the Browning Club when it was first formed in Syracuse, a member of the National Institute of Social Sciences, and president of the Yale Club of Syracuse (1902–12). In 1893 he was appointed head of the department of educational publications for the International Congress. During the next four years he served as director of the National Educational Association. He served as the president of the Educational Press Association of America (1900–24).

REFERENCES: *DAB; WWW* (I); *NYT,* August 20, 1924, p. 13.

Marilyn Meiss

BARNARD, Frederick Augustus Porter. B. May 5, 1809, Sheffield, Massachusetts, to Robert Foster and Augusta (Porter) Barnard. M. December 27, 1847, to Margaret McMurray. Ch. none. D. April 27, 1889, New York, New York.

Frederick Augustus Porter Barnard is also reported as being born on May 25, 1809. He was educated by the Reverend Orville Dewey and in academies at Saratoga, New York, and Stockbridge, Massachusetts. He was graduated from Yale College with the A.B. degree (1828).

Barnard taught in a Hartford, Connecticut, grammar school and was a tutor in Yale College in 1830, where he instituted teaching of classes below senior level by specialists rather than having them in groups instructed in all subjects by a tutor. He suffered increasing deafness and taught at institutions for the deaf in Hartford (1831) and New York City (1832–37).

He was professor of mathematics and natural philosophy (1837–48) and of chemistry (1848–54) at the University of Alabama.

He taught astronomy and mathematics (1854–56) and served as president (1856–61) at the University of Mississippi in Oxford. He resigned in 1861 as a sympathizer of the Union side of the Civil War. While in Oxford, he had been ordained in the Episcopal church in 1855 and served as rector of an Oxford parish to 1861.

Barnard lived in Norfolk, Virginia, from 1861 until its capture by Union troops in 1862. He worked as chief of the map and chart division of the United States Coast Survey (1862–64) and became president of Columbia College (later, University) in 1864, serving to 1889. He developed the concept of elective courses and common examinations for entrance to college. Under Barnard, Columbia became a major American university with admission of women in 1883 and establishment of a women's department that later became Barnard College, named in his honor. Teachers College and a school of mines were established, and the graduate and professional departments and schools were strengthened and enlarged. Enrollment increased from about a hundred and fifty to over two thousand students.

Barnard was the author of many articles and books, including *A Treatise on Arithmetic* (1830), *Analytical Grammar* (1836), *Arithmetic Divested of Its Difficulties* (1843), *Letters on Collegiate Government* (1855), *A History of the United States Coast Survey* (1857), *Recent Progress of Science* (1859), and *Machinery and Processes of the Industrial Arts* (1869). He was editor-in-chief of *Johnson's Cyclopaedia* (1872).

Active in scholarly and professional associations, Barnard was a founder of the National Academy of Sciences (foreign secretary, 1874–80) and president of the American Metrological Society, the American Association for the Advancement of Science, and the American Institute, and an honorary member of many foreign societies. He was awarded the Legion of Honor of France in 1873 and was the recipient of many honorary degrees.

REFERENCES: *AC; DAB; EB; NCAB* (6:347); *TC; WWW* (H); *NYT,* April 28, 1889, p. 5; William J. Chute, "The Life of Frederick A. P. Barnard to His Election As President of Columbia College in 1864" (diss., Columbia University, 1952).   *Foster F. Wilkinson*

BARNARD, Henry. B. January 24, 1811, Hartford, Connecticut, to Chauncey and Elizabeth (Andrus) Barnard. M. September 6, 1847, to Josephine Desnoyers. Ch. five. D. July 5, 1900, Hartford, Connecticut.

Henry Barnard was graduated from Yale College in 1830, taught school for one year, and subsequently studied law. Elected as a Whig delegate to the Connecticut General Assembly (1837–40), he introduced the bill creating the state board of common schools (1837) and a year later became the first secretary of the board, the state's chief school officer. He eventually withdrew from the assembly to establish the political neutrality of the office and never again identified himself with a political party. After the state legislature abolished his office in 1842, he accepted a similar assignment in Rhode Island (1843–49), returning to Connecticut as principal of the state normal school and superintendent of common schools (1850–54).

Barnard served brief terms as chancellor of the University of Wisconsin (1857–59), as president of St. John's College in Annapolis, Maryland (1865–66), and finally as the first United States commissioner of education (1867–70). The work of the United States Office of Education continues to reflect the imprint of Barnard's original design: reform and promotion of education (not schools alone) through federally sponsored experimentation, research and development by scholars, and the collection and dissemination of educational statistics and information.

Barnard made his most lasting contributions as founder and editor of the *American Journal of Education,* a periodical published from 1855 to 1882 that won critical acclaim from scholars in the United States and Europe. A man of moderate wealth, he financed the journal almost entirely with his own resources, ceasing publication when his energy and funds were exhausted. The thirty-two massive volumes constituted, according to a contemporary, a literal encyclopedia of education and ensured Barnard's international reputation as an educational statesman and scholar.

Barnard's publications, some of which were collections from the *American Journal of Education,* included *School Architecture* (1848), *Normal Schools* (1851), *National Education in Europe* (1854), *American Pedagogy* (1860), *Educational Aphorisms and Suggestions, Ancient and Modern* (1861), *Memoirs of Object Teaching* (1861), *Science and Art* (1871), *Pestalozzi and His Educational System* (1874), *American Educational Biography* (1874), and *English Pedagogy* (1876).

Henry Barnard was a preeminent nineteenth-century leader in the early development of American public education. Like many of his contemporary educators, he viewed social change and unrest with strong misgivings. Public education offered the means to control the rate and extent of change and to inculcate a common morality in the nation's young. Barnard avoided controversy, choosing instead to advance his cause through research, publication, and administrative leadership. He believed that educational reform required not merely more public schools but the organization of common school systems that would reduce local, state, and, ultimately, national variations in the quality and quantity of educational opportunity.

REFERENCES: *AC; DAB; NCAB* (1:505); *WWW* (H); *NYT,* July 6, 1900, p. 7; Ralph C. Jenkins and Gertrude C. Warner, *Henry Barnard: An Introduction* (Hartford: Connecticut State Teachers Association, 1937);

Richard Emmons Thursfield, *Henry Barnard's American Journal of Education* (Baltimore: Johns Hopkins Press, 1945); Donald R. Warren, *To Enforce Education: A History of the Founding Years of the U.S. Office of Education* (Detroit: Wayne State University Press, 1974).

Donald R. Warren

BARNES, Earl. B. July 15, 1861, Martville, New York, to James and Minerva A. (Myres) Barnes. M. August 6, 1885, to Mary Downing Sheldon *(q.v.).* M. June 17, 1901, to Anna Kohler. Ch. four. D. May 29, 1935, New Hartford, Connecticut.

Earl Barnes attended the Oswego (New York) Normal School (later, State University of New York College); he received the A.B. degree (1889) from Indiana University and the M.S. degree (1891) from Cornell University in Ithaca, New York. He served as professor of European history at Indiana University (1890–91), professor of education at Stanford (California) University (1891–97), staff lecturer at the London Society for the Extension of University Teaching (1900–01), and, until 1914, staff lecturer for the American Society for the Extension of University Teaching with headquarters in Philadelphia.

Mary Downing Sheldon Barnes *(q.v.),* Barnes's first wife and daughter of Edward Austin Sheldon *(q.v.),* was a distinguished educator and writer and the first woman member of the faculty at Stanford University (1892–96).

As early as 1896 and 1897, Barnes laid the groundwork for a career as a public lecturer. He published a syllabus for eight lectures on the history of European civilization (1897) for the University Extension Club of San Jose, California, and abstracts of six lectures on the development of educational control for the Twentieth Century Club's second session of university lectures (1899–1900).

After a year in London (1900–01), Barnes engaged in a period of extensive writing, including syllabi for courses of six lectures on various subjects for the American Society for the Extension of University Teaching. Two of the most notable were *Syllabus of a Course of Six Lectures on Development and Education of Our Human Hungers* (1906) and *Syllabus of a Course of Six Lectures on Educational Movements and Problems of Today* (1903). He was the author of *Studies in Education Devoted to Child Study* (two volumes, 1902), *Where Knowledge Fails* (1907), *Woman in Modern Society* (1912), and *The Psychology of Childhood and Youth* (1914) and coauthor with his first wife, Mary Sheldon Barnes, of *Studies in American History* (1891).

REFERENCES: *NYT,* May 5, 1935, p. 17; *WWW* (I); *Training School Bulletin* 32 (June 1935): 61.   *John C. Hogan*

BARNES, Harry Elmer. B. June 15, 1889, Auburn, New York, to William Henry and Lulu Carlotta (Short) Barnes. M. June 8, 1916, to Lulu Grace Stone. M. January 26, 1935, to Jean Hutchison Newman. Ch. one. D. August 25, 1968, Malibu, California.

Harry Elmer Barnes began his higher education at Syracuse (New York) University, where he received the A.B. (1913) and A.M. (1915) degrees. He was appointed a teaching fellow at Syracuse, lecturing in sociology (1913–15) and was a fellow in history at Barnard College of Columbia University (1915–16), and a Cutting Fellow (1916–17). He earned the Ph.D. degree from Columbia University (1918).

Barnes lectured at Harvard University (1916–17) and joined the faculty at Clark University in Worcester, Massachusetts, as professor of history of thought and culture (1920–23). He also was history professor at the New School for Social Research in New York City (1922–24 and 1926–37). He was in Massachusetts as professor of history and sociology at Smith College in Northampton (1923–30), Springfield College (1923), and Amherst College (1923–25). He taught at Teachers College of Columbia University in 1928 and lectured there until 1938.

Barnes wrote a column three days a week for the Scripps-Howard newspapers (1929–40). He was the author and coauthor of many books, including *Sociology Before Comte* (1917), *History of the Penal Reformatory and Correctional Institutions of New Jersey* (1918), *The New History and the Social Studies* (1925), *The Genesis of the World War* (1926), *An Economic and Social History of Europe* (with M. M. Knight and F. Fluegal, 1927), *Living in the Twentieth Century* (1928), *World Politics in Modern Civilization* (1930), *History of Western Civilization* (two volumes, 1935), *Intellectual and Cultural History of the Western World* (1937), *Social Institutions* (1942), and *Survey of Western Civilization* (1947). He edited a number of publications, including *The History and Prospects of the Social Sciences* (1925), *An Introduction to Sociology* (1927), *Universal History of the World* (1937), and *Studies in American Investments Abroad* (six volumes, 1928–35). He was author of some two hundred articles in many periodicals and professional journals.

He held memberships in many professional associations. He was an investigator for the State Prison Inquiry Commission of New Jersey (1917–18), a member of the State Committee to Investigate Penal Systems in Pennsylvania (1918–19), special consultant for prison industries to the War Production Board (1943–44), and special consultant and historian to the Smaller War Plants Corporation (1945–46).

REFERENCES: *LE* (III); *NCAB* (C:35); *WW* (XXVIII); *WWAE* (XV).

Joyce McDonnold

BARNES, Mary Downing Sheldon. B. September 15, 1850, Oswego, New York, to Edward Austin *(q.v.)* and Frances Anna Bradford (Stiles) Sheldon. M. August 6, 1885, to Earl Barnes *(q.v.).* Ch. none. D. August 27, 1898, London, England.

Mary Downing Sheldon Barnes began her career as an educator in Oswego, New York, where she attended the famous Pestalozzian-oriented Oswego State Normal and Training School (later, State University of New York College), founded and directed by her father Edward Austin Sheldon *(q.v.).* She completed the classical and advanced courses in 1868. In 1871 she was among the first group of women to attend the University of Michigan, where she enrolled in the classical course. At Michigan she studied under Charles Kendall Adams *(q.v.)* with classmate Alice Freeman Palmer *(q.v.),* who also became influential in educational work. Sheldon was graduated in the classical course in 1874 and received the A.M. degree from Michigan in 1878; she participated in the commencement program, reading a poem, "A Legend of the Amazon," to the alumni.

She returned to Oswego where she taught history, botany, Latin, and Greek at the Normal and Training School (1874–76 and 1882–84). Her ideas on education were unusual at that time. She did not use traditional history textbooks but duplicated materials for use by her students. Open discussions were common in her Wellesley (Massachusetts) College history classes where she taught from 1876 to 1879, leaving because of health problems. Before her return to Oswego, she spent one year in recuperation and two years in travel and study abroad (1879–82).

In 1885 she married a younger former student, Earl Barnes *(q.v.),* with whom she shared an interest in history. Early in their marriage, Mary Barnes spent her time visiting, lecturing, and engaging in historical research. Earl Barnes was appointed head of the department of education at Stanford University in 1891 and Mary Barnes joined the Stanford history department in 1892 where she applied the source method with open discussions to instruction in nineteenth-century European history.

Mary Barnes was the author of *Studies in General History* (1885), *Studies in Greek and Roman History* (1886), *Aids for Teaching General History* (1888), *Studies in American History* (with Earl Barnes, 1891), and *Studies in Historical Method* (1896).

REFERENCES: *DAB; NAW; WC; WWW* (H).   *Rita S. Saslaw*

BARR, Arvil Sylvester. B. January 10, 1892, Selvin, Indiana, to Elisha and Ellen (Bolin) Barr. M. April 18, 1914, to Lillian Whittinghill. Ch. none. D. May 12, 1962, Madison Wisconsin.

A. S. Barr received the A.B. and A.M. degrees from Indiana University in 1915 and the Ph.D. degree from the University of Wisconsin-Madison in 1929. Barr taught in a rural school near Selvin, Indiana (1910–11), and at a high school in Selvin (1913–14). From 1915 to 1917 he was a history teacher and coached athletics and debate at the Yankton (South Dakota) High School. Barr was a history instructor at Indiana University in Bloomington (1917–18) and high school secretary at the Chicago Young Men's Christian Association (1918–20). The next year, he was head of the department of education at Evansville (Indiana) College. He served as assistant director in charge of supervision for the Detroit, Michigan, public schools (1921–24). From 1924 to 1929 he was an associate professor at the University of Wisconsin and a professor from 1929. He was a distinguished professor of education at Southern Illinois University in 1957 and 1961.

Barr contributed many articles to professional journals and was editor of the Appleton series in supervision and teaching (with William H. Burton, *q.v.*), *Journal of Educational Research* (from 1928), and *Journal of Experimental Education* (from 1932). His books include *The Methodology of Educational Research* (with Carter V. Good, *q.v.*, and Douglas E. Scates, *q.v.*, 1935), *Supervision* (with William H. Burton and Leo J. Brueckner, *q.v.*, 1938), *Measurement and Prediction of Teaching Efficiency* (1948), and *Educational Research and Appraisal* (with Robert A. David and Palmer O. Johnson, *q.v.*, 1953).

In 1949 Barr was a delegate to the International Congress of Pedagogy at Santander, Spain. He belonged to numerous professional associations: he was a fellow of the American Association for the Advancement of Science and a member of the American Educational Research Association (president, 1952–53), the American Psychological Association (secretary-treasurer, educational psychology division), the Institute of Mathematics and Statistics, the National Society of College Teachers of Education (president, 1949–50), and the International Society of Pedagogical Studies and Research (vice-president). He received the Kappa Delta Pi award for research.

Barr is best remembered for his many contributions to the fields of educational supervision and educational psychology. His major research contributions were in the areas of the measurement and prediction of teaching efficiency.

REFERENCES: *LE* (III); *WWW* (IV); *WWAE* (XIV); *Journal of Educational Research* 56 (December 1962): 172–173.   *Lawrence S. Master*

BARR, Frank Stringfellow. B. January 15, 1897, Suffolk, Virginia, to William Alexander and Ida (Stringfellow) Barr. M. August 13, 1921, to Gladys Baldwin. Ch. none.

Stringfellow Barr became a leading exponent of traditional liberal education with Robert Maynard Hutchins *(q.v.)*. Barr began his college education at Tulane University in New Orleans, Louisiana (1912–13), transferring to the University of Virginia where he received the B.A. (1916) and M.A. (1917) degrees. He was a Rhodes scholar at Oxford (England) University (1919–21), earning second A.B. and M.A. degrees. In 1922 he received a diploma from the University of Paris and studied at the University of Ghent, Belgium (1922–23).

He returned to the University of Virginia as a specialist in modern European history (1924–37). He was a visiting professor of liberal arts at the University of Chicago (1936–37). He became president of St. John's College at Annapolis, Maryland (1937–46), where he instituted a completely new curriculum consisting of four years of reading great books (about 120 classics), mastering the reading of two foreign languages, spending three hundred hours in laboratory sciences, and becoming competent in liberal arts and proficient in mathematics. Barr believed that colleges should abolish the elective system, relinquish specialized education, and abandon texts in favor of four years of reading the great books.

Barr was president of the Foundation for World Government (1948–58) and a visiting professor of political science at the University of Virginia (1951–53). He was professor of humanities at Newark College of Rutgers University (1955–64) and a fellow at the Center for the Study of Democratic Institutions (1966–69).

Among his publications are the following: *Mazzini, Portrait of an Exile* (1935), *Pilgrimage of Western Man* (1949), *Let's Join the Human Race* (1950), *Citizens of the World* (1952), *Copydog in India* (1955), *The Kitchen Garden Book* (1956), *Purely Academic,* a novel (1958), *The Will of Zeus* (1962), *The Three Worlds of Man* (1963), *The Mask of Jove* (1966), and *Voices That Endured* (1971). He was advisory editor (1926–30 and 1934–37) and editor (1930–34) of the *Virginia Quarterly Review* and advisory editor for the British edition of the Great Books (1944–46).

Barr instituted and conducted the Columbia Broadcasting System's Sunday afternoon radio program "Invitation to Learning," which discussed the great books (1937–40).

In World War I Barr served in the ambulance service and surgeon general's office (1917–19). He was active in world government organizations, including the World Movement for World Federal Government in Paris (executive council), and was a member of the adult education board of the Columbia Broadcasting System (from 1938) and other professional and scholarly groups.

REFERENCES: *CA* (1–4); *CB* (August 1940); *LE* (III); *WW* (XXXVI).

William W. West

BARRETT, Janie Porter. B. August 9, 1865, Athens, Georgia, to Julia Porter. M. October 31, 1889, to Harris Barrett. Ch. four. D. August 27, 1948, Hampton, Virginia.

Janie Porter Barrett was reared in a Macon, Georgia, home where her mother worked for a wealthy white northern family. When she was thirteen years old, her mother sent her to the predominately black Hampton (Virginia) Institute. She was graduated in 1884.

Barrett returned to Georgia and taught in a school in Dawson (1884–86). She accepted an offer to teach domestic science at Hampton Institute (1886–87) and was at Haines Normal and Industrial School in Augusta, Georgia (1887–89). After her marriage in 1889, she founded the Locust Street Social Settlement in Hampton, Virginia (1890), the first black neighborhood settlement house. She held classes in sewing and laundering for girls and in baby care, homemaking, and poultry raising for adults.

In 1915 Barrett, with the support of the State Federation of Colored Women's Clubs, opened the Virginia Industrial School for Colored Girls on a farm near Peake, Virginia. The school was a correctional facility enrolling about one hundred delinquent girls a year.

After her husband's death in 1915, she became superintendent of the school and moved with her daughters to Peake. The school had been financed by state and federal funds and private donations; in 1920, the State Federation of Colored Women's Clubs accepted a state offer of public financing and turned full control of the school over to the state in 1942.

Barrett was a major founder of the Virginia State Federation of Colored Women's Clubs (1908). She was a member of the Southern Commission on Interracial Cooperation, the Virginia Commission on Interracial Cooperation, and the executive board of the Richmond Urban League. She was a delegate to the White House Conference on Child Health and Protection (1930). She received the William E. Harmon Award (1929). The Virginia Industrial School for Colored Girls was named the Janie Porter Barrett School for Girls in 1950.

REFERENCES: *DAB* (supp. 4); *NAW;* Sadie Iola Daniel, *Women Builders* (Washington, D.C.: The Associated Publishers, 1931); Sylvia G. L. Dannett, *Profiles of Negro Womanhood 1619–1900,* vol. 1 Negro Heritage Library. (Philadelphia: Educational Heritage, Inc., 1964); Mary White Ovington, *Portraits in Color* (New York: Viking Press, 1927); Thomas Yenser, ed., *Who's Who in Colored America: 1933–1937,* 4th ed. (Brooklyn: Thomas Yenser Publication, 1937).   *Exyie C. Ryder*

BARROWS, Alice Prentice. B. November 15, 1877, Lowell, Massachusetts, to Charles Dana and Marion (Merrill) Barrows. M. December 30, 1913, to W. G. Tinckon Fernandez. Ch. none. D. October 2, 1954, New York, New York.

Alice Barrows was graduated from Vassar College in Poughkeepsie, New York (1900), and taught English for several years in New York at the Packer Collegiate Institute in Brooklyn, the Ethical Culture School in Manhattan, and Vassar College. In 1907 she began graduate work with John Dewey (*q.v.*) at Teachers College, Columbia University, and from 1908 to 1911 worked as a social investigator with the Russell Sage Foundation, making extensive studies of women workers in the New York City garment trades. In 1911 she returned to educational work as director of the vocational guidance survey sponsored by the Public Education Association of New York City, a private group promoting educational reforms.

From 1914 to 1918 Barrows worked as secretary to William A. Wirt *(q.v.)*, the superintendent of schools of Gary, Indiana. Wirt had been hired as an educational consultant to convert the New York City school system to the Gary, or platoon school, plan, which divided classes into two groups alternating between academic and special subjects. The voters rejected school reform in the mayoralty election of 1917, and Barrows took a position in the City Schools Division of the United States Bureau of Education where she launched a nationwide campaign for the platoon school.

In the 1920s Barrows became the most aggressive national publicist for the platoon school plan. Her job in the bureau as an expert in school building problems involved making surveys of public school systems and recommending desirable curricular and building changes. During the 1920s, she conducted surveys in many cities across the country. In each case, her reports laid out the educational advantages of the platoon school system over traditional curricular and building arrangements. Barrows promoted the platoon plan in articles for *School Life* (the bureau's official monthly journal) and other publications. In 1925 she helped organize and served as secretary of the National Association for the Study of the Platoon or Work-Study-Play School Organization.

She became involved in numerous other political and ideological causes such as civil liberties for radicals, civil rights for blacks, and support for Loyalist Spain. After her retirement from the Office of Education in 1942, Barrows assumed leadership positions in several organizations, including the Congress of American-Soviet Friendship, the National Federation of Constitutional Liberties, and the Progressive Citizens of America. Divorced in 1922, she resumed use of her maiden name.

REFERENCES: *LE* (III); *WWAE* (VIII); Alice P. Barrows Papers, University of Maine; Raymond A. Mohl, "Urban Education in the Twentieth Century; Alice Barrows and the Platoon School Plan," *Urban Education* 9 (October 1974): 213-37; *NYT,* October 3, 1954, p. 86.

Raymond A. Mohl

BARROWS, Anna. B. 1864, Fryeburg, Maine, to George Bradley and Georgiana (Souther) Barrows. M. no. D. February 11, 1948, Fryeburg, Maine.

Anna Barrows was graduated from the Fryeburg (Maine) Academy and the Boston Cooking School (1886). She taught cooking and domestic science at a number of schools, sometimes instructing at more than one school at a time. She taught at the North Bennet Street Industrial School (1886–91) and School of Domestic Science (1891–95) in Boston, Lasell Seminary in Auburndale, Massachusetts (1891–1900), the Robinson Female Seminary in Exeter, New Hampshire (1895–1905), and the Chautauqua (New York) School of Domestic Science (1900–20) and was a lecturer in the School of Practical Arts at Teachers College, Columbia University (1905–32). She engaged in extension work with women for the United States Department of Agriculture (1917–18) and lectured widely on cooking and domestic science.

Barrow's publications include *Eggs: Facts and Fancies About Them* (1890), *The Home Science Cook Book* (with Mary J. B. Lincoln, 1902), *Principles of Cookery* (1907), and *An Outline on the History of Cookery* (with Bertha E. Shapleigh, 1915), and she contributed the section "Principles of Cookery" to the American School of Home Economics' *Handbook of Food and Diet* (1912). She also wrote bulletins for the United States Department of Agriculture. She was editor of *Everyday Housekeeping* (1894–1908).

Barrows was an active member of a number of organizations, including the American Home Economics Association (secretary, 1914–15), and she served on the Boston School Committee from 1900 to 1903.

REFERENCES: *WWW* (III); M. B. Arnsdale, "Well-Remembered Pioneer," *Journal of Home Economics* 40 (May 1948): 261; *NYT,* February 12, 1948, p. 23.   *Barbara Ruth Peltzman*

BARTHOLOMEW, William Nelson. B. February 13, 1822, Boston, Massachusetts, to Erastus Bartholomew and n.a. M. July 19, 1876, to Jennie S. Thurston. Ch. two. D. April 12, 1907, Newton Centre, Massachusetts.

William N. Bartholomew is credited with both Nelson and Newton as his middle name. (The obituary in *The Town Crier* of Newton Centre, Massachusetts, where he lived out his last years, used Nelson.)

Bartholomew was trained to be a cabinetmaker, but after a few years in that trade, he decided to become an artist. His decision to go into art led him, in 1850, to make a trip to California with J. Wesley Jones, the famed daguerreotypist. It appears that it was Jones who encouraged Bartholomew to follow his interest in the field of art.

In 1852 Bartholomew introduced systematic instruction in drawing in several Boston schools. Shortly thereafter, he was put in charge of drawing instruction in all of the Boston high schools. He remained with the Boston school system as a supervisor of instruction in drawing until 1871. After retiring, he lived in Newton Centre to his death at the age of eighty-five.

Among Bartholomew's books were *Bartholomew's Sketches from Nature* (c. 1855), *Linear Perspective Explained* (1859), *Bartholomew's Drawing Book* (c. 1867), *Bartholomew's National System of Industrial Drawing* (1879), *How to Teach Bartholomew's National System of Industrial Drawing* (1881), and *First Lessons in Landscape Drawing* (1894).

REFERENCES: *WWW* (H); George C. Croce and David H. Wallace, *The New-York Historical Society's Dictionary of Artists in America 1564–1860*

(New Haven: Yale University Press, 1957); *Newton* (Massachusetts) *Graphic,* April 15, 1907, p. 2; *The Town Crier* (Newton Centre, Massachusetts), April 12, 1907, p. 2.   *Roger H. Jones*

BARTON, Benjamin Smith. B. February 10, 1766, Lancaster, Pennsylvania, to Thomas and Ester (Rittenhouse) Barton. M. 1797 to Mary Pennington. Ch. two. D. December 19, 1815, New York, New York.

Benjamin Smith Barton was orphaned at the age of fourteen; his older brother William was his guardian and saw to his early education at the academy in York, Pennsylvania. Barton devoted his spare time to his instinctive drive, collecting and classifying natural materials, including plants and insects, and bird watching. These studies were enhanced by his ability to draw and sketch.

He began his medical training in 1784 at the age of eighteen under Dr. William Shippen of Philadelphia. Barton attended the University of Edinburgh, Scotland (1786–87), and later the University of Göttingen, Germany. He was the author of the first botany textbook to be published in the United States, *Elements of Botany* (1803). He published many short papers in the United States and in England on varied and diverse topics.

In spite of a lifetime of ill health, suffering particularly from the gout, Barton invested a generous portion of his energies into the foundation of American education through his influence at the University of Pennsylvania. He was the professor of natural history and botany (1789) at the age of twenty-three, professor of materia medica (1795), and professor of theory and practice of medicine in 1813, succeeding Benjamin Rush *(q.v.).*

Barton served for ten years (1790–1800) as one of the curators of the American Philosophical Society and as a vice-president (1802–15). He was founder and editor for the short-lived *Philadelphia Medical and Physical Journal* (1804–09).

REFERENCES: *DAB; DSB; EB; NCAB* (8:377); *WWW* (H).
Isadore L. Sonnier

BASCOM, John. B. May 1, 1827, Genoa, New York, to John and Laura (Woodbridge) Bascom. M. no. D. October 2, 1911, Williamstown, Massachusetts.

John Bascom received the A.B. (1849) and A.M. (1852) degrees from Williams College. He was graduated from Andover (Massachusetts) Theological Seminary in 1855.

He taught rhetoric and oratory at Williams College in Williamstown, Massachusetts, from 1855 to 1874 when he became president of the University of Wisconsin. Through "spiritual leadership," Bascom established the great tradition of what later became known as the Wisconsin idea—that the university should serve the good of the state. Forced out of his office in 1887, Bascom returned to Williams, where he taught sociology and political science until his retirement in 1903.

Bascom developed a conception of spiritual evolution, in opposition to Darwin and Spencer whose works, he thought, did not account for morality in human existence. He fought vocational trends in higher education because he believed the student would be left with a "microscopic vision" of the world. He argued that college should be based on the study of philosophy so that students achieve a vision of the "rational life." His militant social philosophy frequently led him outside the walls of the university where he engaged in many reform movements of the day. As an early exponent of the social gospel, he championed such causes as regulation of monopolies, progressive taxation, trade unionism, prohibition, women's rights, and university coeducation.

Bascom wrote articles and books on many subjects, including mathematics, theology, psychology, literature, aesthetics, and political economy. Among his books were *Political Economy* (1859), *Aesthetics* (1862), *Philosophy of Rhetoric* (1865), *Principles of Psychology* (1869), *Growth and Grades of Intelligence* (1878), *Problems in Philosophy* (1885), *The New Theology* (1891), *Social Theory* (1895), and *Evolution and Religion* (1897). He was the recipient of several honorary degrees.

REFERENCES: *DAB; EB; NCAB* (8:196); *WWW* (I); Edward A. Birge *(q.v.)*, "President Bascom and the University of Wisconsin," in *Memorial Service in Honor of John Bascom at the University of Wisconsin*, December 13, 1911; Merle Curti *(q.v.)* and Vernon Carstensen, *The University of Wisconsin, 1848–1925: A History*, 2 vols. (Madison: The University of Wisconsin Press, 1949); Sanford Robinson, *John Bascom, Prophet* (New York: G. P. Putnam's Sons, 1922); *NYT*, October 4, 1911, p. 13.

John W. Jenkins

BATEMAN, Newton. B. July 27, 1822, Fairfield, New Jersey, to Bergen and Ruth (Bower) Bateman. M. 1850 to Sarah Dayton. M. 1859 to Annie Newell Tyler. Ch. five. D. October 21, 1897, Galesburg, Illinois.

Newton Bateman's family migrated west to Illinois in 1833. He was graduated from Illinois College in Jacksonville, Illinois (1843), with honors. He entered Lane Theological Seminary in Cincinnati, Ohio, but ill health forced him to leave after one year, and he traveled the country as an agent for a historical chart.

In 1845 he established a private school in St. Louis, Missouri, and two years later went to St. Charles (Missouri) College as professor of mathematics. In 1851 he became principal of West Jacksonville (Illinois) district school and established the first free high school in Illinois, also serving as county superintendent of schools for Morgan County. He assisted in organizing the Illinois Teachers Association (1854), served as its first vice-president, and helped found and often edited *The Illinois Teacher*. In the fall of 1857 he became principal of Jacksonville (Illinois) Female Academy.

Bateman was state superintendent of public instruction (1859–63, 1865–75). Under his administration the common school system of Illinois was started and developed to a high degree of efficiency. He has been credited as the organizer of the public school system in Illinois. Bateman included in his biennial reports a series of essays that led to his recognition as one of the foremost educational leaders of his time at home and abroad. He wrote *Common School Decisions* (1867), which was recognized as authoritative. He served as editor with Paul Selby of the *Historical Encyclopedia of Illinois* (1875).

Bateman was instrumental in establishing Illinois Normal University (later, Illinois State University) and the State Natural History Society (1858). He was a member of the committee that drafted the bill creating the United States Bureau of Education (1867), a member of the state board of health (1877–91, president for four years), and an assay commissioner appointed by President Rutherford B. Hayes in 1878.

Bateman assumed the office of president of Knox College in Galesburg, Illinois (1875), and was credited with having the most progressive administration in the history of the college up to that time. Following his retirement in 1892 he was appointed president emeritus, trustee, and professor of mental and moral science.

REFERENCES: *DAB; NCAB* (27:260); *WWW* (H); Newton Bateman and Paul Selby, eds., *Historical Encyclopedia of Illinois* (Galesburg, Ill.: Galesburg Printing and Publishing Co., 1875).   *Elizabeth S. Oelrich*

BATES, Katharine Lee. B. August 12, 1859, Falmouth, Massachusetts, to William and Cornelia (Lee) Bates. M. no. D. March 28, 1929, Wellesley, Massachusetts.

Katharine Lee Bates was educated in the public schools of Wellesley and Newton, Massachusetts. She received the A.B. (1880) and A.M. (1881) degrees from Wellesley College.

Following graduation from Wellesley, Bates taught one year at the high school in Natick, Massachusetts, and then at Dana Hall, a girls' preparatory school in Wellesley. She joined the faculty of Wellesley College in 1885 as an instructor in English literature and was appointed associate professor in 1888. In 1889 she went to England for fifteen months of graduate study at Oxford University and upon her return was named full professor and head of the English department at Wellesley. During her tenure in this position, the English department became the largest and most important in the college.

Bates wrote stories and sketches that appeared in local publications and poems in magazines, including the *Atlantic Monthly*. As part of her academic work, she edited numerous critical editions of English classics, editions that included works by Shakespeare, Coleridge, Keats, Ruskin, Tennyson, and Thomas Heywood. She visited France and Spain (1898–

99), Switzerland, Italy, Egypt, and Palestine (1906–07), and Norway, Denmark, and Spain (1913–14), trips that provided the source for several well-known travel books. A trip to the American West in the summer of 1893 was the source of Bates's best-known work; while viewing the surrounding countryside from the vantage point of Pikes' Peak, she was inspired to write the poem "America the Beautiful."

An extensive bibliography indicates the many interests Bates pursued. It includes *The College Beautiful and Other Poems* (1887), *Sunshine and Other Verses for Children* (1890), *The English Religious Drama* (1893), *American Literature* (1898), *Spanish Highways and Byways* (1900), *From Gretna Green to Land's End* (1907), *The Story of Chaucer's Canterbury Pilgrims Re-Told for Children* (1909), *America the Beautiful and Other Poems* (1911), *Shakespeare's Selective Bibliography and Biographical Notes* (1913), *In Sunny Spain* (1913), *Fairy Gold* (poems, 1916), *The Retinue and Other Poems* (1918), *Sigurd, Our Golden Collie and Other Comrades of the Road* (1919), *Yellow Clover* (poems, 1922), *Little Robin Stay-Behind and Other Plays in Verse for Children* (1923), *The Pilgrim Ship* (poems, 1926), and *America the Dream* (poems, 1930). She was the editor or coeditor of several collections of selections from English literature.

Bates was a director of the International Institute for Girls in Spain and a member of many professional and literary societies. Honorary degrees were conferred on her by Middlebury, Oberlin, and Wellesley colleges.

REFERENCES: *DAB* (supp. 1); *NCAB* (42:204); *WWW* (I); *NYT,* March 29, 1929, p. 23.   *Carol O'Meara*

BATTLE, Archibald John. B. September 10, 1826, Powelton, Georgia, to Cullen and Jane Andrews (Lamon) Battle. M. December 7, 1846, to Mary Elizabeth Guild. Ch. none. D. September 30, 1907, Macon, Georgia.

Archibald J. Battle was educated at Eufaula (Alabama) Academy and Mercer University, where he graduated in 1842. He attended the University of Alabama, where he received A.B. (1846) and A.M. (1849) degrees.

Principal of Eufaula Academy, Battle was a tutor in ancient languages at the University of Alabama (1847–52) and professor of science and ancient languages at East Alabama Female College in Tuskegee (1852–55). He was ordained in and served as minister of the Tuskegee Baptist Church (1853). He assumed charge of the Tuskaloosa (Alabama) Baptist Church (1856–57) and was professor of Greek language and literature at the University of Alabama in 1857. Battle founded and served as president of the Alabama Central Female College (1860). He reestablished and was president of the Judson Female Institute in Marion, Alabama (1865–71), and was president of Mercer University in Macon, Georgia (1871–90).

Leaving Mercer University, Battle served as president of Shorter College in Rome, Georgia (1891–98), and was founder and president of Anniston (Alabama) College for Young Ladies (1898–1902). Retiring in 1902, he spent the rest of his life in Macon, Georgia.

Battle was author of *A Treatise, Psychological and Theological in the Human Will* (1876). He was a charter member and president of the Athenaeum in Macon, Georgia. He was the recipient of four honorary degrees.

REFERENCES: *NCAB* (6:498); *TC; WWW* (I).   *John F. Ohles*

BAWDEN, William Thomas. B. November 6, 1875, Oberlin, Ohio, to Henry H. and Harriet Newell (Day) Bawden. M. August 17, 1898, to Ora Richardson. M. April 16, 1949, to Maude Mary Firth. Ch. one. D. April 27, 1960, Santa Barbara, California.

William Bawden was graduated from Denison University in Granville, Ohio, in 1896 and taught math, history, and French there for one year. In 1897 he entered the Rochester Athenaeum and Mechanics Institute to prepare for manual training in a special one-year curriculum. In 1903 he received the B.S. degree from Columbia University and credentials to teach industrial arts. He received the Ph.D. degree from Columbia in 1914.

Bawden taught at the Cedar Valley Seminary in Osage, Iowa (1896–97), New York State Reformatory in Elmira (1898), and Buffalo (New York) public schools (1898–1902). He directed the manual training department at Illinois State Normal University (later, Illinois State University) at Normal (1903–10) and was assistant dean in the college of engineering at the University of Illinois (1914–19). He was a specialist in industrial education with the United States Bureau of Education and assistant commissioner (1914–23).

At the bureau, Bawden gained much insight into industrial education across the nation and contributed numerous articles to professional magazines and books. He conducted the first survey of public schools in America.

In the fall of 1923 he returned to education as associate superintendent of the Tulsa, Oklahoma, schools. He was managing editor of the *Industrial Education Magazine* (1928–35). Bawden then became director of the graduate and industrial and vocational education programs at Kansas State College (later, University) in Manhattan, where he stayed until his retirement in 1945.

Bawden spent the majority of his time in retirement as a leading and active member of various conferences and national organizations, including the Four State Conference and the National Society for the Promotion of Industrial Education. He was author of *Leaders in Industrial Education* (1950) and *History of Kansas State Teachers College* (1952) and was coauthor of *Some Problems in City School Administration* (with George D. Strayer *(q.v.)* and others, 1916).

REFERENCES: *LE* (III); *WWW* (V); *Industrial Arts and Vocational Education* 49 (September 1960): 18.   *Lee H. Smalley*

BEADLE, William Henry Harrison. B. January 1, 1838, Parke County, Indiana, to James Ward and Elizabeth (Bright) Beadle. M. May 18, 1863, to Mrs. Ellen S. Chapman. Ch. three. D. November 13, 1915, San Francisco, California.

William Henry Harrison Beadle grew up on a farm in Indiana and, at the age of nineteen, entered the University of Michigan, from which he earned the B.A. (1861), M.A. (1864), and LL.B. (1867) degrees.

He served in the Union Army in the Civil War, reaching the rank of brevet brigadier general. Beadle practiced law in Indiana and Wisconsin before being appointed surveyor-general for the Dakota Territory by President Ulysses S. Grant in 1869. He served as a member of the territorial legislature and was appointed superintendent of public instruction by the territorial governor in 1879, holding the post to 1885. Beadle became president of the State Normal School (later, General Beadle State College) at Madison, South Dakota, in 1889 and served in that capacity until 1905. He remained as professor of history until he retired in 1912.

Beadle's greatest service to the Dakota Territory and South Dakota and to education was his fight to preserve land grants for the exclusive use of the public schools. He took the position that these sections should not be sold rapidly, should be appraised by a responsible board of state officers and not be sold for less than the appraised value, and should not be sold for less than ten dollars per acre. Despite opposition from settlers who felt the lands should be sold early and the proceeds used for current public services, leaving to later generations the problem of providing aid for schools, Beadle's fight was successful. Congress included his provisions for disposition of school lands in the enabling act for North and South Dakota and the same general principles governed states that gained admission to the union after 1889.

Beadle was the author of *Life in Utah* (n.d.), *Geography, History and Resources of Dakota Territory* (1888), *The Natural System of Teaching Geography* (with A. F. Bartlett, 1899), and *Autobiography of William Henry Harrison Beadle* (1906).

Beadle was an organizer of the South Dakota State Educational Association, serving the first two terms as president; he was also president for a third term in 1909.

REFERENCES: *DAB; NCAB* (17:314); *WWW* (I); William H. H. Beadle, *Autobiography of William Henry Harrison Beadle* (Pierre, S.D.: State Historical Society, 1938); O. W. Coursey, *Biography of General Beadle* (Mitchell, S.D.: Educator Supply Co., 1913); *NYT,* November 14, 1915, p. 19.

Bruce G. Milne

BEARD, Charles Austin. B. November 27, 1874, near Knightstown, Indiana, to William and Mary (Payne) Beard. M. March 8, 1900, to Mary Ritter. Ch. two. D. September 1, 1948, New Haven, Connecticut.

Charles Austin Beard grew up on a farm near Knightstown, Indiana, and attended the nearby Spiceland Academy. He attended DePauw University, where he received the Ph.B. degree (1898) and studied at Oxford University in England. On his return in 1899, he enrolled at Cornell University in Ithaca, New York, for one year and transferred to Columbia University where he received the M.A. (1903) and Ph.D. (1904) degrees.

He joined the faculty at Columbia in 1907 as a professor of politics, leaving in 1917 as a matter of principle when the university trustees tried to suppress faculty critcism of American intervention into World War I.

He directed the Training School for Public Service in New York City (1917–22) and advised the Institute of Municipal Research in Tokyo (1922). During the last twenty years of his life, Beard was concerned with foreign policy and American neutrality; he was a defender of academic freedom and civil liberties and opposed naval expansion, universal military training, and the lend-lease program. His concern for the economic influence on history in his earlier writings led to extended controversy.

Beard coauthored with his wife Mary Beard *The History of the United States* (1921), *Rise of American Civilization* (1927), and *A Basic History of the United States* (1944). Among his many other publications were *The Development of Modern Europe* (with J. H. Robinson, *q.v.*, two volumes, 1907), *American Government and Politics* (1910), *Economic Interpretation of the Constitution* (1913), *Economic Origins of Jeffersonian Democracy* (1915), *History of the American People* (with W. C. Bagley, *q.v.*, 1918), *Our Old World Background* (with W. C. Bagley, 1921), *The Idea of National Interest* (with G. H. E. Smith, 1934), *The Open Door at Home* (with G. H. E. Smith, 1934), *The Republic* (1943), *American Foreign Policy in the Making* (1946), and *President Roosevelt and the Coming of the War 1941* (1947). He edited a number of volumes, including *America Faces the Future* (1932) and *The Nature of the Social Sciences* (1934).

Beard was a member of honorary associations and served as president of the American Historical Association (1933), the American Political Science Association (1926), and the National Association for Adult Education (1936).

REFERENCES: *CB* (March 1941 and October 1948); *DAB* (supp. 4); *EB; NCAB* (D:231); *WWW* (II); *NYT,* September 2, 1948, p. 23.

Amelia Lubrano Morrill

BEBERMAN, Max. B. August 20, 1925, New York, New York, to Israel and Lillian (Miller) Beberman. M. January 18, 1947, to Elizabeth F. Chapman. Ch. nine. D. January 24, 1971, London, England.

Max Beberman received the A.B. degree (1944) from City College, New

York and the A.M. (1949) and Ed.D. (1953) degrees from Teachers College, Columbia University. He was interested in mathematics education and, particularly, the ramifications of the "new mathematics."

After receiving his bachelor's degree, Beberman taught mathematics and science in Nome, Alaska (1946–48), and Riverdale Country Day School, New York City (1949–50). Upon completion of his doctorate he was associate professor of education at Florida State University (1954–55) and associate professor and professor of education at the University of Illinois (1955–71). He was director of the Curriculum Laboratory (1965–71) and educational director of the computer-based Education Research Laboratory (1966–71).

While at Illinois, Beberman was involved with the Illinois Mathematics Project and was instrumental in developing a new series of textbooks. He was a pioneer in promoting changes in the ways of teaching mathematics but criticized the new math as being introduced with undue haste in elementary school and hampering teaching of the simple arithmetic skills that children needed.

Beberman was the author, with others, of a number of mathematics textbooks, including *Algebra, Course 1* and *Algebra, Course 2* (1955), *High School Mathematics Units 1–11* (1960–63), *Algebra, First Course* (1962), *Algebra with Trigonometry, Second Course* (1962), *High School Mathematics Course* 1, 2, and 3 (1964–66), *Math Workshop* (1964–66), and *Algebra Course* 1 and 2 (1970).

Beberman was a member of a number of professional associations and was awarded a Gugenheim fellowship for 1970–71; he was in London for study under the award when he died at the age of forty-five.

REFERENCES: *WWW* (V); *NYT,* January 26, 1971, p. 36; *Newsweek,* February 8, 1971, p. 102; *Time,* February 8, 1971, p. 80.

Robert McGinty

BECK, Charles (Karl). B. August 19, 1798, Heidelberg, Germany, to n.a. M. 1827 to Louisa A. Henshaw. M. 1831 to Teresa Henshaw Phillips. Ch. none. D. March 19, 1866, Cambridge, Massachusetts.

Charles Beck, physical educator and classical scholar, came under the influence of Friedrich Ludwig Jahn, the Father of Gymnastics, at an early age in Berlin, Germany. Beck was a classical scholar and student of theology at the University of Berlin. He was ordained to the Lutheran ministry (1822) and received the doctor's degree (1823) in theology from the University of Tübingen. Because of political conditions in Germany, Beck sought refuge in Switzerland, France, and America (1824).

He was appointed instructor in Latin and gymnastics at Round Hill School in Northampton, Massachusetts, a school that sought to simulate the educational system of ancient Greece. Beck's appointment constituted the beginning of German gymnastics in the United States. He established the first public school gymnasium (1825). Beck left the Round Hill School to establish the Phillipstown Boys' Academy across the Hudson River from West Point, New York.

In 1832 Beck was elected professor of Latin and permanent tutor at Harvard University, where he remained until he retired in 1850. He played an important role, introducing German scholarly methods into American universities and enlivening classical studies.

Beck translated into English Jahn's *Treatise on Gymnastics* (1828). He was author of a monograph in Latin in 1835 and *Introduction to the Metres of Horace* (1835) and *A Latin Syntax* (1838) and was editor of Cicero's *Brutus* (1837), Seneca's *Medea* (1834), and Seneca's *Hercules Furens* (1845). He translated Munk's treatise on meters (1844) and collated and described the manuscripts of the *Satyricon* of Petronius Arbiter (1863).

A representative of Cambridge in the Massachusetts legislature, Beck served as a trustee of the Massachusetts School for Idiotic and Feeble-minded Youth (from 1865).

REFERENCES: *AC; DAB; WWW* (H); Fred E. Leonard and George B. Affleck, *A Guide to the History of Physical Education* (Philadelphia: Lea and Febiger, 1947); Emmett A. Rice and John L. Hutchinson, *A Brief History of Physical Education* (New York: A. S. Barnes and Company, 1952); Deobald B. Van Dalen, Elmer D. Mitchell *(q.v.)*, and Bruce Bennett, *A World History of Physical Education* (New York: Prentice-Hall, 1953); Arthur Weston, *The Making of American Physical Education* (New York: Appleton-Century-Crofts, 1962). *Adelaide M. Cole*

BECKER, Carl Lotus. B. September 7, 1873, Black Hawk County, Iowa, to Charles De Witt and Almeda (Sarvay) Becker. M. June 16, 1901, to Maude Hepworth Ranney. Ch. one. D. April 10, 1945, Ithaca, New York.

Carl Lotus Becker attended Cornell College in Mount Vernon, Iowa (1892–93), and received the B.Litt. (1896) and Ph.D. (1907) degrees from the University of Wisconsin. He was a graduate student (1896–97) and fellow (1897–98) at Wisconsin and a fellow (1898–99) at Columbia University.

He taught history at Pennsylvania State College (later, University) from 1899 to 1901, Dartmouth College (1901–02), the University of Kansas (1902–16), and the University of Minnesota (1916–17). He spent most of his career at Cornell University in Ithaca, New York, where he taught from 1917 until he retired in 1941.

Becker taught courses in the intellectual history of Europe, yet much of his historical writing concentrated on the United States. His doctoral dissertation at the University of Wisconsin, published as *The History of Political Parties in the Province of New York* (1909), demonstrated the impact of property distinctions on political development. *The Declaration of Independence* (1922) was an unsurpassed historical analysis of the document. Other books he wrote were *Beginnings of the American People* (1915), *The Eve of the Revolution* (1918), *Our Great Experiment in Democracy* (1924), *Modern History* (1931), *The Heavenly City of the Eighteenth Century Philosophers* (1932), *Progress and Power* (1936), *How New Will the Better World Be* (1944), and *Freedom and Response in the American Way of Life* (1945).

Becker was active in professional associations, serving as president of the American Historical Association (1934–35). He was the recipient of three honorary degrees.

REFERENCES: *DAB* (supp. 3); *LE* (II); *NCAB* (33:504); *WWW* (II).

Donald O. Dewey

BEECHER, Catharine Esther. B. September 6, 1800, East Hampton, New York, to Lyman and Roxanna (Foote) Beecher. M. no. D. May 12, 1878, Elmira, New York.

Catharine Esther Beecher, a pioneer in the education of women, was the sister of Henry Ward Beecher and Harriet Beecher Stowe. She was educated primarily at home and at a private girls' school in Litchfield, Connecticut, which she entered at the age of ten. She took charge of the household at the age of sixteen on the death of her mother. She decided to teach so that she could contribute to the family income and engaged in intensive study of mathematics, Latin, and philosophy.

Beecher was teaching in a school in New Haven, Connecticut, where she met and planned to marry a Yale mathematics professor, Alexander M. Fisher. Returning from a trip to Europe in 1823, he was lost at sea. Beecher turned her attention to a career as a teacher and with a sister opened a school for girls that became the Hartford (Connecticut) Female Seminary. Dissatisfied with the traditional methods of teaching, she proposed small classes, used advanced students to teach others, correlated courses to stress general principles to be learned, and sought to motivate students to seek information beyond the textbook.

Beecher moved to Cincinnati, Ohio, with her father when he became president of Lane Theological Seminary (1832). She established and directed the Western Female Institute (1832–37) in Cincinnati until it closed because of inadequate financial support. She then retired from administrative work.

Beecher founded the Board of National Popular Education with William Slade (1847) and the American Women's Educational Association (1852) to promote education in the Midwest. The American Women's Educational Association founded colleges in Burlington, Iowa, and Quincy, Illinois, and the Milwaukee (Wisconsin) Female Institute (later, Milwaukee-Downer College).

Beecher's writings include *An Essay on Slavery and Abolitionism, with Reference to the Duty of American Females* (1837), *A Treatise on Domes-*

tic Economy for the Use of Young Ladies at Home and at School (1841), *The Duty of American Women to Their Country* (1845), *Miss Beecher's Domestic Receipt Book* (1846), *The Evils Suffered by American Women and American Children: the Causes and Remedy* (1846), *Physiology and Calisthenics for Schools and Families* (1856), and *Woman Suffrage and Woman's Profession* (1871).

REFERENCES: *DAB; NAW; NCAB* (3:128); *WWW* (H); Charles Beecher, ed., *The Autobiography of Lyman Beecher* (New York: Harper and Brother, 1864), vols. 1–2. Lyman Beecher Stowe, *Saints, Sinners and Beechers* (Indianapolis: Bobbs-Merrill, 1934).   *Darlene E. Fisher*

BELFIELD, Henry Holmes. B. November 17, 1837, Philadelphia, Pennsylvania, to William and Selener (Marshall) Belfield. M. July 27, 1869, to Ann Wallace. Ch. five. D. June 5, 1912, Ann Arbor, Michigan.

Henry Belfield was graduated (1858) from Iowa (later, Grinnell) College in Grinnell, Iowa, as valedictorian of the class and winner of the Sargent Gold Medal for scholarship. He was awarded the A.M. (1861) degree from Griswold College in Davenport, Iowa. He received the A.M. (1868) and Ph.D. (1878) degrees from Iowa College.

Belfield was a tutor of Greek at Iowa College upon graduation in 1858 and tutor of Latin at Griswold College (1860–61). He served as principal and superintendent of schools at Dubuque, Iowa (1859–60, 1861–63, and 1865–66).

Belfield fought in the Civil War. Captured while serving with General William T. Sherman, he was imprisoned at Charleston, South Carolina, until September 27, 1864. Following the war he continued his career in education and was a principal of a Chicago, Illinois, grammar school (1866–76) and a high school (1876–83).

Belfield was an early advocate of manual training, writing and lecturing on the subject from 1872. The Chicago Commercial Club, an organization devoted to movements for civic and social betterment, built and financed a manual training school. The Chicago Manual Training School, the first of its kind in the city, was incorporated April 11, 1883. The first classes, for boys only, began on February 4, 1884, with Belfield as the director until 1903. The school was a model for other manual training schools. The University of Chicago became interested in the manual training movement and made the school part of the university in May 1897, locating it in a building named Henry Holmes Belfield Hall.

In 1903 Belfield became principal of University High School, a position he held until 1908. Called from retirement, he accepted an appointment as special commissioner for the United States Department of Labor to visit, inspect, and report on technical schools of the United States and Europe.

With Alfred Kirk, Belfield was the author of *Model Arithmetic* (1875), *Model Business Arithmetic* (1877), and *Model Second Book in Arithmetic*

(1877). He also wrote *Revised Model Elementary Arithmetic* (1887) and *Rational Elementary Arithmetic* (1898) and edited Thomas De Quincey's *Joan of Arc* (1892) and Lord Philip Chesterton's *Letters to His Son and Godson* (1897). Belfield was a charter member of the National Society for the Promotion of Industrial Education.

REFERENCES: *NCAB* (20:174); *WWW* (I). *Paul W. DeVore*

BELL, Alexander Graham. B. March 3, 1847, Edinburgh, Scotland, to Alexander Melville and Eliza (Symonds) Bell. M. July 11, 1877, to Mabel G. Hubbard. Ch. two. D. August 2, 1922, near Baddeck, Nova Scotia, Canada.

Young Alexander Graham Bell received a musical education under August Benoit Bertini but decided to follow his father, who was a famous teacher and author of speech textbooks and inventor of visible speech, a code of symbols indicating the physiological characteristics of speaking. The boy enrolled as a student-teacher at Weston House, a boys' school near Edinburgh, Scotland, where he taught music and elocution and studied other subjects. He studied at the University of Edinburgh and became a fully qualified teacher. From 1862 to 1866, he qualified for study at the University of London and specialized in the anatomy of vocal organs (1868–70) while he worked in a partnership with his father in London.

The death of his two brothers from tuberculosis and concern for Alexander Graham Bell's health caused his family to move to the more favorable climate of Brantford, Ontario, Canada in 1870.

At the age of twenty-four Bell became a teacher of the deaf in Boston at the invitation of Sarah Fuller *(q.v.)*, principal of a school for the deaf. He taught at the Clarke School for the Deaf in Northampton, Massachusetts, and at the Asylum for Deaf Mutes in Hartford, Connecticut. Motivated by his intense interest in the education of the deaf, he founded a school for the deaf in Boston in 1872 but transferred his classes to Boston University where he was professor of vocal physiology (1873–77). Among his pupils was Mabel G. Hubbard, whom he later married.

In 1874 Bell developed the principle of the telephone but was not able to convince the public of its potential value as a communication device. In 1876 he was granted a patent for his invention and had the opportunity to promote it publicly at the centennial exposition in Philadelphia. Bell was a dedicated scientist, inventor of electrical and phonographic apparatus, and interested in the principles of aerodynamics. He moved to Washington, D.C., in 1881.

Bell played a major role in founding *Science,* later the journal of the American Association for the Advancement of Science. His publications include *The Formation of a Deaf Variety of the Human Race* (1884) and *Duration of Life and Conditions Associated with Longevity* (1918).

He had a continuing interest in the education and welfare of the deaf and was considered the outstanding authority of his generation on the education of the deaf in Great Britain and the United States. Bell was an organizer of the Aerial Experiment Association and founder of the Volta Bureau and the American Association to Promote Teaching of Speech to the Deaf (president). He was active with the Smithsonian Institution (regent, 1898–1922) and National Geographic Society (president, 1898–1903). He was president of the Clarke School for the Deaf for many years to his death.

Among Bell's credits were more than five hundred published lectures, addresses, essays, and articles. He was the recipient of many honorary degrees and awards.

REFERENCES: *AC; DAB; DSB; EB; NCAB* (6:220); *TC; WWW* (I); Robert W. Bruce, *Bell: Alexander Graham Bell and the Conquest of Solitude* (Boston: Little, Brown, 1973); *NYT,* August 3, 1922, p. 13.

Octavia B. Knight

BENEDICT, Erastus Cornelius. B. March 19, 1800, Branford, Connecticut, to Joel Taylor and Currance (Wheeler) Benedict. M. May 7, 1833, to Caroline Margaret Bloodgood. Ch. two. D. October 22, 1880, New York, New York.

Erastus Cornelius Benedict received his early education in New York at New Windsor, Franklin, and Chatham, where he attended the district schools. He was a student at Williams College in Williamstown, Massachusetts, graduating in 1821 with high honors. He was principal of the Johnstown and Newburgh (New York) academies (1815–21) and a member of the teaching staff at Williams College (1821–24).

Benedict studied law in his spare time, was admitted to the New York bar in 1824, and moved to New York City where he served as deputy clerk in the United States District Court of Southern New York. He acquired an extensive knowledge of admiralty law and entered a practice specializing in those cases, becoming one of the foremost admiralty lawyers of his day.

He was elected a member of the city common council (1840) and was appointed a school trustee (1842). For nearly forty years, he was a major figure in the development of education in the city and the state. He served a term in the state legislature (1848). In 1850 he was elected to the board of education of New York City and served for a time as president of the board.

As a member of the board (1850–63), he initiated and carried through reforms that led to the consolidation of the public schools into an efficient single system. He was instrumental in the establishment of the Free Academy, which became the College of the City of New York. He was appointed by the state legislature in 1855 to the board of regents of the state university and served as chancellor (1878–80). He resigned from the board of education in 1863 and was elected to another term as a member of the state assembly; he was elected in 1872 to the state senate.

Benedict was prominent in civic, charitable, and scholarly organizations and was the author of *American Admiralty* (1850), *A Run Through Europe* (1860), and *Medieval Hymns* (1861).

REFERENCES: *AC; DAB; NCAB* (5:415); *TC; WWW* (H); *NYT*, October 23, 1880, p. 2; *Webster's Biographical Dictionary* (Springfield, Mass.: G&C Merriam Co., 1971), p. 134.   *Albert S. Weston*

BENEDICT, Ruth Fulton. B. June 5, 1887, New York, New York, to Frederick S. and Beatrice J. (Shattuck) Fulton. M. June 18, 1914, to Stanley R. Benedict. Ch. none. D. September 17, 1948, New York, New York.

Ruth Fulton Benedict attended Vassar College, graduating with the B.A. degree (1909) in English literature. She became interested in anthropology at the New School for Social Research (1919–21) and in 1921 studied with Franz Boas *(q.v.)* at Columbia University, where she received the Ph.D. degree (1923).

A teacher in two girls' schools in California (1911–14), she married Stanley Benedict, professor of biochemistry at Cornell Medical College in New York City. After completing her studies in 1923, she taught anthropology at Columbia University, becoming a professor of anthropology shortly before her death in 1948.

Benedict was active in anthropological field trips, her books reporting on the cultures she studied. Her research with the Serrano Indians of the Southwest and Blackfoot tribes in Canada established her reputation in the field. Her studies of the Japanese were conducted through interviews with Japanese-Americans during World War II.

In addition to many journal articles, she was author of *Patterns of Culture* (1934), *Zuni Mythology* (two volumes, 1935), *Race, Science and Politics* (1940), and *The Chrysanthemum and the Sword* (1946). She wrote poetry under the name Anne Singleton. She was president of the American Anthropological Association (1947).

REFERENCES: *CB* (May 1941 and November 1948); *DAB* (supp. 4); *EB; NCAB* (36: 469); *NAW; WWW* (II); Victor Barnouw, "Ruth Benedict: Apollonian and Dionysian," *University of Toronto Quarterly* 18 (1949): 241-53; Margaret Mead, *Ruth Benedict* (New York: Columbia University Press, 1974); Margaret Mead, "Ruth Fulton Benedict, 1887–1948," *American Anthropologist* 51 (July 1949): 457-68.   *June M. Collins*

BENEZET, Anthony. B. January 31, 1713, St. Quentin, France, to John Stephen and Jean (Etienne) Benezet. M. 1736 to Joyce Marriott. Ch. none. D. May 3, 1784, Philadelphia, Pennsylvania.

Anthony Benezet was the son of Huguenot parents. He was born in France, but because of religious persecution, his family moved to Holland and then to England where they became Quakers. Benezet, who apparently had no formal education, was apprenticed to a merchant. He migrated to America (1731) and was apprenticed to a cooper.

After several years of drifting from vocation to vocation, Benezet began teaching at the Germantown (Pennsylvania) Academy where he remained until 1742; for the remainder of his life he was a teacher. In 1742 he taught in a Quaker school in Philadelphia and later operated schools of his own.

In addition to a campaign against intemperance, Benezet worked to improve the conditions of life for a number of deprived, harassed, or subjugated groups. He befriended the French who had been expelled from Arcadia, worked to eliminate the slave trade, and supported efforts to protect the rights of Indians and women. His concern for these causes was directed toward educating minority groups and writing tracts dealing with their problems. In the early 1750s Benezet opened a female seminary and, later, a school for blacks to which he willed his limited fortune.

He wrote and distributed a number of works dealing with the plight of downtrodden groups and authored several religious and educational works, including *The Pennsylvania Spelling Book* (1779).

REFERENCES: *AC; DAB; NCAB* (5:419); *TC; WWW* (H); George S. Brooks, *Friend Anthony Benezet* (Philadelphia: University of Pennsylvania Press, 1937); Carter G. Woodson *(q.v.),* "Anthony Benezet of Philadelphia," *Journal of Negro History* 2 (January 1917): 37-50.

Samuel A. Farmerie

BENJAMIN, Harold Raymond Wayne. B. March 27, 1893, Gilmanton, Wisconsin, to Harold Samuel and Harriet Louise (Locke) Benjamin. M. August 26, 1919, to Georgiana Kessi. Ch. three. D. January 12, 1969, Baltimore, Maryland.

Harold Raymond Wayne Benjamin moved with his family to Oregon in 1904 and was graduated from Tualatin Academy in Forest Grove (1910). After a brief homesteading adventure in Canada, Benjamin returned to attend the Oregon Normal School (later, Oregon College of Education) at Monmouth, graduating in 1915. He earned the A.B. (1921) and A.M. (1924) degrees from the University of Oregon and the Ph.D. degree (1927) from Stanford (California) University.

Benjamin's professional career spanned more than a half-century. It began as teaching-principal of the rural Salem Heights (Oregon) elementary school (1915). He served in the military on the Mexican border and in France during World War I. He was superintendent of schools (1920–22) at Umatilla, Oregon, and editor of the *Umatilla Spokesman* (1921–22).

Benjamin was assistant professor of education at the University of Oregon (1922–25), a teaching fellow at Stanford (1925–27), and director of Stanford's student teaching program (1927–31). He moved to the University of Minnesota as professor of education and assistant dean of the college of education (1931–36) and director of the center for continuing study (1936–37). Benjamin went to the University of Colorado as director of the college of education (1937–39). He was dean of the college of education at the University of Maryland (1939–51).

Benjamin's work at Maryland was interrupted by a second tour of military duty during World War II. He was professor and chairman of social foundations of education at George Peabody College in Nashville, Tennessee, from 1951 to 1958, when he retired. He continued to teach as a visiting professor at various universities until 1967.

He achieved national attention with *The Saber-Tooth Curriculum,* published under the pseudonym J. Abner Peddiwell (1930). Benjamin also wrote *An Introduction to Human Problems* (1930), *Under Their Own Command* (1947), *The Cultivation of Idiosyncrasy* (1949), *True Faith and Allegiance* (1950), *Building a National System of Education* (1955), and *Higher Education in the American Republics* (1965). He also wrote an autobiographical novel, *The Sage of Petaluma* (1965), and edited *Democracy in the Administration of Higher Education* (1950), the tenth yearbook of the John Dewey Society.

Benjamin was a member of many professional associations and served as a consultant, lecturer, and keynote speaker. He was a technical advisor at the constitutional convention of the United Nations Educational, Scientific, and Cultural Organization in London (1945), organized and directed the International Education Division of the United States Office of Education (1945–46), and served on educational missions to Japan (1946 and 1950), Afghanistan (1949), and South Korea (1954–55).

REFERENCES: *LE* (III); *WW* (XXVIII); George J. Kabat, "In Memoriam: Harold R. W. Benjamin, 1893–1969," *Educational Forum* 34 (May 1970): 505-12; *NYT*, January 14, 1969, p. 45; Franklin Parker, "In Memoriam: Harold R. W. Benjamin, 1893–1969," *Kappa Delta Pi Record* 5 (February 1969): 93. *Erwin H. Goldenstein*

BENNE, Kenneth Dean. B. May 11, 1908, Morrowville, Kansas, to Henry and Bertha Alveen (Thrum) Benne. M. no.

Kenneth D. Benne was graduated from Kansas State College (later, University) with the B.S. degree (1930), the University of Michigan with the A.M. degree (1936), and Columbia University with the Ph.D. degree (1941). He was a scholar at the Advanced School of Education at Columbia (1936–38).

He was a teacher of physical and biological sciences in Concordia (Kansas) High School (1930–35) and of chemistry in Manhattan (Kansas) High School (1935–36). Benne served as an associate professor of social and philosophical foundations at Teachers College, Columbia University (1938–41), and associate professor of education and research at Horace

Mann-Lincoln Institute in New York City (1946–48). He served on the faculty of the University of Illinois (1948–53). He was Berenson Professor of Human Relations at Boston University (1953–73). He served on active duty with the United States Naval Reserve (1942–46). Benne was in great demand as a consultant and participant in sessions throughout the nation concerned with group therapy and laboratory methods, the role of professors of education, and programs for evaluating action and change in groups, organizations, and communities.

Benne's extensive publications on the role of a professor of education included *A Conception of Authority* (1943), and *Education for Tragedy* (1967); he was coauthor of *Discipline of Practical Judgment* (1943), *Group Dynamics and Social Action* (1950), *Improvement of Practical Intelligence* (1950), *Theoretical Foundations of Education* (1950), *Social Foundations of Education* (1955), *The Planning of Change,* (1961), *The University and the National Future* (1966), *Philosophy and Educational Development* (1966), *The Education Professoriate* (1974), and *The Laboratory Method of Changing and Learning* (1975). He was editor of *Adult Leadership* (1952–53).

He was nationally recognized for his contributions to major institutions and movements in American education and for his services as vice-president of the Boston Adult Center (1957–60), fellow of the National Council of Religion in Higher Education, the International Institute of Arts and Letters, the American Association for the Advancement of Science, and the American Educational Research Association. He was president of the Philosophy of Education Society (1950–51), the American Education Fellowship (1949–52), and the Adult Education Association (1955–56). He held memberships in many groups and received the Kilpatrick Award for distinguished contributions to the American philosophy of education in 1943. He was awarded honorary degrees by Lesley College (1969) and Morris Brown College (1971).

REFERENCES: *CA* (33–36); *LE* (III); *WW* (XXXIX); *WWAE* (XXII); *American Men and Women in Science,* 12th ed. (New York: R. R. Bowker, 1973).   *Frances H. Nelson*

BENNETT, Charles Alpheus. B. March 28, 1864, Holden, Massachusetts, to Charles Emerson and Lucy Ann (Howe) Bennett. M. September 9, 1891, to Clara Emily Blodgett. Ch. two. D. June 17, 1942, Peoria, Illinois.

Charles Bennett grew up on his father's farm and attended schools in Holden, Massachusetts. He received the B.S. degree (1886) from Worcester (Massachusetts) Polytechnic Institute and worked for one year as a machinist until he became principal of the St. Paul (Minnesota) Manual Training School in 1887.

Bennett was invited to head and organize the manual arts department at

Teachers College, Columbia University, in 1891. During his six years as department head (1891–97) Bennett created the first two-year course of study for the training of manual arts teachers and the first graduate courses in manual arts teacher training, and he planned and equipped the Macy Manual Arts Building, the first building designed and equipped solely for the training of manual arts teachers.

In 1897 Bennett moved to the Bradley Polytechnic Institute (later, Bradley University) in Peoria, Illinois, to become department head of the manual arts department. Here he developed courses, planned and equipped shops, and organized a faculty; the institute became one of the most famous of its kind in the world. Bennett gained international recognition while at Bradley.

Bennett resigned his position at Bradley in 1919 to devote full time as writer, editor, and publisher of the *Manual Training Magazine* (later, *Industrial Education Magazine* in 1922), which he founded in 1899. He founded the Manual Arts Press in 1903 and published his works and those of others in the field.

Bennett's books include *Problems in Mechanical Drawing* (1908), *Grammar Grade Problems in Mechanical Drawing* (1916), *The Manual Arts* (1917), *Art Training for Life and for Industry* (1923), and *Beginning Problems in Mechanical Drawing* (1934). His most important contributions were as author of *History of Manual and Industrial Education up to 1870* (1926) and *History of Manual and Industrial Education, 1870–1917* (1937), on which he spent thirty years in research and writing.

He founded the Western Drawing and Manual Training Teachers Association in 1893 (later, Western Arts Association) and served as president and chairman of the executive council, and he helped found the Vocational Education Association of the Middle West (president), which merged into the American Vocational Association. He belonged to many professional and social organizations.

REFERENCES: *LE* (II); *NCAB* (33:310); *WWAE* (I); *Industrial Arts and Vocational Education* 31 (September 1942):291-92; *School and Society* 55 (June 27, 1942):721. *Lee H. Smalley*

BENNETT, Charles Edwin. B. April 6, 1858, Providence, Rhode Island, to James L. and Lucia E. (Dyer) Bennett. M. June 29, 1886, to Margaret Gale Hitchcock. Ch. none. D. May 2, 1921, Ithaca, New York.

Charles Bennett was graduated with the A.B. degree (1878) from Brown University in Providence, Rhode Island. He taught school at Milton, Florida (1878–79), and at Sing Sing, New York (1879–81). He was a graduate student at Harvard University (1881–82) and in Germany at Leipzig (1882–83), Berlin (1883–84), and Heidelberg (1884).

He was principal of the preparatory department of the University of

Nebraska (1884–89). He was professor of Latin at the University of Wisconsin (1889–91) and professor of classical philology at Brown University (1891–92). In 1892 he was elected to be professor of Latin at Cornell University in Ithaca, New York, and continued in this position until his death in 1921.

Bennett was editor of the Cornell Studies in Classical Philology (1892–1921) and of the College Latin Series (1895–1905). He published numerous articles in professional periodicals. He wrote *A Latin Grammar* (1895), which was the first successful American adaption of the style of the German Latin grammars. He was also author of *Appendix to Bennett's Latin Grammar* (1895), *A Latin Composition* (1896), *The Foundations of Latin* (1898), *The Quantitative Reading of Latin Poetry* (1899), *The Teaching of Latin and Greek in Secondary Schools* (with George P. Bristol, 1900), *Latin Lesson* (1901), *Preparatory Latin Writer* (1905), *The Latin Language* (1907), *First Year Latin* (1909), *Syntax of Early Latin* (volume 1, 1910, and volume 2, 1914), and *New Latin Composition* (1912). He was editor of *Caesar's Gallic War* (books 1–4, 1903), *Cicero, Selected Orations* (1904), and *Virgil Aeneid* (books 1–4, 1905). He translated *The Characters of Theophrastus* (with William A. Hammond, 1902), *Horace, Odes, and Epodes* (1914) and *Frontinus, The Stratagems and the Aqueducts of Rome* (1925). Bennet's knowledge of Latin syntax and metric earned him an international reputation among scholars.

He was active in professional associations, including the American Philological Association (president, 1907–08).

REFERENCES: *DAB; EB; WWW* (I); *NYT,* May 3, 1921, p. 17.

Walter J. Sanders

BENNION, Milton. B. June 7, 1870, Taylorsville, Utah, to John and Mary (Turpin) Bennion. M. June 22, 1898, to Cora Lindsay. Ch. ten. D. April 15, 1953, Salt Lake City, Utah.

Milton Bennion was graduated from the University of Utah with the B.Sc. degree (1897). He was a student at the University of Chicago (1898) and Columbia University, where he was awarded the M.A. degree (1901). He also studied at the University of Wisconsin (1912–13) and the University of California (1924). Among his eminent instructors were John Dewey *(q.v.)* at the University of Chicago and J. McKeen Cattell *(q.v.)* and James E. Russell *(q.v.)* at Columbia University.

Bennion first taught in a one-room schoolhouse at the age of sixteen. He was principal of the Southern Branch Utah State Normal School (later, Southern State College) in Cedar City (1897–1900) and accepted a position in 1901 at the University of Utah, where he served to his retirement in 1941. He was a professor of education, director of the school of education (1913–41) and the summer school (1914–38), and vice-president of the university (1940–41).

Bennion's major influence at Utah was as dean of the school of education, which he guided for twenty-eight years. He advocated the professional preparation of teachers, strengthened certification requirements, improved the curriculum, instituted a plan for screening prospective teachers, and added new departments in the school. In recognition of his service, the university conferred on him the honorary Ed.D. degree in 1931.

He was recognized as a leader in character education, which he believed was one of the principal objectives of education. His major contribution to ethical education was *Citizenship: An Introduction to Social Ethics* (1917). Among his other writings were *Moral Teachings of the New Testament* (1928) and *New Frontiers for American Youth* (1939). He served as editorial writer of *The Instructor* magazine for several years.

Active in educational, civic, and religious work, Bennion was a member of the Utah Board of Education (1898–1900), chairman of the Utah State Welfare Commission (1921–23), chairman of the committee on character education of the National Council of Education and National Education Association (1921–25), chairman of Group D. on International Ideals of the World Conference on Education at San Francisco, California (1923), and fellow of the American Association for the Advancement of Science. He was general superintendent of the Church of Latter Day Saints Sunday schools (1943–49) and served on the general board of the Sunday school for forty years. After his death in 1953, the Milton Bennion Foundation was established at the University of Utah.

REFERENCES: *LE* (III); *WWAE* (I); *WWW* (V); Reed H. Beckstead, "The Life, Philosophy and Educational Contributions of Milton Bennion" (Master's thesis, University of Utah, 1954); Howard R. Driggs, "Man of Action," *The Instructor* 88 (May 1953): 132.   *Harry P. Bluhm*

BENTON, Thomas Hart. B. September 5, 1816, Williamson County, Tennessee, to Samuel Benton and n.a. M. 1851 to Sarah Culbertson. Ch. none. D. April 10, 1879, St. Louis, Missouri.

Thomas Hart Benton, nephew of the famous Missouri statesman, was educated at Huntington Academy, Tennessee, and was graduated from Marion (Missouri) College.

In 1837 he traveled to Iowa, then part of Wisconsin Territory, and settled in the frontier town of Dubuque in 1838. He organized, taught, and served as principal of Iowa's first classical school (1838–39).

Benton was elected to the senate of the first general assembly of Iowa in 1846 and served as chairman of the committee on schools, which drew up the legislation that provided for the establishment and organization of the Iowa public school system. He was a successful candidate on the Democratic ticket for the office of superintendent of public instruction. During his six-year tenure in office (1848–54) he played an important role in legislation that provided for collection of local taxes to support educational institutions and pay teachers' salaries. Under a new state constitution of 1857, the public schools of Iowa were reorganized under a state board of education. In 1858 Benton took over the duties of the newly created post of secretary of the board. In this position he was active in the organization and management of local school districts and the examination and certification of teachers. He also took a part in the organization of national educational groups of teachers, which later developed into the National Education Association.

With the outbreak of the Civil War, Benton was appointed colonel of the Twenty-ninth Iowa Volunteer Infantry, and by the close of the war, he had attained the rank of brigadier general. He waged an unsuccessful campaign as the Democratic candidate for governor of Iowa in 1865 and was appointed by President Andrew Johnson as assessor of internal revenue in the Sixth Congressional District. He was last employed as a railroad auditor in Cedar Rapids, Iowa.

REFERENCES: *DAB; WWW* (H); Clarence Ray Aurner, *History of Education in Iowa* (Iowa City, Iowa: State Historical Society of Iowa, 1914), vols. 1, 11; Benjamin F. Gue, *History of Iowa* (New York: Century History Co., 1903), vol. 4.   *Marie Della Bella*

BERNARD, Luther Lee. B. October 29, 1881, Russell County, Kentucky, to Hiram Hamilton and Julia Ann (Wilson) Bernard. M. September 16, 1911, to Frances Fenton. M. September 21, 1925, to Jessie Ravage. Ch. four. D. January 23, 1951, State College, Pennsylvania.

Luther Lee Bernard attended public school in Gordon, Texas; he received the B.S. degree (1899) from Pierce City (Missouri) Baptist College and the A.B. degree (1907) from the University of Missouri. He was a fellow at the University of Chicago, where he received the Ph.D. degree in sociology (1910).

Bernard taught natural sciences at Pierce City Baptist College (1901–03), became principal of a rural Missouri school, and was professor of languages at Lamar (Missouri) College (1903–05). In 1910 he taught sociology at Western Reserve University in Cleveland, Ohio, and history and social sciences at the University of Florida (1911–14). Bernard taught sociology at the University of Missouri (1914–17) and held similar posts at the University of Minnesota (1917–25), Cornell University (1925–26), Tulane University in New Orleans, Louisiana (1927–28), University of North Carolina (1928–29), and Washington University in St. Louis, Missouri (1929–47). From his retirement in 1947 to his death in 1951, Bernard taught at Pennsylvania State College (later, University).

He wrote more than two hundred articles for many periodicals in the United States, Mexico, Argentina, France, and China and was an editor of

American Sociologist and *Social Forces.* He authored over a dozen books, including *The Teaching of Sociology in the United States* (1909), *Instinct* (1924), *Introduction to Social Psychology* (1926), *The Development of Methods in Sociology* (1928), *Social Control* (1939), *Introduction to Sociology* (1942), *Origins of American Sociology* (with Jessie Bernard, 1943), and *War and Its Causes* (1944).

While at Florida he was active in the Florida Child Labor Committee (chairman, 1913–14), the Southern Sociological Congregation (director, 1912–16), and the Florida Conference on Charities and Corrections (vice-president, 1911–12; and treasurer, 1912–13). In 1925 and 1926 Bernard was a Social Science Research Council fellow in Argentina, an experience that stimulated his interest in the relation of education and international relations.

Bernard was active in professional associations, including the American Sociological Society (president, 1932), the Association for Historical Studies (Argentina), and the Czechoslovakian Society of Sociologists, which awarded him the Masaryk Medal.

REFERENCES: *LE* (II); *NCAB* (39:308); *WWW* (III); *WWAE* (VIII); *NYT,* January 25, 1951, p. 25.   *Murry R. Nelson*

BERRY, Martha McChesney. B. October 7, 1866, near Rome, Georgia, to Thomas and Frances (Rhea) Berry. M. no. D. February 27, 1942, Atlanta, Georgia.

Martha Berry was born on a plantation in northwestern Georgia. Despite the Civil War, her family was prosperous. She enjoyed the advantages of private tutors and traveled and inherited a small fortune.

The Berry plantation was adjacent to poverty-stricken farms of Georgia mountaineers. In the 1890s Berry began her career as an educator informally by telling Bible stories to rural children, who called her the Sunday Lady. Realizing that the children would grow up illiterate unless something more were done, she used her own funds to open a day school.

In 1902 she started the Mount Berry (Georgia) School for Boys, a log-cabin boarding school, and added the Martha Berry School for Girls in 1909. She established Berry College in 1926. All the Berry schools were dedicated to preparing poor rural children for vocations. Students earned most of their tuition and gained practical experience by performing nearly all the support work of the campus, including farming, forestry, building construction and maintenance, stenography, and nursing. Berry sought to develop in her students a respect for the dignity of manual labor.

Berry financed her schools from her own funds and solicited philanthropic support, receiving nearly $4 million from Henry Ford.

Berry became nationally respected as an educator, and numerous magazines featured articles about her schools. She was the first woman to serve as a regent of the university system of Georgia (1932) and the only woman appointed to the Georgia State Planning Commission (1937). Voted distinguished citizen by the Georgia legislature (1924), she received the Roosevelt Medal (1925) and medals from the Town Club of New York (1931), the Colonial Society of Dames (1933), and the National Institute of Social Sciences (1939).

REFERENCES: *CB* (April 1940); *DAB* (supp. 3); *NAW; NCAB* (C:49); *WWW* (II); Hamilton Basso, "About the Berry Schools," *New Republic* 78 (April 4, 1934): 206–08; Francis R. Bellamy, "Martha Berry," *Good Housekeeping* 73 (October 1921): 21–22; Martha Berry, "A School in the Woods," *Outlook* 77 (August 6, 1904): 838–41; Tracy Byers, *Martha Berry, The Sunday Lady of Possum Trot* (New York: Putnam's, 1932); *NYT*, February 27, 1942, p. 17; "Thanks for Miss Berry," *Life* 39 (October 24, 1955): 91–92.   *Nancy Baldrige Julian*

BESSEY, Charles Edwin. B. May 21, 1845, Wayne County, Ohio, to Adnah and Margaret (Ellensberger) Bessey. M. December 25, 1873, to Lucy Athearn. Ch. one, Ernst Athearn Bessey, professor of botany. D. February 25, 1915, Lincoln, Nebraska.

The son of a schoolteacher who became a farmer, Charles E. Bessey began his education under his father and in the common schools of northern Ohio. Bessey attended Seville (Ohio) Academy but had to leave school on the death of his father and was employed as a teacher. He attended Michigan Agricultural College (later, Michigan State University) in East Lansing, earning the B.S. (1869) and M.S. (1872) degrees. He studied with Asa Gray *(q.v.)* at Harvard University (1872–73 and 1875–76).

Bessey taught botany, horticulture, and zoology at Iowa Agricultural College (later, Iowa State University) from 1870 to 1884 and served as acting president in 1882. In 1884 he went to the University of Nebraska to become professor of botany and horticulture and dean of the Industrial College (college of agriculture), remaining there until his death in 1915. Bessey was largely responsible for changing the basic program of the college of agriculture from a program based on trial and error to one based on science education and sound research. He served as acting chancellor of the University of Nebraska (1888–91, 1899–1900, and 1907–08).

He was instrumental in the creation of the Nebraska National Forest, the passage of the Hatch Act, which established agricultural experiment stations, and the enactment of significant conservation legislation.

Bessey's publications were numerous and widely used; they include *Geography of Iowa* (1876), *Botany for High Schools and Colleges* (1880), *Essentials of Botany* (1884), *Elementary Botanical Exercises* (1892), *New Elementary Agriculture* (with Lawrence Bruner and Goodwin D. Swezey, 1903), *Elementary Botany* (1904), *Plant Migration Studies* (1905), and

Essentials of College Biology (with Ernst A. Bessey, 1914). He also wrote many technical reports and scientific articles for professional journals and was the botanical editor of several encyclopedias.

Bessey was active in professional organizations, including serving as president of the Iowa Academy of Sciences (1875–84), the Nebraska Academy of Sciences (1891–94), the Society for the Promotion of Agricultural Science (1883–85), the American Association for the Advancement of Science (1913), the American Microscopical Society (1902), and the Botanical Society of America (1896–97). He was awarded honorary degrees by the University of Iowa and Iowa College.

REFERENCES: *AC; DAB; NCAB* (8:361); *TC; WWW* (I); R. J. Pool, "Brief Sketch of Life and Work of Charles Edwin Bessey," *American Journal of Botany* 2 (December 1915): 505–18; Thomas R. Walsh, "Charles E. Bessey: Land Grant College Professor" (Ph.D. diss., University of Nebraska, 1972); Thomas R. Walsh, "Charles E. Bessey and the Transformation of the Industrial College," *Nebraska History* 52 (Winter 1971): 383–409; Thomas R. Walsh, "The American Green of Charles Bessey," *Nebraska History* 53 (Spring 1972): 35–57.

Erwin H. Goldenstein

BESTOR, Arthur Eugene. B. May 19, 1879, Dixon, Illinois, to Orson Porter and Laura Ellen (Moore) Bestor. M. May 24, 1905, to Jeanette Louise Lemon. Ch. four, including Arthur Eugene Bestor, Jr., a critic of American education. D. February 3, 1944, Chautauqua, New York.

Arthur Bestor was graduated with the A.B. degree (1901) from the University of Chicago. He started his teaching career as a professor of history and political science at Franklin (Indiana) College (1901–03) and lectured on political science in the extension division of the University of Chicago (1904–12). He was assistant director (1905), director (1907), and president (1915–44) of the Chautauqua Institution in western New York. Founded by John Heyl Vincent *(q.v.)* in 1878, the Chautauqua Institution was a unique experiment in adult education.

During World War I, Bestor was director of the speakers' division of the Committee on Public Information and chairman of the committee on lectures and entertainment of the Young Men's Christian Association work council. He was chairman of the board of trustees of Town Hall, Inc. (1935–43). He was a member of the executive committee of the American School of Sofia, Bulgaria. He was active in the World Association for Adult Education (American member of the council) and the American Association for Adult Education (chairman, international relations committee). He received an honorary degree from Colgate University.

REFERENCES: *CB* (March 1944); *DAB* (supp. 3); *LE* (II); *NCAB* (A:336, 33:507); *WWW* (II); *NYT,* February 5, 1944, p. 15. *Farouk Zalatimo*

BETHUNE, Joanna Graham. B. February 1, 1770, Fort Niagara, Canada, to John and Isabella (Marshall) Graham. M. July, 1795, to Divie Bethune. Ch. six. D. July 28, 1860, New York, New York.

Joanna Graham Bethune was an early leader in the infant school and Sunday school movements in New York City. She was educated in her mother's school for young children in Paisley, Scotland, and in a school for young ladies in Edinburgh, which her mother had opened in 1779. She prepared to be a teacher in a French school in Rotterdam, Holland.

In 1789 the family emigrated to New York City where Mrs. Graham established a school for the daughters of New York's leading citizens; her own daughters taught in the school.

In July 1795 Joanna Graham married Divie Bethune, a prosperous merchant. Mrs. Graham lived with the Bethunes, and mother and daughter engaged in many philanthropic activities. In 1797 Mrs. Graham founded the Society for the Relief of Poor Widows with Children; both women worked with the society.

Bethune became interested in the work of August Hermann Francke, founder of the Orphan House in Halle, Germany. She organized the Orphan Asylum Society in the City of New York in 1806. A house was built, one of the first orphanages in the United States, and Bethune taught in the monitorial school at the asylum. She served for fifty years on the Orphan Asylum Society's board of directors. She took the initiative in organizing the Society for the Promotion of Industry Among the Poor in 1814. The society provided work for poverty-stricken women during the depression following the War of 1812.

About 1803 and after 1816, Bethune put into practice in New York City the Sunday school movement she had observed on a trip to Scotland. She organized the Female Union Society for the Promotion of Sabbath-Schools in 1816.

After the death of her husband in 1824, Bethune became interested in the work of Johann Heinrich Pestalozzi. She had books explaining Pestalozzian theories sent from Europe and founded the Infant School Society in New York City on May 23, 1827, with the assistance of John Griscom *(q.v.)*. She opened a free infant school and eventually superintended nine infant schools in the city and taught in one of them.

Bethune was author of *The Infant School Grammar Consisting of Elementary Lessons in the Analytical Method* (1830), *Memoir of Miss Anna Goodale* (1834), and *The Life of Mrs. Isabella Graham* (1839).

REFERENCES: *NAW;* George W. Bethune, *Memoirs of Mrs. Joanna Bethune* (New York: Harper & Brothers, 1864); Joanna Bethune, diary manuscripts section, Clements Library, University of Michigan, Ann Arbor.   *John W. Jenkins*

BETHUNE, Mary McLeod. B. July 10, 1875, Mayville, South Carolina, to Samuel and Patsy McLeod. M. May 1898 to Albertus Bethune. Ch. one. D. May 18, 1955, Daytona Beach, Florida.

The fifteenth and first free born of seventeen children of former slaves, Mary McLeod Bethune was permitted at the age of eleven to attend a new school for black children sponsored by the Mission Board of the Presbyterian church. A scholarship provided by a Colorado seamstress paid for her further education at Scotia Seminary in Concord, North Carolina, from which she was graduated in 1893, and at the Moody Bible Institute in Chicago, Illinois (1893–95). When her request to be assigned as a missionary to Africa was refused, she became a teacher and was increasingly concerned about the lack of educational opportunity for black girls. She was a senior instructor at the Haines Institute in Augusta, Georgia (1895–96), and taught at the Palatka (Florida) Mission School (1899–1903).

In 1904 she rented a rundown building and set up her own school in Daytona Beach, Florida, enrolling six students, including her own son. The school was called the Daytona Normal and Industrial School for Negro Girls. Bethune and her students sold sweet potato pies and fried fish, gave concerts in resort hotels, and even begged to raise money to keep the school going. By 1912 she had persuaded James N. Gamble, son of the founder of Procter and Gamble, to be a school trustee. Gamble, Thomas H. White of the sewing machine company, and others became lifelong benefactors of the school that became the coeducational Bethune-Cookman College, with Bethune as president.

Bethune gained recognition as a founder of the National Council of Negro Women (1935), appointee of President Franklin D. Roosevelt as director of Negro affairs in the National Youth Administration, and special adviser on minority affairs (1936). She served as special assistant to the secretary of war to help select candidates for the first officer training school for the Women's Auxiliary Army Corps (1942). As special emissary for the department of state, she attended the founding conference for the United Nations in San Francisco (1945).

She was the recipient of eleven honorary degrees and many special awards and was active in various organizations, including the National Association of Colored Women (president), the National Association for the Advancement of Colored People (vice-president), the Commission on Interracial Cooperation (vice-president), the Association for the Study of Negro Life and History (president), and the National Association of Teachers in Colored Schools (president).

REFERENCES: *CB* (January 1942); *EB; LE* (III); *NCAB* (49:118); *WWW* (III); Alice Fleming, *Great Women Teachers* (Philadelphia: J. B. Lippincott Co., 1965); Rackham Holt, *Mary McLeod Bethune* (New York:

Doubleday and Co., 1964); *Newsweek,* May 30, 1955, p. 47; *NYT,* May 20, 1955, p. 25; Catherine Owens Peare, *Mary McLeod Bethune* (New York: The Vanguard Press, 1951); *Time,* May 30, 1955, p. 44.

Joanne L. Schweik

BETTELHEIM, Bruno. B. August 28, 1903, Vienna, Austria, to Anton and Paula (Seidler) Bettelheim. M. May 14, 1941, to Gertrud Weinfeld. Ch. three.

Bruno Bettelheim was born and educated in Vienna, Austria, earning the Ph.D. degree from the University of Vienna in 1938.

He was arrested by the Nazis in 1938 and incarcerated at Buchenwald and Dachau. Released in 1939, he moved to the United States where he became a naturalized citizen in 1944. Drawing on his experiences in concentration camps, Bettelheim first received international recognition when his article "Individual and Mass Behavior in Extreme Situations" was published in 1943. Reprints of the article became required reading for all United States military officers in Europe by order of General Dwight D. Eisenhower.

Bettelheim was a research associate for the Progressive Education Association at the University of Chicago (1939–41), associate professor of psychology, Rockford (Illinois) College (1942–44), and professor of educational psychology (1944–63) and Stella M. Rowley Distinguished Professor of Education (1963–73) at the University of Chicago. Concurrently he served as head of the Sonia Shankman Orthogenic School (1944–73), a resident school established to serve severely disturbed children with exceptional intellectual ability.

Bettelheim was interested in social psychology and the nature of prejudice. He was concerned that modern knowledge of education and psychology be used in the rearing of children, and he authored a series of articles aimed at the education of the public in child-rearing practices. He was also interested in the effects of communal child rearing on personalities and visited kibbutzim in Israel.

Bettelheim was the author of books on education and psychology, including *Love Is Not Enough—The Treatment of Emotionally Disturbed Children* (1950), *Dynamics of Prejudice* (with Morris Janowitz, 1950), *Symbolic Wounds* (1954), *Truants from Life* (1955), *The Informed Heart* (1960), *Dialogues with Mothers* (1962), *The Empty Fortress* (1967), *Children of the Dream* (1969), *Obsolete Youth* (1970), and *A Home for the Heart* (1974).

A fellow of the American Psychological Association and the American Orthopsychiatric Association, Bettelheim was a member of many professional associations.

REFERENCES: *CB* (July 1961); *LE* (II); *WW* (XXXVIII); David Dempsey, "Bruno Bettelheim Is Dr. No," *New York Times Magazine,* January 11,

1970, p. 22; *The International Who's Who,* 38th ed. (London: Europa Publications Limited, 1974). Paul L. Ward

BETTS, Emmett Albert. B. February 1, 1903, Elkhart, Iowa, to Albert Henry and Grace L. (Greenwood) Betts. M. May 24, 1924, to Thelma Marshall. M. July 15, 1950, to Carolyn Welch. Ch. three.

Emmett Albert Betts received the B.S. degree (1925) from Des Moines (Iowa) University and the M.S. (1928) and Ph.D. (1931) degrees from the University of Iowa.

His professional experience began as a school vocational director in Orient, Iowa (1922–24). He was a school psychologist and elementary principal in Shaker Heights, Ohio (1925–29), and served at the State Teachers College (later, State University of New York College) in Oswego, New York (1934–37), where he was director of teacher education, summer sessions, and the reading clinic. He went to Pennsylvania State College (later, University) as a research professor of education and director of the reading clinic (1937–45) and moved to Temple University in Philadelphia, Pennsylvania, where he was professor of psychology and director of the reading clinic (1945–54). In 1954 he opened the Betts Reading Clinic in Haverford, Pennsylvania, which he directed until 1961, when he moved to the University of Miami in Coral Gables, Florida, as research professor of education and lecturer in psychology.

Betts was a member of the summer faculty or a participant in workshops dealing with vision and reading at more than forty colleges and universities. He served as a consultant to public schools throughout the United States and to the Air University, and other educational groups.

Among Betts's books were *Prevention and Correction of Reading Difficulties* (with Mabel O'Donnell, 1936), *Visual Problems of School Children* (1941), *Index to Professional Publications on Reading and Related Topics* (1944), *Foundations of Reading Instruction* (1946), considered a classic in the field of reading textbooks, and *How to Teach Reading* (1963). He coauthored reading, spelling, and language arts textbooks and served in editorial roles for a number of periodicals, instructional materials, and reference works. He published more than five hundred works, including more than three hundred articles in professional journals on reading and vision. He served as editor to a number of journals, including *Highlights for Children* and *Education* (1948–69), was contributing editor to *My Weekly Reader* (1938–69), *Journal of Experimental Education,* and *Reading Teacher,* and was on the editorial board of *Reading Improvement* and the editorial advisory committee of *Annual Progress in Reading.*

He was active in over twenty professional organizations and assumed leadership roles and held various offices in many of them. He was the founder of the International Council for the Improvement of Reading

Instruction (later, the International Reading Association).

Throughout his career Betts championed the cause of reading instruction based on the reading levels and needs of children as opposed to a static curriculum. His procedures and criteria for determining reading levels and needs through informal reading inventories have been widely accepted by reading specialists. He pioneered visual screening procedures that were used in clinics and schools. He was the recipient of honors, including the Apollo Award of the American Optometric Association (1962), Citation of Merit and Founders Award of the International Reading Association (1971), and the Gold Medal Award of *Education* (1971).

REFERENCES: *CA* (33–36); *LE* (III); *WWAE* (XXII); *WW* (XXXVIII).

George H. Maginnis

BETTS, George Herbert. B. April 1, 1868, Clarkesville, Iowa, to Christopher and Lucinda (Elliott) Betts. M. June 21, 1893, to Anna Marie Freelove. Ch. two. D. December 8, 1934, Evanston, Illinois.

George Herbert Betts attended public school in Clarkesville, Iowa, and received the A.B. degree (1899) from Cornell College in Mount Vernon, Iowa. He received the M.Ph. degree (1904) from the University of Chicago and the Ph.D. degree (1909) from Columbia University.

Before attending Cornell College, Betts had served Iowa schools as teacher, principal, and superintendent in Clarkesville and Allison. After receiving his degree, he returned to public school work (1899–1901) before returning to Cornell as a professor of psychology (1901–18). He was active in Iowa teacher associations and in much demand as a speaker.

He served as professor of religious education at Boston (Massachusetts) University (1918–19), Northwestern University in Evanston, Illinois (1919–21 and 1922–26), and University of Southern California in Los Angeles (1921–22). When Northwestern established its school of education in 1926, Betts was appointed professor of education and director of research, a position he held until his death in 1934. He was interested in religious, character, and general education, which he sought to influence through teaching, speaking, and writing.

Betts edited religious education texts for use in schools and a series of readers. He wrote books on a variety of educational topics; among them were *The Mind and Its Education* (1908), *Distribution and Function of Mental Imagery* (1909), *The Recitation* (1911), *Social Principles of Education* (1912), *New Ideals in Rural Schools* (1913), *Better Rural Schools* (with Otis E. Hall, 1914), *Teachers and Mothers* (1915), *Agriculture* (with O. H. Benson, 1915), *Parenthood and Heredity* (1915), *Roots of Disposition and Character* (1915), *Youth's Outlook Upon Life* (1915), *Outlines of Psychology and School Management* (1915), *Classroom Method and Management* (1917), *How to Teach Religion* (1919), *Physiology and*

Hygiene (with C. P. Emerson, 1919), *The New Program of Religious Education* (1921), *Laboratory Studies in Educational Psychology* (with E. M. Turner, 1924), *The Curriculum of Religious Education* (1924), *Method in Teaching Religion* (1925), *Character Outcome of Present Day Religion* (1931), *Teaching Religion Today* (1934), and *Foundations of Character and Personality,* which was published posthumously in 1937.

Betts was a fellow of the American Association for the Advancement of Science and a member of other professional associations.

REFERENCES: *LE* (I); *NCAB* (30:161); *WWW* (I); *Evanston* (Illinois) *Review,* December 13, 1934.   *Darlene E. Fisher*

BEVIER, Isabel. B. November 14, 1860, near Plymouth, Ohio, to Caleb and Cornelia (Brinkerhoff) Bevier. M. no. D. March 17, 1942, Urbana, Illinois.

Isabel Bevier began her career in education at an early age, teaching country school for three summers before she was eighteen. She attended Plymouth (Ohio) High School, Wooster (Ohio) Preparatory School, and the University (later College) of Wooster, Ohio, where she received the Ph.B. (1885) and Ph.M. (1888) degrees. While at Wooster, she was the first state chairman of the Young Women's Christian Association.

Bevier was principal of the Shelby (Ohio) high school (1885–87) and high school instructor of science in Mount Vernon, Ohio (1887–88). When her fiancé drowned in 1888, she sought solace near friends and accepted a position teaching the natural sciences at Pennsylvania College for Women in Pittsburgh. In preparation for the move, she spent the summers of 1888 and 1889 studying chemistry with Albert W. Smith at Case School of Applied Science in Cleveland, the first woman to be admitted to the institution. Convinced of the need for women to study the chemistry of food, she spent summers studying at Harvard University (1891), working as a chemist at the World's Columbian Exposition (1893), and studying with the famous agricultural chemist, Wilbur O. Atwater *(q.v.),* at Wesleyan University in Middletown, Connecticut (1894). Under Atwater's direction she conducted nutrition studies in Pittsburgh and among blacks near Hampton, Virginia, that were published in United States Department of Agriculture bulletins of 1898, 1899, and 1900.

Bevier studied briefly at Western Reserve University (later, Case Western Reserve University) and at Massachusetts Institute of Technology with Ellen H. Richards *(q.v.).* In 1898 she accepted a position as professor of chemistry at Lake Erie College in Painesville, Ohio, and then moved to the University of Illinois in 1900 as professor and director of courses in household science. Bevier considered home economics a part of liberal education as well as a professional study and insisted that students meet entrance requirements equal to those of other departments and that chemistry should be a prerequisite for admission. She originated the idea of using the thermometer in cooking meat in 1907 and the following year established a house on campus as a study laboratory. She left Illinois in 1921 to accept a position as leader of the home economics department at the University of California at Los Angeles (1921–23). She returned from retirement to Illinois in 1928, retiring again in 1930.

Bevier's major publications were *The Home Economics Movement* (with Susannah Usher, 1906), *Food and Nutrition* (with Susannah Usher, 1906), *Selection and Preparation of Food* (with Anna R. Van Meter, 1906), *The House-Plan, Decoration and Care* (1907), and *Home Economics in Education* (1923). She served on the editorial board of the *Journal of Home Economics* (1909–12) and was the author of numerous articles and bulletins.

Bevier served as a vice-chairman of the Lake Placid Conference on Home Economics, which led to the founding of the American Home Economics Association in 1908. She was the first vice-president of the association and president from 1909 to 1912.

REFERENCES: *DAB* (supp. 3); *LE* (II); *NAW; WWW* (II); *NYT,* March 18, 1942, p. 23.   *Darlene E. Fisher*

BICKNELL, Thomas Williams. B. September 6, 1834, Barrington, Rhode Island, to Allin and Harriet Byron (Kinnicutt) Bicknell. M. September 1860 to Amelia D. Blanding. Ch. none. D. October 6, 1925, Providence, Rhode Island.

Thomas Williams Bicknell received his education from Thetford (Vermont) Academy (1853), Amherst (Massachusetts) College (1854), and Brown University in Providence, Rhode Island, where he received the A.M. degree (1860). While a senior at Brown, he represented Barrington in the Rhode Island legislature.

He taught school from 1854 to 1857 and, after graduating from Brown, was principal of the Bristol (Rhode Island) High School and of the Arnold Street grammar school in Providence. He was elected commissioner of public schools of Rhode Island, a position he filled for six years (1869–75). During this time he reestablished the state normal school, set up a state board of education, provided for salaried school superintendents for all school districts in the state, organized evening schools, and saw the enactment of truancy laws.

In 1875 Bicknell became editor of the *New England Journal of Education* and assumed ownership of the journal in 1876. He was founder, editor, and publisher of the *Primary Teacher* (1877) and *Education* (1880). Among his publications were reports as Rhode Island school commissioner (1869–75), *Biography of William L. Noyes* (1867), *Annals of Barrington, Rhode Island* (1870), *The Bicknells* (four volumes, 1880–88), *Barrington in the Revolution* (1898), *History of Rhode Island Normal School* (1912),

Bicknell Family Geneology (1913), *The Story of Dr. John Clarke* (1915), and *History of the State of Rhode Island and Providence Plantations* (five volumes, 1920).

Bicknell was active in civic and professional associations. He was a representative in the legislatures of both Rhode Island (1859–60) and Massachusetts (1888–90). He was a founder of the town of New England, North Dakota, and the Leader Silk Company (1903). He was active in the Rhode Island Institute of Instruction (president, 1867–68), the National Council of Education (founder, 1880 and president, 1880–84), the American Institute of Instruction (president, 1877–78), and National Educational Association (president, 1884).

REFERENCES: *AC; NCAB* (1:421); *TC; WWW* (I); *NYT,* October 7, 1925, p. 27.   *John W. Schifani*

BIGELOW, Harry Augustus. B. September 22, 1874, Norwood, Massachusetts to Erwin Augustus and Amie (Leighton) Bigelow. M. April 12, 1902, to Mary Parker. Ch. none. D. January 8, 1950, Chicago, Illinois.

Harry Augustus Bigelow attended Norwood (Massachusetts) High School, Harvard University, and the Harvard Law School, where he was an editor on the *Law Review.* He received the LL.B. degree in 1899 and worked as a law clerk and part-time instructor in Boston at the Harvard Law School.

In 1900 he left Boston for Hawaii to start his law practice in Honolulu, but in 1904 he accepted a position at the University of Chicago where he, William Rainey Harper *(q.v.),* and Joseph Henry Beale established the university's law school. In 1908 Bigelow was admitted to the bar in Illinois. In 1909 he became professor and in 1929 dean of the school.

Bigelow was well known for his work on real estate and personal property law. He was editor of *May's Criminal Law* (1905). His case books— *The Law of Personal Property* (1917), *The Law of Rights in Land* (1919), and *The Law of Property* (edited with Ralph W. Aigler and Richard R. B. Powell, 1942)—were standard references in law schools across the United States. Another publication, *The Introduction to the Law of Real Property* (1919), was a brief historical survey of the law and was an invaluable tool for students of the law of property.

As dean of the Law School, Bigelow encouraged the development of a tutorial program. Believing that an understanding of law also required a knowledge of economics, accounting, and psychology, he included these subjects in the law school curriculum.

Bigelow was prominent in the preparation of the *Restatement of the Conflict of Laws* (1934) and *Restatement of the Law of Property* (1936) for the American Law Institute. In 1933 he was appointed trustee in the bankruptcy of the Insull Utility Investments, Inc. In 1939 he retired as dean of the University of Chicago Law School but still taught his classes in the law of property and the conflict of law. In 1947 he was appointed by Harry S Truman to the National Loyalty Review Board. The University of Chicago established the Harry A. Bigelow Professorship and the Bigelow Tutorial Fellowship in his memory.

REFERENCES: *DAB* (supp. 4); *LE* (III); *WWW* (II); *NYT,* January 9, 1950, p. 25.   *Thomas Meighan*

BINGHAM, Caleb. B. April 15, 1757, Salisbury, Connecticut, to David and Hannah (Conant) Bingham. M. 1786 to Hannah Kemble. Ch. two. D. April 6, 1819, Boston, Massachusetts.

Caleb Bingham was graduated from Dartmouth College in 1782 and delivered the valedictory address in Latin. Following his graduation he became a teacher at the Master of Moor's Indian Charity School (1782–84).

Bingham moved to Boston in 1784, where he established a school for young ladies (1784–89). A strong advocate of public elementary education, he played an important role in the reorganization of the Boston public schools. In 1789 Bingham took the post of master of a Boston public reading school and continued in this position for seven years. He helped organize the Boston Library and served as the first librarian, holding the unsalaried post for two years.

In 1796 Bingham retired from teaching to become a bookseller and printer. His shop was a popular gathering place for Boston teachers and scholars. Bingham's first book was *The Young Lady's Accidence or a Short and Easy Introduction to English Grammar* (1785), the second English grammar published in the United States. Other school books he wrote and published include *The Child's Companion* (1792), *The American Preceptor* (1794), *The Colombian Orator* (1797), and *The Astronomical and Geographical Catechism* (1803). He was also the author of *Juvenile Letters* (c. 1802) and *The Hunters; or the Sufferings of Hugh and Francis in the Wilderness* (1814).

Bingham, a Jeffersonian Republican, was an unsuccessful candidate for the state senate. He served as director of the Massachusetts state prison for several years.

REFERENCES: *DAB; NCAB* (8:19); *WWW* (H); Max J. Herzberg, *The Reader's Encyclopedia of American Literature* (New York: Thomas Y. Crowell Co., 1962); George Littlefield, *Early Schools and School-Books of New England* (New York: Russell & Russell, 1965).   *Mark Fravel, Jr.*

BIRGE, Edward Asahiel. B. September 7, 1851, Troy, New York, to Edward White and Ann (Stevens) Birge. M. July 15, 1880, to Anna Wilhelmina Grant. Ch. two. D. June 9, 1950, Madison, Wisconsin.

Edward Asahiel Birge received the A.B. degree (1873) from Williams College in Williamstown, Massachusetts, and the A.M. (1876) and Ph.D.

(1878) degrees from Harvard University. He studied histology and physiology on the postdoctoral level at the University of Leipzig, Germany (1880–81).

Birge taught at the University of Wisconsin from 1875 and remained there for fifty years. He was chairman of the department of zoology (1879–1911) and the first dean of the college of letters and sciences (1891–1918). He was acting president of the University of Wisconsin (1900–03) and president of the university (1918–25).

Birge conducted research and became an expert on the taxonomy of water fleas. He was a pioneer in limnology (the study of physical, chemical, and biological conditions in fresh water). As director of the Wisconsin Geological and Natural History Survey (1897–1919), Birge carried out classical studies of the Wisconsin lakes as individual superorganisms. In 1905 he began a long partnership with Chancey Juday, which led to many publications and the establishment of the Trout Lake Limnological Laboratory in 1925. Birge worked at the laboratory on his most important study, the penetration of light and heat into lake water and the different intensities of water coloration. As dean, Birge established laboratory courses in bacteriology and physiology and in 1887 established the first premedical course at Wisconsin.

Birge wrote many articles and papers on zoology and limnology. He participated in many public, professional, and scientific activities; among them he was secretary to the Wisconsin Commission of Fisheries (1895–1915), a member of the state board of Forestry Commission (1905–15), a member of the state Conservation Commission (1908–15), and president of the American Microscopical Society (1902), the Wisconsin Academy of Science and Arts and Letters (1890–91 and 1918–21), and the Central Board of Zoologists (1908–09). He was a fellow of the American Association for the Advancement of Science and a member of many other organizations.

He received the Council Award from the State Medical Society of Wisconsin (1935) and was posthumously awarded the Naumann Medal of the International Association of Limnology. He was the recipient of several honorary degrees.

REFERENCES: *DAB* (supp. 4); *DSB; LE* (III); *NCAB* (12:290); *WWAE* (XI); *WWW* (III); *NYT*, June 10, 1950, p. 17; *School and Society* 71 (June 24, 1950): 398; *Science* 111 (June 23, 1950): 709. *Barbara Ruth Peltzman*

BIRGE, Edward Bailey. B. June 12, 1868, Northampton, Massachusetts, to Edward and Cornelia M. (Day) Birge. M. June 20, 1901, to Mary Thompson. Ch. none. D. July 16, 1952, Bloomington, Indiana.

Edward B. Birge grew up in Providence, Rhode Island, and entered Brown University where he received the A.B. degree (1891). He studied music at Yale University and received the Mus.B. degree in 1904.

Birge served as supervisor of music in state normal schools at New Haven and New Britain, Connecticut (1896–1901), and then moved to Indianapolis, Indiana, where he became director of public school music, a post he held for twenty years (1901–21). He was appointed to the faculty of the school of music, Indiana University, where he was a leading national figure in music circles (1921–38).

While in Indianapolis, Birge organized the People's Chorus in 1912 and served as director until 1921. He also served as superintendent of the American Institute of Normal Methods at Evanston, Illinois (1911–21).

Birge was a member of the Music Teachers National Association, the Music Supervisors' National Conference (president, 1911), the American Guild of Organists, the National Research Council of Music Education (chairman, 1929), the Indiana Music Teacher's Association (president, 1923), the National Education Association, and Delta Upsilon.

He served as editor of the *Silver Song Series No. 7* (1895), *Part Songs and Choruses for High Schools* (1908), and *Supplementary Songs* (1912) and composed "Concert Overture." Birge authored *History of Public School Music in the United States* (1927). He was associate editor of Music Hour Series and New Music Horizon Series. He served as chairman of the editorial board of *Music Educators' Journal*. He wrote overtures, choruses, and other musical selections.

REFERENCES: *LE* (III); *WWW* (III); R. E. Banta, comp., *Indiana Authors and Their Books, 1816–1916* (Crawfordsville, Ind.: Wabash College, 1949); *Bloomington Daily Herald Telephone*, July 17, 1952; Robert Sabin, ed., *The International Cyclopedia of Music and Musicians*, 9th ed. (New York: Dodd, Mead & Co., 1964); *Music Educators Journal* 39 (November 1952): 21.   *Robert L. Doan*

BIRKHOFF, George David. B. March 21, 1884, Overisel, Michigan, to David and Jane (Droppers) Birkhoff. M. September 2, 1908, to Margaret Grafius. Ch. three. D. November 12, 1944, Cambridge, Massachusetts.

George David Birkhoff, the eldest of six children, was born in Michigan and moved to Chicago at the age of two. Beginning his education in Chicago, he earned the A.B. (1905) and A.M. (1906) degrees at Harvard University and the Ph.D. degree (1907) from the University of Chicago, where he studied under E. H. Moore.

While still an undergraduate student, Birkhoff wrote his first mathematics paper in 1904. In 1913 he solved a synamical systems problem that won him worldwide acclaim and in 1931 an ergodic problem that had baffled scientists for more than fifty years.

Birkhoff taught mathematics at the University of Wisconsin (1907–09) and Princeton University (1909–11). He spent the rest of his career at

Harvard University (1912–44) where he was appointed Perkins Professor (1933–44) and served as dean of the faculty of arts and science (1935–39). Many influential mathematicians in the United States in the mid-twentieth century had been doctoral students of Birkhoff or studied on the post-doctoral level with him.

With a wide range of interests, he published in several areas. In addition to many journal articles he wrote *Relativity and Modern Physics* (1923), *The Origin, Nature and Influence of Relativity* (1925), *Dynamical Systems* (1928), *Aesthetic Measure* (1933), and *Basic Geometry* (with Ralph Beatley, 1941). He was the editor of several mathematics journals, including *Annals of Mathematics* (1911–13), *Transactions of American Mathematical Society* (1920–25), and *American Journal of Mathematics* (1943–44).

Birkhoff was a lecturer at the Collège de France in 1930 and was a decorated officer of the French Legion of Honor. During his life he was accorded numerous honors and was awarded several honorary degrees from American and foreign universities. He was a member of many American and foreign professional associations and served as president of the American Mathematical Society (1924–26) and the American Association for the Advancement of Science (1936–37).

REFERENCES: *DAB* (supp. 3); *EB; LE* (II); *NCAB* (F:396); *WWW* (II); *NYT,* January 13, 1944, p. 19.   *Robert McGinty*

BISHOP, Harriet E. B. January 1, 1818, Panton, Vermont, to Putnam and Miranda Bishop. M. 1858 to John McConkey. Ch. none. D. August 8, 1883, St. Paul, Minnesota.

Harriet Bishop, Minnesota's first schoolteacher, was educated in Vergennes, Vermont, and the Fort Edward (New York) Institute. She taught in Essex, New York. With other women teachers, she attended a course in Albany, New York, sponsored by the Board of Popular Education and under the direction of Catharine Beecher *(q.v.)*. Responding to a letter from doctor and missionary Thomas S. Williamson, she traveled to Minnesota in 1847.

Bishop boarded with a family in exchange for one child's tuition. Holding classes in a log-and-mud cabin, she began teaching with a class of two white and five Indian pupils. Instruction was conducted in English with an interpreter for the Indian children. The school became a center of interest, and by 1849 it had been moved into a frame building and had forty students and a second teacher, Mary Scofield.

In 1850 a school district was organized in St. Paul, and Bishop established a seminary and boarding school to train teachers for the newly opened Northwest Territory area. Bishop was author of *Floral Home* (1857), an account of her early years in Minnesota, and *Dakota War Whoop*

(1863), written under the name Harriet Bishop McConkey. She married a widower, John McConkey, in 1858 and was divorced a few years later. She worked in the local Sunday school and among the sick and poor.

REFERENCES: Harriet E. Bishop, *Floral Home* (New York, 1857); Harriet E. Bishop, *Dakota War Whoop*, ed. Dale L. Morgan (1965); "First Schools of the Last Frontier," *Journal of the National Education Association* 22 (January 1933): 25–26; Zylpha S. Morton, "Harriet Bishop, Frontier Teacher," *Minnesota History* 28 (June 1947): 132–41.

Adeline L. Levin

BISHOP, John Remsen. B. September 17, 1860, New Brunswick, New Jersey, to James and Mary Faugères (Ellis) Bishop. M. July 9, 1885, to Anna Bartram Newbold. Ch. none. D. June 28, 1934, White Plains, New York.

John Remsen Bishop attended St. Paul's School in Concord, New Hampshire, where he was graduated with highest honors (1879). He entered the sophomore class at Yale College in 1880 and, on the basis of his scholastic record, was admitted to the senior class at Harvard University in 1881, graduating in 1882. He received the Ph.D. degree from the University of Cincinnati.

Bishop taught Greek and English at St. Paul's School (1882–83) and was principal of the Princeton (New Jersey) Preparatory School, established as a school for boys preparing to enroll in the College of New Jersey (later, Princeton University). Long neglected, the school was reorganized and revitalized during Bishop's administration (1884–87).

Bishop moved to Cincinnati, Ohio, in 1887 and taught Latin and Greek at Hughes High School (1888–95) and served as principal of Walnut Hills High School (1895–1904). He went to Detroit, Michigan, in 1904 where he served as principal of Eastern High School. Fired from his position after controversy with the Detroit superintendent of schools in 1918, he was dean at the Peekskill (New York) Academy from 1918 to his retirement in 1928.

Bishop was author of *Virgil's Georgics Edited for Sight Reading* (1896) and *Story of the Gallic War* (with T. T. Jones, 1916) and translator of Hermann Weiner's *The Way to the Heart of the Pupil* (1913). He contributed articles to professional journals. He was active in professional organizations and was a founder of the Teachers' Association of Ohio.

REFERENCES: *NCAB* (7:187); *WWW* (IV); *NYT,* June 29, 1934, p. 21; *Detroit Free Press,* July 1, 1934.   *Joe Adams*
Edward J. Nussel

BISHOP, Robert Hamilton. B. July 26, 1777, Whitburn County, Scotland, to William and Margaret (Hamilton) Bishop. M. August 26, 1802, to Ann

Ireland. Ch. eight. D. April 29, 1855, College Hill, Ohio.

Robert Hamilton Bishop attended a local Scottish congregational school and entered the University of Edinburgh at the age of sixteen, was graduated in 1798, and attended the Theological Seminary in Selkirk, Scotland (1798–1802).

He went to America with his bride in the fall of 1802 and preached in a Presbyterian church in New York City. He traveled to Chillicothe, Ohio, as a missionary for the Associate Reformed Church of North America. He was a professor of philosophy at Transylvania University in Lexington, Kentucky (1804–24). Following some difficulty with the Associate Reformed synod, Bishop associated with the Central Assembly and accepted the presidency of the newly opened Miami University (Oxford, Ohio) in 1824, serving in that position to 1841. He remained at Miami holding a professorship in history and philosophy of social relations (one of the earliest courses in modern sociology) to 1844. He then accepted the chair of history and political economy at Farmer's College (Ohio Military Institute) at Pleasant Hill (near Cincinnati), Ohio (1844–55).

Among his many publications and sermons were *Sermons* (1808), *An Outline of the History of the Church in the State of Kentucky* (1824), *Elements of Logic* (1833), and *Elements of the Science of Government* (1839).

REFERENCES: *A C; DAB* (supp. 1); *WWW* (H).   *Alfred J. Ciani*

BLACKBURN, William Maxwell. B. December 30, 1828, Carlisle, Indiana, to Alexander and Delilah (Polk) Blackburn. M. August 16, 1854, to Elizabeth Powell. Ch. one. D. December 29, 1898, Pierre, South Dakota.

William Maxwell Blackburn was educated in district schools and in the academy of La Porte, Indiana. He taught school and attended Hanover (Indiana) College from which he was graduated with the bachelor (1850) and A.M. (1854) degrees. After teaching for one more year, he entered Princeton Theological Seminary and spent the next four years studying there. He served Presbyterian pastorates in Erie, Pennsylvania (1856–63), and Trenton, New Jersey (1863–68). He was professor of biblical and ecclesiastical history at the Seminary of the Midwest (later, McCormick Theological Seminary) in Chicago, Illinois (1868–81). He served a church in Cincinnati, Ohio, from 1881 to 1884 when he accepted the presidency of the Territorial University of North Dakota. In 1885 he became president of Pierre (South Dakota) University (later, relocated in Huron, South Dakota, as Huron College), a position he held until his death in 1898.

A prolific writer, Blackburn contributed to the *Princeton Review* and published many major historical and biographical religious works and stories for young people. His publications varied in scope from *History of the Christian Church from Its Origin to the Present Time* (1879) to the

Uncle Aleck six-story series for children, including *Blind Annie Lorrimer, Blood on the Doorposts, Cherry Bounce, Early Watermelons,* and *The Nevers.* Other principal works were *The Holy Child* (1859), *Exile of Madera* (1862), *Judas, the Maccabee and the Asmonean Princes* (1864), *The Rebel Prince* (1864), *College Days of Calvin* (1866), *Geneva's Shield* (1868), *St. Patrick and the Early Irish Church* (1869), *Admiral Coligny and the Rise of the Huguenots* (1869), and *The Theban Legion* (1871).

He received honorary degrees from Princeton and Wooster (Ohio) universities.

REFERENCES: *AC; DAB; NCAB* (9:441); *TC; WWW* (I).

K. J. Balthaser

BLAIR, James. B. 1656, Scotland, to n.a. M. 1687 to Sarah Harrison. Ch. none. D. April 18, 1743, Virginia.

At the age of twelve, James Blair received the Crombie Scholarship and went to Marischal College in Aberdeen, Scotland. In 1673 he received the M.A. degree from the University of Edinburgh and became rector at Cranston, Scotland. He refused to sign King James's test oath imposed by the Scottish Parliament because it conflicted with his beliefs. Because of this refusal, he was denied ecclesiastical appointment in the Scottish church.

Blair settled in London and gained the favor of the bishop of London. He was given a parish in Virginia (1685). He was appointed commissary for the bishop of London in 1689 and worked for the standardization of clergymen's salaries and the establishment of a college in Virginia.

In 1691 Blair traveled to England to promote the founding of a college, returning to Virginia in 1693 with the charter for the College of William and Mary. The charter named Blair as president of the college. Blair devoted most of his time to political matters. In 1687 he married Sarah Harrison, whose family had large political influence. Blair served on the governor's council from 1689 to 1695 when he was suspended for his disputes with Edmund Andros, governor of the colony of Virginia. Blair returned to England in 1697 and worked to get Andros replaced by Francis Nicholson. In 1701 he was reinstated on the council, but Blair and Nicholson disagreed politically and Blair traveled to England in 1703 where he successfully advocated Nicholson's removal. Blair also had political disagreements with Nicholson's successor, Alexander Spotswood.

The College of William and Mary survived a lack of funds and two fires and was a flourishing institution by 1726. Blair's work as its founder and first president was important in the survival and eventual success of the college.

REFERENCES: *DAB; EB; NCAB* (3:231); *WWW* (H); Sadie Bell, *The Church, The State and Education in Virginia* (New York: Arno Press, New York Times Co., 1969); Lawrence Cremin, *American Education: The*

Colonial Experience 1607–1783 (New York: Harper & Row, 1970); H. Hartwell et al., *The Present State of Virginia and the College* (Williamsburg, Va.: Colonial Virginia, 1940); Parke Rouse, *James Blair of Virginia* (Charlotte, N.C.; The University of North Carolina Press, 1971).

Mark Fravel, Jr.

BLAKER, Eliza Ann Cooper. B. March 5, 1854, Philadelphia, Pennsylvania, to Jacob and Mary Jane (Gore) Cooper. M. September 15, 1880, to Louis J. Blaker. Ch. none. D. December 4, 1926, Indianapolis, Indiana.

Eliza Ann Cooper Blaker attended Philadelphia public schools, graduating as valedictorian from the Girls Normal School in 1874. After two years of teaching in city schools, she enrolled in Ruth Burritt's kindergarten training school in Philadelphia and, after completing the course in 1880, began teaching in the Vine Street Kindergarten.

In 1882 Blaker was invited to organize a kindergarten at the Hadley Roberts Academy, a private school in Indianapolis, Indiana. After only a few months she left the academy to open the city's first free kindergarten for a newly founded charitable organization, the Indianapolis Free Kindergarten Society. Under Blaker's leadership the society opened sixty kindergartens during the next several decades. The kindergartens were supported by private funds until 1901. With the support of Blaker a state law was passed that permitted levying local taxes for the support of public kindergartens.

Blaker remained supervisor of kindergartens for the Indianapolis Free Kindergarten Society until the end of her life. She was influential through her work in the education of teachers. When she arrived in Indianapolis she prepared kindergarten teachers in her own home. This early training school became the Teachers College of Indianapolis in 1905 under the sponsorship of the Free Kindergarten Society, with Blaker serving as president. Under her direction, an estimated twenty thousand women completed the teacher preparation course. She influenced the work of the kindergarten movement throughout the country through the college, which was later affiliated with Butler University in Indianapolis.

Blaker was active in association activities as founder and president of the Indianapolis Council of Women, chairman of a women's relief committee after the devastating Indianapolis flood of 1913, and leader in the International Kindergarten Union and the National Education Association. Hanover (Indiana) College conferred upon her an honorary degree (1917). She remained active as president of Teachers College until her death at her home in Indianapolis.

REFERENCES: *NAW;* Emma Lou Thornbrough, *Eliza A. Blaker, Her Life and Work* (Indianapolis: Eliza A. Blaker Club, 1956).

Walter J. Sanders

BLANTON, Annie Webb. B. August 19, 1870, Houston, Texas, to Thomas Lindsay and Eugenia (Webb) Blanton. M. no. D. October 2, 1945, Austin Texas.

Annie Webb Blanton attended elementary and secondary schools in Houston, Texas, and was graduated from high school in La Grange, Texas. She earned the B. Litt. (1899) and M.A. (1923) degrees at the University of Texas. After some graduate work at the University of Chicago, she received the Ph.D. degree (1927) from Cornell University in Ithaca, New York.

Blanton began her teaching career at the age of seventeen at Pine Springs School in Fayette County, Texas. The following year she moved to Austin, where she taught elementary grades and high school. In 1901 she joined the first faculty at North Texas State Normal College (later, State University) in Denton, where she taught English to 1918 and worked with student publications and extracurricular activities.

Blanton was the first woman president of the Texas State Teachers Association (1917–18). In 1919 she was elected the first woman state superintendent of public instruction in Texas. During two terms she was responsible for improvement of schools for rural and minority pupils, free textbooks, increased teachers' salaries, improved certification standards, and equal recognition of men and women.

In 1923 Blanton was appointed adjunct professor of school administration and later associate professor and chairman of the rural education department at the University of Texas (1927–45). She was the third woman full professor at the University of Texas (1933) and continued in this position until her death in 1945.

Her publications include *Review Outline and Exercises in English Grammar* (1903), *Supplementary Exercises in Punctuation and Composition* (1906), *Grammar Outline* (1908), *Hand Book of Information on Education in Texas* (1922), and *The Child of the Texas One-Teacher School* (1936). She was editor of the *Delta Kappa Gamma Bulletin* to 1945.

Blanton belonged to numerous organizations, including the National Council of Education and the National Education Association (vice-president, 1917, 1919, 1921).

Blanton saw a need for a professional society of superior, experienced women educators. On May 11, 1929, she founded the Delta Kappa Gamma Society with eleven other members who were outstanding in the field of education. Under her leadership the society grew to an important national organization with chapters in foreign countries. An Austin, Texas, elementary school and a women's dormitory at the University of Texas were named in her honor.

REFERENCES: *LE* (II); *WWAE* (I); *WWW* (II); *Texas Outlook* 30 (January

1946): 19; *Texan Who's Who* (Dallas: Texian Co., 1937), 1:44.

Mary H. Appleberry

BLEYER, Willard Grosvenor. B. August 27, 1873, Milwaukee, Wisconsin, to Albert J. and Elizabeth (Groshans) Bleyer. M. 1911 to Alice Haskell. Ch. none. D. October 31, 1935, Madison, Wisconsin.

Willard Bleyer was born into a family of journalists; his father was on the staff of the *Milwaukee Sentinel* for many years. Between the ages of nineteen and twenty-five, Bleyer was involved in newspaper work.

Throughout his undergraduate years (1892–96) at the University of Wisconsin, Bleyer participated in numerous journalistic activities. In his first year he founded the University Press Club and the *Daily Cardinal.* He was editor of the latter, as well as of the *Badger,* a yearbook, and the *Aegis,* a literary magazine, during his remaining three years as an undergraduate.

Bleyer remained at Wisconsin as a fellow in English until he received the master's degree (1898). After two years of teaching and newspaper work, he returned as an instructor at the university, earning the Ph.D. degree (1904) and a subsequent appointment as an assistant professor.

He began to publish the *University Press Bulletin* (1904), taught an experimental first class in journalism (1905), and developed a four-year curriculum of courses to prepare students for journalism careers. In 1927 he was appointed director of the University of Wisconsin School of Journalism. In addition to many articles, he wrote *Newspaper Writing and Editing* (1913), *Types of News Writing* (1916), *How to Write Special Feature Articles* (1919), *Main Currents in the History of American Journalism* (1927), and *Journalism* (1929) and was editor of *The Profession of Journalism* (1918).

Bleyer was influential in efforts to establish national standards for journalism instruction and was active as president of the American Teachers of Journalism and the Association of American Schools and Departments of Journalism and honorary national president of Sigma Delta Chi (1920–21). He was chairman of the National Council on Education for Journalism from 1923 and the Council on Research in Journalism (1924–29).

REFERENCES: *DAB* (supp. 1); *LE* (I); *WWW* (I).

Audrey Potter
John M. Ivanoff

BLOOMFIELD, Leonard. B. April 1, 1887, Chicago, Illinois, to Sigmund and Carola (Buber) Bloomfield. M. March 18, 1909, to Alice Sayers. Ch. two. D. April 18, 1949, New Haven, Connecticut.

Leonard Bloomfield received the A.B. degree (1906) from Harvard University and the Ph.D. degree (1909) from the University of Chicago. He also pursued graduate study at the University of Wisconsin and the universities of Leipzig and Göttingen, Germany.

Bloomfield taught German at the University of Wisconsin (1906–08),

University of Chicago (1908–09 and 1927–40), University of Cincinnati (1909–10), University of Illinois (1910–13), and Ohio State University (1921–27). He completed his career as Sterling Professor of Linguistics at Yale University (1940–49).

Bloomfield believed that students should learn to speak languages before becoming proficient in writing them. He developed a system of study that utilized a teaching team, including a native of the language to correct pronunciation and a linguist to teach structure of the language and who was in charge of the instruction. The procedures became widely known and copied.

During World War II, Bloomfield served in the Office of War Information and the armed forces in establishing methods and techniques for teaching Oriental and modern languages to masses of personnel. He advised in the organization and publication of army manuals on the intensive method of teaching foreign languages.

A prolific writer, Bloomfield wrote many articles and books, including *Introduction to the Study of Language* (1914), *Tagalog Texts with Grammatical Analysis* (1917), *First German Book* (1923), *Menomini Texts* (1928), *Sacred Stories of the Sweet Grass Cree* (1930), *Language* (1933), *Plains Cree Texts* (1934), and *Linguistic Aspects of Science* (1939). *Language* was acclaimed as the best summary of the science of linguistics published since the early part of the nineteenth century.

He held memberships in many professional organizations and societies, including the American Association for the Advancement of Science, the Linguistic Society of America, and the Royal Danish Academy of Sciences.

REFERENCES: *DAB* (supp. 4); *LE* (II); *WWW* (II); *NYT,* April 19, 1949, p. 25; *School and Society* 69 (April 30, 1949): 312.   *Lew E. Wise*

BLOW, Susan Elizabeth. B. June 7, 1843, Carondelet, Missouri, to Henry Taylor and Minerva (Grimsley) Blow. M. no. D. March 26, 1916, New York, New York.

Susan Elizabeth Blow was tutored privately until the age of sixteen when she attended Miss Haines' School in New York City. Blow lived fifteen months with her parents in Brazil, where her father was United States minister, and later traveled to Germany, where she stayed until 1871.

While in Germany, Blow was influenced by the work of Friedrich Froebel and acquired some of the teaching devices he used. When she returned to the United States, she met with William T. Harris *(q.v.)* who shared her interest in the development of the kindergarten. In 1872 Blow went to New York to study with Maria Kraus-Boelte *(q.v.).* Private kindergartens had been established in New York in 1871; Blow was the first kindergarten teacher in America trained by Kraus-Boelte.

Blow returned to St. Louis in 1873 and opened the first public kindergarten in the United States in the Des Peres School in Carondelet. The kindergarten movement grew rapidly, and St. Louis became a center of influence. In 1874 she established a training school for kindergarten teachers. She developed programs based on academic backgrounds and student interests that provided stability and direction to the kindergarten movement. Ill health forced her withdrawal from most activities in 1884, and she left St. Louis in 1889, following dissension with students who sought innovations in the kindergarten that Blow opposed.

She established residences in Cazenovia, New York, and Boston, Massachusetts, and, as she regained her health, was active in the International Kindergarten Union and in professional writing.

Blow was author of *A Study of Dante* (1877), *Symbolic Education* (1894), *Poems and Pictures* (1895), *Letters to a Mother on the Philosophy of Froebel* (1899), *Kindergarten Education* (1900), and *Educational Issues in the Kindergarten* (1908). She translated Froebel's *The Mottoes and Commentaries of Friedrich Froebel's Mother Play* (with Henrietta R. Eliot, 1895) and *The Songs and Music of Friedrich Froebel's Mother Play* (1895).

REFERENCES: *DAB; NAW; NYT,* March 29, 1916, p. 11; Nina C. Vandewalker, *The Kindergarten in American Education* (New York: Macmillan Co., 1908).

James R. Layton
Mary Paula Phillips

BLUNT, Katharine. B. May 28, 1876, Philadelphia, Pennsylvania, to Stanhope English and Fanny (Smyth) Blunt. M. no. D. July 29, 1954, New London, Connecticut.

Katharine Blunt was a strong force in the expansion of educational opportunities for women during the first half of the twentieth century. She attended Miss Porter's School in Farmington, Connecticut, and received the A.B. degree (1898) from Vassar College. She studied at the Massachusetts Institute of Technology (1902–03) and received the Ph.D. degree in chemistry (1907) from the University of Chicago.

After teaching at Vassar College (1903–05 and 1908–13) Blunt returned to the University of Chicago in 1913 as a member of the home economics department; she was appointed its chairman in 1925. Her administrative work was directed toward developing home economics as a part of collegiate education and toward developing graduate work in the field.

During World War I, Blunt was granted a leave of absence from Chicago to serve with the Department of Agriculture as United States food administrator. She was responsible for the publication of leaflets on food conservation and nutrition.

In 1929 Blunt left the University of Chicago to become president of Connecticut College in New London, the only Connecticut institution offering a four-year course for women. During her administration, she increased the college's financial resources, physical facilities, and faculty. She supervised development of the curriculum to encourage intellectual self-dependence, citizenship, and interest in public affairs. Students were given opportunities to engage in direct experiences in politics, economics, business, and home economics, including child study. She retired as president of Connecticut College in 1946.

Blunt was coauthor of *Food and the War* (with Florence Powdermaker, 1918) and *Ultra-Violet Light and Vitamin D in Nutrition* (with Ruth Cowan, 1930). She was also the author of articles in professional journals on the education of women, home economics, and biological chemistry.

She was the recipient of several honorary degrees. Blunt served on the Connecticut State Board of Education and the board of trustees of Russell Sage College in Troy, New York. She was a fellow of the American Association for the Advancement of Science and was active in professional associations, including the American Home Economics Association (president, 1924–26 and member of the council) and the Illinois Home Economics Association (president, 1921–22).

REFERENCES: *CB* (December 1946 and October 1954); *LE* (III); *NCAB* (B:385); *WWAE* (VIII); *WWW* (III); *NYT,* July 30, 1954, p. 17.

Doree Dumas Bedwell

BOAS, Franz. B. July 9, 1858, Minden, Westphalia, Germany, to Meier and Sophie (Meyer) Boas. M. March 10, 1887, to Marie Krackowizer. Ch. six. D. December 21, 1942, New York, New York.

While in Germany, Franz Boas studied at the universities of Heidelberg, Bonn, and Kiel (1877–81), receiving the Ph.D. degree in physics from Kiel in 1881. He centered his attention on anthropology, doing fieldwork among the Eskimo of Baffin Island (1883) and visiting the Indians of the Northwest Coast of America (1886). On frequent visits to the Northwest Coast, he gathered a large body of data, especially on Kwakiutl mythology, language, and art. Boas conducted research in every major area of anthropology. He was concerned with human growth and development and introduced the concept of physiological or developmental age. His study of immigrants, for which he collected a large body of biometric data, challenged traditional beliefs about human races. He stressed the importance of fieldwork in the study of anthropology.

He taught at Clark University in Worcester, Massachusetts (1888–92), and was chief assistant of the department of anthropology at the Chicago exposition (1892–95). Boas was associated with the American Museum of Natural History (1896–1905). He accepted a position at Columbia University, where he taught from 1896 to 1937. At Columbia Boas trained many of this country's leading anthropologists; during the first half of this century, most of those working in descriptive linguistics were students of Boas or of one of his students. He encouraged women to enter the field of anthropology.

Boas was a prolific writer, with more than seven hundred publications to his credit. Among his books were *The Central Eskimo* (1888), *The Growth of Children* (1896), *Changes in Bodily Form in Descendants of Immigrants* (1911), *The Mind of Primitive Man* (1911), *Primitive Art* (1927), *Anthropology and Modern Life* (1929), *Race, Language and Culture* (1940), and *Dakota Grammar* (with Ella Deloria, 1941). He established the *International Journal of American Linguistics* and was editor of the *American Journal of Folk-Lore* and Columbia University Contributions to Anthropology. He was contributing editor of the *Handbook of American Indian Languages* (four volumes, 1911).

Boas was a founder of the American Folklore Society (president, 1931), and the American Anthropological Society (president, 1907–08). He was a fellow of the American Association for the Advancement of Science (president, 1931) and a member of many other associations, including the Germanistic Society of America (corresponding secretary, 1914), the Committee for Democracy and Intellectual Freedom (national chairman 1939–40), the New York Academy of Sciences (president, 1910), and anthropological societies in many countries. He was the recipient of honorary degrees from American and foreign universities.

REFERENCES: *CB* (May 1940 and February 1943); *DAB* (supp. 3); *DSB; EB; LE* (II); *NCAB* (12: 509); *WWW* (II); Melville J. Herskovits, *Franz Boas: The Science of Man in the Making* (New York: Charles Scribner's Sons, 1953); Robert Lowie, "Franz Boas (1858–1942)," *Journal of American Folklore* 57 (1944): 59–64; *NYT,* December 22, 1942, p. 22; George W. Stocking (ed.), *The Shaping of American Anthropology, 1883–1911: A Franz Boas Reader* (New York, Basic Books, 1974).

William Engelbrecht

BOBBITT, John Franklin. B. February 16, 1876, English, Indiana, to James and Mary Bobbitt. M. June 2, 1903, to Sarah Annis. M. to Mabel Deiwert. Ch. one. D. March 7, 1956, Shelbyville, Indiana.

Franklin Bobbitt was graduated from Indiana University (1901) and received the Ph.D. degree from Clark University in Worcester, Massachusetts (1909). He taught in village and rural schools in Indiana (1893–1902) and was an instructor in the Philippine Normal School at Manila (1902–07), where he also served as a member of the Commission of Seven, whose task was to plan the curriculum for the new Philippine school system. He became associated with the University of Chicago in 1909 and remained until his retirement in 1941 as professor of school administration.

During leaves of absence from the University of Chicago, he served as assistant superintendent of schools in Los Angeles, California (1922–23), and Toledo, Ohio (1924). He was considered a pioneer in the development and use of the public school survey, especially as it related to curricular planning. He directed surveys and issued reports for schools in Cleveland,

Ohio (1915), Denver, Colorado (1916), and San Antonio, Texas (1915).

He was a leading member of the Committee on Economy of Time, which held that the analysis of contemporary society was the proper basis for public school curriculum development.

Bobbitt was author of *What Schools Teach and Might Teach* (1916), *The Curriculum* (1918), *Curriculum-Making in Los Angeles* (1922), *How to Make a Curriculum* (1924), his major work, and *The Curriculum of Modern Education* (1941). He also was the author of textbooks written for the Philippine schools, including *A First Book in English* (1904), *A Second Book in English* (with Gertrude R. Eagan, 1905), and the Silver-Burdett Philippine Readers series with his first wife Sarah Annis Bobbitt. He also wrote monographs published by the University of Chicago.

REFERENCES: *LE* (III); *WWW* (III); Mary Louise Seguel, *The Curriculum Field* (New York: Teachers College Press, 1966).

Wilma S. Longstreet

BODE, Boyd Henry. B. October 4, 1873, Ridott, Illinois, to Henry and Gertrude (Wienenga) Bode. M. August 20, 1903, to Bernice Ballard. Ch. two. D. March 29, 1953, Gainesville, Florida.

Boyd H. Bode received A.B. degrees from William Penn College in Oskaloosa, Iowa (1896), and the University of Michigan (1897). He was awarded the Ph.D. degree (1900) from Cornell University in Ithaca, New York.

Bode taught philosophy at the University of Wisconsin (1900–09). He was professor of philosophy at the University of Illinois (1909–21) and professor of education and head of the department of principles and practices of education (1921–44) at the Ohio State University. He taught at the Graduate Institute for Education in Cairo, Egypt (1944–45), and at the University of Tennessee and the University of British Columbia. For several years prior to his death, he conducted graduate seminars at his home in Gainesville, Florida, under the auspices of the University of Florida.

Books by Bode include *An Outline of Logic* (1910), *Fundamentals of Education* (1921), *Modern Educational Theories* (1927), *Conflicting Psychologies of Learning* (1929), *Democracy as a Way of Life* (1937), *Progressive Education at the Crossroads* (1938), and *How We Learn* (1940).

A philosopher in the pragmatic mold of John Dewey *(q.v.)*, Bode received the Kilpatrick Medal in 1947 from William Heard Kilpatrick *(q.v.)* at a meeting chaired by Dewey. He was honored by the Ohio State University in the Bode Memorial Lecture series.

REFERENCES: *LE* (III); *WW* (XXII); *WWW* (III); *NŶT,* March 30, 1953, p. 21.

Ernest E. Bayles

BODLEY, Rachel Littler. B. December 7, 1831, Cincinnati, Ohio, to Anthony Prichard and Rebecca Wilson (Talbott) Bodley. M. no. D. June 15, 1888, Philadelphia, Pennsylvania.

Until she was twelve years old, Rachel Littler Bodley attended a private school run by her mother, an English Quaker. Rejected for missionary work because of her delicate health, she studied at the Wesleyan Female College in Cincinnati. Upon graduation in 1849, she accepted a teaching position at the college and served as preceptress in the higher college studies.

With a special interest in physics and chemistry, she enrolled at the Polytechnic College in Philadelphia, Pennsylvania, for advanced study. By 1862 she was teaching natural sciences at the Cincinnati Female Seminary, where she completed a research study involving the classification and mounting of an extensive plant collection bequeathed to the institution by Joseph Clark. Her work was recognized by Asa Gray *(q.v.)*, the eminent botanist.

Bodley was elected to the chair of chemistry and toxicology in the Women's Medical College of Pennsylvania, the first woman professor of chemistry on record. She was active in several scientific societies, including the Academy of Natural Sciences of Philadelphia, the Cincinnati Society of Natural History, the New York Academy of Sciences, the American Chemical Society of New York, and Philadelphia's Franklin Institute. She served as vice-president of the meeting for the centennial celebration of the discovery of oxygen convened in Northumberland, Pennsylvania, the burial place of Joseph Priestley.

In 1874 Bodley became dean of the faculty at the Women's Medical College, a position she held for fourteen years. She lengthened the course of studies and expanded clinical training opportunities, including the use of the surgical amphitheater.

One of the first three alumnae to receive the A.M. degree from the Wesleyan Female College in Cincinnati, she was awarded an honorary M.D. degree from the Medical College of Pennsylvania in 1879. Bodley published *The College Story,* a pamphlet describing the many successes in the professional lives of women who were graduated from the medical college. She was interested in medical missionary work, which led to an exchange between American college graduates who worked in China, India, and other countries and students from those countries who enrolled at the medical school.

Involved in many community services, Bodley was an elected school director in Philadelphia and a state inspector of local charitable institutions.

REFERENCES: *NAW; WC.*   *M. Ann Dirkes*

BOGLE, Sarah Comly Norris. B. November 17, 1870, Milton, Pennsylvania, to John Armstrong and Emma Ridgway (Norris) Bogle. M. no. D. January 11, 1932, White Plains, New York.

Sarah Comly Norris Bogle was privately tutored for six years and then attended Miss M. E. Stevens School in Germantown, Pennsylvania. She studied for a year at the University of Chicago, traveled abroad, and entered the library school of Drexel Institute in Philadelphia at the age of thirty-two. She was graduated with a certificate (1904) and served as a librarian at Juniata College in Huntingdon, Pennsylvania (1904–07).

Bogle accepted a position as a branch librarian at the Carnegie Library of Pittsburgh, Pennsylvania (1909). She was head of the children's department (1911–17) and principal of the training school for children's librarians (1911–20). The training school became the Carnegie Library School, a department of the Carnegie Institute of Technology (later, Carnegie-Mellon University).

Bogle was active in professional association work as president of the Association of American Library Schools (1917–18) and member of the council of the American Library Association (ALA) from 1917 to 1920. She served as assistant secretary of the ALA from 1920 to her death in 1932. She was secretary to the ALA board of education for librarianship, which supported library schools in the United States (1924–32).

Bogle conducted a library course in Paris in the summer of 1923 for the American Committee for Work in Devastated France. This course developed into the Paris Library School, an international school conducted under the direction of the ALA (1924–29). Bogle served as director of the school during that time. She conducted a survey of the needs of the Virgin Islands under the auspices of the Carnegie Corporation (1929). She served as the ALA representative on a University of Chicago library curriculum study, which led to the publication of six textbooks for library education. Bogle was elected to the Library Hall of Fame in 1951.

REFERENCES: *NAW; NCAB* (C:504); *WWW* (I); *NYT,* January 12, 1932, p. 23.   *Darlene E. Fisher*

BOGUE, Benjamin Nathaniel. B. January 31, 1882, Wabash County, Indiana, to Benjamin and Sarah Jane (Heacock) Bogue. M. October 18, 1917, to Corinne Haddox Barth. Ch. one. D. May 17, 1964, Indianapolis, Indiana.

Benjamin Nathaniel Bogue was educated at district schools near Wabash, Indiana, and at the Lincolnville (Indiana) High School. He enrolled in Earlham College at Richmond, Indiana, in 1900 but was forced to discontinue his studies because he stammered, a problem he had since infancy. He entered the Vories Business College in Indianapolis, Indiana, and resolved to correct the problem himself after unsuccessfully trying a number of corrective programs. Intensive study of the anatomy, vocal organs, and principles of speech resulted in a complete and permanent cure, and he spent his life seeking to remedy irregularities in the speech of others.

On March 8, 1901, Bogue founded the Bogue Institute for Stammerers in Indianapolis with the help of Hervey D. Vories, head of the Vories Business College. The school was very successful and gained an international reputation. Students were enrolled from every state and many foreign countries. Bogue accepted only cases that were correctable at the institute.

In an era characterized by a scarcity of literature on the subject, Bogue contributed many articles to journals and published a monthly speech therapy magazine, *The Emancipator*, for several years. Bogue wrote monographs, including *Advice to Stammerers* (1905) and *The Bogue Institute for Stammerers* (1912) and was also the author of *Stammering, Its Cause and Cure* (1919) and *Stammering, Its Cause and Correction* (1939), both regarded for many years as standard works on the subject. He collected a library of publications on stammering that was believed to be the largest individual collection of its kind in the world.

REFERENCES: *NCAB* (B:201); *Indianapolis News,* May 18, 1964.

Robert C. Morris

BOND, Horace Mann. B. November 8, 1904, Nashville, Tennessee, to James and Jane Alice (Browne) Bond. M. October 11, 1930, to Julia Agnes Washington. Ch. three, including (Horace) Julian Bond, civil-rights leader and politician. D. December 19, 1972, Atlanta, Georgia.

Horace Mann Bond prepared for college at the Lincoln Institute near Louisville, Kentucky, graduating at the age of fourteen. He attended Lincoln University in Pennsylvania, graduating with the B.Edn. and A.B. degrees (1923). He attended the University of Chicago where he received the A.M. (1926) and Ph.D. (1936) degrees.

He taught at Lincoln University (1923–24) and served as head of the department of education at the Colored Agricultural and Normal College (later, Langston University) at Langston, Oklahoma (1924–27). He was director of extension at Alabama State College (later, University) in Montgomery (1927–28) and was a member of the faculty at Fisk University in Nashville, Tennessee (1928–33), where he later served as dean (1937–39). He was dean at Dillard University at New Orleans, Louisiana (1934–37), and also served as research assistant for the Julius Rosenwald Fund (1933–36).

Bond was president of Fort Valley (Georgia) State College (1939–45) and Lincoln (Pennsylvania) University (1945–57), the first black to serve in that post at Lincoln. Honorary president of Lincoln from 1957, he served at Atlanta (Georgia) University as dean of the school of education (1957–66) and director of the Bureau of Educational and Social Research (1966–72).

Bond's professional reputation was established in 1934 with the publication of *The Education of the Negro in the American Social Order,* a landmark study in educational sociology applied to blacks. *Negro Education in Alabama: A Study in Cotton and Steel* (1939) was written from his doctoral dissertation at the University of Chicago. He also wrote *Black American Scholars* (1972), a result of his research for the 1959 Howard University lecture, "The Search for Talent." He wrote many articles that were published in popular and professional journals. He served on the editorial staff of the *Journal of Negro Education.*

Bond made several trips to West Africa and conducted an educational survey there. Active in various organizations, he served as chairman of the board of the American Society on African Culture. He received the Susan Colver Rosenberger Prize and an award from the Educational Research Association of America for his doctoral dissertation and its subsequent publication. He received honorary degrees from Lincoln and Temple universities.

REFERENCES: *CA* (1–4); *CB* (March 1954); *LE* (IV); *WWAE* (XXII); *WW* (XXXVI); *WWW* (V); *NYT*, December 22, 1972, p. 34. *Walter C. Daniel*

BONNELL, John Mitchell. B. April 16, 1820, Bucks County, Pennsylvania, to William and Jean (Mitchell) Bonnell. M. 1847 to Mary Ann Morton. Ch. three. D. October 1, 1871, Macon, Georgia.

John Mitchell Bonnell spent his formative years in Philadelphia, Pennsylvania. He attended Jefferson College in Philadelphia, completing his studies at the age of sixteen. Too young to graduate, he took a position with a local academy until 1838, when he returned to Jefferson for graduation.

Bonnell moved to Georgia in 1840. He became a circuit preacher for the Methodist church for the North Georgia circuit, headquartered in the Athens area. Bonnell accepted a position teaching Greek at Emory College in Oxford, Georgia (1848–51), and moved to Wesleyan Female College in Macon, Georgia, in 1851 where he taught until 1853. He served as the president of Tuscaloosa (Alabama) College (1853–59). Bonnell returned to Wesleyan Female College as president in 1859, serving to his death in 1871.

As president of Wesleyan Female College, Bonnell was active in the cause of education in Georgia. He was one of the three organizers of the Georgia Teachers Association (later, Georgia Education Association), serving as vice-president.

He was the author of many articles for Methodist church publications and professional journals. He was author of a textbook, *A Manual of the Art of Prose Composition: For the Use of Colleges and Schools* (1867).

REFERENCES: *NCAB* (5:396); Dorothy Orr, *History of Education in Georgia* (Chapel Hill: University of North Carolina Press, 1950); George G. Smith, *History of Georgia Methodism from 1786 to 1866* (Atlanta: A. B. Caldwell Publisher, 1913).   *Donald C. Stephenson*

BONNEY, Mary Lucinda. See **RAMBAUT, Mary Lucinda Bonney.**

BONSER, Frederick Gordon. B. June 14, 1875, Tower Hill, Illinois, to Aaron and Eliza (Stevens) Bonser. M. August 17, 1902, to Edna Madison MacDonald. Ch. two. D. June 8, 1931, Pompton Lakes, New Jersey.

Frederick G. Bonser received the B.S. (1901) and M.S. (1902) degrees from the University of Illinois at Urbana. He received the Ph.D. degree (1910) from Teachers College, Columbia University.

Bonser was director of the training school at the State Normal School (later, Eastern Washington State College) in Cheyney, Washington (1902–05), and professor and director of the training school at the State Normal School (later, Western Illinois University) at Macomb, Illinois (1906–10). Upon leaving Macomb, Bonser moved to Teachers College of Columbia University as professor of education (1913–31) and director of the Speyer School (1910–13).

Bonser believed in the child-centered concept of education, which considered the interests of children and an understanding of their inner and outer environment paramount. Called the Father of Industrial Arts Education, Bonser evolved a widely published definition of industrial arts, established the activity-oriented curriculum (general shop concept) for the industrial arts, and, with James E. Russell *(q.v.),* developed the industrial-social theory of industrial arts.

Bonser wrote over eighty articles and some ten books, including *The Reasoning Ability of Children* (1911), *Industrial Education* (1914), *Educational Use of Recreation Activities of Children* (1918), *The Elementary School Curriculum* (1920), *Industrial Arts for Elementary Schools* (with L. C. Mossman, 1923), and *Life Needs and Education* (1932).

Bonser was a member of the Columbia University committee on work in rehabilitation of disabled soldiers (1918–19) and served on educational survey commissions of the Philippines (1925) and the states of Virginia (1927) and New Jersey (1929).

REFERENCES: *WWW* (I); *NYT,* July 9, 1931, p. 27; *School and Society* 34 (December 12, 1931); 796–98; *Teachers College Record* 33 (October 1931): 1–8.   *Lee H. Smalley*

BORING, Edwin Garrigues. B. October 23, 1886, Philadelphia, Pennsylvania, to Edwin McCurdy and Elizabeth (Garrigues Truman) Boring. M. June 18, 1914, to Lucy M. Day. Ch. four. D. July 1, 1968, Cambridge, Massachusetts.

Edwin G. Boring followed Wilhelm Wundt and Edward B. Titchener *(q.v.)* as productive experimental psychologists who were as concerned with writing about scientific psychology as they were at conducting basic research. He was graduated from the Friends' Select School in Philadelphia, Pennsylvania (1904), and studied engineering at Cornell University in Ithaca, New York, receiving the bachelor's degree in mechanical engineering (1908). He returned to Cornell to study physics and then psychology, receiving the A.M. (1912) and Ph.D. (1914) degrees.

Boring's first job was with the Bethlehem Steel Company. Dissatisfied with engineering, he taught at the Moravian Parochial School in Bethlehem, Pennsylvania (1909–10). He was a graduate assistant and instructor at Cornell (1913–18). A volunteer for military service in World War I, he was assigned to conduct intelligence testing and was associate editor of the massive research report, *Psychological Testing in the U.S. Army* (1918–19).

Boring took positions at Clark University (1919–22) and in 1922 at Harvard University, where he stayed until retirement in 1957. At Harvard he fought to break psychology away from philosophy, founded the psychology department, and was director of the psychology laboratories.

During his years at Harvard, Boring wrote a number of research reports and books, including *A History of Experimental Psychology* (1929), *The Physical Dimensions of Consciousness* (1933), *Sensation and Perception in the History of Experimental Psychology* (1942), the autobiographical *Psychologist at Large* (1961), *History, Psychology and Science* (1963), and *Source Book in the History of Psychology* (with R. J. Hernstein, 1965). He coedited several textbooks, including *Psychology: A Factual Textbook* (with H. P. Weld and H. S. Langfield, 1935). He was coeditor of the *American Journal of Psychology* (1925–46) and editor of *Contemporary Psychology* (1956–61). He initiated the four-volume *A History of Psychology in Autobiography* (1929).

Boring was active in professional organizations, including the American Psychological Association (secretary, 1920–22 and president, 1928) and the XVII International Congress of Psychology (honorary president, 1963), and was a fellow of the American Association for the Advancement of Science. He was the recipient of several honorary degrees and was awarded the gold medal of the American Psychological Foundation (1959).

REFERENCES: *CA* (1–4); *CB* (March 1962); *LE* (III); *WWW* (V); S. S. Stevens, "Edwin Garrigues Boring: 1886–1968," *American Journal of Psychology* 81 (December 1968): 589–606; *NYT*, July 2, 1968, p. 26; Duane P. Schultz, *A History of Modern Psychology* (New York: Academic Press, 1967).   *Michael L. Davis*

BOWDITCH, Henry Pickering. B. April 4, 1840, Boston, Massachusetts, to Jonathan Ingersoll and Lucy Orne (Nichols) Bowditch. M. September 9, 1871, to Selman Knauth. Ch. seven. D. March 13, 1911, Boston, Massachusetts.

Henry Pickering Bowditch, one of the foremost American physiologists, attended the school of Epes S. Dixwell, where he set up a skeleton from the cadaver of one of his father's horses. He was graduated from Harvard University with the A.B. degree (1861). He enrolled at the Lawrence Scientific School in Cambridge, Massachusetts, where his studies in chemistry and natural history were interrupted by service in the Civil War (1861–65). He returned to Harvard as a student, receiving the A.M. (1866) and M.D. (1868) degrees.

Bowditch spent three years (1868–71) in Europe, studying physiology under Claude Bernard, histology under Louis Antoine Ranvier, and neurology under Jean Martin Charcot. In Leipzig, Germany, he studied in the laboratory of Karl Ludwig.

Bowditch joined the Harvard faculty, teaching physiology, in 1871, served as dean of the Harvard Medical School (1883–93), and was George Higginson Professor of Physiology (1903–06). At Harvard he started the first physiological laboratory in America (1871). He invented new laboratory apparatus and attracted to the laboratory some of the best experimenters of his time. He engaged in some classical research studies in physiology. He was a pioneer in composite photography and in anthropometry, studying the rate of growth in schoolchildren (1872–91).

Bowditch was author of many papers on physiology and wrote *Growth of Children* (1877), *Hints for Teachers of Physiology* (1889), *Is Harvard a University?* (1890), and *Advancement of Medicine by Research* (1896). In 1877 he was coeditor of the *Journal of Physiology (American Journal of Physiology)*.

Bowditch was a founder of the American Physiological Society in 1887 (president, 1888 and 1891–95), a fellow of the American Association for the Advancement of Science (vice-president, 1886, 1900), and a member of the National Academy of Sciences. He was a trustee of the Boston Public Library (1895–1902).

REFERENCES: *DAB; DSB; NCAB* (12:252); *WWW* (I); Ralph H. Major, *A History of Medicine* (Springfield, Ill.: Charles C. Thomas Publishers, 1954), 2:904; *NYT,* March 14, 1911, p. 11.   *Richard M. Coger*

BOWEN, Wilbur Pardon. B. July 28, 1864, Lima, Michigan, to Charles Marshall and Julia (Peirce) Bowen. M. August 25, 1892, to Nellie Stirling. M. August 9, 1898, to Lois E. Knapp. Ch. five. D. September 5, 1928, Ann Arbor, Michigan.

Wilbur Bowen spent his youth in New Jersey but returned to Michigan in 1880 and was graduated from Chelsea (Michigan) High School. He taught for a year in a rural school and, in 1884, entered Michigan State Normal College (later, Eastern Michigan University) at Ypsilanti, receiving two teaching certificates in 1886 and 1887 and the B.Pd. degree (1897). He attended the University of Michigan, receiving the B.S. (1900) and M.S. (1901) degrees.

From 1887 until 1892, Bowen served as an assistant in the department of mathematics at Michigan State Normal College and became interested in physical education. He was head of the department of physical education at the University of Nebraska (1892–94), spending his vacation periods in study at Harvard University and Chautauqua Institution, New York.

Bowen taught at Michigan State Normal College (1894–1900) and was a student in the medical department and an instructor in physiology at the University of Michigan (1900–02). From 1903 until his death in 1928, he was a professor of physical education at Michigan State Normal College.

Bowen directed a program of specialized courses in physical education, the first in the Midwest. One of the first state syllabi for use by teachers was prepared under his direction (1915). His work was important to teacher education institutions when formal and informal physical education programs were being united into their modern status.

Bowen wrote many articles and books, including *A Teacher's Course in Physical Training* (1898), *Mechanics of Bodily Exercise* (1909), *The Teaching of School Gymnastics* (1909), *The Teaching of Gymnastic Games* (1909), *Action of Muscles* (1912), *The Teaching of Play* (1913), *The Mechanism of Muscular Movement* (1917), *Applied Anatomy and Kinesiology* (1919), *The Theory and Practice of Organized Play* (with Elmer D. Mitchell, *q.v.,* 1923), and *The Conduct of Physical Activities in Schools* (1927).

Active in professional associations, Bowen was president of the Athletic Research Society (1914–15).

REFERENCES: *WWW* (I); *American Physical Education Review* 33 (October 1928): 556, Deobald B. Van Dalen, Elmer D. Mitchell, and Bruce Bennett, *A World History of Physical Education* (New York: Prentice-Hall, 1953).   *Adelaide M. Cole*

BOWMAN, Isaiah. B. December 26, 1878, Waterloo, Ontario, Canada, to Samuel and Emily (Shantz) Bowman. M. June 28, 1909, to Cora Goldthwait. Ch. three. D. January 6, 1950, Baltimore, Maryland.

Isaiah Bowman, geographer and president of Johns Hopkins University, was graduated from the State Normal College (later, Eastern Michigan University) in Ypsilanti, Michigan, in 1902. He received the B.Sc. degree (1905) from Harvard University and the Ph.D. degree (1909) from Yale University.

Bowman was an instructor in geography at the Ypsilanti normal school (1903–04) and an assistant in physiology at Harvard (1904–05). He taught geography at Yale (1905–15). While he was director of the American Geographic Society of New York (1915–35), he enlarged the society's membership, staff, and programs so that a small organization became one of worldwide influence. In 1935 Bowman became president of Johns Hopkins University, where he was responsible for many changes in the administrative organization, extending the instructional services of the university by adding departments of aeronautics, geography, and oceanography.

A frequent contributor to journals, Bowman was also author of *Forest Physiography* (1911), *South America* (1915), *The Andes of Southern Peru* (1916), *The New World-Problems in Political Geography* (1921), *Desert Trails of Atacama* (1923), *An American Boundary Dispute* (1923), *The Mohammedan World* (1924), *International Relations* (1930), *The Pioneer Fringe* (1931), *Geographical Thought in Relation to the Social Sciences* (1933), and *Design for Scholarship* (1936). He was editor of *Limits for Land Settlement* (1937) and associate editor and editor of *Journal of Geography* (1918–20), *Bulletin of the American Geographical Society* (1910–15), and *Geographical Review*.

Leader of the first Yale South American expedition (1907) and Central Andes expedition of the American Geographical Society (1913), Bowman was geographer and geologist of the Yale Peruvian expedition (1911). He participated in the American Commission to Negotiate Peace (1918–19) and the Peace Conference in Paris (1919). A frequent adviser to and member of committees of the United States Department of State, he was a member of the American delegation to the Dumbarton Oaks Conference (1944) and the United Nations Conference in San Francisco (1945). He was a member of the board of the American Telephone and Telegraph Company, Council on Foreign Relations, Woods Hole Oceanographic Institution, and American Geographical Society of New York.

A member of many scholarly and professional associations, Bowman was chairman of the National Research Council (1933–35), vice-chairman of the Science Advisory Board (1933–35), and president of the International Geographical Union (1931–34), the Association of American Geographers (1931), and the American Association for the Advancement of Science (1943). He was active in the American Philosophical Society (council, 1935) and the National Academy of Sciences (vice-president, 1941–45). He was a member of many foreign scientific societies and received awards or medals for achievement from six American and foreign organizations and fourteen honorary degrees from American and foreign colleges and universities.

REFERENCES: *CB* (January 1945); *DAB* (supp. 4); *DSB; EB; LE* (III); *NCAB* (40:484); *WWW* (II); *NYT,* January 7, 1950, p. 17.

Gorman L. Miller

BOWMAN, John Bryan. B. October 16, 1824, Mercer County, Kentucky, to John and Mary (Mitchum) Bowman. M. 1845 to Mary Dorcas Williams. Ch. none. D. September 29, 1891, Harrodsburg, Kentucky.

John Bryan Bowman, founder of the University of Kentucky, attended Bacon College in Harrodsburg, Kentucky, where his father was an incorporator and trustee. He was graduated in 1842, studied law, and was admitted to the bar but did not practice law.

Bowman inherited and managed Old Forest Farm in Mercer County, Kentucky, for ten years. Bacon College failed, and Bowman assumed the initiative of organizing an institution to take its place. He raised a fund of $150,000, and the Kentucky legislature granted a charter in 1858 for Kentucky University to be opened in Harrodsburg. It opened as Taylor Academy in 1858, and the College of Arts and Sciences was in operation in 1859. Bowman served as regent and managed the institution through the Civil War. In 1864 an accidental fire destroyed the buildings.

The legislature opened the location of a new college to bids from cities in the state and appointed a committee to establish the institution. Lexington, Kentucky, won the right to locate the college, and the organizing committee suggested to Bowman that his college be merged with the new agricultural and mechanical college into the Kentucky University. The new institution opened in 1865 with the addition of Transylvania University and with Bowman as regent. He was in charge of the total university with each unit administered by its own presiding officer. Bowman resigned in 1874; the legislature reorganized and separated the institutions in 1878. The Agricultural and Mechanical College later became the University of Kentucky.

Bowman was active in Lexington to his death in 1891, participating in the organization of Hooker (later, Hamilton) College, the College of the Bible, and Commercial College.

REFERENCES: *DAB; NCAB* (4:516); *WWW* (H); Henry M. Pyles, "The Life and Work of John Bryan Bowman" (doct. diss., University of Kentucky, 1945).   *John F. Ohles*

BOYD, David French. B. October 5, 1834, Wytheville, Virginia, to Thomas Jefferson and Minerva Ann (French) Boyd. M. October 5, 1865, to Esther Gertrude Wright. Ch. eight. D. May 27, 1899, Baton Rouge, Louisiana.

David French Boyd was educated at Pike Powers, a classical school in Staunton, Virginia, and the University of Virginia, from which he was graduated in 1856.

He taught school in Wytheville, Virginia (1856–57), and Homer and Rocky Mount, Louisiana (1857–60). He was appointed professor of ancient languages at the Louisiana State Seminary of Learning in Pikeville, which was headed by William Tecumseh Sherman. He resigned from the seminary and served in the Confederate Army (1861–65).

Following the war, he was appointed superintendent of the Louisiana State Seminary (later, Louisiana State University). In 1869 and 1870 he aided in getting laws passed by the state legislature providing for racial segregation of parish public schools. The seminary building burned in 1869, and Boyd secured temporary quarters in Baton Rouge at the Louisiana State School for the Deaf and Dumb. In 1876 Boyd was responsible for the merger of the Louisiana Agricultural and Mechanical College with the renamed Louisiana State University.

In 1880 Boyd was removed from his position on false charges of mismanagement of funds; he was recalled to the presidency in 1884. From 1880 to 1884 he had operated private military academies in Virginia and was president of Alabama Polytechnic Institute (later, Auburn University) (1883–84). Returning to Louisiana State University, he served as president (1884–86) and professor of mathematics (1886–88). He was recognized as a pioneer in industrial and technical education in the South.

He served as superintendent of the Kentucky Military Institute at Farmdale (1888–93) and as a professor at Ohio Military Academy at Germantown (1893–94) and Michigan Military Academy at Orchard Lake (1894–97). He returned to Louisiana State University as professor of philosophy and civics (1897–99). Boyd was awarded an honorary degree by Louisiana State University. He was a brother of Thomas Duckett Boyd *(q.v.)*.

REFERENCES: *DAB; NCAB* (13:235); *WWW* (H); *Louisiana State University Bulletin,* ser. 2, no. 2 (June 1904); *New Orleans Daily Picayune,* May 30, 1899; T. M. Owens, *History of Alabama and Dictionary of Alabama Biography* (Chicago: S. J. Clarke Publishing Co., 1921), vol. 3.

S. S. Britt, Jr.

BOYD, David Ross. B. July 31, 1853, Coshocton, Ohio, to James and Mary Ann (Ross) Boyd. M. September 6, 1882, to Jennie Thompson. Ch. one. D. November 17, 1936, Glendale, California.

David Boyd was graduated from the University of Wooster (later, Wooster College) in Ohio with the A.B. (1878) and A.M. (1881) degrees.

He became principal of Van Wert (Ohio) High School (1878) and was appointed superintendent of the Van Wert public schools (1879). He served as superintendent of schools in Arkansas City, Kansas (1888–92). When the University of Oklahoma was founded in 1892, Boyd was named first president of the institution. He laid out the original campus and planned the landscaping for the area. His interest in landscaping and beautification continued throughout his life.

He served as president of the Territorial Board of Education of Oklahoma (1893–1908) and was active in teachers' associations. He petitioned President Grover Cleveland to provide land grants for the use of higher education and public buildings before opening the Cherokee strip to settlement. This policy was observed in later land openings in Oklahoma.

Boyd resigned as president of the University of Oklahoma in 1908 to assume the position of superintendent of education for the Presbyterian Board of Home Missions. In 1912 he became president of the University of

New Mexico and served until his retirement in 1919. At New Mexico, he increased student enrollment and obtained public lands to be used for higher education.

He was a founder of the American Association of University Presidents. He was awarded honorary degrees from the University of Wooster (1900) and the University of New Mexico (1927).

REFERENCES: *LE* (I); *NCAB* (27:13); *WWW* (I); D. F. Hughes, *Pueblo on the Mesa* (Albuquerque: University of New Mexico Press, 1939); *Glendale* (California) *News Press,* November 17, 1936.   *Karen Wertz*

BOYD, Thomas Duckett. B. January 20, 1854, Wytheville, Virginia, to Thomas Jefferson and Minerva Ann (French) Boyd. M. March 15, 1882, to Annie Foules Fuqua. Ch. eight. D. November 2, 1932, Baton Rouge, Louisiana.

Thomas Duckett Boyd attended Howard Shriver's private school in Wytheville, Virginia, and was graduated from Louisiana State University (LSU) with the A.M. degree (1872).

Boyd spent one year surveying and reading law and then became adjunct professor of mathematics at LSU (1874), commandant of cadets (1875), and professor of English (1880). He became acting president of the university in 1886. In 1888 he became president of the State Normal School (later, Northwestern State University) at Natchitoches, serving until 1896, when he returned to LSU as president.

During his tenure as president of LSU, Boyd created the department of education and the law school and moved the Audubon Sugar School from New Orleans to Baton Rouge. He reorganized university departments into colleges and supported agricultural programs of the university. He was able to get a permanent income from taxes for the university, and opened the university to women in 1904.

Boyd was a leader in the development of the public schools of Louisiana. He held teachers' institutes and summer normal schools over the state in his efforts to create interest in the public schools. He helped to change the popular concept of public schools from that of charity institutions to public institutions to assist all people to become efficient citizens. He was able to get a legislative act passed providing local funds for the support of public schools in the parishes.

Boyd was a founder of the Louisiana Chautauqua and was active in professional organizations, serving as president of the National Association of State Universities (1919–20) and the National Association of Land Grant Colleges (1921–22). He was an organizer of the Louisiana Education Association and founded the *Louisiana School Review.* He received an honorary degree from Tulane University. He was a brother of David French Boyd *(q.v.).*

REFERENCES: *DAB* (supp. 1); *LE* (I); *NCAB* (13:236); *WWW* (IV); Charles W. Dabney, *Universal Education in the South,* vol. 1 (Chapel Hill: University of North Carolina Press, 1936); The Louisiana State University, *Alumni News* 9 (December 1933).   *S. S. Britt, Jr.*

BOYDEN, Albert Gardner. B. February 5, 1827, South Walpole, Massachusetts, to Phineas and Harriet (Carroll) Boyden. M. November 18, 1851, to Isabella Whitten Clarke. M. August 24, 1898, to Clara Adelia Armes. Ch. three, including Arthur Clarke Boyden, educator. D. May 31, 1915, Bridgewater, Massachusetts.

While assisting his blacksmith father, Albert Boyden attended the district schools of South Walpole, Massachusetts. He decided at an early age to be a teacher. Without formal training, he taught school for three winters before matriculating at the State Normal School (later, Bridgewater State College) at Bridgewater, from which he was graduated in 1849.

With the exception of the years 1853–1857 when he held teaching or administrative positions in Salem and Boston, Massachusetts, Boyden served the Bridgewater Normal School. He was assistant to the school's first principal, Nicholas Tillinghast (1850–53), and to Marshall Conant (1857–60). Boyden was selected principal of the school in 1860. Until 1906 he was engaged in the formal training of teachers for public service, an innovative concept at the time. The institution realized a significant expansion in enrollment, faculty, program, and physical plant under Boyden.

Boyden was editor of *Massachusetts Teacher* (1865–70) and served as president of various educational associations, including the Massachusetts Teachers Association (1872–73) and the Massachusetts Schoolmasters' Club (1888–89). He was also secretary of the National Council of Education (1884).

Boyden was succeeded by his son Arthur Clarke Boyden as principal and later president of the Bridgewater State Normal School and State Teachers College.

REFERENCES: *NCAB* (14:256); *WWW* (I).   *Richard S. Offenberg*

BOYDEN, Frank Learoyd. B. September 16, 1879, Foxboro, Massachusetts, to Benjamin Franklin and Anna Wales (Cary) Boyden. M. June 17, 1907, to Helen Childs. Ch. three. D. April 25, 1972, Deerfield, Massachusetts.

Frank L. Boyden was graduated from Amherst (Massachusetts) College with the A.B. degree (1902). He received the A.M. degree from Williams College in Williamstown, Massachusetts (1924), and Yale University (1926).

He accepted the principalship of the public town academy of Deerfield, Massachusetts, to raise money for his law studies. His stay, which he intended to be temporary, extended over sixty years. When he retired in 1968, Deerfield Academy was a preeminent American secondary boys' boarding school enrolling about five hundred students; Boyden was the best-known headmaster in the country.

Founded in 1799, the academy had deteriorated and by 1902 it had only fourteen boys and girls studying in one rundown building. Boyden recruited students from nearby farms and began a lifelong campaign to improve and enlarge the school's physical facilities. When the Massachusetts legislature in the 1920s proscribed providing further funds to educational institutions, including Deerfield, the school's continued existence was in doubt. Boyden led a major fund drive to change the institution into a private school.

Boyden placed heavy emphasis on character building, athletics, personal attention to students, and minimal bureaucracy and organization. The school did not have catalogs, student government, or faculty committees. John Gunther wrote of the school in *Death Be Not Proud* (1949), and John McPhee wrote *The Headmaster* (1966), a biography of Boyden.

Boyden served on the boards of trustees of other institutions, including Amherst College, Andover-Newton Theological School, Nichols College, Cushing Academy, Stoneleigh-Burnham School, and Vermont Academy. As the long-time chairman of the board of trustees of the University of Massachusetts, he helped persuade the state legislature to give that institution greater autonomy and support. He received the Shattuck Centennial Citation for service to secondary education (1958), a citation by the President of the United States (1967), and many other honors, including many honorary degrees from American colleges and universities.

REFERENCES: *LE* (III); *WWW* (V); Donald Barr, "The Tale of the Headmaster," *Saturday Review,* April 15, 1967, pp. 70–71; John McPhee, *The Headmaster* (New York: Farrar, Straus and Giroux, 1966); *NYT,* April 26, 1972, p. 48.   *William Kornegay*

BOYNTON, Percy Holmes. B. October 30, 1875, Newark, New Jersey, to George Mills and Julia Hoyt (Holmes) Boynton. M. October 11, 1902, to Lois Damon. M. February 28, 1941, to Florence (Brinkman) Rice. Ch. two. D. July 8, 1946, New London, Connecticut.

After graduating from Amherst (Massachusetts) College with the A.B. (1897) and from Harvard University with the A.M. (1898), Percy Holmes Boynton began his professional career as an instructor in English at Smith Academy in St. Louis, Missouri. In 1902, as a graduate student, he became a reader at the University of Chicago. His association with that institution continued until his retirement in 1941. Starting as an associate in English (1903), Boynton progressed to the rank of professor (1923) and served as dean of the college of arts and literature (1912–23).

Boynton was a prolific writer, specializing in literary criticism, American literature, and English composition. From 1909 to 1928, he contributed more than thirty-five articles to such periodicals as *The Nation, New Republic,* and *The North American Review.* His major contribution was as the author of standard literature and composition textbooks in which he made a point of following suggestions made by classroom teachers. Boynton's books include *London in English Literature* (1913), *Principles of Composition* (1915), *History of American Literature* (college text, 1919), *History of American Literature* (school text, 1923), *Some Contemporary Americans* (1924), *More Contemporary Americans* (1926), *The Rediscovery of the Frontier* (1931), *The Challenge of Modern Criticism* (1933), and *Literature and American Life* (1936).

Boynton served on the advisory board of the *Journal of American Literature* (1928–29) and the *English Journal* (1912–20). Among his other activities was the radio program, "The University of Chicago Round Table." During its first year (1928), the program originated directly from classrooms; later it developed into authoritative discussions of general subjects. After 1934 Boynton was less active in the program because of demands of his weekly series of book talks conducted for station WGN. He was secretary of instruction (1903–14) and principal of summer schools (1914–17) of the Chautauqua Institution. Retiring to Mystic, Connecticut, Boynton was active in war work and civil affairs during World War II.

REFERENCES: *LE* (II); *NCAB* (35:188); *WWW* (II); *NYT,* July 9 1946, p. 21; *School and Society* 64 (July 20, 1946): 41; *Wilson Library Bulletin* 21 (September 1946): 8.   *Mary Harshbarger*

BRACKETT, Anna Callender. B. May 21, 1836, Boston, Massachusetts, to Samuel Eaton and Caroline (Callender) Brackett. M. no. Ch. one adopted. D. March 18, 1911, Summit, New Jersey.

Anna Callender Brackett was educated in Boston, Massachusetts, private schools and Abbott's Academy and was graduated from the State Normal School (later, Framingham State College) at Framingham, Massachusetts, in February 1856.

She was a teacher in a graded school in East Brookfield, Massachusetts, and assistant principal of the Cambridge (Massachusetts) high school. She served as assistant principal of Framingham Normal School and was vice-principal of the Girls' High and Normal School of Charleston, South Carolina. With the outbreak of the Civil War the school was closed, and Brackett was one of the last northerners to leave Charleston. She left for Massachusetts by way of New Orleans and the Mississippi River because of the blockade. Stopping in St. Louis, Missouri, she was offered the principalship of the St. Louis Normal School, the first woman in the United States to hold that position (1861–70). During her nine years there, Brackett helped set high standards for the education of teachers. She left the position in 1872 in a dispute with the school board over the number and quality of students in the program.

With Ida M. Eliot, her assistant in St. Louis, Brackett opened a private school for girls in New York City in 1870, which she continued to conduct to her retirement in 1895. She used no grades or written examinations and did not believe in punishment. She was first to introduce study of German and Latin grammar in a girls' school in the state of New York. Many graduates of the school were enrolled with advanced standing by Vassar and other quality colleges.

Brackett was interested in the theory as well as the practice of education, which is reflected in her books, including *The Relation of School and Home* (1873), *The Education of American Girls* (1874), *Technique of Rest* (1892), and *Women and the Higher Education* (1893). She compiled with Ida M. Eliot *Poetry for Home and School* (1876) and translated Karl Rosenkranz's *Philosophy of Education* as the first book in William T. Harris's *(q.v.)* International Educational Series in 1886. She was drama editor for five years for *Harper's Bazaar*.

Her students raised an endowment fund in her memory, which became a graduate fellowship of the American Association of University Women.

REFERENCES: *DAB; NAW; NCAB* (21:264); *WWW* (I); *NYT,* March 19, 1911, sec. 2, p. 11.   *Linda C. Gardner*

BRACKETT, Jeffrey Richardson. B. October 20, 1860, Quincy, Massachusetts, to Jeffrey Richardson and Sarah Cordelia (Richardson) Brackett. M. June 16, 1866, to Susan Katharine Jones. M. June 22, 1935, to Louisa deBerniere Bacot. Ch. none. D. December 4, 1949, Charleston, South Carolina.

Jeffrey Richardson Brackett received his early education at the Adams Academy in Quincy, Massachusetts, and earned the B.A. degree (1883) at Harvard University. He received the Ph.D. degree (1889) from Johns Hopkins University. He was an instructor in history and government and lecturer on philanthropy and social work at Johns Hopkins (1899–1904).

At the request of Harvard University and Simmons College in Boston, Massachusetts, he founded and directed the school of social work at Simmons (1904–20), the first program to provide instruction in social work under university sponsorship and to provide full-time academic and field-work. Brackett required that his students have a broad academic background as well as schooling in the methods of social work.

Brackett was the author of *The Negro in Maryland* (1889) and a supplement, *Notes on the Progress of the Colored People of Maryland* (1890), *Supervision and Education in Charity* (1903), *Social Service Through the Parish* (1923), and *The Transportation Problem in American Social Work* (1936).

He was chairman of the executive committee of the Charity Organization Society of Baltimore (1897–1904), president of the Baltimore City Department of Charities and Correction with a seat on the city council (1900–04), and president of the National Conference of Charities and Correction (1904) (later, National Conference of Social Welfare). He was a member of the Massachusetts State Board of Welfare (1906–34). He chaired the State Board of Charities (1906–19) and the department of social services of the Protestant Episcopal diocese of Massachusetts (1922–29).

Brackett participated in the development of the pioneering program in medical social work developed at Massachusetts General Hospital in Boston. He was active in the committee for homeless men of the Family Society and the Massachusetts Civic League. He assisted in passage of the Mother's Aid Law (1912) and the Old Age Assistance Law (1931).

REFERENCES: *DAB* (supp. 4); *NCAB* (38:515); *WWW* (IV); *NYT,* December 6, 1949, p. 32.   *Joseph P. Cangemi*
                                                           Thomas E. Kesler

BRADBURY, William Batchelder. B. October 6, 1816, York, Maine, to David and Sophia (Chase) Bradbury. M. no. D. January 7, 1868, Montclair, New Jersey.

William Batchelder Bradbury grew up in York, Maine, where he demonstrated musical talent learning to play the instruments available in the community. When he was fourteen, the family moved to Boston, Massachusetts, where he studied piano and organ and took singing lessons from Lowell Mason *(q.v.)* and joined Mason's singing groups. He was organist in a Boston church (1834–36) but gave up the position to go to Machias, Maine, and, later, to St. John's, New Brunswick, as a music teacher.

In 1840 Bradbury moved to Brooklyn, New York, and again became a church organist at the Baptist Tabernacle in New York City (1841). He organized singing classes for children, which developed into annual singing festivals. With Thomas Hastings, Bradbury began to compile collections of songs (including some of his own) and developed a flourishing and profitable business.

He spent 1847 to 1849 studying and traveling in England and Germany. In Leipzig he studied the organ and harmony with Moritz Hauptmann, Ignaz Moscheles, and Ernst Wenzel. He wrote weekly letters from Leipzig for publication in New York City religious newspapers and the *New York Observer*. In 1854 he joined his brother Eugene and a German immigrant piano maker in establishing the piano manufacturing firm of Lighte, Newton and Bradbury, later the Bradbury Piano Company. On his return from Europe and to his death, he was active in organizing and conducting music festivals, classes, and conventions in the New York–New Jersey area. He taught at the New York Musical Institute with Lowell Mason and George Frederick Root *(q.v.)* and with Thomas Hastings at the New York Musical

Academy (1853–56).

Bradbury edited and published secular and sacred song books and was author or editor of some sixty collections of popular music. Among his books were *The Psalmodist* (1844), *Choralist* (1847), *Musical Gems for Home and School* (1849), *Mendelssohn Collection* (1849), *Psalmistra* (1851), *Golden Chain of Sabbath School Melodies* (1861), *Bradbury's Golden Shower of Sunday School Melodies* (1862), *The Golden Censer* (1864), and, with Thomas Hastings, *The Shawm* (1853), *The Jubilee* (1858), and *Fresh Laurels* (1867). He also composed Sunday school cantatas and wrote the tunes to several church hymns.

REFERENCES: *A C; DAB; NCAB* (5:140); *WWW* (H); John T. Howard, *Our American Music,* 4th ed. (New York: Thomas Y. Crowell Co., 1965).

Thomas A. Barlow

BRADFORD, Edward Hickling. B. June 9, 1848, Roxbury, Massachusetts, to Charles F. and Eliza E. (Hickling) Bradford. M. June 20, 1900, to Edith Fiske. Ch. four. D. May 7, 1926, Boston, Massachusetts.

A graduate of Harvard University with the A.B. degree (1869), Edward Hickling Bradford received the M.A. (1872) and M.D. (1873) degrees from the Harvard Medical School. Following medical studies in Europe, he joined the staff of the Boston Dispensary in 1876. He was a member of the staff of Children's Hospital (1878–1909) and was associated with Boston City Hospital (1880–94).

A brilliant medical pioneer, Bradford sought an academic forum for his talents and insights. From 1881 to 1893 he held various instructorships in orthopedics and surgery at Harvard Medical School. He became the first full professor of orthopedic surgery at the school (1903) and served as dean (1912–18).

Bradford's most significant accomplishments were the cofounding with Augustus Thorndike in 1893 of the Boston Industrial School for Crippled and Deformed Children, the first of its kind in the nation, and his successful efforts to persuade the commonwealth to set up the Massachusetts Hospital School in Canton (1904). He continued to serve as trustee of these pioneer foundations for the education of the handicapped until his death.

Bradford was a founding member of the American Orthopedic Association (president, 1888) and wrote *Treatise on Orthopedic Surgery* (with Robert W. Lovett, 1890), which became a classic in its field. He was a fellow of the American Academy of Arts and Sciences, the American Association for the Advancement of Science, and the American Surgical Association and a member of other professional groups. He served on the general governing board of the Volunteer Medical Service Corps during World War I and was a member of the board of overseers of Harvard University.

REFERENCES: *DAB; WWW* (I); *Boston Evening Transcript,* May 8, 1926; *Boston Daily Globe,* May 8, 1926; E. H. Bradford, *A Review of the Work of the Industrial School for Crippled and Deformed Children* (Boston: Industrial School, 1926); Richard Leonardo, *Lives of Master Surgeons* (New York: Froben Press, 1948).   *Joseph M. McCarthy*

BRADFORD, Mary Carroll Craig. B. August 10, 1862, New York, New York, to James B. and Ann Turk (Carroll) Craig. M. 1878 to Edward Taylor Bradford. Ch. four. D. January 15, 1938, Denver Colorado.

Mary Carroll Craig Bradford received her early education in the public schools of New York City, continued her education in private schools, and attended the University of Paris where she was graduated with the B.A. degree.

After her marriage in 1878 to Lieutenant Edward Taylor Bradford, the couple moved to Colorado where her husband was engaged in the marble business at Leadville. After his death on Christmas Day, 1901, Mary C. C. Bradford taught school and was elected county superintendent of Adams County (1903–04). She was associate editor of *Modern World* in 1907. She was superintendent of schools in the city and county of Denver (1909–12) and state superintendent of public instruction (1913–20 and 1923–26). While state superintendent, Bradford was recognized across the country for her program providing for school standardization, which she first proposed in 1914. The quality of instruction in Colorado elementary schools was improved through a system of school inspection and grading by the state.

Bradford was active in educational and civic organizations. She was a charter member of the Woman's Club of Denver and president of the Colorado Federation of Women's Clubs. She was a member of the Educational Council of Colorado and the Colorado Teacher's Association and president of the National Education Association (1918), the first Colorado woman and second woman to hold that post. She was a leader of the Character Education Association and the National Patriotic Educational movement. Bradford was a frequent lecturer on educational topics and contributed articles to professional journals.

REFERENCES: *NCAB* (B:207); *NYT,* January 16, 1938, sec. 2, p. 9; *WC;* I. J. Lewis, "Tribute to Mrs. Mary C. C. Bradford," *NEA Proceedings* (1938): 17.   *Grace Napier*

BRADLEY, Amy Morris. B. September 12, 1823, East Vassalboro, Maine, to Abired and Jane (Baxter) Bradley. M. no. D. January 15, 1904, Wilmington, North Carolina.

Amy Morris Bradley became a teacher in a private school at the age of fifteen and later in public country schools during the summer and winter and in private homes during the spring and fall to finance studies at an East Vassalboro, Maine, academy.

Appointed principal of a grammar school in Gardiner, Maine, at the age of twenty-one, she taught in several Maine grammar schools until she was forced to move to a warmer climate because of a bronchial condition. After living with a brother in North Carolina for a couple of years, she went to Costa Rica in 1853 to teach English to daughters of a wealthy family. In San José, she started an English school that continued for three years until she returned to New England at the death of her father.

At the onset of the Civil War, Bradley offered her services as a nurse and was assigned to a Maine regiment. She served on a hospital ship, was matron of a convalescent home for soldiers in Washington, D.C., and worked in a convalescent camp near Alexandria, Virginia.

After the war she went to Wilmington, North Carolina, to participate in the education of poor southern white youngsters. With the support of the American Unitarian Association and Soldiers Memorial Society of Boston, she opened a school in Wilmington in 1867. With additional support of the Peabody Fund and the assistance of Mary Porter Tileston Hemenway, a Boston philanthropist, Bradley established a second school and, in 1872, the Tileston Normal School to meet the need for qualified teachers to staff the expanding school system.

By 1891 health problems resulted in Bradley's resignation as administrator of the school. She resided in a cottage provided for her on the school grounds to her death in 1904.

REFERENCES: *NAW; WC.;* C. Lowe, "Amy M. Bradley and Her Schools," *Old and New* 1 (1870): 775.   *Joan Duff Kise*

BRALLEY, Francis Marion. B. March 6, 1867, Honey Grove, Texas, to John and Katharine (White) Bralley. M. March 17, 1892, to Mary Melzina Meade. Ch. four. D. August 23, 1924, Dallas, Texas.

Francis Marion Bralley was graduated from Walcott Institute in Honey Grove, Texas, in 1885. He taught in the Honey Grove public schools (1885–92) and was superintendent of Fannin County schools (1892–98). He assumed the superintendency at Honey Grove (1898) and served there until he became an assistant superintendent of public instruction in 1905.

He became general agent of the Conference for Education in Texas, where he worked successfully for passage of a constitutional amendment permitting local school districts to levy taxes for the support of schools (1908–09). He served as superintendent of the State School for the Blind in Austin (1909–10), state superintendent of public instruction (1910–13), and director of extension at the University of Texas (1913–14).

Bralley was president of the College of Industrial Arts in Denton, Texas, from 1914 to his death in 1924. The college later became the Texas State College for Women and Texas Woman's University.

Bralley served as president of the board of regents for state normal colleges (1911–13) and executive secretary of the Organization for Enlargement by the State of Its Institutions for Higher Education (1912–14). He was active in many professional associations and was awarded an honorary degree by Baylor University.

REFERENCES: *WWW* (I); *Dallas Morning News,* August 24, 1924.

T. J. Kallsen

BRAMELD, Theodore Burghard Hurt. B. January 20, 1904, Neillsville, Wisconsin, to Theodore and Minnie (Dangers) Brameld. M. July 29, 1949, to Ona Margaret Katherine Swanson. M. December 29, 1971, to Midori Matsuyama. Ch. three.

Growing up in Wisconsin, Theodore Brameld was graduated from Ripon (Wisconsin) College with the B.A. degree in English (1926) and was a field secretary for Ripon College for two years. He became a fellow in philosophy at the University of Chicago, graduating with a Ph.D. degree (1931).

Brameld's first teaching positions were in New York at Long Island University (1931–35) and Adelphi College (1935–39). He was invited to establish a program in philosophy of education at the University of Minnesota, where he stayed for eight years (1939–47). He taught at New York University (1947–58), and Boston University (1958–69).

Brameld developed and was the outstanding spokesman for reconstructionism in American education, a view that was shaped by an extended progressivism. He believed that through social consensus, schools and society should set goals, and education should provide the opportunity for learning cooperative methods for achieving those goals.

Brameld developed his views in *Ends and Means in Education* (1950), *Patterns of Educational Philosophy* (1950), and *Toward a Reconstructed Philosophy of Education* (1956). He began studying anthropology in 1952 and made a study of the culture and education of Puerto Rico, which was published as *Philosophies of Education in Cultural Perspective* (1955) and *The Remaking of a Culture—Life and Education in Puerto Rico* (1959). Brameld field-tested a theory of anthropotherapy in Japan and wrote *Japan: Culture, Education, and Change in Two Communities* (1968). He was also the author of *A Philosophic Approach to Communism* (1933), *Design for America* (1945), *Minority Problems in the Public Schools* (1945), *Education for the Emerging Age* (1961), *Education as Power* (1965), *The Use of Explosive Ideas in Education* (1965), *The Climactic Decades: Mandate to Education* (1970), and *The Teacher as World Citizen* (1976). His books have been translated into Spanish, Korean, Italian, Japanese, and Portuguese. He edited or coauthored several books and wrote nearly two hundred articles and book reviews.

Brameld was a Fulbright Research Scholar and a distinguished lecturer and fellow at numerous universities. He was an American delegate to the

International Conference of the New Education Fellowship in Australia (1946), a regional vice-president of the American Education Fellowship (1942–53), secretary-treasurer (1941–47) and president (1947–48) of the Philosophy of Education Society, and a member of many professional associations.

REFERENCES: *CA* (17–18); *CB* (June 1967); *LE* (V); *WW* (XXXIV); Theodore Brameld, "Culturology as the Search for Convergence," in Peter A. Bertocci, ed., *Mid-Twentieth Century American Philosophy: Personal Statements* (Atlantic Highlands, N.J.: Humanities Press, 1974).

Robert R. Sherman

BRANDENBURG, William Aaron. B. October 10, 1869, Clayton County, Iowa, to Francis Marion and Enfield B. (Maxwell) Brandenburg. M. June 22, 1893, to Altana Adeline Penfield. Ch. six. D. October 29, 1940, St. Louis, Missouri.

William A. Brandenburg attended a rural school in Clayton County, Iowa. He received the Ph.B. (1900) and M.A. (1903) degrees from Drake University in Des Moines, Iowa.

Brandenburg was assistant principal of a school in Volga, Iowa (1893–95). He served as superintendent of schools for Capitol Park City schools in Des Moines (1900–05). During part of his tenure as superintendent, he began to teach in the department of education at Drake (1904–06). He became the superintendent of Mason City, Iowa, schools (1905–10) and was superintendent of the Oklahoma City (Oklahoma) schools (1910–13).

Brandenburg was appointed president of Kansas State Manual Training Normal School (later, Kansas State College of Pittsburg) in 1913. The school grew under Brandenburg's presidency and was renamed the Kansas State Teachers College of Pittsburg in 1922. The school had two buildings, 40 teachers, and 450 students in 1913 and fifteen buildings, 140 faculty members, and 1,350 students by 1940. A laboratory school was established. The college developed from an institution where teachers were trained to teach manual arts to a school recognized as an outstanding teacher-education institution in the area.

Brandenburg authored *Outlines of Civics* and *A History of the United States*, wrote articles for professional journals, and lectured widely. He was president of the North Central Association of Colleges and Secondary Schools (1938), the Kansas State Teachers Association (1938), and the American Association of Teachers Colleges (1940). He was awarded an honorary degree by Monmouth (Illinois) College.

REFERENCES: *CB* (1940); *LE* (I); *NCAB* (35:154); *WWAE* (I); *WWW* (I); *NYT,* October 30, 1940, p. 23. *James R. Layton*

BRATTLE, William. B. November 22, 1662, Boston, Massachusetts, to Thomas and Elizabeth (Tyng) Brattle. M. to Elizabeth Hayman. M. to

Elizabeth Gerrish. Ch. one. D. February 26, 1717, Cambridge, Massachusetts.

Like most of the first American educators in the colonial colleges, William Brattle was primarily a theologian, graduating in theology from Harvard College in 1680 at the age of eighteen. The same year he became a tutor in logic at Harvard, a post he held until 1696.

During these years he wrote his well-known *Compendium Logicae Secundum Principia D. Renati Cartesii,* the first American textbook on logic, which was used at Harvard during Brattle's years as tutor and was still the prescribed textbook in logic as late as 1765.

From 1696 to 1700 Brattle was a fellow of the Harvard Corporation. In these four years, while Harvard President Increase Mather *(q.v.)* was in Europe, Brattle and his friend and colleague John Leverett took over the office of directors of principle, along with their work as teachers at Harvard. As directors of principle they adhered to a policy that leaned toward a new order in theological theory. According to Cotton Mather, Harvard College flourished during their regime, and Brattle came to be called Father of the College.

In 1696 Brattle was ordained a pastor of the Congregational church in Cambridge, Massachusetts, where his support of religious reform probably played a significant role in his failure to win reelection to the Harvard Corporation in 1700. In 1703 he was reelected, however, when he and his more liberal followers replaced the stricter Mather group.

REFERENCES: *DAB; WWW* (H); Edward Harris, *An Account of Some of the Descendants of Captain Thomas Brattle* (Boston: D. Clapp, 1867); Josiah Quincy, *The History of Harvard University* (Boston: J. Owen, 1840), vol. 1.   *Walter F. C. Ade*

BRAWLEY, Benjamin Griffith. B. April 22, 1882, Columbia, South Carolina, to Edward McKnight and Margaret (Dickerson) Brawley. M. July 20, 1912, to Hilda Damaris Prowd. Ch. none. D. February 1, 1939, Washington, D.C.

Perhaps the most prolific writer of all Afro-American educators, Benjamin Brawley was born to a well-to-do family. His father who had been born to a free black family, was a graduate of Bucknell University and an influential clergyman who, when Brawley was three years old, became president of the newly created University for Negroes at Selma, Alabama. Under the guidance of his parents, Brawley began to study classical languages and read widely in English and American literature at an early age. He entered Atlanta (Georgia) Baptist College (later, Morehouse College) at the age of thirteen and received the A.B. degree in 1901. He earned the A.B. degree (1906) at the University of Chicago and the A.M. degree (1908) from Harvard University.

Brawley taught in a Florida rural school for a year and returned to

Atlanta Baptist College as a teacher of English (1902–10). He taught English at Howard University in Washington, D.C. (1910–12), and returned to Atlanta Baptist as its first dean in 1912.

In 1920 Brawley gave up his work at Morehouse College and went to Liberia, West Africa, to conduct an educational survey of that republic. In 1921 he was ordained into the ministry at Peoples Baptist Church of Boston and became pastor of the Messiah Baptist Church, Brockton, Massachusetts. In 1923 he accepted a position as professor of English at Shaw University in Raleigh, North Carolina, so he could be near his ailing father who was teaching theology at the same school. In 1931 he returned to Howard University and taught and lectured there until his death in 1939.

Brawley's books include *A Short History of the American Negro* (1913), *History of Morehouse College* (1917), *The Negro in Literature and Art* (1918), *A Social History of the American Negro* (1921), *A Short History of the English Drama* (1921), *A New Survey of English Literature* (1925), *Freshman Year English* (1929), *Doctor Dillard of the Jeanes Fund* (1930), *History of the English Hymn* (1932), *Early Negro American Writers* (1935), *Paul Lawrence Dunbar* (1936), *The Negro Genius* (1937), and *Negro Builders and Heroes* (1937). He wrote nearly a hundred published poems and published three volumes of his own poetry.

Brawley was president of the Association of Colleges for Negro Youth (1919-20). He was the recipient of honorary degrees from Shaw University and Morehouse College.

REFERENCES: *LE* (I); *NCAB* (37:159); *NYT,* February 7, 1939, p. 19; *WWW* (I); Theresa Gunnels Rush et al., *Black American Writers: Past and Present* (Metuchen, N.J.: Scarecrow Press, 1975).   *Walter C. Daniel*

BREASTED, James Henry. B. August 27, 1865, Rockford, Illinois, to Charles and Harriet N. (Garrison) Breasted. M. October 22, 1894, to Frances Hart. M. June 7, 1935, to Imogen Hart Richmond. Ch. three. D. December 2, 1935, New York, New York.

At the age of fifteen, James Henry Breasted enrolled in Northwestern (later, North Central) College in Naperville, Illinois. He attended intermittently and received the A.B. degree in 1888. Interested in the study of drugs, he entered the Chicago College of Pharmacy in 1882, graduating in 1886. He worked for a short period of time as a licensed pharmacist. Changing his professional interest to the ministry, he attended the Congregational Institute at the Chicago Theological Seminary (1888-90) and studied Hebrew at the Yale Graduate School, which awarded him the A.M. degree (1892). He also studied at the University of Berlin, Germany, where he received the Ph.D. degree (1894) upon completion of a Latin thesis on the sun-hymns from the capital of Ikhnaten (Amenhotep IV) at Tell-el-Amarna.

Breasted became assistant director of Haskell Oriental Museum at the University of Chicago (1895) and professor of Egyptology and Oriental history (1905). He was the first teacher of Egyptology in America.

In 1900 Breasted received an invitation from the Prussian Royal Academy of Sciences to collaborate on a dictionary of the Ancient Egyptian language. He gathered notes, which became the four-volume text *Ancient Records of Egypt* (1906–07). His *A History of Egypt* (1905) was accepted by scholars as the standard history of the ancient Egyptians. He coauthored with James Harvey Robinson (*q.v.*) *Outlines of European History* (1914), *A Short Ancient History* (1915), *A General History of Europe* (1926), and *Our World Today and Yesterday* (1934). Among his other books were *Development of Religion and Thought in Ancient Egypt* (1912), *Ancient Times* (1916), *Oriental Forerunners of Byzantine* (1924), *The Conquest of Civilization* (1926), *The Edwin Smith Surgical Papyrus* (two volumes, 1930), *The Dawn of Conscience* (1933), and *The Oriental Institute* (1933).

Breasted was elected a member of the Académie des inscriptions et belles lettres (Institut de France) in 1930 and was the recipient of several honorary degrees and the gold medal of the Geographic Society of Chicago (1929), Rosenberger Gold Medal (1929), the gold medal for the Holland Society of New York (1930), and The Fine Arts Medal of the American Institute of Architects (1934). He was active in professional associations, including serving as president of the American Oriental Society (1918), the History of Science Society (1926), and the American Historical Association (1928).

REFERENCES: *DAB* (supp. 1); *EB; LE* (III); NCAB (B:377); *WWW* (I).
LeRoy Barney

BRECKINRIDGE, Robert Jefferson. B. March 8, 1800, Cabell's Dale, Fayette County, Kentucky, to John and Mary Hopkins (Cabell) Breckinridge. M. March 11, 1823, to Ann Sophronisba Preston. M. 1847 to Virginia (Hart) Shelby. M. 1868 to Margaret White. Ch. several. D. December 27, 1871, Danville, Kentucky.

Robert Jefferson Breckinridge attended Jefferson College in Canonsburg, Pennsylvania (1816-18), and spent part of 1818 at Yale College. He was graduated from Union College in Schenectady, New York (1819). He returned to Lexington, Kentucky, to manage his mother's estate and engaged in the study of law. In 1824 he was admitted to the bar. First elected to the lower house of the Kentucky legislature in 1825, Breckinridge was reelected three times and served in the legislature to 1828.

In 1828 he abandoned the legal profession and became a ruling elder of the Mount Horeb Presbyterian Church of Fayette County (1829). He studied for the ministry (1831-32) and was licensed to preach in 1832. He was enrolled in Princeton Seminary for a short time in 1832. On November 26, 1832, he was ordained at the Second Church of Baltimore, Maryland, where he became a major figure in the controversy that divided the Presbyterian church into two groups: the Old School and the New School.

On April 17, 1845, Breckinridge became president of Jefferson College. He was pastor of the First Presbyterian Church of Lexington, Kentucky (1847–53); at the same time he was state superintendent of instruction for Kentucky (1847–51). Breckinridge played a major role in building a sound structure for public schools of the state and providing for their financial support.

In 1853, when the Presbyterian church established a theological school at Danville, Kentucky, Breckinridge was made professor of exegetic, didactic, and polemic theology. Because of poor health, he resigned that position on September 17, 1869, and retired in December 1869.

Breckinridge was an advocate of emancipation long before the Civil War and presided over the national Republican Convention at Baltimore in 1864, which renominated Abraham Lincoln for the presidency. He was a supporter of Lincoln and a major adviser in Kentucky to the President during the Civil War. Two of his sons served in the Civil War, one on each side.

Breckinridge edited the *Literary and Religious Magazine* while in Baltimore and the *Danville Quarterly Review* from 1861 to 1865. He was author of *Memoranda of Foreign Travel* (1839), *Papism in the Nineteenth Century in the United States* (1841), *Kentucky School Reports* (1848–53); and *The Knowledge of God, Objectively Considered* (1858).

REFERENCES: *AC; DAB; NCAB* (9:242); *TC; WWW* (H); W. H. Vaughan, "Breckinridge, Pioneer-Educational Administrator," *Peabody Journal of Education* 23 (March 1946): 284–305.   *Lawrence S. Master*

BRECKINRIDGE, Sophonisba Preston. B. April 1, 1866, Lexington, Kentucky, to William Campbell Preston and Issa (Desha) Breckinridge. M. no. D. July 30, 1948, Chicago, Illinois.

Sophonisba Preston Breckinridge received her education in Lexington, Kentucky, and was graduated with the B.S. degree (1888) from Wellesley (Massachusetts) College. She taught mathematics in a Washington, D.C., high school for a few years and then returned to Kentucky to study law in her father's law office. In 1895 she became the first woman to be admitted to the Kentucky bar. A graduate student at the University of Chicago, she received the Ph.M. (1897) and Ph.D. (1901) degrees. She was the first woman graduate of the university law school with the J.D. degree (1904).

Breckinridge started her career at the University of Chicago as a docent in political science in 1901, served as assistant dean of women (1902), and was dean of preprofessional social service students and Samuel Deutsch

Professor of Public Welfare Administration (1929–33). She was also dean of the college of arts, literature and science (1923–29). After her retirement in 1933, she continued teaching courses in public welfare until 1942.

Her writings include, *The Delinquent Child and the Home* (1912), *Truancy and Non-Attendance in the Chicago Schools* (1917), *New Homes for Old* (Americanization Studies, 1921), *Madeline McDowell Breckinridge, A Leader in the New South* (1921), *Family Welfare Work in a Metropolitan Community: Selected Case Records* (1924), *Public Welfare Administration: Select Documents* (1927), *Marriage and the Civic Rights of Women: Separate Domicile and Independent Citizenship* (1931), *Women in the Twentieth Century: A Study of Their Political, Social and Economic Activities* (1933), *The Family and the State: Select Documents* (1934), *Social Work and the Courts: Select Statutes and Judicial Decisions* (1934), and *The Illinois Poor Law and Its Administration* (1939).

Breckinridge was a founder of the *Social Service Review* and served as one of its editors from 1927 to 1948. She also edited the Social Services Series, which provided documentary material for advanced students.

She was one of the organizers of the Chicago School of Civics and Philanthropy (1907), became its dean, and helped incorporate the school into the University of Chicago (1920) as the Graduate School of Social Service Administration. It developed into one of the most outstanding schools of its kind in the world. From 1907 to 1920 Breckinridge lived at Hull House part of each year. She promoted use of social workers in the courts, the extension of civil service, and adequate care for residents of state institutions.

In 1908 she organized the Immigrant's Protective League and served as its first director and secretary of the board. She was active in the National Woman's Suffrage Association (vice-president, 1911). She was a delegate to the Women's Peace Congress at the Hague (1915) and helped organize the Women's International League for Peace and Freedom. She was also a delegate to several international conferences. She was president of the American Association of Schools of Social Work (1934), a forty-year member of the National Conference of Social Work, and a member of many other associations. Breckinridge was awarded several honorary degrees. She was voted a special citation for her social work by the Illinois State Welfare Association.

REFERENCES: *DAB* (supp. 4); *LE* (III); *NAW; NCAB* (37:65); *WWW* (II); E. Abbott et al., "Sophonisba Preston Breckinridge over the Years," *Social Service Review* 22 (December 1948): 417–50; K. F. Lenroot, "Sophonisba Preston Breckinridge, Social Pioneer," *Social Service Review* 23 (March 1949): 88–92; *NYT*, July 31, 1948, p. 15; "Sophonisba Preston Breckinridge; A Supplementary Statement," *Social Service Review* 23 (March 1949): 93–96.   *Lawrence S. Master*

BRICKMAN, William Wolfgang. B. June 30, 1913, New York, New York, to David Shalom and Sarah (Shaher) Brickman. M. February 26, 1958, to Sylvia Schnitzer. Ch. three.

William Wolfgang Brickman received the B.A. (1934) and M.S. in education (1935) degrees from City University of New York and the Ph.D. degree (1938) from New York University. He moved through the ranks from instructor to professor at New York University (1940–42 and 1946–62), served in the United States Army during World War II, and moved to the University of Pennylvania in 1962.

Brickman was the author, coauthor, or editor of twenty-two books, including *Guide to Research in Educational History* (1949), *The Changing Soviet School* (1960), *The Countdown on Segregated Education* (1960), *Religion, Government and Education* (1961), *A Century of Higher Education* (1962), *Educational Systems in the United States* (1964), *Automation, Education, and Human Values* (1966), *Conflict and Change on the Campus* (1970), *Education and the Many Faces of the Disadvantaged* (1972), *Comparative Education; Concept, Research, and Application* (1973), *Bibliographical Essays on History and Philosophy of Education* (1975), *Bibliographical Essays on Comparative and International Education* (1975), *Two Millennia of International Relations in Higher Education* (1975), and *Ideas and Issues in Educational Thought* (1976).

Brickman was the first president of the Comparative and International Education Society (1956–59) and also president in 1967–68. Under the society's auspices, he directed school visitation programs with Gerald H. Read (*q.v.*) for educators to West and East Europe, South America, Asia, and Africa. He was visiting professor and guest lecturer at many American and foreign universities and consultant to several state departments of education and the United States Office of Education. He served as editor of *School and Society* (later, *Intellect*) from 1953 to 1976. His articles appeared extensively in the professional literature, and he contributed to *Encyclopaedia Britannica, Encyclopedia Americana, Dictionary of American History, Encyclopedia of Educational Research,* and *Encyclopedia of Education.*

He served on the editorial board of *Paedagogria Historica,* an international journal of the history of education, the National Fulbright Selection Committee, the international education committee of the Institute of International Education, the College Entrance Examination Board, the American Association of Colleges for Teacher Education, the Phi Delta Kappa committee on religion and education, the Academic Advisory Board of Yeshiva University, and the Council of International Associations for the Advancement of Educational Research. Brickman was a member of the Evaluation Board of National Council for Accreditation of Teacher Education, the board of trustees of the Pennsylvania Federation of Citizens for

Educational Freedom and of many professional organizations.

REFERENCES: *CA* (1–4); *LE* (V); *WW* (XXXIX); *Directory of American Scholars* (New York: R. R. Bowker, 1974).   *James J. Van Patten*

BRIGANCE, William Norwood. B. November 17, 1896, Olive Branch, Mississippi, to Benjamin Edgar and Rebecca (Joyner) Brigance. M. August 9, 1922, to Jane Martin. Ch. two. D. January 30, 1960, Crawfordsville, Indiana.

W. Norwood Brigance received the A.B. degree (1916) from the University of South Dakota, the A.M. degree (1920) from the University of Nebraska, and the Ph.D. degree (1930) from the State University of Iowa. He studied at the University of Chicago (1921) and the University of Wisconsin (1922).

Brigance's professional career began as a high school teacher in Dallas, South Dakota (1916–17), Hastings, Nebraska (1920–21), and Chicago, Illinois (1921–22). He served with the United States Army in World War I. From 1922 until his death in 1960 he was a professor of speech at Wabash College in Crawfordsville, Indiana. At Wabash, many of his students won state, interstate, and national oratorical contests. While on leave from Wabash (1936–38), he reorganized the teaching of speech in the Hawaiian schools.

Brigance was coauthor of *A Notebook for Beginning Speech* (with M. G. Phillips, 1927), *Speech* (with W. G. Hedde, 1935), *Speechmaking* (with R. K. Immel, *q.v.*, 1938), *American Speech* (with W. G. Hedde, 1942), *Speech for Military Service* (with R. K. Immel, 1943), and *A Drill Manual for Improving Speech* (with F. M. Henderson, 1955), and author of *The Spoken Word* (1927), *Classified Speech Models* (1928), *Speech Composition* (1937), *Speech Communication* (1947), and *Speech: Techniques and Disciplines in a Free Society* (1952). Brigance also authored a biography, *Jeremiah Sullivan Black: A Defender of the Constitution and the Ten Commandments* (1934). He was editor for the Speech Association of America of a two-volume work, *A History and Criticism of American Public Address* (1943), and edited the *Quarterly Journal of Speech* (1942–45).

In 1951 the Tau Kappa Alpha National Board of Awards chose Brigance as the United States speaker of the year in educational, scientific, and cultural activities. He was the recipient of the Order of Merit, Lambda Chi Alpha (1956) and Distinguished Alumnus Award of Tau Kappa Alpha (1959).

Brigance was a member of professional associations, including the Speech Association of America (vice-president, 1935, 1945, and president, 1946), Indiana Speech Association (president, 1931), and Tau Kappa Alpha (vice-president, 1934–39).

REFERENCES: *LE* (III); *NCAB* (47:249); *WWW* (III); *NYT,* February 1, 1960, p. 27.   *Lew E. Wise*

BRIGGS, Thomas Henry. B. January 25, 1877, Raleigh, North Carolina, to John D. and Florence B. (Dunn) Briggs. M. September 11, 1902, to Helen Hoyt Harriman. M. May 30, 1941, to Ruth G. Sugnet. Ch. two. D. August 12, 1971, Meredith, New Hampshire.

Thomas Henry Briggs received the A.B. degree (1896) from Wake Forest College in North Carolina. He pursued graduate studies at the University of Chicago (1898–1901) and received the Ph.D. degree from Columbia University (1914).

He taught at Atlantic Collegiate Institute in Elizabeth City, North Carolina (1896–98), John B. Stetson University in De Land, Florida (1899–1900), Princeton-Yale Academy in Chicago, Illinois (1900–01), and Eastern Illinois State Normal School (later, Eastern Illinois University) in Charleston (1901–11). He was professor of education at Teachers College, Columbia University, from 1912 to 1942, when he retired and became emeritus professor of education. He was particularly influential in the development of the junior high school.

Briggs was the author of many books, including *Reading in Public Schools* (with Lotus D. Coffman, *q.v.*, 1908), *A First Book of Composition* (with Isabel McKinney, 1913), *Formal Grammar as a Discipline* (1914), *Junior High School English,* books 1 and 2 (with Isabel McKinney and Florence Skeffington, 1920), *The Junior High School* (1920), *Curriculum Problems* (1926), *Secondary Education* (1933), *Improving Instruction* (1938), *Pragmatism and Pedagogy* (1940), and *The Meaning of Democracy* (with W. F. Russell *q.v.*, 1941). He was the editor of junior and senior high school textbooks and a frequent contributor to professional journals.

He served as director of consumer education study for the National Association of Secondary School Principals (1942), and chairman of the board on the Council for Advancement of Secondary Education (1951) and was a delegate to the Pan American Seminars in Secondary Education in Santiago, Chile (1954). He was Ingles Lecturer at Harvard University in 1930, Laureate Lecturer of Kappa Delta Pi in 1940, and Sir John Adams Lecturer at the University of California in 1946. He was a member of various professional organizations and active in community projects.

REFERENCES: *LE* (III); *WW* (XXII); *WWW* (V); Winfield Scott Downs, ed., *Who's Who in New York: City and State* (New York: Lewis Historical Publications Co., 1960); *NYT*, August 15, 1971, p. 66.

Harold J. McKenna

BRIGHAM, Albert Perry. B. June 12, 1855, Perry, New York, to Horace Ames and Julia (Perry) Brigham. M. June 27, 1882, to Flora Winegar. Ch. two. D. March 31, 1932, Washington, D.C.

Albert Perry Brigham, geographer, educator, author, and clergyman, attended the local Perry, New York school. He studied at Madison (later, Colgate) University in Hamilton, New York, from which he received the A.B. (1879) and A.M. (1882) degrees. He studied at Hamilton Theological Seminary from 1879 to 1882, when he was ordained to the Baptist ministry.

Brigham accepted pastorates in Stillwater (1882-85) and Utica (1885-91), New York. In the summer of 1889 he pursued an early interest in geology at the Harvard Summer School of Geology. In 1891 he resigned his pastorate, entered the Harvard Graduate School to study geology, and was graduated in 1892 with the A.M. degree. Brigham was appointed head of the multiple department of natural history, zoology, geology, paleontology, physiography, and, later, geography at Colgate University. He was professor and head of the department until his retirement with emeritus rank in 1925, having earned a worldwide reputation as a scientist, teacher, and leader.

Brigham's chief geological interest was in land forms and glacial geology, but it was as a geographer that he became best known and made his most original contributions. Essentially a humanist, he was especially interested in the study of geographic influences on human history and wrote a number of papers and delivered many lectures on the subject before learned societies in America and England and two international geological congresses.

A clear and effective writer, many of Brigham's books were used as school and college texts. In addition to some ninety papers prepared for scientific journals, he wrote *Text Book of Geology* (1900), *Introduction to Physical Geography* (with G. K. Gilbert, 1902), *Geographic Influences in American History* (1903), *From Trail to Railway Through the Appalachians* (1970), *Ontario High School Physical Geography* (1909), *Commercial Geography* (1911), *Essentials of Geography* (with C. T. McFarlane, 1916), *Cape Cod and the Old Colony* (1920), *A Manual for Teachers of Geography* (1921), and *The United States of America—Studies in Physical, Regional, Industrial, and Human Geography* (1927).

Brigham was one of the founders of the Association of American Geographers in 1904 and served as secretary (1904–11), treasurer (1911–13), and president (1913–14). He was a fellow of the Geological Society of America, the American Association for the Advancement of Science, and the Royal Geographical Society of London (honorary) and a member of the National Education Association, the National Council of Geography Teachers (president, 1929–30), and the New York State Science Teachers' Association (president, 1905).

From 1929 until shortly before his death in 1932, he was honorary consultant in geography to the Library of Congress, spending about half of each year in that activity. In 1930 he was selected by the American Geographical Society to represent American geographers at the centenary of the Royal Geographical Society of London. He received three honorary degrees. On his seventy-fifty birthday, he received the unusual distinction of having the June (1930) issue of the *Annals* of the American Association of American Geographers dedicated to discussions of his work.

REFERENCES: *DAB* (supp. 1); *LE* (I); *NCAB* (24:281); *WWW* (I); *NYT*, April 1, 1932, p. 21; Alger E. Burdick, "The Contributions of Albert Perry Brigham to Geographic Education" (Ph.D. diss., George Peabody College for Teachers, 1951).   *J. Franklin Hunt*

BRITTAIN, Marion Luther. B. November 11, 1865, Wilkes County, Georgia, to Jabez Mercer and Ida (Callaway) Brittain. M. December 20, 1889, to Lettie MacDonald. Ch. three. D. July 1, 1953, Atlanta, Georgia.

Marion Luther Brittain attended Covington (Georgia) High School and was graduated from Emory College (later, University) in Oxford, Georgia, with the A.B. degree (1886) and was a graduate student at the University of Chicago (1898).

Brittain taught in Gordon County, Georgia, schools for a year and was principal of the Crew Street School in Atlanta (1889-90). He was head of the language department at Boys High School in Atlanta (1890-98) and superintendent of Fulton County, Georgia, schools (1900-10).

Appointed state superintendent of public instruction in 1910, Brittain served to 1922, when he was elected president of the Georgia School of Technology (later, Institute of Technology), which he headed to his retirement in 1944. Brittain considered his major accomplishments to be the establishment of the first Reserve Officer Training Corps unit in the South, a gift from the Guggenheim Foundation that established the School of Aeronautics, and organization of a ceramics engineering program.

Brittain was the author of *Introduction to Caesar* (1900), *History and Methods of Sunday School Work* (1901), *History of the Second Baptist Church of Atlanta* (1905), *Blue Book of Stories* (1915), *Lessons for Adult Education* (1922), and *The Story of Georgia Tech* (1948).

Active in professional associations, Brittain was president of the Georgia State Teachers' Association (1906), the Southern Educational Association (1913), the Council of State Superintendents (1917), and the Georgia Baptist Young People's Union (1902), and he served as president of the advisory board of the Techwood Slum Clearance Project. He was an international judge of the Fisher Body Guild (1931-36), a member of the board of visitors of the United States Naval Academy (1934-39), and a member of the Federal Prison Industries Board. He was the recipient of honorary degrees from the University of Georgia and Mercer and Emory universities.

REFERENCES: *LE* (III); *NCAB* (E:324); *NYT*, July 2, 1953, p. 23; *WWAE* (VIII); *WWW* (III); Dorothy Orr, *History of Education in Georgia* (Chapel Hill: University of North Carolina Press, 1950).

John F. Ohles

BROOKS, Charles. B. October 30, 1795, Medford, Massachusetts, to Jonathan and Elizabeth (Albree) Brooks. M. June 27, 1827, to Cecilia Williams. M. August 1, 1839, to Charlotte Ann (Haven) Lord. Ch. three. D. July 7, 1872, Medford, Massachusetts.

Charles Brooks was graduated from Harvard University in 1816, remaining for three years to complete theological studies. He served as pastor of the Third Congregational Church (Unitarian) in Hingham, Massachusetts (1820-39). Appointed professor of natural history at the University of the City of New York, he traveled to Europe to study from 1839 to 1843 in preparation for his new position. Failing eyesight, however, forced him to an early retirement.

Brooks was a longtime advocate of state-controlled common education. He supported peace movements, temperance campaigns, and the antislavery crusade. He sought to win support for the adaptation of the Prussian system of education to America. He campaigned in behalf of an 1837 bill that created the Massachusetts Board of Education, including an address before a joint session of the state legislature. He opposed the appointment of Horace Mann (*q.v.*) as secretary of the board but actively supported Mann's reform efforts. A popular lecturer, he advocated establishment of state normal schools before state legislatures and citizen groups throughout New England and the mid-Atlantic states. He endorsed proposals for a federal education agency as early as 1839 and lobbied for the creation of such an agency to 1867, when the United States Department of Education was established.

Brooks was author of *A Family Prayer-book* (1821), *Prayers for Children and Young People* (1837), *Parisian Linguist* (c. 1841), *Elementary Course of Natural History* (1847), *Elements of Ornithology* (1847), and *History of the Town of Medford* (1855). His "Remarks on Europe Relating to Education, Peace and Labor," which first appeared in the *Knickerbocker* of New York in 1843, was an important statement on European education.

REFERENCES: *AC; DAB: NCAB* (12:287); *TC: WWW* (H); *NYT,* July 12, 1872, p. 2; Donald R. Warren, *To Enforce Education: A History of the Founding Years of the U.S. Office of Education* (Detroit, Mich.: Wayne State University Press, 1974). *Donald R. Warren*

BROOKS, Edward. B. January 16, 1831, Stony Point, New York, to n.a. M. 1855 to H. Marie Dean. Ch. two. D. June 29, 1912, Philadelphia, Pennsylvania.

Edward Brooks, the son of a factory owner, was a contributor to the village newspaper by the age of fourteen. He completed his common school education when he was fifteen and went to work in his father's factory for the next three years. During this time he continued his interest and study in literature, mathematics, science, and writing.

Brooks began his teaching career in Cuddebackville, New York, at the age of eighteen. A student at the Liberty (New York) Normal School (1850), he studied and taught at the University of Northern Pennsylvania, moving from student to teacher to chairman of the department of mathematics (1851-54). He taught literature and mathematics at Monticello (New York) Academy (1854-55) and then went to the new normal school (later, Millersville State College) at Millersville, Pennsylvania, where he developed a nationwide reputation for his instructional methods (1855-66). He was principal from 1866 to 1883, when he moved to Philadelphia. He was elected superintendent of schools for Philadelphia (1891-1906). He provided a department of commerce in the Boys' High School and established the Commercial High School for Girls. He reorganized the Girls' High School and Girls' Normal School, instruction in the elementary grades, and the office of the superintendent of schools. In 1893 he introduced the observance of Flag Day.

Brooks was the author of professional education books, as well as a series of about twenty mathematics textbooks. He reintroduced the use of objectives in the teaching of arithmetic. Among his books were *Methods of Teaching Mental Arithmetic* (1870), *The Philosophy of Arithmetic* (1876), *Normal Methods of Teaching* (1879), *Mental Science and Culture* (1883), *Reading and Elocution* (1878), *The Story of the Iliad* (1889), *The Story of the Odyssey* (1891), *The Story of the Aeneid* (1898), *The Story of King Arthur* (1899), and *The Story of Siegfried* (1903). *Normal Methods of Teaching* included special methods for teaching various subjects, and the history and description of teaching methods. Brooks was said to be the first to use model lessons in a professional book.

Brooks was president of the Pennsylvania State Teachers Association (1868) and the Normal Section of the National Teachers Association (1876). He was awarded several honorary degrees.

REFERENCES: *AC; NCAB* (2:294); *TC: WWW* (I). *Robert L. Hillerich*

BROOKS, Eugene Clyde. B. December 3, 1871, Greene County, North Carolina, to Edward Jones and Martha Eleanor (Brooks) Brooks. M. December 19, 1900, to Ida Sapp. Ch. three. D. October 18, 1947, Raleigh, North Carolina.

Eugene Brooks was graduated from Trinity College (later, Duke University) in Durham, North Carolina, with the A.B. degree (1894) and engaged in research at Columbia University (1913-14).

He was Washington correspondent for the *Raleigh* (North Carolina) *News and Observer* and a clerk in the United States Treasury Department. Returning to North Carolina, he was a school principal in Kingston and superintendent of schools in Monroe (1900-03). In 1902 Brooks was secretary of the educational campaign committee of North Carolina that sought to assist the Southern Education Board in an effort to reduce illiteracy and increase educational opportunities in the South. In 1903-04, he continued as secretary of the committee and was supervisor of rural schools for the state superintendent of public instruction. He was superintendent of the Goldsboro, North Carolina, schools (1904-07) and a member of the faculty of Trinity College as first head of the department of education and professor of the history and science of education (1907-19).

Brooks served as state superintendent of public instruction of North Carolina from 1919 to 1923. Under his leadership, the state department of education was reorganized, the school term was lengthened, summer schools for teacher training were increased, state education laws were codified, consolidation of small school districts was fostered, and teacher's salaries were improved.

In 1923 he resigned as state superintendent to become president of the North Carolina State College of Agriculture and Engineering. Until the merger of North Carolina State College in 1931 with the University of North Carolina and North Carolina Women's College into a new University of North Carolina, Brooks led his college through a period of expansion in courses, programs, departments and schools, and physical plant. After 1931 he continued to head the College of Agriculture and Engineering as a university vice-president until his retirement in 1934.

Brooks was the author of *The Story of Cotton and the Development of the Cotton States* (1911), *The Story of Corn and the Westward Migration* (1916), *Woodrow Wilson as President* (1916), *Education for Democracy* (1919), *Stories of South America* (1922), and *Our Dual Government* (1924). He also edited *North Carolina Poems* (1912) and was the first editor of *North Carolina Education* (1906–23).

Active in civic and professional activities, Brooks was appointed chairman of a state committee to study the needs of county government (1925); he was chairman of a legislative commission on distribution of school equalization funds (1925-26) and a member of the North Carolina Park Commission. He was president of the Association of Southern Agricultural Workers (1931-32), the North Carolina College Conference (1931-32), and the North Carolina Teachers Assembly (1912-13). He was a member of the Committee of Eight to rewrite American history for elementary schools (1904) and of the national finance commission of the American Council of Education and state director of the National Education Association. He received several honorary degrees and was posthumously elected to the North Carolina Educational Hall of Fame in 1948.

REFERENCES: *LE* (II); *NCAB* (36:237); *WWAE* (I); *WWW* (II); Willard B. Gatewood, Jr., *Eugene Clyde Brooks: Educator and Public Servant* (Durham, N.C.: Duke University Press, 1960); *Letters and Personal Papers of Dr. Clyde Brooks* from the North Carolina Department of

Archives, Raleigh, North Carolina; *NYT,* October 20, 1947, p. 23.
Charles A. Reavis

BROOKS, Stratton Duluth. B. September 10, 1869, Everett, Missouri, to Charles Meyers and Marion (McClure) Brooks. M. September 3, 1890, to Marcia E. Stuart. Ch. four. D. January 18, 1949, Kansas City, Missouri.

Stratton Duluth Brooks, educator and president of the University of Oklahoma, was graduated from the Michigan State Normal College (later, Eastern Michigan University) at Ypsilanti with the B.Pd. (1892) and M.Pd. (1899) degrees. He received the A.B. degree (1896) from the University of Michigan and the A.M. degree (1904) from Harvard University.

He taught in Millbrook, Michigan (1887-88), and was principal of the Danville (Illinois) High School (1890-92). He later taught at Mount Pleasant (Michigan) Normal School (1892-93) and at the La Salle (Illinois) High School. He was assistant professor of psychology and education and high school inspector at the University of Illinois (1900-02), assistant superintendent of schools in Boston, Massachusetts (1902-06), superintendent of schools in Cleveland, Ohio (1906), superintendent of schools in Boston (1906-12), and president of the University of Oklahoma (1912-23). During his administration the university experienced a rapid period of growth; enrollment increased fivefold. He was later president of the University of Missouri (1923-31).

Brooks was the author of textbooks on composition, rhetoric, and English composition, and a series of school readers, including *Composition-Rhetoric* (with Marietta Hubbard, 1905), *Brooks's Readers* (eight volumes, 1906), and *English Composition* (two volumes, 1911-12).

He was the president of the National Society for the Scientific Study of Education (1906), the superintendent section of the National Education Association (1909-10), and the Oklahoma State Teachers Association (1913). He was a member of the State Vocational Education Board of Oklahoma and the board of trustees of Massachusetts College and executive officer of the State Geological Society of Oklahoma. He was the recipient of two honorary degrees.

REFERENCES: *LE* (III); *NCAB* (18:277); *WWAE* (XI); *WWW* (II); *NYT,* January 20, 1949, p. 27.   *Joan Duff Kise*

BROUDY, Harry Samuel. B. July 27, 1905, Filipowa, Poland, to Michael and Mollie (Wyzan) Broudy. M. August 15, 1947, to Dorothy L. Hogarth. Ch. one.

Harry Samuel Broudy emigrated to the United States as a small boy with his family from Russian Poland. He attended the public schools of Milford, Massachusetts. He studied chemical engineering at Massachusetts Institute of Technology and worked as a newspaper reporter before completing the A.B. degree as valedictorian (1929) at Boston University. He studied philosophy at Harvard University, receiving the M.A. (1933) and Ph.D. (1935) degrees.

Broudy was a supervisor for the department of education for Massachusetts (1936-37). He taught philosophy and psychology of education at the Massachusetts state teacher's colleges at North Adams (1937-49) and Framingham (1949-57), then became professor of the philosophy of education at the University of Illinois, Urbana-Champaign, from 1957 until his retirement in 1974.

His publications include *Building a Philosophy of Education* (1954), *Psychology for General Education* (with E. L. Freel, 1956), *Paradox and Promise* (1961), *Democracy and Excellence in American Secondary Education* (with B. O. Smith, *q.v.*, and J. R. Burnett, 1964), *Philosophy of Education* (with others, 1967), *The Real World of the Public Schools* (1972), and *Enlightened Cherishing* (1972). He was editor of *Educational Forum* (1964-72).

Internationally recognized as an outstanding exponent of the classical realist viewpoint in the philosophy of education, Broudy made notable contributions to the theories of teacher education and general, aesthetic, and higher education.

Broudy was active in professional organizations, including serving on advisory boards to the Educational Testing Service (1968-71) and the American Association of Colleges of Teacher Education (1966-69) and held memberships in many professional associations, including the Philosophy of Education Society (president, 1953) and the Association for Realistic Philosophy (president, 1955). He was a fellow of the Center for Advanced Study in the Behavioral Sciences (1967-68) and a consultant to the Educational Research Council and the Agency for International Development (Korea, 1970). He was the recipient of several honorary degrees.

REFERENCES: *CA* (1–4); *LE* (V); *WW* (XXXVII); Harry S. Broudy, "Unfinished Business," in P. A. Bertocci, ed., *Mid-Twentieth Century American Philosophy* (Atlantic Highlands, N.J.: Humanities Press, 1974), pp. 84-103.   *Ronald D. Szoke*

BROWN, Alice Van Vechten. B. June 7, 1862, Hanover, New Hampshire, to Samuel Gilman and Sara (Van Vechten) Brown. M. no. D. October 16, 1949, Middletown, New Jersey.

Alice Van Vechten Brown received her early education in the schools of Clinton and Utica, New York, and under private tutors. She studied painting under William M. Chase, Abbott Thayer, and others at the Art Students' League in New York City (1881-85). Interrupted in her studies by prolonged illness in her family, she abandoned her intention to become a creative artist and turned to the study and teaching of art history.

A teacher all of her life, Brown was appointed assistant director of the Norwich (Connecticut) Art School, in 1891 and by 1894 had advanced to the position of director. She was asked to reorganize the art teaching program for Wellesley (Massachusetts) College in 1897, which offered a program of studies in art history that consisted mainly of looking at photographs and reading textbooks. Under her direction and organization, the art department offered laboratory work as a vital part of the study of art history. By 1900 Wellesley was the only college in the country that offered a major in the history of art. The Wellesley method of teaching art history included drawing and modeling from photographs or casts of works of art, developing skills in a manner similar to those learned in laboratory experimentation in science.

Brown served as director of the college's Farnsworth Museum. She established a policy of loan exhibitions (1899-1900) and inaugurated a course in museum training (1911) and the first college course on modern art taught in the United States (1927).

She was the author of *A Short History of Italian Painting* (with William Rankin, 1914). She served on the board of directors of the College Art Association of America and the Committee on Medieval and Renaissance Studies of the Archaeological Institute of America. She was awarded honorary degrees by Wellesley and Hamilton colleges.

REFERENCES: *NAW; WWW* (II); *NYT,* October 19, 1949, p. 29.

Roger H. Jones

BROWN, Charlotte Hawkins. B. June 11, 1883, Henderson, North Carolina, to Edmund Hunter and Carolyn Frances Hawkins. M. June 14, 1911, to Edward S. Brown. Ch. none. D. January 11, 1961, Greensboro, North Carolina.

Charlotte Hawkins Brown moved at an early age to Cambridge, Massachusetts, where she attended public schools. She was a protégé of Alice Freeman Palmer (*q.v.*), president of Wellesley (Massachusetts) College, who sent her to Salem (Massachusetts) Normal School. She was graduated in 1901.

Brown went to North Carolina and in 1901 founded a school for black youngsters. In 1903 it became the Alice Freeman Palmer Memorial Institute, a day and boarding school. The Sedalia Club, organized in Boston, assisted in raising funds. The school was rebuilt after a 1917 fire, and financial help was received from the Julius Rosenwald Fund. Brown headed the school to 1952 and then was finance director to 1955. The school was closed in 1971.

Brown was a prominent lecturer on education in the United States. She was president of the North Carolina Federation of Colored Women's Clubs and secretary of the National Association of Colored Women (1918–22).

Governor Clyde R. Hoey appointed her to the state defense council in 1940. She was the first black woman to serve on the national board of the Young Women's Christian Association. Brown raised six children of relatives. She received several honorary degrees.

REFERENCES: *NYT*, January 12, 1961, p. 29; Benjamin Brawley (*q.v.*), *Negro Builders and Heroes* (Chapel Hill: University of North Carolina Press, 1937), pp. 282-84; Anna S. L. Brown, "Alice Freeman Palmer Memorial Institute," *Opportunity* (August 1923): 246–48; *Journal of Negro History* 46 (April 1961): 130; Constance Hill Marteena, *The Lengthening Shadow of a Woman: A Biography of Charlotte Hawkins Brown* (Hicksville, N.Y.: Exposition, 1977); *Who's Who in Colored America*, 7th ed. (Yonkers, N.Y.: Burckel and Associates, 1950); Wilhelmena S. Robinson, *International Library of Negro Life and History: Historical Negro Biographies* (New York: Publishers Co., 1967), pp. 167-68.

Shirley M. Ohles

BROWN, Clara Maud. See ARNY, Clara Maud Brown.

BROWN, Elmer Ellsworth. B. August 28, 1861, Kiantone, New York, to Russell McCrary and Electa Louisa (Sherman) Brown. M. June 20, 1889, to Fanny Fosten Eddy. Ch. none. D. November 3, 1934, New York, New York.

Although Elmer Ellsworth Brown was not sent to school until he was eight years old, he passed the county examination for a teacher's certificate at the age of thirteen. He received the top score in the group tested but was not able to teach because of his age. He attended the State Normal College (later, Illinois State University) at Normal, Illinois, and was graduated in 1881. He received the A.B. degree (1889) from the University of Michigan and the Ph.D. degree (1890) from the University of Halle-Wittenberg (Germany).

Brown was superintendent of schools in Belvidere County, Illinois (1881-84), and assistant to his brother Isaac E. Brown who was state secretary of the Illinois Young Men's Christian Association (1884-87).

On his return to America from Germany, Brown served as a high school principal in Jackson, Michigan (1890-91), and as an assistant professor in the art and science of teaching at the University of Michigan (1891-92). He joined the faculty of the University of California at Berkeley in 1892 to organize a department of education and continued there to 1906 when he was appointed United States commissioner of education in the Department of the Interior. While commissioner of education, he encouraged rural education, establishment of agricultural high schools, home economics courses for girls, and international education. He was a contributor to the beginnings of the child welfare movement.

He resigned as commissioner in 1911 to become the seventeenth chancellor of New York University (NYU). During his twenty-two years at NYU (1911-33), the university enrollment increased, university standards were raised, medical and law schools were established as postgraduate schools, a dental school was organized, and an undergraduate coeducational college was established at Washington Square in New York City.

Brown was the author of *The Making of Our Middle Schools* (1903), *Origin of American State Universities* (1905), *Government by Influence and Other Addresses* (1909), *Victory and Other Verse* (1923), and *A Few Remarks* (1933).

Brown was active in professional groups, including the National Council of Education (president, 1905-07), the National Education Association (director), and the American Association for the Advancement of Science (vice-president, section on education, 1907). He was the recipient of a number of foreign honorary awards and of honorary degrees by American universities.

REFERENCES: *DAB* (Supp. 1); *LE* (I); *NCAB* (28:323); *WWW* (I); *NYT*, November 4, 1934, p. 1.   *Jordan Greer*

BROWN, Goold. B. March 7, 1791, Providence, Rhode Island, to Smith and Lydia (Gould) Brown. M. to n.a. Ch. two. D. March 31, 1857, Lynn, Massachusetts.

Goold Brown's father was a teacher, essayist, and classicist who taught his son to read Greek at the age of five. Goold Brown attended the Friend's School in Providence, Rhode Island. Family finances did not permit Brown to receive a college education, and he studied independently in his spare time from his work as a merchant's clerk, a job he hated.

Brown taught at a school near Providence, at the Nine Partners Boarding School in Mechanic, New York (1813), and at John Griscom's (*q.v.*) School in New York City (1813). He opened a private academy in New York that prospered for twenty years. As headmaster, Brown gained a reputation as a classical scholar and teacher.

Brown wrote *The Child's First Book* (1882). Dissatisfied with the current strategies of teaching grammar, he wrote *The Institutes of English Grammar* (1823). He also wrote *The First Lines of English Grammar* (1823), *A Catechism of English Grammar* (1827), *A New English Grammar* (1841), and *Brown's Small Grammar Improved* (1856). His greatest contribution was the monumental *Grammar of English Grammars* (1851), called "the most exhaustive, most accurate, and most original treatise on the English language ever written." The bibliography included 548 titles and is said to have taken twenty-three years to prepare. It remains a hallmark to its writer's genius and a monument to scholarship in the history of the English language.

REFERENCES: *AC; DAB; NCAB* (8:265); *TC; WWW* (H); John A. Neitz, *Old Textbooks* (Pittsburgh: University of Pittsburgh Press, 1961).

LeRoy Barney

BROWN, Hallie Quinn. B. March 10, 1850, Pittsburgh, Pennsylvania, to Thomas Arthur and Frances Jane (Scroggins) Brown. M. no. D. September 16, 1949, Wilberforce, Ohio.

Hallie Quinn Brown, lecturer and club woman, was one of six children born to Frances Jane Brown, a freed slave, and Thomas Arthur Brown, a riverboat agent. By the time she was twenty, her family had moved from Pittsburgh, Pennsylvania, to Ontario, Canada, and then to Wilberforce, Ohio, where the children might obtain a good education.

Brown received the B.S. degree (1873) from Wilberforce University. She taught in Mississippi and South Carolina at plantation schools during Reconstruction. Subsequently she taught in public schools in Columbia, South Carolina, was dean of Allen University in Columbia, taught in Dayton, Ohio (1887-91), went back to the South as principal of Tuskegee (Alabama) Institute, and was appointed professor of elocution at Wilberforce in 1893 and again in 1900.

She became a professional lecturer after she was graduated from the Chautauqua Lecture School in 1886. She traveled extensively in the United States and Europe for the benefit of Wilberforce University, a black institution. She lectured abroad on Negro life in America and included Negro songs and folklore in her programs. Besides her lectures for Wilberforce, she supported the Women's Christian Temperance Union and lectured in England for the British Women's Temperance Association. In 1899 she was a representative of the United States to the International Congress of Women in London.

Brown was a founder of the first national organization for Negro women, the Colored Woman's League of Washington, D.C. (a forerunner of the National Association of Colored Women) and was active in the National Association of Colored Women (president, 1920-24). She took part in the 1924 presidential campaign, making campaign speeches, addressing the Republican National Convention in Cleveland, Ohio, and serving as director of Colored Women's Activities in the Chicago national headquarters for the campaign.

Brown was the author of numerous books, including *Bit and Odds: A Choice Selection of Recitations* (1880), *First Lessons in Public Speaking* (1920), *Homespun Heroines and Other Women of Distinction* (1926), and *Pen Pictures of Pioneers of Wilberforce* (1937).

Brown was honored by the dedication of a community house in St. Paul, Minnesota, to her, the Hallie Quinn Brown Memorial Library of Central

State College at Wilberforce, Ohio, and the Hallie Quinn Brown Scholarship at Wilberforce.

REFERENCES: *NAW: Afro-American Encyclopedia* (North Miami: Educational Book Publishers, 1974), 2:412.; John P. Davis, ed., *American Negro Reference Book* (Englewood Cliffs, N.J.: Prentice-Hall, 1966), p. 542. Ruth Neely, ed., *Women of Ohio* (Chicago: Clarke Publishing Co., 1939), 1:237–38.   *Charlotte G. Glashagel*

BROWN, LeRoy Decatur. B. November 3, 1848, Noble County, Ohio, to Jeremiah Byron and Isabella Carey (Harris) Brown. M. November 28, 1878, to Esther Emma Gabel. Ch. six. D. January 13, 1898, San Luis Obispo, California.

LeRoy Decatur Brown received his early education at a Noble County, Ohio, farm community where he worked as a farmer in the summer and attended district school in the winter. He ran away from home at the age of fifteen to serve in the Civil War. On his return from the war, he attended a graded school at Senecaville, Ohio, and an academy in Athens, Ohio (1867–69). He was graduated from Ohio Wesleyan University in Delaware, Ohio, with the bachelor's (1879) and A.M. (1882) degrees. While at Ohio Wesleyan, he spent summers visiting American and European schools.

He taught in several district schools and at Newport, Ohio (1873–74), and with John M. Amos in a normal school in Caldwell. He was superintendent of schools at Belpre (1874–75), Eaton (1875–79), and Hamilton (1879–94), Ohio.

In 1883 he was elected the Ohio state superintendent of public instruction, taking office in 1874 and serving to 1887. During his term of office he secured important reforms in school management, increased the efficiency of school libraries, and provided for increased appropriations for colleges and common schools. When his term of office expired, he worked as a bank cashier in Alliance, Ohio.

In 1887 he became the first president of the University of Nevada in Reno. When he arrived there was one building on a twenty-acre campus of sagebrush; no teachers had been hired, and there were twenty-five students. In two years the enrollment was 150 with a faculty of ten professors. He wrote articles for newspapers to create interest in the university and to get support for public funds. He organized a public library with free reading rooms for the use of students and citizens in Reno.

In 1889 he resigned as president of Nevada University because of ill health. He moved to Los Angeles, California, where he improved the Greek and chemistry curricula of the high schools, enabling them to be accredited by the University of California. He was superintendent of schools at Santa Monica (1890–94) and Los Angeles (1894–95) and later at San Luis Obispo, California, and served on the county board of education.

Brown wrote articles on education for the *Ohio Educational Monthly Magazine* and *New England Journal of Education*. He was awarded an honorary degree by Baker University in Baker City, Kansas.

REFERENCES: *NCAB* (24:257); Samuel Bradford Doten, *An Illustrated History of the University of Nevada* (Reno: University of Nevada, 1924); James W. Hulse, *The University of Nevada: A Centennial History* (Reno: University of Nevada Press, 1974). *Joan Duff Kise*

BROWNE, William Hand. B. December 31, 1828, Baltimore, Maryland, to William and Patience (Hand) Browne. M. 1863 to Mary Catherine Owings. Ch. six. D. December 13, 1912, Baltimore County, Maryland.

William Hand Browne was educated in a private school in Baltimore and a local college. He continued his studies at the University of Maryland, receiving the M.D. degree (1850). He did not practice medicine but pursued a business career, joining with a cousin to form the firm of T. J. Hand and Company, which was primarily engaged in trade with Peru from 1851 to 1861.

His literary career began in 1861 when the *South*, a Baltimore newspaper, published his translation of a German story. With A. T. Bledsoe, Browne founded *The Southern Review* and served as its junior editor (1866–68). He was editor and part owner of *The New Eclectic Magazine,* later *The Southern Magazine* (1868–75). He was also editor-in-chief of a short-lived Baltimore weekly paper, *The Statesman* (1868–69). He was librarian of the Johns Hopkins University (1879–81) and professor of English literature until his retirement in 1910.

Browne was the compiler of *The Clarendon Dictionary* (1882), a translator of Jakob von Falker's *Greece and Rome* (1882), and editor of *Selections from the Early Scottish Poets* (1896), a school edition of Oliver Goldsmith's *The Vicar of Wakefield* (1900), and *The Taell of Rauf Coilyerr* (1903). He was the author of *History of Maryland* (with J. Thomas Scharf, 1877) for use as a school text, *English Literature* (with Richard M. Johnston, 1873), *The Life of Alexander H. Stephens* (with Richard M. Johnson, 1878), *Maryland, the History of a Palatinate* (1884), and *George Calvert and Celius Calvert* (1890). He edited thirty-three volumes of *Archives of Maryland* for the Maryland Historical Society (1882-1912). He was editor of *Maryland Historical Magazine* (1906–10).

REFERENCES: *AC; DAB; NCAB* (11:233); *WWW* (I); James W. Bright, "In Memoriam William Hand Browne, 1828–1912," *Johns Hopkins University Circular* 252 (February 1913): 3–28. *Richard J. Cox*

BROWNELL, Herbert. B. February 12, 1862, Madison, New York, to Nathaniel Stoddard and Abby (Barker) Brownell. M. July 15, 1891, to May Miller. Ch. seven, including Samuel Miller Brownell, United States commissioner of education, and Herbert Brownell, Jr., attorney general of the United States. D. September 15, 1936, Lincoln, Nebraska.

Herbert Brownell attended Colgate Academy in Hamilton, New York. He began his teaching career at the age of sixteen in the rural schools of Madison County, New York. While teaching at Little Compton, Rhode Island, and Bouckeville and Deansboro, New York, he engaged in self-study and passed a New York State examination, receiving a diploma from the state department of public instruction (1889). He attended the New York State Teachers' College (later, State University of New York College) at Oswego, graduating in 1890. He stayed at Oswego to study psychology and science.

Brownell was superintendent of schools at Whitesboro, New York (1891–93), and moved to Peru, Nebraska, where he was professor of physical science at the Nebraska State Teachers' College (later, Peru State College) (1893–1910). Brownell gained recognition at Peru for his pioneering efforts to train teachers to use the inductive method in the teaching of science. In 1910 he accepted an appointment as professor of the technique of science in the teachers college of the University of Nebraska. He organized a department of science and served as chairman of the university's department of secondary education (1921–34).

In addition to his effective teaching, Brownell was widely known for his publications, including *Laboratory Lessons in General Science* (1916), *A Text in General Science* (1918), *The Teaching of Science and the Science Teacher* (with Frank Wade, 1925), *A First Course in Physics* (1930), and *Physical Science* (1931). He also published several series of laboratory lessons and contributed articles to professional periodicals.

Brownell was a member of several professional associations. He was awarded an honorary degree by Hamilton College in 1896.

REFERENCES: *LE* (I); *NCAB* (26:402); *WWAE* (VIII); Erwin H. Goldenstein, *The First Fifty Years: The University of Nebraska Teachers College* (Lincoln: University of Nebraska, 1958).   *Erwin H. Goldenstein*

BROWNELL, Thomas Church. B. October 19, 1779, Westport, Massachusetts, to Sylvester and Nancy (Church) Brownell. M. August 1811 to Charlotte Dickinson. Ch. none. D. January 13, 1865, Hartford, Connecticut.

Thomas Church Brownell entered the College of Rhode Island (later, Brown University) in 1800. He left Rhode Island in 1802 to follow Jonathan Maxcy (*q.v.*), who became president of Union College in Schenectady, New York.

Upon graduation from Union College (1804), Brownell was made a tutor in Latin and Greek by the college's new president, Eliphalet Nott (*q.v.*). He was appointed professor of belles lettres and moral philosophy (1806) and professor of chemistry and mineralogy (1808). During 1809 he traveled abroad, spending the year attending lectures and enjoying a walking tour of England.

Returning to the United States in 1810, Brownell resumed his professorship at Union College where he continued for the next eight years. These were years of spiritual growth in which he left the Congregational church to become a member of the Protestant Episcopal church (1813); he was ordained a deacon in 1816. While serving as a professor at Union College, Brownell engaged in missionary activities in the surrounding countryside. In 1818 he left Union, was ordained a priest, and became assistant minister of Trinity Church in New York City, The following year he was consecrated as the third bishop of Connecticut.

To fill a need for trained lay leaders and clergy, Brownell worked with a group of Episcopal clergymen and Hartford, Connecticut, residents to secure legislative approval of a charter for Washington College in 1823 (the name was changed to Trinity College in 1845). The founding of the college, the second in the state, climaxed a thirty-five year struggle by the state's Episcopalians to break the educational monopoly of Congregationalist-controlled Yale. The charter prohibited the imposition of any religious test on students, faculty members, or other members of the college.

When classes began on September 23, 1824, there were nine students and six faculty members; within a few years, the student body had grown to nearly one hundred. Duties of the episcopate competed with the needs of the fledgling college, and in 1831 Brownell resigned as president. Until his death, he continued to provide advice and encouragement to Trinity College. As bishop of Connecticut, Brownell became ex officio chancellor of the college in 1849.

He was the author of a number of books, including *Bible Class and Family Expositor* (1833) and *Commentary on the Book of Common Prayer* (1841), and editor of a five-volume work, *Religion of the Heart and Life* (1839–40). In addition, he prepared commentaries, position papers, and sermons.

In 1852, he became presiding bishop of the American episcopate and held this position until his death in 1865.

REFERENCES: *AC; DAB; NCAB* (3:495); *WWW* (H); Theodore D. Lockwood, *Trinity College: 150 Years of Quality Education* (New York: The Newcomen Society in North America, 1974).   *Gary C. Ensign*

BROWNELL, William Arthur. B. May 19, 1895, Smethport, Pennsylvania, to Fred William and Hattie Adelaide (Foote) Brownell. M. 1924 to Kathryn Kahn. Ch. three. D. May 24, 1977, Walnut Creek, California.

William A. Brownell attended local schools until 1912 when he entered Allegheny College in Meadville, Pennsylvania, from which he was awarded the A.B. degree summa cum laude (1917). He received the A.B. (1923) and Ph.D. (1926) degrees from the University of Chicago and studied at the University of Illinois from 1923 to 1925.

After teaching for four years at Smethport (Pennsylvania) High School, he spent a year in the United States Army. His first collegiate teaching assignment was as instructor of educational psychology at the University of Illinois (1923–25). He also taught at Cornell University in Ithaca, New York (1926–27), University of Michigan (1927–28), George Peabody College for Teachers in Nashville, Tennessee (1928–29), Duke University in Durham, North Carolina (1930–49), and Northwestern University in Evanston, Illinois (1949–50). He finished his career at the University of California at Berkeley, where he served as professor of educational psychology and dean of the school of education (1950–62).

Brownell conducted research in the psychology of learning, primarily with lower-grade schoolchildren in the study of arithmetic. He was the author of many articles in professional journals, chapters in eight yearbooks of educational organizations, and eight research monographs published in the Duke University Research Studies in Education and as bulletins of the college of education, Bureau of Educational Research of the University of Illinois. Brownell conducted investigations comparing systems of mathematics instruction in England and Scotland. He was coauthor of five series of arithmetic textbooks (1938–66). He sought to encourage a change in the teaching of arithmetic from stress on mechanical memorization by drill to the acquisition of meaning.

He was active in many national professional organizations including the American Educational Research Association (president, 1939), the American Psychological Association (president, division of educational psychology, 1947), the National Society for the Study of Education (director, 1942–48), and the American Association for the Advancement of Science (vice-president, 1947). He was the recipient of an honorary degree from Allegheny College.

REFERENCES: *LE* (IV); *WW* (XXXII); *WWAE* (XV); *Education Magazine* 82 (October 1961): 123.   *Phyllis F. Kavett*

BROWNSON, Josephine Van Dyke. B. June 26, 1880, Detroit, Michigan, to Henry Francis and Josephine (Van Dyke) Brownson. M. no. D. November 10, 1942, Grosse Pointe, Michigan.

Josephine Van Dyke Brownson, daughter of Catholic lay leader Henry Francis Brownson, was educated in Sacred Heart convents, the Detroit Normal Training School, and the University of Michigan, where she earned the B.A. degree (1913). She began teaching in the Detroit public schools in 1903.

Although she continued to teach in the schools for twenty-five years, her major work was planning, implementing, and developing catechetical instruction for children, particularly those of the poor and immigrant families who moved to Detroit to work in the expanding automotive industry. She attracted and held students because she saw that their personal, recreational, and social needs, as well as their spiritual ones, were satisfied.

Brownson and others who had joined her formed the Catholic Instruction League in 1916 for the purpose of teaching religion to public school children. Twenty-four years later, in 1940, when the Confraternity of Christian Doctrine assumed responsibility for this work, there were 454 teachers and over 14,000 students in seventy-four schools of religion.

Brownson wrote *Learn of Me*, a graded series for use in religion classes (1918–38), which corresponded to a standard grade level and avoided the question-and-answer catechisms then in wide use. She wrote *Stopping the Leak* (1925), a teachers' manual that suggested a totally new approach for the teaching of religion. She also wrote *Catholic Bible Stories* (1919) and *Living Forever* (1928).

Brownson resigned from the Detroit public schools in 1928 to work full time for the Catholic Instruction League. In 1939 she was named a member of a commission to advise the Venezuelan government on social service work. She received the Pro-Ecclesia et Pontifice decoration from Pius XI (1933) and an honorary degree from the University of Detroit, and she was named a Laetare Medalist by the University of Notre Dame in 1939.

REFERENCES: *CB* (March 1940); *NAW; NYT*, November 11, 1942, p. 25; Monica Weadlock Porter, *Josephine Van Dyke Brownson, Alumna* (New York: Manhattanville College of the Sacred Heart, 1948); Walker Romig, *Josephine Van Dyke Brownson*. (Detroit: The Gabriel Packard Press, 1955); *New Catholic Encyclopedia* (New York: McGraw-Hill, 1967).

Anne E. Scheerer

BRUBACHER, Abram Royer. B. July 27, 1870, Lebanon, Pennsylvania, to Daniel and Catherine (Royer) Brubacher. M. August 24, 1897, to Rosa Haas. Ch. one, John Seiler Brubacher (*q.v.*), educator. D. August 23, 1939, Albany, New York.

Abram Royer Brubacher was educated at Phillips Academy at Andover, Massachusetts, and was graduated with the B.A. (1897) and Ph.D. (1902) degrees from Yale University. From 1899 to 1900, he had been Soldiers' Memorial Fellow at Yale.

Instructor in Greek at Yale (1900–02), he moved to New York as principal of Gloversville (1902–05) and Schenectady (1905–08) high schools and was superintendent of Schenectady schools (1908–15).

In February 1915 he became president of the New York State College for Teachers (later, State University of New York at Albany) in Albany, where he remained to his death in 1939. The college experienced great growth in students, faculty, and physical plant during Brubacher's presidency. He established a graduate department and introduced summer sessions in 1917 and extension courses in 1918.

Brubacher was the author of many books, including *High School English* (with Dorothy Ermina Snyder, two volumes, 1912), *English: Oral and Written* (1912), *Teaching—Profession and Practice* (1927), *High School Composition and Grammar* (with Katherine E. Wheeling, 1930), *Junior English for Everyday Use* (with Clara E. Springsteed, 1934), and *Senior English for Everyday Use* (with Katherine E. Wheeling, 1935). He edited the four-volume *The Spirit of America* (With Jane Louise Jones, 1920). He contributed many articles to professional and popular periodicals.

He was a member of professional associations and was president of the New York State Teachers Association (1913–14) and the New York State Council of Superintendents (1913). He was a trustee of the Albany Academy and the Albany Home for Children (president, 1923–31). He received an honorary degree from Alfred (New York) University.

REFERENCES: *LE* (I); *NCAB* (30:224); *WWAE* (VIII); *WWW* (I); *NYT*, August 24, 1939, p. 19.   *John F. Ohles*

BRUBACHER, John Seiler. B. October 18, 1898, Easthampton, Massachusetts, to Abram Royer (*q.v.*) and Rosa (Haas) Brubacher. M. August 12, 1924, to Winifred Wemple. M. February 10, 1972, to Dorothy Kohler. Ch. two.

John Seiler Brubacher was graduated from Yale University with the B.A. degree (1920) and continued his education at Harvard University, where he received the J.D. degree (1923), and at Columbia University, where he was awarded the Ph.D. degree (1927).

He was professor of the history and philosophy of education at Dartmouth College (1924–25), Columbia University (1925–28), and Yale University (1928–58). From 1958 to 1969 he was professor at the University of Michigan.

Brubacher's publications include *Modern Philosophies of Education* (1939), *History of the Problems of Education* (1946), *Higher Education in Transition* (with Willis Rudy, 1958), *Bases for Policy in Higher Education* (1965), *The Law and Higher Education—A Case Book* (1971), *Courts and Higher Education* (1971), and *Higher Education: Its Identity Crisis* (1972).

Brubacher was visiting professor at the American University of Beirut, Lebanon (1951–52) and Fulbright Fellow at the University of Kyushu, Japan (1957), and he received the Distinguished Service to Education Award from the John Dewey Society in 1973. He was a member of many educational associations, among them the Philosophy of Education Society (president, 1942–46) and the Society of Professors of Education (president, 1962). He was chairman of the committee that prepared the 1955 yearbook of the National Society for the Study of Education, *Modern Philosophies and Education.*

REFERENCES: *CA* (1–4); *LE* (V); *WW* (XXXVIII); *WWAE* (XVI).

Mary J. Tull

BRUCE, William Herschel. B. April 8, 1856, Troup County, Georgia, to Hilery Sanford and Catherine Rebecca (Pruitt) Bruce. M. November 6, 1879, to Lillie Ora Hart. Ch. four. D. December 30, 1943, Opelika, Alabama.

As mathematician, textbook author, and vigorous administrator, William Herschel Bruce labored to standardize and upgrade teacher education in Texas. After teaching in Alabama rural schools he received the A.B. degree (1883) from Alabama Polytechnic Institute (later Auburn University). He received the A.M. degree (1886) from Baylor University at Waco, Texas, and the Ph.D. degree (1890) from Mercer University in Macon, Georgia.

Bruce spent his early career in Texas as superintendent of schools at Blanco (1884–93), Marble Falls (1893–96), and Athens (1896–99). During this period he organized teachers' institutes and wrote geometry books.

Bruce was president of John Tarleton College in Stephenville, Texas (1899–1900). He was professor of mathematics (1901–06) and president of North Texas State Normal College (later, North Texas State University) in Denton (1906–23). He campaigned for the elevation of his own institution and the other state normal schools to a four-year college status.

Bruce's published works include *Some Noteworthy Properties of the Triangle and Its Circles* (1906), *Elements of Plane Geometry* (1910), *Elements of Solid Geometry* (1912), *Principles and Processes of Education* (1916), and a poem *The Charms of Solitude* (1923). He was coauthor with William Seneca Sutton (*q.v.*) of *Arithmetic* (1906), which was widely adopted as a school text in Texas.

Active in professional associations, Bruce was president of the Texas State Teachers Association (1905), a fellow of the Texas Academy of Science, chairman of the Texas State Board of Examiners (1906–10), and vice-president of the American Association of Colleges. He was awarded honorary degrees by Baylor and Trinity (Texas) universities.

REFERENCES: *LE* (I); *WWAE* (I); *WWW* (II); C. M. Mizell, "Dr. W. H. Bruce: His Contribution to Public Education" (Master's thesis, Southern Methodist University, 1926); James L. Rogers, *The Story of North Texas* (Denton: North Texas State University, 1965). *Walter Doyle*

BRUECKNER, Leo John. B. April 21, 1890, Streator, Illinois, to Herman and Leonore (Schneider) Brueckner. M. December 24, 1917, to Agnes Holland. Ch. four. D. July 23, 1967, Los Angeles, California.

Leo Brueckner attended the University of Michigan (1909-11) and the University of Iowa, where he received the B.A. (1913), M.A. (1915), and Ph.D. (1919) degrees. His first interest (and doctoral dissertation) was in the area of diagnosing reading difficulties, but he later became interested in instruction in arithmetic.

Brueckner was superintendent of schools in Lowden, Iowa (1913–14). On the faculty of the Detroit Teachers College (1916–17 and 1919–20), he served as an assistant dean (1919–22). During World War I, he was a captain in the army (1917–19). He was a professor of education at the University of Minnesota from 1922 until his retirement in 1955.

He was the author of many books, including *Triangle Arithmetic* (with others, 1928), *Diagnostic Tests and Practice Exercises in Arithmetic* (with C. J. Anderson, 1928), *Diagnosis and Remedial Teaching in Arithmetic* (1930), *New Curriculum Arithmetic* (with others, 1935), *The Changing Elementary School* (with others, 1939), *Supervision* (with A. S. Barr, *q.v.* and William H. Burton, *q.v.*, 1938), *How to Make Arithmetic Meaningful* (with Foster E. Grossnickle, 1947), *The Diagnosis and Treatment of Learning Difficulties* (with Guy L. Bond, 1955), *Improving the Arithmetic Program* (1957), *Developing Mathematical Understandings in the Upper Grades* (with others, 1959), *Discovering Meanings in Arithmetic* (with Foster E. Grossnickle, 1959), and *Moving Ahead in Arithmetic* (1963).

While in Minnesota Brueckner advocated the reorganization of the state's curriculum to make it more meaningful to pupils.

Brueckner was a member of several professional associations. He served as an educational consultant to the Office of Military Government in Germany in Berlin (1947–48) and Bavaria (1949).

REFERENCES: *LE* (III); *WWAE* (XXII); *WWW* (IV); *NYT*, July 25, 1967, p. 32.   *Robert McGinty*

BRUMBAUGH, Martin Grove. B. April 14, 1862, Huntingdon County, Pennsylvania, to George B. and Martha (Peightal) Brumbaugh. M. July 30, 1884, to Anna Konigmacher. M. January 29, 1916, to Flora Belle Parks. Ch. two. D. March 14, 1930, Pinehurst, North Carolina.

Martin Grove Brumbaugh combined political office with a distinguished career in education. He received the B.E. degree (1881) from Juniata College in Huntingdon, Pennsylvania, and the M.E. (1883), B.S. (1885), M.S. (1887), and Ph.D. (1895) degrees from the University of Pennsylvania.

He served as superintendent of schools of his native Huntingdon County (1884–90), chairman and first professor of pedagogy at the University of Pennsylvania (1894–1900), president of Juniata College (1895–1906, 1924–30), first commissioner of education in Puerto Rico (1900–02), and Philadelphia superintendent of schools (1906–15). He was conductor of teachers' institutes for the state of Louisiana (1886–91).

In 1900 Brumbaugh was granted a leave from the University of Pennsylvania to be commissioner of education for Puerto Rico. He felt that his task was to democratize and Christianize the people of the island. Brumbaugh organized a public school system, imposing practices found on the continent upon the island commonwealth. He sought to create a functional educational system, in which both teachers and students were bilingual. He established a normal school and a free public library.

As superintendent of schools in Philadelphia, Brumbaugh undertook a building program for the elementary schools. The basic education curriculum was modernized, classes were established for the exceptional child and for the undernourished, evening courses were provided for adults, and industrial and vocational instruction was expanded in the schools. A vocational school for girls and a training school for teachers were established. Brumbaugh was active on citizens' committees that helped to reform Pennsylvania's educational laws.

Largely because of the recognition gained from his accomplishments in Philadelphia, Brumbaugh was elected governor of Pennsylvania on the Republican ticket in 1914. During his tenure (1915–19) he supported humanitarian legislation, considering the greatest achievement of his term the passage of a child labor law in 1915. He was an unsuccessful candidate for nomination for President of the United States for the Republican party in 1916.

Brumbaugh was active in professional activities and the author of *Juniata Bible Lectures* (1897), *Geography of Pennsylvania* (1898), *History of the German Baptist Brethren* (1899), *Standard Readers* (five volumes, 1899–1902), *The Making of a Teacher* (1905), *Life and Works of Christopher Dock* (1908), *Story of Roosevelt* (1922), and, with J. S. Walton, *Stories of Pennsylvania* (1897) and *Liberty Bell Leaflets* (1898–1900). He was editor of the Lippincott educational series of schoolbooks. Brumbaugh was the recipient of several honorary degrees.

REFERENCES: *NCAB* (15:409); *WWW* (I); V. A. Clampa, "Martin Grove Brumbaugh, Pioneering Superintendent of the Philadelphia Public Schools," *Pennsylvania History* 7 (January 1940): 31–41; Salvatore Michael Messina, "Martin Grove Brumbaugh, Educator" (Ph.D. diss., University of Pennsylvania, 1965); *NYT;* March 15, 1930, p. 19.

Robert L. Leight

BRYAN, Anna E. B. July 1858, Louisville, Kentucky, to Parish G. and Eliza H. Belle (Richard) Bryan. M. no. D. February 21, 1901, Chicago, Illinois.

Anna Bryan was born and raised in Kentucky and was graduated from the Louisville Girls High School. On a visit to Chicago, she heard about the Chicago Free Kindergarten Association's training school and enrolled in the program, completing the course (1884) with honors. She was a teacher in the Marie Chapel Charity Kindergarten (1884) and served as its director (1885–87).

In 1887 she returned to Louisville as director of the newly formed Free Kindergarten Association training school for kindergarten teachers. Critical of methods based on the principles outlined by Friedrich Froebel, Bryan sought to evolve alternative procedures. The training school opened in the kindergarten of Steve Holcomb's Mission in Louisville. Under Bryan, the Louisville program expanded from one to eight kindergartens, and the training classes increased in enrollment from five to fifty students.

She presented a paper at the 1890 National Educational Association meeting that indicated a break with Froebelian tradition and attracted visitors and students from all over the country to observe and study at the Louisville school. With the encouragement of Francis Parker (*q.v.*), head of the Cook County Normal School in Chicago, and William Hailmann (*q.v.*) Bryan wrote a series of articles for *Kindergarten Magazine* (1890–93).

She returned to Chicago in 1894 as principal of the kindergarten department at Armour Institute, where she remained to her death in 1901. Ill health had previously required temporary retirements from her post.

Bryan was consulted by John Dewey (*q.v.*) who sought her advice in establishing a kindergarten section at his University of Chicago experimental school. As chairman of the child study committee of the International Kindergarten Union (1897–1901) and a member of the committee on teacher training, she was able to publicize her theories, relating them to the child development research of G. Stanley Hall (*q.v.*).

REFERENCES: *NAW; Pioneers of the Kindergarten in America* (New York: The Century Co., 1924); Agnes Snyder, *Dauntless Women in Childhood Education, 1856–1931* (Washington, D.C.: Association for Childhood Education International, 1972).   *Elizabeth S. Oelrich*

BRYAN, Enoch Albert. B. May 10, 1855, Bloomington, Indiana, to John and Eliza Jane (Philips) Bryan. M. May 1881 to Hattie E. Williams. Ch. three. D. November 6, 1941, Pullman, Washington.

Enoch Albert Bryan attended Indiana University, earning the B.A. (1878) and M.A. (1885) degrees. He received the A.M. degree (1893) in classical studies from Harvard University.

While working on his bachelor's degree, he taught in a public school in southern Indiana for three years and continued to work the family farm. Upon graduation, he assumed the position of superintendent of schools in Grangeville, Illinois (1878–82). He left Illinois in 1882 for Vincennes (Indiana) University where he served as president (1882–93). Bryan became president of Washington Agricultural College and School of Sciences (later, Washington State University) and director of the Agricultural Experimental Station at Pullman in 1893. He took over a school that had been in existence less than two years but was rocked with scandal and whose board of regents had been dismissed; a legislative investigation was underway, and there was a move to establish a new institution in another location in the state. Bryan reorganized the college and developed it into a stable and respected institution.

He worked to upgrade the college by instituting strict admission standards, rewriting the curriculum to include courses to meet students' cultural needs, and building public support of the institution. The Agricultural Research Station became an asset to the agricultural industry. Washington State College was one of the the first in the nation to make agricultural courses academically respectable.

After retiring in 1916, Bryan became state commissioner of education for Idaho until 1923. Returning to Washington State College, he accepted the position of research professor in economics, a post he held until his death in 1941.

He was the author of *The Mark in Europe and America* (1893), *Historical Sketch of the State College of Washington* (1928), and *Occident Meets Orient* (1936). He was president of the Association of Land Grand Colleges and Universities (1915). He held honorary doctorates from several American colleges and universities. He was a brother of William Lowe Bryan (*q.v.*).

REFERENCES: *LE* (I); *NCAB* (35:233); *WWAE* (I); *WWW* (II); *Bellingham Evening Journal*, November 6, 1941; *NYT*, November 7, 1941, p. 23; *Pullman Herald*, February 28, 1930; *Rosalia* (Washington) *Citizen Journal*, November 14, 1941.   *Michael A. Balasa*

BRYAN, William Lowe. B. November 11, 1860, Bloomington, Indiana, to John and Eliza Jane (Philips) Bryan. M. July 13, 1889, to Charlotte A. Lowe. Ch. none. D. November 21, 1955, Indianapolis, Indiana.

William Lowe Bryan began his higher education at Indiana University, receiving the A.B. (1884) and A.M. (1886) degrees. He later studied in Europe at Berlin (Germany) University (1886–87) and Paris, France, and Würzburg, Germany (1900–01). He received the Ph.D. degree (1892) from Clark University in Worcester, Massachusetts.

Bryan was a professor of Greek and psychology at Indiana University (1884–1902). He received recognition for his research on the development of voluntary motor ability and the physiology and psychology of learning.

Bryan was vice-president at Indiana (1893–1902), became president in 1902, and served until 1937.

Bryan authored many noted works, including *Plato the Teacher* (1897), *The Republic of Plato* (with his wife, 1898), *The Spirit of Indiana* (1917), *Paradise* (1927), *The President's Column* (1934), *Farewells* (1938), *Wars of*

Families of Minds (1940), and *The Psychology of Learning a Life Occupation* (with Ernest Hiram Lindley, *q.v.*, and Noble Harter, 1941).

Bryan was active in professional organizations, including the Carnegie Foundation for the Advancement of Science (trustee) and the American Psychological Association (president, 1903). He was the recipient of many honorary degrees. He was a brother of Enoch Albert Bryan (*q.v.*).

REFERENCES: *LE* (I); *NCAB* (13:464): *WWW* (III); Burton D. Myers, *Trustees and Officers of Indiana University 1820 to 1950* (Bloomington: Indiana University, 1950); *NYT*, November 22, 1955, p. 35.

Robert L. Doan

BRYANT, John Collins. B. December 21, 1821, Ebley, Gloucestershire, England, to John and Pormela (Collins) Bryant. M. May 21, 1851, to Hannah M. Clarke. Ch. three. D. November 6, 1901, Buffalo, New York.

John Collins Bryant came to the United States from England with his family in 1829 and settled in Ohio. He attended the public schools and Norwalk (Ohio) Academy. He was graduated from the Cleveland (Ohio) Medical College with the M.D. degree (1846) and practiced medicine in Amherst, Ohio.

In 1853 Henry D. Stratton, a brother-in-law of Bryant, had established a successful business school in Cleveland and a second school in Buffalo, New York, in 1854. Bryant went to Buffalo in 1856, joining his brother Henry B. Bryant and Stratton in conducting the school. Bryant was president of the Buffalo Bryant and Stratton Business College from 1860 to his death in 1901 and participated in the establishment and management of the additional forty-three Bryant and Stratton colleges established in cities throughout the United States and Canada. When his brother died, he sold his interest in all schools, except the one in Buffalo.

Bryant was the author of *Bryant's New Counting-House Bookkeeping* (1880), *Business Forms* (1880), and *Commercial Law* (1880).

REFERENCES: *NCAB* (18:395).   *John F. Ohles*

BRYANT, Joseph Decatur. B. March 12, 1845, East Troy, Wisconsin, to Alonzo Ambrose and Harriet (Adkins) Bryant. M. September 29, 1874, to Annette Amelia Crum. Ch. one. D. April 7, 1914, New York, New York.

Joseph Bryant, American surgeon and medical educator, was brought up on a farm and attended elementary school in his home town. He attended the Norwich (New York) Academy and later studied medicine under Dr. George Avery. He received the M.D. degree (1868) from Bellevue Hospital Medical College in New York City and was a surgical intern at Bellevue Hospital (1869–71).

He served on the faculty of Bellevue Hospital Medical College (1871–1914), first as a professor of anatomy and clinical surgery and later as professor of the principles and practices of surgery. Bryant served as a sanitary inspector for New York City Health Department (1873–79). He was commissioner of both the New York City Health Department and the New York State Board of Health from 1879 to 1893. He served as a surgeon with the New York State National Guard (1873–94).

Bryant became a personal friend and private physician of Grover Cleveland. During Cleveland's presidency, Bryant performed an operation for a malignant growth on Cleveland that was kept secret until after the death of both men. He worked for the eradication of pulmonary tuberculosis, campaigned against overcrowded housing conditions in New York City, and assumed leadership when New York City was threatened with a cholera epidemic in 1892.

Bryant was the author of many medical monographs, including the two-volume *Manual of Operative Surgery* (1884), and coeditor of the eight-volume *American System of Surgery* (with Albert H. Buck, 1906–11).

He was president of the American Medical Association (1907–08), the New York State Medical Association (1899), and the New York Academy of Medicine (1895–97). He was a fellow of the American Surgical Association and Physicians' Aid Society. He received an honorary degree from New York University in 1906.

REFERENCES: *DAB: NCAB* (23:31); *WWW* (I); *NYT,* April 8, 1914, p. 13.   *Richard M. Coger*

BRYANT, Ralph Clement. B. January 22, 1877, Princeton, Illinois, to Arthur and Elizabeth Browning (Hughes) Bryant. M. June 1, 1904, to Alice Joiner. Ch. two. D. February 1, 1939, New Haven, Connecticut.

Ralph Clement Bryant, noted forester, came from a family of poets and foresters. His formal training as a forester started at the University of Illinois (1896–97). He transferred to the newly created School of Forestry at Cornell University in Ithaca, New York, and received the F. Eng. degree in 1900.

Upon graduation from the School of Forestry, he worked for the state of New York in the Forest, Fish and Game Commission for one year. In 1901 he entered the service of the Bureau of Forestry of the Philippine Islands and within two years was promoted to assistant chief. He participated in the pioneer work of organizing and administering public forests in the Philippine Islands and introduced American methods of logging and manufacturing heavy hardwood timber.

In 1905 he returned to the mainland and for a year was an inspector in the United States Forest Service. From 1906 he was an instructor of logging and lumbering and by 1911 professor of lumbering at the School of Forestry at Yale University. At Yale he recognized the importance of field studies in forestry and developed a practical course in which students were trained in lumbering techniques in various field sites throughout the South.

He was president of the Society of American Foresters (1920–21) and chairman of the forestry advisory board of Middlebury College, which awarded him an Sc.D. degree in 1928. In 1911 Yale University conferred an honorary M.A. degree on him. He was a fellow of the American Association for the Advancement of Science and a member of professional associations.

Bryant wrote two books, *Logging* (1913) and *Lumber* (1922), which were long-time standards in the field of forestry.

REFERENCES: *DAB* (supp. 2); *NCAB* (28:191); *WWW* (I); *NYT,* February 3, 1939, p. 15.   *Harold J. McKenna*

BRYSON, Lyman Lloyd. B. July 12, 1888, Valentine, Nebraska, to George E. and Nancy M. (Hayes) Bryson. M. October 4, 1912, to Hope Mersereau. M. May 11, 1945, to Katherine McGrattan. Ch. one. D. November 24, 1959, New York, New York.

Lyman Lloyd Bryson was educated in the public schools of Omaha, Nebraska, and received the A.B. (1910) and M.A. (1915) degrees from the University of Michigan. He studied law at Georgetown and Columbia universities.

Bryson worked as a newspaperman in Omaha and Detroit, Michigan, a Red Cross official (1918–24), a college instructor, and an adult education expert. He was associate director and director of the San Diego Museum of Anthropology and Archaeology (1927–30). He served on the faculties of the University of Michigan (1913–17), University of California at Los Angeles (1925–32), the School of American Research in Albuquerque, New Mexico, (1931), and as adult education forum leader in the Des Moines (Iowa) public school system (1932–34). In 1935 he became professor of education at Teachers College, Columbia University, and remained there until retirement in 1953.

One of his major activities at Columbia was the establishment of the readability laboratory. The purpose of the laboratory was to rewrite books in a simple vocabulary for people with a limited education. He became associated with the Columbia Broadcasting System in 1938 as moderator or director of a number of programs including "Invitation to Learn," "United Nations Casebook," and "Lamp Unto My Feet."

Bryson served as a civilian adviser to the United States military in World Wars I and II and became adviser to the United Nations Educational, Scientific and Cultural Organization in 1947.

He won the Nelson C. Field Poetry Prize as an undergraduate at the University of Michigan. Among his extensive writings were *The Grasshopper* (prize play, 1917), and many books, including *Adult Education*

(1936), *Which Way America?* (1939), *The New Prometheus* (1941), *Communications of Ideas* (1948), and *The Drive Toward Reason* (1954). He was editor of The Peoples' Library.

A member of many organizations, Bryson served as president of the American Association for Adult Education (1944) and the Institute for Intercultural Studies and was honorary president of the Conference on Science, Philosophy, and Religion. He was the recipient of several honorary degrees.

REFERENCES: *CB* (September 1951 and February 1960); *LE* (III); *NCAB* (45:246); *WWAE* (XV); *WWW* (III); *NYT,* November 26, 1959, p. 37.

S. S. Britt, Jr.

BUCKHAM, Matthew Henry. B. July 4, 1832, Hinckley, Leicestershire, England, to James and Margaret (Barnsby) Buckham. M. December 27, 1857, to Elizabeth Wright. M. September 2, 1897, to Martha Goddard Tyler. Ch. six. D. November 29, 1910, Burlington, Vermont.

Matthew Henry Buckham moved to the United States with his family in 1834, settling in Vermont, where his father served as pastor of Congregational churches. Buckham attended the University of Vermont, graduating with the A.B. (1851) and A.M. (1854) degrees. He traveled and studied in Europe (1854–56), attending University College in London, England (1854–55).

Buckham was principal of the Lenox (Massachusetts) Academy (1852–53) and a tutor (1853–54) and professor of English literature (1856), Greek language and literature (1857–63), and rhetoric (1863–71) at the University of Vermont. He was elected president in 1871, serving to his death in 1910.

During his presidency, the student body of the University of Vermont increased four times, the faculty tripled in size, and the endowment funds were doubled. Many new buildings were constructed, and departments of electrical engineering and sanitary science were organized.

Buckham wrote many educational papers that were compiled with addresses and sermons and published as *The Very Elect* in 1912. He was a member of the Vermont Board of Education (1867–74) and a school commissioner in Burlington, Vermont (1869–80). He was awarded several honorary degrees.

REFERENCES: *NCAB* (2:42); *WWW* (I). *John F. Ohles*

BULKLEY, John Williams. B. November 3, 1802, Fairfield, Connecticut, to n.a. M. no. D. June 19, 1888, Brooklyn, New York.

John Williams Bulkley prepared for college and the ministry against his father's plans that he become an artisan. A temporary breakdown in health diverted him to teaching, and he remained an active teacher and administrator from the age of twenty-three until he retired at the age of eighty-three. He taught school in Fairfield, Connecticut (1825–31), and was a teacher and principal at schools in Troy (1831–38) and Albany (1838–50), New York.

He became the first superintendent of schools (1850–73) for the newly formed municipality of Brooklyn, New York, which was a merger of Williamsburg, Bushwick, and Brooklyn. His annual reports promoted improvements, such as Pestallozian object teaching and teacher training. While superintendent, he was principal of the Saturday Normal School, which he had helped organize. He was made assistant superintendent because of his advanced age and continued in that post until 1885.

Bulkley was a pioneer in the organization of professional educational associations. As early as the 1830s, he was an organizer of the Troy (New York) Teacher's Society. In 1845 he was one of the founders and first president (and again in 1851) of the New York State Teachers' Association, the first state organization for teachers. He was chairman of the board of editors of the first state educational journal. He was one of the founders of the National Teachers' Association (later, National Education Association) in 1857, serving as its first secretary and fourth president (1860).

REFERENCES: *DAB; NCAB* (13:520); *WWW* (H).

Joseph C. Bronars, Jr.

BUNNELL, Charles Ernest. B. January 12, 1878, Dimock, Pennsylvania, to Lyman Walton and Ruth Naomi (Tingley) Bunnell. M. July 24, 1901, to Mary Ann Kline. Ch. one. D. November 1, 1956, Burlingame, California.

Charles Ernest Bunnell excelled at his studies and learned to read at an early age using the Bible, *the Farmers' Almanac,* and the *Youths' Companion* as texts. At the age of twelve he passed an examination for the certification of teachers in Pennsylvania's rural schools. After graduating from Montrose (Pennsylvania) High School he spent two years at Keystone Academy to improve his Latin and Greek. Bunnell entered Bucknell University in Lewisburg, Pennsylvania, graduating summa cum laude with the B.A. degree (1900) with supplementary honors courses in Greek. He received the A.M. degree (1902) from Bucknell.

In the fall of 1900 Bunnell signed for a job in Alaska teaching forty-eight children of mixed blood at Woody Island in the Aleutian chain. He went home to Pennsylvania in the summer of 1901 to marry his college sweetheart, Mary Ann Kline, and returned with her to Alaska; both of them taught school in Kodiak.

After teaching four years in Valdez, he passed the Alaska bar examination in 1908. In 1915 President Woodrow Wilson (*q.v.*) appointed Bunnell judge of the district court in Fairbanks, where he served six years. He was an unsuccessful candidate for Alaska delegate to the United States Congress in 1914.

In 1921 Bunnell was asked to be the first president of the proposed Alaska Agricultural College and School of Mines (renamed University of Alaska in 1935). The college started with four courses (agriculture, general science, home economics, and mining) in the fall of 1922 with one building, six faculty members, and six students. Bunnell helped many students find jobs so they would be able to attend college. The school grew steadily with the exception of the war years. Bunnell retired in 1948 and became president emeritus.

REFERENCES: *LE* (III); *WWAE* (XI); *WWW* (III); William R. Cashen, *Farthest North College President* (Fairbanks: University of Alaska Press, 1972); *NYT,* November 3, 1956, p. 23.   *Marjorie Tillotson*

BURCHENAL, Elizabeth. B. 1877, Richmond, Indiana, to Charles Henry and Mary E. (Day) Burchenal. M. no. D. November 21, 1959, Brooklyn, New York.

Elizabeth Burchenal's interest in folk art began in the home of her parents where her mother was a musician, and her father, a judge, was especially concerned with folklore.

Burchenal was graduated from Earlham College in Richmond, Indiana, with the A.B. in English and Sargent Normal School of Cambridge, Massachusetts, in 1898. She attended the Gilbert Normal School of Dancing and became convinced that dance should be an important part of the physical education curriculum.

Burchenal taught at Teachers College, Columbia University (1902–05), where she began her pioneer research on folk dances of Canada, Europe, and the United States. From 1904 she traveled around the world gathering folk arts at their sources. Many folk dances she collected were published in fifteen books and numerous articles that were recognized as basic authoritative sources for folk dance and folk music in the English language.

Burchenal was executive secretary of the New York City Girl's Branch, Public Schools Athletic League (1905–16), where she was credited with the development of folk dance in American education and became known as America's foremost folk-dance authority. She was associated with the New York City Department of Education (1909–16). She was organizer of the American Folk Dance Society (1916), which was later expanded into the Folk Arts Center.

Burchenal was the author of *Athletics for Girls* (with Mrs. Frank M. Roessing, 1909) and *Folk Dancing as a Popular Recreation* (1919) and compiler and editor of dance and song books, including *Folk Dances of Finland* (1915), *American Country Dances* (1918), *Folk Dances of Old Homelands* (1922), *Rinnce na Eirann: National Dances of Ireland* (1924), *Dances of the People* (1934), *Folk Dances of Germany* (1938), *American Country Dance Music* (1941), and *Folk Dances of the U.S.* (1950).

She was a delegate to the first International Congress of Folk Arts convened by the League of Nations in Prague, Czechoslovakia (1928), and the second congress in Belgium (1930), and she was United States chairman of the International Commission on Folk Arts and Folklore. She was a fellow of the American Association for Health, Physical Education and Recreation, a charter member and fellow of the American Academy of Physical Education, and a member of the American Folk Lore Society (council member), the National Institute for the Social Sciences, and various foreign folk societies. She received the Luther Gulick Medal in 1950 and was awarded an honorary degree by Boston University in 1943.

REFERENCES: *WW* (XXVIII); Anatole Chujoy, *Dance Encyclopedia* (New York: A. S. Barnes and Co., 1949); Ellen W. Gerber, *Innovators and Institutions in Physical Education* (Philadelphia: Lea and Febiger, 1971); Doris Hering, ed., *Twenty-five Years of American Dance* (New York: Dance Magazine, 1954); Christine Leahy, "In Memoriam," *Journal of Health, Physical Education* 31 (May–June 1960: 43); *NYT,* November 22, 1959, p. 86.   *Adelaide M. Cole*

BURGESS, John William. B. August 26, 1844, Giles County, Tennessee, to Thomas T. and Mary J. (Edwards) Burgess. M. August 24, 1869, to Augusta Thayer Jones. M. September 2, 1885, to Ruth Payne Jewett. Ch. one. D. January 13, 1931, Brookline, Massachusetts.

John William Burgess attended Cumberland University near Nashville, Tennessee (1859–62). He received the A.B. degree (1867) from Amherst (Massachusetts) College. He studied law in Springfield, Massachusetts, and was admitted to the bar in 1869. He studied in Germany at the universities of Berlin, Leipzig, and Göttingen (1871–73).

Burgess taught English literature and political economy at Knox College in Galesburg, Illinois (1869–71), and was a professor at Amherst College (1873–76). He left Amherst in 1876 to teach constitutional law and political science at the law school of Columbia College (later, University). In 1880 he organized the first department of political science in the United States and became dean in 1890. He was appointed graduate dean at Columbia (1890–1912). He promoted the development of programs for independent research, the education of teachers, and the preparation of students for public service positions. He retired in 1912.

Burgess was the author of *The American University* (1884), *Political Science and Comparative Law* (two volumes, 1890–91), *The Civil War and the Constitution, 1859–65* (two volumes, 1901), *Reconstruction and the Constitution, 1866–76* (1902), *The European War of 1914* (1915), *The Reconciliation of Government with Liberty* (1915), *America's Relations to the Great War* (1916), *Recent Changes in American Constitutional Theory* (1923), and *Reminiscences of an American Scholar* (1934). He founded the

Political Science Quarterly (1886), which was the first journal of its type in the United States, and also initiated *Studies in History, Economics, and Public Law* (1892).

Burgess was the first Theodore Roosevelt Professor of American History and Institutions lecturing in German universities under a program to provide closer academic relations with Germany (1906–07). He received honorary degrees from American and German universities.

REFERENCES: *DAB* (supp. 1); *NCAB* (23:39); *WWW* (I); *NYT,* January 14, 1931, p. 23; R. Gordon Hoxie, "John W. Burgess, American Scholar" (Ph.D. diss., Columbia University, 1951).

C. Kenneth Murray

BURGESS, Theodore Chalon. B. April 27, 1859, Little Valley, New York, to Chalon and Emma (Johnston) Burgess. M. August 17, 1887, to Laura May Briggs. Ch. one. D. February 26, 1925, Peoria, Illinois.

Theodore Chalon Burgess was graduated from the Fredonia (New York) State Normal School (later, State University of New York College) in 1879 and received the A.B. (1883) and A.M. (1886) degrees from Hamilton College in Clinton, New York, and the Ph.D. degree (1898) from the University of Chicago.

He was head of the classical department at the Fredonia State Normal School (1883–96) and spent the rest of his career at Bradley Polytechnic Institute (later, Bradley University) in Peoria, Illinois. He joined the institution on its founding as head of the department of ancient languages (1897–1925) and was dean (1899–1903), acting director (1903–04), and director and president (1904–25). The institution flourished under Burgess and granted its first baccalaureate degree in 1920. He extended both the academic and vocational curricula.

Burgess was the author of *Epideictic Literature* (1902) and *Elementary Greek* (1907). He was active in professional associations, serving as secretary and president of the Classical Association of the Middle West and South and of the Schoolmaster Club. He received an honorary degree from Hamilton College.

REFERENCES: *NCAB* (20:170); *WWW* (I).   *John F. Ohles*

BURK, Frederic Lister. B. September 1, 1862, Blenheim, Ontario, Canada, to Erastus and Matilda (Turner) Burk. M. September 30, 1898, to Carolyn Frear. Ch. none. D. June 12, 1924, Kentfield, California.

Frederic Lister Burk moved with his family from his native Canada to El Dorado County, California, in 1869. After graduating from Sacramento, (California) High School, he earned the B.L. degree (1883) from the University of California and was among the first to receive the M.A. degree (1892) from Stanford (California) University. He studied at Clark University in Worcester, Massachusetts, where he received the Ph.D. degree (1898).

Burk wrote feature articles for various San Francisco publications (1883–89). Journalism led Burk to an interest in psychology and his studies with G. Stanley Hall (*q.v.*) at Clark University. He taught in several public and private schools in California (1889–91). He was superintendent of Santa Rosa (California) schools and was the first president of the State Normal School (later, San Francisco State University) at San Francisco in 1899. He held the position until his death in 1924.

Although criticized by William T. Harris (*q.v.*) and Francis Parker (*q.v.*), Burk developed a self-drill and self-correction program of instruction. He produced self-instructive bulletins in elementary subjects that brought him recognition as a progressive educator who protested against lockstep schooling. Among his followers who developed laboratory plans and implemented his individualized system during the 1920s and 1930s were Helen Parkhurst (*q.v.*) in Dalton, Massachusetts, and Carleton W. Washburne (*q.v.*) in Winnetka, Illinois.

Burk wrote *A Study of the Kindergarten Problems* (with Carolyn Frear Burk, 1899), *Lockstep Schooling* (1913), *Every Child a Minor* (1915), courses of study with others, and articles in professional journals. As normal school president, Burk was a member of the California State Board of Education (1899–1912).

REFERENCES: *DAB; WWW* (I); Lawrence Cremin, *The Transformation of the School: Progressivism in American Education, 1876–1957* (New York: Vintage Press, 1961); *Harvard Studies in Education* (Cambridge: Harvard University Press, 1928), vol. 2.   *Alda A. Harper*

BURNHAM, William Henry. B. December 3, 1855, Dunbarton, New Hampshire, to Samuel and Hannah (Dane) Burnham. M. no. D. June 25, 1941, Dunbarton, New Hampshire.

William Henry Burnham, father of the school mental hygiene movement, attended Harvard University, where he received the A.B. degree (1882). He earned the Ph.D. degree from Johns Hopkins University (1888).

Burnham was an instructor at Wittenberg College (later, University) in Springfield, Ohio (1882–83), the State Normal School (later, State University of New York College) in Potsdam, New York (1883–85), and Johns Hopkins University in Baltimore, Maryland (1888–89). He joined the faculty at Clark University in Worcester, Massachusetts, as a docent in 1890 and continued there, serving as professor of pedagogy and school hygiene from 1906 to 1926.

Burnham was the author of *The Normal Mind* (1924) and *Great Teachers and Mental Health* (1926). He was an assistant editor of *Paedagogical Seminary,* departmental editor for hygiene of the *Cyclo-*

pedia of Education, and wrote articles on school hygiene for the *Universal Cyclopedia.* He was active in professional associations, as a fellow of the American Association for the Advancement of Science and a member of the permanent committee of the International Congress for School Hygiene (honorary president of group B of the 1st International Congress), the council of the American School Hygiene Association, and other organizations. He was an original member (1894) of the department of child study (merged with the department of physical and health education, 1924) of the National Educational Association.

REFERENCES: *LE* (I); *WWW* (I); *NYT,* June 26, 1941, p. 23.

John F. Ohles

BURNS, James Aloysius. B. February 13, 1867, Michigan City, Indiana, to Patrick and Bridget (Connolly) Burns. M. no. D. September 9, 1940, Notre Dame, Indiana.

Considered the first major American Catholic educational historian, James A. Burns began his studies at Notre Dame (Indiana) University at the age of sixteen in 1883, entered the congregation of the Holy Cross (1888), and was ordained to the priesthood (1893). Burns was awarded the A.B. (1888) and A.M. (1894) degrees at Notre Dame.

Burns first taught and engaged in theological study at Watertown, Wisconsin (1889–91). He was a teacher of chemistry at the University of Notre Dame from 1893. He was religious superior at Notre Dame (1898–1901) and was made superior of Holy Cross College in Washington, D.C., which served as the house of studies for his order. He upgraded the preparation of the faculty and set an example, receiving the Ph.D. degree (1906) from Catholic University of America in Washington.

In 1919 Burns was named president of Notre Dame and served until 1922, when he assumed the full-time task of managing the program of expansion and the drive for endowment support. He reorganized the university into four colleges, raised faculty salaries, initiated a successful fund-raising effort, and closed the preparatory division. He returned to Holy Cross in 1926, and was named provincial of the Indiana Province (1927) and first-assistant superior general of the congregation (1938).

Burns was the author of significant studies of Catholic education in the United States, including *Principles, Origin and Establishment of the Catholic School System* (1908), *Growth and Development of the Catholic School System* (1912), and *Catholic Education—a Study of Conditions* (1917).

Burns was instrumental in founding the National Catholic Education Association in 1904 and was its first vice-president.

REFERENCES: *CB* (October 1940); *LE* (I); *NCAB* (38:325); *WWW* (I); *New Catholic Encyclopedia* (New York: McGraw-Hill, 1967); *NYT,* September 10, 1940, p. 23.

James M. Vosper

BURNZ, Eliza Boardman. B. October 31, 1823, Rayne, England, to n.a. M. twice n.a. Ch. four. D. June 20, 1903, Walters Park, Pennsylvania.

Eliza Burnz (sometimes spelled Burns), the Mother of Women Stenographers, was instrumental in the promotion of Pitman shorthand in the United States.

She came to the United States from England with her parents in 1837. She started teaching in Salem, Massachusetts, at the age of fifteen and later taught in Tennessee, Mississippi, and Alabama, and in the Cincinnati, Ohio, public schools.

Burnz was first acquainted with Pitman shorthand in 1846 and developed an interest in promoting phonography (shorthand) and simplified spelling. She sought to teach freedmen in Nashville, Tennessee, to read using books printed with a phonetic alphabet. She returned to New York City in 1869 and created the Burnz system of shorthand. She taught shorthand at the Mercantile Library (1869–72), free classes (at her suggestion) at the Cooper Institute (1872–89), and daily classes at the Young Women's Christian Association, and at the Burnz School of Shorthand.

Burnz was a writer of books, including *Childhood Hours* (1850), *Reading Lessons in Steno-Phonography* (1870), *First Lessons in Steno-Phonography* (1872), *Burnz' Phonic Shorthand* (1873), *How to Write Shorthand* (1878), *The Liberal Hymn Book* (1880), *Help for Young Reporters* (1881), and *Pure Phonics for Home and Kindergarten* (1903). In 1892 she published *Step by Step Primer,* which advocated a systematic spelling reform. She was editor of the *American Journal of Phonography.*

Burnz was a member of the New York State Stenographers' Association and its first librarian. She was one of the organizers of the Spelling Reform Association in Philadelphia (1876) and served as vice-president for several years. She organized the League for Short Spelling and served as its secretary.

REFERENCES: *NCAB* (6:46); *WC; NYT,* June 23, 1903, p. 7.

Elizabeth S. Oelrich

BURROWES, Thomas Henry. B. November 16, 1805, Strasburg, Pennsylvania, to Thomas and Anne (Smith) Burrowes. M. April 6, 1837, to Salome Carpenter. Ch. fifteen. D. February 25, 1871, State College, Pennsylvania.

Thomas Burrowes resided twice in Ireland and once in Canada before returning to his native Lancaster County, Pennsylvania. He read law with Amos Ellmaker (1826), studied at Yale Law School, and was admitted to the Lancaster County bar (1829).

Burrowes entered politics and was elected to the Pennsylvania state legislature in 1831. He was appointed secretary of the commonwealth and superintendent of common schools when his party won the gubernatorial election of 1835. Previously opposed to school legislation, as superintendent he played a leading role in the establishment of public education in Pennsylvania. He supported agricultural education, manual training, and coeducation.

When his party was removed from control of the state government, Burrowes went into semiretirement as a farmer from 1838 to 1845. He returned to the practice of law in 1845 and became a member of the local school board. He had an impact on the development of education in the state. Seeking to improve the quality of education in Pennyslvania, he worked for the upgrading of teacher training and promoted the development of a professional attitude by teachers. He organized teachers' institutes, drew up and fought for the Normal School Act, and participated in the founding of Millersville State Normal School (later, Millersville State College).

Burrowes was mayor of Lancaster, Pennsylvania (1858–59), and served again as state superintendent of schools (1860–63). He organized and was superintendent of the Soldier's Orphans Schools of the state (1865–68) and president of the Agricultural College of Pennsylvania (later, Pennsylvania State University) from 1868 to 1871, seeing the college through a critical period and restoring the institution to stability and growth.

Burrowes founded and edited (1852–70) *The Pennsylvania School Journal.* In addition to reports as state superintendent, he was the author of *State-Book of Pennsylvania* (1846) and *The Army and Navy of America* (with Jacob K. Neff, 1866) and editor of *Pennsylvania School Architecture* (1855).

Burrowes was a founder of the Pennsylvania State Education Association and the American Association for the Advancement of Education and was active in the movement to establish the United States Bureau (later, Office) of Education.

REFERENCES: *DAB; NCAB* (25:439); *WWW* (H); Albert O. Michener, "Thomas Henry Burrowes, LLD., Champion of the Common Schools of Pennsylvania" (Master's thesis, Temple University, 1932); Robert L. Mohr, *Thomas Henry Burrowes* (Philadelphia: University of Pennsylvania Press, 1946); James P. Wickersham (*q.v.*), "Thomas Henry Burrowes, LL.D." *The Pennsylvania School Journal* 19 (April 1871): 281-85.

Samuel A. Farmerie

BURTON, Warren. B. November 23, 1800, Wilton, New Hampshire, to Jonathan and Persis (Warren) Burton. M. 1828 to Sarah Flint. M. 1845 to Mary Merritt. Ch. none. D. June 6, 1866, Salem, Massachusetts.

Warren Burton was educated in a district school and then through his own efforts and the aid of interested persons in the community prepared for admission to Harvard University. After graduation in 1821, he apprenticed himself as a schoolteacher. He enrolled at the Cambridge (Massachusetts)

Divinity School, from which he was graduated in 1826.

Burton was ordained (1826) in the Congregational church (later, he became a Swedenborgian) and embarked on a forty-year career as a clergyman, writer, and lecturer. He served churches in Massachusetts at East Cambridge (1828–29), South Hingham (1833–35), Waltham (1835–37), and as a minister preaching in Boston but not assigned to a church (1844–48). He was a lecturer and writer (1829–33) and with the Brook Farm Association (1841–44). He served as chaplain at the prison in Worcester (1849) and for the Massachusetts Senate (1852), constitutional convention (1853), and House of Representatives (1853, 1860).

Burton sought social reform through education and spent most of his time lecturing and writing on the subject. He recognized the importance of the home in the educational process and believed that lack of proper home education thwarted the efforts of the school. He was influential in promoting the movement that developed parent-teacher organizations.

Burton wrote books in the fields of phrenology, transcendentalism, and education. Among them were *My Religious Experience in My Home* (1829), *Cheering Views of Man and Providence* (1832), *The District School as It Was* (1833), *Uncle Sam's Recommendations of Phrenology to His Millions of Friends in the United States* (1842), *Helps to Education in the Homes of Our Country* (1863), and *The Culture of the Observing Faculties in the Family and the School* (1865).

REFERENCES: *AC; DAB; NCAB* (7:516); *WWW* (H); "Home Education" *Barnard's American Journal of Education* 2 (1856): 333-36; "Warren Burton," *Barnard's American Journal of Education* 16 (1871): 430.

Samuel A. Farmerie

BURTON, William Henry. B. October 9, 1890, Fort Worth, Texas, to George Charles and Agnes Ann (Selbie) Burton. M. August 4, 1920, to Virginia Nottingham. Ch. none. D. April 3, 1964, Portland, Oregon.

William Henry Burton received the B.A. and B.Edn. degrees (1915) from the University of Oregon, the A.M. degree (1917) from Teachers College, Columbia University, and the Ph.D. degree (1924) from the University of Chicago.

Burton taught in rural elementary and secondary schools of Oregon. He became assistant professor of education at the Washington State College (later, University) in Pullman (1918–21); director of the Training School of the State Teachers College (later, Winona State College) in Winona, Minnesota (1921–23); director in charge of training of teachers of the Cincinnati (Ohio) public schools; professor of education at the University of Cincinnati (1924–26), the University of Chicago (1926–31), and the University of Southern California (1931–39); and director of apprenticeship at the Harvard Graduate School of Education (1939–55). From the time of his retirement from Harvard in 1955 until his death in 1964, he was a part-time faculty member of the Oregon College at Monmouth and consultant to the Oregon State Department of Education. Burton advocated shared responsibility in teaching and supervision.

For over forty years, Burton was a curriculum consultant to a number of states and local school systems, author, and editor. He was author of many books, including *Supervision and the Improvement of Teaching* (1922), *Supervision of Instruction* (with A. S. Barr, *q.v.*, 1926), *Nature and Direction of Learning* (1929), *Supervision of Elementary Subjects* (1929), *Introduction to Education* (1934), *Supervision* (with L. J. Brueckner, *q.v.*, and A. S. Barr, 1938), *The Guidance of Learning Activities* (1944), *Growth and Development of the Preadolescent* (with A. W. Blair, 1951), and a series, Reading for Living (with Clara B. Baker and Grace Kemp, 1950–51). He was the author and coauthor of more than a dozen tests.

Burton was active in professional organizations, including the National Department of Supervision and Curriculum Development of the National Education Association (president, 1927–28) and the American Education Fellowship (New England vice-president, 1946–49). He received an honorary degree from Pacific University of Forest Grove, Oregon.

REFERENCES: *CA* (1–4); *LE* (III); *WWAE* (XVII); *WWW* (IV).

Robert C. Laserte

BUSHEE, James. B. October 15, 1805, Smithfield, Rhode Island, to n.a. M. to Lucy Aldrich. M. to Harriet Mowry. Ch. three. D. December 20, 1888, North Smithfield, Rhode Island.

James Bushee attended the academy at Woonsocket, Rhode Island (1826–28), and taught in Somerset and Fall River, Massachusetts. In 1831 he returned to Woonsocket, where he served as principal of Old Smithfield Academy to 1852. He moved the school into his spacious home where he introduced the conversational style of teaching.

In 1852 Bushee moved to Worcester, Massachusetts, where he taught at the Worcester Academy and at a private girls' school. He was a professor of chemistry at the Worcester Medical College and headed the science department at the Highland Military School for ten years. He returned to Woonsocket in 1879 and taught for six years, retiring at the age of eighty.

Bushee was an outstanding teacher of mathematics and science. He constructed and made use of unusual and imaginative equipment, including some revolutionary astronomical models. He was author of *Synopsis of Precession with New Precession Apparatus* (1862).

In August 1866 Bushee was honored at a gathering of his former pupils in Worcester, Massachusetts, and in 1885 on his eightieth birthday at a reunion of his former students.

REFERENCES: Edward Field, ed., *State of Rhode Island and Providence*

Plantations at the End of the Century (Boston: Mason, 1902), p. 359; *Representative Men and Old Families of Southern Massachusetts* (Chicago: J. H. Beers, 1912), p. 179; Woonsocket (Rhode Island) *Evening Reporter,* December 21, 1888.   *John F. Ohles*

BUTCHER, Thomas Walter. B. July 3, 1867, Industry, Illinois, to Bowman Rilea and Adaline (Vail) Butcher. M. July 3, 1900, to Mary Whitmore Peck. Ch. three. D. July 14, 1947, Emporia, Kansas.

Thomas Walter Butcher attended Garfield University in Wichita, Kansas (1887–90), and was graduated with the A.B. degree (1894) from the University of Kansas. He received the A.M. degree (1904) from Harvard University. He studied at the University of Berlin, Germany (1908–09).

Butcher's career began as a teacher in a Kansas country school (1890–91). In 1894 he became a high school teacher in Wellington, Kansas. He organized the Sumner County (Kansas) High School and was principal to 1906. He served as the president of the Central State Normal School (later, University) in Edmond, Oklahoma (1906–08), and was superintendent of schools in Enid, Oklahoma (1909–13).

In 1913 Butcher became president of Kansas State Normal School (later, Emporia Kansas State College) in Emporia and continued in that capacity until his retirement in 1943. During the three decades that Butcher held the post, the school became the Kansas State Teachers College, the student enrollment increased more than threefold, and the physical plant was enlarged. Master's degrees were awarded from 1929. Providing leadership in public school music, the school originated public school music contests. A bureau of educational measurements provided trained personnel who established statewide public school testing programs and provided a national testing program for elementary and secondary schools.

Butcher wrote *The Common Sense Spelling Book* (1913) and coauthored an arithmetic textbook series. He served in many civic and professional organizations. He was a delegate to the Citizens Conference on Education in Kansas City, Missouri (1920), and to the Illiteracy Conference in Denver, Colorado (1923). He was a member of the National Council of Normal School Presidents and Principals (president, 1919–20), the Kansas State Teachers Association (president, 1905), and the Oklahoma State Teachers Association (president, 1911). He was a member and the secretary of the International Jury of Awards on Social and Industrial Betterment of the Louisiana Purchase Exposition in St. Louis, Missouri (1904). He was a member of the board of regents of the University of Kansas (1902–06) and the Kansas State Board of Education (1913–33). He was a member of the Wellington, Kansas, City Council (1900–06).

He received an honorary degree from the College of Emporia (Kansas). The Kansas State Teachers College honored him posthumously by naming its elementary laboratory school the Thomas W. Butcher Children's School.

REFERENCES: *LE* (II); *NCAB* (39:526); *WWW* (V).   *Jerry L. Johns*

BUTLER, Edward Mann. B. July, 1784, Baltimore, Maryland, to n.a. M. August 1806 to Martha Dedman. Ch. one. D. November 1, 1855, St. Louis, Missouri.

(Edward) Mann Butler, early nineteenth-century Kentucky educator, received his early education in Chelsea, New London, England, between the ages of three and fourteen. Uncorroborated reports suggest that he studied medicine and law at St. Mary's College in Georgetown, District of Columbia. He moved to Kentucky in April 1806; the Fayette County Bar Association admitted him to practice that year. Overpowered by his legal contemporaries (including Henry Clay), Butler abandoned the legal profession for the classroom.

Butler founded private academies and seminaries in Kentucky at Versailles, Maysville, Washington, and Frankfort. He taught mathematics at Transylvania University in Lexington where he headed the grammar school.

In 1813 Butler became the first principal of the Jefferson Seminary, which had been authorized by the 1798 Kentucky General Assembly. In 1829 he became the first principal of Kentucky's first free public school. Located in Louisville, the school was the forerunner of Kentucky's public school system incorporated in 1834–35.

While living in various Kentucky frontier towns and settlements (1806–13), he started several libraries and helped incorporate the Louisville Library Company. His Louisville Lyceum (with five hundred volumes) eventually evolved into the Louisville Free Public Library.

The Kentucky General Assembly twice authorized the secretary of state and the governor to lend Butler official documents for the preparation of his 1834 *History of Kentucky,* a landmark book of early historiographic method. He also wrote essays and books about the Ohio River Valley, the Mississippi trails to Natchez, and Missouri-Kentucky frontier life and customs. He compiled a biography of George Rogers Clark and contributed a history of Lousiville in the city's first directory (1832). Butler owned, edited, or wrote for several newspapers, including the *Western Courier, Louisville Correspondent,* and *Frankfort Commentator.*

Butler helped establish the First Unitarian Church in Louisville and served on the church's first board of trustees. In 1833 he became the first president of the Kentucky Association of Professional Teachers, the probable antecedent of the Kentucky Common School Society (1835) and later the Kentucky Education Association of 1857.

Butler moved to St. Louis, Missouri, in 1840, where he continued his scholastic enterprises. Little is known about his Missouri work and activities. Butler died on November 1, 1855, in a Missouri Pacific Railroad accident near St. Louis.

REFERENCES: Lewis Collins, *History of Kentucky* (Frankfort: Kentucky Historical Society, 1966); William Eley Connelley and E. M. Coulter, *History of Kentucky* (Chicago: American Historical Society, 1922), vol. 2; Porter H. Hopkins, *KEA: The First One Hundred Years* (Lexington, Ky: Transylvania Printing Co., 1957); J. Stoddard Johnston, ed., *Memorial History of Louisville from Its First Settlement to the Year 1896* (Chicago: American Publishing Co., 1896), vols. 1–2; *Louisville Herald,* October 1, 1922, January 28, 1923; *Louisville Journal,* November 3, 1855; Henry McMurtrie, *Sketches of Louisville and Its Environs* (Louisville, Ky.: S. Penn, Jr., 1819); Frank LeRond McVey (*q.v.*), *The Gates Open Slowly* (Lexington, Ky.: The University of Kentucky Press, 1949).

Robert D. Neill

BUTLER, Howard Crosby. B. March 7, 1872, Croton Falls, New York, to Edward Marchant and Helen Belden (Crosby) Butler. M. no. D. August 13, 1922, Neuilly, France.

Howard Crosby Butler learned Latin from his mother and studied with private tutors at the Lyons Collegiate Institute and the Berkeley School in New York City. He received the A.B. (1892) and A.M. (1893) degrees from the College of New Jersey (later, Princeton University). He pursued his studies at the Columbia University School of Architecture and the American School of Classical Studies in Rome, Italy.

He organized and conducted archeological expeditions to Syria from 1899 to 1900, 1904 to 1905, and in 1909. He was on the Princeton faculty from 1897 to 1922. He was lecturer on architecture (1895–97) and professor of art and archeology (1901–22). He was first master in residence of the graduate college (1905–22) and director of the school of archaeology (1920–22). Butler directed the American excavations of Sardis (1910–14, 1922). He died in Neuilly, France, probably on August 13, 1922, on his return to the United States from Sardis.

Butler was the author of books on architecture and archeology, including *Scotland's Ruined Abbeys* (1900), *The Story of Athens* (1902), *Architecture and Other Arts* (1903), *Architecture* (1925), *Early Churches in Syria* (1929), and many reports on the Syrian archeological expeditions. He was a member of the Archeological Institute of America. He was a trustee of the American Schools of Oriental Research. He won the Drexel Gold Medal in 1910.

REFERENCES: *DAB; NCAB* (20:56); *WWW* (I); *NYT,* August 16, 1922, p. 9; Henry Fairfield Osborn, *Impressions of Great Naturalists* (New York: Charles Scribner's Sons, 1928), pp. 221–26.   *Roger H. Jones*

BUTLER, Marie Joseph. B. July 22, 1860, Ballynunnery, County Kilkenny, Ireland, to John and Ellen (Forrestal) Butler. M. no. D. April 23, 1940, Tarrytown, New York.

Marie Joseph Butler, a Roman Catholic sister, was the founder of the Marymount schools and colleges in the United States and Europe. She was born in Ireland, christened Joanna, and educated both in public schools and in a day school conducted by the Sisters of Mercy. At the age of sixteen, she entered the congregation of the Sacred Heart of Mary at Beziers, France. She taught at Oporto, Portugal, and then at Braga, Portugal, before being sent to teach in the congregation's school at Sag Harbor, New York.

In 1907 James Butler, Mother Butler's cousin, gave the order some property in Tarrytown, New York, for a school, and she opened the Marymount School there in 1908. Her long-range plan was to found a Catholic women's college, and this goal was attained in 1918 when Marymount College opened. In the succeeding twenty years, new Marymount schools were begun in Los Angeles, Paris, New York, and Rome.

Butler established courses in political science and law in her colleges and encouraged her students and graduates to participate in charitable and social service work with the poor. She was president of Marymount College in Tarrytown from 1918 to 1926, then was elected mother general of the order, an office she held until her death in 1940.

Mother Marie Joseph Butler was the founder of fourteen American schools, including six Marymounts, of which three were colleges.

REFERENCES: *NAW;* Katherine Burton, *Mother Butler of Marymount* (New York: Longman, Green, 1944); *Dictionary of Catholic Biography* (New York: Doubleday and Co., 1961); *New Catholic Encyclopedia* (New York: McGraw-Hill, 1967). *Sister Stephanie Sloyan*

BUTLER, Nicholas Murray. B. April 2, 1862, Elizabeth, New Jersey, to Henry L. and Mary Jones (Murray) Butler. M. February 7, 1887, to Susanna Edwards Schuyler. M. March 5, 1907, to Kate La Montagne. Ch. one. D. December 7, 1947, New York, New York.

Nicholas Murray Butler received the A.B. degree with honors (1882) and the A.M. (1883) and Ph.D. (1884) degrees from Columbia College (later, University). He studied at the universities of Berlin, Germany, and Paris, France (1884–85).

Butler became a teacher of philosophy at Columbia University in 1885, was appointed professor of philosophy, first dean of the faculty of philosophy (1890), and president of the university in 1901, retiring in 1945. He was a major organizer and first president of the New York College for the Training of Teachers, which became Teachers College of Columbia University in 1898. He was president of other components of Columbia, including Barnard College and the College of Pharmacy (1904), New York Post-Graduate Medical School (1931), and Bard College from 1928 until its separation from Columbia in 1944.

Butler drafted New Jersey legislation for the organization and support of public libraries (1886) and for the introduction of manual training in schools (1887). As a member of the New Jersey State Board of Education, Butler campaigned for the reorganization of the state normal school, improved methods of school administration, opposed conflict of interest in the superintendency, and authored legislation for nonpartisan boards of education (1888–95).

Among Butler's three thousand published books, articles, essays, reports, and speeches were *The Meaning of Education* (1898), *True and False Democracy* (1907), *The American As He Is* (1908), *Education in the United States* (1910), *Philosophy* (1911), *The International Mind* (1913), *A World in Ferment* (1918), *Is America Worth Saving?* (1920), *Scholarship and Service* (1921), *Building the American Nation* (1923), *The Faith of a Liberal* (1924), *The Path to Peace* (1930), *Looking Forward* (1932), *Between Two Worlds* (1934), *The Family of Nations* (1938), *Across the Busy Years* (1939), *Why War?* (1940), *Liberty, Equality, Fraternity* (1942), and *The World Today* (1946). He was founder and editor of *Educational Review* (1889–1920), the Great Educators Series (1892–1901), the Teachers Professional Library (1894–1929), and Columbia University Contributions to Philosophy and Education (1888–1902).

He worked with Pope Pius XI in 1928 to modernize the Vatican Library, was an original trustee of the Carnegie Foundation for the Advancement of Teaching, and was trustee of Carnegie Corporation of New York (chairman, 1937–45) and Columbia University Press. He was chairman of the National Committee on Reconstruction of the University of Louvain, Belgium (1915–25), and president of the Carnegie Endowment for International Peace (1925–45). Butler was a member of the Commission of Reorganization of the Government of the State of New York (1925–26), the American Academy of Arts and Letters (chancellor, 1924–28 and president, 1928–41), the National Educational Association (president, 1895), the Germanistic Society (president, 1906–07), the American Scandinavian Society (first president, 1908–11), the France-America Society (president, 1914–24), the American Hellenic Society (president), and the Italy American Society (president of the board of trustees, 1929–35), and he belonged to many other cultural, educational, and political organizations throughout the world.

Butler worked for international understanding and cooperation. He was personally acquainted with many European leaders and with presidents of the United States. His correspondence with presidents filled seventeen volumes. He attended every Republican national convention from 1880 to

1932 and played an active role in drafting Republican party platforms. He supported women's suffrage and opposed prohibition.

Butler spoke at universities and before governmental bodies and other organizations throughout the world. His reports as president of Columbia University are important documents in the history of education. He was awarded over forty honorary degrees from universities in the United States and abroad and received decorations and awards from many foreign nations. Butler shared the Nobel Peace Prize in 1931 with Jane Addams.

REFERENCES: *DAB* (supp. 4); *EB; NCAB* (34:1); *WWW* (II); Laurence A. Cremin, David A. Shannon, and Mary Evelyn Townsend, *A History of Teachers College, Columbia University* (New York: Columbia University Press, 1954); *NYT,* December 7, 1947, p. 1, December 8, 1947, p. 1; Albert Marrin, *Nicholas Murray Butler* (Boston: Twayne Pub., 1976).

Barbara Ruth Peltzman

BUTLER, Noble. B. July 17, 1810, Chester County, Pennsylvania, to Jonathan and Nancy (Hopkins) Butler. M. 1839 to Lucinda Harney. Ch. five. D. February 12, 1882, Louisville, Kentucky.

When Noble Butler was seven years old his family moved from Chester County, Pennsylvania, to a settlement that became Hanover, Indiana. He received his early education in log schoolhouses. In 1825 a school was established a mile from his home; in four years it expanded into Hanover College. Butler was one of the first to enroll; he was graduated in 1836.

Butler was appointed professor of Greek and Latin at Hanover in 1836. He was at Louisville, Kentucky (1839–43), as professor of foreign languages in the Louisville College, a forerunner of the University of Louisville. He attended the Harvard Divinity School, graduating in 1845. Returning to Louisville, he conducted a school for young ladies and was principal of Louisville High School.

During the Civil War period Butler continued to teach in schools for young women. In 1866 Butler and Dr. E. A. Grant opened the School for Young Ladies and Girls in Louisville, which included a kindergarten and a class for resident graduates. Unlike most education for women of this period that was aimed to give young ladies social graces, this move toward higher education caused wide comment. Butler was an advocate of education for women and supported the temperance movement.

Butler was the author of many popular textbooks, including *Introductory Lessons in English and Grammar* (1846), *A Practical Grammar of the English Language* (1846), and *A Practical and Critical Grammar of the English Language* (1874) and editor of revisions of the Goodrich's Readers series (1847) and the American Standard School series (1866–75). In 1880 Butler published *Butler's Miscellanies,* a collection of essays and observations.

REFERENCES: *AC;* Sam Adkins and M. R. Holtzman, *The First Hundred Years* (Louisville: Jobson Printing Co., 1956); Charles Carpenter, *History of American School Books* (Philadelphia: University of Pennsylvania Press, 1963); Elizabeth Hummel, "Noble Butler" (Master's thesis, University of Louisville, 1963).   *Frank H. Stallings*

BUTTERFIELD, Kenyon Leech. B. June 11, 1868, Lapeer, Michigan, to Ira Howard and Olive F. (Davison) Butterfield. M. November 28, 1895, to Harriet E. Millard. Ch. two. D. November 26, 1935, Amherst, Massachusetts.

Kenyon Leech Butterfield attended local Lapeer, Michigan, public schools, was graduated first in the class of 1891 with the B.S. degree from Michigan Agricultural College, and received the A.M. degree (1902) from the University of Michigan.

Butterfield edited the *Michigan Grange Visitor* (1892–96) and was superintendent of the Michigan Farmers' Institute and field agent of the Michigan Agricultural College (later, State University) from 1895 to 1899. He was an instructor of rural sociology at the University of Michigan in 1902, but left to become president of the Rhode Island College of Agriculture and Mechanic Arts (later, University) and professor of political economy. Butterfield was president of the Massachusetts Agricultural College (later, University of Massachusetts) from 1906 to 1924 and the Michigan State College (later, University) from 1924 to 1928. He pioneered in agricultural education and was an early advocate of programs in adult education. He served as a counselor on rural work to the International Missionary Council (1928–32), visiting mission fields across the world.

A leader in the international country life movement, he was the author of *Chapters in Rural Progress* (1908), *The Country Church and the Rural College* (1911), *The Farmer and the New Day* (1919), and *A Christian Program for the Rural Community* (1923). He edited the Farmers' Book Shelf series.

President Theodore Roosevelt appointed Butterfield to the Commission on Country Life (1908), and President Woodrow Wilson *(q.v.)* appointed him to investigate and study agricultural credits in Europe (1913). He was chairman of the Massachusetts Food Supply Commission (1917) and during World War I served as a member of the Army Educational Commission of the Young Men's Christian Association in charge of agricultural, vocational, and general technical instruction with the American Expeditionary Forces in France. He organized and was president of the World Agricultural Society and the American Country Life Association.

He was a member of many American and foreign associations. He received honorary degrees from Amherst College and Rhode Island State College and received honors from Belgium and France.

REFERENCES: *DAB* (supp. 1); *LE* (I); *NCAB* (B:27, 27:138); *WWW* (I); *NYT*, November 27, 1935, p. 21.   *Barbara Ruth Peltzman*

BUTTRICK, Wallace. B. October 23, 1853, Potsdam, New York, to Charles Henry and Polly Dodge (Warren) Buttrick. M. December 1, 1875, to Isabella Allen. Ch. three. D. May 27, 1926, Baltimore, Maryland.

Wallace Buttrick received his early schooling at Ogdensburg (New York) Academy (1868–69) and Potsdam (New York) Normal School (later, State University of New York) (1871–72). In 1875 he took a job as a railway clerk while he worked his way through the Rochester (New York) Theological Seminary, from which he was graduated in 1883.

He became minister of the First Baptist Church in New Haven, Connecticut (1883–89), and continued his ministry in St. Paul, Minnesota (1889–92), and Albany, New York (1892–1902).

In 1902 Buttrick was named secretary and executive officer of the General Education Board established by John D. Rockefeller. The board surveyed the nation's educational needs, endowed established colleges, and worked to upgrade primary and secondary education in the South, particularly among blacks. It also provided for demonstrations of better farming methods in cooperation with the United States Department of Agriculture. Concern was also shown for better professional training, especially for doctors. Buttrick was president (1917–23) and chairman (1923–26) of the board.

Buttrick was a trustee of the Rockefeller Foundation, the University of Rochester, Rochester Theological Seminary, and Peking (China) Union Medical College. He was chairman of the International Education Board (1924–26) and a director of the Rockefeller Foundation's China Medical Board. He was a member of the board of the American Baptist Home Mission Society and chairman of its committee on education. He was the recipient of several honorary degrees.

REFERENCES: *DAB; NCAB* (22:419); *WWW* (I); *NYT*, May 28, 1926, p. 21.   *Mark Fravel, Jr.*

BUTTS, Robert Freeman. B. May 14, 1910, Springfield, Illinois, to Robert Freeman and Cornelia A. (Paddock) Butts. M. May 30, 1936, to Florence Randolph. Ch. two.

R. Freeman Butts was graduated from the University of Wisconsin, receiving the A.B. (1931), M.A. (1932), and Ph.D. (1935). He joined the faculty of Teachers College, Columbia University, in 1936 where he spent some forty years; in 1958 he was appointed William F. Russell Professor in the Foundations of Education. From 1965 to his retirement in 1975, he served as director of the Institute of International Studies; he also was a member of the faculty of international affairs (Columbia University) and associate dean for international studies.

R. Freeman Butts's career was long and distinguished: he was Fulbright Research Scholar with the Australian Council for Educational Research in Melbourne (1954); educational adviser at the Central Institute of Education, University of Delhi in India (1959); recipient of a Carnegie travel grant for research in newly independent countries of Africa and Asia (1961–62); senior specialist at the East-West Center of the University of Hawaii (1965); and special scholar-in-residence at the Aspen Institute for Humanistic Studies (1973). He was president of the Comparative and International Education Society (1964–65), the National Society of College Teachers of Education (1953), and the American Educational Studies Association (1968–69) and director of the History of Education Society. The American Educational Studies Association established the R. Freeman Butts Lecture in 1974 to be delivered at its annual conventions.

His books include *The College Charts Its Course* (1939), *A Cultural History of Western Education* (1947), *The American Tradition in Religion and Education* (1950), *Assumptions Underlying Australian Education* (1955), *A Cultural History of Western Education* (1955), *A History of Education in American Culture* (with Lawrence A. Cremin, 1953), *American Education in International Development* (a John Dewey Society lecture, 1963), and *The Education of the West: A Formative Chapter in the History of Civilization* (1973).

REFERENCES: *CA* (13–16); *LE* (V); *WW* (XXXIX); *WWAE* (XXII).

Francesco Cordasco

BYERLY, William Elwood. B. December 13, 1849, Philadelphia, Pennsylvania, to Elwood and Rebecca (Wayne) Byerly. M. May 28, 1885, to Alice Worcester Parsons. M. July 23, 1921, to Anne Carter Wickham Renshaw. Ch. two. D. December 20, 1935, Swarthmore, Pennsylvania.

William Byerly was raised in Orange, New Jersey, and schooled by a private tutor. He attended Harvard University and was graduated with the A.B. degree (1871). Byerly received one of the first two Ph.D. degrees granted by Harvard in 1873. One of his professors, Benjamin Peirce *(q.v.)*, greatly influenced Byerly, who became one of the most noted mathematicians in America.

Byerly was an assistant professor of mathematics at Cornell University (1873–76) and taught mathematics at Harvard (1876–1913), being named Perkins Professor of Mathematics in 1901. Threatened with blindness, he retired as professor emeritus in 1913.

He promoted higher education for women and was the first member of the Harvard faculty to agree to give courses to women. Byerly was characterized as the person most responsible for the growth and development of Radcliffe College; a hall was named for him at Radcliffe.

His devotion to mathematics produced several textbooks, of which his two companion volumes on calculus were considered to be the best at that time. Among his writings were *Elements of Differential Calculus* (1879), *Elements of Integral Calculus* (1881), *An Elementary Treatise on Fourier Series and Spherical, Cylindrical, and Ellipsoidal Harmonics* (1895), *Generalized Coordinates* (1916), and *Introduction to the Calculus of Variation* (1917). He was editor of *Annals of Mathematics* (1899–1911).

REFERENCES: *AC; DAB* (supp. 1); *NCAB* (27:348); *WWW* (I); *NYT,* December 21, 1935, p. 17.   *Robert McGinty*

C

CADY, Calvin Brainerd. B. June 21, 1851, Barry, Illinois, to Cornelius Sydney and Rebecca T. (Morgan) Cady. M. August 12, 1872, to Josephine Upson. M. June 5, 1915, to Elizabeth Hoar. Ch. four. D. May 29, 1928, Portland, Oregon.

Calvin Brainerd Cady was educated at the Oberlin (Ohio) College Conservatory and the Leipzig (Germany) Conservatory from 1872 to 1874. He studied organ under B. R. Papperitz and harmony, counterpoint, and piano under E. F. Richter and Oscar Paul.

Cady was a music teacher in the public schools of Oberlin, Ohio (1871–72), before going to Germany. After his return, he taught harmony and piano at the Oberlin College Conservatory (1874–79). In 1880 he was professor of music at the University of Michigan, where he established the first music degree program at Michigan and was the first in the United States to teach music as a major subject for the degrees of bachelor of arts and master of arts.

He taught at the Chicago Conservatory (later, Chicago College of Music) from 1888 to 1901 and gave private lessons in Boston, Massachusetts, to 1907. He was a lecturer in the music extension department at Teachers College, Columbia University (1907–10), and a lecturer on pedagogy at the Institute of Musical Art in New York City (1908–13). He was director of the Music Education School, an elementary school for boys and girls, in Portland, Oregon (1913–16). He was appointed dean of the normal department of the Cornish School in Seattle, Washington, in 1916.

Cady was a pioneer in establishing music degree programs in American universities. As a teacher he believed that music should be taught as a means to further understanding of the liberal arts. He was the author of *Music Education* (three volumes, 1902–07) and *The New Students' Refer-*

ence Work and editor of the *Musical Yearbook* (1884) and *New Music Review* in Chicago from 1892 to 1894. He was a contributor to the *Encyclopedia of Education* and to many music and educational periodicals.

REFERENCES: *NCAB* (21:425); *WWW* (IV); *The Oregonian* (Portland, Oregon), May 30, 1928; Robert Sabin, ed., *The International Cyclopedia of Music and Musicians,* 9th ed. (New York: Dodd, Mead & Co., 1964).   *Donald Corwin Jones*

CADY, Sarah Louise Ensign. B. September 13, 1829, Northampton, Massachusetts, to Salmon and Melinda (Cobb) Ensign. M. 1850 to Henry Stearns Cady. Ch. four. D. November 8, 1912, New York, New York.

Before the age of two, Sarah Louise Ensign Cady was placed in a Pestalozzi-inspired infant school. When she was three and a half, the family moved to Westfield, Massachusetts, and entered her in a district school. She was graduated from the Westfield Academy and Westfield Normal School (later, State College) at the age of seventeen.

She taught in public schools until her marriage to her second cousin, Henry Cady, in 1850. Left a widow with four children and a meager income in 1864, Cady returned to teaching. She conducted a school for two years in Westfield, then was associate principal of Maplewood Hall, a large boarding school for young women in Pittsfield, Massachusetts. Moving to Connecticut in 1870, she established the West End Institute in New Haven (later, Mrs. Cady's School for Girls). Cady was highly successful; graduates of her school were able to enter colleges without examination. She employed high-quality teachers who were college graduates or native in foreign languages and special lecturers and instructors. Cady was credited with establishing one of the earliest kindergartens at her school. The school was moved to a building owned by Yale University. Cady closed the school when she experienced difficulty in finding a new location when her lease was not renewed in 1899.

Sarah Cady spent her last dozen years in New York City where she was active in club and church work and served on executive boards and committees of the Young Women's Christian Association and the Women's Christian Temperance Union. In 1920 the Alumnae Association of Connecticut College established an annual prize for reading and public speaking as a memorial to Sarah Louise Ensign Cady, who had pioneered in establishing a preparatory school for girls that was equal to the boys' schools in the country.

REFERENCES: *DAB; NCAB* (9:373).   *M. Jane Dowd*

CAIN, William. B. May 14, 1847, Hillsboro, North Carolina, to William and Sarah Jane (Bailey) Cain. M. no. D. December 7, 1930, Chapel Hill, North Carolina.

William Cain attended Hillsboro (North Carolina) Academy. Although only fourteen years old, Cain, along with other cadets, assisted the Civil War effort by drilling Confederate troops. He was graduated with the A.M. degree (1866) from the North Carolina Military and Polytechnic Institute, the former Hillsboro Academy.

Cain possessed a keen grasp of mathematics, which enabled him to analyze a variety of engineering problems from the standpoint of the theorist. He was in charge of railroad location surveys from 1868 to 1874 and 1880 to 1882. Cain was professor of mathematics and engineering in the Carolina Military Institute at Charlotte, North Carolina (1874–80). In 1882 he accepted a similar position at the Citadel in Charleston, South Carolina. He was elected professor and head of the department of mathematics and engineering in 1888 at the University of North Carolina and held the position until his retirement (1920).

Cain was a pioneer in writing American civil engineering textbooks. Six of his writings were popular compact handbooks: *A Practical Theory of Voussoir Arches* (1874), *Maximum Stresses in Framed Bridges* (1878), *Voussoir Arches, Applied to Stone Bridges, Tunnels, Domes and Groined Arches* (1879, which was republished in 1902 under the title *Theory of Steel-Concrete Arches and of Vaulted Structures*), *Theory of Solid and Braced Elastic Arches* (1879), *Symbolic Algebra* (1884), and *Practical Designing of Retaining Walls* (1888). He also wrote *A Brief Course in the Calculus* (1905) and *Earth Pressure, Retaining Walls and Bins* (1916).

William Cain was one of the original five Kenan professors appointed at the University of North Carolina in 1918. Until his death, Cain was sought as counsel in the engineering field. Formulas he developed were named for him, and engineers in the United States and abroad used his methods of analysis. In 1923 Cain was awarded the J. James R. Croes Medal by the American Society of Civil Engineers for his paper "The Circular Arch Under Normal Loads."

REFERENCES: *DAB* (supp. 1); *NCAB* (A:290); *WWW* (I).

Dennis G. Wiseman

CAJORI, Florian. B. February 28, 1859, St. Aignan, Switzerland, to George and Catherine (Camenisch) Cajori. M. September 3, 1890, to Elizabeth Edwards. Ch. one. D. August 14, 1930, Berkeley, California.

Florian Cajori was the first professor of the history of mathematics in the United States, and he established a model for research and writing in the field. A native of St. Aignan, Switzerland, Cajori emigrated to the United States, settling in Whitewater, Wisconsin. He studied at Whitewater State Normal School (later, University of Wisconsin-Whitewater) and received the B.S. (1883) and M.S. (1886) degrees from the University of Wisconsin. He studied at Johns Hopkins University in Baltimore, Maryland (1886), and Tulane University in New Orleans, Louisiana, where he earned the Ph.D. degree (1894).

Cajori was assistant professor of mathematics and professor of applied mathematics at Tulane University (1885–88). He was professor of physics (1889–98) and mathematics (1898–1918) and dean of the department of engineering (1903–18) at Colorado College in Colorado Springs. He was professor of the history of mathematics (1918–29) at the University of California at Berkeley.

Among more than a dozen published books, Cajori's most prominent were *Teaching and History of Mathematics in the United States* (1890), *History of Mathematics* (1894), *History of Elementary Mathematics* (1896), *History of Physics* (1899), *Introduction to the Modern Theory of Equations* (1904), *History of the Logarithmic Slide Rule* (1909), *William Oughtred* (1916), *History of the Conceptions of Limits and Fluxions in Great Britain from Newton to Woodhouse* (1919), *Early Mathematical Sciences in North and South America* (1928), *History of Mathematical Notations* (two volumes, 1928–29), and *The Chequered Career of Ferdinand Randolph Hassler* (1929). Nearly two hundred of his articles were published in mathematical and scientific journals in the United States and abroad.

Cajori served as a member of several committees on mathematics education for the National Education Association. He was president of the Mathematical Association of America (1917) and Comité international d'histoire des sciences (1929), vice-president of the History of Science Society (1924–25), and a member of numerous other national and international scientific and mathematical organizations. He was awarded honorary degrees by Colorado College and the universities of Colorado and Wisconsin.

REFERENCES: *DAB* (supp. 1); *EB; NCAB* (27:178); *WWW* (I); Lav G. Simons, "Florian Cajori," *The American Mathematical Monthly* 37 (November 1930): 460–62; David Eugene Smith *(q.v.)*, "Florian Cajori," *Bulletin of the American Mathematical Society* 36 (November 1930): 777–80.   *D. Richard Bowles*

CALDERONE, Mary Steichen. B. July 1, 1904, New York, New York, to Edward J. and Clara (Smith) Steichen. M. 1926 to n.a. Martin. M. November 27, 1941, to Frank A. Calderone. Ch. three.

Mary Steichen Calderone was the daughter of Edward Steichen, the famous photographer. She spent her early years in France and New York City. She was graduated from the Brearley School in New York (1922) and received the B.A. degree (1925) from Vassar College in Poughkeepsie, New York. Calderone first tried acting as a career and eventually decided on a medical education and practice in the field of public health.

She received the M.D. degree (1939) from the University of Rochester (New York) Medical School and the M.P.H. degree (1942) from Columbia University.

She was medical director of Planned Parenthood-World Population (1953–64), where she was credited with being a major influence in persuading the American Medical Association in 1964 to permit physicians to dispense birth control information.

She noted a large number of requests for information about sexual problems beyond just birth control. With five colleagues, she planned an organization to be concerned with problems of human sexuality; the result was the Sex Information and Education Council of the United States (SIECUS) in 1964 with Calderone as the executive director. She became a frequent lecturer on human sexuality to various groups across the country. Calderone was an advocate of sex education in the schools beginning at the kindergarten level.

Calderone produced the *First Picture Book* (1930) and the *Second Picture Book* (1931) pioneering in the use of photographs in children's books. She edited *Abortion in the United States* (1958) and the *Manual of Family Planning and Contraceptive Practice* (1964) and wrote *Release from Sexual Tensions* (1960).

Calderone was a fellow of the American Public Health Association, and a member of many other organizations, including the American Medical Association, the American Association of Marriage Counselors, the National Council on Family Relations, the National Health Council (director), the National Council of Church of Christ (commission on family life), the American College of Obstetricians and Gynecologists (liaison committee on family life education), and the Mental Health Association of Nassau County, New York (board of directors). She received a number of awards, including the distinguished service award of the Mental Health Association of Nassau County (1958), the fourth annual award for distinguished service to humanity of the women's auxiliary of the Albert Einstein Medical Center in Philadelphia (1966), the Woman of Conscience Award of the National Council of Women (1968), a citation of the Merrill-Palmer Institute (1969), and the Woman of Achievement Award of the Albert Einstein College of Medicine of Yeshiva University (1969).

REFERENCES: *CB* (November 1967); *WW* (XXXVI); *New York Post,* January 9, 1965; *Newsday,* February 22, 1966; John G. Rogers, "Dr. Mary Calderone: Sex Educator," *Parade,* June 18, 1967; *Washington* (D.C.) *Post,* July 10, 1966; *Who's Who of American Women 1974–1975* (Chicago: Marquis, 1975).   *Reese Danley Kilgo*

CALDWELL, David. B. March 22, 1725, Lancaster County, Pennsylvania, to Andrew and Ann (Stewart) Caldwell. M. 1766 to Rachel Craighead. Ch.

none. D. August 25, 1824, Guilford County, North Carolina.

David Caldwell received a basic education, was apprenticed as a carpenter, and worked at his trade for four years. He started to prepare himself for the Presbyterian ministry and was graduated from the College of New Jersey (later, Princeton University) in 1761. He taught school in Cape May, New Jersey, for a year; at the same time, he completed his theological studies and served as an instructor of languages in the college. He was licensed to preach by the New Brunswick, New Jersey, presbytery in 1763, served as a missionary in North Carolina, and was ordained in 1765. He was installed as pastor of the Buffalo and Alamance, North Carolina, churches in 1768 and continued there until he retired a few years before his death.

Caldwell studied and practiced medicine. He attempted unsuccessfully to thwart the battle of Alamance (May 16, 1771). He was a member of the Halifax convention (1776) and the state convention of 1788.

Caldwell conducted a classical school in his home for sixty years. His school was famous, drawing students from all southern states, including those who later served as governors (five), members of Congress, and statesmen, lawyers, jurists, physicians, and clergymen.

REFERENCES: *AC; DAB; NCAB* (10:203); *WWW* (H).

Joseph P. Cangemi
Thomas E. Kesler

CALDWELL, Joseph. B. April 21, 1773, Lammington, New Jersey, to Joseph and Rachel (Harker) Caldwell. M. 1804 to Susan Rowan. M. 1809 to Helen (Hogg) Hooper. Ch. none. D. January 27, 1835, Chapel Hill, North Carolina.

Joseph Caldwell studied at a local grammar school in Princeton, New Jersey, and was admitted to the College of New Jersey (later, Princeton University) at the age of fourteen. He completed his degree in 1791 and delivered the Latin salutatory address at graduation. He studied theology and was licensed to preach by the Presbyterian church.

He taught school in his home town of Lammington, New Jersey, and in Elizabethtown (later, Elizabeth). He was a tutor at the College of New Jersey (1795–96). In 1796 he was appointed professor of mathematics at the University of North Carolina.

At the age of thirty-one, Caldwell was named president of the University of North Carolina. He resigned as president in 1812 to return to the teaching of mathematics and to continue his studies. He was the scientific expert for North Carolina in the surveying of the boundary line between North Carolina and South Carolina in 1813. Caldwell was persuaded to return to the office of president of the university in 1817; he continued in this position until his death in 1835.

Seeking to provide equipment for the university's programs in science and to improve the library, he visited Europe in 1824 to obtain scientific apparatus and books. The equipment included a telescope and other astronomical instruments, and Caldwell used personal funds to build an observatory (1836). He was refunded the money shortly before his death. This was the first observatory established in connection with an American institution of higher education.

Caldwell advocated internal improvement for North Carolina, especially better transportation and more common schools. He was a strong supporter of the Lancastrian system of instruction by monitors in the schools as economical and effective. He criticized the state for its failure to provide schools. He proposed public elementary and secondary schools and a system of higher education and a teacher-training program.

Caldwell wrote *A Compendious System of Elementary Geometry* (1822). His letters to the *Raleigh Register* advocating better transportation were signed "Carlton" and were published as the *Letters of Carlton*. A monument was erected at the University of North Carolina to his memory in 1858. The College of New Jersey awarded him an honorary degree in 1816.

REFERENCES: *AC; DAB; NCAB* (13:241); *WWW* (H); Luther L. Gobbel, *Church-State Relationships in Education in North Carolina Since 1776* (Durham, N.C.: Duke University Press, 1938).   *Earl W. Thomas*

CALDWELL, Otis William. B. December 18, 1869, Lebanon, Indiana, to Theodore Robert and Isabelle (Brenton) Caldwell. M. August 25, 1897, to Cora Burke. Ch. two. D. July 5, 1947, near New Milford, Connecticut.

Otis William Caldwell was graduated with the B.S. degree (1894) from Franklin College in Indiana. He enrolled in the University of Chicago, where he was graduated in 1898 with the Ph.D. degree in botany.

Caldwell was a teaching principal of Ninevah (Indiana) High School (1894–95). He became professor of botany and head of the biology department at Eastern Illinois State Normal School (later, Eastern Illinois University) in Charleston, a position he held from 1899 to 1907, when he was appointed associate professor of botany and head of the department of natural sciences of the school of education, University of Chicago. He was dean of University College, University of Chicago (1913–17).

While studying the science program at the Gary, Indiana, schools, Caldwell became acquainted with Abraham Flexner *(q.v.)* who hired Caldwell in 1917 to serve as the first director of the Lincoln School and professor of education at Teachers College, Columbia University. In 1920 Caldwell became director of the division of school experimentation of the Institute of Educational Research at Teachers College. During his tenure, the Lincoln School became one of the finest progressive schools in the country. He hired the most able faculty and encouraged their experimentation.

In 1927 Caldwell was appointed director of the Institute of School Experimentation, a position he held until 1928, when he was given an extended leave of absence. He retired from Teachers College in 1935 as professor emeritus. After his retirement, he served as general secretary of the American Association for the Advancement of Science until his death in 1947.

In addition to writing numerous textbooks, Caldwell authored several popular science books. He contributed to journals of both education and science. His books include *Laboratory and Field Manual of Botany* (1901), *Plant Morphology* (1903), *Practical Botany* (with J. Y. Bergen, 1911), *Elements of General Science* (with William L. Eiklenberry, 1914), *Introduction to Botany* (with J. Y. Bergen, 1914), *Laboratory Manual of General Science* (with others, 1915), *Biology in the Public Press* (with Charles W. Finley, 1923), *Then and Now in Education* (with Stuart A. Courtis, *q.v.*, 1923), *Open Doors to Science, with Experiments* (with W. H. D. Meier, 1926), *Introduction to Science* (with F. D. Curtis, 1929), *Biological Foundations of Education* (with Charles C. Skinner and J. Winfield Tietz, 1931), *An Experimental Story of Superstitions and Other Unfounded Beliefs Related to Certain Units of General Science* (1932), *Biology for Today* (with F. D. Curtis and N. H. Sherman, 1933), *Do You Believe It?* (with Gerhard E. Lundeen, 1934), *Everyday Biology* (with F. D. Curtis and N. H. Sherman, 1940), and *Everyday Science* (with F. D. Curtis, 1943). He was editor of *Science Remaking the World* (with E. E. Slosson, 1923).

Caldwell was a fellow and a life member of the American Association for the Advancement of Science. He was president of the National Association for Research in Science Teaching (1940).

REFERENCES: *LE* (II); *DAB* (supp. 4); *NCAB* (35:495); *WWAE* (I); *WWW* (II); *NYT*, July 6, 1947, p. 40.   *Dennis M. Wint*

CALIVER, Ambrose. B. February 25, 1894, Saltville, Virginia, to Ambrose and Cora (Saunders) Caliver. M. December 24, 1916, to Rosalie Evelyn Rucker. Ch. one. D. January 29, 1962, Washington, D.C.

Ambrose Caliver was educated in the public schools of Virginia and Knoxville, Tennessee, and was graduated from Knoxville College with the B.A. degree (1916). He received the M.A. degree (1920) from the University of Wisconsin and the Ph.D. degree (1930) from Teachers College, Columbia University. He received a diploma in cabinet making from Tuskegee (Alabama) Institute (1915) and a personnel management certificate from Harvard University (1918).

Caliver was a high school principal in Rockwood, Tennessee (1916), and an instructor and assistant principal of Douglass High School in El Paso, Texas (1917). He joined the faculty at Fisk University in Nashville, Tennessee, to develop a manual arts program in 1919 and became publicity director (1925), dean of the scholastic department (1926), and dean of the university (1927). In 1930 he became a specialist in the education of Negroes for the United States Office of Education and served as specialist in higher education of Negroes (1946–50). He became assistant to the commissioner in 1950 and also chief of the adult education section in 1955.

As the first specialist in the education of blacks in the Office of Education, Caliver conducted surveys on the education of blacks, produced important bulletins, and compiled bibliographies on black education. He was influential in the organizing of the National Advisory Committee on the Education of Negroes (1931) and participated in national conferences. After World War II he became director of the Project for Literacy Education (1946). Programs to improve reading of adult blacks led to an interest in adult education. He directed a project for the adult education of Negroes from 1946.

Caliver was the author of *Bibliography on Education of the Negro* (1931), *Background Study of Negro College Students* (1933), *Secondary Education for Negroes* (1933), *Education of Negro Teachers in Rural Communities* (1933), *Availability of Education to Negroes in Rural Communities* (1935), *Fundamentals in the Education of Negroes* (1935), *Education of Negroes* (1937), *Education of Teachers for Improving Majority-Minority Relationships* (1944), and *Education of Negro Leaders* (1949).

He was a member of professional associations and was active in the Adult Education Association of the U.S.A. (president, 1960–62, chairman of the section on literacy and fundamental education, 1954–56, and founder, 1955, and consultant to the national commission on literacy, 1955–62). He was a delegate to the Inter-American Cultural Council (1951), board member of the Southern Educational Foundation and the Council of National Organizations, trustee of Knoxville College, and a member of the White House Conference on Children in a Democracy (1941). He was president of the National Association of Collegiate Deans and Registrars in Negro Schools (1928). He received honorary degrees from Tuskegee Institute and Virginia State, Knoxville, and Morgan State colleges.

REFERENCES: *LE* (III); *WWAE* (XIV); *WWW* (IV); Walter C. Daniel and John B. Holden, *Ambrose Caliver: Adult Educator and Civil Servant* (Washington: Adult Education Association of the U.S.A., 1966); *Who's Who in Colored America,* 7th ed. (Brooklyn, N.Y.: Burckel and Associates, 1950).   *John F. Ohles*

CALKINS, Mary Whiton. B. March 30, 1863, Hartford, Connecticut, to Wolcott and Charlotte Grosvenor (Whiton) Calkins. M. no. D. February 26, 1930, Newton, Massachusetts.

The eldest of a minister's five children, Mary Whiton Calkins attended

Buffalo (New York) elementary schools. Her father accepted a parish in Newton, Massachusetts, where she was graduated from high school. In 1882 she entered Smith College as a sophomore, spent a year at home, and was graduated from Smith, receiving the A.B. (1885) and A.M. (1887) degrees. She attended Clark University (1890–91) and Harvard University (1893–95), where she studied under Josiah Royce, Hugo Munsterberg, and William James *(q.v.)*. After passing the Ph.D. oral examination with distinction and completing a thesis, she was denied the degree because she was a woman. Later she declined an offer of Radcliffe College to grant her the degree.

In 1887 she became a tutor in Greek at Wellesley College; at the end of forty-two years of service at Wellesley, she was a research professor of philosophy and psychology. In addition to teaching at Wellesley, Calkins worked in the Harvard psychology laboratory from 1892 to 1895.

Calkins set up the first psychology laboratory in a women's college at Wellesley in 1891. Her experimental work centered on dreams, color theory, memory, space-time consciousness, emotion, and association. Her emphasis on the conscious self and the social reference of self-consciousness foreshadowed the work of later investigators in the field of personality. Calkins's interest in metaphysics led to a philosophy of personalistic absolutism.

Philosophy dominated her teaching and writing during her last twenty years. In addition to thirty-seven articles in American and foreign periodicals, she was the author of *Introduction to Psychology* (1901), *The Persistent Problems of Philosophy* (1907), *A First Book in Psychology* (1910), and *The Good Man and the Good* (1918).

Calkins was the first woman president of the American Psychological Association (1905) and was president of the American Philosophical Association (1918). She lectured at the University of London in 1927 and was made an honorary member of the British Psychological Association. She received honorary degrees from Columbia University and Smith College.

REFERENCES: *DAB* (supp. 1): *NAW; NCAB* (13:75); *NYT,* February 27, 1930, p. 24; *WWW* (I).   *M. Jane Dowd*

CALKINS, Norman Allison. B. September 9, 1822, Gainesville, New York, to Elisha Deming and Abigail (Lockwood) Calkins. M. 1854 to Mary Hoosier. Ch. two. D. December 23, 1895, New York, New York.

Norman Allison Calkins's education was received in the local district common school and in a classical academy. He started teaching at the age of eighteen during the winter term in Castile, New York, while continuing his own studies. Within six years he was principal of Centre School in Gainesville and the local superintendent of schools (1845–46). In 1846 he resigned his position as superintendent to become the editor of *Student* (later, *Student and Schoolmate),* a monthly educational journal in New York City (1846–56). Calkins conducted teachers' institutes in New York, New Jersey, Pennsylvania, and Connecticut.

Calkins became assistant superintendent of schools in New York City in charge of the primary schools (1862–95). In 1864 he also was employed as an instructor of methods and principles of education in the Saturday classes of the New York City Normal School. The school became the Normal College in 1871, and he continued as professor of methods and principles until Saturday classes were discontinued about 1882.

Calkins was interested in the Pestalozzian movement in education and had studied the experiment of Robert Owen at New Harmony, Indiana. He interpreted the object method of instruction in his books, advocated using graduated exercises, and put emphasis on practical skills and impressions and object recognition rather than formal grammar. He wrote *Primary Object Lessons* (1861), *Teaching Color* (1877), *Manual of Object-Teaching* (1882), *First Reading from Blackboard to Books* (1883), and *How to Teach Phonics* (1889).

Calkins was active in the National Educational Association as president of the department of elementary schools (1873), president of the department of school superintendents (1883), treasurer (1883–85), president (1886), and chairman of the board of trustees (1886–95). He was treasurer (1857–83) of the American Congregational Union, which sought to encourage the establishment of Congregational churches in the West. He received an honorary degree from Marietta (Ohio) College.

REFERENCES: *AC; DAB; NCAB* (10:86); *WWW* (H); Will S. Monroe *(q.v.), History of the Pestalozzian Movement in the U.S.* (New York: Arno Press and the New York Times, 1969); *NYT,* December 25, 1895, p. 5.

Mark Fravel, Jr.

CAMP, David Nelson. B. October 3, 1820, Durham, Connecticut, to Elah and Orit (Lee) Camp. M. June 25, 1844, to Sarah Adaline Howd. Ch. two. D. October 19, 1916, New Haven, Connecticut.

David Nelson Camp received his earliest education from the Bible and religious books. Because of family illnesses and farm responsibilities, his formal education took place intermittently in a variety of Connecticut district public schools and private academies, including the private school of Mrs. Goodwin; Durham, Hartford, and Meriden academies; and the temporary normal school established by Henry Barnard *(q.v.)* in 1839. His education was supplemented by private tutors. He received the A.M. degree (1853) from Yale College.

At the age of eighteen, Camp accepted a teaching position at North Guilford, Connecticut, which he held for one term (three months). Camp taught public school in Connecticut at Cromwell, Branford, and Meriden for several years and after 1845 taught several teachers' institutes. He was appointed a teacher of the Connecticut State Normal School (later, Central Connecticut State College) at New Britain in 1849 and later was associate principal (1855). In 1857 he became commissioner of common schools and principal of the state normal school, holding this position until 1866 when forced by ill health to resign. He traveled in Europe (1866–67).

Camp returned from his travels to accept an appointment at St. John's College in Annapolis, Maryland, in 1867, but became the assistant to Henry Barnard, who was appointed the first United States commissioner of education. Camp resigned from that position on the death of his father in the winter of 1868. Later he founded the New Britain (Connecticut) Seminary in 1870, where he and his daughter Ellen taught until the end of his active career in 1880.

Camp was the author of *Globe Manual* (1864), *Manual of Illustrative Teaching* (1868), and *History of New Britain, Farmington, and Berlin* (1889). He wrote several *Camp's Outline Maps and Geographies* and was compiler and editor of *The American Year Book* and revised *Outline Maps* and *Government Instructor* by S. Augustus Mitchell *(q.v.)*. Camp's autobiographical notes were published by his grandchildren as *Recollections of a Long and Active Life* (1917).

Upon retirement, Camp took part in religious, financial, and civil activities. He held positions of leadership in the Congregational church, the Connecticut Temperance Union, and the New Britain Young Men's Christian Association. He served as an executive for several business firms. Camp was elected to the New Britain Council (1871) and the board of aldermen (1872–76) and was mayor (1877–79). He was elected to the Connecticut legislature in 1889 and chaired the committee on education. He was a charter member of the National Council of Education and served as secretary of the National Teachers' Association (later, National Education Association) in 1864.

REFERENCES: *DAB; NCAB* (2:520); *TC; WWW* (I); David Nelson Camp, *Recollections of a Long and Active Life* (New Britain, Conn., 1917); *NYT,* October 20, 1916, p. 9.   *Norman H. Calaway*

CAMPA, Arthur Leon. B. February 20, 1905, Guaymas, Mexico, to Daniel and Delfina (López) Campa. M. April 23, 1943, to Lucille Cushing. Ch. five.

Arthur Leon Campa attended the University of New Mexico where he received both the A.B. and A.M. degrees in 1930. He received the Ph.D. degree (1940) from Columbia University.

Campa taught modern languages at Albuquerque (New Mexico) High School (1928) and at the University of New Mexico (1929–46). He became chairman of the division of modern languages and literature at the University of Denver (Colorado) in 1946.

Author of bulletins on Spanish folklore and articles in professional and learned journals, Campa wrote *Spanish Folklore in New Mexico* (1930), *Acquiring Spanish* (1944), *Mastering Spanish* (1945), *Spanish Commercial Correspondence* (coauthor, 1945), *Spanish Folk Poetry in New Mexico* (1946), and *Treasure of the Sangre de Cristos* (1963).

Campa was active in many associations, including the American Folklore Society (councillor) and folklore societies of Brazil, Venezuela, Argentina, Mexico, and other countries. He was president of the American Folklore Festival Association and the Folklore Society of Colorado (1950). He was cultural attaché at the United States Embassy at Lima, Peru (1955–57), and director of fiestas for the United States Coronado Exposition Commission (1940). He served with the United States Army Air Corps during World War II.

REFERENCES: *CA* (17–18); *WW* (XXXVI); *Directory of American Scholars* (New York: R. R. Bowker, 1957); *Who Is Who in the West United States and Canada* (Chicago: Marquis, 1971).   *A. Rolando Andrade*

CAMPBELL, Douglas Houghton. B. December 16, 1859, Detroit, Michigan, to James Valentine and Cornelia (Hotchkiss) Campbell. M. no. D. February 24, 1953, Palo Alto, California.

Douglas Houghton Campbell, distinguished botanist and son of a Michigan supreme court judge, attended the University of Michigan and was graduated with the Ph.M. (1882) and Ph.D. (1886) degrees. His thesis, "The Development of the Ostrich Fern," received the Walker Prize of the Boston Society of Natural History in 1886. He studied cell structure, microtechnique, and staining living plant tissue in Germany at Bonn, Tübingen, and Berlin (1886–88).

Campbell taught zoology and botany at Detroit High School (1882–86). Upon returning to the United States from Germany, he was professor of botany at Indiana University (1888–91) and then accepted the chair of botany at newly founded Stanford University in California. Campbell remained at Stanford until retirement in 1925 and was emeritus professor until his death in 1953.

Campbell published more than a hundred and fifty papers and reviews, six books, one monograph, and a few pamphlets contributing to the knowledge of morphology and the life history of various plants. He was the author of *Elements of Structural and Systematic Botany for High School and Elementary College Courses* (1890), *The Structure and Development of Mosses and Ferns* (1895), *Lectures on the Evolution of Plants* (1899), *A University Textbook of Botany* (1902), *An Outline of Plant Geography* (1926), and *The Evolution of Land Plants* (1940).

Campbell was editor of the *American Naturalist,* a member of the National Academy of Sciences, the Royal Society of Edinburgh, and the Linnaean Society of London and president of the Botanical Society of America (1913) and the Pacific section of the American Association for the Advancement of Science (1930). He received an honorary degree from the University of Michigan.

REFERENCES: *DSB; LE* (II); *NCAB* (A:284); *WWW* (III); Harry Baker Humphrey, *Makers of North American Botany* (New York: Ronald Press, 1961); *NYT,* February 25, 1953, p. 27.   *Stratton F. Caldwell*

CAMPBELL, Prince Lucien. B. October 10, 1861, Newmarket, Missouri, to Thomas Franklin and Jane Eliza (Campbell) Campbell. M. September 12, 1887, to Eugenia J. Zieber. M. August 20, 1908, to Susan (Campbell) Church. Ch. one. D. August 14, 1925, Eugene, Oregon.

Prince Lucien Campbell moved with his parents from Missouri to Monmouth, Oregon, where his father took the position of president of Christian College. Campbell enrolled in Christian College and completed the required curriculum in 1879. He received the A.B. degree (1886) from Harvard University.

He taught at Christian College for three years and went to Kansas in 1882 as a reporter for the *Kansas City Star* for fourteen months.

Campbell returned to Monmouth, Oregon, from his studies at Harvard and became a professor of classics at Oregon State Normal College (previously Christian College). In 1890 he was elected president of Oregon State Normal (later, Oregon College of Education), with the task of encouraging the conservative faculty of Christian College to accept the new ideas developed by the normal school leadership. His success led to his election in 1902 as president of the University of Oregon in Eugene.

When he took office, the university was a minor institution of 250 students. Through Campbell's efforts, a school of music was added (1902), as were the division of correspondence and extension (1907) and schools of education (1910), journalism (1912), architecture, allied arts and business administration (1914), sociology (1920), and physical education (1921). He reorganized the school of law from a night school to a regular division of the university.

Campbell helped organize the American Council on Education (first secretary-treasurer, 1917–18) and was active in the Association of State Colleges (vice-president and acting president, 1916–17), the State Textbook Commission, the Bureau of Mines and Geology, the State Library Commission, the Oregon Social Hygiene Society, the Oregon Association for the Prevention of Tuberculosis, and the regional committee for the Young Men's Christian Association in Oregon and Idaho. He received honorary degrees from Pacific University and the University of Colorado.

After his death, *Education and the State,* a statement of his philosophy of education, was published by his former students in 1927 with a limited edition of 150 copies.

REFERENCES: *DAB; NCAB* (21:231); *WWW* (I); Henry D. Sheldon, *History of the University of Oregon* (Portland: Binfords & Mort, 1940). *James J. O'Connor*

CAPEN, Elmer Hewitt. B. April 5, 1838, Stoughton, Massachusetts, to Samuel and n.a. (Shepard) Capen. M. to Letitia H. Mussey. M. 1877 to Mary L. Edwards. Ch. three, including Samuel Paul Capen, educator. D. March 22, 1905, Medford, Massachusetts.

Elmer Hewitt Capen was educated in the local Stoughton, Massachusetts, district school, the Pierce Academy at Middleborough, Massachusetts, and the Green Mountain Institute at South Woodstock, Vermont, and he received the B.A. degree from Tufts College (later, University) in Medford, Massachusetts (1860). Capen studied law at Harvard University, was admitted to the bar in 1864, and practiced law for a while at Stoughton. He studied theology and was ordained an Episcopalian minister in 1865, when he became pastor of the Independent Christian Church of Gloucester, Massachusetts. Capen was pastor of churches in St. Paul, Minnesota (1869–70), and Providence, Rhode Island (1870–75).

In 1878 Capen was inaugurated president of Tufts College, a position he held for twenty-seven years. During his presidency, there was a large increase in the student population and the faculty. New departments were added and existing ones enlarged, and preparatory and medical schools were established. Tufts developed the elective system to its fullest extent and was the first New England college to offer a degree without requiring students to study Greek. A civil engineering degree program was offered and enlarged to include electrical and mechanical engineering degrees. Capen advocated equality for women in education, and women were admitted to Tufts on the same terms as men in 1892. Capen taught courses in political economics and ethics and served as the college chaplain.

He was the author of many articles, *Occasional Addresses* (1902), and *The College and the Higher Life* (1905). Capen was active in civic and educational affairs as chairman of the state board of education and of the board of visitors of the Salem Normal School. He was president of the New England Commission on Admissions Examinations and the Law and Order League of Massachusetts. He was a trustee of the Universalist General Convention. While an undergraduate at Tufts, Capen was elected to one term in the state legislature (1859–60); he was a delegate to the national Republican convention in 1888.

Capen received an honorary degree from St. Lawrence University (1877).

REFERENCES: *AC; DAB; NCAB* (6:241); *WWW* (I); *NYT*, March 23, 1905, p. 9.   *Barbara Ruth Peltzman*

CARMICHAEL, Leonard. B. November 9, 1898, Philadelphia, Pennsylvania, to Thomas Harrison and Emily Henrietta (Leonard) Carmichael. M. June 30, 1932, to Pearl Kidston. Ch. one. D. September 16, 1973, Washington, D.C.

Leonard Carmichael studied at the Germantown Friends School in Philadelphia (1917) and attended Tufts College (later, University) in Medford, Massachusetts, graduating with the B.S. degree in 1921. He received the Ph.D. degree (1924) from Harvard University and studied at the University of Berlin under a Sheldon Fellowship (1924).

He was an instructor at Tufts (1923–24) and taught at Princeton University (1924–27) and at Brown University in Providence, Rhode Island (1927–36), where he was director of the psychological laboratory (1927–36) and the laboratory of sensory physiology (1934–36). He was chairman of the department of psychology and dean of the faculty of arts and sciences at the University of Rochester (1936–38). His major interest was the study of human behavior.

In 1938 he accepted the presidency of Tufts College, where he also served as director of the research laboratory of sensory psychology and physiology. During his administration the college curriculum was reorganized, and the advising system was changed to deal more effectively with student educational needs.

Carmichael was called to Washington, D.C., during World War II as director of the National Roster of Scientific and Specialized Personnel, which he organized to place highly trained Americans in positions that needed their particular skills (1941–43), and as a member of the War Manpower Commission, the Natural Resources Planning Board, and the National Research Council. He served on a special commission to aid the vocational rehabilitation, education, and training problems of the returning veterans (1945–52).

He resigned as president of Tufts in 1953 to become the seventh secretary of the Smithsonian Institution. He cleaned out "the nation's attic," as he called it, modernized its exhibits, established the Museum of History and Technology, expanded the Museum of Natural History, and renovated the National Zoo. He retired in 1964 to join the National Geographic Society as vice-president for research and exploration. He joined Jacques Yves Cousteau in exploring ocean depths and accompanied an expedition that climbed Mount Everest.

Carmichael wrote *Basic Psychology* (1957) and coauthored *Read and Write* (with others, 1924), *Elements of Human Psychology* (with Howard C. Warren, 1930), and *Reading and Visual Fatigue* (with Walter F. Dearborn, 1947). He was editor of *Manual of Child Psychology* (1946) and coeditor of *The Selection of Military Manpower* (with Leonard C. Mead, 1952). He was cooperating editor of *Psychological Index* (1931–36), associate editor of the *Journal of Genetic Psychology, Psychology Monographs,* and *British Journal of Educational Psychology.* He was editor of a series of books on psychology for Houghton Mifflin Company. He contributed a chapter, "The Physiological Correlates of Intelligence," to the thirty-ninth yearbook of the National Society for the Study of Education.

Working with Herbert Jasper at Brown University, Carmichael developed electroencephology, the measurement of brain waves, when medical research doubted that the brain transmitted electrical impulses.

During his lifetime he accrued many honors, held dozens of professional offices, received honorary degrees from some twenty-one colleges and universities and many awards, including the Hartley Public Welfare Medal from the National Academy of Science (1972) "for eminence in application of science to public welfare" and the presidential Citation of Merit (1942), and was decorated by governments of the Federal Republic of Germany, Spain, Denmark, and Italy.

He was a fellow of the American Association for the Advancement of Science and the American Academy of Arts and Sciences. He held membership in the International Primatological Society (president, 1964–68), the National Academy of Sciences (chairman of the section of psychology, 1950–53), the National Research Council, the American Psychological Association (president, 1939–40), the International Union of Biological Sciences (section president), and the American Philosophical Society (president, 1970–73). He served on many delegations, commissions, and boards of directors and was vice-chairman of the Harvard Foundation for Advanced Study and Research (1951–54 and 1956–58).

REFERENCES: *CA* (41–44); *LE* (III); *NCAB* (F:200); *WW* (XXXVIII); *WWAE* (XVI); *WWW* (VI); *Brittanica Book of the Year 1974,* p. 516; *NYT,* September 17, 1973, p. 36.   *Stephen J. Clarke*

CARMICHAEL, Oliver Cromwell. B. October 3, 1891, Goodwater, Alabama, to Daniel Monroe and Amanda Delight (Lessley) Carmichael. M. July 13, 1918, to Mae Crabtree. Ch. two. D. September 25, 1966, Asheville, North Carolina.

Oliver Cromwell Carmichael studied for two years at Alabama Presbyterian College. He transferred to the University of Alabama and received the A.B. (1911) and M.A. (1914) degrees. He taught German and French at the University of Alabama (1911–12) and at Florence (Alabama) Normal School (later, University of North Alabama) in 1912–1913 before going to Oxford, England, as a Rhodes scholar in 1913. He spent a year with the Commission for Relief in Belgium before returning to Oxford for one term in April 1915. Carmichael's academic career was interrupted by service in the British Young Men's Christian Association, the British Army, and the United States Army. He was decorated for his war service.

In Birmingham, Alabama, Carmichael was chairman of the French department at Central High School (1919–20) and principal of Henry (1920–21) and Woodlawn (1921–22) high schools. In 1922 he became dean and assistant to the president of Alabama College (later, University of Montevallo) at Montevallo and was president from 1926 to 1935. He obtained a 200 percent increase in the state's annual appropriation and added $1 million to the value of the college plant.

Carmichael moved to Vanderbilt University in Nashville, Tennessee, in 1935, to be dean of the graduate school and senior college (1935–37), vice-chancellor (1936–37), and chancellor (1937–46). At Vanderbilt he promoted a $9 million building and endowment fund campaign, enhanced the liberal arts program, organized a college of law, constructed a central library, and developed a cooperative curriculum arrangement with George Peabody College for Teachers.

Carmichael was president of the Carnegie Foundation for the Advancement of Teaching (1946–53). In 1953 he became president of the University of Alabama. During his presidency controversies arose concerning the desegregation of the university. In 1957 he became affiliated with the Ford Foundation for the Advancement of Education.

Carmichael wrote *The Changing Role of Higher Education* (1949), *Universities: Commonwealth and American* (1959), and *Graduate Education, a Critique and a Program* (1961). He was active in professional organizations and served as president of the Southern Association of Colleges for Women and the Southern Association of Colleges and Secondary Schools (1955–56). He was a member of the White House Conference on Child Health and Protection (1931), the advisory committee to the Manpower Commission (1942–43), the advisory council for the Southern Research Institute (1945), and the President's Commission on Higher Education (1946–47). He was chairman of the board of trustees of the State University of New York (1948–53) and chairman of the board of the Learning Resources Institute (1959). In 1960 he was appointed to the commission established by the Southern Regional Educational Board to chart a course for higher education in the south. Carmichael received many honorary degrees from colleges and universities.

REFERENCES: *CA* (9–10); *CB* (January 1946 and December 1966); *LE* (III); *NCAB* (F:312); *WWAE* (XVI); *WWW* (IV); *NYT,* September 27, 1966, p. 47.   *Erwin H. Goldenstein*

CARMICHAEL, Omer. B. March 7, 1893, Hollins, Alabama, to William and Lucy (Wilson) Carmichael. M. 1926 to Elnora Blanchard. Ch. three. D. January 9, 1960, Louisville, Kentucky.

Omer Carmichael was graduated from the University of Alabama with the A.B. degree (1914) and received the A.M. degree (1924) from Columbia University.

Carmichael served in Alabama as a teacher in Tallapoosa County (1911–12) and as a teacher (1914–16) and principal (1916–19) in Selma. He was superintendent of schools in Talladega (1919–20) and Selma (1920–26), Alabama, Tampa, Florida (1926–30), Lynchburg, Virginia (1932–45), and Louisville, Kentucky (1945–60).

In Louisville Carmichael found a school system typical of the southern racial segregation pattern of separate schools, faculties, and administrative staffs and where educational meetings and committee activities were always separated by race. Carmichael broke this pattern and laid the groundwork for responding to what he considered an inevitable court decision striking down the separate-but-equal doctrine. When the 1954 Supreme Court decision was announced, he reiterated his readiness to comply, and the board of education supported his position. The smooth transition to a free choice of schools made Carmichael a national figure. In 1956 President Dwight D. Eisenhower paid tribute to Carmichael's leadership, commenting on the calm that characterized the Louisville community during the transition.

Carmichael was the author of *The Lousville Story* (with Weldon James, 1957). He was a trustee of Lynchburg (Virginia) College and a member of many associations, including the American Association of School Administrators (vice-president, 1954–55), the Alabama Education Association (president, 1926), and the Kentucky Association of Colleges and Secondary Schools (president).

He was the recipient of many awards, including the Fiorella H. LaGuardia Award (1957) and the Brotherhood Award of the National Conference of Christians and Jews. He received honorary degrees from Harvard, Yale, and Kentucky universities and Dartmouth College.

REFERENCES: *LE* (III); *WWAE* (XV); *WWW* (III); Omer Carmichael and Weldon James, *The Louisville Story* (New York: Simon and Schuster, 1957); *NYT,* January 10, 1960, p. 86.   *Frank H. Stallings*

CARPENTER, George Rice. B. October 25, 1863, Eskimo River Mission Station, Labrador, Canada, to Charles Carroll and Feronia N. (Rice) Carpenter. M. 1890 to Mary Seymour. Ch. one. D. April 8, 1909, New York, New York.

George Rice Carpenter was born while his parents were in the pioneer missionary service at Eskimo River Mission Station on the coast of Labrador. After preparation for college at Phillips Academy in Andover, Massachusetts, he entered Harvard University and was graduated in 1886. He was awarded the Rogers Fellowship, which enabled him to study for two years throughout Europe; he spent most of the time in Paris, France, and Berlin, Germany.

He was appointed an instructor in English upon his return to Harvard (1888–90). The Massachusetts Institute of Technology awarded him an assistant professorship in 1890, and he remained there until 1893 when he accepted the chair of rhetoric at Columbia University. Carpenter was professor of rhetoric and English composition at Columbia for sixteen years to his death in 1909.

While at Columbia, Carpenter attained a reputation as an eminent rhetorician and a prolific writer and critic of literature. He was the author of *Elements of Rhetoric* (1899), *Life of Longfellow* (1901), *Life of Whittier* (1903), and *Teaching of English* (1903). He was editor of *Lantham's Letters of Dante* (1891), *American Prose* (1898), *Modern English Prose* (with W. T. Brewster, 1904), and *Model English Prose* (1905). He received an award from the Dante Society and an honorary degree from the University of the South.

REFERENCES: *DAB; NCAB* (23: 328); *WWW* (I); *NYT,* April 9, 1909, p. 9.   *Alfred J. Ciani*

CARPENTER, William Weston. B. March 2, 1889, Lawrence, Kansas, to William Thomas and Helen Eva (Weston) Carpenter. M. December 27, 1914, to Doris Melvina Cotey. Ch. three. D. September 28, 1968, Columbia, Missouri.

William Weston Carpenter was graduated from the University of Kansas, receiving the A.B. (1912) and A.M. (1917) degrees. He studied at the University of Arizona and received the Ph.D. degree (1926) from Columbia University.

Carpenter was a teacher of science in Arizona high schools and head of the science department of Phoenix Union High School to 1920. He was dean of Phoenix Junior College (1920–23) and became a professor of science teaching (1925–27) and school administration (1927–28) at George Peabody College for Teachers in Nashville, Tennessee. He joined the faculty of the University of Missouri in 1928 as professor of education, serving to his retirement in 1959. Carpenter was in the United States Army in World War I and was an educational reorganization adviser in Japan (1948–50).

Carpenter was the author of many articles, reports, and books, including *The Teacher and Secondary School Administration* (with John Rufi, 1931), *State and National School Administration* (with Ralph Yakel, 1932), *Community School Administration* (with L. G. Townsend, 1936), *Community School Building Problems* (with N. E. Viles, 1937), *The Organization and Administration of the Junior College* (1939), *Schoolhouse Planning and Construction* (1946), *Evaluating the Educational Services in the*

Local School District (with others, 1955), and *Syllabus for School Building Problems* (1956).

A national secretary of Phi Delta Kappa, Carpenter was a member of professional associations. He served as chairman of the research committee of the American Association of Junior Colleges. Active in the Boy Scouts, he was a recipient of the Silver Beaver award.

REFERENCES: *LE* (III); *WW* (XXXI); *Columbia Missourian,* September 29, 1968.   *John F. Ohles*

CARR, William George. B. June 1, 1901, Northampton, England, to Alfred S. and Alice (Bailey) Carr. M. August 20, 1924, to Elizabeth Vaughan. Ch. one.

William George Carr received the B.A. (1924), M.A. (1926), and Ph.D. (1929) degrees from Stanford University.

He was a teacher at Roosevelt Junior High School in Glendale, California (1924–25), and professor of education at Pacific University in Forest Grove, Oregon (1926–27). He was a director of research for the California Teachers Association (1928–29) and the assistant director of research (1929–31), director of research (1931–40), associate secretary (1940–52), and executive secretary (1952–67) of the National Education Association (NEA). On his retirement, he was president of the International Council of Nontheatrical Events.

As executive secretary, Carr guided the NEA through a major period of development as a classroom teacher-oriented organization and an aggressive and militant advocate for the rights and benefits of teachers. He was instrumental in effecting the merger of the NEA and the black American Teachers Association in 1966. Carr was a frequent visiting professor to many American colleges and universities.

Carr was the author of *Education for World Citizenship* (1928), *County Unit of School Administration* (1931), *The Lesson Assignment* (with John Waage, 1931), *School Finance* (1933), *John Swett: The Biography of An Educational Pioneer* (1933), *Purposes of Education* (1938), *Learning the Ways of Democracy* (with others, 1940), *Educational Leadership* (1942), *Education and the People's Peace* (1943), *Only by Understanding* (1945), *One World in the Making* (1946), and *The Waging of Peace* (1946).

In addition to his contributions to American education, Carr was instrumental in the formation of the United Nations Educational, Scientific, and Cultural Organization (UNESCO). He served as deputy secretary of UNESCO and helped write the preamble and statement of purposes in its constitution. He was active in the World Confederation of Organizations of the Teaching Profession (secretary-general, 1946–70, and president, 1970–72) and the Sino-American Cultural Society (president from 1969). He was a frequent delegate for the United States to international education conferences and was the recipient of awards from several foreign countries and honorary degrees from several American universities.

REFERENCES: *CA* (53–56); *CB* (September 1952); *LE* (V); *WWAE* (XIV); *WW* (XXXI); Robert J. Havighurst *(q.v.)*, ed., *Leaders in American Education* (Chicago: University of Chicago Press, 1971).

Robert E. Conner
Jeffrey Martin

CARRICK, Samuel. B. July 17, 1760, York (later, Adams) County, Pennsylvania, to n.a. M. to Elizabeth Moore. M. 1794 to Annis McClellan. ch. n.a. D. August 17, 1809, Knoxville, Tennessee.

Samuel Carrick, a frontier preacher and educator, moved to the Shenandoah Valley in Virginia at an early age. He studied for the Presbyterian ministry under William Graham. In 1782 he was licensed to preach and served as pastor at Rocky Spring, Virginia.

Early in his ministry Carrick began to go to the Tennessee frontier as a traveling missionary. He often spoke to small groups of people gathered outside. By 1791 he had moved to the area near the junction of the Holston and French Broad rivers and organized the Lebanon Presbyterian Church. He also organized the first church in the newly formed town of Knoxville, Tennessee, and served as its pastor.

In 1793 Carrick established a seminary in his home where instruction was offered in Latin, Greek, English, geography, logic, philosophy, astronomy, and rhetoric. In 1794 Blount College, named in honor of Governor William Blount, was granted a charter by the Tennessee territorial legislature. Carrick was appointed president of the college, which later became East Tennessee College and, eventually, the University of Tennessee. He continued in the post to his death in 1809.

REFERENCES: *DAB; WWW* (H). *Harold D. Lehman*

CARRINGTON, William Thomas. B. January 23, 1854, Calloway County, Missouri, to William and Susan (Fisher) Carrington. M. August 19, 1879, to Mary Holloway. M. 1932 to Willa Howard. Ch. two. D. January 21, 1937, Jefferson City, Missouri.

William Thomas Carrington spent part of his childhood roughing it with his father in the forests of Missouri, helping to supply railroad ties and timbers to the railroad company. His father was also a county judge in Calloway County for thirty years (1854–84). Carrington's education began at Sugar Grove Academy in Missouri and continued at McGee College in College Mound, Missouri, where he received the A.M. degree. Carrington attended Kirksville (Missouri) Normal School (later, Northeast Missouri State University), where he received a Master of Scientific Didactics degree. He also studied at the University of Missouri.

Carrington first taught in Calloway County (1872–75) beginning at the

CARTER, James Gordon   [243]

age of seventeen. He was principal of Missouri schools in Piedmont (1876–78), Arrow Rock (1878–79), and Oak Ridge (1879–81), and was superintendent of schools for Cape Girardeau (1881–83). He served as chief clerk with the Missouri State Department of Education (1883–87). In 1887 he returned to the Missouri public schools as principal in Springfield (1887–92) and Mexico (1892–95).

In 1899 Carrington became state superintendent of public schools of Missouri, serving until 1907. He was the first president of Southwest Missouri Normal School (later, State University) in Springfield from 1907 to 1918. During World War I, he served in Washington, D.C., in the Department of War Risk Insurance. He returned to the Missouri State Department of Education as supervisor of vocational education (1919–32).

He thought cultural studies were more important than formal studies and sought to remove abstractions, formalities, and authority from education. He favored concrete learning situations and the reading of literature.

Carrington's writings, both professional and personal, include *Missouri School Reports* (1899–1907), *Elements of Agriculture for Public Schools* (1904), *Course of Study for Rural and Village Schools* (n.d.), *Mary (Holloway) Carrington as Her Husband Knew Her* (1930), and *History of Education in Missouri* (1931). Carrington founded and edited the *Missouri School Journal* when he was state superintendent.

He was president of the Missouri State Teachers Association (1889) and state director for the National Educational Association (1889–1903). He established county teachers' associations, helped establish the Springfield and Maryville normal schools, and fought for library funds for all public schools.

REFERENCES: *LE* (I); *WWW* (I); William T. Carrington, *History of Education in Missouri* (1931); Roy Ellis, *Shrine of the Ozarks: A History of Southwest Missouri State University* (Springfield: Southwest Missouri State University, 1968); Claude A. Phillips, *A History of Education in Missouri* (Jefferson City, Mo.: Hugh Stephens Printing Co., 1911).

James R. Layton

CARTER, James Gordon. B. September 7, 1795, Leominster, Massachusetts, to James and Betsy (Hale) Carter. M. 1827 to Anne M. Packard. Ch. one. D. July 21, 1849, Chicago, Illinois.

James Gordon Carter was graduated with honors from Harvard University in 1820. He taught school at Leominster, Massachusetts (1820–30), where he supported the Pestalozzian principles that pupils should discover truth inductively rather than memorize instruction from books or teachers. He applied the inductive method in writing geography texts.

Carter took an active role in supporting reform of public education. He wrote a series of articles published in the *Boston Transcript* and in the *Boston Patriot,* signing the articles "Franklin." His views were published in pamphlet form, widely distributed, and frequently discussed. An important aspect of Carter's suggestions for improving the schools was the establishment of normal schools for teacher training. In 1830 Carter assisted in organizing the American Institute of Instruction, of which he was an influential member and, for some time, an officer.

Carter was a member of the Massachusetts legislature, serving in the house (1835–38) and in the senate (1839–40), and he was chairman of the legislative committee on education. Among the measures reported from the committee were those proposing instruction of youth employed in factories, providing funds for training common-school teachers, establishing a state board of education, and providing a state secretary of public schools. Although disappointed in not being selected as secretary, Carter was first to be appointed to the Massachusetts Board of Education.

He was author of pamphlets containing his letters to the *Boston Transcript and Boston Patriot* and *Geography of Massachusetts* (1830) and *Geography of New Hampshire* (1831), and was editor of the *Literary Gazette, United States Gazette* (1824), and *New York Review* (1826).

REFERENCES: *AC; DAB; NCAB* (10:507); *WWW* (H); Grace Taylor Brown, "The Importance and Influence of James Gordon Carter, Pioneer Educator in Massachusetts, 1795–1849" (doct. diss., Boston University, 1957).   *Thomas F. Reidy*

CARTWRIGHT, Morse Adams. B. November 3, 1890, Omaha, Nebraska, to Theodore Parker and Isabella Titus (Hudson) Cartwright. M. August 15, 1914, to Myrtle Lenore Salsig. ch. two. D. April 21, 1974, Pasadena, California.

Morse Adams Cartwright was graduated from Manual Training High School in Denver, Colorado, in 1907. He received the B.S. degree in jurisprudence (1912) from the University of California at Berkeley and studied at California under a teaching fellowship in the English department (1912–13). Cartwright taught English at the University of California (1913–14).

In 1914 he became city editor of the Riverside, California, daily newspaper. He managed the University of California Press (1917–20 and 1923–24) and served as a journalism instructor (1918–20).

In 1918 Cartwright assumed the position of assistant to the president and executive secretary of the University of California. He was assistant director of the University of California Extension Division (1923–24) and was assistant to the president of the Carnegie Corporation in New York (1924–26). He helped organize and became director (1926–49) and president (1950) of the American Association for Adult Education. He was executive officer of the Institute of Adult Education (1941–49) and professor of education at Teachers College, Columbia University (1941–51). He was a consultant to the federal government on adult education programs (1942–43).

Cartwright was author of *Ten Years of Adult Education* (1935), *Adult Adjustment* (with Glen Burch, 1945) and a number of pamphlets, including *Unemployment and Adult Education* (1931), and *Marching Home* (1944). He was editor of *Adult Education Journal* (1927–49).

Cartwright was official United States representative at the World Conference on Adult Education in England in 1929 and was a trustee of the Belgian-American Educational Foundation and the National Parks Commission. He was a member of the United States National Commission for the United Nations Educational, Scientific, and Cultural Organization. Cartwright received honorary degrees from Southwestern University in Memphis, Tennessee, and Mount Allison University, Canada.

REFERENCES: *CB* (September 1947 and June 1974); *LE* (III); *WW* (XXVII); *WWW* (VI); D. C. Fisher, "Morse A. Cartwright," *Adult Education Journal* (July 1949): 150–52; *NYT,* April 22, 1974, p. 38.

S. S. Britt, Jr.

CASE, Adelaide Teague. B. January 10, 1887, St. Louis, Missouri, to Charles Lyman and Lois Adelaide (Teague) Case. M. no. D. June 19, 1948, Boston, Massachusetts.

Adelaide Case grew up in New York City where she attended the Brearley School. After receiving the A.B. (1908) from Bryn Mawr (Pennsylvania) College, she taught at St. Faith's School in Poughkeepsie, New York (1908–09), and was librarian at the Episcopal Church Mission House in New York City (1914–16).

Choosing religious education as a vocation, Case began teaching at the New York Training School for Deaconesses (1917–19) and studying at Teachers College, Columbia University, where she received the A.M. (1919) and Ph.D. (1924) degrees. She taught at Teachers College for over twenty years (1920–41), becoming head of the department of religious education in 1938. The Episcopal Theological Seminary in Cambridge, Massachusetts, named her professor of Christian education (1941–48), a particular honor since she was the first woman professor in an Episcopal seminary.

Case spoke frequently in churches and at professional meetings and wrote numerous articles and several books, including *As Modern Writers See Jesus: A Descriptive Bibliography* (1927), and *Liberal Christianity and Religious Education* (1924).

Case helped promote church-related vocations for women and favored their ordination. Among the first women on the National Council of the Episcopal Church, she was a member of many educational, religious, and pacifist organizations. She was a member of governing boards of the Religious Education Association, the Church League for Industrial Democracy (later, the Episcopal League for Social Action), the Childhood Education Association, and the International Council of Religious Education. She received an honorary degree from Hobart College (1934).

REFERENCES: *LE* (III); *NAW;* Adelaide T. Case, "Teaching Christian Education: A Week from a Professor's Diary," *Religious Education* 43 (September-October 1948): 304–07; *NYT,* June 20, 1948, p. 62; *School and Society* 68 (July 3, 1948): 10.   *Natalie A. Naylor*

CASE, Charles Orlando. B. July 9, 1860, near Rock Island, Illinois, to Charles Harrison and Sarah Jane (Taylor) Case. M. 1892 to Angie M. Jackson. Ch. four. D. November 25, 1933, Phoenix, Arizona.

Charles Orlando Case was orphaned and forced to fend for himself before he reached the age of nine. From 1879 to 1883 he attended Hillsdale College in Michigan.

He settled in Arizona in 1889. He worked as a teacher, principal, and superintendent of schools in Globe, Alma, Mesa, Prescott, Phoenix, and Jerome. Many of his students aided him in his political campaigns. When Arizona became a state in 1912, Case was elected the first superintendent of public instruction. With the exception of one term, he served in that capacity until 1933. His ability and vision contributed greatly to the development of the educational system of the new state.

Case was a member of Arizona's state board of education and on the boards of education of the state teachers' colleges in Tempe and Flagstaff. He was a regent of the University of Arizona and served on the state board of pardons and paroles. He was a member of the National Education Association and the Arizona State Education Association. In 1928 the University of Arizona granted him the honorary degree of Ped.D.

REFERENCES: *LE* (I); *NCAB* (24:25); *WWW* (IV).

Nancy Baldrige Julian

CASSIDY, Rosalind. B. July 17, 1895, Quincy, Illinois, to John Warren and Margaret (Ashbrook) Cassidy. M. no.

Rosalind Cassidy was graduated from Mills College in Oakland, California, with the B.S. degree (1918), and received the A.M. (1924), and Ed.D. (1937) degrees from Columbia University.

Cassidy was an instructor in physical education at Mills College in 1918 and chairman of the physical education department (1925–39). From 1939 until 1947 she served as convenor of the school of education and community services and as director of summer sessions (1939–42). While at Mills she provided leadership in promoting the development of modern dance and organized camping and social group work movements on the

West Coast and a democratic and humane physical education nationally.

In 1947 she joined the staff of the department of physical education at the University of California at Los Angeles (UCLA) where she administered the graduate program and established the department as a national center of professional preparation. She retired from UCLA in 1962.

Her major publications include *The New Physical Education* (with Thomas D. Wood, *q.v.*, 1927), *New Directions in Physical Education for the Adolescent Girl in High School and College* (1938), *Physical Fitness for Girls* (with Hilda C. Kozman, 1943), *Group Experience: The Democratic Way* (with Bernice Baxter, 1943), *Counseling Girls in a Changing Society* (with Hilda C. Kozman, 1947), and *Methods of Physical Education* (with others, 1947). While at UCLA Cassidy wrote *Curriculum Development in Physical Education* (1954), *Supervision in Physical Education* (1956), and *Counseling in the Physical Education Program* (1959). She coauthored *Theory in Physical Education* (with Hilda C. Kozman, 1963), *Methods in Physical Education* (with Hilda C. Kozman, 1967), and *Humanizing Physical Education* (with S. F. Caldwell, 1974).

Cassidy was director of the California Youth Authority Workshop (1947), a member of the board of the Girl Scouts of America (1947–51), and a fellow of the general education board of the Rockefeller Foundation (1936–37) and the American Association of Health, Physical Education and Recreation. She was a member of the American Academy of Physical Education (president, 1950–51) and the American Association of University Women (higher education committee, 1958). She was awarded the Luther Halsey Gulick Award in 1956.

REFERENCES: *LE* (II); *NAW; WW* (XXXI); Stratton F. Caldwell, "Conceptions of Physical Education in Twentieth Century America: Rosalind Cassidy" (Ph.D. diss., University of Southern California, 1966); Russell Holmes Fletcher, ed., *Who's Who in California: A Biographical Reference Work of Notable Living Men and Women of California* (Los Angeles: Who's Who Publications Co., 1941); Alberta Lawrence, ed., *Who's Who Among North American Authors* (Los Angeles: Golden Syndicate Publishing Co., 1929). *Stratton F. Caldwell*

CASTAÑEDA, Carlos Eduardo. B. November 11, 1896, Camargo, Mexico, to Timoteo and Elise (Leroux) Castañeda. M. December 27, 1921, to Elisa Rios. Ch. three. D. April 3, 1958, Austin, Texas.

Carlos Eduardo Castañeda came to the United States from Mexico with his parents in 1908. He received the A.B. (1921), A.M. (1923), and Ph.D. (1932) degrees from the University of Texas. He also studied at the universities of Mexico and Havana and the College of William and Mary.

Castañeda taught Spanish in Texas public high schools in Beaumont (1921) and San Antonio at Brackenridge High School (1922–23) and in the

College of William and Mary (1923–27). At the University of Texas from 1927 to 1958, he served as professor of history and in various other capacities, including librarian for Latin American studies. He taught summers at a number of American universities and at the University of Mexico.

Castañeda was a prolific writer; his books include *The Mexican Side of the Texan Revolution* (1928), *The Finding of Texas* (1936), *The Winning of Texas* (1936), *The Missions at Work* (1938), *The Passing of the Missions* (1939), *End of the Spanish Regime in Texas* (1942), *The Land of Middle America* (1947), and *The Fight for Liberty* (1948). He was coauthor, compiler, and translator of many other works, including the two-volume *History of Texas, 1673–1719* (by Fray Juan Augustin Morfi). He was associate editor of *The Americas*.

He received national and international honors from many professional associations and was decorated as knight commander of the Order of Isabella la Católica by Spain and was a corresponding member of the Academy de la Historia, Academy de Ceiencias Politicas de Venezuela. He was active in a variety of associations, including the American Catholic History Association (president, 1939) and the League of Latin-American Citizens (director-general of education). He was a member of the executive committee of the Institute for Latin American Studies. On leave from the University of Texas, he served on the Fair Employment Practices Commission (1943–45). He was an honorary member of historical associations in France, Mexico, Guatemala and Argentina and the recipient of honorary degrees.

REFERENCES: *NYT*, April 6, 1958, p. 88; *WWW* (III); *Directory of American Scholars*, 3d ed. (New York: R. R. Bowker, 1957).

C. Len Ainsworth

CASWELL, Hollis Leland. B. October 22, 1901, Woodruff, Kansas, to Hollis Leland and Lotta (Hood) Caswell. M. February 12, 1928, to Ruth Allen. Ch. two.

Hollis Leland Caswell attended Kansas State College (later, Fort Hays Kansas State College) in Hays and the University of Nebraska where he received the A.B. degree (1922). He was awarded the A.M. (1927) and Ph.D. (1929) degrees from Teachers College, Columbia University. Caswell served as high school principal in Auburn, Nebraska (1922–24), and was superintendent of the Syracuse (Nebraska) public schools (1924–26).

Upon graduation from Teachers College, Caswell was appointed assistant professor at George Peabody College for Teachers in Nashville, Tennessee; he was promoted to professor in 1931. He served as associate director of the division of surveys and field studies, where he became a consultant to several states, including Alabama, Florida, and Virginia, and a number of city school systems in the reform of school curricula. In 1937 Caswell joined the faculty at Teachers College, where he became director of the division of instruction (1938–50), director of schools and school experimentation:1943–48), associate dean (1946–49), dean (1949–54), and president (1954–61).

Caswell was active in professional associations, particularly the Society of Curriculum (chairman of the executive committee, 1936–37) and, after its merger with the Department of Supervisors and Directors of Instruction in 1942, the newly formed Department of Supervision and Curriculum Development of the National Education Association (president, 1944–46). Later the department became the Association for Supervision and Curriculum Development. Caswell was active in the John Dewey Society (vice-president, 1948–49) and was editor of its eighth yearbook, *The American High School* (1946).

He contributed to professional journals and wrote a number of books in the curriculum field, including *Curriculum Development* (with Doak S. Campbell, 1935), *Readings in Curriculum Development* (1937), and *Curriculum Improvement in Public Schools* (with associates, 1950).

REFERENCES: *CB* (July 1956); *LE* (III); *NYT,* September 30, 1961, p. 22; *WWAE* (XVI); *WW* (XXXI); Mary Louise Seguel, *The Curriculum Field* (New York: Teachers College Press, 1966). *John F. Ohles*

CATTELL, James McKeen. B. May 25, 1860, Easton, Pennsylvania, to William Cassady and Elizabeth (McKeen) Cattell. M. December 11, 1888, to Josephine C. Owen. Ch. seven. D. January 20, 1944, Lancaster, Pennsylvania.

James McKeen Cattell's father William was president of Lafayette College in Easton, Pennsylvania. Cattell received the B.A. (1880) and M.A. (1883) degrees from Lafayette. He studied in Europe with Wilhelm Wundt and Hermann Lotze (1880–82) and at Johns Hopkins University in Baltimore, Maryland (1882–83). He returned to work with Wundt in 1883 and earned the Ph.D. degree in 1886 from the University of Leipzig, Germany. In the fall of 1886, he studied at St. John's College, Cambridge, England, where his association with Francis Galton, James Ward, and Alexander Bain clarified his ideas and influenced his subsequent work.

Returning to America in 1887, Cattell lectured in psychology at the University of Pennsylvania and Bryn Mawr (Pennsylvania) College. In 1888 he lectured and developed a laboratory in England at Cambridge University. He returned to the University of Pennsylvania as first professor of psychology there and chairman of the department of psychology (1888–91). Cattell became head of the department of psychology at Columbia University in 1891 and served as head of the departments of anthropology (1896–1902) and philosophy (1902–05). Under his direction psychology at Columbia became one of the strongest departments of research and advanced teaching, and Cattell was a major influence in psychology in the United States.

Cattell's stance on an independent position for the university professor led to many controversies, which probably contributed to his departure from Columbia in 1917. A letter he wrote protesting sending conscientious objectors to combat duty was interpreted as an act of treason, and he was dismissed. Cattell sued Columbia, and the case was settled by granting him a large annuity.

Upon leaving Columbia, Cattell spent more time in editorial work. His first editorial experience was with the *Psychological Review* (1894–1904), which he founded with J. Mark Baldwin *(q.v.)*. He also founded the *Archives of Psychology*. Cattell bought *Science* from Alexander Graham Bell *(q.v.)* in 1895; it was made the official organ of the American Association for the Advancement of Science in 1900 and was given to the association at Cattell's death. He acquired *Scientific Monthly* (1900) and *American Naturalist* (1908). He founded *School and Society* in 1915 as a weekly medium of communication for American education. He established the *Biographical Directory of American Men of Science* (1908) and *Leaders in Education* (1932). Cattell founded the Science Press in 1923 to publish his journals and books.

Cattell was active in many general and special scientific organizations. He was a founder in 1892 of the American Psychological Association (president, 1895). He was president of the American Association for the Advancement of Science (1924 and vice-president, 1898 and 1913), the New York Academy of Sciences (1902), the American Society of Naturalists (1902), the Eugenics Research Association (1914), and Sigma Xi (1913–15). He presided over the Ninth International Congress of Psychology (1929). In 1921 he founded the Psychological Corporation, a nonprofit stock corporation organized to apply psychology to industry. He was the recipient of several honorary degrees.

REFERENCES: *DAB* (supp. 3); *LE* (I); *NCAB* (34:377, D:94); *WWW* (II); *NYT,* January 21, 1944, p. 16; W. B. Pillsbury *(q.v.),* "James McKeen Cattell," *National Academy of Sciences Biographical Memoirs* (Washington, D.C.: National Academy of Sciences, 1949), vol. 25; "The Psychological Researches of James McKeen Cattell: A Review by Some of His Pupils," *Archives of Psychology* 4 (April 1914): 1–101.

Harold G. MacDermot

CHADBOURNE, Paul Ansel. B. October 21, 1823, North Berwick, Maine, to Isaiah and Pandora (Dennett) Chadbourne. M. October 9, 1850, to Elizabeth Sawyer Page. Ch. two. D. February 23, 1883, New York, New York.

An orphan by the time he was thirteen, Paul Ansel Chadbourne learned farming and carpentry while he resided with friends. At the age of seventeen, he moved to Great Falls, New Hampshire, where he attended the district school and was apprenticed as a druggist's clerk. He attended Phillips Academy in Exeter, New Hampshire, and matriculated at Williams College in Williamstown, Massachusetts, entering as a sophomore in 1845 and graduating first in his class in 1848.

He was a teacher and principal in the schools of Freehold, New Jersey (1848–50), Great Falls, New Hampshire (1850–51), and East Windsor Hill, Connecticut (1851–53) where he pursued theological studies at the Theological Seminary of Connecticut (later, the Hartford Theological Seminary).

He accepted an appointment at Williams College as professor of botany and chemistry in 1853 and later taught natural history. In 1858 he accepted a similar position at Bowdoin College and taught at both Williams and Bowdoin, while serving the Maine Medical School as dean and teaching at the Berkshire (Maine) Medical Institute until it was discontinued. He delivered lectures for twelve years at the Mount Holyoke (Massachusetts) Seminary and Western Reserve College in Ohio and delivered a series of lectures at the Lowell (Massachusetts) Institute and the Smithsonian Institution in Washington, D.C.

In 1866 Chadbourne became the first president of the Agricultural College at Amherst (later, the University of Massachusetts). Poor health forced him to resign this position after seven months, and he moved to Wisconsin, where he assumed the presidency of the University of Wisconsin (1867–70). In 1870 he moved to Utah, staying there until 1872 in an effort to renew his health. Chadbourne returned to Massachusetts in 1872 to succeed Mark Hopkins *(q.v.)* as president of Williams College. He served the college until 1881 when he returned to Amherst as president of the Agricultural College (1882–83).

Chadbourne's publications include *Lectures in Natural History: Its Relations to Intellect, Taste, Wealth and Religion* (the Smithsonian Institution lectures, 1860), *Lectures on Natural Theology* (the Lowell Institute lectures, 1867), *Instinct in Animals and Men* (1872), and *The Public Service of the State of New York* (three volumes, 1882).

Chadbourne participated in professional and civic activities. He conducted scientific expeditions to Newfoundland (1855), Florida (1857), Scandinavia (1859), and Greenland (1861). He was a member of the Massachusetts State Senate (1865–66) and succeeded Louis Agassiz *(q.v.)* on the Massachusetts State Board of Agriculture in 1874. He was awarded honorary degrees by Williams and Amherst colleges.

REFERENCES: *AC; DAB; NCAB* (6:238); *WWW* (H); *NYT,* February 24, 1883, p. 5.   *Richard S. Offenberg*

CHADWICK, George Whitfield. B. November 13, 1854, Lowell, Massachusetts, to Alonzo C. and Hannah Godfrey (Fitts) Chadwick. M. June 17,

1888, to Ida Brooks. Ch. two. D. April 4, 1931, Boston, Massachusetts.

George Whitfield Chadwick attended high school in Lawrence, Massachusetts, and studied piano and organ with an older brother. While quite young, he wrote waltzes and light overtures. He worked for his father in the insurance business and studied piano under Carlyle Petersilea. He was a student at the New England Conservatory of Music in Boston, where he studied organ with George Whiting (1872) and continued instruction in the organ with Dudley Buck (1873) and Eugene Thayer (1874–75). He studied in Europe (1877–80) at Berlin with Karl August Haupt, Leipzig with Solomon Jadassohn, Dresden with Gustav Merkel, and Munich with Josef Rheinberger.

In 1876 Chadwick left Massachusetts to head the music department at Olivet (Michigan) College, where he remained a year. While in Europe he composed some string quartets, which were played in public, and for a thesis composed an overture, *Rip Van Winkle* (1879), which was called the best work produced that year in the conservatory. He returned to the United States in 1880 and taught private lessons until 1882 when he became an instructor in music theory at the New England Conservatory; in 1897 he became its director and held the post until his death in 1931. He played an important role as an educator in American music, instructing such artists as Horatio Parker *(q.v.)*, Henry Hadley, and F. S. Converse.

Chadwick's compositions include overtures: *The Miller's Daughter, Thalia* (1883), *Second Symphony* (1885), *Melpomene* (1885), *Adonais* (1898), *Euterpe* (1903); symphonic poems: *Aphrodite* (1912), *Tom O'Shanter* (1915), and *The Angel of Death* (1917); symphonic sketches: *Pastoral Prelude* and *Columbian Ode,* written for the exposition in Chicago in 1893; cantatas: *Phoenix Expirans* (1892), *Ballad of the Lovely Rosabelle, The Viking's Last Voyage, The Pilgrims' Hymn, The Lily Nymph* (1893); and the lyric drama *Judith* (1901). He also composed chamber music, the comic opera *Tabasco* (1894), nearly seventy songs, and many pieces of church music and some music for the organ.

Chadwick authored a textbook, *Harmony* (1897). He received an honorary degree from Yale University in 1897. He was a member of the American Academy of Arts and Letters.

REFERENCES: *AC; DAB* (supp. 1); *EB; NCAB* (7:326); *WWW* (I).

Renaldo E. Rivera

CHAMBERLAIN, Joshua Lawrence. B. September 8, 1828, Brewster, Maine, to Joshua and Sarah Dupee (Brastow) Chamberlain. M. December 7, 1855, to Frances Caroline Adams. Ch. none. D. February 24, 1914, Brunswick, Maine.

Joshua Lawrence Chamberlain was graduated from Bowdoin College in 1852 and from the Bangor (Maine) Theological Seminary in 1855. He taught

CHAMBERS, *Henry Edward*   [253]

rhetoric and modern languages at Bowdoin until 1862, when he became lieutenant colonel of the Twentieth Maine Infantry. He won the Congressional Medal of Honor defending the Little Round Top at Gettysburg, was brevetted major general, and was chosen by Grant to receive the formal surrender of weapons and colors of Lee's army at Appomattox. After being mustered out of the army, he served four successive terms as governor of Maine (1866–71).

Returning to Bowdoin, he assumed the presidency (1871–83); he was professor of mental and moral science (1874–79) and lecturer in political science and public law (1883–85). Following a series of business ventures in Florida, he became surveyor of customs in Portland, Maine, in 1900, a post he held for the remainder of his life.

Chamberlain was one of the American commissioners to the Paris Exposition (1878) and was honored by the French government for his participation. He wrote a notable report on the educational exhibit at the exposition. Among his other writings were *Maine: Her Place in History* (1877), *The Passing of the Armies* (1915), and a history of New York University for the six-volume *Universities and their Sons* (1898–1923) for which he was one of the editors-in-chief.

REFERENCES: *AC; DAB; NCAB* (1:419); *NYT*, February 25, 1914, p. 9; *WWW* (I).   *Joseph M. McCarthy*

CHAMBERS, Henry Edward. B. November 28, 1860, New Orleans, Louisiana, to Joseph A. and Maria (Charles) Chambers. M. December 27, 1883, to Ellen White Taylor. Ch. two. D. March 8, 1929, New Orleans, Louisiana.

Henry Edward Chambers attended public and private schools and Tulane University in New Orleans, Louisiana, and was a fellow at Johns Hopkins University (1893–94). During his lifetime he was engaged first in education and then in business.

Chambers was a teacher in rural Louisiana schools (1877–81) and was principal in Arkansas at Mineral Springs (1881–82) and Monticello (1883–84) and McDonough School in New Orleans (1885–87). He was president of the Monticello (Arkansas) Male and Female College (1882–83) and superintendent of the Beaumont, Texas, public schools (1884–85). He was professor of science at the New Orleans' Boys High School (1887–90). He was assistant professor of science at Tulane University (1890–93) and principal of the Monroe (Louisiana) High School (1894–96); he returned to the New Orleans' Boys' High School (1896–1901 and 1902–05). He was a writer and businessman from 1905 to his death.

He was the author of *Twenty Lessons in Bookkeeping* (1885), *Primary Speller* (1888), *A School History of the United States* (1887), *A Higher History of the United States* (1889), *Search Questions in American His-*

tory (1890), *Constitutional History of Hawaii* (1896), *West Florida* (1898), *An Introduction to Louisiana History* (1896), *A Baratarian Elaine* (1900), *Under the Stars and Bars* (a play, 1907), *The Legend of the God Votan* (1909), *The Territory of Louisiana, 1803–1812, and Modern Louisiana, 1876–1910* (volume 3 of *The South in the Building of the Nation*, 1910), *Mississippi Valley Beginnings* (1922), *Subjectivity of Certain Economic Concepts* (1924), and *History of Louisiana State and People* (three volumes, 1925). His history of the United States was included in braille books. He was editor of *Progressive Teacher* (1885–89) and founder and editor (1893–94) and business manager (1907–08) of the *Louisiana State Review*.

Chambers organized the Louisiana State Chautauqua in 1893, was its first superintendent (1893–1903), vice-president (1897), and president (1902). He was president of the Department of Secondary Education of the National Educational Association (1890). He conducted the Louisiana Teachers' Institute at the Louisiana Normal School (later, Northwestern State University of Louisiana) from 1901 to 1902.

REFERENCES: *WWW* (I); *The Times Picayune* (New Orleans, Louisiana), March 9, 10, 1929.   *S. S. Britt, Jr.*

CHAMBERS, Merritt Madison. B. January 26, 1899, Knox County, Ohio, to Rufus Ward and Etta Amelia (Miller) Chambers. M. no.

Merritt Madison Chambers received a primary and secondary education in the public schools of Ohio. He received the B.A. degree (1922) from Ohio Wesleyan University in Delaware, Ohio, and the M.A. (1927) and Ph.D. (1931) degrees from Ohio State University.

Chambers taught political science at the University of North Dakota (1926–27) and Oregon State College (later, University) in Corvallis (1927–30). He was head of the department of social science at Teacher's College in Kansas City, Missouri (1931–32). He worked as a research associate at Purdue University in Lafayette, Indiana, in association with the Carnegie Foundation (1932–34) and the Brookings Institution in Washington, D.C. (1934–35).

Chambers was on the research staff of the American Council on Education in Washington, D.C., from 1935 to 1951. He participated in conducting national surveys on educational practices within the states and served on several national commissions. After retirement in 1951, he was the owner-operator of Lafayette Farms in Mount Vernon, Ohio, to 1958. He was a consultant to the United States Office of Education and held visiting professorships at several universities (1963–69). He continued to be active in the study of higher education, especially its legal aspects.

Chambers was author of many publications, including *Youth-Serving Organizations* (1947), *Universities of the World Outside the U.S.* (1950), *The Campus and the People* (1960), *Voluntary Statewide Coordination in*

Public Higher Education (1961), *Chance and Choice in Higher Education* (1962), *Financing Higher Education* (1963), *The College and the Courts Since 1950* (1964), *Freedom and Repression in Higher Education* (1965), *Bibliography on Higher Education* (1966), *The Colleges and the Courts, 1962–1966* (1967), *Higher Education: Who Pays, Who Gains* (1968), *Higher Education in The Fifty States* (1970), *Above High School* (1970), *The Developing Law of the Student and College* (1972), *Faculty and Staff Before the Bench* (1973), and *Higher Education and State Governments* (1974).

Chambers was active in a number of professional and civic associations and organizations, including fellow of the American Association for the Advancement of Science and a member of the National Organization of Legal Problems in Education (executive committee, 1964–65).

REFERENCES: *CA* (9–12); *LE* (V); *WW* (XXXVIII); *WWAE* (XXIII); *Who's Who in the Midwest*, 13th (Chicago: Marquis).   *J. K. Ward*

CHANDLER, Joe Albert. B. March 26, 1903, Colfax, Washington, to William and Mary (Wilkie) Chandler. M. July 3, 1928, to Marie Barlow. Ch. two. D. August 11, 1974, Seattle, Washington.

Joe A. Chandler attended Walla Walla, Washington, public schools, was an all-state high school athlete, and was graduated from Washington State College (later, University) at Pullman in 1925.

Chandler was a teacher and coach at La Conner, Washington, and served as La Conner superintendent of schools (1931–38). He joined the Washington Education Association in 1938 as assistant executive secretary and became executive secretary in 1940, serving to his retirement in 1965. While he served the association, the membership tripled. He was credited with playing a major role in the enactment of legislation in Washington providing for continuing teacher contracts, improved retirement benefits, and increased funds for public education. He was influential in opening the membership in teacher associations to black teachers on the national level.

Chandler was a frequent contributor to professional journals. He served as vice-president of the National Education Association (1941–42) and president of the National Association of Secretaries of State Teachers Associations (1945–46). He was a member of the joint committee of the National Education Association and the National Congress of Parents and Teachers (1958), the White House Conference on Education (1960), and the National Education Association Special Project on Instruction (1961–64). He served on committees evaluating education associations of Utah (1959), Hawaii (1962), and California (1963). He was awarded an honorary degree by Pacific Lutheran University (1960).

REFERENCES: *LE* (III); *WWAE* (XIV).

John F. Ohles

CHANNING, Edward Tyrrell. B. December 12, 1790, Newport, Rhode Island, to William and Lucy (Ellery) Channing. M. 1826 to Henrietta A. S. Ellery. Ch. none. D. February 8, 1856, Cambridge, Massachusetts.

Edward Tyrrell Channing entered Harvard University at the age of thirteen or fourteen and demonstrated an interest in arts and letters. Because of his participation in a student rebellion of 1807, he was not awarded a degree with his class, although Harvard later awarded him honorary A.M. (1819) and LL.D. (1847) degrees.

For a time, Channing read law with his brother Francis but turned to scholarly interests. In 1814 and 1815, Channing joined with some literary colleagues to form a group to publish the *North American Review*. First edited by William Tudor and Jared Sparks *(q.v.)*, Channing, with Richard H. Dana as his assistant, assumed the editorship for volumes seven, eight, and nine. He was succeeded by Edward Everett.

In 1819 Channing became Boylston Professor of Rhetoric and Oratory at Harvard, where he remained for thirty-two years. He retired at the age of sixty and lived his remaining five years in Cambridge, Massachusetts. Though he wrote little, he contributed the "Life of William Ellery" (his grandfather) in 1836 to Jared Sparks's the Library of American Biography series, and in 1856 his *Lectures Read to the Seniors in Harvard College* was issued posthumously.

REFERENCES: *AC; DAB; NCAB* (13:150); *WWW* (H). *William W. West*

CHAPIN, Aaron Lucius. B. February 6, 1817, Hartford, Connecticut, to Laertes and Laura (Colton) Chapin. M. August 23, 1843, to Martha Colton. M. August 26, 1861, to Fanny Coit. Ch. none. D. July 22, 1892, Beloit, Wisconsin.

Aaron Lucius Chapin's boyhood and youth were spent in Hartford, Connecticut, where he prepared for college at the Hartford Grammar School under the guidance of F. A. P. Barnard *(q.v.)*, later president of Columbia College (later, University). Chapin entered Yale College in 1833 and was graduated in 1837. He pursued theological studies at the Union Theological Seminary in New York.

While studying in New York, Chapin taught at the New York Institute for the Deaf and Dumb. On the completion of the theological course, he accepted an assignment from the American Home Missionary Society. He arrived in Milwaukee, Wisconsin, in 1843 and was ordained in the Presbyterian church in 1844. He was one of a group that made plans to establish Beloit (Wisconsin) College. A charter member of the corporation, he was elected president of the college in 1849.

He was inaugurated first president of Beloit in 1850 and also headed the department of social science and political economy. He held office until his resignation in 1886 when he became president emeritus and professor of civil polity.

Chapin wrote sermons and addresses and *First Principles of Political Economy* (1879), and he edited *Wayland's Political Economy* (1878). He was an associate editor of *Johnson's Cyclopedia* (1875–78) and edited the *Congregational Review* (1870–71) and *The New Englander* (1872–73).

Chapin was among the founders of Rockford (Illinois) College, the Chicago (Illinois) Theological Seminary, the Wisconsin Academy of Science, Arts and Letters, and the National Council of Education. He was a trustee of the Wisconsin Institute at Delavan (1865–81) and for several years president of the board. He was a member of the American Board for Foreign Missions (1851–89), a director of the American Home Missionary Society (1850–83), president of the Wisconsin Academy of Science (1870), and on the board of examiners at the United States Naval Academy in Annapolis, Maryland (1872–73), and the United States Military Academy in West Point, New York (1873). He received two honorary degrees.

REFERENCES: *AC; DAB; NCAB* (3:184); *WWW* (H); *The Biographical Dictionary of Representative Men of Chicago and Wisconsin* (Chicago: American Biographical Publishing Co., 1895); *Dictionary of Wisconsin Biography* (Madison: The State Historical Society of Wisconsin, 1960); *Milwaukee Sentinel,* July 23, 1892; *Transactions of the Wisconsin Academy of Science* 9 (1893): 52–54. *Lawrence S. Master*

CHAPMAN, John Gadsby. B. December 8, 1808, Alexandria, Virginia, to n.a. M. no. D. November 28, 1889, Brooklyn, New York.

In his boyhood, John Chapman was encouraged by friends to develop his artistic talent. He began to work in oils at the age of sixteen and went to Winchester, Virginia, as a professional artist in 1827, when he also studied at the Pennsylvania Academy of Fine Arts. He studied in Rome and Florence, Italy (c. 1828–31). He copied old masters and painted "Hager and Ishmael Fainting in the Wilderness," which was the first American painting engraved in Italy (1830).

On his return to the United States in 1831, Chapman held a successful exhibition in Alexandria, Virginia, and located in New York City, where he helped found the Century Club. He showed versatility in art forms, having success in various media. He taught and engaged in wood engraving, painting portraits, and illustrating for publications. He returned to Italy in 1848 where he spent most of the rest of his life.

Chapman wrote *The American Drawing Book* (1847), which was said to have been the finest drawing book published, *The Elements of Art* (1848), and *Elementary Drawing-Book* (1872). He illustrated many books, including Harpers *Bible* (1846), *The Grammatic Reader* by Edward Hazen, and Samuel Griswold Goodrich's *(q.v.)* annual, *The Token.*

Chapman's painting "The Baptism of Pocahontas" is one of eight large paintings hanging in the rotunda of the Capitol in Washington, D.C. He was a member of the National Academy of Design.

REFERENCES: *AC; DAB; NCAB* (7:460); *WWW* (H); George C. Croce and David H. Wallace, *The New-York Historical Society's Dictionary of Artists in America* (New Haven: Yale University Press, 1957).

M. Jane Dowd

CHAPMAN, Paul Wilber. B. February 10, 1891, Brookfield, Missouri, to George Wolcott and Henrietta (Wilber) Chapman. M. August 10, 1916, to Elizabeth Lewis. Ch. two. D. April 28, 1953, Athens, Georgia.

Paul Wilber Chapman received his early education in Missouri local schools and the University of Missouri, where he received the B.S.A. (1914) and B.S.Ed. (1916) degrees. He received the M.S. degree (1931) from the University of Georgia.

He began his teaching career in 1915 in Macon, Missouri. He was superintendent of schools in Missouri at Queen City (1916–17) and New London (1917–19). He was state supervisor of agricultural education in Missouri (1919–20) and Georgia (1920–33) and also was professor of rural journalism at the Georgia State College of Agriculture (1921–29). He was state director of the Georgia State Board of Vocational Education (1925–33).

In 1933 Chapman became dean of the college of agriculture at the University of Georgia, a position he held until 1950, when he became associate dean in charge of instruction. The last years of his life (1950–53) were devoted to writing and speaking on farm subjects.

He was the author of many books, including *The Green Hand* (1932), which was made into a movie and printed in braille. Among other books he wrote were *Farm Crops* (with others, 1925), *Livestock Farming* (with L. M. Scheffer, 1936), *Occupational Guidance* (1937), *Southern Crops* (with Ray Thomas, 1938), *Successful Farming in the South* (1939), *Better Farm Living* (1941), *Better Rural Communities* (1941), *Better Rural Careers* (1941), *Victory Barnyard* (1943), and *Efficient Farm Management* (with others, 1948). He was department editor of *The Progressive Farmer*.

Chapman was a consultant to the United States Office of Education, consultant to the Agriculture Committee of the Americas and the Bankers Association, a director of the American Foundation for Agriculture, and a member of the National Advisory Committee on Education, the National Education Association (president of the department of vocational education, 1928), the American Vocational Association (president, 1930), and the National Association of State Directors of Vocational Education (president, 1929). He was awarded an honorary degree by Clemson College.

REFERENCES: *LE* (III); *NCAB* (46:256); *WWW* (III); *The Story of Georgia* (New York: The American Historical Society, 1938), vol. 4; *NYT,* April 29, 1953, p. 29.   *Donald C. Stephenson*

CHARTERS, Werrett Wallace. B. October 24, 1875, Hartford, Ontario, Canada, to Alexander and Mary Ann (Mealley) Charters. M. December 21, 1907, to Jessie B. Allen. Ch. four. D. March 8, 1952, Livingston, Alabama.

W. W. Charters earned the A.B. degree (1898) from McMaster University in Canada, was graduated from the Ontario Normal College (1899), and received the B.Pd. degree from the University of Toronto, Canada, and the M.Ph. (1903) and Ph.D. (1904) degrees from the University of Chicago.

He began teaching in Canada in a rural school at Rockford, Ontario (1894–95), and was principal of the Model School in Hamilton, Ontario (1899–1901). He moved to the United States to serve as principal of the elementary school and director of student teaching at the State Normal School (later, Winona State College) in Winona, Minnesota (1904–07). He taught the theory of teaching (1907–17) and was dean of the school of education at the University of Missouri (1910–17). He was professor of education (1917–19) and dean of the school of education (1918–19) at the University of Illinois. He was director of the research bureau for retail training at the Carnegie Institute of Technology (1919–23) and served at the University of Pittsburgh as a professor of education (1925–28), dean of the graduate school (1924–25), and director of the research bureau for retail training. He joined the University of Chicago as a professor of education (1925–28).

In 1928 Charters joined Ohio State University as director of the bureau of research and held this position until his retirement in 1947. Charters became prominent in the field of audiovisual technology. He directed the Payne Fund studies on the effect of radio and films and reported that the motion picture was a potent medium of education. He was a pioneer in radio instruction. In 1929 he was appointed to the Advisory Committee on Education by Radio; in 1930 he analyzed the work of the Federal Radio Commission as it pertained to the use of radio for instruction; and he also established the Institute for Education by Radio through a Payne Fund grant.

Charters wrote on various phases of education; his books include *Method of Teaching* (1910), *Teaching the Common Branches* (1913), *Curriculum Construction* (1923), *The Teaching of Ideals* (1927), and *Motion Pictures and Youth* (1933). He coauthored many books, including *Essential Language Habits* (with others, 1924), *Analysis of Secretarial Duties and Traits* (with Isadore B. Whitley, 1924), *Basic Material for a Pharmaceutical Curriculum* (with others, 1927), *The Commonwealth Teacher-Training Study* (with Douglas Waples, 1929), *Democracy Readers* (with Prudence Cartright, 1940), *Latin America* (with others, 1944), and *The Day Before Yesterday* (with others, 1946). He also was coauthor with Dean F. Smiley and Ruth Strang *(q.v.)* of the Health and Growth Series

(1935–39). He explored relationships in education and with media and curriculum design, and he wrote extensively in these fields.

Charters was director of the bureau of training of the War Manpower Commission (1942–43), chairman of the board of trustees of the Northern Baptist Convention's Board of Education, and a member of many professional associations. He was awarded an honorary degree by Muskingum (Ohio) College.

REFERENCES: *LE* (III); *WWAE* (XII); *WWW* (III); *NYT,* March 10, 1952, p. 21; Paul Saettler, *A History of Instructional Technology* (New York: McGraw-Hill, 1968).   *Paul Woodworth*

CHASE, William Merritt. B. November 1, 1849, Williamsburg, Indiana, to David Hester and Sarah (Swaim) Chase. M. 1886 to Alice Bremond Gerson. Ch. eight. D. October 25, 1916, New York, New York.

William Merritt Chase showed an early interest in art; as a child he began to copy woodcuts and other pictures and made profile portraits of friends and members of his family. His early education was in the schools in Indianapolis. His first formal study of art was under B. F. Hayes, a portrait painter in Indianapolis. In 1869 Chase went to New York City to study with J. O. Eaton and to attend the National Academy of Design. Later he opened a studio in St. Louis, Missouri, with the painter James S. Patterson and painted fruit and flower pieces, which enabled him to earn enough money to travel to Europe in 1874.

In Europe Chase attended the Munich (Germany) Academy, where for several years he was a student of Alexander von Wagner and Karl von Piloty. He won the praise of European art critics for copies he made of masterpieces of great painters, notably Velasquez. He spent a year in Venice, Italy (1877), traveling with two other American artists, Frank Duveneck *(q.v.)* and John Twachtman.

After his return to the United States, Chase opened a studio in New York and taught at the Art Students' League. He also taught at the Pennsylvania Academy of Fine Arts and Brooklyn Art School. In the summer of 1891 he conducted an art school in Chinnecock, Long Island, and took groups of students to Europe for summer classes (1903–13). For a time he maintained a studio in his villa in Florence, Italy, where he taught and painted.

Chase was a member of the American Academy of Arts and Sciences. He received many awards, including a medal at the Centennial Exposition in Philadelphia (1876), a silver medal from the Paris Salon (1889), first prize from the Cleveland Art Association (1894), Shaw Prize of the Society of American Artists (1895), and gold medals from the Philadelphia Academy of Fine Arts (1895) and the Paris Exposition (1900).

REFERENCES: *DAB; NCAB* (13:28); *WWW* (I); *NYT,* October 26, 1916, p. 11.   *Roger H. Jones*

CHAUVENET, William. B. May 24, 1820, Milford, Pennsylvania, to William Mare and Mary B. (Kerr) Chauvenet. M. 1841 to Catherine Hemple. Ch. five, including Regis Chauvenet, president of the Colorado School of Mines. D. December 13, 1870, St. Paul, Minnesota.

Willaim Chauvenet attended school in Philadelphia. He entered Yale College at the age of sixteen, at the end of his freshman year won a first prize for Latin composition, and was graduated with high honors in 1840.

For a brief period he assisted Professor Alexander Dallas Bache *(q.v.)* in observations on magnetism at Girard College in Philadelphia. He became professor of mathematics for the United States Navy and served on the U.S.S. *Mississippi* (1841). In 1842 he took charge of the Naval Asylum in Philadelphia and sought to raise standards of instruction. He participated in establishing the four-year United States Naval Academy at Fort Severn at Annapolis, Maryland, where he taught mathematics, astronomy, navigation, and surveying. He taught mathematics at Washington University in St. Louis, Missouri (1859–62). He became chancellor of the university in 1862 and resigned in 1869 because of ill health.

Chauvenet was the author of *Binomial Theorem and Logarithms* (1843), *A Treatise on Plane and Spherical Trigonometry* (1850), *A Manual of Spherical and Practical Astronomy* (1863), and *A Treatise on Elementary Geometry* (1870).

He was one of the original members of the American Association for the Advancement of Science (general secretary, 1859). He helped found the National Academy of Sciences (vice-president, 1868–70) and was elected to the American Philosophical Society and the American Academy of Arts and Sciences. The Naval Academy honored Chauvenet's memory with a bronze tablet on July 31, 1916. The Mathematical Association of America established a biennial award, the Chauvenet Prize for Mathematical Exposition.

REFERENCES: *AC; DAB; NCAB* (11:210); *WWW* (H).

> *Joseph P. Cangemi*
> *Thomas E. Kesler*

CHAVIS, John. B. 1762 or 1763, probably in Mecklenburg County, Virginia, to n.a. M. to Fanny or Frances Chavis. D. June 15, 1838, Orange County, North Carolina.

It is likely that John Chavis was the "indentured servant named John Chavis" mentioned in the estate inventory of attorney John Milner in 1773. The beneficiary of Milner's Greek and Latin volumes, Reverend William Willie of Sussex, Virginia, may have had a role in the early training and education of John Chavis after Milner's death. Chavis enlisted in December 1778 in the Fifth Virginia Regiment, serving three years. In 1789 he was employed as a tutor, and the Mecklenburg County tax list showed he was a free Negro whose property consisted of one horse.

Chavis was educated at Washington Academy in Lexington, Virginia (later, Washington and Lee University), and perhaps as a private student of Dr. John Witherspoon *(q.v.)*, president of what became Princeton University. Chavis was licensed to preach on November 19, 1800, by the presbytery of Lexington (Virginia). He served as a missionary to slaves in Maryland, Virginia, and North Carolina for the general assembly of the Presbyterian church (1801–07). He preached to and moved freely among white Presbyterians, who attended his services.

In 1807 or 1808 Chavis settled in Raleigh, North Carolina, where he was recognized for his teaching. His school was organized on a dual plan with white students in attendance during the day and black students in the evening. He was called a "good Latin and a fair Greek scholar." Some white students were said to have boarded in the Chavis home while attending the school.

Chavis Park in Raleigh is named in his honor and is located near the site of Chavis's school.

REFERENCES: *DAB; NCAB* (7:123); *WWW* (H); Daniel L. Boyd, *Freeborn Negro: The Life of John Chavis* (Princeton, N.J.: Princeton University Press, 1974); Margaret Burr DesChamps, "John Chavis as a Preacher to Whites," *The North Carolina Historical Review* 32 (April 1955): 165–72; Edgar W. Knight *(q.v.)*, "Notes on John Chavis," *The North Carolina Historical Review* 7 (July 1930): 326–45; G. C. Shaw, *John Chavis, 1763–1838: A Remarkable Negro Who Conducted a School in North Carolina for White Boys and Girls* (Binghampton, N.Y.: n.p., 1931); Charles Lee Smith, *The History of Education in North Carolina* (Washington, D.C.: Government Printing Office, 1888); Stephen B. Weeks, "John Chavis, Ante-Bellum Negro Preacher and Teacher," *The Southern Workman* (February 1914).   *Barbara M. Parramore*

CHEEVER, Ezekiel. B. January 25, 1614, London, England, to William Cheever and n.a. M. 1638 to Mary (n.a.). M. 1652 to Ellen Lathrop. Ch. ten. D. August 21, 1708, Boston, Massachusetts.

A graduate of Cambridge (England) University, where he had attended Emmanuel College, Ezekiel Cheever emigrated to Boston in 1637. A year later he moved to a region where he and others founded the New Haven colony in 1639. He opened a school in his home for the instruction of Latin to boys; later he moved to a schoolhouse provided by the town. During his tenure at New Haven he wrote *A Short Introduction to the Latin Tongue; for the Use of the Lower Forms in the Latin School Being the Accidence,* generally referred to as Cheever's *Accidence*. It was issued in eighteen editions before the American Revolution and was published as late as 1838.

Cheever left New Haven in 1650 to serve as master of the grammar school in Ipswich, Massachusetts. In 1661 he moved to Charlestown, and he became master of the Boston Latin School in January 1671. Cheever remained there until his death in 1708.

In addition to his teaching, Cheever had served as a member of the New Haven colony court for the plantation in its first session and had been a deputy to the general court. He was the foremost educator of the early colonial period.

REFERENCES: *AC; DAB; NCAB* (12:439); *TC.*   *John F. Ohles*

CHERRY, Henry Hardin. B. November 16, 1864, near Bowling Green, Kentucky, to George Washington and Frances Martha (Stahl) Cherry. M. April 3, 1896, to Bessie Lysle Fayne. Ch. three. D. August 1, 1937, Bowling Green, Kentucky.

Henry Hardin Cherry grew up on a farm near Bowling Green, Kentucky, and attended local district schools. He was graduated in 1889 from the Southern Normal and Business College in Bowling Green. He worked as a farm hand and taught penmanship in adult and evening classes to finance his education.

Cherry's brother Thomas had been president of Acadia College in Crowley, Louisiana (1889–92), and the two brothers purchased the Southern Normal and Business College in 1892, with Henry teaching the business courses and Thomas the literary curriculum. They changed the name to Bowling Green Business College and Literary Institute but reverted to Southern Normal School and Bowling Green Business College in 1893, when they struggled through the financial depression. In 1898 Henry Cherry bought his brother's interest in the school, and Thomas Cherry became a distinguished superintendent of the Bowling Green public schools. Cherry separated the two instructional programs into the Southern Normal School and the Bowling Green Business College, which was sold in 1907. The business college became the Bowling Green College of Commerce and merged with Western Kentucky State Teachers College in 1963.

Cherry sought to have his institution organized as a state normal school; in 1907 it became the Western Kentucky State Normal School (later, Western Kentucky University) with Cherry as president until his death in 1937. Western Kentucky rapidly expanded, becoming the largest institution of its kind in 1934. Cherry was an exponent of the work ethic and was not interested in the development of many extracurricular activities; athletics and fraternities were not part of the school life until the last years of his administration.

Cherry was the author of *Our Civic Image and Our Government* (1906), *Education: The Basis of Democracy* (1926), and pamphlets, and he was editor of a quarterly, *The Southern Educator.* He was active in professional organizations, including the Kentucky Education Association (president, 1902 and 1926), and was a member of the State Educational

Commission and the State Council for Defense during World War I. He organized the Farmer's Chautauqua in 1913, which brought speakers and musical performances to the western Kentucky rural areas. He was president of the College Heights Foundation in which he began a student loan fund to assist poor students in pursuing their educations. He raised funds for the Kentucky Building, a museum of Kentucky history. A building was named in his honor at Western Kentucky, and he was awarded an honorary degree by the University of Kentucky in 1911.

REFERENCES: *LE* (I); *NCAB* (39:66); *WWAE* (I); *WWW* (I); James P. Cornette, "History of the Western Kentucky State Teachers College" (Ph.D. diss., George Peabody College, 1939); Benjamin LaBree, ed., *Press Reference Book of Prominent Kentuckians* (Louisville: The Standard Printing Co., 1916); Mary T. Moore, "History of the Western Kentucky State Teachers College," *Filson Club History Quarterly* 28 (Fall 1954): 328–40; Mary Young Southard and Ernest C. Miller, eds., *Who's Who in Kentucky* (Louisville: The Standard Printing Co., 1936).

Robert D. Neill

CHEYNEY, Edward Potts. B. January 17, 1861, Wallingford, Pennsylvania, to Waldron J. and Fannie (Potts) Cheyney. M. June 8, 1886, to Gertrude Levis Squires. Ch. three. D. February 1, 1947, Chester, Pennsylvania.

Son of a prosperous businessman, Edward Potts Cheyney attended country schools, Philadelphia's Penn Charter School, and the University of Pennsylvania, where he received the B.A. degree (1883) and a bachelor of finance degree (1884) from the new Wharton School. He traveled in Europe and studied at German universities and the British Museum (1884, 1894, 1904–05).

Cheyney taught in the University of Pennsylvania as an instructor of history and then of Latin and mathematics; he was professor of history (1890) and Henry Charles Lee Professor (1929–34). His belief in evolution, order, and progress led to his formulation of six laws of history, presented as an address on his election to the presidency of the American Historical Association (1923).

His first publications were monographs on American history; he then turned to English history. He wrote *Changes in England in the Sixteenth Century* (1895), *Introduction to Industrial and Social History of England* (1901), *A Short History of England* (1904), *Readings in English History* (1908), *A History of England from the Defeat of the Spanish Armada to the Death of Elizabeth* (two volumes, 1914–26), *Law in History and Other Essays* (1927), *Modern English Reform, From Individualism to Socialism* (1931), *Dawn of a New Era* (1936), and *History of the University of Pennsylvania* (1940).

Cheyney coedited *Translations and Reprints from Original Sources of*

European History (with others, 1890s), making them available in attractive form and at modest prices for classroom use. He was editor of *American Historical Review* (1912–20) and was instrumental in its acquisition in 1915 by the American Historical Association. He received an honorary degree from the University of Pennsylvania in 1911.

REFERENCES: *DAB* (supp. 4); *LE* (II); *WWW* (II); *American Historical Review* 52 (April 1947): 647–48; *NYT,* February 2, 1947, p. 57.

M. Jane Dowd

CHITTENDEN, Russell Henry. B. February 18, 1856, New Haven, Connecticut, to Horace Horatio and Emily Eliza (Doane) Chittenden. M. June 20, 1877, to Gertrude Louise Baldwin. Ch. three. D. December 26, 1943, New Haven, Connecticut.

Russell Henry Chittenden, educator and one of the founders of biochemistry in America, studied in the local public and private schools of New Haven, Connecticut. He enrolled in the Sheffield Scientific School at Yale College where he studied chemistry and received the Ph.B. (1875) and Ph.D. (1880) degrees. He continued his study of physiological chemistry in Heidelberg, Germany (1878–79 and 1882).

Chittenden was an instructor in physiological chemistry at the Sheffield Scientific School in 1875 as the first to teach the course in the United States. He was appointed to the newly founded professorship of physiological chemistry in the Sheffield Scientific School (1882) and was its director (1898–1922).

Chittenden was the author of numerous papers in scientific journals, principally on physiological chemistry and toxicology. He was editor of *Studies in Physiological Chemistry,* the results of research conducted in his laboratory (four volumes, 1884, 1901). He wrote *Digestive Proteolysis* (1895), *Physiological Economy in Nutrition* (1905), *Nutrition of Man* (1907), *History of the Sheffield School* (two volumes, 1928), *Development of Physiological Chemistry in the United States* (1930), and *The First Twenty-five Years of the American Society of Biological Chemists* (1945).

In 1893 Chittenden was appointed to the Committee of Fifty, which was set up in reaction to the campaign of Mary H. H. Hunt *(q.v.)* of the Women's Christian Temperance Union for "scientific temperance instruction." Chittenden's experiments on the effects of alcohol on the human body showed that many of the harmful effects ascribed to alcohol were not confirmed in the laboratory. This work was incorporated in the two-volume publication entitled *Physiological Aspects of the Liquor Problem* (1903).

He was elected a member of the National Academy of Sciences (1890) and was a member of many organizations, including the American Society of Naturalists (president, 1893) and the American Physiological Society (president, 1895–1904). He was an organizer and first president of the

American Society of Biological Chemists (1906). He was a fellow of the American Academy of Arts and Sciences and an honorary fellow of the New York Academy of Medicine. He received five honorary degrees from American and foreign universities.

REFERENCES: *DAB* (supp. 3); *DSB; LE* (II); *NCAB* (10:181); *WWW* (II); *NYT,* December 27, 1943, p. 19.   *C. Roy Rylander*

CHRISTIANSEN, Fredrik Melius. B. April 1, 1871, Eidsvold, Norway, to Anders and Oleana (Braaten) Christiansen. M. July 14, 1897, to Edith Lindem. Ch. seven. D. June 1, 1955, Northfield, Minnesota.

F. Melius Christiansen came from a Norwegian family of amateur musicians. As a youth he learned to play the violin, cornet, and piano. At the age of seventeen, he emigrated to the United States. Settling in Wisconsin, he became director of a Scandinavian band while still in his teens. He moved to Minneapolis, Minnesota, where he attended Augsburg College and Northwestern Conservatory of Music, from which he was graduated in 1894. With his bride and brother, he traveled to Europe (1897) to study at the Royal Conservatory in Leipzig, Germany, where he was awarded a diploma in 1899.

From 1894 to 1897 Christiansen taught, played the violin and organ, and directed choirs in Minneapolis. On his return from Europe in 1899, he resumed his musical career in Minneapolis. In 1903 Christiansen agreed to a one-year trial as head of the music department at St. Olaf College in Northfield, Minnesota; he stayed for forty more years.

Christiansen was best known as director of the St. Olaf choir, which, under his leadership, became one of the finest in the country. In 1912 the choir made the first of its many successful annual American concert tours, went to Norway in 1913, and toured Europe in 1930. In 1935 he founded the summer Christiansen Choral School, which for years trained directors from across the country in his methods. When he retired in 1944 he had done much to popularize a cappella singing and had made the St. Olaf choir world famous.

Christiansen was author or compiler of *Augsburg Collection of Sacred Music* (n.d.), *Fifty Famous Hymns Arranged for Ladies' Voices* (1914), *School of Choir Singing* (1916), *Practical Modulation* (1916), *Anthems for Women's and Mixed Voices* (1919–42), *St. Olaf Choir Series* (1919–32), and *Organ Music for Church and Home* (1942).

REFERENCES: *WWW* (III); Leola Nelson Bergmann, *Music Master of the Middle West: The Story of F. Melius Christiansen and the St. Olaf Choir* (Minneapolis: University of Minnesota Press, 1944); *NYT,* June 2, 1955, p. 29.   *Frederik F. Ohles*

CLAP, Thomas. B. June 26, 1703, Scituate, Massachusetts, to Stephen and Temperance (Gorham) Clap. M. November 23, 1727, to Mary Whiting. M.

February 5, 1740, to Mary Haynes. Ch. five. D. January 7, 1767, New Haven, Connecticut.

Thomas Clap, rector and president of Yale College, grew up in Scituate, Massachusetts, on the south shore of Massachusetts Bay. He prepared for Harvard College with a local minister. He was graduated from Harvard in 1722 and studied divinity in Scituate with the minister who prepared him for college. He returned to Harvard in 1725 to receive the Master of Arts degree.

Clap taught school in 1722 and in 1725 preached in Norwich, Connecticut. He took charge of a church in Windham, Connecticut (1726–39). When Elisha Williams resigned as rector of Yale College in 1739, Clap was appointed to the post and was installed in April 1740. While rector, Clap classified the books in the library, issued a catalog in 1743, and drew up new college laws and had them printed in 1748. In 1745 the trustees adopted a new charter; among the changes was establishment of the office of president in place of rector. The first orrery (planetarium) for astronomical instruction in America was built under Clap's supervision.

He came into conflict with some members of the college corporation and the colonial assembly over control of the college and, later, with students on matters of discipline. In the spring of 1766, students demanded his removal, and he resigned in July.

Among Clap's publications were *An Introduction to the Study of Philosophy* (1743), *Constitution of Colleges* (1754), *A Brief History and Vindication of the Doctrine Received and Established in the Churches of New England* (1755), *An Essay on the Nature and Foundation of Moral Virtue and Obligation: Being a Short Introduction to the Study of Ethics* (1765), *The Annals or History of Yale-College, in New-Haven, in the Colony of Connecticut* (1766), the first history of the college, and *Conjectures upon the Nature and Motion of Meteors* (1781).

REFERENCES: *AC; DAB; NCAB* (1:166); *WWW* (H); Napthali Daggett, *The Faithful Serving of God and Our Generation, the Only Way to a Peaceful and Happy Death: A Sermon Occasioned by the Death of the Reverend Thomas Clap* (New Haven: B. Mecom, 1767); Clifford K. Shipton, *Biographical Sketches of Those Who Have Attended Harvard College in the Classes 1722–1725* (Boston: Historical Society, 1945); Louis L. Tucker, *Puritan Protagonist: President Thomas Clap of Yale College* (Chapel Hill: University of North Carolina Press, 1962).

Richard G. Durnin

CLAPP, Cornelia Maria. B. March 17, 1849, Montague, Massachusetts, to Richard and Eunice Amelia (Slate) Clapp. M. no. D. January 1, 1935, Mount Dora, Florida.

Cornelia Maria Clapp attended local schools near Montague, Massachusetts, and entered Mount Holyoke Seminary (later, College) at South

Hadley, Massachusetts, where she was graduated in 1871. She received the Ph.B. (1888) and Ph.D. (1889) degrees from Syracuse (New York) University. She also studied at the University of Chicago, where she received the Ph.D. degree in 1896.

Clapp taught in Andalusia, Pennsylvania, in 1872. She began teaching various subjects at Mount Holyoke and became particularly interested in natural history. She was selected to study at the Anderson School of Natural History at Penikese Island in Buzzards Bay (1874). She accepted the theory that learning should take place from observations rather than from books. She implemented the theory at Mount Holyoke, where she urged her students to learn through self-observation in the laboratory.

Clapp also studied at the Massachusetts Institute of Technology, Williams College, and Syracuse University in the 1880s and at the newly opened Marine Biological Laboratory in Woods Hole, Massachusetts, in 1888. She took part in research projects and conducted investigations during her summer vacations from Mount Holyoke. A distinguished teacher of women, Clapp was influential in the growth of Mount Holyoke, in its change from a seminary to a college, and in establishing the role of women as scholars and teachers in higher education.

Clapp was designated one of the most important zoologists in the country by *American Men of Science* (1906) and received an honorary degree from Mount Holyoke in 1921. A new science laboratory at Mount Holyoke was named in her honor in 1929.

REFERENCES: *LE* (I); *NAW; NYT*, January 2, 1935, p. 25; *WWW* (I).

Evelyn Patricia Flowers

CLAPP, Margaret Antionette. B. April 11, 1910, East Orange, New Jersey, to Alfred Chapin and Anna (Roth) Clapp. M. no. D. May 3, 1974, Tyringham, Massachusetts.

Margaret Clapp grew up in East Orange, New Jersey. She majored in economics at Wellesley (Massachusetts) College and was graduated with the A.B. degree (1930). She earned the M.A. (1937) and Ph.D. (1946) degrees from Columbia University.

Clapp taught in New York City at the Todhunter School (1930–39) and the Dalton School (1939–41). She was research assistant to the British Broadcasting System (1942–43) and for the American Red Cross (1945).

She was an instructor of history at New Jersey College for Women (later, Douglass College) in 1945, and at Columbia University (1946). Clapp was an assistant professor of history at Brooklyn College from 1947 until she was selected president of Wellesley in 1949.

While she was at Columbia, Allan Nevins *(q.v.)* suggested John Bigelow as a subject for a dissertation. It was published as *Forgotten First Citizen: John Bigelow* and earned the Pulitzer Prize for American Biography for Clapp in 1948.

Clapp contributed a chapter, "The Social and Cultural Scene," to *The Greater City* (1948) edited by Nevins; she edited *The Modern University* (1950).

Clapp's presidency at Wellesley was one of the college's most notable. She advocated a well-balanced liberal arts education, maintained a stable enrollment, and increased college endowment funds, the size of the faculty, and the amount of student financial aid.

In 1966 Clapp resigned to head Lady Doak College in Madurai, India. She was counselor for cultural affairs at the United States embassy in New Delhi, the first woman to hold that rank (1970–71).

Clapp was active in professional organizations and was a member of the American Historical Association, served on the Problems and Policies Committee of the American Council on Education and the Board of Foreign Scholarship of the State Department, was a trustee of the Carnegie Endowment for International Peace, and was a director of the Council for Financial Aid to Education. She was the recipient of several honorary degrees.

REFERENCES: *CB* (June 1948 and June 1974); *NCAB* (H:189); *WWAE* (XXIII); *WWW* (VI); *NYT,* May 4, 1974, p. 44; *Time,* May 13, 1974, p. 100.   *Mary Harshbarger*

CLAXTON, Philander Priestley. B. September 28, 1862, near Shelbyville, Tennessee, to Joshua Calvin and Anne Elizabeth (Jones) Claxton. M. December 1885 to Varina Staunton Moore. M. September 1894 to Anne Elizabeth Porter. M. April 23, 1912, to Mary Hannah Johnson. Ch. four. D. January 12, 1957, Knoxville, Tennessee.

Philander Priestley Claxton received his education in the public schools of Bedford County, Tennessee, and the Turrentine Academy. He attended the University of Tennessee in Knoxville where he received the A.B. (1882) and A.M. (1887) degrees. He studied at Johns Hopkins University in Baltimore, Maryland (1884–85), and in Germany (1885–86). He visited European schools in 1897, 1925, and 1930.

Claxton taught at Goldsboro, North Carolina (1882), and was a superintendent of North Carolina schools at Kinston (1883–84), Wilson (1886–87), and Asheville (1887–93). He was professor of pedagogy and German (1893–96) and director of the practice and observation school (1896–1902) at the North Carolina State Normal and Industrial College (later, North Carolina State University). He was professor of education (1902–06) and professor of secondary education and inspector of high schools at the University of Tennessee.

Claxton was appointed by President William Howard Taft in 1911 to be United States commissioner of education. He served in that position more than ten years through the Taft administration and the two administrations of Woodrow Wilson *(q.v.)* to 1921. As commissioner he traveled widely, advocating better teaching facilities and better trained teachers with higher salaries. He was chairman of the committee that wrote the bill to rehabilitate disabled World War I veterans and participated in developing the first plan for federal aid for vocational education in the public schools.

After service as commissioner, Claxton was provost of the University of Alabama (1921–23) and superintendent of schools at Tulsa, Oklahoma (1923–29). He served as president of Austin Peay Normal School (later, State University) in Clarksville, Tennessee (1930–46).

Claxton wrote with James McGinniss *Effective English* (1917) and *Effective English, Junior* (1921), and he was editor of *North Carolina Journal of Education* (1897–1901) and *Atlantic Educational Journal* (1901–03).

Claxton was a member of the Southern Education Board (chief of the bureau of investigation and information, 1902–03), president of the Southern Educational Association, superintendent of the Summer School of the South (1902–11), member of the Rockefeller Sanitary Commission, director of the Moral Education Board, member of the council of the National Education Association, and chairman of the National Student Forum on the Paris Pact (1929–38). He was the recipient of five honorary degrees.

REFERENCES: *LE* (III); *NCAB* (15:270); *WWAE* (VIII); *WWW* (III); Charles Lee Lewis, *Crusader for Public Education* (Nashville: University of Tennessee Press, 1948); *NYT*, January 13, 1957, p. 84.

Vincent Giardina

CLEAVELAND, Parker. B. January 15, 1780, Rowley, Massachusetts, to Parker and Elizabeth (Jackman) Cleaveland. M. September 9, 1806, to Martha Bush. Ch. none. D. October 15, 1858, Brunswick, Maine.

Parker Cleaveland attended the Dummer Academy near his home and entered Harvard University before the age of sixteen (1795). After graduation from Harvard (1799), he taught school in Haverhill, Massachusetts, and York, Maine (1799–1803). He read and prepared himself in law but decided to study for the ministry. After spending a few months studying theology, he received a tutorship in mathematics and natural philosophy at Harvard (1803–05). He accepted a position at Bowdoin College (Brunswick, Maine) in mathematics and natural philosophy, where he remained until his death in 1858.

In 1820 the Medical School of Maine was established and administered by Bowdoin College; Cleaveland was named instructor in materia medica and was responsible for many administrative duties for the school. In 1828 Cleaveland's department at Bowdoin was changed to a department of chemistry, mineralogy, and natural philosophy.

Cleaveland developed interests in meteorological phenomena and fossil shells and, after the exploitation of local mineral deposits, lectured in mineralogy and chemistry (1808). With a growing interest in mineralogy,

Cleaveland sought to fill a need for an elementary book on American minerals. He wrote the first American work on the subject, *Elementary Treatise on Mineralogy and Geology* (1816). He wrote a larger, two-volume edition (1822). He also wrote *Agricultural Queries* (1827).

Cleaveland was a fellow of the American Academy of Arts and Sciences and a member of the American Philosophical Society, the Imperial Mineralogical Society of St. Petersburg, Russia, and the Geological Society of London, England. He received honorary degrees from Dartmouth College and Bowdoin. The mineral Cleavelandite was named in his honor in 1936.

REFERENCES: *AC; DAB; DSB; NCAB* (13:56); *WWW* (H).

Isadore L. Sonnier

CLEMENT, Rufus Early. B. June 26, 1900, Salisbury, North Carolina, to George Clinton and Emma Clarissa (Williams) Clement. M. December 23, 1919, to Pearl Anne Johnson. Ch. one. D. November 7, 1967, New York, New York.

Rufus Early Clement received the B.A. degree (1919) from Livingstone College in Salisbury, North Carolina, the B.D. degree (1922) from Garrett Biblical Institute in Evanston, Illinois, and the M.A. (1922) and Ph.D. (1930) degrees from Northwestern University in Evanston.

He was a member of the faculty of Livingstone College (1922–31) and was promoted to professor and dean in 1925. He served as dean of the Louisville (Kentucky) Municipal College for Negroes (1931–37) and became president of Atlanta (Georgia) University, where he served from 1937 to 1967. Under Clement, Atlanta University gained accreditation and added schools of library science (1941), education (1944), and business administration (1946); in 1947 the Atlanta School of Social Work was made an integral part of Atlanta University after having been one of six institutions originally affiliated in a cooperative endeavor. In 1941 a project in adult education, the People's College, was begun.

Clement was active in professional associations, serving as a delegate for the National Education Association to the World Confederation of the Teaching Profession (1949) and as president of the National Association of Teachers in Colored Schools (1935–36), the Association of Colleges and Secondary Schools for Negroes (1938–39), and the National Association of Deans and Registrars (1932–34). In 1953 his election to the Atlanta Board of Education was the first time a black had been elected to office in Atlanta since 1871; he was reelected in 1957. He served as a trustee to Livingstone, Morehouse (Atlanta), and Spelman (Atlanta) colleges.

A contributing editor to the *Journal of Negro Education* and a contributor to the *Dictionary of American Biography,* Clement was the author of articles on Negro education. He was the recipient of several honorary degrees, including one from the University of Liberia (1956).

REFERENCES: *CB* (June 1946 and January 1968); *LE* (III); *NCAB* (I:338); *WWAE* (XXII); *WWW* (IV); *NYT,* November 8, 1967, p. 40.

Anne R. Gayles

CLERC, Laurent. B. December 26, 1785, La Balme, France, to Joseph François and Mary Elizabeth (Candy) Clerc. M. 1819 to Elizabeth Crocker Boardman. Ch. several. D. July 18, 1869, Hartford, Connecticut.

Falling into a hearth fire destroyed Laurent Clerc's hearing when he was a year old. His father, mayor of La Balme, France, was able to send the boy at the age of twelve to be educated in Paris. At the Institute for the Deaf and Dumb, director Abbé Roch A. C. Sicard took great interest in Clerc, personally instructing him for eight years. At twenty he became an assistant teacher and later an instructor of the upper grades.

Sicard took Clerc to London in 1815 to help demonstrate their instructional methods; there they met Thomas Hopkins Gallaudet *(q.v.),* an American searching on behalf of a Hartford, Connecticut, surgeon for information about teaching the deaf. The abbé invited Gallaudet to Paris, where he attended classes for several months at the institute. Sicard agreed to let Clerc go to Connecticut to help establish a school for the deaf. During a two-month voyage, Clerc taught Gallaudet the single-hand alphabet and sign language (developed by the founder of the Paris school, Abbé de l'Epée), and the American taught English to Clerc.

On arrival in Boston, Clerc presented an address written in perfect English, outlining the needs of the deaf. Gallaudet and Clerc spent several months visiting large cities and appearing before state legislatures to promote education of the deaf. They raised enough money to start in Hartford, Connecticut, the American Asylum for the Instruction of the Deaf and Dumb (later, the American School for the Deaf). Gallaudet was the school's principal and Clerc was a teacher. Clerc addressed the United States Congress in 1819, which authorized a grant of twenty thousand acres of land for the school.

Clerc retired after teaching forty-one years in the Hartford school but maintained an active interest in the institution, authoring numerous addresses and articles on the education of the deaf, which appeared in the *American Annals of the Deaf.*

REFERENCES: *AC; DAB; NCAB* (22:253); *WWW* (H); Albert W. Atwood, *Gallaudet College: Its First Hundred Years* (Lancaster, Pa.: Intelligencer Printing Co., 1964); *NYT,* July 19, 1869, p. 1.

M. Jane Dowd

CLINTON, De Witt. B. May 2, 1769, Little Britain, New York, to James and Mary (De Witt) Clinton. M. February 13, 1796, to Maria Franklin. M. May 8, 1819, to Catherine Jones. Ch. ten. D. February 11, 1828, Albany, New York.

De Witt Clinton was educated at the local grammar school, Kingston Academy, and Columbia College (later, University), from which he received the A.B. degree (1786) as head of his class. He studied law with Samuel Jones, Jr., and was admitted to the bar in 1789.

Clinton did not practice law but became a private secretary to his uncle, Governor George Clinton. Among his responsibilities, De Witt Clinton was secretary of the board of regents of the University of the State of New York and of the board of fortification of New York harbor. When his uncle lost the election for governor in 1795, Clinton returned to Columbia to study natural sciences.

He was a member of the state legislature (1797) and state senate (1798–1802 and 1806–11). He was also elected to the Council of Appointments, which filled some fifteen thousand civil and military appointive offices. He was appointed United States senator from New York in 1802 to fill an unexpired term, but resigned to become mayor of New York City (1803–06, 1809, and 1812–15). While mayor, he was chief organizer of the Public School Society (1805) and chief patron of the New York Orphan Asylum and the New York City Hospital.

Clinton was the most powerful political leader in the state and the head of the Republican party. He served as lieutenant governor of New York (1811–15). In 1812 he was nominated for the office of President of the United States by New York Republicans supported by a strong delegation of Federalist leaders, but he was defeated by James Madison. Clinton promoted building a state canal from the Great Lakes to the Hudson River. In 1816 his proposal was adopted by the legislature, and he was named to the canal commission. In March 1817 the incumbent governor resigned to become vice-president, and Clinton was elected governor of New York (1817–23 and 1825–28).

As governor Clinton saw the beginning of construction of the canal. He proposed gradual abolition of slavery in the state, sought to provide help for the poor, and supported state normal schools for the training of teachers. Clinton was respected for his liberal ideas and administrative competence and was the most effective force for public education in the history of the state. He was a competent naturalist who discovered a native American wheat strain and a new fish.

Clinton published many scientific papers on a variety of subjects. He also wrote *Introductory Discourse: A Summary of the State of Scientific Knowledge in America* (1814), *Memoir on Antiquities of the Western Parts of the State of New York* (1820), and *Letters on the Natural History and Internal Resources of New York* (1822).

He was the first president of the Public School Society of New York City (1805) and a leading promoter of the Lancastrian school methodology in America. He served as president of the American Academy of Art (1816) and was founder and president of the New-York Historical Society (1817), cofounder and president of the Literary and Philosophical Society (1816), and vice-president of the American Bible Society and the Education Society of the Presbyterian Church.

REFERENCES: *AC; DAB; EB; NCAB* (3:43); *WWW* (H).

J. Franklin Hunt

CLOUD, Henry Roe. B. December 28, 1886, Winnebago, Nebraska, to Na-Xi-Lay-Hunk-Kay and Hard-To-See. M. June 12, 1916, to Elizabeth Bender. Ch. five. D. February 9, 1950, Siletz, Oregon.

Henry Roe Cloud was born on the Winnebago reservation in Nebraska and named Wa-Na-Xi-Lay-Hunka (War Chief). He adopted "Henry" when he entered school and later added the "Roe" in honor of the missionaries who were his adoptive parents. He attended an Indian school at Genoa, Nebraska, and Mount Hermon school near Northfield, Massachusetts. He was the first full-blooded Indian to graduate from Yale University with the A.B. (1910) and A.M. (1912) degrees. He received the B.D. degree (1913) from Auburn (New York) Theological Seminary and was ordained a Presbyterian minister in 1913. In 1932 he earned a Doctor of Divinity degree from Emporia (Kansas) College.

Cloud's professional career was spent in bettering the conditions of Indians. In 1913 he chaired an official delegation of the Winnebago tribe to the President of the United States and in 1915 he founded the Roe (later, American) Indian Institute in Wichita, Kansas, and was its superintendent (1915–30). The school sought to teach Indians to become leaders. Throughout those years he also served as editor of *The Indian Outlook* and as a member of several committees concerned with Indian affairs. In 1925 he was appointed a member of the Committee of One-Hundred by the secretary of the interior.

He was the Indian member of a field survey team of the Brookings Institution (1926–27 and 1928–30) and coauthored the Meriam Survey report, which revealed the acute poverty of Indian groups, a report that led to some notable reforms. He became a special representative of the United States Indian Service in 1931, an association he maintained throughout the rest of his life.

In 1933 President Franklin D. Roosevelt appointed Cloud superintendent of the Haskell Institute in Lawrence, Kansas. He left Haskell Institute in 1936 to serve as assistant supervisor of Indian education in the Indian Bureau Service. He was superintendent of the Umatilla Reservation in Pendleton, Oregon (1947–50), and regional representative for the Grande Ronde and Siletz Indians (1948–50). He traced family histories of Oregon coastal Indians to determine their eligibility to share in a $16 million award in payment of an early-day land seizure by the government.

He was a prominent writer and lecturer on Indian affairs, particularly as they pertained to education.

REFERENCES: *DAB* (supp. 4); *WWAE* (I); *WWW* (II); *Contemporary American Indian Leaders* (New York: Dodd, Mead & Co., 1972); *The Indian Leader* 53 (February 24, 1950); *Indian Truth* 27 (January-March 1950); *NYT,* February 12, 1950, p. 84; (Portland) *Oregon Journal,* February 12, 1950.   *Anne E. Scheerer*

COBB, Lyman. B. September 18, 1800, Lenox, Massachusetts, to Elijah William and Sally (Whitney) Cobb. M. April 7, 1822, to Harriet Chambers. Ch. eight. D. October 26, 1864, Colesburg, Pennsylvania.

Lyman Cobb was one of a group of brilliant self-made educators who emerged in the first half of the nineteenth century. Born in Massachusetts, he spent most of his life in New York State. He attended country schools until the age of sixteen, when he became a teacher.

Cobb was a significant writer and publisher of school books. He published the highly popular *Cobb's Spelling Book* in about 1821. He moved to New York City where he edited and published textbooks.

Among his other schoolbooks were *Just Standard for Pronouncing the English Language* (1825), *Spelling-Book* (1826), *First Book* (1830), *Expositor* (1835), *Miniature Lexicon of the English Language* (1835–54), *Arithmetical Rules and Tables* (1835), and *New Pronouncing School Dictionary* (1843). He published several readers including the Juvenile Reader series (first through third readers, 1831), *Sequel to the Juvenile Reader* (1832), New Juvenile Reader series (first through third readers, 1842), *New Sequel or Fourth Reading Book* (1843), and *New North American Reader* (1844).

He also wrote *A Critical Review of Noah Webster's Spelling Book* (1828) and *Evil Tendency of Corporal Punishment* (1847).

Cobb was Pestalozzian in his approach to teaching, which was reflected in his books. He sought to make school reading interesting and to move away from the traditional monotonous repetition.

REFERENCES: *DAB; NCAB* (22:290).   *Robert H. Hoexter*

COBB, Stanwood. B. November 6, 1881, Newton, Massachusetts, to F. Darius and Laura Maria (Lillie) Cobb. M. 1919 to Ida Nayan Whitland. Ch. none.

Stanwood Cobb was graduated as valedictorian with the A.B. degree (1903) from Dartmouth College and received the A.M. degree (1910) from Harvard Divinity School.

Cobb was a teacher at a nautical preparatory school (1904) and an instructor in history and Latin at Robert College in Constantinople, Turkey (1907–10). Returning to the United States, he engaged in private instruction in Washington, D.C. (1910–12), toured Europe with Sargent's Travel School for Boys (1912–13), and served as a traveling tutor (1913–14). Back in the United States, he was head of the English department at St. John's

College in Annapolis, Maryland (1914–15), a teacher at the Asheville (North Carolina) School for Boys (1915–16), and an instructor of English and history at the United States Naval Academy at Annapolis, Maryland (1916–19).

In 1919 Cobb founded and was principal of the Chevy Chase (Maryland), Country Day School, where he served until his retirement. He founded and directed the Mast Cove Camp (1926).

Cobb was the author of many books, including *The Real Turk* (1914), *Ayesha of the Bosphorus* (1915), *The Essential Mysticism* (1918), *Simia, A Tale in Verse* (1919), *The New Leaven* (1928), *Discovering the Genius Within You* (1932), *New Horizons for the Child* (1934), *Character—A Sequence in Spiritual Psychology* (1938), *The Way of Life of Wu Ming Fu* (1942), *Tomorrow and Tomorrow* (1951), *What Is Man?* (1952), *Magnificent Partnership* (1954), *What Is God?* (1955), *Life with Nayan* (1969), and *Radiant Living* (1970).

He was the founder (1919) and chairman of the executive committee (1919–30) of the Progressive Education Association (president, 1927–30). He was a member of several literary associations.

REFERENCES: *LE* (III); *WW* (XXII); *WWAE* (I); Walter H. Drost, "A Visit with Stanwood Cobb," *Educational Forum* 35 (March 1971): 287–94; Patricia Albjerg Graham, *Progressive Education from Arcady to Academe: A History of the Progressive Education Association, 1919–1955* (New York: Teachers College, Columbia University, 1965). *Paul Unger*

COCHRAN, David Henry. B. July 5, 1828, Springville, New York, to Samuel and Catherine (Gallup) Cochran. M. 1851 to Harriet Stryker Rawson. Ch. four. D. October 4, 1909, Brooklyn, New York.

Teacher, professor, and college president, David Cochran began his teaching career at the age of fifteen. By teaching and lecturing, he worked his way through Hamilton College in Clinton, New York, from which he was graduated in 1850. He served in New York State as professor of natural science at Clinton Liberal Institute (1850–52), principal of Fredonia Academy (1852–54), professor of chemistry at the New York State Normal College (later, State University of New York at Albany) at Albany (1854), and principal (1855–64) and second president of Brooklyn Collegiate and Polytechnic Institute (later, Polytechnic Institute of New York) (1864–99).

Although his years at Albany were relatively uneventful, his long tenure at Brooklyn saw major changes in the institution. Originally a preparatory school, the institute was authorized to grant degrees in 1869. In 1890 it received a broad collegiate charter as the Polytechnic Institute of Brooklyn with a preparatory academic department and a collegiate department with admission requirements similar to those of other colleges. Cochran continued his interest in chemistry, and largely through his efforts, it was said,

Brooklyn Polytechnic Institute offered more pure mathematics than Yale and Harvard universities, more engineering fieldwork than the United States Military Academy at West Point, and more laboratory analysis than Yale University's Sheffield Scientific School. He was a strong opponent of athletics but was never successful in eliminating them.

Cochran was president of the American Society for the Regulation of Vivisection, a member of the Brooklyn Institute of Arts and Sciences, and vice-president of the American Humane Association. He was a trustee of Hamilton College for thirty years. He was the recipient of honorary degrees.

REFERENCES: *AC; NCAB* (3:397); *WWW* (I); William Marshall French and Florence Smith French, *College of the Empire State: A Centennial History of the New York State College for Teachers at Albany* (Albany, 1944); Miles Merwin Kastendieck, *The Story of Poly* (Wilmington, Del.: Harvey Matthews and Co., 1940); *NYT,* March 5, 1899, p. 22, and October 5, 1909, p. 9.   *Carey W. Brush*

COCKING, Walter Dewey. B. December 10, 1891, Manchester, Iowa, to Jesse E. and Emily (Hixson) Cocking. M. August 10, 1915, to Eva O. Van Kirk. Ch. none. D. January 14, 1964, Mamaroneck, New York.

Walter Dewey Cocking was educated in a one-room local school and at the Strawberry Point (Iowa) high school. He received the A.B. degree (1913) from Des Moines (Iowa) College, the M.A. degree (1923) from the State University of Iowa, and the Ph.D. degree (1928) from Columbia University.

He was a teacher and administrator in public schools in Iowa (1913–18) and was superintendent of the Storm Lake, Iowa, public schools (1918–22). He was director of junior high schools in San Antonio, Texas (1923–25), and director of the division of curriculum, books, and supplies in St. Louis, Missouri (1925–27).

Cocking was professor of education and school administration at George Peabody College for Teachers in Nashville, Tennessee (1928–33). From 1933 to 1937 he was commissioner of education for the state of Tennessee. He was dean of the College of Education at the University of Georgia (1937–41), consultant in program planning for the Federal Security Agency (1941), and chief of educational services for the Office of Price Administration (1942–43). From 1943 to his retirement in 1960, he was associated with the Buttenheim Publishing Corporation in New York City and taught courses on school physical plant and administration to many American colleges and universities as a visiting professor. He was an early proponent of language laboratories, special classroom furniture, and areas for individual study.

He was the author of numerous school surveys and articles and of

Administrative Procedures in Curriculum Making (1928), *Organization and Administration of Public Education* (with C. H. Gilmore, 1938), *The American Schools* (with L. B. Perkins, 1949), and *As I See It* (1955). He was editor (1943–60) of *The School Executive, Educational Business,* and *The American School and University* yearbook.

Cocking was active in professional organizations and served as chairman of the Tennessee Educational Commission (1934–35), chief specialist on school administration for the President's Advisory Committee on Education (1937), and consultant to the Tennessee Valley Authority. He was a member of the science committee of the National Resources Committee (1936–40) and chairman of the National Council on Economic Education. He was the organizer of the National Conference of Professors of Educational Administration (1947), which established the Cocking Loan Fund and Annual Cocking Lecture. He was an officer or board member of the National Committee on Scouting in the Schools, the Outdoor Education Association, and other civic organizations. He was the recipient of two honorary degrees.

REFERENCES: *LE* (III); *NCAB* (52:102); *WWAE* (VIII); *WWW* (IV); W. R. Flesher and A. L. Knoblauch, *A Decade in Educational Leadership: The First Ten Years of NCPEA, 1947–1956* (National Conference of Professors of Educational Administration, 1958), p. 78; Dale K. Hayes and William L. Pharis, *National Conference of Professors of Educational Administration: The Second Ten Years, 1957–1967* (NCPEA, 1967), p. 135; *NYT,* January 15, 1964, p. 31.   *Charles M. Achilles*

COE, George Albert. B. March 26, 1862, Monroe County, New York, to George W. and Harriet (Van Voorhis) Coe. M. September 3, 1888, to Sadie E. Knowland. Ch. none. D. November 9, 1951, Claremont, California.

George Albert Coe was graduated with the A.B. (1884) and A.M. (1888) degrees from the University of Rochester, New York. He received the S.T.B. (1887) and Ph.D. (1891) degrees from Boston (Massachusetts) University. He studied at the University of Berlin, Germany (1890–91).

He was a member of the faculty at the University of Southern California in Los Angeles (1888–93), and was John Evans Professor of Philosophy at Northwestern University in Evanston, Illinois (1893–1909). Coe was professor of religious education at Union Theological Seminary in New York City (1909–22) and at Teachers College, Columbia University (1922–27).

He wrote *The Spiritual Life—Studies in the Science of Religion* (1900), *The Religion of the Mature Mind* (1902), *Psychology of Religion* (1916), *A Social Theory of Religious Education* (1917), *Law and Freedom in the School* (1923), and *What Ails Our Youth?* (1924).

Coe was active in professional associations and was president of the Religious Education Association (1909–10). He led the fight against military activities in education, opposing compulsory military training proposals and Reserve Officers Training Corps units at schools and colleges. He was chairman of the Committee on Militarism in Education and the Citizens Committee of One Hundred, which defended three New York City teachers accused of leftist political activities in 1926.

REFERENCES: *LE* (III); *WWW* (III); *NYT,* November 10, 1951, p. 10; "In Memoriam: George Albert Coe," *Religious Education* 47 (March-April 1952): 67–125; *School and Society* 74 (November 17, 1951): 318.

Albert S. Weston

COFFMAN, Lotus Delta. B. January 7, 1875, near Salem, Indiana, to Mansford E. and Laura Ellen (David) Coffman. M. December 28, 1899, to Mary Emma Farrell. Ch. two. D. September 22, 1938, Minneapolis, Minnesota.

After graduating from high school, Lotus Delta Coffman taught in a country school. He attended Indiana Normal School (later, Indiana State University), Terre Haute, from which he was graduated in 1896. After teaching several years, he returned to the University of Indiana where he received the A.B. (1906) and A.M. (1910) degrees. In 1911 he received the Ph.D. degree from Columbia University.

From 1896 and while a student at Indiana, Coffman was a teacher and superintendent of schools in Salem and Connersville, Indiana, director of teacher training at Illinois State College (later, Eastern Illinois University) at Charleston (1907–09, 1911–12), lecturer at Columbia University (1909–11), and professor of education at the University of Illinois (1912–15). He served at the University of Minnesota (1915–38) as dean of the college of education (1915–20) and president, a position he occupied from 1920 until his death in 1938.

Coffman, one of the first major university presidents to come from the field of education, ranked as an outstanding contributor to public education and university administration. While president at Minnesota, he established many new programs that influenced higher education throughout the country, including a two-year general college, the Center for Continuation Study, which offered short courses for graduates in various professions, a university college for gifted students, an institute of child welfare, an institute of technology, a fine arts department with an art gallery, a school of journalism, and a graduate school of business. He pioneered the scientific approach to supervision at all levels of instruction and furthered interest in guidance and student personnel work.

Coffman coauthored one of the first textbooks on the teaching of reading, *Reading in Public Schools* (with T. H. Briggs, *q.v.,* 1908) and two books on the teaching of arithmetic, *How to Teach Arithmetic* (with J. C. Brown, 1913) and *The Supervision of Arithmetic* (with W. A. Jessup, *q.v.,*

1915), and was the author of *The Social Composition of the Teaching Population* (1911) and *The State University: Its Work and Problems* (1934). He edited a series of educational books for D. C. Heath and was a coeditor of *Educational Administration and Supervision* (1915–38).

Nationally and internationally recognized for his administrative skills, Coffman served in many professional organizations, including the National Education Association (secretary of the Commission on the Emergency in Education, 1918–20, and chairman of the Educational Policies Commission, 1935–38). He was president of the National Society of College Teachers of Education (1917–18), the North Central Association of Colleges and Secondary Schools (1921–22), the Association of Urban Universities (1921–22), the American Council on Schools (1921–23), and the National Association of State Universities (1930). He was secretary of the board of trustees of the Carnegie Foundation for the Advancement of Teaching and the Carnegie Corporation and chairman of the American Council on Education. He conducted many educational surveys in the United States, the Soviet Union, Australia, New Zealand, the Philippines, and at the Yenching University in Peking, China. He received many honorary degrees from American colleges and universities.

REFERENCES: *DAB* (supp. 2); *LE* (I); *NCAB* (C:241, 35:253); *WWAE* (VIII); *WWW* (I); William C. Bagley *(q.v.)*, "Lotus D. Coffman as I Knew Him," *The Educational Forum* (January 1939): 151–59; Thomas H. Briggs, "Lotus Delta Coffman—1875–1938," *Educational Administration and Supervision Including Teacher Training* (October 1938): 481–84; Ernest H. Lindley *(q.v.)*, "Lotus Delta Coffman—An Interpretation," *School and Society* (December 31, 1938): 837–40; "Lotus Delta Coffman, 1875–1938," *The North Central Association Quarterly* (January 1939): 255–60; *NYT,* September 23, 1938, p. 27; Malcom M. Willey, "Lotus Delta Coffman: Educational Statesman, 1875–1938," *The Educational Record* (January 1939): 10–27.   *Lawrence Byron Smelser*

COLBURN, Dana Pond. B. September 29, 1823, West Dedham, Massachusetts, to Isaac and Mary Colburn. M. no. D. December 15, 1859, Bristol, Rhode Island.

The youngest of fifteen children, Dana Colburn attended the common schools in Dedham, Massachusetts, where his proficiency in arithmetic was soon evident. After a short term as a shoemaker's apprentice, Colburn studied at home under Joseph Underwood, Jr., who persuaded him to attend the Normal School (later, Bridgewater State College) at Bridgewater, Massachusetts. He completed the course of study there in 1843, having been particularly influenced by his mathematics teacher, N. Tillinghast, later principal of the normal school.

Colburn taught in Dover and Sharon, Massachusetts, East Greenwich,

Rhode Island, and Brookline, Massachusetts. In 1847 he was invited by Horace Mann *(q.v.),* secretary of the Massachusetts Board of Education, to become an instructor in the Massachusetts teachers' institutes. In 1848 he took a position teaching arithmetic and serving as assistant principal at Bridgewater Normal School, despite a reduction in salary from his position in Brookline.

He was a teacher at a private school in Providence, Rhode Island (1852–54). In 1854 the school became the Rhode Island State Normal School (later, Rhode Island College) with Colburn as its first principal. He continued there until his death in 1859.

Colburn became nationally known for his institute work, as a contributor to educational journals, especially *The Rhode Island Schoolmaster,* and for his series of arithmetic textbooks. Colburn's arithmetic texts established his place in the history of American education. They include *The First Steps in Numbers* (with George A. Walton, 1849), *The Decimal System of Numbers* (1852), *Interest, Discount, Equation of Payments* (1853), *Arithmetic, Its Application* (1855), *The First Book of Arithmetic* (1856), *The Common-School Arithmetic* (1858), *The Child's Book of Arithmetic* (1859), and *Inductive Lessons in Intellectual Arithmetic* (1863).

REFERENCES: *DAB; NCAB* (12:267); *WWW* (H); *American Journal of Education* (March 1862): 289–304; *The Rhode Island Schoolmaster* 6 (1860): 26–28. *Stephen J. Clarke*

COLBURN, Warren. B. March 1, 1793, Dedham, Massachusetts, to Richard and Joanna (Eaton) Colburn. M. August 28, 1823, to Temperance C. Horton. Ch. seven. D. September 13, 1833, Lowell, Massachusetts.

Warren Colburn attended local district schools. He worked in factories, studied mathematics, and became a machinist. After being employed for five years, he began to prepare for Harvard University with the Reverend Edward Richmond of Stoughton, Massachusetts. He was graduated from Harvard in 1820 after showing a strong interest in mathematics and physical science.

In 1820 Colburn opened a tuition school in Boston and developed a system of teaching arithmetic. In 1823 he came to the attention of manufacturer Francis Cabot Lowell, who hired him as superintendent of a cotton factory at Waltham, Massachusetts. He moved to the Merrimack Manufacturing Company at Lowell, where he was superintendent and invented parts to improve the machinery. He founded a lyceum at Lowell, where he delivered a series of popular lectures which continued for many years. He lectured on commerce, nature, physics, and astronomy and demonstrated the magic lantern and telescope.

While headmaster of the Boston school, Colburn wrote his textbooks in arithmetic: *First Lessons in Arithmetic on the Plan of Pestalozzi* (1821), *Arithmetic: Being a Sequel to First Lessons in Arithmetic* (1822), and *An Introduction to Algebra* (1825). *First Lessons in Arithmetic* was republished in 1826 with the title *Intellectual Arithmetic Upon the Inductive Method of Instruction.* He wrote a graded series, *Lessons in Reading and Grammar,* from 1830 to 1833.

Colburn was a member of the first school board of Lowell, Massachusetts (1826–29). A cofounder of the American Institute of Instruction in Boston, he was a member of the American Academy of Arts and Sciences and was on the examining committee for mathematics for Harvard University for a number of years.

REFERENCES: *AC; DAB; NCAB* (10:445): *WWW* (H).   *Billy G. Dixon*

COLEMAN, Satis Narrona Barton. B. June 12, 1878, Tyler, Texas, to John Henry Martin and Catherine Wilson (McCarley) Barton. M. March 13, 1896, to Walter Moore Coleman. Ch. two. D. April 17, 1961, Cedar Falls, Iowa.

Satis Narrona Barton Coleman was educated at the Texas State Normal School (later, Sam Houston State University) in Huntsville and studied music under private tutors. She attended Columbia University, where she received the B.S. (1927), A.M. (1928), and Ph.D. (1931) degrees.

Coleman taught music in New York City and Washington, D.C. She was a music teacher and researcher at Lincoln School of Teachers College, Columbia University (1925–42). Her major fields of interest and contributions to education were in creativity and music. Coleman demonstrated the possibilities of creative work for children in music.

Coleman was a major author of articles and books in the field of music, including *Creative Music for Children* (1922), *Bells: Their History, Legends, Making, and Uses* (1927), *Creative Music in the Home* (1927), *Singing Time* (with Alice G. Thorn, 1929), *The Drum Book* (1930), *A Children's Symphony* (1931), *The Gingerbread Man and Other Songs* (1931), *Christmas* (pageant, 1933), *Christmas Carols of Many Countries* (with E. K. Jorgenson, 1935), *Another Singing Time* (with Alice G. Thorn, 1939), *Your Child's Music* (1940), *Songs of American Folks* (with Adolph Gregman, 1942), *Volcanoes New and Old* (1949), *The New Singing Time* (1950), and *Dancing Time* (1952). She was author of the Creative Music for School series (1925–27).

She was national chairman of the music committee for the Association for Childhood Education (1940–42).

REFERENCES: *WW* (XV); *WWW* (IV); *NYT,* April 19, 1961, p. 39.

John F. Ohles

COLLAR, William Coe. B. September 11, 1833, Ashford, Connecticut, to Charles and Mary Ann (Coe) Collar. M. February 24, 1858, to Hannah

Caroline Averill. M. January 5, 1892, to Mary Evelyn Cornwell. Ch. four. D. February 27, 1916, Waban, Massachusetts.

When William Coe Collar became the headmaster of Roxbury (Massachusetts) Latin School in 1867, it was already a good preparatory school; when he relinquished the position forty years later, it was one of the most distinguished in the nation. He received the A.B. (1859) and A.M. (1864) degrees from Amherst (Massachusetts) College.

As headmaster, Collar introduced new subjects to Roxbury Latin School that were being included in the curriculum in other secondary schools, such as chemistry, physics, music, drawing, and physical training. He pioneered in the use of laboratories and experimental methods in teaching physics and chemistry. By the 1890s the school was well known and received many visitors from normal schools and university departments of education.

Collar made innovations in the instruction of Latin and promoted these changes in textbooks, which became standards in American schools. He collaborated with Moses Grant Daniell in writing *The Beginner's Latin Book* (1886) and *First Latin Book* (1894), particularly popular texts. They also coauthored *The Beginner's Greek Composition* (1893). Collar wrote *Practical Latin Composition* (1889) and *First Year German* (1905) and was a contributor to *Methods of Teaching History* (1895). He edited Vergil's *Aeneid* and William Eysenbach's *A Practical German Grammar* (1893).

Collar was a leader in the effort to improve relations between preparatory schools and colleges, with special concern for college entrance requirements. In 1885 he was a founder of the New England Association of Colleges and Preparatory Schools, the first regional accrediting association in the country. He was a member of the Latin Conference of the Committee of Ten (1892), which sought to reform the American secondary school curriculum. Collar was a member of many other organizations, including the Headmaster's Association of the United States, the Harvard Teacher's Association, the Modern Language Association, and the Boston School Committee (1878–81).

REFERENCES: *NCAB* (21:253); *WWW* (I); Richard W. Hale, Jr., *Tercentenary History of the Roxbury Latin School, 1645–1945* (Cambridge, Mass.: Riverside Press, 1946); Theodore R. Sizer, *Secondary Schools at the Turn of the Century* (New Haven: Yale University Press, 1964).

William Kornegay

COLLINS, Mauney Douglass. B. July 5, 1885, Choestoe, Georgia, to Archibald B. and Mary L. (Jackson) Collins. M. 1911 to Winnie Louise Byrd. M. September 15, 1921, to Mary Jeannette Cochran. Ch. one. D. March 9, 1967, Atlanta, Georgia.

Mauney D. Collins was educated in the public schools of Choestoe, Georgia, and in the high school at Hiawassee, Georgia, from which he was graduated in 1906. He was graduated from Hiawassee Junior College in

1908 and attended Mercer College in Macon, Georgia (1908–09), Columbia University (1915), the University of Georgia (1915–16), and Oglethorpe University in Atlanta, Georgia, where he received the B.A. (1931) and M.A. (1932) degrees and an honorary Ped.D. degree (1933).

Collins began his teaching career in Choestoe in 1903, was ordained to the ministry in 1909, and was editor of the *Campbell* (Georgia) *News* (1919–23). He served as the Campbell County superintendent of schools (1921–32). In 1932 the Campbell and Fulton County schools merged, and Collins served as a supervisor in the combined system for a year. He was elected Georgia state superintendent of schools (1933–58). During Collins's long tenure in the office of state superintendent, study groups of teachers and parents were organized to plan improved educational facilities and programs, teacher education was strengthened, visiting teacher services were initiated, and the state established vocational guidance, counseling, and testing programs.

Collins was active in his church and community. In 1921 he served as pastor of five churches in addition to his position as superintendent of the Union City schools. In the early 1930s he was pastor of the Fairburn Baptist Church, Fairburn, Georgia, and editor of the *Fairburn Messenger* for five years. He also engaged in a successful real-estate business.

Collins was active in professional and civic activities, including the National Educational Legislative Committee of the Georgia Democratic Committee (1919–24), the National Education Association (state director, from 1935), the National Council of Chief State School Officers (president and member of the legislative committee), and the Locust Grove Institute and Georgia Odd Fellow Orphans' Home (trustee). He received a medal from Oglethorpe University (1936) and honorary degrees from Mercer University and Bob Jones University.

REFERENCES: *LE* (III); *WWAE* (XVI); *WWW* (IV); *Atlanta Constitution*, March 10, 1967; *History of Georgia* (Chicago: The S. J. Clarke Publishing Co., 1926), vol. 11; *The Story of Georgia* (New York: The American Historical Society, 1938).

Donald C. Stephenson

COLLITZ, Hermann. B. February 4, 1855, Bleckede, Hanover, Germany, to Christian and Friederike (Schäfer) Collitz. M. August 13, 1904, to Klara Hechtenberg *(q.v.)*. Ch. none. D. May 13, 1935, Baltimore, Maryland.

Hermann Collitz was educated in Germany in a private school in Bleckede, the Johanneum Lyceum at Lüneburg, and the University of Göttingen. He studied comparative philosophy, Sanskrit, and Slavic languages at the University of Berlin in 1878 and received the Ph.D. degree (1879) from Göttingen. He was granted a stipend to continue his research work in 1879 while continuing his studies of Indo-European linguistics. At the

University of Berlin, he edited a collection of Greek dialect inscriptions, the first of which appeared in 1883. He also edited a German low-dialect dictionary by Karl Bauer.

In 1883 he received an appointment at the University of Halle (Germany) library and in 1885 was granted the "Venia Docendi" for Sanskrit and comparative philosophy. He was associate professor of German and comparative philosophy at the newly founded Bryn Mawr (Pennsylvania) College (1886–1907). He was professor of Germanic philosophy at Johns Hopkins University in Baltimore, Maryland, from 1907 until 1927, when he retired as professor emeritus. The courses he conducted at Johns Hopkins employed manuscripts and interpretation of works in the antecedent old German languages, including Gothic, Old High German, Norse, Frisian, and Saxon. Some of these courses were the first given regularly at any American university.

Collitz was the author of *Die Verwantschaftsverhältnisse der Griechschen* (1885), *Die neueste Sprachforschung* (1886), and *Das Schwache Praeteritum und sein Vorgeschichte* (1912), and he wrote scholarly books, including *Problems in Comparative Germanic Philosophy* (1906), *Early Germanic Vocalism* (1918), *The Scope and Aims of Linguistic Science* (1925), and *World Languages* (1926). He was editor of *Sammlung der Griechischen Dialekt Inschrifter* (four volumes, 1884–1915) and of journals, including *Modern Language Notes* (1902–13), *American Journal of Philology,* and *Journal of English and German Philology.*

Johns Hopkins University honored Collitz on his seventy-fifth birthday by publishing *Studies in Honor of Hermann Collitz,* compiled by former students and colleagues. He was a founder of the American Linguistic Society in 1925 and was a member of many other associations, including the Modern Language Association of America (president, 1925). He received an honorary degree from the University of Chicago (1916).

REFERENCES: *LE* (I); *NCAB* (D:284); *NYT,* May 14, 1935, p. 21; *WWW* (I).   *Kenneth Sipser*

COLLITZ, Klara Hechtenberg. B. 1863, Rheydt, Rhineland, Germany, to Wilhelm and Maria (Friederichs) Hechtenberg. M. August 13, 1904, to Hermann Collitz *(q.v.).* Ch. none. D. November 23, 1944, Baltimore, Maryland.

Klara Hechtenberg Collitz was graduated from Höhere Leherinner-Bildungsanstalt, Neuwied on Rhein in 1881. She continued her education in Lausanne, Switzerland (1889–92), and Oxford University, where she won first-class honors in 1895. She also studied at the University of Chicago (1897), the University of Bonn (1898), and the University of Heidelberg, where she received the Ph.D. degree (1901). She was a graduate student in Greek and German at Johns Hopkins University (1908–11).

She was a lecturer in French philology at Victoria College in Belfast, Ireland (1895–96), and taught French and German at Smith College in Northampton, Massachusetts, where she became chairman of the department of Germanic philology (1897–99). She lectured on Germanic philology to women students at Oxford University, England (1901–04). She retired from teaching after her marriage to Hermann Collitz.

Collitz was a member of many American and foreign professional organizations. She addressed the Pan-American Congress in Washington, D.C., on "University Education for Women" (1915).

Her publications include *Das Fremdwort bei Grimmelshausen* (1901), *Der Briefstil im 17. Jahrhundert* (1903), *Fremdwörterbuch des 17. Jahrhunderts* (1904), *Selections from Early German Literature* (1910), *Selections from Classical German Literature* (1914), *Biographical Sketch of Hermann Collitz and Bibliography of Prof. Collitz's Writings* (1930), *Verbs of Motion in Their Semantic Divergence* (1931), *The History of Alliteratives in German* (1933), *Clipped Appellatives in German* (1936), and *Verba Dicendi* (1937). She contributed articles to philological journals.

REFERENCES: *NCAB* (A:90); *WWW* (II); *NYT,* November 24, 1944, p. 23.   *Barbara Ruth Peltzman*

COLTON, Elizabeth Avery. B. December 30, 1872, Choctaw Nation, Indian Territory (Oklahoma), to James Hooper and Harriet Eloise (Avery) Colton. M. no. D. August 15, 1924, Clifton Springs, New York.

Elizabeth Avery Colton, professor of English, worked for the improvement of women's colleges in the South. Daughter of missionary parents, she was raised in Indian Territory and a succession of North Carolina communities where her father was a supply pastor, evangelist, and professor. Colton desired to obtain a college education but was forced to alternate study with teaching school. She was graduated from the Statesville (North Carolina) Female College with the B.A. degree and attended Mount Holyoke College in South Hadley, Massachusetts (1891–93). Returning to North Carolina on the death of her father, she taught at Queen's College in Charlotte for six years and then attended Teachers College, Columbia University, where she received the B.S. (1903) and A.M. (1905) degrees.

She taught at Wellesley (Massachusetts) College (1905–08) and returned to North Carolina, where she headed the English department at Meredith College in Raleigh (1908–20). Colton worked to raise the standards of her own and other women's colleges in the South. All southern higher education, in particular the education of women, was in a depressed condition. There were only four accredited women's colleges in the entire South, and most of the others were little more than finishing or preparatory schools.

Colton conducted research on southern women's colleges and published her findings in pamphlets: *Southern Colleges for Women* (1911), *Standards* of Southern Colleges for Women (1911), Improvements in Standards of Southern Colleges Since 1900 (1913), The Approximate Value of Recent Degrees from Southern Colleges (1913), The Junior College Problem in the South (1914), and The Various Types of Southern Colleges for Women (1916). Her research provided guidelines for the Southern Association of College Women to accredit institutions and criteria by which schools could raise their standards.

Colton sought to unite the Southern Association of College Women and the Association of Collegiate Alumnae. The merged American Association of University Women passed a resolution in 1921, praising Colton's work in making the merger possible.

REFERENCES: DAB; NAW; WWW (I); Mary Lynch Johnson, Elizabeth Avery Colton, An Educational Pioneer in the South (North Carolina Division and the South Atlantic Section of the American Association of University Women, n.d.).   Linda C. Gardner

COLVIN, Stephen Sheldon. B. March 28, 1869, Phenix, Rhode Island, to Stephen and Clara Anna (Turner) Colvin. M. October 18, 1891, to Edna F. Boothman. M. July 18, 1895, to Eva Mable Collins. Ch. one. D. July 15, 1923, New York, New York.

Stephen Sheldon Colvin was an American pioneer in intelligence testing. He was graduated from Worcester (Massachusetts) Academy in 1887 and received the Ph.B. (1891) and A.M. (1894) degrees from Brown University in Providence, Rhode Island. He studied in Germany at the University of Berlin (1895–96) and received the Ph.D. degree (1897) from the University of Strassburg.

Colvin was on the staff of the Providence (Rhode Island) Journal (1891–93) and was an instructor of rhetoric at Brown University (1892–95). He taught English in Worcester, Massachusetts, high schools (1897–1901) while studying under G. Stanley Hall (q.v.) of Clark University. In 1901 Colvin became assistant professor of psychology at the University of Illinois, where he remained until 1912, except for a year as assistant professor of philosophy at Brown University (1903–04). The years at Urbana were significant for Colvin. He became professor of psychology and then department head, and he was a close collaborator of William C. Bagley (q.v.).

He was professor of educational psychology at Brown University (1912–23) and also served as director of the school of education (1919–23). As inspector of secondary schools in Rhode Island, he played an important role in developing public high schools in the state. In 1923 he accepted an appointment as professor of education at Teachers College, Columbia University, but succumbed to a heart ailment soon after beginning his new assignment.

Colvin inaugurated the use of intelligence tests for students at Brown

University. In 1922 he directed a survey to measure the intelligence of high school seniors in Massachusetts as part of a national testing program conducted by the United States Bureau of Education. Although he was one of the first American educators to use group mental tests extensively, he viewed them as providing only some of the data needed for determining students' abilities.

Colvin was the author of *The Thing-in-Itself of Schopenhauer* (1897), *Some Facts in Partial Justification of the Dogma of Formal Discipline* (1909), *The Learning Process* (1911), *Human Behavior* (with W. C. Bagley, 1913), and *Introduction to High School Teaching* (1917). He was a fellow of the American Association for the Advancement of Science and a member of professional associations.

REFERENCES: *DAB; NCAB* (27:198); *WWW* (I); *NYT,* July 16, 1923, p. 11. *Donald R. Warren*

COMFORT, George Fisk. B. September 20, 1833, Berkshire, New York, to Silas C. and Electra (Smith) Comfort. M. January 19, 1871, to Anna Manning. Ch. one. D. May 5, 1910, Montclair, New Jersey.

George Fisk Comfort prepared for college at Wyoming Seminary in Kingston, Pennsylvania, and Cazenovia (New York) Seminary. He took the classical course at Wesleyan University in Middletown, Connecticut, and was graduated with the A.B. (1857) and A.M. (1860) degrees.

Comfort taught natural sciences, drawing, and painting at the Amenia and Fort Plain seminaries in New York and studied in Europe for five years (1860–65), including two years in Berlin, Germany, at the University of Berlin, Academy of Fine Arts, and Royal Library. He also traveled and studied in the Orient (1879, 1887, and 1891).

Upon his return to the United States in 1865, Comfort accepted the chair of modern languages and aesthetics at Allegheny College in Meadville, Pennsylvania. He left in 1868 to become lecturer in Christian archaeology at Drew Theological Seminary in Madison, New Jersey, and was professor of modern languages and archaeology (1872–73).

Comfort organized the college of fine arts at Syracuse (New York) University and served as dean (1873–93). He originated the granting of degrees in the fine arts, including architecture, painting, sculpture, and music. Comfort was elected president of the Southern College of Fine Arts in LaPorte, Texas in 1891.

He was the author of *Modern Languages in Education* (1886) and the series of language instruction books, the German Course (1870), as well as several essays. He was editor of *Northern Christian Advocate* (1872–93). Active in professional and civic associations, Comfort was an organizer of the American Philological Society (secretary, 1869–76) and the Central New York Society of Artists (1901). He was a founder of the Metropolitan

Museum of Art in New York City (1869) and the Syracuse Museum of Fine Arts (1896), which he served as director. He received honorary degrees from the University of the State of New York and Syracuse University.

REFERENCES: *AC; NCAB* (3:162); *WWW* (I); *NYT,* May 6, 1910, p. 9.   *Roger H. Jones*

COMMAGER, Henry Steele. B. October 25, 1902, Pittsburgh, Pennsylvania, to James Williams and Anna Elisabeth (Dan) Commager. M. July 3, 1928, to Evan Carroll. Ch. three.

Henry Steele Commager was graduated from high school in Chicago, Illinois, and attended the University of Chicago, where he received the Ph.B. (1922), M.A. (1923), and Ph.D. (1928) degrees. He studied at the University of Copenhagen, Denmark (1924–25).

Commager was a member of the faculty at New York University (1926–38) and at Columbia University (1939–56). He was professor of history at Amherst (Massachusetts) College from 1956. He was lecturer on American history (1942–43) and Pitt Professor of American History (1947–48) at Cambridge (England) University and Harmsworth Professor of American History at Oxford (England) University and lecturer at many other American and foreign universities.

A major contributor to historical literature, Commager's books include *The Growth of the American Republic* (1931), *Our Nation's Development* (with others, 1934), *Theodore Parker* (1936), *The Heritage of America* (with Allan Nevins, *q.v.,* 1939), *Our Nation* (with Eugene C. Barker, 1941), *America: The Story of a Free People* (with Allan Nevins, 1942), *Majority Rule and Minority Rights* (1943), *The Story of the Second World War* (1945), *The American Mind* (1951), *Living Ideas in America* (1952), *Freedom, Loyalty, Dissent* (1954), *Joseph Story* (1954), *Europe and America since 1942)* (with G. Brunn, 1954), *The Spirit of Seventy-six* (two volumes, 1958), *The Era of Reform* (1960), *The Great Proclamation* (1960), *Crusaders for Freedom* (1962), *Lester Ward and the Welfare State* (1965), and editor of many others. He was coeditor with James B. Conant *(q.v.)* of Oxford (England) University's Home University Library, associate editor of *American Scholar,* and contributing editor of *Scholastic* magazine.

Commager was trustee of the American Scandinavian Foundation, a fellow of the American Scandinavian Society, a Guggenheim Fellow (1960–61), and a member of many other organizations. He received the Herbert B. Adams Award of the American Historical Society (1929), was decorated Knight Order of Dannebrog by Denmark, and received many honorary degrees from American and foreign universities.

REFERENCES: *CA* (21–22); *CB* (January 1946); *NCAB* (G:335); *WW* (XXXVI).

John F. Ohles

COMPTON, Arthur Holly. B. September 10, 1892, Wooster, Ohio, to Elias and Otelia Catherine (Augspurger) Compton. M. June 28, 1916, to Betty Charity McCloskey. Ch. two. D. March 15, 1962, Berkeley, California.

Arthur H. Compton attended the College of Wooster (Ohio), where his father was a member of the faculty, and received the B.S. degree (1913). He studied at Princeton University (1913–16), was a Porter Ogden Jacobus Fellow (1915–16), and received the M.A. (1914) and Ph.D. (1916) degrees.

Compton taught physics at the University of Minnesota (1916–17) and was a research engineer at the Westinghouse Lamp Company in East Pittsburgh, Pennsylvania (1917–19), and a National Research Fellow at the Cavendish Laboratory, Cambridge (England) University (1919–20). He was professor and head of the physics department at Washington University in St. Louis, Missouri (1920–23). At the University of Chicago, he was professor of physics (1923–29), Charles H. Swift Distinguished Science Professor (1929–45), and chairman of the department of physics and dean of the division of physical sciences (1940–45). Compton directed the Metallurgical Laboratory of the Manhattan Project at the University of Chicago (1942–45), where the chain reaction was achieved that made the atomic bomb a possibility. He served as chancellor of Washington University in St. Louis (1945–53) and continued there as professor of natural history (1953–61).

Compton was the author of *X-Rays and Electrons* (1926), *The Freedom of Man* (1935), *X-Rays in Theory and Experiment* (with S. K. Allison, 1935), *The Religion of a Scientist* (1938), *Human Meaning of Science* (1940), and *Atomic Quest: A Personal Narrative* (1956). He was associate editor of *Physical Review* and served on the editorial boards of other journals.

Consulting physicist to the General Electric Company (1926–45), Compton also served as governor of the Argonne National Laboratory (1945), member of the President's Commission on Higher Education (1946–48), United States delegate to United Nations Educational, Scientific, and Cultural Organization meetings in Paris, France (1946), and Mexico (1947). He was general chairman of the Laymen's Missionary Movement (1937–41) and cochairman of the National Conference of Christians and Jews (1938–47). He was a trustee of the College of Wooster, Brookings Institution, and Fisk University and a regent of the Smithsonian Institution. He was a member of the National Cancer Advisory Board (1937–44), vice-president of the Chicago Tumor Institute (1937–45) and president of the American Association of Science Workers (1939–40). He was awarded the Nobel Prize for physics (1927) and received many awards and medals. He was the recipient of many honorary degrees from American and foreign colleges and universities. He was a brother of Karl T. Compton *(q.v.).*

REFERENCES: *CB* (August 1940, September 1958, May 1962); *DSB; LE*

(III); *NCAB* (G:363); *NYT,* March 16, 1962, p. 1; *WWAE* (XVI); *WWW* (IV).   *John F. Ohles*

COMPTON, Karl Taylor. B. September 14, 1887, Wooster, Ohio, to Elias and Otelia Catherine (Augspurger) Compton. M. to Rawena Rayman. M. to Margaret Hutchinson. Ch. three. D. June 22, 1954, New York, New York.

Karl T. Compton attended the College of Wooster (Ohio), where his father was a professor of philosophy and psychology. Compton received the B.A. (1908) and M.S. (1909) degrees from Wooster and the Ph.D. degree (1912) from Princeton University.

Compton taught chemistry at the College of Wooster (1909–10) and was instructor of physics at Reed College in Portland, Oregon (1913–15). He returned to Princeton as assistant professor and professor of physics (1915–30) and chairman of the department of physics (1929–30).

Compton was president of the Massachusetts Institute of Technology (MIT) from 1930 to 1948 and was president of the MIT Corporation from 1948 to his death in 1954. He was credited with leading MIT from the status of an undergraduate engineering college to one of the leading centers of graduate scientific education in the world. He introduced a five-year program of study and industrial experience there.

Compton was active in governmental affairs as a member of advisory committees to the United States Department of Agriculture (1924–30), Bureau of Standards (1931–41), Department of Commerce (1933–36), and Weather Bureau (1935–48). He served on several governmental boards during and after World War II, including the special advisory committee on the atomic bomb (1945), and was chairman of the Research Board for National Security (1945–46), the Joint Chiefs of Staff Evaluation Board on Atomic Bomb Tests (1946), the Research and Development Board (1948–49), the New England Committee on Atomic Energy (1954), and the President's Advisory Committee on Universal Training (1946–47). He was a trustee of a number of philanthropic foundations and the Brookings Institution (1940–50), Norwich University (1935–50), Princeton University (1952–54), and Western College for Women (1953–54).

A member of many civic, professional, and scholarly organizations, Compton was president of the American Association for the Advancement of Science (1935–36), the American Society for Engineering Education (1938–39), and the American Physical Society (1927–29). He received many awards and medals and was granted honorary degrees by over thirty American and foreign colleges and universities. He was the brother of Arthur H. Compton *(q.v.).*

REFERENCES: *CB* (March 1941 and September 1954); *DSB; LE* (III); *NCAB* (C:81, 42:3); *NYT,* June 23, 1954, p. 1; *WWAE* (XV); *WWW* (III).
John F. Ohles

COMSTOCK, Ada Louise. B. December 11, 1876, Moorhead, Minnesota, to Solomon Gilman and Sarah (Ball) Comstock. M. June 14, 1943, to Wallace Notestein. Ch. none. D. December 12, 1973, New Haven, Connecticut.

Ada Louise Comstock (Notestein) was the daughter of Solomon Gilman Comstock who migrated from Maine to Minnesota in 1870 and settled in Moorhead, where he became a successful attorney and a leading citizen. He was probably the single greatest influence upon her life.

Ada Comstock was graduated from Moorhead High School in 1892. Since she was only fifteen years old, her father thought she should attend the University of Minnesota in Minneapolis, close to home (1892–94). She transferred to Smith College in Northampton, Massachusetts, where she received the B.L. degree (1897). She returned to Moorhead State Normal School in Minnesota, where she received a teaching diploma (1898). She received the M.A. degree (1899) in English, history, and education from Columbia University. She studied at the Sorbonne in Paris, France (1904–05).

Comstock began her career in 1899 as an assistant in the department of rhetoric at the University of Minnesota. She was appointed first dean of women at the University of Minnesota (1907). She left Minnesota in 1912 to become the first academic dean at Smith College where she concerned herself with women's educational experiences from housing to instruction. She became the first full-time president of Radcliffe College in Cambridge, Massachusetts (1923–43). By the end of her administration, Radcliffe had established academic and financial stability, and Harvard University had accepted regular classroom coeducation with Radcliffe.

Comstock was active in professional associations, including the Association of Deans of Women (president, 1908), the American Association of University Women (president, 1921), the Commission on Direction of Investigation of History and Other Social Studies in the Schools of the American Historical Association (1929–34), the Institute of Pacific Relations, and the International Federation of University Women (member of the council). She was appointed by President Herbert Hoover to the National Commission on Law Observance and Enforcement (1929).

Upon her retirement from Radcliffe in 1943, she married Wallace Notestein, Sterling Professor of History at Yale. She continued her activities on behalf of education and improved international relations for many years and was sought as a public speaker when she was over eighty years old. She received fourteen honorary degrees and other honors, including the Jane Addams Medal awarded by Rockford (Illinois) College, a Radcliffe scholarship endowed in her name, and three dormitories named after her.

REFERENCES: *LE* (III); *NCAB* (C:21); *WW* (XXII); *WWAE* (VIII); *WWW* (VI); *NYT,* December 13, 1973, p. 50; Susan Margot Smith, "Ada

Louise Comstock,'' in Barbara Stuhler and Gretchen Kreuter, eds., *Women of Minnesota: A Beginning History* (St. Paul: Minnesota Historical Society, 1977).

Susan Margot Smith

COMSTOCK, Anna Botsford. B. September 1, 1854, Otto, New York, to Marvin and Phebe (Irish) Botsford. M. October 7, 1878, to John Henry Comstock, *(q.v.)*. Ch. none. D. August 24, 1930, Ithaca, New York.

Anna Botsford Comstock was graduated from the Chamberlain Institute in Randolph, New York (1873), and Cornell University, where she received the B.S. degree (1885).

As a student at Cornell, she met her future husband, a professor of entomology. They moved to Washington, D.C., in 1879 where he took a job in the United States Department of Agriculture and where she worked for a time. They returned to Cornell in 1882.

Comstock studied wood engraving at the Cooper Union in New York City to illustrate books that she and her husband wrote. Her work won a bronze medal at the Pan-American Exposition in Buffalo, New York, in 1901.

Comstock was appointed assistant in nature study in Cornell's extension department in 1897 where she worked to introduce nature study to rural schools. She taught nature study as assistant professor and professor at Cornell (1913–22). She taught summers at the state teachers' institute at Chautauqua, New York.

While at Cornell, Comstock wrote many leaflets on nature study and *The Nature Quarterly*, a publication for teachers. Unable to find a publisher for her text, *The Handbook of Nature Study* (1911), she and her husband founded the Comstock Publishing Company of Ithaca, New York. The *Handbook* went through many editions and was used in schools throughout the world. From 1917 to 1923 Comstock edited *Nature Study Review*, which was later incorporated with *Nature Magazine*.

She was also author of *Ways of the Six-Footed* (1903), *How to Know the Butterflies* (with J. H. Comstock, 1904), *How to Keep Bees* (1905), *The Pet Book* (1914), *Nature Notebooks on Birds, Plants, Trees and Animals* (1914), and a novel, *Confessions to a Heathen Idol* (1906).

Comstock was the third woman elected to the American Society of Wood Engravers and was associate director of the American Nature Association. In 1923 Comstock was chosen by the National League of Women Voters as one of the twelve greatest living American women. She was a trustee of Hobart and William Smith colleges and received an honorary degree from Hobart College.

REFERENCES: *NAW; NCAB* (22:11); *WWW* (I).   *Bonnie B. Barr*

COMSTOCK, George Cary. B. February 12, 1855, Madison, Wisconsin, to Charles Henry and Mercy (Bronston) Comstock. M. June 12, 1894, to Esther Cecile Everett. Ch. one. D. May 11, 1934, Madison, Wisconsin.

George Cary Comstock was educated in the public schools and received his Ph.B. degree (1877) from the University of Michigan and the LL.B. degree (1883) from the University of Wisconsin.

After graduation from Michigan Comstock worked as a recorder and assistant engineer for the Army Corps of Engineers on the Great Lakes and Mississippi River surveys. In 1879 his former astronomy teacher at Michigan, James Craig Watson, persuaded him to become assistant director of Wisconsin University's Washburn Observatory at Madison. Although he studied law, received his law degree at Wisconsin, and was admitted to the bar, he never practiced law. Comstock taught astronomy and mathematics at Ohio State University (1885–87) and returned to Madison as professor of astronomy in 1887. He became director of the Washburn Observatory in 1889. From 1906 to 1920 he was director and dean of the graduate school. He continued to teach astronomy and direct the observatory to his retirement in 1922.

He was the author of *An Elementary Treatise upon the Method of Least Squares* (1890), *A Text-Book of Astronomy* (1901), *A Text-Book of Field Astronomy for Engineers* (1902), and *The Sumner Line as an Aid to Navigation* (1919).

Comstock conducted significant research in astronomy. He was elected to the National Academy of Sciences in 1899. He helped organize the American Astronomical Society and served as secretary and president. He was elected to the American Academy of Arts and Sciences, the Astronomische Gesellschaft (Germany), and the Société astronomique (France). He was a fellow in the American Association for the Advancement of Science and received honorary degrees.

REFERENCES: *DAB* (supp. 1); *DSB; LE* (I); *NCAB* (12:454); *WWW* (I); *The Capital Times* (Madison, Wisconsin), May 11, 1934.

Thomas Meighan

COMSTOCK, John Henry. B. February 24, 1849, Janesville, Wisconsin, to Ebenezer and Susan (Allen) Comstock. M. October 7, 1878, to Anna Botsford *(q.v.).* Ch. none. D. March 20, 1931, Ithaca, New York.

When John Henry Comstock was a baby, his father joined a group going to California in search of gold. The group was stricken with cholera and the father died on the journey. Comstock worked as a sailor on the Great Lakes as a youth. With the money he earned, he attended academies and Cornell University in Ithaca, New York, where he received the B.S. degree (1874). He studied at Yale College (1874–75) and the University of Leipzig, Germany (1888–89).

On petition of fellow students, Comstock taught a course in entomology at Cornell in 1872 and was an instructor in entomology at Cornell from 1874. He was a lecturer of zoology at Vassar College in Poughkeepsie, New York (1877), and an entomologist with the United States Department of Agriculture in Washington, D.C. (1879–82). He returned to Cornell in 1882 as professor of entomology and invertebrate zoology and served to his retirement in 1914. Comstock married Anna Botsford, who was a noted author of nature study books, a wood engraver, and a natural history artist.

Comstock was the author of several books on entomology, including *Notes on Entomology* (1875), *Introduction to Entomology* (1888), *A Manual on the Study of Insects* (1895), *Insect Life* (1897), *How to Know the Butterflies* (with Anna Botsford Comstock, 1904), *The Spider Book* (1912), and *Wings of Insects* (1918). He was a member of many scientific and scholarly organizations, including the Entomological Society of London, of which he was a fellow. The Comstock Memorial Library of Entomology was established in his honor at Cornell University.

REFERENCES: *AC; DAB* (supp. 1); *NCAB* (22:10); *WWW* (I).

Albert Nissman

COMSTOCK, John Lee. B. September 25, 1787, Lynne, Connecticut, to Samuel and Esther (Lee) Comstock. M. n.a. D. November 21, 1858, Hartford, Connecticut.

John Lee Comstock received a common school education and engaged in the study of medicine. He was awarded a diploma in medicine and became a surgeon in the War of 1812. He served at Fort Trumbull in New London, Connecticut, and was in charge of three hospitals on the northern frontier.

At the close of the war, Comstock lived in Hartford, Connecticut, where he practiced medicine. He began to write schoolbooks, primarily in the sciences, which he also illustrated. *A Grammar of Chemistry* (1822) was published by Samuel Griswold Goodrich *(q.v.)*. *Outlines of Physiology* (1836) was the first physiology text to be widely used as a school text and continued to be reprinted to 1893. *A System of Natural Philosophy* (1830) was translated into several languages.

Among other texts Comstock wrote were *Elements of Mineralogy* (1827), *History of the Greek Revolution* (1828), *Natural History of Birds* (1830), *Elements of Chemistry* (1831), *An Introduction to the Study of Mineralogy* (1832), *An Introduction to the Study of Botany* (1832), *Outlines of Geology* (1834), *The Young Botanist* (1835), *Youth's Book of Astronomy* (1835), *A Treatise on Mathematical and Physical Geography* (1837), *Comstock's Common School Philosophy* (1839), *Manual of Natural Philosophy* (with Richard D. Hoblyn, 1846), *The Illustrated Botany* (1847), *Elements of Geology* (1847), *The Flora Belle or Gems from Nature* (1847), and *A History of Precious Metals* (1849).

REFERENCES: *AC;* John A. Nietz, *Old Textbooks* (Pittsburgh, Pa.: University of Pittsburgh Press, 1961).   *John F. Ohles*

CONANT, James Bryant. B. March 26, 1893, Boston, Massachusetts, to James Scott and Jennett Orr (Bryant) Conant. M. April 17, 1921, to Grace Thayer Richards. Ch. two.

James Bryant Conant received the A.B. degree from Harvard University in 1913 and the Ph.D. degree in chemistry there in 1916. That autumn he began teaching organic chemistry at Harvard, was a professor at age thirty-four (1927), and head of the chemistry department in 1931.

Known and respected as a research chemist, he was named president of Harvard in 1933. During his tenure, Harvard broadened the geographic and social representation of its student body, opened all departments of the university to women students, and required students to engage in general education studies, following the guidelines established in the report of a special faculty committee, *General Education in a Free Society* (1946).

Following his retirement from Harvard in 1953, Conant served four years in the Federal Republic of Germany, first as United States high commissioner (1953–55) and later as ambassador (1955–57). He conducted studies for the Carnegie Corporation on the American high school (1957–62) and the education of American teachers (1962–63). He advised the Ford Foundation on education in Berlin, Germany (1963–65).

He wrote many books, including *Practical Chemistry* (with N. H. Black, 1920), *Organic Chemistry* (1928), *The Chemistry of Organic Compounds* (1933), *Our Fighting Faith* (1942), *On Understanding Science* (1947), *Education in a Divided World* (1948), *Education and Liberty* (1953), *The American High School Today* (1959), *Education in the Junior High School Years* (1960), *Slums and Suburbs* (1961), *The Education of American Teachers* (1963), *Shaping Educational Policy* (1964), and *The Comprehensive High School: A Second Report to Interested Citizens* (1967). He was editor of *Harvard Case Studies in Experimental Science* (two volumes, 1957).

Among Conant's books, those reporting on educational studies and providing recommendations for educational reform are of particular significance. *The American High School Today,* a study of the comprehensive high school, included twenty-one recommendations for the improvement of the high school. *Education in the Junior High School Years* critically examined the early secondary school years, and *The Comprehensive High School* raised particular questions about financial inequities among school districts. *Slums and Suburbs* argued against token integration across attendance boundaries and for decentralized school administration. *The Education of American Teachers* included twenty-seven recommendations for improving the preparation of American teachers.

Conant served with the United States Army in World War I. He was chairman of the National Defense Research Committee (1941–46) and a member of the general advisory committee to the Atomic Energy Commission (1947–52) and the Educational Policies Commission (1941–46), on the board of science advisors to the Rockefeller Institution (1930–49) and the National Science Foundation (chairman, 1951), and on the board of trustees of the Carnegie Foundation for the Advancement of Teaching. He received some fifty honorary degrees from American and foreign universities.

REFERENCES: *CA* (13–16); *CB* (February 1951); *EB; LE* (III); *NCAB* (D:48); *WW* (XXXVI); *WWAE* (XV); Merle Borrowman, "Conant, the Man," *Saturday Review* (September 21, 1963): 58–60; Thomas Grissom, "Education and the Cold War: The Role of James B. Conant," in Clarence J. Karier, Paul Violas, and Joel Spring, eds., *Roots of Crisis: American Education in the Twentieth Century* (Chicago: Rand McNally and Co., 1973); Robert J. Havighurst, ed., *Leaders in American Education* (Chicago: The University of Chicago Press, 1971).   *Norman J. Bauer*

CONATY, Thomas James. B. August 1, 1847, Kilmallough, Ireland, to Patrick and Alice (Lynch) Conaty. M. no. D. September 18, 1915, Coronado, California.

Thomas James Conaty completed the bachelor's degree at the College of St. Sulpice in Montreal, Quebec, in 1867, spent two years at the Jesuit College of the Holy Cross in Worcester, Massachusetts (1867–69), and studied at the Montreal (Canada) Theological Seminary.

After his ordination in 1872 in Springfield, Massachusetts, Conaty served two parishes in Worcester (1880–96). He was appointed the second rector of the Catholic University of America in Washington, D.C. (1897–1903). The new university, established in 1889, was unsettled; by the time he stepped down as rector, it had grown and become important in American Catholic education. In 1896 Pope Leo XIII conferred on him the title of domestic prelate and nominated him as titular bishop of Samos in 1901. He was bishop of Monterrey and Los Angeles from 1903 to 1915 and worked to improve Catholic education in California.

Conaty helped to establish the Catholic Summer School for religious professionals at Plattsburgh, New York, in 1892 and started a monthly journal, *Catholic Home and School.* He was president of the National Catholic Education Association from 1899 to 1903. In 1898 he published *New Testament Studies,* a student guide to significant events in the life of Christ. He received honorary degrees from Georgetown (Washington, D.C.) and Laval (Quebec, Canada) universities.

REFERENCES: *DAB; NCAB* (12:407); *WWW* (I); *The Catholic News,* September 25, 1915; John Delaney and James E. Tobin, *Dictionary of Catholic Biography* (Garden City, N.Y.: Doubleday and Co., 1961); Peter

Hogan, *The Catholic University of America, 1896–1903: The Rectorship of Thomas J. Conaty* (Washington, D.C.: Catholic University of America, 1949); *NYT,* September 19, 1915, p. 15.   *George J. Michel*

COOK, Albert Samuel. B. January 12, 1873, Greencastle, Pennsylvania, to Samuel Hassler and Nannie A. (Fahrney) Cook. M. December 27, 1898, to Helen J. Earnshaw. Ch. three. D. March 10, 1952, Towson, Maryland.

The person most responsible for the modernization of the Maryland public school system in the first half of the twentieth century was Albert S. Cook. He was a country schoolteacher in 1889 following graduation from the Cumberland Valley State Normal School (later, Shippensburg State College) in Shippensburg, Pennsylvania. Cook continued his training at Gettysburg (Pennsylvania) College (1892–93) and Princeton (New Jersey) University, where he received the A.B. degree (1895). He received the A.M. degree from Princeton (1906), and took some postgraduate courses in education at Teachers College, Columbia University (1904–08).

In 1895 Cook became principal of the Bel Air (Maryland) Academy and Graded School and principal of Franklin High School in Reistertown, Maryland, in 1898. His able leadership attracted attention, and in 1900 he was appointed the school examiner for Baltimore County.

In Baltimore County Cook inherited a school system that had experienced little growth despite a rapid increase in population. The original duties of the school examiner had been to visit each school annually and examine pupils in various subjects. Cook determined there was need for a more professional teaching staff and began to hold teacher meetings, often inviting leading educators to address them. His title was changed to superintendent in 1904, reflecting a concept of supervision as the continued training of teachers in service. Cook eventually obtained financial aid for teachers to attend summer school, was given more specialized supervisors to assist him, and developed a written course of study. The 653-page report, *Baltimore County Course of Study* (1921), had widespread influence.

Because of his performance in Baltimore County, Cook was appointed state superintendent of schools in 1920. His most significant achievement was the introduction of a school equalization program to ensure that children in rural areas would receive the same educational opportunities as those in urban centers. After his retirement in 1942, he remained active in numerous professional organizations. He published a number of articles on education, concerned primarily with roles and duties of educational supervisors. He received several honorary degrees.

REFERENCES: *LE* (III); *WWW* (III); Thomas H. Briggs *(q.v.),* "Albert Samuel Cook: Educational Leader and Friend," *Educational Administration and Supervision* 28 (October 1942): 481–92; E. Cheever, "Albert

S. Cook—Schoolman,'' *Educational Administration and Supervision* 28 (February 1942): 209–12; Amy C. Crewe, *No Backward Step Was Taken: Highlights in the History of the Public Elementary Schools of Baltimore County* (Baltimore: Teachers Association of Baltimore County, 1949).

Richard J. Cox

COOK, Albert Stanburrough. B. March 6, 1853, Montville, New Jersey, to Frederick Weissenfels and Sarah (Barmore) Cook. M. June 1, 1886, to Emily Chamberlain. M. June 7, 1911, to Elizabeth Merrill. Ch. two. D. September 1, 1927, New Haven, Connecticut.

Albert Stanburrough Cook was a precocious child who read the Bible by the age of five and later taught himself French and Hebrew. Although his early schooling was sporadic, with some private tutelage at the age of six and brief attendance at the age of twelve at Miss Crane's School in Boonton, New Jersey, Cook showed an outstanding aptitude for literary study. He went to work for a year in New York City and at the age of fifteen taught in a country school in Towaco, New Jersey.

He graduated with the B.S. (1872) and M.S. (1875) degrees from Rutgers College (later, the State University) in New Brunswick, New Jersey. He studied in Germany at Göttingen and Leipzig (1877–78) and in London, England, and Jena, Germany (1881–82), and he received the Ph.D. degree (1882) from the University of Jena.

Cook taught mathematics at Rutgers (1872–73) and was a teacher at the Freehold (New Jersey) Institute (1873–77). On his return from Europe, he expected to return to Rutgers but was denied the position because he had been a critic of mismanagement of the Rutgers Grammar School.

Cook became an associate in English and organizer of the department at Johns Hopkins University in Baltimore, Maryland (1879). On his second trip to Europe he had studied Old English first with H. Sweet in London and later with Georg Eduard Sievers in Jena. Cook held a professorship at the University of California (1882–89) and took an active part both in university academic affairs and in public-school leadership, speaking on and demonstrating educational improvements. In 1889 Cook went to Yale University, where he remained for thirty-two years as professor of English language and literature. He retired in 1921, continuing to be active in literary scholarship, publishing some of his most incisive work in Old English poetry and Chaucer after that time.

Cook is most famous for more than seventy-five volumes of the Yale Studies in English, which he initiated in 1898, and for his development of literary scholars in the Yale program. His bibliography includes some three hundred titles, including *The Art of Poetry* (1892), *The Bible and English Prose Style* (1892), *First Book of Anglo Saxon* (1894), *Christ of Cynewulf* (1900), *The Dream of the Road* (1905), *Elene, Phoenix, and Physiologues*

(1919), and *Literary Middle English Reader* (1915). He was coeditor for English of the *Journal of English and Germanic Philology* (1897–1905). He was secretary of the National Committee on Entrance Examinations in English (1897–99), a member of the Modern Language Association (president, 1887–88), and a fellow of the Medieval Academy. He was the recipient of five honorary degrees.

REFERENCES: *DAB; NCAB* (38:517); *WWW* (I).

William W. West

COOK, John Williston. B. April 20, 1844, near Oneida, New York, to Harry De Witt and Joanna (Hall) Cook. M. August 26, 1867, to Lydia Farnham Spofford. Ch. two. D. July 16, 1922, Chicago, Illinois.

John Williston Cook's mother was a former teacher who inspired her son to engage in a career in education. He spent his boyhood in Kappa, Illinois, and, upon finishing his schooling there, entered Illinois State Normal University (later, Illinois State University) at Normal in 1862. He was graduated in 1865 and taught for one year in the Brimfield, Illinois, public schools.

Cook returned to Illinois State Normal as principal of the grammar department of the model school and spent thirty-six years there—twenty-four as a teacher (1866–90) and nine as president (1890–99).

In 1899, at the age of fifty-five, Cook left Normal to become president of the newly established state normal school at De Kalb, Illinois. He was particularly interested in the opportunity to improve practice teaching as an essential part of teacher education and set up the De Kalb plan, which made extensive use of public schools. Public-school critic teachers and the superintendent of schools were made members of the normal school faculty. He retired from Northern Illinois Normal School (later, Northern Illinois University) in 1919 and continued there as a lecturer.

Cook became widely known as a speaker at teachers' institutes. He served as editor and publisher of the *Illinois Schoolmaster* (with E. C. Hewitt, 1874–76) and *Illinois School Journal* (with E. C. Hewitt, 1883–84, and R. R. Reeder, 1884–86). He was author of *Educational History of Illinois* (1912). He was president of the Illinois State Teachers' Association (1880) and the National Educational Association (1904). Cook was an outstanding spokesman for the normal schools and their achievements in American teacher education.

REFERENCES: *DAB; NCAB* (27:428); *WWW* (I); Earl W. Hayter, *Education in Transition: The History of Northern Illinois University* (De Kalb: Northern Illinois University Press, 1974). *Leo J. Alilunas*

COOKE, John Esten. B. March 2, 1783, Bermuda, to Stephen and Catherine (Esten) Cooke. M. no. D. October 19, 1853, near Louisville, Kentucky.

John Esten Cooke moved with his family from the Bermuda Islands to Alexandria, Virginia, in 1791 and later settled in Leesburg, Virginia. He studied medicine under his father and at the University of Pennsylvania, where he received the M.D. degree (1805).

Cooke practiced medicine in Warrenton (1805–21) and Winchester, Virginia (1821–27). He accepted an offer to teach theory and practice of medicine at the Transylvania University Medical School in Lexington, Kentucky, in 1827, where he wrote *Treatise on Pathology and Therapeutics* (1828), said to be the first American systematic medical textbook. He was also professor of church history and polity at the new Episcopalian Seminary in Lexington (1832–37).

In 1837 he moved to Louisville, Kentucky, where he was a cofounder of the Louisville Medical Institute (later part of the University of Louisville). He was dismissed from his post in 1844 because of his discredited medical beliefs and practices, including the bleeding of patients and treatment of the liver as a cause of most human illness. He lived on a farm near the Ohio River for the rest of his life.

In addition to the *Treatise* of 1828, Cooke was the author of *Essays on the Autumnal and Winter Epidemics* (1829) and *Essay on the Invalidity of Presbyterian Ordination* (1829). He founded, with C. W. Short, the *Transylvania Journal of Medicine and the Associate Sciences* in 1828.

REFERENCES: *AC; DAB; NCAB* (4:518); *WWW* (H).   *John F. Ohles*

COOKE, Josiah Parsons. B. October 12, 1827, Boston, Massachusetts, to Josiah Parsons and Mary (Pratt) Cooke. M. 1860 to Mary Hinckley Huntington. Ch. none. D. September 3, 1894, Newport, Rhode Island.

Josiah Parsons Cooke introduced laboratory instruction into undergraduate chemistry courses in the United States and is credited with giving chemistry its proper status in the undergraduate curriculum. He was graduated from Harvard University in 1848. His formal training in chemistry consisted of a few lectures by Benjamin Silliman *(q.v.)* at the Lowell Institute of Boston and a few months of study with Jean Baptist André Dumas and Henri Victor Regnault during the year he spent in Europe following his graduation (1848–49).

On his return from Europe he was appointed a tutor in mathematics at Harvard. He was appointed Erving Professor of Chemistry and Mineralogy in 1850. He remained at Harvard as department chairman as well as a teacher during his entire career, a period of more than forty years. During this time Harvard's chemistry department grew to become one of the most outstanding in the world.

The Erving professorship at Harvard had been established in 1792, but Cooke was the first appointee who engaged in serious chemical research. Among his notable chemical investigations was determination of the atomic weight of antimony. He was an enthusiastic user of the laboratory method of instruction. He also gave courses of popular lectures in Lowell and Worcester, Massachusetts, New York City, and Washington, D.C.

Cooke was the author of *Chemical Problems and Reactions* (1857), *Elements of General Physics* (1860), *Religion and Chemistry* (1864), *First Principles of Chemical Philosophy* (1868), *The New Chemistry* (1873), *Contributions from the Chemistry Laboratory at Harvard College* (1877), *Scientific Culture* (1881), *Credentials of Science* (1888), and *Laboratory Practice* (1891).

Cooke was a member of the American Academy of Arts and Sciences and an honorary member of the Chemical Society of London. He received honorary degrees from Cambridge (England) University and Harvard University.

REFERENCES: *AC; DAB; DSB; NCAB* (6:12); *WWW* (H); B. Harrow, *Eminent Chemists of Our Time* (New York: D. Van Nostrand Co., 1929); *Scientific American* 71 (1894): 234.   *B. Richard Siebring*

COOLEY, Edwin Gilbert. B. March 12, 1857, Strawberry Point, Iowa, to Gilbert and Martha (Hanon) Cooley. M. January 1, 1878, to Lydia A. Stanley. Ch. six. D. September 28, 1923, La Grange, Illinois.

Edwin Cooley entered Iowa State University in 1872 but his studies were interrupted by work as an apprentice to a wagon maker. He attended the University of Chicago, where he received the Ph.B. degree (1895).

In 1882 he became principal of a school at Strawberry Point, Iowa, and went to Cresco, Iowa, as superintendent in 1885. He moved to Illinois as principal at East Side (Aurora) High School (1891) and Lyon's Township High School in La Grange (1893). He was elected head of Chicago Normal School but chose to accept instead the superintendency of the Chicago public schools (1900–09). In 1909 he became president of the D. C. Heath and Company publishing firm for a year. Cooley traveled in the United States and Europe studying industrial schools as educational commissioner of the Commercial Club of Chicago (1910–15). In December 1918 he became head of the continuation schools in Chicago, serving to his death in 1923.

Cooley was the author of *Some Continuation Schools in Europe* (1912), *The Need of Vocational Schools in the United States* (1912), and *Vocational Education in Europe* (two volumes, 1912–15).

Active in professional organizations, Cooley was a member of the National Council of Education, the Illinois State Teachers Association (president, 1894) and the National Educational Association (president, 1907, and head of the department of superintendence, 1904). He served on the Iowa State Normal Board (1890–96). He received an honorary degree from the University of Illinois and was decorated with the Order of Franz Josef by the government of Austria.

REFERENCES: *DAB* (supp. 1); *NCAB* (14:136); *WWW* (I); Forest Crissey, *The Making of an American School-Teacher* (Chicago: C. M. Barnes, 1906).   *D. Eugene Meyer*

COOLEY, LeRoy Clark. B. October 7, 1833, Point Peninsula, New York, to James and Sally (Clark) Cooley. M. May 30, 1859, to Rossabella Flack. Ch. none. D. September 20, 1916, Poughkeepsie, New York.

LeRoy Clark Cooley, physicist and educator, was graduated from the New York State Normal College (later, State University of New York at Albany) in Albany (1855). He received the A.B. (1858), M.A. (1861), and Ph.D. (1870) degrees from Union College in Schenectady, New York.

He was professor of mathematics at Fairfield (New York) Academy (1858–59). He was a professor of physical science at the New York State Normal College (1860–74). From 1874 he taught physics and chemistry at Vassar College in Poughkeepsie, New York, until he retired in 1907.

His writings include *A Textbook of Physics* (1868), *A Textbook of Chemistry* (1869), *Easy Experiments in Physical Science* (1870), *Natural Philosophy for High Schools* (1871), *Elements of Chemistry for High Schools* (1873), *New Textbook of Physics* (1880), *New Textbook for Chemistry* (1881), *Beginner's Guide to Chemistry* (1886), *Laboratory Studies in Chemistry* (1894), and *The Student's Manual of Physics* (1897). He presented addresses and wrote papers on the promotion of science teaching in secondary schools.

Cooley was a member of the American Physics Society, the National Education Association, and the New York State Teachers Association (president, 1899) and a fellow of the American Association for the Advancement of Science.

REFERENCES: *AC; NCAB* (11:263); *WWW* (I).   *Richard W. Gates*

COOLIDGE, Julian Lowell. B. September 28, 1873, Brookline, Massachusetts, to Joseph Randolph and Julia (Gardner) Coolidge. M. January 17, 1901, to Theresa Reynolds. Ch. eight. D. March 5, 1954, Cambridge, Massachusetts.

Julian Lowell Coolidge attended Phillips Academy in Exeter, New Hampshire, and Harvard University, receiving the A.B. degree in 1895. He was a member of the Harvard track team and set an intercollegiate record for the mile in 1895. He received the B.S. degree (1897) from Oxford University (England). He studied from 1902 to 1904 with Corrado Segre at Turin, Italy, and Eduard Study at Bonn, Germany. He received the Ph.D. degree (1904) from the University of Bonn.

He taught at the Groton (Massachusetts) School (1897–99) and joined the faculty at Harvard as a teacher of mathematics (1900–40). He was master of Lowell House at Harvard (1929–40).

During World War I, Coolidge served as a major in the United States

Army Ordnance and was a liaison officer attached to the French general staff in Paris (1918–19). In 1919 he organized courses at the Sorbonne for American servicemen, and served as commandant of the American Expeditionary Force detachment at the University of Paris. The French government awarded him the decorations of officer of the Cross of the Legion of Honor and Officer d'instruction publique.

Coolidge was author of *Elements of Non-Euclidean Geometry* (1909), *Treatise on the Circle and the Sphere* (1916), *Geometry of the Complex Domain* (1924), *Introduction to Mathematical Probability* (1925), one of the first modern English texts on the subject, *Algebraic Plane Curves* (1931), *A History of Geometrical Methods* (1940), *A History of the Conic Sections and Quadric Surfaces* (1943), and *Mathematics of Great Amateurs* (1949). He also contributed many articles to learned journals.

He was a fellow of the American Academy of Arts and Sciences and a member of the American Mathematical Society (vice-president), the Mathematical Association of America (president, 1925), and the Association of Mathematical Teachers of New England (president). He was an exchange professor to the Sorbonne (France) in 1927. He received honorary degrees from Lehigh and Harvard universities.

REFERENCES: *DSB; LE* (II); *NCAB* (46:459); *WWW* (III); M. Hammond et al., "J. L. Coolidge," *Harvard University Gazette* (February 26, 1955): 136–38; *NYT,* March 6, 1954, p. 15; Dirk J. Struik, "J. L. Coolidge (1873–1954)," *American Mathematical Monthly* 62 (1955): 669-82.

Daniel S. Yates

COOPER, Hermann. B. December 31, 1895, Wilbraham, Massachusetts, to Richard Watson and Emma (White) Cooper. M. August 22, 1923, to Nelle Virginia Asbury. M. September 22, 1958, to Abbie Haug. Ch. none.

Early and continuing exposure to campuses where his father served as a faculty member or administrator undoubtedly influenced Hermann Cooper's choice of career. He received the B.A. (1916) and Bachelor of Music (1917) degrees from Upper Iowa University in Fayette where his father was president. Cooper chose to pursue education rather than music as a career and accepted an appointment as principal of the high school at Crosby, North Dakota (1916–17). He was awarded the M.A. (1921) and Ph.D. (1930) degrees from Columbia University.

Following service in the United States Army during World War I, Cooper was appointed director of research of the Bureau of Educational Services for Citizens of Delaware where he directed studies of significant aspects of Delaware's public-school system. He accepted his first position in the state where he would become known to his colleagues as Mr. Teacher Education as head of the education department and director of training at the State Normal School (later, State University of New York

College) at Geneseo, New York (1925–29). He served as principal of the normal school (later, State University of New York College) at Fredonia, New York (1929–31).

Cooper joined the New York State Education Department as an associate in 1931 and two years later was appointed assistant commissioner for teacher education and certification. He was responsible for the preparation of teachers at the eleven publicly supported campuses that reported to the State Education Department and for formulating and administering the regulations and procedures by which all candidates qualified for certification. Under Cooper's direction, normal schools became degree-granting colleges with the addition of a fourth year of study restricted to arts and sciences. This established the basis for their later conversion to multi-purpose liberal arts colleges. These colleges were absorbed into the newly formed State University of New York in 1948, and Cooper became the university's executive dean for teacher education, continuing his responsibility for these campuses. He played a prominent role in the rapidly expanding state university to his retirement on December 31, 1962.

Cooper was coauthor with Richard Watson Cooper of *Negro School Attendance in Delaware* (1923) and *The One-Teacher School in Delaware* (1925) and author of *An Accounting of Progress and Attendance of Rural School Children in Delaware* (1930).

Cooper was active in teacher certification, serving on the law and licensing committee of the board of superintendents of New York City (1935–49) and on the executive committee for the National Teachers Examinations of the Educational Testing Service. A member of professional associations, he was the recipient of several citations for distinguished service and several honorary degrees.

REFERENCES: *LE* (III); *WW* (XXXI); "Dr. Hermann Cooper Appointed Director of State College Education," *New York State Education* 19 (December 1931): 297; *NYT,* June 22, 1962, p. 7; John F. Ohles, "The Historical Development of New York State University College at Fredonia" (Ed.D. diss., State University of New York at Buffalo, 1964), pp. 232–42.   *Frank T. Lane*

COOPER, Myles. B. February 1735 or 1737, Wha House Estate, Cumberland County, England, to William and Elizabeth Cooper. M. no. D. May 1 or 20, 1785, Edinburgh, Scotland.

Myles Cooper, an English Loyalist, clergyman, and educator, entered Queen's College, Oxford, England, at the age of sixteen. He received the B.A (1756) and M.A. (1760) degrees. He served as a fellow of Queen's College, where he became a distinguished classical scholar. Ordained a deacon in 1760 and an Anglican priest in 1761, he was elected chaplain of Queen's College.

Cooper was acting as curate of a church near Oxford in 1762 when he was appointed assistant to the president, professor of moral philosophy, and a fellow at King's College (later, Columbia University) in New York City by the archbishop of Canterbury. Moving to New York, he was chosen president of King's College after the resignation of Samuel Johnson *(q.v.)* in 1763. During Cooper's administration, the college expanded, a medical school and hospital were founded, and the college received large grants of land. A laboratory grammar school was established to prepare young men for college. The college was tailored in the image of Oxford through changes in the curricula and rules of discipline. Support for the college in the form of material and monetary gifts was received from England.

Cooper was a leading clergyman in the colonies. He presided at the Convention of Episcopal Clergymen in 1765 and sought support of the clergy for an American episcopate. He was an active member of the Society for the Propagation of the Gospel in Foreign Parts. He wrote for the paper, *Whip for the Whig,* which was begun in 1768.

Cooper was a strong supporter of the royal government and was the author of a series of papers and pamphlets proposing "Proper Respect that was due to the Mother Country." Accused of writing nearly all of the Loyalist materials that were published, he became a symbol of the Loyalists in New York. Cooper was forced to flee his enemies and left New York on May 25, 1775, as hostilities grew between England and the colonies. He never returned.

In England Cooper returned to his place in the church, was a fellow at Queen's College, and served as senior minister in the English chapel at Cowgate near the University of Edinburgh, Scotland (1778–85).

REFERENCES: *AC; DAB; NCAB* (6:341); *WWW* (H); *Encyclopedia Americana* (New York: Americana Corp., 1966).   *Richard M. Coger*

COOPER, Oscar Henry. B. November 22, 1852, near Carthage, Texas, to William Henry and Katherine (Hunter) Cooper. M. November 24, 1886, to Mary Bryan Stewart. Ch. four. D. August 22, 1932, Abilene, Texas.

Oscar Henry Cooper attended Marshall University (Texas) for one year and was graduated with an A.B. degree from Yale College (later, University) in 1872. He engaged in graduate study at Yale (1881–84) and the University of Berlin, Germany (1884–85), where he studied philosophy and philology.

Cooper was a teacher in 1871 at Woods Post Office in Panola County, Texas. For six years following his graduation he served as president of Henderson (Texas) Male and Female College. He served on the first faculty of Sam Houston Normal Institute (later, State University) in Huntsville, Texas (1879–81). Upon returning to Texas in 1885, he became principal of Houston High School and was state superintendent of public instruction (1886–91). He was superintendent of the Galveston public schools (1896–99).

Cooper served as president of Baylor University in Waco, Texas (1899–1902), and of Simmons College (later Hardin-Simmons University) in Abilene, Texas (1902–09). He organized Cooper's Boys School in Abilene (1909). When the school closed in 1915, he rejoined the faculty of Simmons College as head of the department of education and philosophy and chairman of the faculty. He taught part time at the University of Texas in Austin (1928–30) but continued to be associated with Simmons until his death in 1932.

Cooper was an advocate of improved quality in public schools and was a participant in state-sponsored programs to improve methods of instruction in the schools. He played a major role in drafting a proposal for the creation of a state university in Texas and in passage of the legislation. He was a fellow of the Texas State Historical Association, member of the executive board of the Conference for Education in Texas (1907), chairman of a committee that surveyed the state school system (1921), on the advisory group of the Simplified Spelling Board, and president of the Association of Texas Colleges (1923). He wrote *History of Our Country* (with others, 1895), a popular public school text, four volumes of educational reports, and about a hundred published addresses. He was a member of many professional associations and the recipient of three honorary degrees.

REFERENCES: *LE* (I); *NCAB* (30:512); *WWW* (I); Frederick Eby *(q.v.)*, *The Development of Education in Texas* (New York: The Macmillan Co., 1925); C. E. Evans, *The Story of Texas Schools* (Austin: The Steck Co., 1955). *Jack W. Humphries*

COOPER, Sarah Brown Ingersoll. B. December 12, 1835, Cazenovia, New York, to Samuel Clark and Laura (Case) Ingersoll. M. September 4, 1855, to Halsey Fenimore Cooper. Ch. four. D. December 11, 1896, San Francisco, California.

Sarah Brown Ingersoll Cooper was graduated from Cazenovia (New York) Seminary in 1853. She taught for a short time in Eagle Village, New York, and attended the Troy Female Seminary (1854). She was a governess in the family of Governor William Schley in Augusta, Georgia.

In 1855 she married a classmate from the Cazenovia Seminary who was a surveyor, customs inspector, and internal revenue assessor in Chattanooga and Memphis, Tennessee. In Memphis she conducted a Bible class for soldiers in the Union Army and was president of the Society for the Protection of Refugees.

In 1869 the Coopers moved to San Francisco where Halsey Cooper died in 1885. After visiting the Silver Street Kindergarten conducted by Kate Douglas Smith Wiggin *(q.v.)*, Cooper organized the Jackson Street Kindergarten (1878) for the children of San Francisco's poor. She founded more kindergartens, which were organized under the Golden Gate Kindergarten

Association in 1884, and the Golden Gate Kindergarten Free Normal Training School in 1891.

Cooper was first president of the International Kindergarten Union (1892) and president of the Women's Congress in San Francisco (1895) and the Women's Press Association. She was one of five women named as a delegate to the Pan-Republic Congress at the World's Columbian Exposition in Chicago (1893) and was treasurer of the General Federation of Women's Clubs (1894–96).

REFERENCES: *DAB; NAW; NCAB* (3:132); *WC; WWW* (H); *San Francisco Chronicle,* December 12, 1896; Agnes Snyder, *Dauntless Women in Childhood Education, 1856–1931* (Washington, D.C.: Association for Childhood Education International, 1972).   *Marlis Mann*

COOPER, Thomas. B. October 22, 1759, Westminster, England, to Thomas Cooper and n.a. M. August 12, 1779, to Alice Greenwood. M. about 1811 to Elizabeth Pratt Hemming. Ch. eight. D. May 11, 1839 (recorded as May 12 on his tombstone), Columbia, South Carolina.

Thomas Cooper studied at Oxford University in England but did not receive a degree, probably because he would not sign the thirty-nine articles of religion, the dogma of the Church of England. He continued his study of law, medicine, chemistry, and philosophy and became a lawyer in 1787. His knowledge of chemistry led to a successful business career in cloth dyeing, but he was a victim of an economic recession in the early 1790s.

After a short stay in France and an involvement with the Jacobin Society, Cooper followed Joseph Priestley, another Free-Thinker and discoverer of oxygen, to the United States. Cooper settled in Northumberland, Pennsylvania, near Priestley. Cooper was a supporter of Thomas Jefferson *(q.v.)* and was convicted of violating the sedition laws for a written attack on President John Adams.

Cooper practiced law and medicine until he was appointed judge of the Fourth Common Pleas District of Pennsylvania in 1806. In 1811 he was impeached for overbearing conduct and removed from office. He was appointed professor of chemistry at Carlisle (later, Dickinson) College in Carlisle, Pennsylvania, where he served until 1815. He was professor of chemistry and mineralogy at the University of Pennsylvania (1815–19).

In March 1819 Cooper was appointed professor of chemistry, mineralogy, natural philosophy, and law at the University of Virginia with the support of Jefferson. He never served because of opposition to his religious beliefs. In December 1819 Cooper accepted a one-year appointment as professor of chemistry at South Carolina College. He was appointed temporary president in 1820 and was elected president in 1821. Cooper's writings and religious beliefs continued to make him a center of controversy, and an effort was made in the legislature for his dismissal. The controversy continued for two years, and he resigned as president and later (1834) as professor of chemistry.

At South Carolina Cooper taught what was probably the first course of political economy offered in a college in the United States. He helped establish the Medical University in Charleston and provided leadership to improve the public schools.

He was the author of many pamphlets and books, including *Some Information Respecting America* (1794), *The Bankrupt Law of America* (1801), *A Practical Treatise on Dyeing and Callicoe Printing* (1815), *Some Information Concerning Gas Lights* (1816), *Consolidation* (two volumes, 1824 and 1834), *Lectures on the Elements of Political Economy* (1826), *The Fabrication of the Pentateuch* (1829), and *A Manual of Political Economy* (1833). He was editor of *The Thomson System of Chemistry* (four volumes, 1818), *Statutes at Large of South Carolina* (five volumes, 1836–39), and *The Emporium of Arts and Sciences* (1812–14).

He was the recipient of an honorary degree.

REFERENCES: *AC; DAB; EB; NCAB (11:31); WWW* (H); Edwin L. Green, *History of the University of South Carolina* (Columbia, S.C.: The State Company, 1916); Helen Kohn Hennig, *Great South Carolinians* (Chapel Hill: The University of North Carolina Press, 1940), pp. 220–21; Charles F. Himes, *Life and Times of Judge Thomas Cooper, Jurist, Scientist, Educator, Author, Publicist* (Carlisle, Pa.: Dickinson School of Law, 1918); Daniel W. Hollis, *South Carolina College* (Columbia: University of South Carolina Press, 1951); Dumas Malone, *The Public Life of Thomas Cooper, 1783–1839* (Columbia: University of South Carolina Press, 1961). *Ishmael C. Benton*

COPPÉE, Henry. B. October 13, 1821, Savannah, Georgia, to Edward and Carolina Eugenia (Raingeard De Lavillate) Coppée. M. 1848 to Julia de Witt. Ch. five. D. March 21, 1895, Bethlehem, Pennsylvania.

Henry Coppée was a leader and author in education and military affairs. He attended Yale College (1835–37) and entered the Military Academy at West Point, New York, from which he was graduated in 1845.

He served with distinction in the war with Mexico (1846–48). He taught geography, history, and ethics at the United States Military Academy and had charge of the library from 1850 to 1855. He taught English literature and history at the University of Pennsylvania (1855–66). From 1866 to 1875 Coppée served as the first president and professor of history and literature of Lehigh University at Bethlehem, Pennsylvania. He left the presidency to pursue full-time teaching and writing (1875–93) but served as acting president on the death of his successor (1893–95).

Coppée was the author of many books, including *Elements of Logic*

(1857), *Elements of Rhetoric* (1858), *Gallery of Famous Poets* (1858), *Gallery of Distinguished English and American Female Poets* (1860), *Manual of Battalion Drill* (1862), *Manual of Evolutions of the Line* (1863), *Manual of Court-Martial* (1863), *Grant and His Campaigns: A Military Biography* (1866), *Lectures in English Literature* (1872), and *English Literature Considered as an Interpreter of English History* (1873). His *History of the Conquest of Spain by the Arab Moors,* which first appeared in *The Penn Monthly* in 1873, was considered his best literary effort and was published in two volumes in 1881. He edited *The Classic and the Beautiful from the Literature of Three Thousand Years by the Authors and Orators of All Countries* (six volumes, 1888–92). He was editor of *The United States Service Magazine,* a scholarly military periodical (1864–65).

Coppée was a member of many learned societies and served as a member of the Assay Commission of the United States Mint (1874–76) and a regent of the Smithsonian Institution (1874–95). He received honorary degrees from the University of Georgia and the University of Pennsylvania.

REFERENCES: *AC; DAB; NCAB* (7:111); *WWW* (H); *Daily Globe* (South Bethlehem, Penn.), March 21, 1895, p. 1.   *Donavon Lumpkin*

COPPENS, Charles. B. May 24, 1835, Turnhout, Belgium, to Peter H. and Caroline (Vaes) Coppens. M. no. D. December 14, 1920, Chicago, Illinois.

Charles Coppens spent over half a century as a college professor in Catholic higher education. He obtained the bachelor's degree from St. Joseph's College in Turnhout, Belgium, and in 1853 joined the Society of Jesus, becoming ordained as a priest in New York State. He studied on the graduate level at Fordham University in New York City and St. Louis (Missouri) University.

He was a professor of Latin and Greek at St. Louis University (1855–59), St. Xavier College in Cincinnati, Ohio (1859–62), and the Normal School at Florissant, Missouri (1865–75). He returned to St. Louis University as professor of Latin, Greek, and English (1875–80). He was professor of philosophy at Detroit (Michigan) College (later, University of Detroit) from 1886 to 1891, Creighton University in Omaha, Nebraska (1896–1905), and Loyola University in Chicago, Illinois. He was president of St. Mary's College in St. Mary's, Kansas (1881–84).

Coppens exerted a strong influence over Jesuit education and Catholic education through his writings and his scholarship; his books were widely used in Catholic colleges and schools. Besides writing numerous articles for well-known Catholic periodicals of his time, he wrote books, including *The Art of Oratorical Composition* (1885), *A Practical Introduction to English Rhetoric* (1886), *A Brief Textbook of Logic and Mental Philosophy* (1895), *Moral Principles and Medical Practice* (1897), *The Living Church of the Living God* (1902), *A Systematic Study of the Catholic Religion*

(1903), *Mystic Treasures of the Holy Mass* (1904), *The Protestant Reformation* (1907), *Choice Morsels of the Bread of Life* (1909), *A Brief History of Philosophy* (1909), *Who Are the Jesuits?* (1911), *Spiritual Instructions for the Religious* (1914), *Office of the Immaculate Conception of the Blessed Virgin Mary* (1916), and *The Spiritual Exercises of St. Ignatius Adapted to an Eight Day Retreat* (1916).

REFERENCES: *DAB; WWW* (I); *Catholic Encyclopedia and Its Makers* (New York: The Cyclopedia Press, 1917), p. 34; "Death of Father Coppens," *America* 24 (December 25, 1920): 248; *Guide to Catholic Literature, 1888–1940* (Detroit: Romig and Co., 1940), pp. 264–65.

George J. Michel

COPPIN, Fanny Marion Jackson. B. c. 1837, Washington, D.C., to n.a. and Lucy Jackson. M. 1881 to Levi Jenkins Coppin. Ch. none. D. January 21, 1913, Philadelphia, Pennsylvania.

Fanny Jackson Coppin was born a slave; it was said that Ora Clark, an aunt, purchased her freedom for $125. Her decision to become a teacher led her to enter Oberlin (Ohio) College in 1860 where she received the A.B. degree (1865). While in college, she conducted a class to teach freedmen from the South as they came to Ohio.

She received an invitation from the Institute for Colored Youth (later, Cheyney State College) in Cheyney, Pennsylvania, to teach Greek, Latin, and math. She began work there in 1865 and became principal of the institute in 1869. She ran the school with Richard T. Greener, the first black graduate of Harvard University, and Octavius V. Catto.

Coppin discovered that the only place a black could learn a trade was "in the house of refuge" or the penitentiary. Therefore, she expanded the institute's curriculum from the cultural and academic subjects to those of trades and other skills. Her industrial education plan soon grew to include girls in cooking and sewing. The industrial building provided for bricklaying, plastering, carpentry, shoemaking, printing, tailoring, dressmaking, millinery, typewriting, stenography, and cooking. Years of success for the highly academic curriculum made it easy to add the industrial segment to the school. To find jobs and to popularize the skills of the students, works of the students were placed on public display on Industrial Exchange Day. To further publicize industrial education and improve conditions of blacks, Coppin joined in working on the *Christian Recorder,* a paper published by blacks.

In 1900 her husband, Levi Coppin, was elected bishop of the African Methodist Episcopal (AME) church. He chose South Africa as a place to serve as a missionary. In 1902 Fanny Coppin entered missionary work at Cape Town and organized Miti societies among the African women.

She wrote *Biographical Sketches of Institute Teachers, Graduate and*

Undergraduate (n.d.), and *Reminiscences of School Life, and Hints on Teaching* (published by her husband, 1913). She was president of the Women's Home and Foreign Missionary Society of the AME church and a delegate to the Centenary Conference on the Protestant Missions of the World in London, England (1888).

REFERENCES: *NAW; Afro-American,* (Baltimore, Md.), December 1975.   *Deborah Staton*

CORBIN, Joseph Carter. B. March 26, 1833, Chillicothe, Ohio, to William and Susan Corbin. M. September 11, 1866, to Mary J. Ward. Ch. six. D. January 9, 1911, Pine Bluff, Arkansas.

Joseph Carter Corbin, black college president and state superintendent of education, was educated in "pay schools" (schools that charged tuition) in Ohio and Kentucky. He extended his education with home study of Caesar, Cicero, and analytical geometry. He entered Ohio University in Athens, from which he received the A.B. (1853) and two master's degrees (1856 and 1889). He later received an honorary degree from a southern Baptist institution.

Corbin was employed as a clearinghouse clerk in the Bank of the Ohio Valley in Cincinnati, a reporter for the *Arkansas Republican* newspaper, and a money order clerk in the Little Rock, Arkansas, post office. He was elected Arkansas superintendent of public instruction and ex officio president of the university board of trustees in 1873. He taught at Lincoln Institute in Jefferson City, Missouri. He returned to Arkansas to accept the position of principal of Branch Normal College (later, University of Arkansas at Pine Bluff) in Pine Bluff (1875–1905). Many university buildings were erected, and a library was established under Corbin's leadership. He later served as principal of the Merrill public school in Pine Bluff.

Corbin was active in professional associations, serving as president of the Arkansas State Colored Teachers Association. He contributed many articles on mathematics and educational topics to professional journals. Active in the masonic lodge, he wrote *Minutes of Masonry of the Grand Lodge of Arkansas, 1873–1902* and *The Status of Colored Freemasons.*

REFERENCES: *WWW* (IV); J. H. Reynolds and D. Y. Thomas, *History of the University of Arkansas* (Fayetteville: University of Arkansas, 1910).   *Don C. Locke*

CORDERO Y MOLINA, Rafael. B. October, 1790, San Juan, Puerto Rico, to n.a. D. July 5, 1868, San Juan, Puerto Rico.

Rafael Cordero y Molina was born to poor free black parents in 1790. He received no formal education because the elementary schools on the island would not accept black children. One of his parents was literate and taught him how to read and write and encouraged him to become an avid reader. He is reported to have mastered two trades, cigar making and shoemaking.

In 1810 Cordero opened a school in San German. In his small house he plied his trade and had his living quarters and a schoolroom, where he accepted children without regard to race, sex, or parental income. He instructed, fed, and housed boys and girls from the canefields. By 1814 Cordero's sister Celestina joined him to teach the girls. They moved to San Juan and set up a workshop, school, and home. Great men of Puerto Rican history were taught in this school, including novelist Alejandro Tapis and Baldorioty de Castro, the Autonomist party leader.

A modest man, Cordero never charged a fee in fifty-eight years of teaching. He did not acknowledge he was making a contribution to society, even though families moved to San Juan so that their children could attend his school.

Cordero was called El Maestro in later years. A civic organization, La Sociedad Economics, rewarded him with a prize of a hundred pesos, of which he spent half to purchase books and clothing for his students and distributed the rest among the beggars of San Juan. In his last years, the society gave him a salary of fifteen pesos each month. When he died on July 5, 1868, his coffin was carried through the streets of San Juan on the shoulders of men he had taught as children. Thousands joined the procession.

Today, Calle de la Luna has become Calle Rafael Cordero y Molina, and his house is a national monument; a large elementary school in Santurce bears his name.

REFERENCES: María Teresa Babín, *The Puerto Ricans' Spirit: Their History, Life and Culture* (New York: Collier Books, 1971); Paul G. Miller *(q.v.), Historia de Puerto Rico* (New York: Rand McNally, 1939); Salvador Brau, *Historia de Puerto Rico* (New York: Appleton & Co., 1904); Frederico Torar Ribes, *A Chronological History of Puerto Rico* (New York: Plus Ultra Educational Publishers, 1973); Jay Nelson Tucu and Norma C. Vergora, *Heroes of Puerto Rico* (New York: Fleet, 1970).

Rafael L. Cortada
Jean Challman

CORLET, Elijah. B. 1611, London, England, to n.a. D. February 24, 1687, Cambridge, Massachusetts.

Elijah Corlet grew up in London and was educated at Lincoln College, Oxford University, which admitted him in 1626 or 1627. He emigrated to Cambridge, Massachusetts Bay colony, as early as 1641 and was admitted as a freeman of the colony on May 14, 1645.

He may have been employed at the College (Harvard) in 1639 and 1640. He had gained a reputation as a teacher by 1643 and was the first schoolmaster whose salary was partly paid by the town treasury, voted at a town meeting on November 13, 1648.

For forty years, Corlett taught in a stone building built in Cambridge in 1647 and razed in 1769. The school was a boys' Latin grammar school preparing students for the college. Indian pupils were taught at the school and were paid either by the Society for the Propagation of the Gospel or by the Commissioners of the United Colonies of New England.

Corlet died at the age of seventy-seven after having taught in Cambridge for about forty-six years.

REFERENCES: *AC;* George E. Littlefield, "Elijah Corlet and the 'Faire Grammar Schoole' at Cambridge," *Publications of the Colonial Society of Massachusetts* 16 (April 1913): 131–40.   *John F. Ohles*

CORSON, Juliet. B. January 14, 1841, Mt. Pleasant, Roxbury, Massachusetts, to Peter R. and Mary Ann (Henderson) Corson. M. no. D. June 18, 1897, New York, New York.

Juliet Corson, pioneer in cookery education, dietetics, and vocational training, moved to New York City when she was six years old. Ill health kept her from attending school on a regular basis, but she read Greek and Roman history and classical poetry at home.

Corson began to earn a living after her mother's death and her father's remarriage. One of her first positions was as librarian in the Working Women's Library at New York University (1860–73). She wrote poems and sketches for newspapers to supplement her salary and eventually wrote a weekly column for the *New York Leader* on music, books, pictures, and other items relating to women's interests. She was then employed by the *National Quarterly Review* to prepare its semiannual index and was asked to join its regular publication staff.

In 1873 the Women's Educational and Industrial Society of New York, of which Corson was secretary, opened the Free Training School for Women where sewing, shorthand, bookkeeping, and proofreading were taught. Originally established in Corson's home, this school became popular and had to find larger quarters. Corson added a course in cooking after studying French and German books on the subject and hiring a chef to demonstrate to classes.

At the request of John Eaton *(q.v.)*, United States commissioner of education, Corson wrote a brochure for the Bureau of Education on the history and management of cooking schools in the United States and Europe. He also requested that she lecture before the Training School for Nurses in Washington, D.C., and other groups across the country. She demonstrated teaching domestic science as regular instruction in the public schools to boards of education and educators in major cities. She presented a six-week course to Montreal, Quebec, Canada, high-school girls in 1880; this experience has been called the first lesson in cookery in a public school on the North American continent. Her influence led to the establishment of home economics instruction in many major American cities.

Corson was also concerned with instruction in dietetics and cooking for medical patients. She taught a course in cooking for invalids to many schools of nursing. With a major concern for the poorer classes of society, her efforts were frequently directed toward free instruction to many groups, and her content emphasized dietary programs for lower-income groups.

In addition to writing for the *New York Leader* and *National Quarterly Review,* Corson wrote a pamphlet, *Fifteen Cent Dinners for Families of Six* (1877), which was translated into foreign languages and distributed and read across the world. She wrote the *Cooking Manual* (1877), *Cooking School Text Book and Housekeeper's Guide* (1879), *New Family Cook-Book* (1885), *Local American Cookery* (1885), *Practical American Cookery* (1886), *Diet for Invalids and Children* (1886), and *Family Living on $500 a Year* (1887). She was editor of *Household Monthly* (1890–91). She was awarded a prize at the Chicago, Illinois, World's Columbian Exposition in 1893 for scientific cookery and sanitary dietetics.

Ill health forced Corson to an early retirement and confinement as an invalid in New York City. Her time was primarily spent in writing until her death in 1897.

REFERENCES: *AC; DAB; NAW; NCAB* (8:453); *TC; WWW* (H); *NYT,* June 20, 1897, p. 5.   *Gertrude Langsam*

COTTINGHAM, Harold Fred. B. December 11, 1913, Charleston, Illinois, to Fred Hervey and Francis (Coon) Cottingham. M. June 4, 1941, to Violet Costello. Ch. two.

Harold Cottingham earned the B.Ed. degree (1935) from Eastern Illinois State University in Charleston, the M.A. degree (1940) from the University of Iowa, and the Ed.D. degree (1947) from Indiana University. He was a teacher in Illinois high schools at Paris (1936–41) and Hinsdale (1941–42) and an instructor in the United States Navy at Indiana University (1942–44).

After leaving the navy, Cottingham became guidance director and instructor of psychology at William Woods College in Fulton, Missouri (1944–45), and served as director of guidance and research for the Moline (Illinois) public schools (1945–48). He became associated with Florida State University in 1948 as associate professor of psychology and guidance and professor of education and guidance. He was head of the department of guidance and counseling (1958–68). He was John Mosler Professor at Fordham University in New York City (1968–69). From 1963 to 1967 and from 1969 to 1970 he was a consulting member of the subcommittee on counseling and testing for the National Manpower Advisory Committee of the United States Department of Labor.

A leader in elementary school counseling, Cottingham was the author of *Guidance in Elementary Schools* (with W. E. Hopke, 1961), *Guidance in Junior High School* (1961), and *Counseling and Accountability* (1973) and coeditor of *Directed Readings in Guidance and Personnel Services* (with others, 1964). He was editor of the *Guidance Bulletin* (1953–63).

Cottingham was a member of many professional associations and served as a diplomate of the American Board of Professional Psychology and was president of the National Vocational Guidance Association (1962–63), the American Personnel and Guidance Association (1964–65), the Florida Association of Deans and Counselors (1954–56), and the Southern Association of Counselor Education and Supervision (1971–72).

REFERENCES: *LE* (III); *WWAE* (XXII); *WW* (XXXIX).

Vincent Giardina

COTTON, Fassett Allen. B. May 1, 1862, Nineveh, Indiana, to Marion Irwin and Rachel Amanda (Wright) Cotton. M. November 5, 1885, to Florence N. Wright. M. October 14, 1903, to Lena L. Dobson. Ch. two. D. April 2, 1942, Flagstaff, Arizona.

Fassett Cotton was graduated from the Nineveh (Indiana) township high school (1880). He attended Spiceland (Indiana) Academy and enrolled at the Terre Haute State Normal School (later, Indiana State University) in 1888–89. He received the A.B. degree (1902) from Butler University in Indianapolis, Indiana, and the Ph.B. degree (1903) from the University of Chicago.

Cotton taught in various Indiana schools (1880–89). He served as county superintendent of schools (1889–95) and deputy Indiana state superintendent of public instruction (1895–1901). He was state superintendent of public instruction (1903–09). Under his administration at the state level, consolidation of public schools advanced, and the study of agriculture became an important part of the public school curriculum. Cotton was successful in organizing community interest in the schools.

Following his career in public school administration, Cotton became a college president. He served as the first president of the State Normal School (later, University of Wisconsin—La Crosse) in La Crosse, Wisconsin (1909–24). He selected a faculty, organized recruitment of students, and planned a curriculum that included a course of study for rural school-teachers, as well as the traditional classical studies. He supported physical education, which became the major area of study at the school. Faculty dissatisfied with the uncertain financial position of the school forced his resignation in 1924.

He was appointed president of the Northern Arizona Normal School (later, Northern Arizona University) at Flagstaff (1924–26). During his two years in Arizona, the normal school became Northern Arizona State

Teachers College. He established departments of physical education, public-school music, and rural education.

Cotton was the author of *Agriculture for Common Schools* (with Martin L. Fisher, 1909) and *Education in Indiana: 1793–1934* (1934) and editor of *Manual Training for Common Schools* (with Eldrith G. Allen, 1910). He received an honorary degree from Franklin College in 1905.

REFERENCES: *WWAE* (IX); *WWW* (IV); R. E. Banta, *Indiana Authors and Their Books, 1816–1916* (Crawfordsville, Ind.: Wabash College, 1949), p. 73.   *David Alan Gilman*

COULTER, John Merle. B. November 20, 1851, Ning-Po, China, to Moses Stanley and Caroline (Crowe) Coulter. M. January 1, 1874, to Georgie Margaret Gaylord. Ch. four. D. December 23, 1928, Yonkers, New York.

John Merle Coulter's missionary father died when he was two years old, and he and his mother returned to Indiana to live with her father, a professor at Hanover College. Coulter received the A.B. (1870), A.M. (1873), and Ph.D. (1882) degrees from Hanover. He received the Ph.D. degree (1884) from Indiana University.

In 1872 he was appointed an assistant geologist on the Hayden Rocky Mountain survey. While the expedition was camped in the mountains waiting for F. V. Hayden, Coulter tramped the surrounding area looking for plants. When Hayden arrived, he was so impressed with Coulter's collections he appointed him botanist of the expedition, which was looking for hot springs and geysers in what is now known as Yellowstone National Park. As the youngest member of the team, Coulter was given one of the smallest holes to study; it was later named Old Faithful.

He taught natural sciences at Hanover College (1874–79) and biology at Wabash (Indiana) College (1879–91). He was president of the University of Indiana (1891–93). He became president of Lake Forest (Illinois) University (later, College) (1893–96), an institution he thought to be well endowed so there would be less pressure about money. Dissatisfied with administrative demands upon his time, he resigned from Lake Forest and went to the University of Chicago to head the department of biology (1896–1925). He trained well-qualified men and women who attained leadership roles in botany.

Coulter founded, edited, managed, and often financed the *Botanical Gazette* (1875–1919), one of the leading scientific journals in the country. He also wrote *Synopsis of the Flora of Colorado* (1873), *Manual of Rocky Mountain Botany* (1885), *Handbook of Plant Dissection* (1886), *Revision of North American Umbellifarae* (1888), *Manual of the Flora of Western Texas* (1891), a series of three textbooks—*Plant Relations, Plant Structures,* and *Plants* (1899)—*Plant Studies* (1900), *Monograph of North American Umbelliferae* (1900), *Morphology of Spermatophytes* (with

Charles J. Chamberlain, 1901), *Morphology of Angiesperms* (with Charles J. Chamberlain, 1903), *Botany* (1906), *Elementary Studies in Botany* (1913), *Fundamentals of Plant Breeding* (1914), *Evolution of Sex in Plants* (1914), and *Plant Genetics* (1918). What was to be Coulter's greatest work, a history of botany, was unfinished on his death in 1928. He was editor of *Nature and Art* (1898). He edited and revised the sixth edition of *Gray's Manual of Botany* (1890).

After retirement in 1925 Coulter became an adviser to Boyce Thompson Institute for Plant Research at Yonkers, New York, a foundation for which he was largely responsible.

Coulter was active in professional and scientific organizations as a fellow of the American Academy of Arts and Sciences (president, 1918) and of the American Association for the Advancement of Science (vice-president, 1891). He was president of the American Botanical Society (1897).

REFERENCES: *AC; DAB; NCAB* (11:68); *WWW* (I); *NYT,* December 24, 1928, p. 13.   *LeRoy Barney*

COUNCILL, William Hooper. B. July 12, 1848, Fayetteville, North Carolina, to William and Mary Jane Councill. M. to n.a. M. September 5, 1885, to Maria H. Weeden. Ch. four. D. April 17, 1909, Normal, Alabama.

William Councill was born a slave and became a teacher and college president. As a young child, he, his mother, and his brother were sold by their master and traded in 1857 through the Richmond (Virginia) Slave Pen to an Alabama slaveholder. During the Civil War, they fled to Union Army protection in Stevenson, Alabama, where Councill attended one of the first schools established for blacks by northerners (1865–67). He was self-educated, reading at night by the light of a pine knot, a practice he later referred to as study at "Pine Knot College." He taught school in Alabama from 1867 at Stevenson and Jonesville, and was principal of the Huntsville Colored School. While teaching, he studied law and was admitted to the Alabama bar in 1883.

Councill was a chief enrolling clerk for the Alabama House of Representatives (1872–74) and was receiver of the general land office for the northern district of Alabama (1875). He founded and edited the *Huntsville* (Alabama) *Herald* (1877–84). In 1875 he organized the Alabama Normal School for Negroes at Normal (later, the Alabama Agricultural and Mechanical College). He headed the institution from 1875 to his death in 1909; he had reduced his participation in administering the college a year before because of ill health.

Under Councill, the Agricultural and Mechanical College developed into a substantial black institution. He was an early proponent of industrial training for black men and was a skilled mediator between blacks and whites in Alabama. He was associated with Bishop Henry MacNeal

Turner, a civil-rights leader and advocate of the return of blacks to Africa. He was a contributor of articles to journals, including the *Arena* and *Forum*.

REFERENCES: *WWW* (I); *NYT,* April 18, 1909, p. 13. *Anne R. Gayles*

COUNTS, George Sylvester. B. December 9, 1889, Baldwin City, Kansas, to James Wilson and Mertie Fiorella (Gamble) Counts. M. September 24, 1913, to Lois Hagel Bailey. Ch. two. D. November 10, 1974, Belleville, Illinois.

George S. Counts attended Baker University in Baldwin City, Kansas, and received the A.B. degree in 1911. He received the Ph.D. degree with honors from the University of Chicago in 1916.

Counts's professional career began in 1916 at Delaware College (later, University of Delaware) in Newark, Delaware, as the head of the department of education and director of the summer school. He taught educational sociology at Harris College in St. Louis, Missouri (1918–19), secondary education at the University of Washington (1919–20) and education at Yale University (1920–26) and the University of Chicago (1926–27). He spent the major portion of his professional career at Teachers College, Columbia University, from 1927 to 1956. After retirement from Teachers College, he served as a visiting professor at the University of Pittsburgh (1959), Michigan State University (1960), and Southern Illinois University (1962–71).

Counts was active in politics. He served as New York State chairman of the American Labor party (1942–44). He helped establish the Liberal party in New York, ran as its candidate for the United States Senate in 1952, and was its chairman from 1954 to 1959. He was a member of the National Committee of the American Civil Liberties Union (1940–73).

Counts was the author of twenty-nine books and hundreds of articles. Among his principal works were *The Selective Character of American Secondary Education* (1922), *Principles of Education* (1924), *The Social Composition of Boards of Education* (1927), *The Soviet Challenge to America* (1931), *The Social Foundations of Education* (1934), *I Want to Be Like Stalin* (1947), *The Country of the Blind: The Soviet System of Mind Control* (with N. Lodge, 1949), *American Education Through the Soviet Looking Glass* (1951), *Education and American Civilization* (1952), *Decision-Making and American Values in School Administration* (1954), *The Challenge of Soviet Education* (1957), *Krushchev and the Central Committee Speak on Education* (1959), *Education and Human Freedom in the Age of Technology* (1958), and *Education and the Foundations of Human Freedom* (1962). He was editor of *Social Frontiers* for the Educational Policies Commission of the National Education Association (1936–42).

He was active in professional organizations, including the American Federation of Teachers (president, 1939–42), and was a member of the executive committee of the National Commission on Education and Defense (1940–42), the Commission on Motion Pictures in Education (1942–48), the United States Educational Mission to Japan (1946), and the Commission of International Exchange of Persons (1948–50).

Counts was a recipient of many honors and awards, including honorary degrees from Baker University (1935) and Southern Illinois University (1971). He received the Annual Educator's Award of B'nai B'rith (1953), the Teacher's College Medal of Distinguished Service (1954), the John Dewey Society Award (1967), the Phi Delta Kappa Award (1967), and an award for distinguished service from the American Association of School Administrators (1968).

REFERENCES: *CA* (5–8); *CB* (December 1941 and January 1975); *LE* (III); *NCAB* (F:190); *WWAE* (XI); *WWW* (VI); *NYT,* November 11, 1974, p. 32.   *Ralph E. Ackerman*

COURTIS, Stuart Appleton. B. May 15, 1874, Wyandotte, Michigan, to William Munroe and Lizzie Easton (Folger) Courtis. M. June 12, 1901, to Margaret Alice Weber. Ch. four. D. October 19, 1969, Cupertino, California.

Stuart Appleton Courtis was a student at Central High School in Detroit, Michigan, and Detroit Business University. He attended the Massachusetts Institute of Technology for two years, studied summers at the University of Chicago and Columbia University, and received the B.S. (1919) and M.A. (1921) degrees from Columbia. He received the Ph.D. degree (1925) from the University of Michigan.

Courtis was head of the department of science and mathematics at the Liggett School in Detroit (1898–1914) and was director of educational research for the Detroit public schools (1914–19). He was director of instruction and dean of the Detroit Teachers College (1920–24) and served as consultant to public schools in Detroit (1924–31) and Hamtramck, Michigan (1926–30) and the Culver (Indiana) Military Academy (1930–35). He was professor in the school of education at the University of Michigan (1921–44) and also professor of education at Wayne University (later, Wayne State University) in Detroit (1931–44). He also was president of the Detroit Thermo Electric Power Company and the Courtis Research Foundation.

Courtis developed Courtis standardized tests and was the author of *Then and Now in Education* (with Otis W. Caldwell, *q.v.*, 1924), *Why Children Succeed* (1925), *The Measurement of Growth* (1932), *Philosophy of Education* (1933), and *A Picture Dictionary for Children* (with Garnette Walters, 1939). He participated in school surveys of Gary, Indiana, and New

York City. He was a member of the Hanus Committee on a School Inquiry of New York City (1911) and was in charge of testing for the public schools of Boston, Massachusetts (1912). He was a fellow of the American Association for the Advancement of Science (secretary, 1913–17, and president, 1918–19 and 1932–33, of section L). He was secretary of the College Teachers of Education (1925–31) and president of the National Association of Directors of Educational Research (1917–18).

REFERENCES: *LE* (III); *WW* (XXII); *WWAE* (XIII); *WWW* (V).

John F. Ohles

COVELLO, Leonard. B. November 26, 1887, Avigliano (Potenza), Italy, to Pietro and Clementina (Genovese) Covello. M. June 15, 1923, to Rose Accurso. Ch. none.

Leonard Covello was brought to the United States by his parents, who settled in East Harlem in 1895. Covello's life (and the forces that influenced it) was linked to East Harlem, an immigrant enclave located in the northeast sector of Manhattan Island, New York City. He went to school in East Harlem at P.S. No. 83 and Morris High School.

Following graduation from Columbia University with the B.S. degree (1911), Covello served as a teacher of French and Spanish at De Witt Clinton High School and as chairman of the department of Italian (1926–34). He was principal of Benjamin Franklin High School (1934–56). He began study for the Ph.D. degree at New York University in 1930 and received the degree in 1944 with a major in educational sociology. His dissertation, "The Social Background of the Italo-American School Child," a massive sociocultural chronicle, had taken over a decade to write. He taught at New York University (1929–42) where his course "The Social Background and Educational Problems of the Italian Family in America" represented the earliest systematic enquiry at the university level of Italian family mores in the United States.

Covello played an important role in the Italian community in New York City. In 1910 he and John Shedd organized the Lincoln Club of Little Italy in East Harlem. At De Witt Clinton High School, a *Circolo Italiano* was established (1914) under Covello's sponsorship. He participated in the work of the Italian League for Social Service (organized in 1915), and the Young Men's Italian Educational League (organized, 1916), early efforts to improve the lot of Italian-Americans. Covello served from 1912 as the first vice-president of the Italian Teachers Association in New York City, a major force in stimulating Italian language study. He was a leader of the Italian Parents Association (organized in 1927), which provided a bridge between the schools and the Italian community. Covello played an important role in 1922 when the New York City Board of Education granted parity to Italian with other modern languages in the city schools. He was active in the Italian Educational League, the Italy-America Society, the Casa Italiana Educational Bureau, and the Instituto di Cultura Italiana (later, the Casa Italiana of Columbia University). Covello was the founder of the American Italian Historical Association in the mid-1960s.

REFERENCES: *LE* (III); *WWAE* (XXII); Francesco Cordasco, *Studies in Italian American Social History: Essays in Honor of Leonard Covello* (New York: Rowman and Littlefield, 1975).   *Francesco Cordasco*

COWLES, LeRoy Eugene. B. April 30, 1880, Chester, Utah, to William Henry and Sarepta Evelyn (Judkins) Cowles. M. March 3, 1904, to Cecilia Etta Brown. Ch. five. D. January 2, 1957, Orem, Utah.

LeRoy Eugene Cowles was educated in the public schools in Weber County, Utah, and at the Weber Academy in Ogden, Utah. He attended the University of Chicago, where he received the Ph.B. (1910) and M.A. (1913) degrees. He received the Ph.D. degree (1926) from the University of California in Berkeley.

At the age of sixteen, Cowles drove mule teams in a Wyoming mine. He was a teacher at the Heber City (Utah) public schools (1903–05), an instructor at Weber Academy (1905–08 and 1910–13), and principal of Carbon County High School at Price, Utah (1913–14). He served the University of Utah teaching education courses (1915–21) and was professor and head of the department of educational administration (1921–41). He was dean of the lower division of the university (1932–41) and president of the university (1941–46). After his retirement in 1946, he was guest professor and acting head of the department of secondary education at the University of New Mexico (1947–48) and director of secondary education of the Utah State Department of Public Instruction (1949–50).

Cowles was the author of *Utah Educational Program of 1919* (1926), *Provo School System* (with L. John Nuttall, 1929), *Organization and Administration of Education in Utah* (1934), and *University of Utah and World War II* (1949). He was active in professional organizations and was chairman of the Utah Teachers Retirement Board (1935–41) and president of the Utah Education Association (1927–28). He received an honorary degree from the University of Utah (1946).

REFERENCES: *LE* (III); *NCAB* (42:285); *NYT,* January 3, 1957, p. 31; *WWAE* (XIV); *WWW* (III).   *John F. Ohles*

COWLING, Donald John. B. August 21, 1880, Trevalga, Cornwall, England, to John P. and Mary K. (Stephens) Cowling. M. June 27, 1907, to Elizabeth L. Stehman. Ch. four. D. November 27, 1965, Minneapolis, Minnesota.

Donald John Cowling emigrated to the United States with his family in 1882. He received the A.B. degree (1902) from Lebanon Valley College in Annville, Pennsylvania, and attended Yale University, from which he received the A.B. (1903), A.M. (1904), B.D. (1906), and Ph.D. (1909) degrees.

Cowling taught philosophy and biblical literature at Baker University in Baldwin City, Kansas (1906–09), and was appointed president of Carleton College in Northfield, Minnesota (1909–45). The student body tripled in size while Cowling was president and benefited from his effectiveness in fund-raising. It developed as one of the major small liberal arts colleges in the country.

Cowling was the author of articles and *Colleges for Freedom* (with Carter Davidson, 1947). He was active in professional educational associations, including serving as president of the Association of American Colleges (1918–19), the American Council on Education (1918–19), and the Religious Education Association (1924–26). He served on special committees for the North Central Association of Colleges and Secondary Schools (1939–44). Active in the Congregational church, he was chairman of commissions for the tercentenary celebration, the Pilgrim Memorial Fund, and the Commission on Missions and was a trustee of the national council and foundation for education. He was a director of the Congregational Education Society (1925–34). He was on the national executive committee of the League to Enforce Peace (1918–22), a member of the American University Union in Europe (1923–26), a member of the American educational delegation to Russia (1928), on the executive committee of the World Alliance for International Friendship (1928–36), and vice-president of Americans United for World Government (1944–47). He served on state agencies for unemployed youth, crime, and education and was a trustee of many institutions, including the Chicago Theological Seminary (1912–42), Breck School in St. Paul, Minnesota (from 1936), Walker Art Center, Minneapolis, Minnesota (1939–45), Minneapolis Symphony Orchestra (1937–47), and St. Paul Institute and Museum (from 1937).

He received many awards, was decorated an Officer of Public Instruction of France, and was granted eleven honorary degrees from American colleges and universities.

REFERENCES: *LE* (III); *WWAE* (XIV); *WWW* (IV); *NYT,* November 29, 1965, p. 35.   *John F. Ohles*

CRABBE, John Grant. B. November 29, 1865, Mt. Sterling, Ohio, to Thomas W. and Julia Catherine (Baughman) Crabbe. M. January 29, 1889, to Jennie Florence Graffe. Ch. none. D. January 30, 1924, Greeley, Colorado.

John Grant Crabbe received the A.B. (1889) and A.M. (1892) degrees from Ohio Wesleyan University in Delaware, Ohio, and the Ph.M. degree (1897) from Ohio State University.

Prior to 1889 he spent two years teaching in rural schools. He was professor of Latin and Greek at Flint (Michigan) Normal College (1889–90) and served as superintendent of Ashland (Kentucky) public schools (1890–1907). He was elected superintendent of public instruction for the state of Kentucky in 1908 and served in that position until 1910 when he accepted an appointment as president of Eastern Kentucky State Normal School (later, Eastern Kentucky University) at Richmond. From this position he moved to the presidency of Colorado State Teachers College (later, University of Northern Colorado) in Greeley, Colorado, in 1916. He died while in this office in 1924.

During his years in Kentucky, Crabbe sought to reduce the state's illiteracy rate and was a strong supporter of "moonlight schools," which were organized for this purpose. He was instrumental in the development of Colorado State Teachers College as one of the outstanding teacher preparation institutions west of the Mississippi. During his seven-year tenure the budget, enrollment, and size of the faculty were doubled. He sought to raise teaching to the status of other professions.

He served as president of the Kentucky Education Association (1899), the Kentucky Schoolmasters Club (1909–16), the Department of Normal Schools of the Southern Education Association (1912), and the National Education Association (1913–14). He was secretary of the North Central Council of Normal School Presidents (1916–23) and secretary-treasurer (1917–21) and president (1921–23) of the American Association of Teachers' Colleges.

Crabbe was active in Sunday school work in Ashland, Kentucky, and in Greeley, Colorado, where he organized and taught Crabbe's International Bible Class, one of the largest Bible classes in the state. He was the author of numerous bulletins and monographs on subjects in education and a writer of songs, including three that became popular, "Beauty for Ashes," "If I Forget Thee," and "Kentucky Schools." He received several honorary degrees.

REFERENCES: *NCAB* (19:43); *WWW* (I); *Denver Post,* January 30, 1924; *NYT,* January 31, 1924, p. 15.   *Thomas A. Barlow*

CRABTREE, James William. B. April 18, 1864, Crabtree, Ohio, to Peter and Sarah Catherine (Williams) Crabtree. M. July 6, 1899, to Donna A. Wilson. Ch. three. D. June 9, 1945, Washington, D.C.

James William Crabtree received his early education in the local schools. He moved to Nebraska with his parents in the 1870s and continued his education at Peru State Normal School (later, Peru State College), from which he was graduated in 1887. He earned a B.S. degree (1890) from Bloomfield Scientific Institute and the B.A. and M.A. degrees from the University of Nebraska in 1908.

Crabtree taught in Nebraska rural schools for six years before becoming superintendent of the Ashland, Nebraska, public schools (1889–95). He was an assistant teacher of mathematics at the University of Nebraska (1895–96), leaving that position to become principal of the Beatrice, Nebraska, high school (1896–97). He returned to the University of Nebraska as inspector for the high schools of the state (1897–1904). He was president of Peru State Normal School (1904–10) and served as Nebraska superintendent of public instruction (1910–11). He was president of the River Falls (Wisconsin) State Teachers College (later, University of Wisconsin—River Falls) from 1911 to 1917. Crabtree became secretary of the National Education Association (NEA) in 1917, a position he held until 1935.

While secretary of the NEA, Crabtree opened association headquarters in Washington, D.C., expanded services to members, started a research division, began publication of the *NEA Journal,* and saw membership grow from fewer than eight thousand in 1917 to nearly two hundred thousand in 1935. After his retirement from the NEA, he accepted the position of secretary general of the World Federation of Education (1935–38).

Crabtree was the author of *Roll of Honor Wordbook* (1899), *The Crabtree Speller* (1908), and the autobiographical *What Counted Most* (1935). He also wrote the pamphlet *The Canvasser and His Victims* and others in the field of education.

Crabtree was active in professional organizations, including the Nebraska State Teachers Association (president, 1897–98), and he was treasurer of the NEA in 1904. He was secretary of the Central Association of the State Normal School Presidents (1908) and of President Herbert Hoover's Advisory Committee on Education (1931–32). He was awarded an honorary degree by the University of Nebraska.

REFERENCES: *CB* (July 1945); *LE* (II); *WWW* (II); *WWAE* (VIII); *NEA Journal* 24 (January 1935): 1–3; "The Service of Secretary J. W. Crabtree," *NEA Journal* 34 (October 1945): 130; *NYT,* June 11, 1945, p. 15.   *Erwin H. Goldenstein*

CRAIG, Clara Elizabeth. B. c. 1873, Providence, Rhode Island, to Bernard and Mary (McCormick) Craig. M. no. D. January 24, 1943, Providence, Rhode Island.

Clara Elizabeth Craig attended the public schools of Providence, Rhode Island, and was graduated from Clark University in Worcester, Massachusetts.

Craig joined the faculty at the Rhode Island Normal School in 1893 as a teacher in the demonstration classes. A new building was opened in 1898, and she became supervisor of the Children's School; she was later appointed director of the training school. The normal school was renamed the Rhode Island College of Education in 1920 and later became Rhode Island

College. Craig was director of training and dean of the college (1936–40).

In 1913 Craig was sent to Italy by the Rhode Island State Department of Education to study the methods of Maria Montessori, who had gained international recognition for her system of educating preschool youngsters. Craig was graduated from the Montessori International Institute and returned to Rhode Island Normal School, where she introduced the Montessori method in the Children's School. She received national attention, and her adaptations of the Montessori method to the primary grades were imitated in schools across the country. She retired from the Rhode Island College of Education in 1940.

Craig was awarded honorary degrees by Rhode Island College of Education, Brown University, and Bryant and Catholic Teachers colleges. A building at the new campus of Rhode Island College was named in her honor in 1958.

REFERENCES: *NYT,* January 25, 1943, p. 13; Providence, Rhode Island *Evening Bulletin,* January 25, 1943; *Quarterly Journal of the Rhode Island Institute of Instruction* (April 1943): 14–20.   *John F. Ohles*

CRAIG, Oscar John. B. April 18, 1846, near Madison, Indiana, to Miles William and Mary Stuart (Feather) Craig. M. August 20, 1875, to Narcissa Eudora Gassaway. Ch. three. D. March 5, 1911, San Diego, California.

Oscar John Craig served in the Civil War and attended Asbury University (later, DePauw University) in Greencastle, Indiana, from which he received the A.B. (1881) and A.M. (1884) degrees. He received the Ph.D. degree from Wooster (Ohio) University (later, College of Wooster) in 1887.

Craig was superintendent of schools in Sullivan, Indiana (1880–84), and was on the Purdue University faculty in Lafayette, Indiana, as principal of the preparatory department (1884–87) and professor of history and political economy (1887–95).

In 1895 he was the first president of the University of Montana in Missoula. Under his direction, the university was organized, courses of study established, buildings constructed, and the first faculty of two other members hired. He resigned because of ill health in 1908 with the university firmly established.

Craig was the author of *Ouiatanon: A Study in Indiana History* (1893), *The Effect of the Bible on Civilization* (n.d.), and *The Prohibition of the Constitution* (n.d.). He was the author of articles published in journals and a well-known lecturer at teachers' institutes and association meetings.

REFERENCES: *NCAB* (15:218); *TC; WWW* (I).   *John F. Ohles*

CRANDALL, Prudence. B. September 3, 1803, Hopkinton, Rhode Island, to Pardon and Esther Crandall. M. 1834 to Calvin Philleo. Ch. none. D. January 28, 1889, Elk Falls, Kansas.

Prudence Crandall (Philleo) received her education in a Friends' school in Providence, Rhode Island, and taught school in Plainfield, Connecticut.

Prominent citizens of Canterbury, Connecticut, encouraged her to open a school for their daughters. She opened the Canterbury Female Boarding School in 1831 and conducted it with outstanding success. A friend of Crandall's black maid sought admission to the school in preparation for teaching black children. Crandall decided to admit the child over the vigorous objections of a majority of the townspeople. In the face of a growing crisis, white parents withdrew pupils, and the school was forced to close.

Crandall decided to open a school for "young ladies and little misses of colour" as advertised in William Lloyd Garrison's *Liberator* on March 2, 1833. Black girls were attracted to the school, and conflict between Crandall and the community escalated. On May 24, 1833, the Connecticut legislature passed a law requiring that schools for blacks could not be established without the consent of local authorities. Crandall was arrested, tried, and convicted on her resistance to the law, but the conviction was set aside on an appeal. Crandall was finally forced to close the school in September 1834 when local citizens threatened to burn her house and wrecked it with clubs and iron bars.

Crandall married the Reverend Calvin Philleo in 1834 and accompanied him to Illinois, moving to Kansas after her husband's death in 1874. In 1886, at the age of eighty-seven, she was granted a pension of four hundred dollars a year by the state of Connecticut. She retained a great interest in causes such as women's rights and suffrage until her death in 1889 in Elk Falls, Kansas.

REFERENCES: *AC; DAB; EB; NAW; NCAB* (2:307); *WWW* (H); Edmund Fuller, *Prudence Crandall* (Middletown, Conn.: Wesleyan University Press, 1971); Mae Norton Morris, "Prudence Crandall—A Pioneer in Equal Rights," *Connecticut Teacher* (March 1964): 4–5. *Audrey Potter*

CRANE, Julia Ettie. B. May 19, 1855, Hewittville, New York, to Samuel Coggeshall and Harriet K. (Bissell) Crane. M. no. D. June 11, 1923, Potsdam, New York.

The daughter of a Forty-niner in California who returned to the East to operate a chair factory and serve as justice of the peace in Potsdam, New York, Julia E. Crane was graduated from the Potsdam State Normal School (later, State University of New York College at Potsdam) in 1874. She continued her study of voice in summer schools and with Marcel Garcia in London.

She taught in a district school (1874–77) and moved to Pennsylvania where she taught mathematics, calisthenics, and vocal music at the Pennsylvania State Normal School at Shippensburg (later, Shippensburg State

College) from 1877 to 1880. On her return from Europe she was employed as a private vocal teacher and in 1884 joined the faculty of the Potsdam State Normal School as a music teacher, a position she retained until her death.

Dissatisfied with the program of studies provided for supervisors of public school music, she established the Crane Normal Institute in Potsdam in 1886. The school graduated as many as twenty-five students a year and acquired a national reputation. It was the first music education program associated with a regular normal school. Students studied the psychology of learning and the techniques of teaching music. She maintained positions in both the Crane and state normal schools to her death in 1923. In 1926 the institute was incorporated as a department of the state normal school.

A national figure in music education, Crane was the author of *Music Teacher's Manual* (1887), in which she developed a philosophy, widely accepted by music educators, that music provides an essential mental and social discipline necessary for children to become productive and cultured citizens. She was a frequent lecturer and contributor of articles to professional journals on music education.

Crane was active in professional associations and was frequently invited to teach music methods at major American universities during the summers.

REFERENCES: *NCAB* (6:522); William D. Claudson, "The Philosophy of Julia E. Crane and the Origin of Music Teacher Training," *Journal of Research in Music Education* 17 (1969): 399–404.   *Pamela G. Massey*

CRANE, Thomas Frederick. B. July 12, 1844, New York, New York, to Thomas Sexton and Charlotte (Nuttman) Crane. M. July 10, 1872, to Sarah Fay Tourtellot. Ch. one. D. December 9, 1927, DeLand, Florida.

Thomas Frederick Crane was graduated from the College of New Jersey (later, Princeton University) with the A.B. (1864), A.M. (1867), and Ph.D. (1883) degrees.

Crane was appointed professor of Romance languages at Cornell University in Ithaca, New York, where he remained to his retirement in 1909. He served as dean of the college of arts (1896–1902), dean of the faculty (1902–09), and acting president (1899–1900 and 1912–13). He conducted particularly significant research on the development of European folklore and was a leading authority in the field.

Crane was author of many books, including *Tableaux de la Revolution Française* (1884), *Italian Popular Tales* (1885), *La société française au dix-septième siècle* (1889), *The Exempla* (1890), *Chansons populaires de la France* (1891), and *Italian Social Customs of the Sixteenth Century* (1920) and edited *Le romantisme français* (1887).

Crane was a member of many American and foreign scholarly organizations and was a founder of the American Folk-Lore Society in 1888. He received an honorary degree from Princeton University in 1903.

REFERENCES: *DAB; NCAB* (B:103); *TC; WWW* (I); *NYT*, December 11, 1927, p. 31.   *John F. Ohles*

CRARY, Isaac Edwin. B. October 2, 1804, Preston, Connecticut, to Elisha and Nabby (Avery) Crary. M. Jane Elizabeth Hitchcock. M. 1841 to Bellona Pratt. Ch. none. D. May 8, 1854, Marshall, Michigan.

After spending his early life on a farm in Connecticut, Isaac Edwin Crary attended Bacon Academy in Colchester, Connecticut, and was graduated from Trinity College in Hartford, Connecticut, in its first graduating class (1827).

He became a lawyer and practiced law for two years in Connecticut and assisted in editing the *New England Weekly Review*. In 1832 he moved to Bellevue, Michigan, and purchased 240 acres of land. He was admitted to the Michigan bar in 1833 and practiced law in Marshall, Michigan. He served as a school commissioner, justice of the peace, commissioner of highways, and editor of the *Marshall Democratic Expounder*.

Crary served as territorial delegate to Congress from Michigan (1835–37) and was elected Michigan's first representative in Congress (1835–41). He was a member of the Michigan House of Representatives (1842–46) and served as speaker in 1846.

Crary and John D. Pierce *(q.v.)*, a close friend and onetime business partner, were the most influential men in the field of education during the early years of development of the territory and state of Michigan. Crary served as chairman of the committee on education in the constitutional convention of 1835. He prepared the article that proposed a state superintendent of public instruction. He had studied reports of the Prussian system of education and formulated plans for the state superintendent to provide for the broad powers he found in the Prussian cultural ministry. He submitted a plan for organizing and providing support for common schools. He also proposed a plan for the development of a state university at the 1835 convention, and in March 1837 the Michigan legislature authorized the development of the University of Michigan. The institution was to have branches in centers convenient to the population of the state. A board of regents was created to provide leadership and exercise control over higher and secondary education. Crary served on the board of regents (1837–44), and the state board of education (1850–54).

REFERENCES: *DAB; WWW* (H); James V. Campbell, *Outlines of the Political History of Michigan* (Detroit: Schober & Co., 1876); Silas Farmer, *History of Detroit and Wayne County and Early Michigan*, 3d ed. (Detroit: Silas Farmer & Co., 1890); George N. Fuller, ed., *Historic*

Michigan, 2 vols. (Lansing: National Historical Association, 1924).
H. J. Prince

CRAVEN, Braxton. B. August 22, 1822, Randolph County, North Carolina, to Braxton York (?) and Ann Craven. M. to Irene Leach. Ch. four. D. November 7, 1882, Trinity College, North Carolina.

Braxton Craven was believed to be the illegitimate son of Braxton York, a cousin of Brantley York, the founder of Union Institute (later, Duke University in Durham, North Carolina).

At the age of seven, Craven was orphaned, and he grew up with the farm family of Nathan Cox. He supplemented a few months' attendance at a neighborhood school with intensive self-instruction. He taught briefly in a school supported by public subscription of funds before attending a Quaker school at New Garden, North Carolina, for two years. In 1840 he was licensed to preach by the Methodist Episcopal church and became an assistant teacher at Union Institute, founded two years earlier by Methodists and Quakers. He received the B.A. degree by examination from Randolph-Macon College in Ashland, Virginia, in 1850.

After two years as a teacher at Union Institute (1841–42), he became principal and remained there to his death in 1882, except for three years (1863–66) during the Civil War when he engaged in the ministry. In 1851 the school was rechartered by the North Carolina legislature as the state's first normal school. It received little financial support and had limited success as a normal school but continued to train ministers for the Methodist church. The legislature returned the school to the Methodist church in 1859 when the name was changed to Trinity College.

Craven established an educational journal, *Southern Index,* in 1850, which later became the literary magazine *Evergreen.* He wrote *Theory of Common Schools* (1850) and *An Historical Sketch of Trinity College* (1876), and published a revised *Bullion's English Grammar* (1864). He was awarded several honorary degrees.

REFERENCES: *DAB; NCAB* (3:445); *TC; WWW* (H); Jerome Dowd, *The Life of Braxton Craven* (Durham, N.C.: Duke University Press, 1939); Thomas N. Ivey, "Braxton Craven," *Biographical History of North Carolina from Colonial Times to the Present* (Greensboro: Charles L. Van Noppen, 1906), vol. 4.   *D. Richard Bowles*

CRAWFORD, James Pyle Wickersham. B. February 19, 1882, Lancaster, Pennsylvania, to James and Corinne (Wickersham) Crawford. M. June 3, 1909, to Florence May Wickersham. Ch. one. D. September 22, 1939, Philadelphia, Pennsylvania.

James Pyle Wickersham Crawford was named after his maternal grandfather, James Pyle Wickersham *(q.v.),* a major figure in the development of education in Pennsylvania. Crawford attended Friends' Central School in Lancaster, Pennsylvania. He received the B.A. (1902) and Ph.D. (1906) degrees from the University of Pennsylvania. He studied in Europe at the universities of Grenoble, France, Madrid, Spain, and Freiburg, Germany (1904–06).

Crawford joined the University of Pennsylvania faculty as an instructor in Romance languages in 1906, remaining on the staff until his death in 1939; he also served as department chairman. He was a prominent textbook author, philologist, teacher, scholar of Spanish drama and lyric poetry, Hispanist, and leader in Spanish-language education.

He was the founder and editor of the *Hispanic Review* (1933–39) and editor of the *Modern Language Journal* (1920–24). His articles appeared in American and foreign journals and discussed French, Italian, and Spanish literature and pedagogy. Among his books were *Life and Works of Suarez de Figueroa* (1907), *Spanish Composition (1910)*, *Spanish Pastoral Drama* (1915), *First Book in Spanish* (1919), *Temas Españoles* (1922), *Spanish Drama before Lope de Vega* (1923), and *Un Viaje por España* (1931). He edited *Tragedia de Narciso* (1909).

Crawford served in the United States Army (1918–19). He was a member of many American and foreign professional associations and was awarded an honorary degree by Franklin and Marshall College.

REFERENCES: *DAB* (supp. 2); *LE* (I); *NCAB* (29:309); *WWW* (I); Henry G. Doyle, "In Memorium: J. P. Wickersham Crawford," *Modern Language Journal* 24 (March 1940): 457–58; *NYT,* September 23, 1939, p. 17.

Samuel A. Farmerie

CROCKER, Lucretia. B. December 31, 1829, Barnstable, Massachusetts, to Henry and Lydia E. (Ferris) Crocker. M. no. D. October 9, 1886, Boston, Massachusetts.

Lucretia Crocker was educated in the Boston public schools and was graduated from the State Normal School of West Newton, Massachusetts (later, Framingham State College), in 1850.

She was instructor in geography, math, and general science at the West Newton Normal School in 1850, but ill health forced her to resign in 1854. She joined the faculty of Antioch College in Yellow Springs, Ohio, as a professor of mathematics and astronomy in 1857, resigning in 1859 to return to Boston. She taught botany and mathematics at the Newbury Street School. She was head of the science department (1873–76) of the Society to Encourage Studies at Home, a correspondence school founded by Anna Eliot Ticknor, widow of George Ticknor *(q.v.)*.

In 1873 Crocker and three other women were elected to the Boston School Committee but were kept from taking office through legal maneuvers by the men on the committee. Elected in 1874 under new legislation, she and the other women were seated on the committee. Under a reorganization of the Boston schools in 1876, Crocker was elected to a new board of supervisors. In this position, she oversaw broad changes in teaching science in the Boston schools. She introduced new subjects and, with Ellen H. Richards *(q.v.)*, established a course in mineralogy. She supported the Teachers' School of Science, a lecture series seeking to improve science teaching.

Crocker was the coauthor of a geography text, *Our World* (with Mary L. Hall, 1864), and wrote *Methods of Teaching Geography: Notes on Lessons* (1883).

She served on a committee of the American Unitarian Association that selected books for Sunday school libraries (1866–75). She was an active member of the committee on teachers of New England Freedman's Aid Society and in 1869 made an extensive tour of freedmen's schools in the South. During the early 1870s she was secretary and chairman of the executive committee of Sarah Fuller's *(q.v.)* Boston School for Deaf Mutes. She founded the Women's Education Association (1872).

In 1880 she was elected to the American Association for the Advancement of Science, a particular honor for one who was not a working scientist. A school in the Jamaica Plain section of Boston and Crocker Hall at the State College at Framingham were named in her honor.

REFERENCES: *NAW; Boston Transcript,* October 11, 1866.

Marilyn Meiss

CROSBY, Alpheus. B. October 13, 1810, Sandwich, New Hampshire, to Asa and Abigail (Russell) Crosby. M. August 27, 1834, to Abigail Grant Jones Cutler. M. February 12, 1861, to Martha Kingman. Ch. none. D. April 17, 1874, Salem, Massachusetts.

Reading Latin and Greek at eight years of age, Alpheus Crosby prepared for college in New Hampshire at Gilmanton and Phillips Exeter academies and under several Dartmouth College tutors. He entered Dartmouth College in Hanover, New Hampshire, in 1823 as the youngest and academically highest in his graduating class (1827). He studied at Andover (Massachusetts) Theological Seminary (1831–33) and was licensed to preach.

He spent a year teaching at Moor's Indian Charity School in Hanover, New Hampshire, and for three years at Dartmouth as a tutor in Latin and Greek. After further study he returned to Dartmouth as professor of Latin and Greek languages in 1833. By 1837 his wife had become an invalid, and Crosby toured Europe with her; she died in Paris, France.

Returning to Dartmouth in 1839, Crosby taught Greek languages and literature until his father-in-law's death in 1849, when he moved to Newburyport, Massachusetts, to care for his invalid mother-in-law. He served as superintendent of schools of Newburyport and became an agent for the

Massachusetts Board of Education under Horace Mann *(q.v.)* in 1854. He was appointed principal of the State Normal School (later, Salem State College) at Salem in its third year of operation. He served in that capacity from 1857 to his retirement in 1865.

Crosby was recognized for his scholarly activities in several fields. He wrote books on Latin, Greek, mathematics, and social questions, including, *A Grammar of the Greek Language* (1842), *First Lessons in Geometry* (1847), and *A Lexicon to Xenophon's Anabasis* (1873). At the time of his death he was working on a Greek dictionary. He was editor of *The Right Way* (1865–67), an abolitionist paper, and *Massachusetts Teacher.* He also wrote a series of elementary lessons for teaching freedmen of the South to read.

While at Salem, Crosby became a prominent citizen and was a lifelong member of the Essex Institute, president of the Salem Atheneum, and a trustee of the Salem Lyceum. He served as an examiner of Harvard University in academic departments, especially ancient languages, and was a life member and director of the American Peace Society.

REFERENCES: *AC; NCAB* (9:97); *TC; WWW* (H); *NYT,* April 19, 1874, p. 1; *Salem Observer,* April 18, 1874.   *Stephen J. Clarke*

CROSS, Anson Kent. B. December 6, 1862, Lawrence, Massachusetts, to George Osgood and Abigail Attwood (Brown) Cross. M. July 27, 1903, to Sarah (Wilkinson) Martin. M. July 14, 1913, to Gertrude Whipple. Ch. none. D. June 14, 1944, St. Petersburg, Florida.

Anson Kent Cross, art educator, author, and inventor, received his preliminary education in the public schools of Lawrence, Massachusetts. He was graduated in 1883 from the Massachusetts Normal Art School (later, Massachusetts College of Art) in Boston.

Cross was employed as an assistant in mechanical drawing and an instructor in freehand drawing at an evening drawing school in Lawrence (1881–83). He was a teacher of drawing in the Boston Evening Drawing Schools (1885) and principal from 1886 to 1900. He also served as an instructor in the Massachusetts Normal Art School. He was an instructor in the school of drawing and painting of the Boston Museum of Fine Arts from 1891 to 1926 when he received an appointment from Columbia University. At Columbia he served until 1936 as director of the university extension art department in charge of the classes in freehand drawing and painting. Cross was the director of the Anson Kent Cross Art School, located during summers in Booth Bay Harbor, Maine, and winters in St. Petersburg, Florida. He believed any person could be taught to draw and paint and developed a method of teaching art that included the training of vision through self-criticism, aided by an instructor, of quick sketches for picture making.

Cross held twenty-three patents primarily for instruments to aid the production or teaching of art; they included different forms of easels, a drawing glass (1912), drawing compasses, a crayon for drawing on glass, an artist's level, and a drawing and painting glass (1921). He was the author of a number of books and articles produced to aid art teachers, including *Free-hand Drawing, Light and Shade and Free-hand Perspective* (1892), *Drawing in Public Schools* (1893), *Mechanical Drawing* (1895), *Color Study* (1896), *Free-hand Drawing* (1896), *Primary Lessons* (1896), *National Drawing Cards* (1896), *National Drawing Books for Grammar Grades* (1896), *Light and Shade* (1897), and *Drawing and Painting, Self-Taught* (1922). Most of his works were translated into Japanese and were used for art instruction in the government art school in Tokyo.

Cross was awarded medals by the Massachusetts Charitable Mechanic Institute for his work in landscape painting and for his innovations in artists' easels and at the International Universal Exposition, Paris (1900), for his easels and the Panama Pacific International Exposition in San Francisco (1915) for his drawing glass.

REFERENCES: *LE* (II); *NCAB* (38:27); *WWW* (II); *NYT,* June 18, 1944, p. 36.   *Roger H. Jones*

CROSS, Wilbur Lucius. B. April 10, 1862, Mansfield, Connecticut, to Samuel and Harriet M. (Gurley) Cross. M. July 17, 1889, to Helen B. Avery. Ch. four. D. October 5, 1948, New Haven, Connecticut.

Wilbur Lucius Cross taught high school for one year in Willimantic, Connecticut, before entering Yale College in 1881. Upon receiving the A.B. degree (1885), he was principal of Staples High School in Westport, Connecticut. Returning to Yale, he studied literature under Henry A. Beers and Thomas Lounsbury, earning the Ph.D. degree (1889). He was master of English at Shady Side Academy in Pittsburgh, Pennsylvania (1889–94), before returning to Yale as an instructor in the Sheffield Scientific School. He taught English at Yale (1894–1921), was dean of the graduate school (1916–30), acting provost (1922–23), and Sterling Professor of English (1921–30).

On his retirement from Yale in 1930, Cross was nominated as the Democratic candidate for governor of Connecticut. In a major electoral surprise, he was elected and served for four terms (1931–39). During his tenure, he established significant public works and relief programs to combat the depression of the 1930s, abolished child labor, established minimum wage scales and working standards for women, lowered public utility rates and strengthened regulation of utilities, promoted a civil-service act, established programs for the development of a building program for state institutions, promoted a highway system, and reorganized the management of financing and budgeting.

His books include *The Development of the English Novel* (1899), *The Life and Times of Laurence Sterne* (1909), *History of Henry Fielding* (1918), *An Outline of Biography* (1924), *The Modern English Novel* (1929), *Four Contemporary Novelists* (1930), and his autobiography, *Connecticut Yankee* (1943). He edited many textbooks and served as editor of the *Yale Review,* The Yale Shakespeare, and the Department of English Literature in the *New International Encyclopedia* (1901–03).

Cross was active in professional associations as president of National Institute of Arts and Letters, chancellor of the American Academy of Arts and Letters, and a member of other groups. He was awarded honorary degrees by many American universities and colleges. He was awarded the French Legion of Honor. Connecticut named the Wilbur L. Cross Parkway in his honor.

REFERENCES: *DAB* (supp. 4); *LE* (III); *NCAB* (C:451); *WWW* (II); *NYT,* October 5, 1948, p. 1; Wilbur Lucius Cross, *Connecticut Yankee* (New Haven: Yale University Press, 1943).   *William W. West*

CROZET, Claude. B. January 1, 1790, Villenbrauche, France, to n.a. M. to Mademoiselle de Camp. Ch. none. D. January 29, 1864, Richmond, Virginia.

Claude (also, Claudius) Crozet was educated at the Ecole Polytechnique in Paris and received a commission in the French artillery in 1807. He fought for Napoleon and was captured during the Russian campaign. After the Battle of Waterloo, he ended his military career and emigrated to the United States in 1816. He worked as an engineer with the United States Army and was appointed to the engineering staff of the United States Military Academy at West Point, New York.

Crozet introduced the use of the blackboard at West Point and a system of analysis and demonstration instead of relying only on lecture and models. He established a more demanding requirement in mathematics with an emphasis on descriptive geometry. Crozet wrote the first American textbook on descriptive geometry, *A Treatise of Descriptive Geometry for the Use of Cadets of the U.S.M.A.* (1821). Later he authored another textbook, *Arithmetic for Colleges and Schools* (1848).

Crozet resigned as professor and became the state engineer of Virginia in 1823. From 1832 to 1839 he was president of Jefferson College in Louisiana. He returned to Virginia in 1839 and was president of the board of visitors at the newly organized Virginia Military Institute (VMI). Because the board had control over the institution Crozet exerted an important influence on the development of VMI, which was patterned closely after West Point with similar regulations and uniforms and an emphasis on military and mathematical subjects.

Crozet planned a system of inland communication for the state of Virginia, including roads, canals, and railroads. His greatest engineering feat was the location and construction of a railroad through the Blue Ridge Mountains, which was later part of the Chesapeake and Ohio Company. He assisted in the construction of the aqueduct that supplied Washington, D.C., with water from the Great Falls of the Potomac River and was credited with designing and building the Aqueduct Bridge across the Potomac River into Washington. In 1859 Crozet became principal of Richmond (Virginia) Academy, a position he held until his death in 1864.

REFERENCES: *AC; DAB; NCAB* (18:393); *WWW* (H).

Harold D. Lehman

CUBBERLY, Elwood Patterson. B. June 6, 1868, Antioch, Indiana, to Edwin Blanchard and Catherine (Biles) Cubberly. M. June 15, 1892, to Helen Van Uxem. Ch. none. D. September 14, 1941, Palo Alto, California.

Elwood Patterson Cubberly received the A.B. degree (1891) from Indiana University and the A.M. (1902) and Ph.D. (1905) degrees from Columbia University.

He first taught in a one-room Indiana school in 1888 and was a professor and the youngest college president in the United States at Vincennes (Indiana) University (1891–96). He was superintendent of schools in San Diego, California (1896–98), and joined the faculty of Stanford (California) University in 1898; he served out his career there as a professor of education (1906–33) and dean of the school of education (1917–33). At Stanford he pioneered in the development of new fields of education, often preparing and teaching the courses himself. His most important and most controversial contribution was as an educational historian.

Cubberly was the author of many books in education, including *Syllabus of Lectures on the History of Education* (1902), *School Funds and Their Apportionment* (1905), *Certification of Teachers* (1906), *Changing Conceptions of Education* (1909), *The Improvement of Rural Schools* (1911), *Rural Life and Education* (1913), *Public School Administration* (1915), *School Organization and Administration* (1916), *Public Education in the United States* (1919), *A History of Education* (1921), *Readings in the History of Education* (1921), *The Principal and His School* (1923), *An Introduction to the Study of Education* (1925), *State School Administration* (1927), and *Readings in Public Education in the United States* (1934). He was a department editor of *Monroe's Cyclopedia of Education* (1911–13) and editor of the Riverside Text Books in Education Series.

Cubberly was a member of the Baltimore Educational Commission (1911), and he participated in school surveys in Butte, Montana (1914), and the National School Finance Inquiry (1921–24). He directed school surveys, including those of Portland, Oregon, Salt Lake City, Utah, and Oakland, California. He was a member of the Educational Research Committee of the Commonwealth Fund (1920–25) and an adviser to state legislative commissions, including California, New Mexico, and Washington. He was a fellow of the American Association for the Advancement of Science and a member of many other professional associations. He was awarded the Butler Silver Medal of Columbia University (1915) and the University Medal (1933). He was awarded honorary degrees by the universities of Iowa and Indiana.

REFERENCES: *DAB* (supp. 3); *LE* (I); *NCAB* (30:12); *WWW* (I); *WWAE* (VIII); Lawrence A. Cremin, *The Wonderful World of Ellwood Patterson Cubberly* (New York: Teachers College, Columbia, 1965); *NYT,* September 15, 1941, p. 17; Jesse B. Sears and Adin D. Henderson, *Cubberly of Stanford* (Stanford: Stanford University Press, 1957). *Alan H. Eder*

CUMMINGS, Joseph. B. March 3, 1817, Falmouth, Maine, to Cyrus and Elizabeth (Curtis) Cummings. M. August 15, 1842, to Deborah S. Haskell. Ch. three. D. May 7, 1890, Evanston, Illinois.

Joseph Cummings received his preparatory education at Kent's Hill, Maine, and was graduated from Wesleyan University in Middletown, Connecticut (1849). He had supported himself in part by teaching school while studying. Following graduation he taught natural science and mathematics in Amenia (New York) Seminary for three years. After receiving the M.A. degree in 1843, he became principal of that seminary for another three years.

In 1846 Cummings was ordained by the New England Conference of the Methodist Episcopal church. He preached in various churches in the Greater Boston area for seven years, was an editor of *Zion's Herald,* and served as professor of theology, Concord Biblical Institute (1853–54).

Cummings's most significant work was as a college president. He was president of Genesee College in Lima, New York (1854–57), and in 1857 became the first alumnus chosen president of Wesleyan University. His administration was credited with two major innovations: the enlargement of the curriculum through an increased number of electives and the admission of women, a bold step for its time. He resigned the presidency in 1875 but remained two years more as professor of mental philosophy and political economy.

Cummings returned to the ministry for a few years. He was elected president of Northwestern University in Evanston, Illinois, on June 21, 1881, and also served as professor of moral and intellectual philosophy. During his administration a large debt was paid, schools of dentistry and pharmacy were established, and a science hall and an astronomical observatory were built. The school moved from a period of declining student population to extensive growth.

REFERENCES: *DAB; NCAB* (9:430); *WWW* (H); Charles B. Atwell, ed.,

Alumni Record of the College of Liberal Arts (Evanston, Ill.: Northwestern University, 1903); Estelle Frances Ward, *The Story of Northwestern University* (New York: Dodd, Mead & Co., 1924).

Darlene E. Fisher

CURME, George Oliver. B. January 14, 1860, Richmond, Indiana, to Arthur Allen and Elizabeth Jane (Nicholas) Curme. M. July 14, 1881, to Caroline Cheneweth Smith. Ch. four, including George Oliver Curme, industrial chemist. D. April 29, 1948, White Plains, New York.

George Oliver Curme came from a religious home. His father was in the leather business and was a Methodist minister, and his mother was the daughter of a minister of the United Brethren church. His preparatory schooling was completed in local institutions. During the years 1876 to 1881 he attended DePauw University in Greencastle, Indiana, irregularly because of reverses in his father's business. He was graduated with the A.B. degree (1882) from the University of Michigan. He returned to DePauw and was graduated with the A.M. degree (1885). He studied at the University of Berlin, Germany, in 1890.

Curme became an instructor in French and German languages at Jennings Seminary in Aurora, Illinois (1882–84), and professor of modern languages at the University of Washington (1884–86). He taught German language and literature at Cornell College in Mount Vernon, Iowa (1886–96). He was professor of German philology at Northwestern University in Evanston, Illinois, from 1896 until he retired in 1933. He was a lecturer in German at the University of Southern California (1934–39).

Curme's books were well known in educational circles. The two works that won him international acclaim were *Grammar of the German Language* (1905), which was acknowledged as one of the finest works in English, and *A First German Grammar* (1913). He also wrote *College English Grammar* (1925). *Grammar of the English Language,* which was published in two volumes titled *Syntax* (1931) and *Parts of Speech and Accidence* (1935), and *Principles and Practices of English Grammar* (1946).

Curme received several honorary degrees.

REFERENCES: *DAB* (supp. 4); *EB; LE* (I); *NCAB* (D:53, 36:272); *WWW* (II); *NYT,* April 30, 1948, p. 23.   *LeRoy Barney*

CURRIER, Enoch Henry. B. August 22, 1849, Newburyport, Massachusetts, to Enoch Gerrish and Jane (Wiggin) Currier. M. July 2, 1878, to Charlotte Lewis. Ch. none. D. August 19, 1917, Essex, New York.

Enoch Henry Currier was preparing to enter the ministry when an accident to one of his eyes prevented him from entering college, and he decided to become a teacher of the deaf. He studied the methods of teaching the deaf with Isaac Lewis Peet *(q.v.)* and others.

Currier invented the duplex conico-cylindrical ear tube through which partially deaf students could be instructed in groups of four or more. He became principal of the New York Institution for the Instruction of the Deaf and Dumb, succeeding Peet in 1893, and remained in that position until his death in 1917. He was instrumental in the passage of legislation in New York that ensured the education of deaf children from five years of age. He introduced into his school the wearing of uniforms, military drill, a band, and field music, music played on drums, fifes, bugles, and pipes for military formations. He instituted a kindergarten and instruction in home economics. He used Montesorri methods of instruction in his school.

Currier was the author of *The History of Articulation Teaching* (1894), *Aural Development* (1907), and *The Manual Alphabet in the Public School* (n.d.).

Currier was a member of the New England Society of the City of New York, the American Geographic Society, the National Geographical Society, the Association for the Promotion of Speech to the Deaf, and the Institution of American Instructors of the Deaf. He received an honorary degree from Gallaudet College (1892).

REFERENCES: *NCAB* (18:210); *NYT,* August 21, 1917, p. 7.

Thomas Meighan

CURRY, Jabez Lamar Monroe. B. June 5, 1825, Lincoln County, Georgia, to William and Susan (Winn) Curry. M. March 4, 1847, to Ann Bowie. M. June 25, 1867, to Mary Wortham Thomas. Ch. four. D. February 12, 1903, Ashville, North Carolina.

Jabez Lamar Monroe Curry was the son of a Georgia planter. He was graduated from the University of Georgia (1843) and Dane Law School at Harvard University (1845).

Curry practiced law and was a long-time legislator in the Alabama legislature (1847–48, 1853–54, and 1855–56). He was a member of the United States House of Representatives (1857–61) and a member of the Confederate Congress (1861–65). He was an aide to General Joseph E. Johnston and General Joseph Wheeler as a lieutenant-colonel in the Confederate cavalry (1864–65). He was ordained a Baptist minister in 1865.

Curry was president of Howard College (later, Samford University) in Birmingham, Alabama (1866–68). He served as professor of English philosophy and constitutional and international law at Richmond (Virginia) College (1868–81). He served as president of the board of trustees for Richmond College. Curry was American minister to Spain (1885–88) and again in 1902 at the request of the Spanish government.

Curry's major educational achievements were realized through his service as an agent with the George Peabody Fund and the Slater Fund. He succeeded Barnas Sears *(q.v.)* as general agent of the Peabody Fund in 1881 and was credited with the establishment of state normal schools for both races in twelve southern states, the acceptance by legislatures of responsibility for improving rural schools, the development of racially segregated public graded schools in the South, and contributions to educational literature in his reports and addresses on education.

In 1899 Curry was elected president of a conference of persons interested in promoting education in the South. The group evolved into the Southern Education Board in 1901, with Curry its supervising director until his death in 1903.

Curry was the author of *Gladstone* (1891), *The Southern States of the American Union* (1895), *Establishment and Disestablishment in America* (1899), and *The Civil History of the Government of the Confederate States* (1901).

REFERENCES: *DAB; NCAB* (4:357); *TC; WWW* (I); *NYT,* February 13, 1903, p. 1; Dorothy Orr, *A History of Education in Georgia* (Chapel Hill: University of North Carolina Press, 1950); Richard Connelley Peck, "Jabez Lamar Curry: Educational Crusader" (doct. diss., George Peabody College for Teachers, 1943).

Foster F. Wilkinson

CURTI, Merle Eugene. B. September 15, 1897, Papillion, Nebraska, to John Eugene and Alice (Hunt) Curti. M. June 16, 1925, to Margaret Wooster. M. March 9, 1968, to Francis Bennett Becker. Ch. two.

Merle Eugene Curti received the A.B. summa cum laude (1920), A.M. (1921), and Ph.D. (1927) degrees from Harvard University. He studied at the Sorbonne in Paris, France (1924–25).

He taught history at Beloit (Wisconsin) College (1921–22), Smith College in Northampton, Massachusetts (1925–37), and Teachers College, Columbia University (1937–42). He was professor of history at the University of Wisconsin (1942–68).

Curti was a prolific writer; some of his published works include *Austria and the U.S., 1848–1852* (1927), *American Peace Crusade* (1929), *Bryan and World Peace* (1931), *Social Ideas of American Educators* (1935), *The Learned Blacksmith: Letters and Journals of Elihu Burritt* (1937), *Growth of American Thought* (1943), *Introduction to America* (1944), *Roots of American Loyalty* (with Vernon Carstensen, 1946), *University of Wisconsin: A History* (with Paul Todd, 1949), *America's History* (with W. Thorp and C. Baker, 1950), *American Issues* (with others, 1950), *An American History* (with others, 1950), *American Scholarship in the Twentieth Century* (1953), *Prelude to Point Four* (1954), *Probing Our Past* (1955), *The American Paradox* (1956), *The Making of an American Community* (with Paul Todd, 1959), *Rise of the American Nation* (1960),

American Philanthropy Abroad: A History (with Roderick Nash, 1963), *Philanthropy in the Shaping of American Higher Education* (1965), and *Human Nature in American Historical Thought* (1969). He was a contributor to many scholarly periodicals.

Curti was a Guggenheim Fellow (1929–30) and a visiting professor to universities in India (1946–47), the University of Tokyo, Japan (1959–60), and the University of Melbourne, Australia (1964). He was on the board of directors of the Harry S. Truman Library (1958–61) and a fellow at the Center for Advanced Study in Behavioral Sciences (1956). He was the recipient of an award for distinguished scholarship from the American Council of Learned Societies in 1960. He won a Pulitzer Prize for *Growth of American Thought.*

He was active in many organizations, including the Wisconsin Historical Society (board of curators), the American Historical Association (president, 1953–54), the Mississippi Valley Historical Association (board of editors, 1936–40, and president, 1951–52), the American Council of Learned Societies (vice-chairman, board of directors, 1958–59), the American Academy of Arts and Sciences, and Phi Beta Kappa (senator, 1947–52, president, Wisconsin, 1957–58). He was an honorary fellow in the Wisconsin Academy of Science, Arts and Letters.

REFERENCES: *CA* (5–8); *NCAB* (H:196); *WW* (XXXVIII).

Lawrence S. Master

CUSHMAN, Frank. B. July 15, 1879, Boston, Massachusetts, to Frank and Carrie E. (Prince) Cushman. M. October 5, 1901, to Susan Abbie Wood. Ch. two. D. April 27, 1953, Long Beach, California.

Frank Cushman, industrial educator, studied at the Massachusetts Institute of Technology, the Junior College of Kansas City, Missouri, and the University of Kansas. Cushman's career in education started in 1898 at the Massachusetts Institute of Technology where he served as an assistant instructor (1898–1903). He was a teacher and later vice-principal at Manual Training High School in Kansas City (1901–13). He taught in Kansas City as head of mechanic arts at Northeast High School (1914) and head of the vocational department at Central High School (1915), was in charge of the Mechanic Arts Polytechnic Institute (1916–18) and was in charge of war training work for the Kansas City public schools (1917–18).

In 1918 Cushman took a position with the federal government as agent for industrial education for the West Central states (1918–19), East Central states (1919–20), and the North Atlantic states (1920–22). He returned to Kansas City as principal of Lathrop High School for a short time and then went to Washington, D.C., as chief of the Industrial Arts Service under the Federal Board of Vocational Education in the United States Office of Education, where he was influential in the development of vocational education. He served in Washington from 1922 to 1938. He was a consultant in vocational education after 1938.

Cushman was a pioneer in the development of foreman training and preparing conference leaders. He authored *Mathematics and the Machinist's Job* (1926) and *Foremanship and Supervision* (1927) and contributed many articles and papers to educational and technical journals.

REFERENCES: *LE* (III); *WW* (XVIII); *WWW* (III); *Industrial Arts and Vocational Education* 42 (June 1953): 20.   *Ralph Dirksen*

CUTLER, Elliott Carr. B. July 30, 1888, Bangor, Maine, to George Chalmers and Mary Franklin (Wilson) Cutler. M. May 24, 1919, to Caroline Pollard Parker. Ch. five. D. August 16, 1947, Brookline, Massachusetts.

Elliott Carr Cutler, surgeon and teacher, moved with his parents from Maine to Brookline, Massachusetts. He enrolled at Harvard University where he received the B.A. (1909) and M.D. (1913) degrees. He studied pathology for a summer in Heidelberg, Germany, was a resident surgeon with the Harvard unit of the American Ambulance Hospital in Paris, France (1915), and studied immunology at the Rockefeller Institute in New York City (1916–17).

When the United States entered World War I, Cutler was commissioned a captain and was sent to France as a member of the American Expeditionary Force. He returned to Boston at the end of the war and became a resident surgeon under Harvey Cushing at Brigham Hospital.

Cutler was appointed associate in surgery at Brigham Hospital (1921) and served as director of the laboratory for surgical research and chairman of the department of surgery at Harvard Medical School (1923–24). He was professor of surgery at Western Reserve University Medical School in Cleveland, Ohio (1924–32). He was active in the development of the school and helped establish Lakeside Hospital (now a division of the University Hospitals in Cleveland) and was director of the surgical service.

When Cushing retired in 1932, Cutler returned to Harvard as Moseley Professor of Surgery and surgeon-in-chief at Peter Bent Brigham Hospital. He held both of these positions until his death in 1947. He was recalled to active military duty during World War II. He held the rank of colonel and served as chief surgical consultant and chief of the professional services division of the European theater of operations. He pioneered surgical methods and disaster and emergency practices in hospitals and was promoted to brigadier general in 1945. He was awarded the Distinguished Service Medal with an Oak Leaf Cluster, the Legion of Merit, the Order of the British Empire, the croix de guerre, and the Liberation Cross of Norway.

Cutler returned from military service in poor health; he continued to teach, conduct research, write, and practice medicine until his death in 1947.

Cutler published more than 260 papers and coauthored with Robert Zollinger *Atlas of Surgical Operations* (1939), a valuable reference for surgeons in training. He received honorary degrees from the universities of Strasbourg (France), Vermont, and Rochester and belonged to many professional societies in the United States and abroad, including the American Surgical Association (president, 1947). He was a fellow of the American College of Surgeons, member of the American-Soviet Medical Society (regional vice-president, 1945–47), the American Committee for the Protection of Medical Research (chairman, 1926–42), the Society for Clinical Surgery (president, 1941–46), and the United States Medical Consultants of World War II (president, 1946).

REFERENCES: *DAB* (supp. 4); *NCAB* (36:327); *WWAE* (I); *WWW* (II); Ralph H. Major, *A History of Medicine* (Springfield, Ill.: Charles C. Thomas Publisher, 1954), 2: 954; *NYT,* August 17, 1947, p. 52.

Richard M. Coger

CUTLER, Mary Salome. See **FAIRCHILD, Mary Salome Cutler.**

CUTTER, Calvin. B. May 1, 1807, Jaffrey, New Hampshire, to John and Mary (Batchelder) Cutter. M. n.a. D. June 20, 1872, Warren, Massachusetts.

Calvin Cutter attended the New Ipswich (New Hampshire) Academy. He taught at Wilton, New Hampshire, and Ashby, Massachusetts, and began to study medicine (1829) with an uncle, Nehemiah Cutter of Pepperell, Massachusetts. He attended lectures at Bowdoin and Dartmouth colleges and Harvard University, receiving the M.D. degree from Dartmouth in 1831. He studied privately with Valentine Mott in New York City and George McClellan in Philadelphia.

Cutter practiced medicine in New Hampshire at Rochester (1831–33), Nashua (1834–37), and Dover (1838–41). In 1842 he began a career as a public lecturer on anatomy, physiology, and hygiene (1842–56). He traveled to twenty-nine states lecturing to schools, colleges, teachers' institutes, and lyceums using mannequins and other apparatus in his demonstrations. In the 1840s he began to write schoolbooks.

An early abolitionist, Cutter was selected by a group in Boston, Massachusetts, to transport a supply of Sharp's rifles to a group of Free-Staters in Kansas during the violent struggle over that territory; the rifles were successfully delivered. He stayed in the territory for a year as commander of a company and leader of Jim Lane's army. During the Civil War, he was surgeon of the Twenty-first Massachusetts infantry and became surgeon-in-chief of the Ninth Corps of the Army of the Potomac. He was wounded twice and taken prisoner at Bull Run.

Among Cutter's books were *Cutter's Anatomy and Physiology* (1845), written as a school and college text, *The Physiological Family* (1845),

Physiology Family Physician (1845), *Physiology for Children* (1846), and
First Book on Anatomy and Physiology (1848).

REFERENCES:*AC; TC; Report of the Commissioner of Education for the
Year 1872* (Washington, D.C.: Government Printing Office, 1873), p. 182.

John F. Ohles

D

DABNEY, Charles William. B. June 19, 1855, Hampden-Sydney, Virginia,
to Robert Lewis and Margaretta Lavinia (Morrison) Dabney. M. August
24, 1881, to Mary Chilton Brent. Ch. three. D. June 15, 1945, Asheville,
North Carolina.

Charles William Dabney was an important educator, university president, and government official. He received the A.B. degree (1873) from
Hampden-Sydney (Virginia) College and studied chemistry at the University of Virginia (1874–77) and the University of Göttingen, Germany,
where he received the Ph.D. degree (1880).

He served as professor of chemistry at Emory and Henry College in
Emory, Virginia (1877–78). He accepted an appointment at the University
of North Carolina in 1880 as a professor of chemistry, but taught only
briefly before resigning to become state chemist and director of the North
Carolina Agriculture Experimental Station (1880–87). While at the experimental station, Dabney discovered phosphate deposits in eastern North
Carolina, which became important in the improvement of southern agriculture. His work and influence during this period gave impetus to the
founding of the College of Agriculture and Mechanics Arts (later, North
Carolina State University) as a land-grant institution.

He was director of the Tennessee Experiment Station (1887–90) and was
president of the University of Tennessee (1887–1904). He served as assistant secretary of agriculture (1893–97). At Tennessee, he presided during a
period of rapid growth of the university, organized a summer school for
teacher preparation, and was influential with Philander P. Claxton *(q.v.)* in
the passage of the High School Act in Tennessee.

He assumed the presidency of the University of Cincinnati and was
instrumental in bringing national recognition to the institution as a leading
municipal university (1904–20). After retiring from Cincinnati, Dabney
organized a firm of geologists and engineers for mineral and oil exploration
and wrote about the development of education in the South.

Dabney was the author of reports of the North Carolina and University of Tennessee experiment stations and *Old College and New* (1894), *A National Department of Science* (1897), *A National University* (1897), *Washington's Interest in Education* (1900), *History of Agricultural Education* (1900), *Man in the Democracy* (1904), *The Meaning of the Solid South* (1909), *Washington–Educationist* (1911), *The South Renationalized by Education* (1911), *Fighting for a New World* (1919), and *Universal Education in the South* (two volumes, 1936).

Dabney was active in professional associations; he was a fellow of the American Association for the Advancement of Science, president of the Summer School of the South at Knoxville, Tennessee (1902–04), an organizer of the Southern Education Board (1901), and in charge of government and state exhibits at exhibitions at New Orleans, Louisiana (1883), Atlanta, Georgia (1895), and the Tennessee Centennial Exhibition (1897). He received several honorary degrees.

REFERENCES: *AC; DAB* (supp. 3); *LE* (I); *NCAB* (13:310, E:323); *TC; WWW* (II); Charles W. Dabney, *Universal Education in the South* (Chapel Hill: University of North Carolina Press, 1936); Franklin R. Jones, "The Curriculum Development in Educational Administration in Eight Selected Southern Institutions Preparing School Administrators" (Ed.D. diss., Duke University, 1960); *NYT,* June 16, 1945, p. 28. *Franklin Ross Jones*

DABOLL, Nathan. B. April 24, 1750, Groton, Connecticut, to Nathan and Anna (Lynn) Daboll. M. 1804 to Elizabeth Daboll. M. to Elizabeth Brown. Ch. one, Nathan Daboll, publisher. D. March 9, 1818, Groton, Connecticut.

Nathan Daboll's early formal education was limited to the local school and special tutorage from the village parson, Reverend Jonathan Barber. With a natural aptitude in mathematics, he mastered the concepts of several branches of mathematics through self-instruction while working as a cooper. He also developed a proficiency in astronomy and navigation.

At about twenty years of age, Daboll discovered an error in the calculation of some astronomical data published in a popular almanac. The publisher, Timothy Green, employed Daboll to check other calculations in the almanac. In 1773 Green published the *New England Almanack by Nathan Daboll, Philomath.* Daboll's name appeared on the title page for the years of 1773, 1774, and 1775 and appeared again in 1793. It was continued in publication by his son Nathan and his grandson David Austin Daboll to 1896.

Daboll was a teacher of mathematics, astronomy, and navigation in Connecticut. He conducted schools in navigation at Groton and New London during the Revolutionary War and taught mathematics and astronomy at Plainfield (Connecticut) Academy (1783–88). He returned to Groton in 1788 and resumed his work as a nautical instructor to men of the merchant marine and navy. In 1811, at the invitation of Commodore John Rodgers, he taught a class of midshipmen in navigation and mathematics on the frigate *President*.

In 1799 Daboll published *Daboll's Complete Schoolmaster's Assistant*, an early United States arithmetic textbook. He prepared a navigation text, *Daboll's Practical Navigation*, which was published in 1820, two years after his death.

REFERENCES: *AC; DAB; NCAB* (23:403); *TC; WWW* (H).

H. Keith Stumpff

DALE, Edgar. B. April 17, 1900, Benson, Minnesota, to Eric and Mary Dorothy (Romfo) Dale. M. August 7, 1926, to Elizabeth Kirchner. Ch. two.

Edgar Dale was acknowledged as a major contributor to the study of educational communications. He earned the B.A. (1921) and M.A. (1924) degrees from the University of North Dakota. In 1928 he received the Ph.D. degree from the University of Chicago.

He was a teacher in a small rural school in North Dakota (1918–19). He was superintendent of schools at Webster, North Dakota (1921–24), and a teacher at the junior high school at Winnetka, Illinois (1924–26). His interest in film led to a position with Eastman Kodak as a member of the editorial staff of Eastman Teaching Films (1928–29). He took a position with Ohio State University as research associate in the Bureau of Educational Research and continued as professor of education (1929–70). He was responsible for the simplification and clarification of educational reading materials and the development of a readability formula for measuring grade levels of reading materials.

During World War II, Dale was in charge of the coordination division of the Bureau of Motion Pictures, Office of War Information. He was a consultant to the War Department on the production of instructional training films and technical adviser to the first motion picture unit in Hollywood for the film *Instructional Methods in the Army Air Forces*.

Dale wrote many books and articles, including *How to Appreciate Motion Pictures* (1935), *Teaching with Motion Pictures* (1937), *How to Read a Newspaper* (1941), *Audio Visual Methods in Teaching* (1946), *Can You Give the Public What It Wants?* (1967), *Techniques of Teaching Vocabulary* (1971), and *Building a Learning Environment* (1972). He produced three readers used in the literacy program of the armed services and chaired the committee that produced *Mass Media and Education*, the fifty-third yearbook of the National Society for the Study of Education (1954). Dale was editor of *The News Letter* for some thirty-six years until his retirement. He served on the editorial board of *Read Magazine* and the advisory board of World Book Encyclopedia.

He was the Educational Film Library Association's representative to the

United States National Commission for the United Nations Educational, Scientific, and Cultural Organization (1947–51), served on the Commission on Technical Needs in Press, Film and Radio (chairman, 1949), was president of the Department of Audio-Visual Instruction of the National Education Association (1937–38), and a member of boards of the National Society for the Study of Education, the Educational Policies Commission, and the National Association for Better Broadcasting. He was chairman of the Motion Picture Committee of the National Congress of Parents and Teachers.

Dale received the first Educational Film Library Association Award (1961), the Eastman Kodak Gold Medal Award (1968), and the Distinguished Services Award by the Association for Educational Communications and Technology (1972).

REFERENCES: *LE* (III); *WW* (XXXVIII); *WWAE* (XIII); J. B. Fullen, "Leaders in Education," *Education* 80 (May 1960): 572; "Interview with Edgar Dale," *Theory into Practice* 9 (April 1970): 107–09; "Leader in Education," *Education* 87 (April 1967): 502; Keith I. Tyler and Catharine M. Williams, eds., *Educational Communication in a Revolutionary Age* (Worthington, Ohio: Charles A. Jones Publishing Co., 1973); R. W. Wagner, "Edgar Dale, Professional," *Theory into Practice* 9 (April 1970): 89–95. *Charles L. Maynard*

DALTON, John Call. B. February 2, 1825, Chelmsford, Massachusetts, to John Call and Julia Ann (Spalding) Dalton. M. no. D. February 12, 1889, New York, New York.

John Call Dalton was graduated from Harvard University (1844) and received the M.D. degree from Harvard Medical School (1847). He went to Paris, France, where he studied under the French physiologist Claude Bernard. He became the first physician in the United States to devote his life to experimental physiology and was the first to illustrate lectures with living animals, an experimental method made possible by the discovery of ether. In 1851 he won a prize from the American Medical Association for an essay, "Corpus Luteam."

Dalton served as professor of physiology in the medical department of the University of Buffalo, New York (1851–54), Vermont Medical College at Woodstock (1854–56), Long Island (New York) College Hospital (1859–61), and the College of Physicians and Surgeons in New York City (1855–83). He was president of the College of Physicians and Surgeons from 1884 until his death in 1889.

His publications, based on experiments, include *Treatise on Human Physiology* (1859), *A Treatise on Physiology and Hygiene* (1868), *Experimentation on Animals as a Means of Knowledge, in Physiology, Pathology, and Practical Medicine* (1875), *The Experimental Method in Medical*

Science (1882), *Doctrines of the Circulation* (1884), and *Topographical Anatomy of the Brain* (1885). He contributed extensively to medical journals. His most important physiological research, "Sugar Formation in the Liver," was published in *Transactions of the New York Academy of Medicine* (1871), in which he confirmed the work of Claude Bernard.

Dalton served as brigadier general of the medical corps of the volunteer army during the Civil War and in the last year of his life wrote of this experience. Though uncompleted, it was privately published in 1892 under the title *John Call Dalton, M.D. U.S.V.* He was a member of many American and European societies. He was elected a member of the National Academy of Sciences (1864) and the New York Academy of Medicine (vice-president, 1874–77).

REFERENCES: *AC; DAB; NCAB* (10:500); *TC; WWW* (H); *NYT,* February 13, 1889, p. 2.   *C. Roy Rylander*

DAMROSCH, Frank Heino. B. June 22, 1859, Breslau, Germany, to Leopold and Helene (von Heimburg) Damrosch. M. January 10, 1888, to Hetty Mosenthal. Ch. none. D. October 22, 1937, New York, New York.

Frank Heino Damrosch, son of Leopold Damrosch, leading Wagnerian conductor and director of the Metropolitan Opera Company, was a student of piano at the age of seven. He moved to New York with his family in 1871, where he attended New York City public schools and the College of the City of New York. He studied music under his father and other eminent musicians.

Damrosch chose a commercial career and clerked in a Denver, Colorado, hat store but gradually became involved in music as a church organist, conductor, and music teacher. He conducted the Denver Chorus Club (1882–84) and was the first supervisor of music in the Denver public schools (1884–85). On the death of his father, he returned to New York as chorusmaster of the Metropolitan Opera House (1885–91).

Damrosch was conductor of the Newark (New Jersey) Harmonic Society (1886–87). He organized the People's Singing Classes (1892) that developed into the People's Choral Union, where he instructed workers in sight reading and choral singing. He continued this group to 1912 and was the conductor of other singing groups in New York and Philadelphia, Pennsylvania. He was a founder of the Musical Art Society and its conductor to 1920. He was supervisor of music for the New York City public schools (1897–1905) and succeeded his brother Walter as conductor of the Oratorio Society (1898–1912), founded by Leopold Damrosch in 1874. He was the director of the Institute of Musical Art in New York at its inception in 1905 and continued as dean (1926–33) when it became affiliated with the Juilliard School of Music and served as the undergraduate branch of instruction. He was a brother of Clara Damrosch Mannes *(q.v.).*

Damrosch was the author of *Popular Method of Sight Singing* (1894), *Some Essentials in the Teaching of Music* (1916), and *Institute of Musical Art 1905–26* (1936). He received an honorary degree from Yale University in 1904.

REFERENCES: *DAB* (supp. 2); *LE* (I); *NCAB* (31:209); *NYT*, October 23, 1937, p. 17; *WWW* (I); Nicholas Slonimsky, *Baker's Biographical Dictionary of Musicians*, 5th ed. (New York: G. Schirmer, 1958).

John F. Ohles

DANA, James Dwight. B. February 13, 1813, Utica, New York, to James and Harriet (Dwight) Dana. M. June 5, 1844, to Henrietta Frances Silliman. Ch. four, including Edward S. Dana, American mineralogist. D. April 14, 1895, New Haven, Connecticut.

James Dwight Dana was an outstanding authority in the fields of geology, zoology, and mineralogy. The oldest of ten children, he spent his childhood in Utica, New York, and enrolled in the Charles Bartlett Academy. An excellent student, he showed an aptitude for mathematics and the natural sciences. He was graduated from Yale College with honors in 1833 but left before the graduation ceremony to accept an appointment as instructor of mathematics to midshipmen aboard the U.S.S. *Delaware* in the Mediterranean. Three years later he returned to Yale and for a short period served as an assistant to Benjamin Silliman (*q.v.*), professor of natural history, who became his lifelong friend and whose daughter, Henrietta, he married.

On Silliman's retirement in 1849, Dana was appointed Silliman Professor of Natural History at Yale and began his duties there in 1855. In 1864 his professorship was changed to geology and mineralogy, a position he held until his resignation in 1893 because of ill health.

In addition to his forty-four years as a professor at Yale, Dana's scientific expeditions and writings were highly significant. In 1837 he was appointed geologist and mineralogist on the United States exploratory expedition to the South Seas under Captain Charles Wilkes (1838–42). For thirteen years after his return Dana spent a considerable amount of his time in Washington writing up the reports of the expedition.

Dana was the author of major scientific and academic works. His first paper on geology, which described a visit to Vesuvius volcano on his Mediterranean expedition, appeared in the *American Journal of Science* (1835). His major publications were reports of the Wilkes expedition illustrated with his own drawings: *Report on Zoöphytes* (1846), *Report on the Geology of the Pacific* (1849), and *Report on Crustacea* (1852–54). Dana also wrote *System of Mineralogy* (1837), *Manual of Geology* (1862), *Textbook of Geology* (1864), *Corals and Coral Islands* (1872), and *Characteristics of Volcanoes* (1890) at the age of seventy-seven.

He served as the editor of the *American Journal of Science* (1846–95).

Dana received many American and international awards and high honors. He was president of the American Association for the Advancement of Science (1854). He was awarded the Walleston Medal by the Geological Society of London (1872), the Copley Medal by the Royal Society of London (1877), and the Walker Prize by the Boston Society of Natural History (1892). He was a charter member of the National Academy of Sciences in the United States and an honorary member of several foreign academies. He received honorary degrees from the University of Munich, Harvard University, and the University of Edinburgh.

In spite of poor health during the last thirty-five years of his life, James Dwight Dana was an energetic and tireless writer and educator. He was acknowledged as America's foremost natural scientist throughout his active life.

REFERENCES: *AC; DAB; DSB; NCAB* (30:330); *TC; WWW* (H); C. E. Beecher, "James Dwight Dana," *American Geologist* 17 (1896); Edward S. Dana, "James Dwight Dana," *American Journal of Science* 49 (1895); Daniel Coit Gilman (*q.v.*), *The Life of James Dwight Dana* (New York: Harper & Bros., 1899); *NYT,* April 15, 1895, p. 1.   *Walter F. C. Ade*

DANN, Hollis Ellsworth. B. May 1, 1861, Canton, Pennsylvania, to Judson and Harriet (Harding) Dann. M. July 10, 1890, to Lois Hanford. Ch. four. D. January 3, 1939, New York, New York.

Hollis Ellsworth Dann was graduated from Canton (Pennsylvania) High School (1879) and Elmira (New York) Business College (1887), and he attended a Rochester, New York, music school (1879–80) and engaged in private instruction in Boston, Massachusetts (1881–83).

A teacher of voice and piano from 1884 to 1886, he was principal of the Havana (New York) Academy (1886–87). He was director of music for the Ithaca (New York) public schools (1887–1905). Dann was a member of the faculty of Cornell University in Ithaca, New York (1903–21), and head of the department of music (1906–21). He was director of music for the state of Pennsylvania (1921–25) and head of the department of music education at New York University (1925–36). He gained national recognition in the field of music education.

Dann was involved in the direction of musical performance and education programs as director of the Ithaca Choral Club (1890–1900), member of the faculty of the New School of Methods in Boston, Massachusetts (1896–1906), conductor of the Sage Chapel Choir at Cornell (1903–21), conductor of Annual Music Festivals at Cornell (1904–21), director of the Pennsylvania Summer Session for Supervisors of Music at West Chester (1922–24), and conductor of the first National High School Chorus in Chicago, Illinois, in 1928 and again in 1930.

Dann was the author of many papers and pamphlets on music in the public schools; he also wrote *Complete Manual for Teachers* (1912), *Hollis Dann Music Course* (1915–19), and *New Manual for Teachers* (1929) and compiled *Christmas Carols and Hymns* (1910), *School Hymnal* (1910), *Assembly Songs* (two volumes, 1911, 1914), *Standard Anthems* (four volumes; 1917, 1921, 1924), Hollis Dann Song Series (1935), and *Conductors Book* (1935).

Active in professional associations, Dann was president of the Music Educators National Conference (1920–21) and chairman of the music council for the New York Board of Regents (1910–21). He conducted the National Supervisors Chorus in Chicago (1934). Dann received an honorary degree from Alfred (New York) University in 1906.

REFERENCES: *LE* (I); *WWW* (I); Louis Woodson Curtis, "Hollis Dann," *Music Educators Journal* 25 (February 1939): 24; Osbourne McConathy *(q.v.)*, "Recollections of Hollis Dann," *Music Educators Journal* 26 (September 1939): 17–18; *NYT*, January 4, 1939, p. 21. *John F. Ohles*

DAVENPORT, Charles Benedict. B. June 1, 1866, Stamford, Connecticut, to Amzi Benedict and Jane Joralemon (Dimon) Davenport. M. June 23, 1894, to Gertrude Crotty. Ch. three. D. February 18, 1944, Huntington, New York.

Charles Benedict Davenport's father founded and taught at a private academy in Brooklyn, New York, and was responsible for his son's early education. At the age of thirteen, Davenport entered the Polytechnic Institute of Brooklyn, where he was an outstanding student. He was graduated with a B.S. degree (1886) in civil engineering. Enrolling in Harvard University, he majored in zoology, receiving the A.B. (1889) and Ph.D. (1892) degrees. He became an instructor at Harvard and remained there until 1899 when he taught zoology and embryology and was curator of the zoological museum at the University of Chicago (1899–1904). He was affiliated with the Carnegie Institution as director of the Station for Environmental Evolution (Cold Spring Harbor, Long Island, New York, 1904–34) and director of the department of eugenics and the Eugenic Record Office (1910–34).

Among the over four hundred publications credited to Davenport were *Statistical Methods with Reference to Biological Variation* (1899), *Inheritance in Poultry* (1909), *Inheritance of Characteristics of Fowl* (1909), *Eugenics* (1910), *Elements of Zoology* (1911), *Heredity in Relation to Eugenics* (1911), *Heredity of Skin Color in Negro-White Crosses* (1913), *Defects Found in Drafted Men* (1920), *Body Build and Its Inheritance* (1923), *Genetical Factor in Endemic Goiter* (1932), and *How We Came by Our Bodies* (1936).

A fellow of the American Academy of Arts and Sciences and the American Association for the Advancement of Science, Davenport was a member of many scientific societies, including the American Philosophical Society, the National Academy of Sciences, the American Society of Zoologists (president, 1902–03, 1920–30), the American Genetic Association, the Eugenics Research Association (honorary president, 1937), the Galton Society (president, 1918–30), and the International Federation of Eugenic Organizations (president, 1927–32). He received the gold medal of the National Institute of Social Sciences (1923). He presided over the Third International Congress of Eugenics in 1932.

REFERENCES: *CB* (April 1944); *DAB* (supp. 3); *DSB; LE* (I); *NCAB* (15:397); *NYT,* February 19, 1944, p. 13; *WWW* (II).   *Lew E. Wise*

DAVENPORT, Eugene. B. June 20, 1856, Woodland, Michigan, to George Martin and Esther (Sutton) Davenport. M. November 2, 1881, to Emma Jane Coats. Ch. two. D. March 31, 1941, Woodland, Michigan.

Eugene Davenport attended the Michigan Agricultural College (later, Michigan State University) where he received the B.S. (1878), M.S. (1884), and M.Agr. (1895) degrees.

Davenport was assistant botanist at the experiment station at the Michigan Agricultural College (1888–89) and professor of practical agriculture and superintendent of the college farm (1889–91). He was president of Collegio Agronomica in São Paulo, Brazil (1891–92) and became dean of the college of agriculture of the University of Illinois (1895–1922) and director of the agricultural experiment station and professor of thremmatology (1896–1922). An outstanding contributor to the development of agriculture in Illinois, Davenport organized farm associations and was a major influence in establishing crop rotation practices. From 1895 to 1922, the college of agriculture increased from nine students to twelve hundred students. Experimental stations were established at Urbana and in other parts of the state; there were forty by 1922.

Writer of many journal articles, Davenport also was the author of *Principles of Breeding* (1907), *Education for Efficiency* (1909), *Domesticated Animals and Plants* (1910), *Vacation on the Trail* (1923), and *The Farm* (1927). He was a fellow of the American Association for the Advancement of Science and a member of other organizations. He was the single antirepeal delegate to the Michigan Constitutional Convention that passed the resolution to repeal the Eighteenth Amendment, the first state to do so. Davenport was the recipient of four honorary degrees.

REFERENCES: *CB* (May 1941); *LE* (I); *NYT,* April 1, 1941, p. 23; *WWAE* (VIII); *WWW* (I); *School and Society* 53 (April 5, 1941): 440.   *John F. Ohles*

DAVIDSON, Charles. B. July 29, 1852, Streetsboro, Ohio, to David Botsford and Jeanette (Parker) Davidson. M. August 21, 1878, to Hannah Amelia Noyes *(q.v.).* Ch. one. D. November 24, 1919, Claremont, California.

Charles Davidson received his early education in Ohio district schools and at Grinnell (Iowa) Academy. He received the B.A. (1875) and A.M. (1878) degrees from Iowa (later, Grinnell) College. He was a student at Yale College (1876–77 and 1891–92) and the University of California (1887–90) with Albert Stanburrough Cook *(q.v.)*. He received the Ph.D. degree (1892) from Yale. His doctoral dissertation, "Studies in the English Mystery Plays," was published in 1892 and given a wide distribution.

At the age of sixteen, Davidson was a teacher of a district school located in his father's house in Chester, Iowa. While a graduate student at Iowa College, he taught in the college preparatory school (1877–78). He taught languages in the Mitchell (Iowa) Seminary (1878–79) and moved to Minneapolis, Minnesota, where he founded and was principal of the Minneapolis Academy (1879–84). He was superintendent of schools in Dalles City, Oregon (1884–86), and taught English at the Belmont (California) School (1889–93).

Davidson taught English at the University of Indiana (1893–94) and Adelbert College of Western Reserve University (later, Case Western Reserve) in Cleveland, Ohio (1894–96). He served as English inspector for the regents of the University of the State of New York (1896–1904). He reorganized the teaching of English in the New York schools. He was professor at the University of Maine (1906–11) and established courses for high school teachers and the preparation of principals and school superintendents. He retired to Claremont, California, in 1911.

Davidson was the author of many books, including *Phonology of the Stressed Vowels in Beowulf* (1891), *English in the Secondary School* (1896), *Leaves from an English Inspector's Note-Book* (1903), *The Aims and Organization of Instruction in Composition* (1904), *The Necessary Equipment of Teachers of English* (1904), *English a Factor in the Training of the Business Man* (1904), *English Composition in the Grades* (1905), *Motor Work and Formal Studies in the Primary Grades* (1911), and *Active Citizenship* (1915).

REFERENCES: *NCAB* (19:211); *TC; WWW* (I).   *John F. Ohles*

DAVIDSON, Hannah Amelia Noyes. B. October 29, 1852, Campello, Massachusetts, to Spencer Williams and Mary (Packard) Noyes. M. August 21, 1878, to Charles Davidson *(q.v.)*. Ch. one. D. November 29, 1932, Claremont, California.

Hannah Noyes Davidson attended Iowa (later, Grinnell) College where she received the A.B. (1878) and A.M. (1881) degrees. She was a student of politics, finance, and economics at the University of Minnesota (1886–87) and studied at the University of California (1887–88). She enrolled at the University of Chicago during the summer terms of 1894 and 1895.

She studied Sanskrit and taught at Mitchell (Iowa) Seminary (1878–79) and was principal and teacher at the Minneapolis (Minnesota) Academy

(1879–84). She taught history and English composition in the Dalles City (Oregon) high school (1885–86) and English and history at the Belmont (California) School (1887–93). Davidson lectured on literary art in fiction and drama at Wellesley and Mount Holyoke colleges. From 1902, she directed summer classes for the study of English.

Davidson was the author of *Reference History of the United States* (1892), *Franklin's Services in the Cause of American Independence* (1909), *Value and Use of Biography in the Formation of Character* (1912), and *Studies in Modern Plays* (1915). She also edited *Autobiography and Memoir of David Otis Mears, D.D.* (1919). She produced the Riverside Series of *Silas Marner, Vicar of Wakefield, House of Seven Gables,* and others. She was author, editor, and publisher of the Study-Guide Series of ten books and Study-Guide Courses.

REFERENCES: *NCAB* (19:212); *WWW* (I); *NYT,* November 30, 1932, p. 15.   *John F. Ohles*

DAVIDSON, Thomas. B. October 25, 1840, Deer, Aberdeenshire, Scotland, to Thomas and Mary (Warrender) Davidson. M. no. D. September 14, 1900, Montreal, Canada.

After graduation from Aberdeen (Scotland) University with highest honors in Greek (1860), Thomas Davidson was master of schools in Scotland and England until 1866. He taught for one year at the Collegiate Institute in London, Ontario, Canada (1866–67), and moved to St. Louis, Missouri, where he taught briefly. He went to Boston, Massachusetts, where he became acquainted with William James *(q.v.)* and remained in the United States until 1878, earning a modest income tutoring, lecturing, and writing.

Davidson lived and studied in Europe from 1878 until 1884, founding the Fellowship of the New Life in 1883, a precursor of the Fabian Society. He returned to the United States where he founded two innovative schools, the Summer School of Cultural Sciences in New York's Adirondack Mountains and the Bread Winner's College on the Lower East Side of New York City (1898). It was founded on the belief that the wage earner should have opportunities to acquire an education.

He was the author of *The Philosophical System of Antonio Rosmini-Serbati* (1882), *The Parthenon Frieze and Other Essays* (1882), *Scartayini's Handbook to Dante* (1887), *Prolegomena to in Memoriam* (1892), *Education of the Greek People and Its Influence on Civilization* (1894), *Rousseau and Education According to Nature* (1898), and *A History of Education* (1900). He translated Rosmini's *Psychology* (1883) and was a frequent contributor to philosophical periodicals.

REFERENCES: *DAB; NCAB* (23:311); *WWW* (I); Louis I. Diblin, "Thomas Davidson: Educator for Democracy," *The American Scholar* (Spring 1948): 201; *NYT,* September 22, 1900.   *Karen L. Hadley*

DAVIES, Charles. B. January 22, 1798, Washington, Connecticut, to Thomas John and Ruth (Foote) Davies. M. to Mary Anne Mansfield. Ch. one. D. September 17, 1876, Fishkill-on-Hudson, New York.

Charles Davies attended public schools until he was fifteen years old, when he was admitted to the United States Military Academy at West Point, New York. He was graduated on December 11, 1815, and was commissioned as a brevet second lieutenant. He was assigned to the Corps of Engineers in 1816 but resigned to become a subordinate tutor for one year and principal assistant professor of mathematics at the Military Academy (1816–21). He was assistant professor of natural philosophy (1821–23) and professor of mathematics from 1823 to 1837 when ill health forced him to leave West Point. He traveled for a year in Europe to regain his health and served as professor of mathematics at Trinity College in Hartford, Connecticut (1837–41). Davies returned to West Point in 1841 as paymaster of the academy and a member of the board of visitors until 1846, when he moved to New York City.

Davies was professor of mathematics and natural philosophy at the University of New York (later, New York University) in 1848–49. He retired to Fishkill Landing on the Hudson River to engage in writing textbooks and taught at the New York Normal School (later, State University of New York at Albany) in Albany and taught higher mathematics at Columbia College (later, University) from 1857 to 1865.

Davies was a prolific writer of mathematical textbooks, including seven different arithmetics, four algebras, three geometries, a calculus book, a combined geometry and trigonometry, a general mathematics book, and one dealing with survey of navigation. The more notable of his books are *Elements of Descriptive Geometry* (1826), *Elements of Surveying* (1830), *The Common School Arithmetic* (1831), *Shades, Shadows, and Perspectives* (1832), *Differential and Integral Calculus* (1836), *Elements of Analytical Geometry* (1836), *First Lessons in Algebra* (1838), *The Logic and Utility of Mathematics with the Best Methods of Instruction Explained and Illustrated* (1850), *Mathematical Dictionary* (with his son-in-law, William G. Peck, *q.v.*, 1855), and *The Metric System* (1870). Nearly every school and academy in the United States during the mid-1800s used a Davies' mathematics textbook.

Davies was active in education associations, serving as president of the Teachers' Association of New York and a fellow of the American Academy of Arts and Sciences. He was employed by Congress to report on mathematical questions relating to legislative issues. He was the recipient of several honorary degrees.

REFERENCES: *AC; NCAB* (3:26); *TC; WWW* (H); Charles Carpenter, *History of American School Books* (Philadelphia: University of Pennsylvania Press, 1976), *NYT,* September 19, 1876, p. 4.

Earl E. Keese

DAVIS, Calvin Olin. B. February 5, 1871, Macomb, Michigan, to Calvin and Roselia (Phillips) Davis. M. December 27, 1904, to Winifred Ellen Mack. Ch. one. D. June 22, 1954, Ann Arbor, Michigan.

After attending Utica (Michigan) High School, Calvin Davis began his teaching career at the age of sixteen in the public schools of Macomb County. With five years' teaching experience, he entered the University of Michigan in 1892 and was graduated with the A.B. degree (1895). He later received the A.M. degree (1904) from Michigan and the Ph.D. degree (1910) from Harvard University.

He was a high school teacher (1895–1905) and principal (1905) of the South Bend, Indiana, high school. He was an instructor in the science and art of teaching, inspector of high schools, and professor of education at the University of Michigan (1905–41) and secretary of the school of education when it was organized in 1921 until his retirement in 1941. He played a major role in the development of the junior high school.

Davis was a prolific author of articles and books, including *The Six-Three-Three Plan of Administration of Schools* (1917), which was one of the earliest books on the junior high school movement. He also wrote *High School Education* (with others, 1912), *High School Courses of Study* (1914), *A Guide to Methods and Observation in History* (1914), *The Modern High School* (with others, 1914), *Public Secondary Education* (1917), *Junior High School Education* (1924), *Problems of the Junior High School* (with E. E. Lewis, 1925), *Our Secondary Schools* (1925), *Our Evolving High School Curriculum* (1927), and *History of the North Central Association of Colleges and Secondary Schools* (1944). He was editor of the *North Central Association Proceedings* (1918–25) and *North Central Association Quarterly* (1926–41) and an associate editor of *Clearing House*.

REFERENCES: *LE* (III); *WWW* (III); *WWAE* (XIII); *Ann Arbor* (Michigan) *News,* June 23, 1954, p. 19; "Memorial: Calvin Olin Davis," *University of Michigan School of Education Bulletin* 26 (October 1954): 3–4.   *Charles V. Partridge*

DAVIS, Henry. B. September 15, 1771, Easthampton, New York, to John and Mary (Conkling) Davis. M. September 22, 1801, to Hannah Phoenix Treadwell. Ch. four, including Thomas Treadwell Davis, lawyer and congressman. D. March 8, 1852, Clinton, New York.

Henry Davis's family lived at Stonington, Connecticut, during the Revolutionary War and returned to Easthampton, Long Island, New York, in 1784. Davis received his early education at Clinton Academy at Easthampton. He planned for a career in medicine but changed to the ministry. He studied classics independently, was admitted to the sophomore class at Yale College in 1793, and was graduated with honors in 1796. He served as a tutor at Williams College in Williamstown, Massachusetts (1796–98). Davis studied theology with Charles Backus and was licensed to preach by the association of Tolland County.

He was a tutor at Yale College and was appointed professor of divinity in 1801 but resigned because of poor health in 1803. When his health improved, he was professor of Greek at Union College in Schenectady, New York (1806–09). He was president of Middlebury (Vermont) College (1809–17) and of Hamilton College in Clinton, New York (1817–23), and served as a trustee of Hamilton until 1847. His term of office encompassed some of the stormiest and most critical times of Hamilton's history.

Davis was active in many educational and religious associations, such as the American Board of Commissions for Foreign Missions. He helped establish the Auburn (New York) Theological Seminary and served on the board of trustees until 1834 (president, 1820–24). He was the author of many published sermons and of *Narrative of the Embarrassments and Decline of Hamilton College* (1833).

REFERENCES: *DAB; NCAB* (7:405); *WWW* (H); Walter Pilkington, *Hamilton College: A History, 1812–1962* (Clinton, N.Y.: Hamilton College, 1962).   *J. Franklin Hunt*

DAVIS, Jesse Buttrick. B. March 2, 1871, Chicago, Illinois, to Simon L. and Sarah W. (Buttrick) Davis. M. September 2, 1897, to Lillian B. Drewery. Ch. three. D. November 2, 1955, Newton, Massachusetts.

Jesse B. Davis was born in Chicago, but his family moved to Keeseville, New York, after the death of his father. In 1876 his mother married John Mathews, a Baptist minister who was influential in directing Davis toward a career helping others. When he was twelve years old, his family left upstate New York and moved to Detroit, Michigan. Upon completion of elementary and high school, Davis attended Colgate University in Hamilton, New York, and was graduated with the A.B. degree (1895).

After graduation, he returned to Detroit to teach in his old high school (1895–1907). He moved to Grand Rapids, Michigan, in 1907 as principal of the high school (1907–20) and director of vocational guidance (1912–20).

Davis played a major role in the establishment of a junior college in Grand Rapids in 1914. Supported by the University of Michigan, he presented a plan to the state board of education, which appropriated the funds for the first year of the college. He was president of the Grand Rapids Junior College (1914–20) and supervisor of secondary education for the state of Connecticut (1920–24). He was professor of secondary education at Boston University (1924–50), dean of the school of education (1935–42), and administrative assistant (1942–51). Davis was a frequent lecturer in education, including at the Yale (1921–24) and Harvard (1924–32) graduate schools of education.

Davis was identified with the guidance and counseling movement. His first guidance efforts were at Detroit Central High School where he sought to aid students in selecting occupational fields and studies leading to that goal. He developed a systematic guidance program in Grand Rapids. As school enrollments increased, he employed more counselors and was concerned about the character, ideals, and personality of people seeking these positions. He has been credited with establishing the first guidance programs in public schools.

Davis was the author of *Vocational and Moral Guidance* (1914) and the autobiographical *The Saga of a Schoolmaster,* which was published posthumously in 1956. He was active in professional associations, including helping found the National Vocational Guidance Association (president, 1914–16) and the National Education Association Department of Secondary School Principals (president, 1917).

REFERENCES: *LE* (III); *WWW* (III); *WWAE* (I); Jesse Buttrick Davis, *The Saga of a Schoolmaster* (Boston: Boston University Press, 1956); *NYT,* November 3, 1955, p. 31.   *Gary M. Miller*

DAVIS, John Warren. B. February 11, 1888, Milledgeville, Georgia, to Robert Marion and Katie (Mann) Davis. M. August 24, 1916, to Bessie Rucker. M. September 2, 1932, to Ethel McGhee. Ch. three.

John Warren Davis was graduated from Morehouse College in Atlanta, Georgia, with the A.B. (1911) and A.M. (1920) degrees. He studied at the University of Chicago (1911–13) before returning to Morehouse to teach (1911–15) and serve as registrar (1914–17).

Davis was executive secretary of the 12th Street Young Men's Christian Association in Washington, D.C. (1917–19). At the age of thirty-one (1919), he became president of West Virginia State College, retiring as president emeritus in 1953. The college was considered a model of black public higher education. Under Davis's leadership it was the first historically black college to enroll large numbers of white students.

Davis was the author of two bulletins published by West Virginia State College, *Land-grant Colleges for Negroes* (1934) and *Problems in the Collegiate Education of Negroes* (1937). He was president of the Association of Teachers in Colored Schools (1928), vice-president from 1948 of the National Freedom Day Association, chairman of the National Education Association Committee for the Defense of Democracy through Education (1950–52), and a member of the United States National Commission for the United Nations Educational, Scientific, and Cultural Organization (1960–62), the North Central Association of Colleges and Secondary Schools, and other professional organizations.

He received the James Weldon Johnson Award (1954), was decorated by the government of Haiti, and was awarded honorary degrees from many colleges and universities, including the University of Liberia.

REFERENCES: *LE* (III); *WW* (XXXVI); Wilhelmena S. Robinson, *International Library of Negro Life and History: Historical Negro Biographies* (New York: Publishers Co., 1967), pp. 179–80. *Walter C. Daniel*

DAVIS, Nathan Smith. B. January 9, 1817, Greene, New York, to Dow and Eleanor (Smith) Davis. M. March 5, 1838, to Anna Maria Parker. Ch. three. D. June 16, 1904, Chicago, Illinois.

Nathan Smith Davis, Father of the American Medical Association, received his early education in Chenango and Madison counties, New York. At the age of seventeen he started studying medicine under Dr. Daniel Clark in Smithville Flats, New York. He took three courses in medicine at the College of Physicians and Surgeons of the Western District of New York at Fairfield and was graduated in January 1837.

Davis started practicing medicine in Vienna, New York, and moved to Binghamton, New York, in 1838. He was secretary of the Broome County Medical Society (1841–43), and he represented the county society at the New York State Medical Society (1843–46). At the 1843 meeting of the state society, he presented a resolution concerning the standards of medical education, which led to the organization of the American Medical Association.

Davis went to New York City in 1847, where he was associated with the College of Physicians and Surgeons and lectured on medical jurisprudence. He moved to Chicago in 1849 and became a professor in physiology and pathology at Rush Medical College. In 1850 he was chairman of the department of principles and practice of medicine and of clinical medicine. While at Rush, he headed a movement for the introduction of a sewage system, an adequate water supply, and the establishment of a public hospital in the city of Chicago. He was influential in the establishment of Mercy Hospital.

In 1859 Davis and others from the faculty of Rush Medical College founded the medical department of Lind University (later, the Chicago Medical College and medical school at Northwestern University). Davis was professor of principles and practice of medicine (1859–89). He was dean of the faculty (1859–98) and was able to put into practice many of his ideas on medical education.

Among the books he wrote were *A Text Book on Agriculture* (1848), *History of Medical Education and Institutions in the United States* (1851), *History of the American Medical Association* (1855), *Clinical Lectures on Various Important Diseases* (1873), *Lectures on the Principles and Practice of Medicine* (1884), and *History of Medicine, with the Code of Medical Ethics* (1903). Davis was the founder and editor of *Chicago Medical Examiner* (1860–73) and editor of several other professional journals, including the *Annalist* (1847–49), *Chicago Medical Journal* (1855–59), *Northwestern Journal of Education and Literary Review, American Medi-*

cal *Temperance Quarterly,* and *The Journal of the American Medical Association.*

Davis was among those who organized the Illinois Medical Society and the Chicago Medical Society. He was a founder of the Chicago Academy of Science, the Chicago Historical Society, the Union College of Law, and a founder and trustee of Northwestern University. He was an honorary member of many medical and scientific societies in America and abroad.

REFERENCES: *AC; DAB; NCAB* (35:26); *TC; WWW* (III); *NYT,* June 17, 1904, p. 9.   *Richard M. Coger*

DAVIS, Noah Knowles. B. May 15, 1830, Philadelphia, Pennsylvania, to Noah and Mary (Young) Davis. M. November 25, 1856, to Ella Hunt. Ch. none. D. May 3, 1910, Charlottesville, Virginia.

Noah Knowles Davis's father died two months after his birth, and his mother married another Baptist minister, the Reverend John L. Dagg. The family moved to Alabama where Dagg became the president of Mercer University in 1844. Davis was graduated from Mercer with the A.B. (1849) and A.M. (1853) degrees. He studied chemistry, was a teacher, and worked in an architect's office for several years.

Davis was associated with several Baptist institutions in the South as a teacher of natural science at Howard College (later, Samford University) at Birmingham, Alabama (1852–59), principal of Judson Female Institute at Marion, Alabama (1859–65), and president of Bethel College of Russellville, Kentucky (1868–73). During these years he gave increasing attention to metaphysical studies. He assumed the chair of moral philosophy at the University of Virginia (1873–1906).

He gave a religious discourse each Sunday for many years to a university audience; these were later published in three religious volumes. Davis wrote extensively on metaphysical topics. He wrote *The Theory of Thought* (1880), reputed to be the most comprehensive treatise on logic in English. Several of his books were widely used as undergraduate textbooks, such as *Elements of Deductive Logic* (1890), *Elements of Inductive Logic* (1895), and *Elements on Ethics* (1900). He also wrote *Elements of Psychology* (1892), *Juda's Jewels, a Study in the Hebrew Ethics* (1895), *Synopsis of Events in the Life of Jesus of Nazareth* (1900), and *The Story of the Nazarene* (1903).

REFERENCES: *AC; DAB; NCAB* (4:76); *TC; WWW* (I).

Harold D. Lehman

DAVIS, William Morris. B. February 12, 1850, Philadelphia, Pennsylvania, to Edward M. and Martha (Mott) Davis. M. November 28, 1879, to Ellen B. Warner. M. December 12, 1914, to Mary M. Wyman. M. August 13, 1928, to Lucy L. Tennant. Ch. none. D. February 5, 1934, Pasadena, California.

William Morris Davis entered the Lawrence Scientific School at Harvard University at the age of sixteen, receiving the S.B. degree (1869) and the master of engineering degree with honors (1870). He served for three years as a meteorologist for the Argentine Meteorological Observatory at Cordoba. Davis taught at Harvard University, serving as professor of physical geography and geology (1876–1912).

Davis authored over five hundred published works during his career. He wrote *Elementary Meteorology* in 1894, which was a standard college textbook. In *The Rivers and Valleys of Pennsylvania* (1889) he introduced the Davisian system of landscape analysis, a process to describe the origin of a landscape; *Physical Geography* (1898) and *Geographical Essays* (1909) followed. He was visiting professor to the University of Berlin, Germany (1908–09), and the Sorbonne, Paris, France (1911–12). His German lectures were published in the classic *Die erklärende Beschreibung der Landformen* (1912), possibly the most comprehensive statement of his philosophy.

Davis also wrote *Illustrations of the Earth's Surface* (with Nathaniel Southgate Shaler, *q.v.*, 1881), *Whirlwinds, Cyclones and Tornadoes* (1884), *Elementary Meteorology* (1894), *Physical Geography* (with William H. Snyder, 1898), *Elementary Physical Geography* (1902), *Practical Exercises in Physical Geography* (1908), *Atlas* (1908), *A Handbook of Northern Europe* (1918), and *The Lesser Antilles* (1926). He edited with Douglas W. Johnson *Geographical Essays* (1909) and contributed a chapter to the first National Society for the Study of Education yearbook (1902).

Davis helped found the Geological Society of America, the Association of American Geographers (1904), and the National Council for Geography Teachers (1914). He belonged to many scientific societies and received more than a dozen medals and citations for his achievements.

After retirement, his fieldwork and writing continued. His last years were spent primarily on the Pacific Coast where he continued his studies and lectured at various western universities. Davis has been credited with having made geography a science in the United States.

REFERENCES: *DAB* (supp. 1); *DSB; EB; LE* (III); *NCAB* (24:32, B:93); *WWW* (I); Robert E. Dickinson, *The Makers of Modern Geography* (New York: Frederick A. Praeger, 1969); Preston E. James and Clarence F. Jones, eds., *American Geography: Inventory and Prospect* (Syracuse: Syracuse University Press, 1954).   *Haig A. Rushdoony*

DAY, Henry Noble. B. August 4, 1808, New Preston, Connecticut, to Noble and Elizabeth (Jones) Day. M. April 27, 1836, to Jane Louisa Marble. Ch. none. D. January 12, 1890, New Haven, Connecticut.

Henry Noble Day received his early education at Bethlehem, Connecticut, at Reverend John Langdon's school and the Hopkins Grammar

School. He was graduated from Yale College (1828) where his uncle, Jeremiah Day *(q.v.)*, was president.

After teaching for one year at John Gummere's *(q.v.)* seminary in Burlington, New Jersey, and studying law with Charles Chauncey in Philadelphia, he returned to Yale as a tutor (1831–34). He traveled in Europe (1835), was ordained, and became pastor of the First Congregational Church of Waterbury, Connecticut (1836–40).

Day was professor of rhetoric and homiletics at Western Reserve College in Hudson, Ohio (later, Case Western Reserve University in Cleveland) (1840–58), and also helped manage the Cleveland and Pittsburgh Railroad. He was president of the Ohio Female College near Cincinnati (1858–64) and returned to New Haven, Connecticut, to write textbooks.

His works include *Elements of the Art of Rhetoric* (1850), *Rhetorical Praxis* (1861), *The Systematic Accountant* (1861), *Elements of Logic* (1867), *The Art of Composition* (1867), *Introduction to the Study of English Literature* (1866), *The Art of Discourse* (1867), *Grammatical Synthesis* (1867), *The American Speller* (1869), *The Young Composer* (1870), *The Science of Aesthetics* (1872), *The Elements of Psychology* (1876), *The Science of Ethics* (1876), *The Science of Thought* (1886), *The Elements of Mental Science* (1886), and *The Science of Education* (1889). He was editor of the *Ohio Observer*.

Day received three honorary degrees.

REFERENCES: *AC; DAB; NCAB* (22:309); *WWW* (H); *NYT,* January 13, 1890, p. 2.   *Alfred J. Ciani*

DAY, James Roscoe. B. October 17, 1845, Whitneyville, Maine, to Thomas and Mary Plummer (Hillman) Day. M. July 14, 1873, to Anna E. Richards. Ch. one. D. March 13, 1923, Atlantic City, New Jersey.

James Roscoe Day worked as a steamboat roustabout, stage driver, and cattle herder for about five years in the Pacific Northwest. When an accident took the sight of one eye, he returned to Maine. He began studying for the ministry at Kent's Hill Seminary and was assigned to a charge in Auburn, Maine (1871–72). He was ordained in 1872.

He was said to have been the most popular Methodist minister in Maine at the time, serving churches at Bath (1872–74), Biddeford (1874–76), and Portland (1876–79). He also served churches at Nashua, New Hampshire (1879–81), Boston, Massachusetts (1881–82), New York City (1883–85 and 1889–93), and Newburgh, New York (1885–89). After he left the active ministry he was an influential force in the Methodist church. In 1904 he was elected a bishop but refused the position, explaining that his real interest was in education.

Upon his retirement from the ministry, Day was appointed chancellor of Syracuse (New York) University in 1893. Under Day, Syracuse flourished. From three departments in 1904, it grew to eight colleges and eight schools and from an enrollment of seven hundred and fifty to more than five thousand in 1922. Long-range financial problems faced the university. Day conducted an unsuccessful attempt to raise an endowment fund and resigned his position in 1922.

He wrote *The Raid on Prosperity* (1907) and *My Friend the Workingman* (1920). He was the recipient of honorary degrees from Dickinson College and Wesleyan University.

REFERENCES: *DAB; NCAB* (12:418); *TC; WWW* (I); *NYT*, March 14, 1923, p. 19. *Kenneth Sipser*

DAY, Jeremiah. B. August 3, 1773, New Preston, Connecticut, to Jeremiah Osborn and Abigail (Noble) Day. M. January 14, 1805, to Martha Sherman. M. September 24, 1811, to Olivia Jones. Ch. none. D. August 22, 1867, New Haven, Connecticut.

Jeremiah Day entered Yale College in 1789, but dropped out in 1791 because of pulmonary trouble. He reentered in 1793 and was graduated in 1795.

Upon graduation, he succeeded Timothy Dwight *(q.v.)* as principal of Greenfield Academy (1795–96), which Dwight had established in Fairfield, Connecticut. He served as a tutor at Williams College in Williamstown, Massachusetts (1796–98), and then accepted a similar position at Yale. In 1800 he was licensed to preach by the New Haven West Association of Ministers. Suffering from tuberculosis, he traveled to Bermuda in 1801, where he convalesced for nearly a year. He returned to Connecticut and became professor of mathematics and natural philosophy at Yale in 1803, a position to which he had been elected shortly after his departure for Bermuda.

Day wrote *Introduction to Algebra* (1814), *Mensuration of Superficies and Solids* (1814), *An Examination of President Edward's Inquiry as to the Freedom of Will* (1814), *Plane Trigonometry* (1815), *Navigation and Surveying* (1817), and *Inquiry on the Self-determining Power of the Will* (1838). The algebra text was widely used and went through many revisions. Outside Connecticut, he was known primarily through his textbooks.

Timothy Dwight, president of Yale, endorsed Day as his successor, and Day was ordained and inducted as the ninth president of Yale College at the same time. Although Day was not a healthy man, his term as president (1817–47) was the longest in the history of the college. Quiet and reticent, he built slowly on the foundation laid by his predecessor. After 1820 he taught mental and moral philosophy. He insisted on resigning when he was seventy-four years old and was immediately elected a member of the corporation, serving until a month before his death in August 1867 when he was ninety-four.

REFERENCES: *AC; DAB; NCAB* (1:169); *TC; WWW* (H); *NYT*, August 24, 1867, p. 1. *Daniel S. Yates*

DEARMONT, Washington Strother. B. September 22, 1859, Clark County, Virginia, to Peter and Mary Eliza Ferguson (Bell) Dearmont. M. May 29, 1890, to Julia Lee McKee. Ch. none. D. July 17, 1944, Cape Girardeau, Missouri.

Washington Strother Dearmont moved with his family from Virginia to Missouri shortly after the close of the Civil War. He was graduated from the University of Missouri at Columbia in 1885 with A.B. and B.Pd. degrees and the A.M. degree (1890).

Dearmont began his career in educational administration as superintendent of schools in Mound City, Missouri (1888–93), and served concurrently as the county commissioner of schools for Holt County. In 1893 Dearmont assumed the role of superintendent for the Kirksville, Missouri, schools. He remained in that position until he was appointed president of the State Normal School (later, Southeast Missouri State College) at Cape Girardeau in 1899, a position he had previously refused.

When Dearmont accepted the presidency, there was a movement by some Missouri educators to establish normal schools as four-year, fully accredited schools, which was strongly opposed, especially by President Samuel S. Laws of the University of Missouri. In 1919 a bill that redesignated the normal schools in Missouri as teachers' colleges was approved and credited to Dearmont. He remained at Cape Girardeau as president of the former normal school, later the Southeast Missouri State Teachers College, until 1921. He accepted a position as professor of psychology at Southwestern Louisiana Institute (later, University of Southwestern Louisiana) at Lafayette in 1922 and was dean of the college of education in 1931.

Dearmont played an important role in the development of teacher education in Missouri. Before 1899, normal schools in Missouri offered two years of review and drill exercises as preparation for elementary school teaching. Dearmont redesigned the curriculum to include four years of liberal arts education and intensive professional training in teaching techniques. He was given credit for the preparation of secondary as well as elementary teachers by normal schools.

Dearmont was active in professional associations, including the Missouri State Teachers Association (president, 1901). He was a founder of the American Association of Teachers' Colleges and the North Central Association of Normal School Presidents (president, 1915). In 1925 he assisted in the establishment of the North Central Association of Colleges and Secondary Schools. He was the author of articles in educational journals.

REFERENCES: *LE* (II); *WWW* (II); Mark Scully, "Washington Strother Dearmont," *School and Community* 23 (February 1937): 68–74; Jonas Viles, *The University of Missouri* (Columbia, Mo.: E. W. Stephens Co., 1939).   *James R. Layton*

DE BOER, John James. B. October 12, 1903, Chicago, Illinois, to James and Maria (Wezeman) De Boer. M. September 3, 1931, to Henrietta Geerdes. Ch. one. D. May 21, 1969, Urbana, Illinois.

John J. De Boer studied at Calvin College in Grand Rapids, Michigan (1919–21), and Wheaton (Illinois) College (1921–23). He received the A.M. (1927) and Ph.D. (1938) degrees from the University of Chicago.

He began his teaching career as a teacher of English at Chicago Christian High School (1923–31). He served as director of student teachers at Chicago Teachers College (later, State University) from 1931 to 1944.

De Boer accepted a position in the English department at Herzl Junior College (1944–45), was assigned a chairmanship in the education department at Roosevelt College in Chicago (1945–47), and was appointed to the University of Illinois (1947–68).

Awards De Boer received include the Susan Colver Rosenberg Prize for educational research (1940) and the Wilbur Hatfield Award of the National Council of Teachers of English (NCTE) in 1960. He served as president of the NCTE (1942–43), the American Education Fellowship (1946–47), and the National Conference on Research in English (1951–52). He was the author and coauthor of a number of books, including *Design for Elementary Education* (1945), *Building Better English* (1948), *Creative Writing* (1950), *Teaching Secondary English* (1951), *Reading for Living* (1953), and *The Teaching of Reading* (1960).

De Boer served as the editor of *The Elementary English Review* and was assistant editor of *The English Journal* and coeditor of *Secondary Education* (1966). He was chairman of the committee to prepare the language arts section of *Sequential Tests of Educational Progress*.

REFERENCES: *CA* (1–4); *LE* (I); *WWW* (V); *College English* 31 (October 1969): 64; *English Journal* 58 (September 1969): 937.   *LeRoy Barney*

DE GARMO, Charles. B. January 17, 1849, Muckwonago, Wisconsin, to Rufus and Laura (Wilbur) De Garmo. M. December 29, 1875, to Ida Witbeck. Ch. one. D. May 14, 1934, Miami, Florida.

Charles De Garmo was graduated from Illinois State Normal University (later, State University) in 1873 and received the Ph.D. degree from the University of Halle, Germany, in 1886, where he was influenced by the Herbartian movement. Because of his commitment to Herbartism, which was at its height in the United States between 1875 and 1925, and through his writings, speeches, and prestigious academic positions, he exerted a strong influence upon American education. He advocated ethical training in the public schools but not religious education. Character development was to be the ultimate goal of the school.

De Garmo began his professional career as principal in the Naples, Illinois, public schools (1873–76). He was assistant training teacher

(1876–83) and professor of modern languages (1886–90) at Illinois State Normal University in Normal, Illinois, professor of psychology at the University of Illinois (1890–91), president of Swarthmore (Pennsylvania) College (1891–98), and professor of the science and art of education at Cornell University in Ithaca, New York (1898–1914).

De Garmo was the author of an impressive and varied number of books, including *Essentials of Methods* (1890), *Translation of Lindner's Psychology* (1890), *(English) Language Series* (1898), *Herbart and the Herbartians* (1898), *Interest and Education* (1902), *Principles of Secondary Education* (1907), and *Aesthetic Education* (1913). He was coauthor with Leon L. Winslow of *Essentials of Design in the Industrial Arts* (1923).

De Garmo served as president of the normal department of the National Education Association (1891), a member of the executive committee of the newly formed National Herbartian Society for the Scientific Study of Education (1895), first president of the Society of Professors of Education (1902, reelected 1908), and member of the executive committee of the National Society for the Scientific Study of Education (1905).

REFERENCES: *AC; NCAB* (6:354); *TC; WW* (XVIII). *Carl H. Gross*

DEMIASHKEVICH, Michael John. B. November 8, 1891, Mohilev, Russia, to Ivan A. and Anna S. (Isaeva) Demiashkevich. M. no. D. August 26, 1938, Rockport, Maine.

Michael John Demiashkevich was educated in Russia. He was graduated from the Imperial Historical-Philological and the Imperial Archaeological Institute, Petrograd, in June 1914. He taught at the Alexander I Gymnasium (1914–17), the Deutsche Hauptschule zu St. Petri (1914–21), and the Navy College, Petrograd (1920–23).

He emigrated to the United States, where he received the Ph.D. degree (1926) from Columbia University. He served as assistant in the International Institute of Teachers College, Columbia University (1926–27). He spent two years (1927–29) as a visiting scholar at the universities of Grenoble and Paris (Sorbonne), France, Munich and Berlin, Germany, and London, England. He was a member of the faculty at George Peabody College for Teachers in Nashville, Tennessee, from 1929 to his death in 1938. He espoused the educational philosophy of essentialism, which holds that there are basic concepts or ideas (essentials) that must be transmitted to the young of each generation to preserve the cultural heritage.

His articles appeared in leading national journals and yearbooks. He was a member of the editorial board of *The Educational Forum*. He was the author of *The Activity School* (1926), *Shackled Diplomacy: The Permanent Factors of Foreign Policies of Nations* (1934), *An Introduction to the Philosophy of Education* (1935), in which he explained the concept of essentialism, and *The National Mind: English, French, German* (1938).

In 1934 he was honored by the French government with the title of officier d'académie for his work in comparative education, and in April of the same year he became an honorary corresponding member of the Institut littéraire et artistique de France. His professional organization membership included Phi Delta Kappa, Kappa Delta Pi, the Southern Society for Philosophy and Psychology, the American Sociological Society, and the American Academy of Political and Social Science.

REFERENCES: *WWAE* (VIII); *WWW* (I); B. Harris, "Bibliography of Writings by Michael Demiashkevich," *Educational Forum* 4 (November 1939): 126–28; "In Memoriam: Dr. Michael John Demiashkevich, 1891–1938," *Educational Forum* 3 (November 1938): 125–29; C. S. Pendle, "Peabody's Modern Founders," *Peabody Journal of Education* 22 (March 1945): 280–82.   *Leon W. Brownlee*

DETT, Robert Nathaniel. B. October 11, 1882, Drummondville, Quebec, Canada, to Robert Tue and Charlotte (Johnson) Dett. M. December 27, 1916, to Helen Elise Smith. Ch. two. D. October 2, 1943, Battle Creek, Michigan.

Robert Nathaniel Dett, distinguished black musician and music educator, grew up in Niagara Falls, New York. The youngest of three sons of educated parents, he studied piano privately before attending the Oliver Willis Halstead Conservatory in Lockport, New York (1901–03). He was graduated (1908) from the Oberlin (Ohio) Conservatory of Music, the first black to be awarded the Bachelor of Music degree in composition. He received the Master of Music degree (1932) from the Eastman School of Music in Rochester, New York. He also studied at Columbia and Harvard universities, the University of Pennsylvania, the American Conservatory of Music in Chicago, and under the famous piano teacher, Nadia Boulanger, in France.

Dett was a pianist in Niagara Falls, New York (1898–1903), but his musical career was centered in black colleges throughout the South, where he held significant positions in the music departments of Lane College of Jackson, Tennessee (1908–11), Lincoln Institute at Jefferson City, Missouri (1911–13), and Hampton (Virginia) Institute (1913–32). He composed, taught, and lectured in Rochester, New York. He was married in 1916 to Helen Elise Smith, the first black to be graduated from the Julliard School of Music in New York City.

While in the South, Dett became more acquainted with the Negro spiritual and sought to preserve it. By refining the spiritual and presenting it in an artistic setting, he hoped that Negro folk music would be more readily accepted and appreciated. College choirs he conducted frequently performed his stylized arrangements of spirituals and became the medium through which sophisticated versions of the spirituals were introduced to the public. In 1930 he directed the Hampton Institute Choir to international acclaim as it toured the United States and seven European countries.

Among his better-known piano compositions were *Magnolia Suite* (1911) and "Dance: Juba" from *In the Bottoms Suite* (1913). Two of his more familiar choral compositions were *Don't Be Weary Traveler*, a motet, for which he won the Francis Boott Prize in 1920, and *Listen to the Lambs* (1941). His complete works include many published and unpublished scores. He edited *Religious Folk-Songs of the Negro* (1927) and authored *The Dett Collection of Negro Spirituals* (1936).

Dett received many awards and honors, including the Bowdoin Prize for an essay entitled "The Emancipation of Negro Music," written in 1920 while studying at Harvard. He was awarded honorary degrees by Howard University and Oberlin College. He was president of the National Association of Negro Musicians (1924–26) and was the first in the field of music to receive the Harmon Award (1930).

Dett died in 1943, shortly after he assumed a position as musical consultant with the United Service Organization in Battle Creek, Michigan.

REFERENCES: *CB* (November 1943); *DAB* (supp. 3); *WWW* (II); *American Society of Composers, Authors and Publishers Biographical Dictionary*, 3d ed. (New York: The Lynn Farnol Group, 1966); *The Collected Piano Works of R. Nathaniel Dett* (Evanston, Ill.: Summy-Birchard Co., 1973); Maud Cuney-Hare, *Negro Musicians and Their Music* (New York: Da Capo Press, 1974); *NYT*, October 4, 1943, p. 17; May Stanley, "In Retrospect: R. N. Dett of Hampton Institute," *The Black Perspective in Music* 1 (Spring 1973): 65–69.   *Exyie C. Ryder*

DE VANE, William Clyde. B. June 17, 1898, Savannah, Georgia, to William Clyde and Sarah Charlotte (Peck) De Vane. M. June 20, 1925, to Mabel Phillips. Ch. three. D. August 16, 1965, Greensboro, Vermont.

William Clyde De Vane studied at Furman University in Greenville, South Carolina (1915–16), and Yale University (1917–20), where he received the A.B. (1920) and Ph.D. (1926) degrees.

He was an instructor in English at Yale (1922–26) and remained there to 1934, when he became professor of English and head of the department at Cornell University in Ithaca, New York. He was Goldwyn Smith Professor of English at Cornell (1937–38) and returned to Yale as professor of English and dean (1938–63). As dean, De Vane reorganized the undergraduate curriculum after World War II, emphasizing liberal arts and deemphasizing extracurricular activities. Yale was a model followed by many other liberal arts colleges seeking more effective programs. De Vane also served as director of the division of humanities and social sciences (1946–56). He stepped down as dean in 1963 and was Emily Sanford Professor of English Literature (1944–65).

De Vane was a contributor to the fields of English literature and higher education, including *Browning's Parleyings–The Autobiography of a Mind* (1927), *Charlotte Bronte's Legends of Angria* (with Fanny Ratchford, 1933), *Browning's Shorter Poems* (1934), *A Browning Handbook* (1935), *Selections from Tennyson* (with Mabel Phillips De Vane, 1940), *New Letters of Robert Browning* (with L. L. Knickerbocker, 1950), *American Universities in the Twentieth Century* (1958), and *Higher Education in the Twentieth Century* (1965). He was the literary editor and member of the editorial board of the *Yale Review* (1940–54).

De Vane served in the United States Army in World War I (1918). He was active in scholarly and professional associations; he was president of the Connecticut Council of Higher Education (1951–52) and the College English Association (1939–40) and chairman of the American Council of Learned Societies (1947–49). He was a member of the Modern Language Association of America (executive council, 1938–49). De Vane was a Guggenheim Fellow (1953–54), a trustee of Wells College (1940–65), and president of Foote School Association and Prospect Hill School. He received many honorary degrees from American colleges and universities and the French Legion of Honor (1949).

REFERENCES: *LE* (III); *NCAB* (52:298); *WWAE* (XVI); *WWW* (IV); *NYT,* August 17, 1965, p. 33. *Earl W. Thomas*

DEWEY, Chester. B. October 25, 1784, Sheffield, Massachusetts, to Stephen and Elizabeth (Owen) Dewey. M. 1810 to Sarah Dewey. M. 1825 to Olivia Hart Pomeroy. Ch. fifteen. D. December 15, 1867, Rochester, New York.

Chester Dewey entered Williams College in Williamstown, Massachusetts, in 1802 and was graduated in 1806. He was licensed to preach as a Congregational minister in 1807 and served churches at Tyringham and Stockbridge, Massachusetts, in 1808.

From 1810 until 1827 Dewey taught mathematics, physics, chemistry, and natural history (botany and zoology) at Williams College. He built up collections of botanical and mineral specimens needed to carry on science teaching. He was a principal at the Berkshire Gymnasium in Pittsfield, Massachusetts (1827–36), and the Rochester (New York) Collegiate Institute (1836–50), where he prepared students for college and business occupations. He also lectured at various times on chemistry and botany at the Berkshire Medical Institute at Pittsfield, Massachusetts, and lectured at the Medical School at Woodstock, Vermont (1842–49). He returned to higher education as the first professor of chemistry and natural sciences at the newly founded University of Rochester (1850–61).

One of the first American naturalists, Dewey was a specialist in grasses and contributed to the field of meteorology. Concerned with social problems, he organized the first anti-slavery society in Massachusetts among the students at Williams College (1823). He was the author of many scientific articles in scholarly journals and of *Reports on the Herbaceous Plants and the Quadrupeds of Massachusetts* (1840). His major monograph, *Caricography,* on North American sedges, was serialized from 1824 to 1866 in the *American Journal of Science.* A genus of umbilliferous plants of California was designated Deweya. He received honorary degrees, including the M.D. from Yale (1825).

REFERENCES: *AC; DAB; NCAB* (6:328); *WWW* (H); Asa Gray *(q.v.),* "Chester Dewey," *American Journal of Science* 45 (1868): 122–23.

Jay L. Lemke

DEWEY, Henry Bingham. B. July 26, 1864, Niles, Michigan, to George Martin and Emma (Bingham) Dewey. M. 1897 to Harriette L. White. Ch. two. D. October 30, 1931, Boston, Massachusetts.

Henry Bingham Dewey attended local Michigan public schools and was graduated with the A.B. degree (1890) from the University of Michigan.

Dewey was superintendent of the Shiawassee County, Michigan, public schools (1890–91) and moved to the state of Washington, where he was superintendent of the Sumner public schools (1891–94). After a year of travel and study in Europe, he became a school principal in Tacoma, Washington, serving in different schools to 1898, when he was elected superintendent of the Pierce County (Washington) schools.

In 1904 Dewey was appointed to the state department of education and was assistant state superintendent under R. B. Bryan; he became state superintendent of public instruction in 1908 on the death of Bryan. Dewey served as state superintendent to 1913. He was an unsuccessful candidate for Congress in 1912. Dewey was credited with reorganizing the state department under a law passed in 1909, which organized the department into a structure that continued into the 1970s. He promoted standardization of the schools in the state, vocational education, improvement of rural schools, and greater cooperation between schools and local communities.

Dewey became managing editor of the education department for the Houghton Mifflin publishing company in Boston, Massachusetts. He had been editor and publisher of the *Northwest Journal of Education* from 1905 to 1908.

REFERENCES: *WWW* (I); Jim B. Pearson and Edgar Fuller, eds., *Education in the States* (Washington, D.C.: National Education Association, 1969); *Manual of the Eleventh Session of the Washington State Legislature, 1909* (Seattle: The Pacific Press, 1909); Frederick E. Bolton and Thomas W. Bibb, *History of Education in Washington* (Washington, D.C.: Government Printing Office, 1935).   *John F. Ohles*

DEWEY, John. B. October 20, 1859, Burlington, Vermont, to Archibald S. and Lucina A. (Rich) Dewey. M. July 28, 1886, to Alice Chipman. M. 1946 to Roberta Lowitz Grant. Ch. nine. D. June 2, 1952, New York, New York.

John Dewey was the dean of twentieth-century American educators as a philosopher, psychologist, and practicing educator. He developed and practiced educational reforms that had a profound effect on education throughout the world. He was graduated from the University of Vermont with the A.B. degree (1879) and from Johns Hopkins University with the Ph.D. degree (1884).

He taught philosophy at the University of Michigan (1884–88) and the University of Minnesota (1888–89). In 1889 he returned to Michigan to teach philosophy until 1894, when he went to the University of Chicago to head the department of philosophy and education (1894–1904). While at Chicago he initiated his reform movements in educational theory and practice, testing them in the university high school. In 1904 he became professor of philosophy at Columbia University in New York City. He retired in 1930 but continued to be active at Columbia for many years.

Dewey was the author of many articles and books, including *Psychology* (1887), *Applied Psychology* (with J. A. McLellan, 1889), *Outlines of Ethics* (with James Tufts, 1891), *School and Society* (1899), *Studies in Logical Theory* (1903), *Child and Curriculum* (1906), *Ethics* (1908), *How We Think* (1910), *Interest and Effort* (1913), *Democracy and Education* (1916), *Essays in Experimental Logic* (1916), *Creative Intelligence* (1917), *Reconstruction in Philosophy* (1920), *Human Nature and Conduct* (1922), *Experience and Nature* (1925), *The Public and Its Problems* (1927), *The Quest for Certainty* (1929), *Characters and Events* (1929), *Philosophy and Civilization* (1931), *Art as Experience* (1934), *Liberalism and Social Action* (1935), *Logic: The Theory of Inquiry* (1938), *Freedom and Culture* (1939), *Problems of Man* (1946), and *Knowing and the Known* (with Arthur Bently, 1949).

His teaching and writing, much of it promoting learning by doing, made him the chief prophet of progressive education. He was active in professional associations, serving as president of the American Psychological Association (1899–1900) and the American Philosophical Society (1905–06), a fellow of the National Academy of Sciences, and a corresponding member of L'institut de France. He helped found the New School for Social Research, and he was a charter member of the first teachers' union in New York City and a founder and president of the American Association of University Professors. He visited many countries to study school systems and prepared a report for the reorganization of Turkish schools. He received many honorary degrees from American and foreign universities and was decorated by the governments of China (1939) and Chile (1949). He was made honorary president of the National Education Association (1932) and the American Philosophical Association (1938) and honorary vice-president of the New York State Liberal party (1952).

REFERENCES: *CB* (August 1944 and July 1952); *EB; LE* (III); *NCAB* (A:547, 40:1); *WWW* (III); *WWAE* (XI); William W. Brickman *(q.v.)* and Stanley Lehrer, eds., *John Dewey: Master Educator* (New York: Society for the Advancement of Education, 1959); George Dykhuizen, *The Life and Mind of John Dewey* (Carbondale: Southern Illinois University Press, 1973); *NYT,* June 2, 1952, p. 1.   *Jerome E. Leavitt*

DEWEY, Melvil. B. December 10, 1851, Adams Center, New York, to Joel and Eliza (Green) Dewey. M. October 19, 1878, to Annie Roberts Godfrey. M. May 28, 1924, to Emily McKay Beal. Ch. one. D. December 26, 1931, Lake Placid, Florida.

Early in life, Melville Louis Kossuth Dewey dropped his middle names and shortened his first name, beginning what was to be a lifelong obsession with simplified spelling. He studied at the Hungerford Collegiate Institute in Adams, New York, and the Oneida (New York) Seminary. He taught for a year at Bernhard's Bay, New York, and entered Amherst (Massachusetts) College in 1870. He was graduated with the A.B. degree (1874).

Dewey stayed at Amherst as acting librarian (1874–76). It was there that he published *A Classification and Subject Index for Cataloging and Arranging the Books and Pamphlets of a Library* (1876). Because of its simple logic and ease of application, the Dewey decimal system soon gained wide acceptance in all types of libraries. Dewey's lifelong friend and assistant, Walter T. Biscoe, was instrumental in working out the details of the classification scheme.

Leaving Amherst in 1876, Dewey went to Boston and helped organize the founding and first meeting of the American Library Association. In Boston he managed three societies, the American Library Association, the Metric Buro to establish metric weights and measures, and the Spelling Reform Association. He had assisted in the organizing of all three groups. In 1876 he joined Richard R. Bowker and Frederick Leypoldt in establishing the *Library Journal* and served as editor for the first five volumes.

In 1883 Dewey became the librarian at Columbia College in New York City. In 1887 he started the School of Library Economy at Columbia, the first library school in the United States. Dewey left Columbia in 1889 having come into conflict with the trustees for allowing women to enroll in the program. He moved the school to Albany, New York, renamed it the New York State Library School, and directed it until 1906. Dewey was appointed state librarian and elected by the regents of the University of the State of New York (the state education department) as their secretary and chief executive officer (1889–1900). He headed the home education department (1891–1906) and was director of the New York State Library (1889–1906). While at Albany, Dewey developed traveling libraries to serve small rural communities and aided in establishing the library extension division of the New York State Library, which set standards for libraries throughout the state. He gave women librarians an equal share in all phases of library activity and granted them the recognition they earned. By 1910 Dewey had dropped out of library work. His retirement was devoted to the maintenance of the Lake Placid (New York) Club, a resort he had build especially for the use of educators of modest means. He established the Lake Placid Club in Florida in 1927.

In addition to the decimal system publications (1879–1929), Dewey wrote *Library School Rules* (1871) and bulletins for the University of the State of New York. He served the American Library Association as president (1890–91 and 1892–93) and treasurer. While at Columbia, he was a founder of the New York Library Club (first president), the New York Language Club (secretary and treasurer), and the Children's Library Association (1888). He was active in the founding of the New York State Library Association, the Library Department of the National Educational Association, and the Association of State Librarians (president). He was a trustee of the Chautauqua Institution and the Carnegie Simplified Spelling Board. He received two honorary degrees.

REFERENCES: *AC; DAB* (supp. 1); *NCAB* (23:14); *TC; WWW* (I); *NYT,* December 27, 1931, Sec. II, p. 6; Fremont Rider, *Melvil Dewey* (Chicago: American Library Association, 1944). *Gary D. Barber*

DEXTER, Edwin Grant. B. July 21, 1868, Calais, Maine, to Henry Vaughan and Mary Edna (Boardman) Dexter. M. June 7, 1895, to Allie Martin Hodge. Ch. five. D. December 5, 1938, Linthicum Heights, Maryland.

Edwin Grant Dexter's youth was spent in Templeton, Massachusetts. At the age of sixteen he enrolled in Worcester (Massachusetts) Academy and studied at Brown University in Providence, Rhode Island, from which he was graduated with the Ph.B. (1891) and A.M. (1892) degrees. He received the Ph.D. degree from Columbia University (1899).

He taught applied mathematics at Brown (1891–92) and moved to Colorado Springs, Colorado, where he was the high school science teacher (1892–95). He taught psychology at the Colorado State Normal School (later, University of Northern Colorado) in Greeley (1895–1900).

During the fall of 1899, President Andrew Sloan Draper *(q.v.)* of the University of Illinois offered Dexter a position as professor of education (1900–07). He also was director of the summer session (1901–07) and dean of the school of education (1905–07). At Illinois, he established a psychological laboratory and assumed responsibility for work in psychology, as well as pedagogy. He introduced statistics into the graduate program and designed courses for practicing teachers and administrators.

President Theodore Roosevelt appointed him commissioner of education for Puerto Rico (1907–12). He also served as chancellor of the University of Puerto Rico and president of the Insular Library Board, and he sat in the upper house of the legislature. He was president of the National Institute of Panama (1912–18) and served in the American Red Cross during and after World War I.

Dexter was a member of the Civilian Advisory Board, United States War Department (1920–22), serving as an educational specialist for the Ninth Corps area. He was president of the United States Veterans' Bureau Vocational School at Camp Sheridan, Ohio (1922–24), and chief of the vocational unit of the United States Veterans' Bureau (1924–25). He went to Washington, D.C., as chief of the policy subdivision of the United States Veterans' Bureau (1925–30) and historian for the bureau (1930–38).

Dexter wrote many articles, *A History of Education in the United States* (1904), and *Weather Influences: An Empirical Study of the Mental Effects of Definite Meteorological Conditions* (1904).

Dexter was active in state and national organizations. He was president of the child study section of the Colorado State Teachers' Association. In 1905 he was elected president of the National Society for the Scientific Study of Education. He served as president of the child study section of the Illinois State Teachers' Association and the National Education Association. He was a member of the Société Jean-Jacques Rosseau, a fellow of the American Association for the Advancement of Science and the American Geographical Association, and a collaborating editor of the journal sponsored by the Internationalen Societie für Schulhygiene. He was awarded a medal for an educational exhibit at the World's Columbian Exposition in Chicago (1893) and received an honorary degree from the University of Puerto Rico (1912).

REFERENCES: *NCAB* (36:367); *WWW* (I); *Brown Alumni Monthly* 6 (January 1906); Henry C. Johnson and E. V. Johanningmeier, *Teachers for the Prairie: The University of Illinois and the Schools, 1868–1945* (Urbana: University of Illinois Press, 1972).   *E. V. Johanningmeier*

DEYOE, George Percy. B. March 31, 1901, Mason City, Iowa, to George M. and Mabel (Gillette) Deyoe. M. July 26, 1924, to Edna Katherine Zimmerman. Ch. one. D. July 14, 1961, Champaign, Illinois.

George Percy Deyoe was an outstanding agricultural educator and a prolific writer on agriculture. He received the B.S. degree (1923) from Iowa State College (later, University) in Ames and the M.A. degree (1928) from the University of Chicago. He completed the Ph.D. degree (1934) at Teachers College, Columbia University. His dissertation was published as *Certain Trends in Curriculum Practice and Policies in State Normal Schools and Teachers Colleges* (1934).

Deyoe was a high school teacher of vocational agriculture at Belle Plaine and Vinton, Iowa (1923–27). He was a member of the faculty of the Wisconsin State Teachers College at Platteville (later, University of Wisconsin—Platteville) from 1928 to 1937 and Michigan State College (later, University) at East Lansing (1937–47), and he ended his career at the University of Illinois (1947–61).

His publications include *Getting Acquainted with Agriculture* (with Fred T. Ullrich, 1941), *Supervised Farming in Vocational Agriculture* (1943), *Raising Livestock* (with W. A. Ross and W. H. Peters, 1946), *Living on a Little Land* (1948), a handbook of practical suggestions for small-scale and part-time farming, *Raising Swine* (with J. L. Krider, 1952), *Methods and Materials for Teaching Vocational Agriculture to High-School Students* (1954), and *Agriculture in Our Lives* (1956), a book whose main purpose was "to help people become acquainted with the importance of agriculture in their lives." He authored several bulletins and reports issued by the Division of Agricultural Education of Illinois' colleges of education. He served on the editing-managing boards of *American Vocational Journal* and *Agricultural Education Magazine*.

Deyoe was a postdoctoral fellow of the American Council on Education (1941–42). He was a member of numerous national professional organizations and was frequently appointed to state and national commissions on the evaluation of teacher education and agricultural education, including serving as chairman of the Illinois Council on Community Schools and the Michigan State Committee on Evaluation of Teacher Education. He was a member of the National Technical Committee on Evaluation of Agricultural Education, the National Study Committee for Future Farmers of America Contests, and the American Vocational Association (chairman of the national committee on agricultural educational policy and standards).

REFERENCES: *LE* (III); *WWAE* (I); *WWW* (IV); *Agricultural Education Magazine* 34 (October 1961): 93; *American Vocational Journal* 36 (September 1961): 36.   *Ronald D. Szoke*

DICKEY, Sarah Ann. B. April 25, 1838, near Dayton, Ohio, to Isaac and n.a. (Tryon) Dickey. M. no. D. January 23, 1904, Clinton, Mississippi.

One of eight children scattered among relatives on their mother's death in 1846, Sarah Ann Dickey endured drudgery and extreme privation. At the age of sixteen, able to read and spell a little but not to write, she decided to become a teacher and earned her teacher's certificate in three years. She taught in country schools near Dayton, Ohio (1857–63).

In 1858 she joined the Church of the United Brethren in Christ, which sent her to teach freedmen in Vicksburg, Mississippi (1863–65). Dickey attended Mount Holyoke (Massachusetts) Seminary where she was graduated in 1869. She returned to Mississippi where she taught one year in a freedmen's school in Raymond. She was a teacher for two years in a black public school in Clinton where she was ostracized by whites and threatened by the Ku Klux Klan. She organized a board of trustees of both races for a school of her own, secured a charter in 1873, and purchased a large house in 1874.

The Mount Hermon Female Seminary, a nonsectarian boarding school for black girls, opened in 1875. Dickey faced continual financial problems and made fund-raising trips to northern states for one to three months every year.

Mount Hermon was modeled on the Mount Holyoke domestic work system but the academic work differed greatly, offering a four-year primary course in basic literacy and household arts. Some students took a four-year normal course, and Mount Hermon furnished teachers for black elementary schools throughout Mississippi.

Dickey came to be respected by the white community. She was licensed to preach in 1893 and in 1896 was ordained a minister in the United Brethren in Christ church. On her death, the school was taken over by the American Missionary Association. It was closed in 1924.

REFERENCES: *NAW;* Helen Griffith, *Dauntless in Mississippi, The Life of Sarah A. Dickey* (South Hadley, Mass.: Dinosaur Press, 1966).

M. Jane Dowd

DICKINSON, George Sherman. B. February 9, 1888, St. Paul, Minnesota, to George Richardson and Annette C. (Thomas) Dickinson. M. September 9, 1913, to Bessie May McClure. Ch. none. D. November 6, 1964, Chapel Hill, North Carolina.

George Dickinson received his preliminary education in the public schools of Zanesville, Ohio. He was graduated from Oberlin (Ohio) College with the A.B. (1909) and Mus.B. (1910) degrees and from Harvard University with the A.M. degree (1912). He studied musical theory, composition, and orchestration in Berlin, London, Vienna, and Paris at various times from 1913 to 1935.

He began his teaching career as a music instructor at Oberlin in 1910 and moved to Vassar College in Poughkeepsie, New York, in 1916 where he taught music history, theory, and appreciation. He initiated many changes in the music department, dealing with course content and presentation. The general introductory course for music was changed from appreciation and factual history of music to the study of music as a literary progression of styles. The study included opera, symphony, song, and contemporary music. He planned the Belle Skinner Hall of Music at Vassar, acclaimed for its beauty, special effects, and teaching devices.

Dickinson was the author of *Fortokens of the Tonal Principle* (1923), *Growth and Use of Harmony* (1927), *Classification of Musical Compositions; Decimal-Symbol System* (1938), and *Pattern of Music* (1939). He contributed many articles to journals and was an editor of Columbia University's Studies in Musicology (1933–53).

Dickinson was an associate in the American Guild of Organists. He belonged to many professional organizations, including the American Musicological Society (president, 1947–48), the Music Library Association (president, 1939–41), and the Music Teachers National Association (vice-president, 1938). He was awarded an honorary degree from Oberlin College, and several memorial scholarships at Vassar College were established in his name.

REFERENCES: *LE* (III); *NCAB* (51:71); *WWW* (IV); *NYT,* November 8, 1964, p. 88. *Marilyn Meiss*

DICKINSON, John Woodbridge. B. October 12, 1825, Chester, Massachusetts, to William and Elizabeth (Worthington) Dickinson. M. 1857 to Arexene G. Parsons. Ch. two. D. February 16, 1901, Newton, Massachusetts.

John Woodbridge Dickinson was graduated from Williams College in Williamstown, Massachusetts, with classical honors in 1852. He became an assistant teacher at Westfield (Massachusetts) State Normal School (later, State College) in 1852 and succeeded William H. Wells *(q.v.)* as principal (1857–77). Under his leadership the school gained a national reputation for excellence in teacher training. He introduced the analytic objective method of instruction.

He was appointed secretary of the board of education of Massachusetts in 1877 and held the post until 1893. During his term Massachusetts substituted town control of schools for the older district system, provided free texts and supplies for school children, established schools for truants in each county, reorganized the annual teachers' institutes, established institutes for superintendents and school committees, and introduced a co-partnership system of superintendencies by which poorer communities could share with more affluent communities.

After retirement, Dickinson became active on the Newton School Committee and was an instructor at the Emerson School of Oratory in Boston. Among his books were *Our Republic: A Text-book upon the Civil Government of the United States* (with M. B. C. True, 1888), *The Limits of Oral Training* (1890), *Principles and Method of Teaching, Derived from a Knowledge of the Mind* (1899), and *Rhetoric and Principles of Written Composition* (1901).

REFERENCES: *DAB; WWW* (H); *Boston Globe,* February 17, 1901; *Boston Herald,* February 17, 1901. *Joseph M. McCarthy*

DILLARD, James Hardy. B. October 24, 1856, Nansemond County, Virginia, to James and Sarah Brownrigg (Cross) Dillard. M. July 5, 1882, to

Mary Harmanson. M. November 18, 1899, to Avarene Lippincott Budd. Ch. ten. D. August 2, 1940, Charlottesville, Virginia.

James Hardy Dillard's father was a well-educated man who saw that his son had access to a stimulating intellectual environment during his early years. At the age of twelve Dillard was sent to Norfolk, Virginia, where he attended a classical secondary school. At seventeen, he matriculated at Washington and Lee University in Lexington, Virginia, from which he was graduated with highest honors in 1876.

Dillard served in numerous posts as teacher and school administrator, including Rodman School in Norfolk, Norfolk (Virginia) Academy, the University of Vermont, Phillips Academy in Exeter, New Hampshire, the State Normal School (later, State University of New York College) in Oswego, New York, and Mary Institute, the women's division of Washington University in St. Louis, Missouri. In 1891 he accepted a Latin professorship at Tulane University in New Orleans, Louisiana, where he remained until 1907 as dean of academic colleges.

Dillard's educational, civic, and religious leadership made him a leading citizen of Louisiana. He was active in the Child Welfare Association and the Free Kindergarten Association; he served as president of the public library and succeeded in obtaining a branch for the city's black population. He served on the state board of education as well as the boards of trustees of several state institutions.

In 1907 Dillard was chosen the first president and director of the Negro Rural School Fund, founded and endowed by Anna T. Jeanes. He remained in this position until 1931. He served as president of the closely related John F. Slater Fund (1917–31), vice-president of the Phelps-Stokes Fund, and was a member of the Southern Education Board and the General Education Board. He was a member of the board of visitors of the College of William and Mary (rector, 1917–40), the board of trustees of General Theological Seminary, the Phelps-Stokes Fund Educational Commission to Africa (1924), the Near East Survey Committee, and the University Commission of Southern Race Questions.

Dillard received numerous honors, including honorary doctorates from several universities. He was a recipient of the Harmon Foundation Gold Medal and the Roosevelt Medal. In 1930 two black colleges in New Orleans merged to form Dillard University, an institution serving as a memorial to the humanitarian and educational achievements of James Hardy Dillard.

REFERENCES: *CB* (September 1940); *DAB* (supp. 2); *LE* (I); *NCAB* (34:233); *WWW* (I); Benjamin Brawley *(q.v.)*, *Doctor Dillard of the Jeanes Fund* (New York: Fleming H. Revell Co., 1930); *NYT,* August 3, 1940, p. 15.   *Joe L. Green*

DIMITRY, Alexander. B. February 7, 1805, New Orleans, Louisiana, to Andrea and Marianne Celeste (Dragon) Dimitry. M. 1835 to Mary Powell

Mills. Ch. eight. D. January 30, 1883, New Orleans, Louisiana.

Alexander Dimitry was educated by tutors and at private schools in New Orleans, Louisiana. He was an honors graduate (c. 1829) in the classics at Georgetown (District of Columbia) College (later, University).

After teaching at Baton Rouge (Louisiana) College for two years he became editor of the *New Orleans Bee* in about 1830, issuing the paper in English instead of French as it had been. In 1834 he returned to Washington, D.C., where he was a clerk with the Post Office Department (1834–42).

Dimitry established the St. Charles (Louisiana) Institute in 1842, heading it until his appointment as the first state superintendent of public education in 1847. As superintendent (1847–51) he organized the public schools of Louisiana.

Dimitry was a translator with the United States Department of State from 1854 or 1856 until 1859. He was United States minister to Nicaragua and Costa Rica (1859–61), resigning upon Louisiana's secession from the Union. He was head of the finance section of the Confederate Post Office (1861–65). He was assistant superintendent of schools in New Orleans in 1868 and was professor of ancient languages for a short time in 1870 at Christian Brothers College in Pass Christian, Mississippi.

Dimitry wrote short stories and articles published in periodicals. He was an organizer of the Hebrew Education Society in New Orleans, a member of the Union Literary Society in Washington, D.C., and the recipient of an honorary degree from Georgetown College.

REFERENCES: *AC; DAB; NCAB* (10:176); *NYT,* January 31, 1883, p. 5; *TC; WWW* (H); Rodney Cline, *Education in Louisiana–History and Development* (Baton Rouge: Claitor's Publishing Division, 1974); Rodney Cline, *Pioneer Leaders and Early Institutions in Louisiana Education* (Baton Rouge: Claitor's Publishing Division, 1969); E. W. Fay, *History of Education in Louisiana* (Washington, D.C.: United States Government Printing Office, 1898); Carmen Marie Mouton, "Alexander Dimitry" (Master's thesis, Louisiana State University, 1944).   *Joe L. Green*

DINWIDDIE, Albert Bledsoe. B. April 3, 1871, Lexington, Kentucky, to William and Emily Albertine (Bledsoe) Dinwiddie. M. July 22, 1897, to Caroline Arthur Summey. Ch. six. D. November 21, 1935, New Orleans, Louisiana.

Albert Bledsoe Dinwiddie, son of a Presbyterian minister, moved from Kentucky to Albermarle County, Virginia, at an early age. He attended Potomac Academy in Alexandria, Virginia, and entered the University of Virginia in 1886, from which he received the A.B. (1889), M.A. (1890), and Ph.D. (1892) degrees. He was principal of the family-owned Greenwood

(Virginia) Academy (1891–93) and first assistant principal of University School in Richmond, Virginia (1895–96).

He was professor of mathematics at Southwestern Presbyterian University in Clarksville, Tennessee (1896–1906), except for the year 1902–03 when he studied higher mathematics at the University of Göttingen, Germany. In 1906 he went to Tulane University in New Orleans, Louisiana, to teach applied mathematics and astronomy; in 1910 he became department head. He supplemented his income by writing book reviews for a New Orleans newspaper. He served as dean of the college of arts and sciences (1910–18) and as director of the summer school (1910–21). He was president of Tulane from 1918 until his death in 1935.

During his presidency the Middle America Research Institute and the school of social work were organized, extensive curriculum changes were made, and scholarship and research improved. He improved the financial resources of the university, increased the endowment, and instituted a retirement and group insurance program. During World War I, he was director of war training at Tulane, organizing and training young men in the mechanical arts.

Dinwiddie was a member of many organizations, a fellow of the American Geographical Society, trustee of the Carnegie Foundation for the Advancement of Teaching, director of the New Orleans Public School Alliance, and member of the President's Committee of Fifty on College Hygiene. He received an honorary degree from Southwestern Presbyterian University in 1911.

REFERENCES: *DAB* (supp. 1); *LE* (I); *NCAB* (D:268, 28:124); *WWW* (I).   *S. S. Britt, Jr.*

DIX, Dorothea Lynde. B. April 4, 1802, Hampden, Maine, to Joseph and Mary (Bigelow) Dix. M. no. D. July 17, 1887, Trenton, New Jersey.

Daughter of an improvident father and invalid mother, Dorothea Dix left home as an adolescent and lived with relatives. She opened a "dame school" in Worcester, Massachusetts, at the age of fourteen. Charging a small fee, she taught natural science by telling stories of the earth and stars and conducted instruction in reading, writing, and arithmetic.

In 1819 she moved to Boston where she started a school for young ladies in her grandmother's house. She established a charity school for poor children, called the Hope, in the hayloft of the carriage house. The major emphasis of her schools was to develop good moral character, but she also placed a greater than usual emphasis on the natural sciences. She served for several summers as a governess of the daughters of William Ellery Channing. Suffering from exhaustion, she closed her schools in 1836 and traveled to Europe.

As a Sunday school teacher in a Cambridge jail, Dix was shocked to find the insane locked in with criminals in foul and unheated quarters, and she worked from 1841 for humane treatment of the mentally ill. She investigated conditions of the insane in Massachusetts (1841–43) and was successful in lobbying the state legislature for passage of legislation to improve conditions. She continued her work throughout the United States and Europe. She was credited with restructuring or enlarging state mental hospitals in Massachusetts, Rhode Island, New Jersey, Pennsylvania, and Toronto, Ontario, Canada, and with founding state hospitals in eleven other states (1845–52). On a trip to Europe (1854–57), she was successful in persuading the British and Italian governments to open mental hospitals.

She was superintendent of women nurses for the United States during the Civil War. Dix was the author of books for children, including *Conversations on Common Things* (1824), *Hymns for Children, Selected and Altered* (1825), and *Meditations for Private Hours* (1828).

REFERENCES: *DAB; NCAB* (3:438); *NAW; NYT,* July 20, 1887, p. 5; *WC; WWW* (H); Helen E. Marshall, *Dorothea Dix, Forgotten Samaritan* (Chapel Hill: University of North Carolina Press, 1937); Hope Stoddard, *Famous American Women* (New York: Crowell, 1970).

Nancy Baldrige Julian

DOAK, Samuel. B. August 1, 1749, Augusta County, Virginia, to Samuel and Jane Elizabeth (Mitchel) Doak. M. 1776 to Esther H. Montgomery. M. to Margaretta H. McEwen. Ch. seven, including John Whitefield Doak, second president of Washington College in Tennessee, and Samuel Witherspoon Doak, president of Tusculum College in Greeneville, Tennessee. D. December 12, 1829, Greene County, Tennessee.

The Father of Education in Tennessee, Samuel Doak was among the first of many Presbyterian ministers who taught in the Appalachian mountains in log schoolhouses. Despite the poverty of his Scotch-Irish immigrant parents and over the objections of his father, Doak attended academies at Lexington, Virginia, and Colora, Maryland. He studied at the College of New Jersey (later, Princeton University) under John Witherspoon *(q.v.),* who influenced his religious and educational thought. He was graduated in 1775. He studied theology in Virginia at Prince Edward Academy (later, Hampden-Sydney College) and was ordained a minister by the Hanover (Virginia) presbytery in 1777. A classical scholar and lifelong student, he began to study Hebrew and chemistry in his seventies in order to teach students.

Doak preached in frontier settlements of east Tennessee. In 1780 he was invited to settle near Jonesboro, where he purchased a farm and built a log schoolhouse and the Salem Congregational Church. In 1783 the school was chartered by the general assembly of North Carolina of the Presbyterian church as Martin Academy, which has been called the first seat of higher learning west of the Alleghenies. The school operated under charters granted by the state of Franklin (the territory of the United States south of the Ohio River) and the state of Tennessee. In 1795 it was given college status and renamed Washington College (it was later a preparatory school).

In 1818, at the age of sixty-nine, he resigned the presidency of Washington College and joined his younger son, Samuel Witherspoon Doak, in administering Tusculum Academy (later, College) in Greeneville, where he taught until his death at the age of eighty. He received honorary degrees from Washington and Greeneville colleges.

REFERENCES: *AC; DAB; NCAB* (7:340); *TC; WWW* (H); Esther Pritchett Pridgen, "The Influence of Doctor Samuel Doak upon Education in Early East Tennessee" (Master's thesis, East Tennessee State College, 1952).   *Clinton B. Allison*

DOBBS, Ella Victoria. B. June 11, 1866, Cedar Rapids, Iowa, to Edward O'Hail and Jane Jackson (Forsythe) Dobbs. M. no. D. April 13, 1952, Columbia, Missouri.

The elementary and high school education of Ella Victoria Dobbs in the Cedar Rapids, Iowa, public schools was often interrupted because of her ill health. She earned a diploma from Throop Polytechnic Institute (later, California Institute of Technology) in Pasadena, California (1900), the B.S. degree (1909) and diplomas for teaching and for teaching manual training from Columbia University (1909), and the M.A. degree (1913) from the University of Missouri.

Dobbs first taught in one- and two-room rural schools in Silver Ridge, Nebraska (1885–86), Rock Island, Illinois (1886), Salina, Utah, and in a Mormon mission school in Hyrum, Utah. She taught in Logan, Utah, until she left in 1895 to attend Throop Institute. She was a supervisor for handwork in Los Angeles, California (1900–02), and from 1902 to 1907 taught at Throop Institute, was supervisor of manual training in Helena, Montana, and returned to Throop in 1907. Dobbs joined the faculty of the University of Missouri in 1911 as a teacher of manual arts in the school of education, and remained there to her retirement in 1936.

While at Missouri, Dobbs developed a complete curriculum for educational handwork for the elementary grades as a separate department of applied arts (1924) and served as departmental chairman. She was among the first to advocate teaching children, rather than subjects, and to correlate art and handwork with other school classes.

Dobbs was the author of manual arts books, including *Primary Handwork* (1914), *Illustrative Handwork for Elementary School Subjects* (1917), *Our Playhouse* (1924), *First Steps in Art and Handwork* (1932), *First Steps in Weaving* (1938), and *The Place of Art Activities in a Program of General Education* (1939). She coauthored *History of the National Council of Primary Education* (with Lucy Gage, *q.v.*, and Julia L. Hahn, 1932).

She was credited with founding Pi Lambda Theta, an honor society for women in 1911 (president, 1921–25), the National Council of Primary Education in 1915 (president, 1915–25), and in Columbia, Missouri, the first parent-teacher group, the Equal Suffrage Association (1912), and a branch of the League of Women Voters (1920). She was president of the Missouri State Teachers Association (1925). Dobbs was honored through a Pi Lambda Theta scholarship (1923) by the state of Missouri as one of fifty-five women who helped achieve woman suffrage and by the Association for Childhood Education on the Roll of Honor of leaders of early childhood education. In 1940 the Women's Centennial Congress recognized her as one of one hundred women successful in careers not open to women in 1840.

REFERENCES: *LE* (II); *WWAE* (IX); Agnes Snyder, *Dauntless Women in Childhood Education, 1856–1931* (Washington, D.C.: Association for Childhood Education International, 1972); Verna Wulfekammer, *Ella Victoria Dobbs–Portrait Biography* (Pi Lambda Theta, 1961).

Elizabeth S. Oelrich

DOCK, Christopher. B. 1698, Germany, to n.a. M. to n.a. Ch. two. D. 1771, Skippack, Pennsylvania.

Christopher Dock was born sometime in 1698 in Germany. There is no information about his parents, and no report is made of his wife, although the records show that he had two daughters. He was found dead in the schoolhouse in which he taught during the fall of 1771.

Dock, a German Mennonite, arrived in Germantown, Pennsylvania, in 1714. He operated a school among the Mennonites at Skippack, Pennsylvania (1718–28). He farmed from 1728 to 1738 and returned to teaching in two schools at Skippack and Salford.

Christopher Saur, the Germantown publisher, recognized the superior methods Dock used in his schools and convinced Dock in 1750 to write a description of his method of keeping school. Under the agreement with Saur, the manuscript was to be published after Dock's death, but Dock relented and it was published in 1770, one year before his death. *Schulordnung* [School management] was written in German and is the earliest known book published in America about professional education. Demand for the book was great, and a second edition was printed in the same year.

In 1764 the *Geistliches Magazien* published a lengthy presentation by Dock directed at his former pupils. The same magazine later published Dock's *One Hundred Rules of Conduct for Children*. He also wrote a number of hymns used in the Mennonite churches of Pennsylvania for more than a hundred years after his death.

REFERENCES: *DAB; WWW* (H); Martin G. Brumbaugh *(q.v.)*, *The Life and Works of Christopher Dock* (Philadelphia: J. B. Lippincott Co., 1908); Paul Monroe *(q.v.)*, *Cyclopedia of Education* (New York: Macmillan Co.,

1915); Samuel W. Pennypacker, *Historical and Biographical Sketches* (Philadelphia: Robert A. Tripple, 1883).   *J. Marc Jantzen*

DOD, Thaddeus. B. March 7, 1740, Newark, New Jersey, to Stephen and Deborah (Brown) Dod. M. c. 1773 to Phoebe Baldwin. Ch. none. D. May 20, 1793, Ten Mile, Pennsylvania.

Thaddeus Dod was graduated from the College of New Jersey (later, Princeton University) in 1773. He studied theology, was licensed as a Presbyterian minister in 1775, and was ordained by the presbytery of New York for work on the western frontier in 1777.

After spending two years at Patterson's Creek, Virginia (later in Hampshire County, West Virginia), Dod established a church at Ten Mile, Pennsylvania, in 1779. He was the second minister to settle west of the Monongahela River and the first to establish a presbytery beyond the Alleghenies.

Dod opened a school for thirteen pupils in a log cabin near his new home in 1782, the first classical school west of the Alleghenies. The curriculum included English, the classics, mathematics, and surveying. Dod was a classical scholar who knew Hebrew and had a special interest in mathematics. His log cabin academy closed in 1785.

He was one of the trustees who received a charter to establish an academy at Washington, Pennsylvania. The school opened on April 1, 1789, with Dod as first principal. The courthouse in which the academy was housed burned during the winter of 1790–91 and Dod lost most of his books, but Washington Academy continued and became Washington College in 1806. Dod helped organize a school at nearby Canonsburg, Pennsylvania, which developed into Jefferson College. In subsequent years the two institutions merged as Washington and Jefferson College, and a medical school that had developed at Canonsburg moved to Philadelphia.

REFERENCES: *AC; DAB; NCAB* (7:536); *TC; WWW* (H).
Harold D. Lehman

DODDS, Harold Willis. B. June 28, 1889, Utica, Pennsylvania, to Samuel and Alice (Dunn) Dodds. M. December 25, 1917, to Margaret Murray. Ch. none.

Harold Willis Dodds received the A.B. degree (1909) from Grove City (Pennsylvania) College, and A.M. degree (1914) from Princeton (New Jersey) University, and the Ph.D. degree (1917) from the University of Pennsylvania.

He served as an instructor in economics at Purdue University in Lafayette, Indiana (1914–16), assistant professor of political science at Western Reserve University (later, Case Western Reserve University) in Cleveland, Ohio (1916–20), secretary of the National Municipal League (1920–28), and professor of politics at Princeton University (1927–34).

Dodds was president of Princeton University (1933–57), and the university's programs and physical plant expanded significantly during his presidency. The James Forrestal Research Center was established in 1951 and the Council of the Humanities in 1953. Research programs were initiated and expanded. In a new program of studies initiated in 1947, freshmen studied in four liberal arts areas, sophomores chose their area of concentration, and seniors engaged in original research.

Author of *Out of This Nettle–Danger* (1943) and *The Academic President–Educator or Caretaker?* (1962) and editor of *National Municipal Review* (1920–33), Dodds wrote many articles, surveys, and reports in political science. He was a consultant to several foreign governments and executive secretary in Pennsylvania for the United States Food Administration (1917–19). He was a trustee of the Carnegie Foundation for the Advancement of Teaching (1935) and Danforth Foundation (1957–64) and member and trustee of the General Education Board (1937). He was chairman of the President's Committee on Integration of Medical Services of the Government (1946), of the task force on personnel of the Second Hoover Commission (1954–55), and of the American delegation to the Anglo-American Conference on the Refugee Problem in Bermuda (1943). He was the recipient of over thirty honorary degrees from American and foreign universities.

REFERENCES: *CB* (December 1945); *LE* (III); *NCAB* (D:59); *WW* (XXXVI); *WWAE* (XVI); *National Municipal Review* 46 (July 1957): 387.

John F. Ohles

DODGE, Ebenezer. B. April 22, 1819, Salem, Massachusetts, to Ebenezer and Joanna (Appleton) Dodge. M. 1846 to Sarah Abbot Putnam. M. 1863 to Eleanor F. Rogers. Ch. none. D. January 5, 1890, Hamilton, New York.

Ebenezer Dodge was graduated from Brown University in Providence, Rhode Island, in 1840 and from Newton (Massachusetts) Theological Institution in 1845. After serving churches in New Hampton and New London, New Hampshire, he became professor of biblical criticism and interpretation at Hamilton (New York) Theological Seminary and, professor of evidences of Christianity at Madison University, Hamilton, New York (1853). In 1861 he was professor of Christian theology at Hamilton Seminary.

He was president and professor of philosophy of Madison University and president of Hamilton Theological Seminary from 1868 to his death in 1890. During his years as president, Dodge guided Madison University with marked success, academically and financially. Two supporters of the institution, James B. Colgate and John B. Trevor, contributed substantially to the college. The increase in financial resources enabled Dodge to enlarge the instructional facilities, increase the size of the faculty, and erect buildings, including a new library. In 1890 the name of the university was changed to Colgate University. In 1891 James H. Colgate established the Dodge Memorial Fund for general endowment purposes, a gift that strengthened the financial base of the university.

In addition to articles in various periodicals, Dodge was the author of *Christian Evidences* (1868) and *Theological Lectures* (1883).

REFERENCES: *AC; DAB; NCAB* (5:428); *WWW* (H). *J. Franklin Hunt*

DODGE, Grace Hoadley. B. May 21, 1856, New York, New York, to William Earl and Sarah (Hoadley) Dodge. M. no. D. December 27, 1914, New York, New York.

Eldest of six children born to a wealthy New York City family distinguished in business and humanitarian activities, Grace Hoadley Dodge was educated by tutors, finishing with two years at Miss Porter's School in Farmington, Connecticut (1872–74).

Dodge chose to engage in social work rather than enjoy a life in New York's affluent society. While teaching Sunday school in the industrial school of the Children's Aid Society, she developed a fellowship and discussion group for factory girls, which grew into a club with classes in cooking and sewing and a resident doctor available for health care.

She became a teacher in "kitchen garden classes," which used kindergarten methods to teach household arts to young working-class girls. She helped form the Kitchen Garden Association in 1880; reorganized in 1884 into the Industrial Education Association (IEA), the association was broadened to include manual training for boys and to encourage domestic and industrial classes in the public schools. Although her title was vice-president of the association, she was its real leader. She was one of the first two women appointed to city board of education in 1886. As a member of the board, she promoted manual training, blocked efforts to curtail evening classes for working girls, and became the spokesman of New York's 3,500 women teachers.

The IEA sought to meet a growing demand by placing special emphasis on teacher training, and in 1887 Dodge raised funds and made a young Columbia professor, Nicholas Murray Butler *(q.v.)*, the salaried head of the association. In 1889 the IEA was reorganized into the New York College for Training of Teachers (later, Teachers College); it became part of Columbia University in 1898.

Interested in the welfare of underprivileged young women, Dodge established the Girls' Public School Athletic League in 1905. She promoted the merger of several groups into the American Social Hygiene Association in 1912 and consolidated several church-supported groups into the New York Travelers Aid Society (1907). Dodge was named president of the national board of the Young Women's Christian Association of the United States (1906) and served as president of the trustees of the American College for

Girls at Constantinople, Turkey. She was the treasurer and a member of the board of Teachers College (1892–1911). She donated money for a home economics building that was later named after her.

REFERENCES: *AC; DAB; NAW; NCAB* (18:310); *WC; WWW* (I); *NYT,* December 18, 1914, p. 9, Abbie Graham, *Grace H. Dodge, Merchant of Dreams* (New York: The Woman's Press, 1926). *M. Jane Dowd*

DODGE, Richard Elwood. B. March 30, 1868, Wenham, Massachusetts, to Robert Francis and Sarah Elizabeth (Wood) Dodge. M. August 19, 1896, to Stella Pomeroy Dalton. Ch. two. D. April 2, 1952, Mansfield Center, Connecticut.

Richard Elwood Dodge received his education at the Phillips grammar school, Salem High School and Harvard University, from which he received the A.B. (1890) and A.M. (1894) degrees.

While a college student he became interested in geology and following graduation was an assistant in the Atlantic Coast division of the United States Geological Survey (1890–93). He was an instructor in geology at Harvard (1894–95); he spent his summers as an assistant in the Appalachian division of the Geological Survey.

In 1895 Dodge became an instructor in geology at Teachers College in New York City, which was affiliated with Columbia University in 1898. He left Columbia in 1916. He was with the extension service of the state of Connecticut and served as dean of Connecticut State College (1920–30) and professor of geology (1926–38).

Dodge founded and was a coeditor of the *Journal of School Geography* (1897), which became the *Journal of Geography* in 1902. He wrote numerous papers on the subject of geology and geography and was the author of *Reader in Physical Geography for Beginners* (1900), *Dodge's Geographies* (1903), *Dodge's Geographical Note Books* (1912), and *Dodge-Lackey Geographies* (1927). He coauthored *Teaching of Geography in the Elementary Schools* (with Clara B. Kirchevey, 1913), *The World and Its People* (with Earl E. Lackey, 1932), and *United States* (two volumes, with others, 1934).

Dodge belonged to many geological and geographic societies, including the Association of American Geographers (president, 1915), and received the Distinguished Award from the National Council of Geography Teachers in 1946. He was a district governor of Rotary International (1930–31).

REFERENCES: *LE* (I); *NCAB* (13:549); *WWAE* (I); *WWW* (III); *NYT,* April 3, 1952, p. 35. *Gorman L. Miller*

DORSEY, Susan Almira Miller. B. February 16, 1857, Penn Yan, New York, to James and Hannah (Benedict) Miller. M. June 4, 1881, to Patrick

William Dorsey. Ch. one. D. February 5, 1946, Los Angeles, California.

Susan Almira Miller Dorsey studied in the local Penn Yan, New York, public schools and Penn Yan Academy. She was graduated with the A.B. degree (1877) from Vassar College in Poughkeepsie, New York.

She taught Latin and Greek at Wilson College in Chambersburg, Pennsylvania (1877–78), and taught at Vassar College (1878–81). After her marriage in 1881, she went to Los Angeles, California, where her husband was pastor of the First Baptist Church. Dorsey was a social welfare worker and a charter member of the Los Angeles chapter of the Women's Christian Temperance Union. She began to teach at the Baptist College in Los Angeles (1893–96).

Deserted by her husband and young son in 1894, Dorsey continued to teach and joined the faculty of Los Angeles High School as a teacher (1896–1903), department chairman (1903–07), and vice-principal (1902–13). She was the first woman assistant superintendent of schools (1913–20), the first woman superintendent of schools in Los Angeles (1920–29), and one of the first women superintendents of a major American city.

While Dorsey was superintendent, the Los Angeles schools expanded at a rapid rate, increasing enrollment almost two and one-half times, requiring passage of bond issues and the building of new schools. She supported higher teachers' salaries and job tenure.

Dorsey was active in professional organizations, serving as president of the southern section of the California Teachers Association (1914). She was chairman of the Southern California Committee on the Cause and Cure of War and vice-president of the Women's Law Observance Association. She was a trustee of Scripps College (1927) and the University of Redlands (1929–33). She was made an honorary life president of the National Education Association (1933) and was the recipient of several honorary degrees. A Los Angeles high school was named for her in 1937.

REFERENCES: *LE*(I); *NAW; WW* (XVI); *NYT,* February 6, 1946, p. 23.   *Joan Duff Kise*

DOUGHERTY, Blanford Barnard. B. October 21, 1870, Boone, North Carolina, to Daniel and Ellen Caroline (Bartlette) Dougherty. M. no. D. May 27, 1957, Boone, North Carolina.

Blanford Barnard Dougherty attended a local Boone, North Carolina, one-room school, New River Academy, near Boone, Boone Academy, and Globe Academy in Caldwell County, North Carolina. He studied at Wake Forest College at Raleigh, North Carolina (1892), Holly Springs College in Butler, Tennessee (1893), and Carson-Newman College in Mossy Creek, Tennessee, from which he received the B.S. degree (1896). He received the Ph.B. degree (1899) from the University of North Carolina.

While Dougherty was moving from one college to another, he taught school in North Carolina at Shell's Mills (1890), Zionville Academy (1891–92), and Blowing Rock (1892). He was principal of Hamilton Institute at Beaver Creek (1892) and Globe Academy (1893–95 and 1896–97). He taught Latin and mathematics at Holly Springs College (1897–98).

At the urging of their father, Dougherty and his brother Dauphin opened Watauga Academy in Boone, North Carolina, in the old Boone Academy building in 1899. Dougherty served as superintendent of Watauga County schools from 1899 to 1915.

In 1903 the Appalachian Training School opened in the Watauga Academy building to serve North Carolina mountain youth with Dougherty as superintendent. The school offered a public school, high school, and teacher-training course. By 1920 the school consisted of eight buildings, including classrooms, administration offices, and dormitories. There were also cottages for workers, barns, and shops. In 1921 the institution became a state center for training teachers and in 1925 became the Appalachian State Normal School (later, State University) with Dougherty the president. In 1929 the Appalachian State Teachers College was granted authority by the state to provide four-year programs and confer degrees. Dougherty retired in 1955 at the age of eighty-five.

In addition to his educational responsibilities, Dougherty was president of the Watauga County Bank (1929–34). He served on the state board of education (1945–57), state board of equalization, state school commission (1933–43), and state textbook commission. He was a member of the North Carolina Education Association (committee member, 1925). Dougherty was awarded honorary degrees by Elon College (1926) and the University of North Carolina.

REFERENCES: *LE* (III); *WWW* (III); *WWAE* (XVI); Ruby J. Lanier, *Blanford Barnard Dougherty; Mountain Educator* (Durham, N.C.: Duke University Press, 1974).   *John F. Ohles*

DOUGLASS, Harl Roy. B. June 22, 1892, Richmond, Missouri, to Joseph Allen and Gorda Ann (Lester) Douglass. M. August 1912 to Zanna Mae Mitchell. Ch. three. D. August 19, 1972, Boulder Colorado.

Harl Roy Douglass received the B.S. (1915), A.M. (1921), and Ph.D. (1927) degrees from Stanford University.

Early in his career he taught mathematics at the University of Missouri high school (1913) and was superintendent of schools in Perry, Missouri (1914–17), and Ontario, Oregon (1917–19).

Douglass was on the faculty of the University of Oregon as professor of education and superintendent of the university high school (1919–28). On leave from Oregon, he was acting associate professor of education at Stanford University (1923–24). He was a lecturer in education at the University of Pennsylvania (1928–29) and professor of education at the

University of Minnesota (1929–38). In 1938 he became Kenan Professor of Secondary Education and chairman of the division of teaching at the University of North Carolina.

Douglass was director of the college of education at the University of Colorado from 1940 to 1958, retiring from the university in 1968. He continued to be active as a speaker, writer, and consultant. He believed that the arts and sciences must be prominent in teacher education. In 1936 he was a consultant to the American Youth Commission of the American Council on Education.

He was the author of seventy-five books and monographs. He edited the Douglass Series on Education (five volumes, 1947–52) and was the author of three volumes in the series, *Teaching in High School* (with Hubert H. Mills, 1948), *American Public Education* (with Calvin Grieder, 1948), and *Secondary Education for Life Adjustment* (1952). Among his other books were *Modern Methods in High School Teaching* (1926), *Organization and Administration of Secondary Schools* (1932), *Junior Mathematics* (three volumes, with Lucien B. Kenney, 1940), *Everyday Arithmetic* (two volumes, with Lucien B. Kenney and Donald W. Lentz, 1950), *Trends and Issues in Secondary Education* (1962), and *Modern Administration of Secondary Schools* (1963).

Douglass edited *The High School* (1920–28) and served on the boards of editors of the *Journal of Educational Research, Journal of Experimental Education, Clearing House,* and *Secondary Education.*

He was president of the Society of College Teachers of Education in 1938 and a member of many other professional associations. He was awarded an honorary degree by the University of Maine (1960).

REFERENCES: *LE* (III); *WWAE* (XXII); *WW* (XXX).

Vernon E. Anderson

DOUGLASS, Mabel Smith. B. February 11, 1877, Jersey City, New Jersey, to James Weaver and Wilhelmine Joanne (Midlige) Smith. M. April 14, 1903, to William Shipman Douglass. Ch. two. D. September 21, 1933, Lake Placid, New York.

Mabel Smith Douglass received a public school education through the secondary level in Jersey City, New Jersey, and was graduated from Barnard College of Columbia University in 1899. She taught in the New York public schools until 1903. She married merchant William Shipman Douglass in 1903; after his death in 1917, she operated the W. S. Douglass & Co., a butter, egg, and cheese business.

An energetic and persistent organizer, Douglass wanted to make Rutgers University a coeducational college. Failing that, she accepted the establishment by the Rutgers' trustees of an affiliate, the New Jersey College for Women, in New Brunswick. She served as dean, where she held much power and authority, from its founding in 1918 until 1932, when she took a leave of absence, followed in 1933 by her resignation. The college had developed extensively during her tenure.

Mabel Smith Douglass served as a member of the New Jersey State Board of Education. She wrote *The Early History of New Jersey College for Women* (1929). Honors she received included honorary degrees from Rutgers (1924), Russell Sage College (1932), officier d'académie designation from the French government (1932), and a medal from Columbia University (1931). New Jersey College was renamed Douglass College in 1955.

REFERENCES: *LE* (I); *NAW; WWW* (V); *NYT,* May 23, September 22, October 29, 1933, September 27, 1963. *Joan Williams*

DOVE, David James. B. c. 1696, Portsmouth, England, to David and Mary Dove. M. to n.a. Ch. n.a. D. April 4, 1769, Philadelphia, Pennsylvania.

David James Dove was a pamphleteer and educator of colonial America. His early life is obscure, but he taught grammar in England for sixteen years before coming to America. He arrived in Philadelphia, Pennsylvania, in 1750 and was a teacher of English in the Philadelphia Academy where he was appointed English master (1750).

In September 1751 he opened an academy for young ladies as one of the first American educators to provide higher education for women. Dove was elected as the English master of the new Germantown (Pennsylvania) Union School in 1761 and served there until 1763. He built his own school next to the Union School and opened it in 1763. He continued his school at Germantown until 1768, when he taught at a school in Philadelphia.

Dove used chastisement in place of corporal punishment in his schools and generally was in advance of the pedagogy of his time. He was the author of *Labour in Vain* (1757) and *The Quaker Unmask'd* (1764). He also wrote *The Lottery* (1757), which attacked lotteries employed by educational institutions to raise funds.

REFERENCES: *DAB; WWW* (H). *Michael R. Cioffi*

DOW, Arthur Wesley. B. 1857, Ipswich, Massachusetts, to David F. and Mary P. Annable Dow. M. 1893 to Eleanor Pearson. Ch. none. D. December 13, 1922, Ipswich, Massachusetts.

An artist, teacher, and author, Arthur Wesley Dow received his early education at Ipswich (Massachusetts) High School and Putnam High School in Newburyport, Massachusetts. He was privately tutored in the classics. He studied art in Boston and in Paris, France, where he was a pupil of Gustave Rodolphe Clarence Boulanger and Jules Joseph Lefebvre. During his student years he was awarded medals at the Buffalo, Pan-American, and Panama-Pacific expositions. His pictures were exhibited in the Salon, Paris (1886–87), and he received honorable mention on his work in Paris (1889).

Dow was curator of Japanese art at the Boston Museum of Fine Arts. He was an instructor of art at Pratt Institute, Brooklyn, New York (1895–1904), and instructor of composition at the Art Students' League in New York (1897–1903). For a number of years he directed the Summer School of Art at Ipswich, Massachusetts.

He was head of the department of fine arts at Teachers College, Columbia University, from 1904 to his death in 1922. The art department grew from one section of thirty-five students to more than seven times that number. At Teachers College, Dow worked with John Dewey (*q.v.*) who introduced Dow to progressive educational philosophy. Their students later provided leadership in elementary and secondary art education.

Dow changed the direction of art education in the United States. He first introduced the Japanese wood block method into schools, and he was the first to study the art methods of primitive people. He did much to increase the importance of art in the curriculum of public schools and colleges.

Dow was the author of a number of articles and books, including *Composition* (1899) and *The Theory and Practice of Teaching Art* (1908).

REFERENCES: *WWW* (I); Frederick M. Logan, *Growth of Art in American Schools* (New York: Harper & Brothers, 1955), *NYT,* December 14, 1922, p. 21; *School and Society* 17 (January 6, 1923): 17.

Roger H. Jones

DOWNEY, John. B. 1765, Germantown, Pennsylvania, to John and Sarah Downey. M. to Alice Ann Beatty. Ch. n.a. D. July 26, 1826, Harrisburg, Pennsylvania.

John Downey spent his early life in the vicinity of his birth, Germantown, Pennsylvania. Although his father, head of the English School of the Germantown Academy, was killed in 1774, his mother's efforts made it possible for him to receive a classical education. In 1795 Downey moved to Harrisburg, where he opened a school. While he taught school, he served the city and the commonwealth in various positions as justice of peace, town clerk, and member of the legislature. He was treasurer of a company that built a bridge across the Susquehanna River at Harrisburg, and, under his direction, the Harrisburg and Middleton Turnpike Company was incorporated.

Downey is best known for a plan of education he submitted to the governor of Pennsylvania in 1797. The plan proposed the establishment of elementary schools in townships, advanced schools (high schools), and academies for the teaching of liberal science courses. The system was to have its major support in a property tax system. Attendance in the school would be required. Although his plan was not used at the time, it was later considered to have great merit and influenced future school organization.

Downey was the author of numerous political sketches of a humorous vein, which were written under the pen names of Simon the Wagoner, Simon Slim, or Simon Easy. A compilation of the sketches was made in *Justice's Assistant*.

REFERENCES: *AC; DAB; WWW* (H). *Gorman L. Miller*

DOWNING, Elliot Rowland. B. November 21, 1868, Boston, Massachusetts, to Orrien Elliot and Mary Jane (Rowland) Downing. M. June 24, 1902, to Grace Emma Manning. Ch. three. D. September 10, 1944, Williams Bay, Wisconsin.

Elliot Rowland Downing attended Ishpeming, Michigan, public schools and Albion (Michigan) College, where he received the B.S. (1889) and M.S. (1894) degrees. He was a fellow at the University of Chicago (1899–1901), where he received the Ph.D. degree (1901), and studied at Columbia University (1907–08), the University of Würzburg, Germany, and the Naples (Italy) Aquarium (1908).

Downing was an instructor at the Fort Payne (Alabama) Academy (1890–91) and the Beloit (Wisconsin) College Academy (1891–96). He was superintendent of the Disciplinary Training School for Boys in Brooklyn, New York (1896–98), and secretary of the Brooklyn Children's Aid Society (1898–99). He was professor of biology at the Northern State Normal School (later, Northern Michigan University) at Marquette, Michigan (1901–11). In 1911 he joined the faculty of the University of Chicago as an assistant and associate professor of natural science and served as assistant dean of the school of education (1913–16). He retired in 1934.

Downing was the author of a number of books, including *A Field and Laboratory Guide in Biological Nature-Study* (1918), *The Third and Fourth Generation* (1918), *A Source Book of Biological Nature-Study* (1919), *A Field and Laboratory Guide in Physical Nature-Study* (1920), *A Naturalist in the Great Lakes Region* (1922), *Our Physical World* (1924), *Our Living World* (1924), *Teaching Science in the Schools* (1925), *Elementary Eugenics* (1928), *Science in the Service of Health* (1930), *Introduction to the Teaching of Science* (1934), *A Learning Guide in Biology* (with Veva H. McAtee, 1936), and *Living Things and You* (with Veva H. McAtee, 1940). He served as editor of the *Nature Study Review* (1907–11).

A fellow of the American Association for the Advancement of Science and a member of several professional and scientific organizations, he was president of the National Association of Research in Science Society (1930–32).

REFERENCES: *LE* (I); *NCAB* (37:205); *WWW* (II); *School Science and Mathematics* 45 (February 1945): 101–02; *Science Education* 28 (December 1944): 289. *John F. Ohles*

DOYNE, John James. B. October 28, 1858, Farmville, Virginia, to John and Agnes (Stratton) Doyne. M. November 1, 1882, to Ida Beard. Ch. three. D. September 6, 1944, Lonoke, Arkansas.

John James Doyne was graduated from the local Farmville high school and studied for three years at the University of Virginia. He moved to the small village of Lonoke, Arkansas, in 1879 where he was a teacher in the village schools (1879–88), taught at Fort Smith (1888–90), and returned to Lonoke as teacher and administrator (1890–99) and as the county examiner for Lonoke County for fourteen years and Sebastian County for one year.

He was elected to the office of state superintendent of public instruction of Arkansas and served from 1898 to 1902 and 1906 to 1908; in the intervening years (1902–06) he was deputy state superintendent. In 1908 he became the first president of the new State Normal School (later, the State College of Arkansas) at Conway. He was president for nine years and was instrumental in establishing and formulating its curriculum and organization as a teacher-training institution.

Doyne became superintendent of the Lonoke schools in 1917 and served until he was seventy-nine years old. He was superintendent of the Arkansas State School for the Blind (1937–39). He retired from active work in 1939 and died in 1944, the dean of Arkansas educators of his time.

Doyne was a life member of the Arkansas Education Association (president, 1888 and 1897). For five years he was editor of *The Arkansas Teacher,* a state publication.

REFERENCES: *LE* (I); WW (IX); *Arkansas Gazette* (Little Rock), September 7, 1944; *Centennial History of Arkansas* (Chicago: S. J. Clarke Publishing Co., 1922), vol. 2; T. M. Stinnett and Clara B. Kennan, *All This and Tomorrow Too* (Little Rock: Arkansas Education Association, 1969).

Carl F. Vaupel, Jr.

DRAKE, Daniel. B. October 20, 1785, near Plainfield, New Jersey, to Isaac and Elizabeth (Shotwell) Drake. M. April 10, 1807, to Harriet Sisson. Ch. four, including Charles Daniel Drake, lawyer, jurist, and United States senator. D. November 6, 1852, Cincinnati, Ohio.

Daniel Drake, an important medical educator, was the son of poor parents who left New Jersey in 1788 and migrated to Kentucky. They settled on a farm on the Ohio River in an area called Mays Lick, Kentucky.

Drake was sent to Fort Washington (now Cincinnati, Ohio) in 1800 to study medicine and Latin under the tutelage of Dr. William Goforth, a leading physician of the town. Drake received his diploma from Goforth and became his partner in 1804. He studied for one term at the Medical College of the University of Pennsylvania in 1805 and returned to Mays Lick to practice medicine. In 1807 he went back to Cincinnati in partnership with Goforth. Drake developed an extensive medical practice, and he became proprietor of a drugstore and later of a general store.

Drake's desire was to teach medicine, and he returned to the University of Pennsylvania medical school in 1815. He received the M.D. degree (1816) and returned to practice medicine in Cincinnati. He taught materia medica in the medical department at Transylvania University in Lexington, Kentucky (1817–18). He returned to Cincinnati in 1818 to establish a medical school. In 1819 Drake obtained a charter and founded the Ohio Medical College (later, Medical College of the University of Cincinnati). He was a professor of medicine and first president of the school. Internal troubles in the school led to his removal from the presidency on March 6, 1822. Reinstated a week later on the insistence of people in the community, he resigned and left the college.

Drake returned to Transylvania University in 1823 as a professor and was dean of the school from 1825 to 1827. On the death of his wife in 1827, Drake returned to Cincinnati and established the first eye and ear clinic in the Mississippi Valley. In 1828 he joined the faculty at Jefferson Medical School in Philadelphia, returned to Cincinnati in 1829, and organized a medical school as a department of Miami University (Ohio). The school experienced many difficulties and closed in 1830; Drake again joined the faculty at the Ohio Medical College and left in 1831.

He established a medical department at Cincinnati College that was in operation from 1831 to 1839. He moved to Louisville, Kentucky, and became a professor at the Louisville Medical Institute and in 1849 was again president of the Ohio Medical College. He returned to Louisville Medical Institute in 1850 and for the third time was president of the Ohio Medical College in 1852, but died shortly after taking the position.

Drake was the author of many articles in professional journals and *Notices Concerning Cincinnati* (1810), *Natural and Statistical View or Picture of Cincinnati* (1815), *A Practical Treatise on the History, Prevention, and Treatment of Epidemic Cholera* (1832), and *A Systematic Treatise, Historical, Etiological, and Practical, on the Diseases of the Interior Valley of North America* (1850). He founded and edited the *Western Medical and Physical Journal* (1827). He was a member of several medical and scholarly societies and was active in many civic enterprises.

REFERENCES: *DAB; NCAB* (5:110); *WWW* (H); John H. Talbott, *A Biographical History of Medicine* (New York: Grune and Stratton, 1954).

Richard M. Coger

DRAPER, Andrew Sloan. B. June 21, 1848, Westford, New York, to Sylvester Bigelow and Jane (Sloan) Draper. M. May 8, 1872, to Abbie Louise Lyon. Ch. two. D. April 27, 1913, Albany, New York.

Andrew Sloan Draper was educated in the Albany, New York, public schools and was graduated from the Albany Academy in 1866. He received the LL.B. degree (1871) from the Albany Law School.

While studying law, Draper had taught at the Albany Academy and a private school in Westford (1866–70). He practiced law in Albany (1871–84), was active in Republican politics and served in the state legislature (1881), and was a member of the Albany board of education (1879–81 and 1890–92). He had been appointed judge of the United States court of commissioners on the Alabama Claims case (1884–86). He was superintendent of schools in Cleveland, Ohio (1892–94).

Draper's greatest contributions were made during his six years as New York State superintendent of public instruction (1886–92) and nine years as commissioner of education (1904–13). He worked to establish uniformity among the state normal schools in admissions, methods, practice teaching, and graduation requirements. The school year was extended from twenty to thirty-two weeks, written contracts for teachers were mandated, and a system of uniform teachers' examinations was instituted.

He was the first state commissioner of education, a position created by the merger of the department of public instruction and the board of regents, and organized the new department and obtained a new building to house it. He reorganized the state normal school system with a new curriculum that emphasized professionalized subject matter and required a high school diploma for admission. The Albany Normal College (later, State University of New York at Albany) was granted full collegiate status, local school commissioners were replaced by district superintendents with administrative training, all elementary and secondary school courses of study were reorganized, teacher certification requirements were revised, and a statewide teachers' retirement system was established.

Between terms as superintendent of public instruction and commissioner of education, Draper served as president of the University of Illinois (1894–1904). He introduced many educational reforms and a rapid expansion of the institution with seven colleges, ten schools, and a complete university reorganization.

Draper wrote many monographs and was the author of *The Rescue of Cuba* (1899), *Origin and Development of the Common School System of New York State* (1903), *American Education* (1909), and *Agriculture and Its Educational Needs* (1909). He was editor of the ten-volume *Draper's Self Culture* (1907). He received a silver medal from the Paris Exposition of 1900 for the monograph *Educational Administration and Organization in the United States* (1900).

Draper was president of the National Association of School Superintendents (1889–91) and the North Central Association of Colleges and Secondary Schools (1903). He was appointed a member of the United States Board of Indian Commissioners (1902). He received honorary degrees from Colgate and Columbia universities and the University of Illinois.

REFERENCES: *AC; DAB; NCAB* (12:498); *TC; WWW* (I); Carey W.

Brush, "The Cortland State Normal School: Response to Changing Needs and Professional Standards, 1866–1942" (Ph.D. diss. Columbia University, 1961); Harlan H. Horner, *The Life and Work of Andrew Sloan Draper* (Urbana: University of Illinois Press, 1934); *NYT*, April 28, 1913, p. 11. *Carey W. Brush*

DRAPER, John William. B. May 5, 1811, St. Helen's, England, to John Christopher and Sarah (Ripley) Draper. M.c. 1830 to Antonia Coetana de Paiva Pereira Gardner. Ch. five. D. January 4, 1882, Hastings-on-Hudson, New York.

John William Draper received his early education in England at home under private tutors and at a public school, where he developed a fondness for science. In 1829 he enrolled in the University of London to study chemistry, but the death of his father in 1832 prevented his completing the program. He emigrated to the United States in 1833, settled in Christianville, Virginia, and operated a scientific laboratory. He studied at the University of Pennsylvania and received the M.D. degree (1836).

Draper became professor of chemistry and natural philosophy at Hampden-Sydney (Virginia) College (1836). Two years later he was professor of chemistry at the Free Academy, which became the City College of New York (later, part of the City University of New York). In 1840 he helped organize the medical department and was professor of chemistry.

As a chemist, Draper investigated capillary action and osmosis. His work on radiant energy was among his most significant. He contributed to spectrum analysis and, following Daguerre's discovery of the action of sunlight on silver and its application to the permanent preservation of images, he made the first complete portrait of a person by sunlight. In 1856 he wrote *Human Physiology, Statical and Dynamical,* which contained the first photomicrographs published. In association with Samuel F. B. Morse, he was the first to establish with certainty the practicability of using electricity for sending messages over long distances.

He also wrote *History of the Intellectual Development of Europe* (1863), *Thoughts on the Future Civil Policy of America* (1865), the authoritative three-volume *History of the American Civil War* (1867–70), and *History of the Conflict Between Religion and Science* (1874), a work translated into many languages.

A member of many learned societies of the United States and Europe, Draper was elected to the American Philosophical Society (1843) and the National Academy of Sciences (1877) and was elected the first president of the American Chemical Society (1876). He was awarded an honorary degree.

REFERENCES: *AC; DAB; DSB; NCAB* (3:406); *WWW* (H); *NYT,* January 5, 1882, p. 8. *Norman J. Bauer*

DRISLER, Henry. B. December 27, 1818, Staten Island, New York, to Henry and Catherine Drisler. M. no. D. November 30, 1897, New York, New York.

Henry Drisler was educated on Staten Island, New York, and was graduated from Columbia College (later, University) in 1839. He taught Greek and Latin in the Columbia Grammar School (1839–45). In 1845 he became adjunct professor of Latin at Columbia College, in 1857 became Columbia's first professor of Latin as a separate field of study, and in 1867 became professor of Greek. Drisler served as acting president (1878, 1888–90) and was appointed the first dean of Columbia College (1890–94).

Drisler was editor of the Riddle and Arnold *Copious and Critical English-Latin Lexicon* (1849), assisted Charles Anthon (*q.v.*) in preparing *Latin-English Dictionary for the Use of Schools* (1852), and edited a revision of Henry George Liddel and Robert Scott's *Greek-English Lexicon* and an enlarged edition of Charles D. Yonge's *English-Greek Lexicon* (1870). He was an assistant editor of *Johnson's New Universal Cyclopedia* (1875–78) and general editor of the Harper Series of Classical Texts.

Drisler was a trustee of the Astor Library, the New York Public Library, the American School of Classical Studies in Athens, Greece, the Trinity School, the General Theological Seminary, and the Leake and Watts Orphan Asylum. He was president of the Columbia Alumni Association (1872–80), vice-president of the Archaeological Institute of America (1886–89), and vice-president of the Society for Promoting Religion and Learning.

On his retirement, he was awarded a gold medal, and the Henry Drisler Fellowship in Classical Philosophy and Henry Drisler Classical Fund for the purchase of books and materials for classical study were established. He was awarded two honorary degrees.

REFERENCES: *AC; DAB; NCAB* (4:254); *TC; WWW* (H).

Barbara Ruth Peltzman

DU BOIS, William Edward Burghardt. B. February 23, 1868, Great Barrington, Massachusetts, to Alfred and Mary (Burghardt) Du Bois. M. May 12, 1896, to Nina Gomer. M. February 14, 1951, to Shirley Graham. Ch. two. D. August 27, 1963, Accra, Ghana.

William E. B. Du Bois was an educator, editor, historian, and a pioneer in Negro culture. He was graduated from Fisk University in Nashville, Tennessee, with the A.B. degree (1888) and entered Harvard University, from which he received the A.B. (1890), M.A. (1891), and Ph.D. (1895) degrees.

His teaching career began at Wilberforce (Ohio) University (1894–96). He taught one year at the University of Pennsylvania (1896–97) before accepting a position as professor of history and economics at Atlanta

(Georgia) University (1897–1910). He was director of publications and editor of *Crisis* for the National Association for the Advancement of Colored People (1910–32). He resigned in 1932 because of ideological differences and returned to Atlanta University as professor of sociology and head of the sociology department (1932–44).

During the early years of his career, Du Bois's advice was widely sought by educators and political leaders. He disagreed with Booker T. Washington's philosophy of accommodation and was an outspoken advocate of complete equality of opportunity for blacks. He viewed agitation and protest as viable means of focusing attention on Negro problems.

His principal written works include *The Suppression of the African Slave-trade to the United States of America, 1638–1870* (1896), *The Study of the Negro Problems* (1898), *The Philadelphia Negro* (1899), *The Talented Tenth* (1903), *The Souls of Black Folk* (1903), *John Brown* (1909), *Quest of the Silver Fleece* (1911), *The Negro* (1915), *Dark Waters* (1920), *The Dark Princess* (1928), *Black Reconstruction* (1935), *Black Folks: Then and Now* (1939), *Dusk of Dawn* (1940), *Color and Democracy* (1945), *The World and Africa* (1947), *In Battle for Peace* (1952), and *Black Flame* (1957–61). He was editor of *Phylon* and editor-in-chief of the *Encyclopedia of the Negro* (1933–45).

Du Bois was one of the founders of the Niagara Movement (1905), a forerunner of the National Association for the Advancement of Colored People. He was a fellow of the American Association for the Advancement of Science, vice-chairman of the Council for African Affairs (1945–49), and chairman of the Peace Information Bureau. In 1940 he founded *Phylon: A Review of Race and Culture*.

His disenchantment with American policies and with the Negro leadership in the United States motivated him to revive the Pan African Congress in 1945, which had first convened in Paris in 1919; he was cochairman of the congress with Kwame Nkrumah of Ghana. His efforts earned for him recognition as Father of Pan-Africanism.

He traveled extensively in communist countries during the 1950s and lectured at universities in Sofia, Bulgaria, Prague, Czechoslovakia, Moscow, U.S.S.R., and Berlin, Germany, He went to Ghana in 1962 where he began editing the first *African Encyclopedia,* joined the Communist party, and became a citizen of Ghana.

He was the first Negro elected to the National Institute of Arts and Letters (1943). Other honors included election to Phi Beta Kappa, honorary degrees conferred by several American universities, and the receipt of the International Peace Price (1952) and Lenin International Peace Prize (1959). He received the Knight Commander of the Liberian Order of African Redemption.

REFERENCES: *CB* (January–June 1940, October 1963); *EB; NCAB*

(13:307); *TC; WWW* (IV); *NYT,* August 28, 1963, p. 33; David L. Sills, ed., *International Encyclopedia of the Social Sciences* (New York: Macmillan and Free Press, 1968), vol. 4; *Who's Who in Colored America*, 7th ed. (Brooklyn, N.Y.: Burckel & Associates, 1950).   *Octavia B. Knight*

DUCHESNE, Rose Philippine. B. August 29, 1769, Grenoble, France, to Pierre François and Rose Euphrosine (Perier) Duchesne. M. no. D. November 18, 1852, St. Charles, Missouri.

The daughter of a prominent family, Rose Philippine Duchesne was born and reared in Grenoble, France. Against the wishes of her family, she entered the visitation novitiate at Saint Marie-d-'en-Haut (Grenoble) in 1788. In two years she was back at home as her father foresaw the coming French Revolution.

After the revolution was over, she gained title to her former convent in 1801 and tried unsuccessfully to reestablish the community. In 1804 Mother (later, Saint) Madeline Sophie Barat, founder of the Society of the Sacred Heart whose primary mission was the education of girls, came to Saint Marie and accepted its residents, including Mother Duchesne, into her congregation. In 1815 Duchesne was elected secretary-general of the society and moved to Paris to oversee the establishment of a motherhouse.

In 1817 when Bishop Louis DuBourg of the Missouri Territories called at the Paris house seeking religious to establish a school for girls in St. Louis, Missouri, Duchesne asked to be allowed to go. As head of a community with four younger sisters, she set sail for the New World at the age of forty-nine. The sisters arrived in Saint Louis in August 1818 and moved to Saint Charles, Missouri. On September 14 they opened the first free non-public school for girls west of the Mississippi River, the first school of the Religious of the Sacred Heart in the United States. The community and the schools were transferred to Florissant, Missouri, in 1819. An increase in the number of French and American sisters and financial support from local families enabled Mother Duchesne to open schools in Louisiana (1821 and 1825), to establish an orphanage, an academy, and a parish school in St. Louis (1827), and to reopen the mission at St. Charles (1828).

At the age of seventy-one and in fragile health, she joined a small group of missionaries serving the Potawatomi Indians at Sugar Creek, Kansas, but returned to St. Charles the following year. She died in 1852 and was beatified by Pope Pius XII in 1940.

REFERENCES: *AC; DAB; NAW; TC; WWW* (H); Marion Bascom, *Blessed Philippine Duchesne, Pioneer Missionary of the New World* (New York: Manhattanville College of the Sacred Heart, 1944); Louise Callen, *Philippine Duchesne* (Westminster, Md.: The Newman Press, 1965); Marjory Erskine, *Mother Philippine Duchesne* (New York: Longman, Green and Co., 1926).   *Anne E. Scheerer*

DUDLEY, James Benson. B. November 3, 1859, Wilmington, North Carolina, to John B. and Annie J. D. Dudley. M. February 23, 1882, to Susie Wright Samson. Ch. none. D. April 4, 1925, Greensboro, North Carolina.

James Benson Dudley, college president, was educated by private teachers until public schools were opened for blacks in North Carolina. He studied at the Philadelphia Institute for Colored Youth and received the A.B. degree from Shaw University in Raleigh, North Carolina (1880), and the A.M. degree from Livingstone College in Salisbury, North Carolina. He also studied at Harvard University and other institutions during the summers.

He served as principal of the Peabody School in Wilmington, North Carolina, from 1880 to 1896, when he was appointed president of North Carolina Agricultural and Technical College (later, State University) in Greensboro, a position he held until his death in 1925. His main interest at the school was in agriculture, and he was always anxious to aid the agricultural interests of the state. In 1912 he was one of the organizers of the State Farmers' Union and Cooperative Society, whose purpose was to help black farmers in North Carolina. He received an honorary degree from Wilberforce (Ohio) University.

REFERENCES: *WWW* (I); Benjamin Brawley *(q.v.)*, *Negro Builders and Heroes* (Chapel Hill: University of North Carolina Press, 1937), Charles H. Hamlin, *Ninety Bits of North Carolina Biography* (New Bern, N.C.: Owen G. Dunn Co., 1946.)   *Don C. Locke*

DUER, William Alexander. B. September 8, 1780, Rhinebeck, New York, to William and Catherine (Alexander) Duer. M. September 11, 1806, to Hannah Maria Denning. Ch. one. D. May 30, 1858, New York, New York.

Son of an American Revolutionary patriot and signer of the Articles of Confederation, William Alexander Duer studied law in Philadelphia and with Nathaniel Pendleton in New York. Admitted to the bar in 1802, he began practice in New York City, moved to New Orleans, Louisiana, to practice, and returned to New York, where he opened an office in Rhinebeck.

Duer was elected to the New York State Assembly in 1814 and served as chairman of a legislative committee on colleges and academies. He served as a judge on the New York State Supreme Court (1822–29) but resigned from the bench to accept the presidency of Columbia College (1829–42).

At Columbia, Duer abolished traditional rank-order class seating. He modified and added courses to the curriculum, including a "scientific and literary course" of study that did not require Latin or Greek for entrance. He established professorships in Hebrew, French, German, Italian, and Spanish and taught a freshman composition course.

Retiring to his country home near Morristown, New Jersey, Duer devoted his time to writing the biography of his grandfather, *The Life of
William Alexander* (1847). He was also the author of *Outlines of the
Constitutional Jurisprudence of the United States* (1833), *A Course of
Lectures on the Constitutional Jurisprudence of the United States* (1843),
and *Reminiscences of an Old Yorker* (1867), which was published posthumously.

REFERENCES: *AC: DAB; NCAB* (6:344); *WWW* (H); Horace Coon,
Columbia—Colossus on the Hudson (New York: E. P. Dutton, 1947).

Ruth Ledbetter Galaz

DUGGAN, Stephen Pierce. B. December 20, 1870, New York, New York,
to Hugh and Mary (Hayden) Duggan. M. January 2, 1902, to Sarah Alice
Elsesser. Ch. four. D. August 18, 1950, Stamford, Connecticut.

Stephen Pierce Duggan was known as the Apostle of Internationalism in
the United States and abroad. He received the B.S. (1890) and M.S. (1896)
degrees from the College of the City of New York (CCNY) and the M.A.
(1898) and Ph.D. (1902) degrees from Columbia University.

Duggan taught international law and then the history of education at
CCNY from 1896 and served as chairman of the education department from
1906. He was organizer and head of the teachers' extension and evening
division and was professor of political science from 1910 until 1928, when
he resigned to work full time on organizations dealing with international
affairs.

Duggan was an organizer of the Institute of International Education at
Columbia University to establish two-way scholarships between American
and foreign universities; he was its first director (1919–46). He was president of the Academy of Public Education in New York City for one year
(1922–23). He was the author of *The Eastern Question* (1902), *A History of
Education* (1916), *The League of Nations* (1919), *The Two Americas*
(1933), *Professor at Large* (1943), an autobiography, and *The Rescue of
Science and Learning* (with Betty Druary, 1948).

Duggan was a founder and director of the Foreign Policy Association,
director of the Council on Foreign Relations, and trustee of the Institute of
Pacific Relations, Vassar College, and World Peace Foundation. He was a
member of the Philippine Education Commission, the League of Nations'
committee on international cooperation, the American Brazilian Conciliation Commission and many other national and international organizations.
He was decorated by the governments of France, the Netherlands, Italy,
Czechoslovakia, Hungary, and Chile and was awarded seven honorary
degrees. He was the first recipient of the John Finley Medal for service to
New York City. The Stephen Duggan Memorial Lectures at the Institute of
International Education were founded in 1950.

REFERENCES: *LE* (III); *NCAB* (38:308, C:61); *WWAE* (XIV); *WWW* (III); *Educational Forum* 15 (November 1950): 128; *Institute of International Education News Bulletin* 26 (October 1950): 3-7; *NYT,* August 29, 1950, p. 13; *School and Society* 92 (August 26, 1950): 143.

E. C. Condon

DUNGLISON, Robley. B. January 1, 1798, Keswick, England, to William and Elizabeth (Robley) Dunglison. M. October 5, 1824, to Harriette Leadham. Ch. seven, including Richard James Dunglison, prominent physician. D. April 1, 1869, Philadelphia, Pennsylvania.

Robley Dunglison has been referred to as the Father of American Physiology. He began the study of medicine in 1814 and passed his examinations at the Royal College of Surgeons in London in 1819, where he had studied for several years. He received a diploma from the Society of Apothecaries and began practice as a surgeon-apothecary. The University of Erlangen, Germany, awarded him the M.D. degree (1823) by examination. One year later (1824), his earliest publication, *Commentaries on the Disease of the Stomach and Bowels of Children,* was published.

As a result of attention created by the book he was invited by Thomas Jefferson *(q.v.)* to be professor of medicine at the University of Virginia and served from 1825 to 1833. He held the chair of materia medica, therapeutics, hygiene, and medical jurisprudence at the University of Maryland (1833–35). He was also professor of the institutes of medicine at Jefferson Medical College, Philadelphia (1836–68). While Dunglison was at Jefferson Medical College, it outranked all other institutions of its kind in America.

A writer on many subjects outside the field of medicine, Dunglison translated and edited many foreign works. Among his medical books were *Human Physiology* (1832), *A New Dictionary of Medical Science and Literature* (1833), *Element of Hygiene* (1835), *General Therapeutics, or Principles of Medical Practice; with Tables of the Chief Remedial Agents, etc.* (1836), *New Remedies; the Method of Preparing and Administering Them* (1839), *The Practice of Medicine* (1842), and *A Dictionary of the English Language for the Use of the Blind* (1860). The medical dictionary was revised by his son in 1874 under the title *Medical Lexicon: A Dictionary of Medical Science.* He was editor of the *American Medical Intelligencer* (1837–44) and *Dunglison's College and Clinical Record* (with Frank Woodbury, 1880–83).

Dunglison was active in many organizations and was particularly active in the cause of the blind, serving as vice-president of the Pennsylvania Institution for the Blind. He was also president of the Philadelphia Musical Fund Society and vice-president of the American Philosophical Society. He received two honorary degrees.

REFERENCES: *AC; DAB; NCAB* (10:270); *WWW* (H); *NYT,* April 4, 1869, p. 3.   *Gorman L. Miller*

DUNSTER, Henry. B. 1609 (baptism November 26), Lancashire, England, to Henry Dunster and his wife (n.a.), M. June 1641 to Elizabeth Harris Glover. M. 1644 to Elizabeth Atkinson. Ch. five. D. February 27, 1659, Scituate, Massachusetts.

Henry Dunster was the first president of Harvard College. He came from a yeoman family in the parish of Bury, Lancashire, England. He attended Magdalene College of Cambridge University, as a sizar (a deserving poor boy who worked his way) and was graduated with the A.B. (1631) and M.A. (1640) degrees. After his first degree he returned to his village to teach in the Latin grammar school and serve as a curate in the local parish.

His Puritan views led to his emigration to Massachusetts in the summer of 1640. Nathaniel Eaton, the head of the new Harvard College, had been dismissed in 1639. On August 27, 1640, Dunster was elected president. He found the college without students, teachers, funds, or buildings, but he was an able administrator and reestablished the college.

Dunster brought from Cambridge University ideas that set a pattern for Harvard (and for other early American colonial colleges). The first commencement was held in the new college hall in September 1642, with nine students receiving degrees. The college library was first supplied with books that were donated by educated people in the colony and especially from the legacy (four hundred volumes) of the Reverend John Harvard, for whom the college was named in 1639.

The college seal, veritas, was accepted in 1643. The most important event of the Dunster years was the charter of 1650, obtained from the general court of Massachusetts, in which the basic purposes of Harvard were set forth and the governance of the institution established.

Dunster was a Hebrew scholar. He was credited with a revision of the Bay Psalm Book, with the help of Richard Lyon, printed in Cambridge in 1651 as *The Psalms, Hymns and Spiritual Songs of the Old and New Testament, Faithfully Translated into English Metre.* This work was widely used in the New England churches.

The first printing press in the English colonies came to Cambridge in 1638. Dunster married the widow of Jose Glover who died on his way to America with this first press and font of type. Stephen Day was the first printer, and Dunster assisted in management of the press. The press was later the property of the college.

Henry Dunster came into conflict with the orthodox Puritan establishment over adult baptism. In 1654 he was removed from his post as president of Harvard and retired to Scituate in the Massachusetts Plymouth Colony.

REFERENCES: *AC; DAB; EB; NCAB* (6:409); *TC; WWW* (H); Samuel

Eliot Morison, *The Founding of Harvard College* (Cambridge: Harvard University Press, 1935); Samuel Eliot Morison, *Three Centuries of Harvard* (Cambridge: Harvard University Press, 1942). *Richard G. Durnin*

DURANT, Henry. B. June, 1802, Acton, Massachusetts, to Henry and Lucy (Hunt) Durant. M. December 10, 1833, to Mary E. Buffet. Ch. one. D. January 22, 1875, Oakland, California.

Henry Durant attended Phillips Academy in Andover, Massachusetts, and was graduated from Yale College in 1827.

He was principal of Garrison Forrest Academy in Baltimore County, Maryland (1827–29), and returned to Yale, where he served as tutor (1829–33) and completed theological studies at Yale Theological Seminary.

He was pastor of the Byfield (Massachusetts) Congregational Church (1833–49). Durant served as a trustee of Governor Dummer Academy in Byfield and was named principal of the academy in 1847, in addition to his duties as minister. In 1849 he resigned from both the church and academy and engaged in the furniture manufacturing business.

Leaving Massachusetts, he arrived in San Francisco, California, on May 1, 1853. He established the Contra Costa Academy in Oakland on June 6, 1853, and served as the principal until 1860. Through Durant's influence, the board of directors of the academy requested and was granted a charter from the state board of education on April 13, 1855, for permission to establish the College of California. By 1860 a class was enrolled with Durant as professor of Greek and mental and moral philosophy.

On March 23, 1868, the legislature provided for the establishment of a state-supported University of California, and the College of California buildings and faculty were turned over to the university. The first president of the University of California was Henry Durant, who was elected to the office on August 16, 1870. Advanced age and failing strength prompted his resignation in 1872. He served as mayor of Oakland from 1873 to his death.

REFERENCES: *DAB; NCAB* (7:228); *TC; WWW* (H); Richard G. Durnin, "Henry Durant: From Byfield to Berkeley," *Essex Institute Historical Collections* 108 (January 1972): 58–74. *Richard G. Durnin*

DuSHANE, Donald. B. June 5, 1885, South Bend, Indiana, to James and Emma (Anderson) DuShane. M. June 29, 1907, to Harriette McLelland. Ch. three. D. March 11, 1947, Washington, D.C.

After attending elementary and secondary schools in South Bend, Indiana, Donald DuShane received the B.S. degree (1906) from Hanover (Indiana) College and the M.S. degree (1913) from the University of Wisconsin.

DuShane began his career teaching at South Bend High School (1906–10). He was named principal of Shelbyville (Illinois) High School (1910–

11), followed by superintendencies in Indiana at Madison (1911–16), Clinton (1916–18), and Columbus (1918–41).

A long-time member of the National Education Association (NEA) DuShane chaired the organization's Committee on Tenure (1934–40). He was author of Indiana's tenure law, which served as a model for many other states. His vigorous pursuit of laws promoting the interests of pupils and teachers led to his election as president of the NEA (1940–41).

From September 1941 until his death, DuShane was the executive secretary of the newly formed National Commission for the Defense of Democracy Through Education. Through this office he vigorously pursued the enhancement of public education, particularly in his investigations of political tampering in the public schools of New York and Chicago. The Chicago investigation ultimately led to the resignation of Superintendent William Johnson and a shakeup of the board of education.

DuShane also served as trustee of the Indiana State Teachers' Retirement Fund (1921–33), and was president of the board of the Southern Indiana Tuberculosis Hospital (1938–41) and of the Indiana Conference on Social Work (1926), Indiana Tuberculosis Association (1937), Indiana State Teachers' Association (1921), and Indiana Society on Mental Hygiene.

In 1949 the NEA established the Donald DuShane Memorial Defense Fund to aid teachers unjustly treated in cases important to the welfare of the profession. He was awarded two honorary doctorates.

REFERENCES; *LE* (II); *WWW* (II); "Donald DuShane," *Nations Schools* 39 (May 1947): 17; "Donald DuShane," *National Education Association Journal* 36 (April 1947): 328; *NYT,* March 13, 1947, p. 28; "Portrait of Donald DuShane," *School and Society* 65 (March 22, 1947): 208; "Tribute to Donald DuShane," *Adult Education Bulletin* 11 (April 1947): 99.

Gerald G. Szymanski

DUTTON, Samuel Train. B. October 16, 1849, Hillsboro, New Hampshire, to Jeremiah and Rebecca (Train) Dutton. M. October 8, 1874, to Cornelia North. Ch. two. D. March 28, 1919, Atlantic City, New Jersey.

Samuel Train Dutton was a pioneering city superintendent and professor of school administration. He began to prepare for the ministry, but on graduation from Yale College with the A.B. degree (1873), he accepted a position as a school principal in South Norwalk, Connecticut. He moved to New Haven as city superintendent in 1882. He later received the A.M. degree (1890) from Yale.

Dutton became superintendent of the Brookline, Massachusetts, schools in 1890, where he established an unusual amount of cooperation between the school, home, and community. He was one of the earliest advocates of the idea that the public school should become a community center.

He was appointed superintendent of the Horace Mann schools in New York City and professor of school administration at Teachers College, Columbia University, in 1900. He became increasingly interested in international education after 1905. He retired in 1915, becoming the first professor emeritus of Teachers College.

Dutton was the author of *Social Phases of Education* (1892), *The Morse Speller* (1896), *School Management* (1903), and *The Administration of Public Education in the United States* (with David Snedden, *q.v.*, 1908).

He was prominent in several peace organizations as a founder of the New York Peace Society (1906), director of the American Peace Society, secretary of the World's Court League, and trustee of the World Peace Foundation. He was among those instrumental in persuading Andrew Carnegie to fund the Carnegie Endowment for International Peace (1910) and was a member of its commission of inquiry into the Balkan War of 1913. He was a trustee of the College for Women in Constantinople, Turkey, and Christian College in Canton, China. He was awarded an honorary degree by Baylor University in 1912.

REFERENCES: *DAB; NCAB* (23:105); *WWW* (I); C. H. Levermore, *Samuel Train Dutton: A Biography* (New York: Macmillan Co., 1922); *NYT,* March 29, 1919, p. 13. *Ronald D. Szoke*

DUVENECK, Frank. B. October 9, 1848, Covington, Kentucky, to Bernard and Katherine (Siemers) Decker. M. March 25, 1886, to Elizabeth Boott. Ch. one. D. January 3, 1919, Cincinnati, Ohio.

Frank (Decker) Duveneck's father died in 1849; his mother married, and the boy adopted the name of his stepfather. He attended Covington, Kentucky, and Cincinnati, Ohio, public schools.

As a youth, Duveneck painted in Latrobe, Pennsylvania, and in Quebec, Canada (1862), and returned to Kentucky where he was involved in the decoration of Catholic churches in Covington. In Cincinnati he worked with a German-trained decorator, Wilhelm Lamprecht (1866). He went to Munich, Germany, to attend the Royal Academy where he studied painting under Wilhelm von Diez and was influenced by Wilhelm Leibl Ludwig Loefftz and Wilhelm Trubner (1870).

Duveneck opened his first school of painting in Munich in 1878 where his pupils and followers were called Duveneck boys. In 1890 he returned to Cincinnati where, during the winter and for several winters following, he taught painting classes in the art museum. In 1900 he taught at the Art Academy of Cincinnati and served until his death in 1919.

His better-known paintings include *He Lives by His Wits, Cobbler's Apprentice, Turkish Page,* and *Whistling Boy.* During his life, Duveneck's work was exhibited widely, showing at the Boston Arts Club, the National Academy of Design in New York, the Society of Painters-Etchers, the

Louisiana Purchase Exposition, and the Exhibition of American Art in Berlin.

He received numerous awards, including medals from the Columbian Exposition in Chicago (1893), the Pan-American Exposition in Buffalo (1901), the National Academy (1906), and a special gold medal of honor at the Panama-Pacific Exposition in San Francisco (1915). He was honored by appointments to various panels and juries and was awarded an honorary degree by the University of Cincinnati (1917).

REFERENCES: *DAB; NCAB* (20:87); *WWW* (I); *NYT,* January 4, 1919, p. 11; Walter H. Siple, *Frank Duveneck: Catalog: Exhibition of the Works of Frank Duveneck* (Cincinnati, Ohio: Cincinnati Art Museum, May 1936).   *Roger H. Jones*

DWIGHT, Francis. B. March 14, 1808, Springfield, Massachusetts, to James Scutt and Mary (Sanford) Dwight. M. July 24, 1834, to Catherine Van Rensselaer Schermerhorn. M. April 20, 1843, to Catherine Waters Yates. Ch. none. D. December 15, 1845, Albany, New York.

Francis Dwight, the eighth of twelve children, was the son of a wealthy Springfield (Massachusetts) businessman. He was graduated from Phillips Academy in Exeter, New Hampshire, and Harvard University (1827) and studied law at Northampton, Massachusetts, and at Harvard Law School under John Hooker Ashmun (1827–30).

Dwight practiced law in Massachusetts, Michigan Territory, and Geneva, New York (1834–38). He became interested in the field of education and moved to Albany, New York.

John Canfield Spencer, the secretary of state of New York and superintendent of common schools, encouraged Dwight to publish a paper, which was later to become the official organ of the state common school system, *The District School Journal of the State of New York.* It was first published in March 1840, and for many years the paper was sent by the state legislature to every school district in New York and was credited with influencing the establishment of the code of public instruction in the state.

Dwight was appointed superintendent of schools for the city and county of Albany and was a member of the board of directors of the Albany Normal School (later, State University of New York at Albany). He helped establish teacher-training institutions in New York State, encouraged supervision of schools on the county level, and promoted teacher conventions. He died in Albany at the age of thirty-seven.

REFERENCES: *AC; DAB; NCAB* (12:268): *WWW* (H). *Jerome F. Megna*

DWIGHT, Theodore William. B. July 18, 1822, Catskill, New York, to Benjamin Woolsey and Sophia Woodbridge (Strong) Dwight. M. August 24, 1847, to Mary Bond. Ch. three. D. June 29, 1892, Clinton, New York.

Theodore William Dwight, founder of the Columbia University Law School, was from an illustrious family, with a grandfather and a cousin who were presidents of Yale College. After graduating from Hamilton College in Clinton, New York (1840), he studied physics in New York City and entered the Yale Law School in 1841.

Dwight was an instructor in classics at Utica (New York) Academy and was a tutor at Hamilton College (1842–46). Admitted to the bar in 1845, he was named Maynard Professor of Law, History, Civil Polity, and Political Economy at Hamilton in 1846. He established a department of law in 1853 and founded a law school in 1855, which he headed until he went to Columbia University in 1858. At Columbia, he was professor of municipal law and founder of the Columbia Law School, which he headed until his retirement in 1891.

Dwight engaged in public affairs and was particularly concerned with judicial, prison, and municipal reform. At the time, he was regarded as the greatest living professor of law, in England as well as in the United States. He conducted at Columbia what was almost a proprietary school; he was essentially the only professor. He demonstrated the superiority of law school instruction to reading law in a lawyer's office and also encouraged students to work in law offices and courts. Dwight located instruction near law offices and courts and arranged schedules to accommodate student involvement.

As Columbia became a university, the trustees decided to expand law instruction to more scholarly objectives than mere admission to the bar. When the changes were put into effect in 1891, Dwight retired, two other faculty members resigned, and most of the students followed to the newly established New York Law School. There the faculty continued the Dwight method of teaching, as contrasted to the case method, which was being imported from Harvard University to Columbia.

Dwight was the author with E. C. Wines of *Report on the Prisons and Reformatories of the United States and Canada* (1867), *Cases Extracted from the Reports of the Commissions of Charities* (1863), and *James Harrington and His Influence upon American Political Institutions and Political Thought* (1887). He was associate editor of the *American Law Register* and legal editor of *Johnson's Cyclopedia of Literature and Science*.

Dwight and E. C. Wines were appointed to examine the prison systems of New York (1866), and Dwight was a delegate to the New York state constitutional convention (1867). He was chairman of the legislative committee of the Committee of Seventy (1873), vice-president of the state board of public charities, president of the state prison association, and state representative to the International Prison Congress in Stockholm, Sweden (1878). He received two honorary degrees.

REFERENCES: *AC; DAB; EB; NCAB* (6:346); *TC; WWW* (H); John W. Burgess, *Reminiscences of an American Scholar* (New York: Columbia University Press, 1934); Horace Coon, *Columbia: Colossus on the Hudson* (New York: E. P. Dutton & Co., 1947); *A History of Columbia University 1754–1904* (New York: Columbia University Press, 1904); *NYT,* June 30, 1892, p. 8.   *Joseph C. Bronars, Jr.*

DWIGHT, Timothy. B. May 14, 1752, Northampton, Massachusetts, to Timothy and Mary (Edwards) Dwight. M. March 3, 1777, to Mary Woolsey. Ch. eight. D. January 11, 1817, New Haven, Connecticut.

Timothy Dwight was one of the most influential intellectual leaders in the early history of the United States. He was graduated from Yale College in 1769. He taught in a New Haven grammar school and returned to Yale as a tutor in 1771. He received the M.A. from Yale in 1772.

Licensed to preach in 1777, Dwight spent a year as a chaplain in the Revolutionary Army before assuming a pulpit in Northampton, Massachusetts (1778). He opened a successful coeducational school in Northampton and, when called to another pulpit in Greenfield Hill, Connecticut, in 1783, founded another coeducational school that attracted pupils from outside New England.

On the death of Ezra Stiles *(q.v.)* in 1795, Dwight was selected president of Yale College, a position he held until his death in 1817. Keeping his religious, social, and political ideas, Dwight realized that intellectual developments in science and other fields could not be ignored. He led Yale in important new directions. He established a professorship of chemistry (1802) and filled the position with Benjamin Silliman *(q.v.),* who became a major figure in the growth of American science. Dwight and Silliman established the Yale Medical Institution in 1813. Dwight was also influential in ministerial training; the Yale theological department was set up a few years after his death.

Dwight promoted educational activities outside Yale. He was instrumental in the founding of Andover (Massachusetts) Theological Seminary. He promoted educational activities on the frontier and abroad through the Missionary Society of Connecticut, the American Home Missionary Society, and the American Board of Commissioners for Foreign Missions. He was a founder of the Connecticut Academy of Arts and Sciences.

Dwight was a well-known author. Among his books were poems, including an epic in eleven volumes, *Conquest of Canaan* (finished in 1775 and published in 1785), *The Triumph of Infidelity* (1788), and *Greenfield Hills* (1794). Other books were *True Means of Establishing Public Happiness* (1795), *The Duty of Americans* (1798), and *Discourse on Events of the Last Century* (1801). Published posthumously were *Theology Explained and Defended* (five volumes, 1818–19), *Travels in New England and New*

York (four volumes, 1821–22), and *Sermons by Timothy Dwight* (two volumes, 1828).

Dwight's grandson Timothy Dwight (1828–1916, *q.v.*) was president of Yale from 1886 to 1899.

REFERENCES: *AC; DAB; EB; NCAB* (1:168); *TC; WWW* (H); Lewis E. Buchanan, "The Ethical Ideas of Timothy Dwight," *Research Studies of the State College of Washington* 13 (September 1945): 185–99; Charles E. Cunningham, *Timothy Dwight, 1752–1817: A Biography* (New York: Macmillan Co., 1942); Benjamin Woodbridge Dwight, *The History of the Descendants of John Dwight, of Dedham, Mass.* (New York: Printed for the author, 1874); Brooks Mather Kelley, *Yale: A History* (New Haven: Yale University Press, 1974); Denison Olmsted *(q.v.)*, "Timothy Dwight as a Teacher," *American Journal of Education* 5 (1858): 567–85; Kenneth Silverman, *Timothy Dwight* (New York: Twayne Publishers, 1969).

Roger Lehecka

DWIGHT, Timothy. B. November 16, 1828, Norwich, Connecticut, to James and Susan (Breed) Dwight. M. December 31, 1866, to Jane Wakeman Skinner. Ch. none. D. May 26, 1916, New Haven, Connecticut.

Timothy Dwight was the second man of that name to become president of Yale College. His grandfather, Timothy Dwight (1752–1817, *q.v.*), a well-known theologian, was president from 1795 to 1817. Dwight's earlier education was received at home, at Norwich Academy, and at Hopkins Grammar School in New Haven. He was graduated from Yale College with the B.A. (1849) and M.A. (1852) degrees. He studied theology at Yale Divinity School (1850–53) and from 1856 to 1858 traveled in Germany to engage in classical studies at the University of Bonn and New Testament studies at the University of Berlin.

Dwight was a tutor in Latin at Yale (1851–55). After his study in Germany, he taught biblical literature (New Testament) at Yale Divinity School. He was licensed to preach in 1855 and was ordained a minister in 1861. Dwight became president of Yale in 1886 and served in that capacity until 1899. For the first two years of his presidency, he also was acting treasurer of Yale.

From 1866 to 1874 Dwight was an editor of the *New Englander*. He published in that journal "Yale College—Some Thoughts Respecting Its Future," in which he emphasized the need for smaller teaching units, closer contact between faculty and students, less emphasis on the marking system, and greater responsibility on the student rather than the instructor to maintain class attendance. He believed the purpose of education is to stimulate intellectual interest and curiosity and present means to satisfy that interest once it is aroused. He carried these views into his administration as president of Yale. Dwight thought the most striking change during his administration was the adoption of the elective system. The central idea of his administration was a university in which all departments were coequal and coordinate, rather than the departments being subordinate to the collegiate program. During the first year of his presidency (1887), Yale College was renamed Yale University.

Dwight translated and edited F. Godet's *Commentary on the Gospel of John* (1886) and was the author of *Thoughts of and for the Inner Life* (1899) and *Memories of Yale Life and Men, 1845–1889* (1903). He edited several volumes of *Meyer's Commentary on the New Testament* (1884–87). He was awarded four honorary degrees. He was a member of the American Committee for the Revision of the English Version of the Bible (1871–81).

REFERENCES: *AC; DAB; NCAB* (1:173); *NYT,* May 27, 1916, p. 11; *TC; WWW* (I); Timothy Dwight, *Memories of Yale Life and Men* (New York: Dodd, Mead and Co., 1903); Francis Parsons, *Six Men of Yale* (New Haven: Yale University Press, 1939). *Robert R. Sherman*

DYER, Franklin Benjamin. B. January 27, 1858, Warren County, Ohio, to John M. and Margaret (Martin) Dyer. M. 1888 to May Archibald. Ch. three. D. May 10, 1938, Cincinnati, Ohio.

Franklin Benjamin Dyer attended local county schools and Maineville Academy. He received the A.B. degree (1879) from Ohio Wesleyan University in Delaware, Ohio. He also studied at Syracuse (New York) University and Harvard University.

Dyer was a teacher in a Warren County, Ohio, rural school (1880) and served as superintendent of schools in Ohio at Loveland, Batavia, and Madisonville (1881–1901). He was assistant superintendent of the Cincinnati (Ohio) public schools (1902) and served as the first dean of the Ohio State Normal School at Oxford (1902–03). He was superintendent of the Cincinnati public schools (1903–12) and the Boston (Massachusetts) public schools (1912–18).

Dyer gained a national reputation for his reorganization of the Cincinnati schools. He introduced vocational education into the school program and cooperated with the University of Cincinnati to establish a college for teachers. He removed teacher appointment from political patronage and placed it on a professional basis. He instituted the first citywide public school system of guidance and counseling.

Active in professional associations, particularly the National Education Association, Dyer also became well known throughout the state of Ohio for his participation in teachers' institutes. Returning in retirement to Cincinnati, he served for twelve years as a member of the Cincinnati board of education.

REFERENCES: *LE* (I); *WWW* (IV); James J. Burns, *Educational History of Ohio* (Columbus: Historical Publishing Co., 1905), p. 491; "F. B. Dyer

Dies in Cincinnati,'' *Ohio Schools* (June 1938): 300.   *Marjorie Muntz*

DYKEMA, Peter William. B. November 25, 1873, Grand Rapids, Michigan, to Cornelius and Henrietta (Nutting) Dykema. M. December 24, 1903, to Jessie Dunning. Ch. five. D. May 13, 1951, Hastings-on-Hudson, New York.

Peter W. Dykema was a leader in American music education during the era of its greatest growth. After earning the B.S. (1895) and M.L. (1896) degrees from the University of Michigan, he studied with Franz Arens (voice) and Frank Shephard (theory). He also studied in Berlin, Germany, and at the New York City Institute of Musical Art (1911–12).

He taught English and German at Aurora (Illinois) High School (1896–98), was principal of Indianapolis (Indiana) Junior High School (1898–1901), and was music supervisor at the New York Ethical Culture School (1901–13). He was appointed professor of music and chairman of the department of public-school music at the University of Wisconsin (1913–24) and also directed the Madison (Wisconsin) Choral Union. He was professor of music education at Teachers College, Columbia University, from 1924 to 1940, when he was appointed professor emeritus.

Dykema authored and edited many song books and instructional materials, which include *Twice 55 Community Song Book* (seven volumes), the New Laurel Library, Modern Orchestra Series, Modern Band Series (with Norwal L. Church), Singing Youth, and Music Series Singing School. In 1929 he and Jacob Kwalwasser published the Music Tests Series. Dykema also wrote textbooks on music education, including *New School Music Handbook* (with Hannah M. Cundiff, 1923), *Music for School Administrators* (1931), *The Teaching and Administration of High School Music* (with Karl W. Gehrkens, *q.v.*, 1941), and *The Supervision and Administration of Music Education* (1949). He was editor of the *Music Supervisors Journal* (1914–21).

Dykema helped to organize, develop, and influence music on local and national levels. Active in the Music Supervisors National Conference, he was president (1916) and also served as chairman of the national research council, the past presidents' committee (1948), and the community music committee (1925–39). He was national president of Phi Mu Alpha Sinfonia (1922–28) and a member of the board of control of the National Bureau of the Advancement of Music (1932–43).

REFERENCES: *LE* (III); *NCAB* (40:68); *WWAE* (X); *WWW* (III); *NYT,* May 15, 1951, p. 31; Robert Sabin, ed., *The International Cyclopedia of Music and Musicians,* 9th ed. (New York: Dodd, Mead, 1964).

Richard Bancroft

E

EAKINS, Thomas. B. July 25, 1844, Philadelphia, Pennsylvania, to Benjamin and Caroline (Cowperthwait) Eakins. M. January 1884 to Susan Hannah Macdowell. Ch. none. D. June 25, 1916, Philadelphia, Pennsylvania.

Thomas Eakins was graduated from Central High School in Philadelphia, Pennsylvania, in 1861. He studied drawing at the Pennsylvania Academy of the Fine Arts and anatomy at Jefferson Medical College. He traveled to Paris where he spent three years (1866–69) studying painting at the École des beaux arts under Jean Léon Gerome and sculpture with Augustin Alexandre Dumont. He spent most of 1870 in Spain.

Eakins returned to Philadelphia in 1870 where he began the study of anatomy at the Jefferson Medical College. He assisted Christian Schussele in painting classes at the Pennsylvania Academy of Fine Arts in 1873. During the next few years he served the academy as its director of instruction, although it was the summer of 1882 before he was officially named professor of drawing and painting. In 1882 he was formally elected director of the Art School at the Pennsylvania Academy. As director of the academy he instituted a curriculum based on the thorough study of the nude figure; this included an emphasis on anatomy, dissection, and scientific perspective, innovations that revolutionized American art teaching.

The students at the academy were responsive to Eakins's innovations, but the public was not receptive to his use of nude figures, and he was forced to resign as director in 1886. The majority of his male students left the academy at this time and formed the Art Students League of Philadelphia, where Eakins served as the unpaid head for six or seven years. Eakins was an expert photographer, and he collaborated with Eadweard Muybridge in photographing human and animal movement in 1844.

While Eakins did not receive the recognition he deserved by his place in American art and education, he received awards from the Chicago Exposition (1893), the Paris Exposition (1900), and the Buffalo Exposition (1901), gold medals from the St. Louis Exposition (1904), the Temple Gold Medal from the Philadelphia Academy of Fine Arts, and the Proctor Prize from the National Academy of Design.

REFERENCES: *AC; DAB; NCAB* (5:421); *WWW* (I); Sylvan Schendler, *Eakins* (Boston: Little, Brown and Co., 1967).   *Roger H. Jones*

EARHART, Will. B. April 1, 1871, Franklin, Ohio, to Martin Washington and Hanna Jane (Corwin) Earhart. M. December 29, 1897, to Birdelle M. Darling. Ch. one. D. April 23, 1960, Los Angeles, California.

Will Earhart received a public school education and private music lessons. He was supervisor of music in the public schools of Greenville, Ohio (1896–98), and Richmond, Indiana (1898–1912), where he also was a conductor of a festival chorus and symphony orchestra. He was director of music for the Pittsburgh (Pennsylvania) public schools (1912–40). He also was a lecturer (1913–18) and professor (1918–21) of music in the school of education at the University of Pennsylvania. He was a lecturer at the Carnegie Institute of Technology (later, Carnegie Mellon University) in Pittsburgh (1916–18 and 1921–40). Earhart advocated granting high school credit for music study that was conducted outside of school.

Earhart was the author of many books, including *Music in the Public Schools* (1914), *Music in Secondary Schools* (with Osbourne McConathy, *q.v.*, 1917), *The Eloquent Baton* (1931), *Music to the Listening Ear* (1932), *The Meaning and Teaching of Music* (1935), *Choral Techniques* (1937), and *Elements of Music Theory* (two volumes, with C. N. Boyd, 1938). He was editor of *Art Songs for High Schools* (1910), *The Congdon Music Primer, No. 1* (with C. H. Congdon), *The Congdon Music Primer, No. 4* (with C. H. Congdon), and *The School Credit Piano Course* (with others, 1918).

A member of many organizations, Earhart was president of the Music Educators National Conference. He served on the Pittsburgh Municipal Band Concert Committee (1925–30) and the national advisory committee of the Federal Music Project of the Works Project Administration (1935–36). He received an honorary degree from the University of Pittsburgh (1920).

REFERENCES: *LE* (III); *WWW* (V); Nicholas Slonimsky, ed., *Baker's Biographical Dictionary of Musicians,* 5th ed. (New York: G. Schirmer, 1958); Nicholas Slonimsky, ed., *The International Cyclopedia of Music and Musicians,* 5th ed. (New York: Dodd, Mead, 1949). *John F. Ohles*

EATON, Amos. B. May 17, 1776, Chatham, New York, to Abel and Azuba (Hurd) Eaton. M. October 16, 1799, to Polly Thomas. M. September 16, 1803, to Sally Caddy. M. October 20, 1816, to Ann Bradley. M. August 5, 1827, to Alice Johnson. Ch. ten. D. May 10, 1842, Troy, New York.

Amos Eaton, noted botanist, geologist, and science educator, came from a farm family and was raised in western New York State. He was graduated (1799) from Williams College in Williamstown, Massachusetts, and taught for a brief period in a country school after graduation.

He studied law in New York City and was admitted to the New York State bar (1802). He practiced law and was a land agent and surveyor in Catskill, New York. While in Catskill he gave lectures on botany.

His law career ended in 1810 over an alleged forgery; he spent five years in a New York City jail. On his release at the age of forty, he entered Yale College to study science (1815–17) with Benjamin Silliman *(q.v.)* and Eli

Ives. After his study at Yale, he returned to Williams College (1817) where he introduced a popular course in science.

He moved to the Troy-Albany area in New York where he became associated with Governor De Witt Clinton *(q.v.)* and Stephen Van Rensselaer, patrons and promoters of science and public improvement. Eaton was hired to work on a survey of the area along the Erie Canal route. This experience helped him develop his botanical and geologic interests. Eaton lectured in villages and schools throughout the Northeast. He sponsored the Troy Lyceum of Natural History and compiled many textbooks in the areas of chemistry, zoology, and geology.

Eaton made important contributions to science education. He developed a theory of practical science education for students. Students learned by doing rather than through rote memorization. He developed scientific experiments and field studies as supplements to science lessons. In 1824 Eaton persuaded Stephen Van Rensselaer to establish the Rensselaer School in Troy where Eaton was senior professor, emphasizing and testing his practical education theory. In 1835 the program was expanded and the school was renamed Rensselaer Institute (later, Rensselaer Polytechnic Institute) emphasizing science and engineering. It was the first school in America to offer the bachelor of natural science and civil engineering degrees.

Eaton was the author of *An Index to the Geology of the Northern States* (1818), *Chemical Instructor* (1822), *Philosophical Instructor* (1824), *Zoological Text-Book* (1826), and *Geological Text-Book* (1830) and the translator of Louis-Claude Richard's *A Botanical Dictionary* (1816).

REFERENCES: *DAB; DSB; NCAB* (5:312); *TC;WWW* (H).

Harold J. McKenna

EATON, John. B. December 5, 1829, Sutton, New Hampshire, to John and Janet (Andrews) Eaton. M. September 29, 1864, to Alice Eugenia Shirley. Ch. three. D. February 9, 1906, Washington, D.C.

John Eaton's early life was spent on the farm where he was born. He attended the local school and at the age of sixteen began to teach in that school to earn money to continue his education at Thetford (Vermont) Academy and Dartmouth College, from which he was graduated in 1854.

He was principal of the Ward School in Cleveland, Ohio (1854–56), and superintendent of schools at Toledo, Ohio (1856–59), a position from which he resigned to study theology at Andover (Massachusetts) Theological Seminary.

In 1861 he became a Union army chaplain during the Civil War. In 1862 General Ulysses S. Grant ordered Eaton to gather ex-slaves together into camps where they could be taught skills that would enable them to become self-supporting. This came to be the model for the Freedmen's Bureau and, when the bureau was formally organized in 1865, Eaton was appointed assistant commissioner in charge of the District of Columbia, Maryland, and parts of Virginia.

After his resignation from the army in December 1865, he founded the *Memphis* (Tennessee) *Post*, which he edited (1866–67). The *Post* supported Grant for the presidency and advocated a system of free public schools. Eaton served as state superintendent of schools in Tennessee (1867–69). He had limited success in that post because of public opposition to spending money for free public education.

President Grant appointed Eaton to the board of visitors of the United States Military Academy at West Point (1869) and later United States commissioner of education (1870–86). The Bureau of Education was suffering from financial neglect, but with Grant's support, Eaton gained widespread congressional acceptance for it and helped it to become a valuable agency in the collection and dissemination of educational information and practices.

He resigned as commissioner in 1886 because of his health but soon reentered active professional life as president of Marietta (Ohio) College, a position he held until 1891. He was president of Sheldon Jackson College in Salt Lake City, Utah (1895–99). He was the first American superintendent of schools in Puerto Rico where he was instrumental in bringing about significant educational reforms. He retired in 1900.

Eaton was the author of reports on the Freedmen's Bureau, on Tennessee schools, and for the Bureau of Education. He edited *Thetford Academy* (1895) and wrote *Grant, Lincoln and the Freedmen* (with Ethel Mason, 1907). He was a councillor of the American Public Health Association, vice-president of the American Association for the Advancement of Science, and president of the American Social Science Association (twice), the National Congress of Education (1855), and the American Society for Religious Education. He was awarded two honorary degrees. He was an honorary member of the French ministry of education and received the order of the Commander of the Rose from Brazil.

REFERENCES: *AC; DAB; NCAB* (8:390); *TC; WWW* (I); *NYT*, February 10, 1906, p. 9.   *Richard L. Hart*

EBY, Frederick. B. October 26, 1874, Berlin (later, Kitchener), Ontario, Canada, to Aaron and Matilda Croft (Bowers) Eby. M. December 26, 1900, to Elizabeth Nuckolls Newman. Ch. five. D. February 11, 1968, Austin, Texas.

Frederick Eby was a student at the Stratford (Ontario) Collegiate Institute (1888–91) and was graduated with the A.B. degree (1895) from McMaster University. He was a graduate student at the University of Chicago (1895–97) and received the Ph.D. degree (1900) from Clark University in Worcester, Massachusetts. He spent the 1905–06 academic year doing graduate work at the University of Berlin, Germany.

Eby's career as a professional educator began in 1897 as a teacher at Morgan Park Academy in Chicago, Illinois. He moved to Texas, where he was professor of philosophy and education at Baylor University in Waco (1900–09). He went to the University of Texas at Austin in 1909, became professor of philosophy and history of education, and retired in 1959 as professor emeritus.

Eby pioneered in the junior college movement and was active in the fields of religious and aesthetic education. He studied under John Dewey *(q.v.)* at Chicago but broke from Dewey's philosophy and became a proponent of spiritual emphasis in education. His interest in the junior college movement began at the University of Chicago where he became acquainted with President William Rainey Harper *(q.v.)*

After going to Texas, much of Eby's work involved research, program and course development, teaching, lectures, and conferences relating to the junior college movement. He was instrumental in founding the junior college system in Texas and the eventual financial support of junior college programs by the state of Texas.

Among books Eby authored were *Christianity and Education* (1914), *Education in Texas—Source Materials* (1918), *Development of Education in Texas* (1925), *Early Protestant Educators* (1931), *The Development of Modern Education* (with C. F. Arrowood, 1934), *The History and Philosophy of Education, Ancient and Medieval* (with C. F. Arrowood, 1940), and *Albert Henry Newman: The Church Historian* (1940).

Eby's contributions to education were recognized by a lecture series in his honor at the University of Texas (1950) and the establishment of the Frederick Eby Research Prize. He was awarded honorary degrees from McMaster (1921) and Baylor (1945) universities.

REFERENCES: *LE* (III); *WWAE* (VII); *WWW*(V); "Frederick Eby and the Junior College," *Junior College Journal* 28 (October 1957): 73; "Frederick Eby Honored by Lecture Series," *School and Society* 71 (May 27, 1950): 332; *NYT*, February 12, 1968, p. 53; *Time*, July 15, 1957, p. 54.

Fred W. Tanner

EDWARDS, Newton. B. September 12, 1889, Carthage, North Carolina, to Isaac Newton and Lucy Ann (Knight) Edwards. M. August 11, 1914, to Anza Supple. Ch. two. D. October 15, 1969, Liberty, North Carolina.

Newton Edwards studied history at the University of South Carolina where he received the A.B. degree (1910). He received the A.M. degree (1913) from Columbia University and the Ph.D. degree (1923) from the University of Chicago.

He first taught in 1910 and was on the faculty of Lander College at Greenwood, South Carolina (1914–18), before moving to the University of

Chicago, where he taught and pursued doctoral studies. In 1923 he moved to the university's school of education, where he spent the next thirty-two years teaching the history, law, and politics of education.

Beginning in 1948 Edwards divided his time between the University of Chicago and the University of Texas at Austin to his retirement in 1955. After retiring, he returned to his native Carolinas to serve (1955–60) on the faculty of the University of South Carolina and then moved to Liberty, North Carolina, where he was a part-time teacher at Duke University until his death in 1969.

Edwards's interest in the legal questions of education led him to write the widely acclaimed *The Courts and the Public Schools* (1933), which was cited as an outstanding contribution to educational research by the American Educational Research Association in 1939. In the 1960s he collaborated with Lee O. Garber in publishing eight volumes in the School Law Casebook Series. Edwards was also the author of *The Extent of Equalization Secured Through State School Funds* (with H. G. Richey, 1938), *Equal Educational Opportunity for Youth* (1939), and *The School in the American Social Order* (with H. G. Richey, 1947). He edited *Education in a Democracy* (1941) and was editor of the *Elementary School Journal* (1930–40).

Edwards was a member of many professional associations. He served as secretary to the Illinois Educational Commission (1923) and to the Committee on the Place of National Organizations in American Education, and he was a member of the technical staff of the President's Advisory Committee (1937) and the American Educational Research Association (president, 1943–44).

REFERENCES: *LE* (III); *WW* (XXVIII); *WWAE* (XV); "Newton Edwards, 1889–1969," *Elementary School Journal* 70 (February 1970): 237–38; *Who's Who in Chicago and Illinois* (Chicago: Marquis, 1945).

William E. Eaton

EELLS, Cushing. B. February 16, 1810, Blandford, Massachusetts, to Joseph and Elizabeth (Warner) Eells. M. March 5, 1838, to Myra Fairbank. Ch. two. D. February 16, 1893, Tacoma, Washington.

Cushing Eells grew up in western Massachusetts in a Puritan family. His early life was centered around farm work and participation in church activities where he was especially impressed by visiting missionaries. He was graduated from Williams College in Williamstown, Massachusetts, in 1834 and entered what was later the Hartford (Connecticut) Theological Seminary, where he studied for the ministry and taught school part-time.

Shortly after their marriage in 1838, Eells and his bride left for Washington Territory to work with the Spokane Indians. After nine years of fruitless missionary work near the present site of Spokane, Washington, the Eells mission ended with the news that Marcus Whitman and thirteen others had been massacred by Indians at a mission near what is now Walla Walla, Washington. Eells fled with his family to western Oregon and settled in Forest Grove, where he was the first teacher of what has become Pacific University. Eells moved back to eastern Washington in 1859 and settled at the site of the Whitman Mission. He bought the land from the missionary society and established a seminary named after his martyred friends, Marcus Whitman and his wife.

Eells struggled for ten years to bring civilization to Walla Walla, which had grown from a military outpost to a bustling frontier town with rampant crime and vice. He was principal and teacher at the seminary, county superintendent of schools, and a farmer. Eells and his wife worked untiringly to keep the seminary open, selling farm produce to raise cash. Eventually they donated half the proceeds of the sale of their land and other cash grants to the seminary. In 1883 the seminary was reorganized; the next year the territorial legislature amended the original charter, making Whitman College the first chartered college in Washington.

Eells left the Walla Walla area in 1872 to settle in western Washington where his sons were living. He stayed for the next few years working as a missionary to the Skokomish Indians. In 1874 he began frequent trips to the interior of eastern Washington, establishing churches at several locations, including Colfax, Washington, where he stayed until 1881. Eells returned to western Washington in 1888 to be near his family, continuing to preach on a regular basis until his death in 1893.

REFERENCES: Myron Eells, *Father Eells* (Boston: Congregational Sunday-school and Publishing Co., 1894); C. S. Kingston, "Cushing Eells," in *Where the Saints Have Trod. Proceedings of the Washington Congregational Conference, May 1938* (Seattle: Frayn Printing Co., 1938); W. D. Lyman, "The Chief Features of the Life of Father Eells," *The Whitman College Quarterly* 1 (April 1897): 3-16.   *Michael A. Balasa*

EELLS, Walter Crosby. B. March 6, 1886, Mason County, Washington, to Myron and Sarah (Crosby) Eells. M. January 1, 1912, to Natalie Esther Soules. M. 1947 to May Washington. Ch. three. D. December 15, 1962, Washington, D.C.

Walter Crosby Eells received the baccaulaureate degree from Whitman College (1908), the A.M. degree from the University of Chicago (1911), and the Ph.D. degree from Stanford University (1927). He began as a high school teacher (1908–10) and taught mathematics at Whitworth College in Tacoma, Washington (1911–13) and the United States Naval Academy (1913–16). Eells taught and served as the Whitman College Alumni Association secretary (1916–27).

He was a member of the Stanford University faculty (1927–38) where he gained national repute as a scholar and writer in junior college education.

Eells assumed the editorship of the *Junior College Journal* in 1930, serving for fifteen years. He was instrumental in the development of policy formulation and philosophical bases of junior college education. He was elected the first full-time executive secretary of the American Association of Junior Colleges (1938–45).

In 1945 Eells became chief of the Foreign Education Division of the Veterans Administration. From 1947 until his retirement in 1951 he served on the staff of General Douglas MacArthur, supreme commander for the Allied powers, as adviser on higher education to the Japanese government. He was a professor of education at Catholic University in Washington, D.C. (1953–54).

Eells was the author of *The Junior College* (1931), *Alaska Natives* (with H. D. Anderson, 1935), *Surveys of American Higher Education* (1937), *Present Status of Junior College Terminal Education* (1941), *Why Junior College Terminal Education?* (1941), *College Teachers and College Teaching* (1957), *American Dissertations on Foreign Education* (1959), *Academic Degrees* (with H. A. Haswell, 1960), *Administration of Higher Education* (with E. V. Hollis, 1960), *The College Presidency, 1900–1960* (1961), *Sabbatical Leaves in American Education* (1962), and *Degrees in Higher Education* (1963).

After his retirement, he spent two and one-half years visiting sixty-three countries, observing educational conditions. From these experiences and travels emerged extensive, significant works dealing with foreign education, including *Education in the New Japan* (two volumes, 1948), *Educational Progress in Japan* (1951), *Communism in Education in Asia, Africa and the Far Pacific* (1954), and *The Literature of Japanese Education, 1945–54* (1956). He was editor of the *Whitman Alumnus* (1917–27).

Upon his return to the United States, Eells worked on a number of private projects in Washington, D.C., and with the American Council on Education, the Southern Regional Education Board, and the United States Office of Education. He was awarded an honorary degree by Whitman College (1938).

REFERENCES: *LE* (III); *WWAE* (XII); *WWW* (IV); Ernest V. Hollis, "Walter Crosby Eells, 1886–1962," *School and Society* 91 (Summer 1963): 242; Curtis Richer, "Walter C. Eells," *Junior College Journal* 35 (February 1963): 3.   *Haig A. Rushdoony*

EGGLESTON, Joseph Dupuy, Jr. B. November 13, 1867, Prince Edward County, Virginia, to Joseph Dupuy and Anne Carrington (Booker) Eggleston. M. December 18, 1895, to Julia Jane Johnson. Ch. two. D. March 13, 1953, Hampden-Sydney, Virginia.

Joseph D. Eggleston, Jr., attended Hampden-Sydney (Virginia) College from which he received the A.B. (1886) and M.A. (1891) degrees.

Following his graduation, Eggleston taught in Missouri, Georgia, and North Carolina public schools (1886–89). He was employed as an instructor (1891–93) and superintendent (1893–1900) of the Asheville, North Carolina, public schools.

Eggleston accepted an editorial position on the staff of the Johnson Publishing Company in Richmond, Virginia (1900–01), and served as editor and secretary of the Bureau of Information and Publicity of the Southern Education Board located at the University of Tennessee (1902–03). He returned to his home county, Prince Edward (Virginia), to become county superintendent of schools (1903–05). He was active in the campaign for better schools, which was credited with passage of the High School Act of 1906 providing state tax support for the establishment of high schools in the state.

In 1905 he ran successfully for state superintendent and held this post from 1906 to January 1913. Under his leadership, many rural high schools were established, and the number of one-room schools was reduced by more than 10 percent. In January 1913 Eggleston became chief of field service in rural education in the United States Bureau of Education but resigned the post six months later to become president of Virginia Polytechnic Institute (later, Virginia Polytechnic Institute and State University) in Blacksburg (1913–19). His administration was characterized by resolving the differences of diverse factions of the staff, founding an education extension in the state, and developing an agricultural extension program.

In 1919 Eggleston assumed the presidency of Hampden-Sydney College. He remained there until 1939, retiring at the age of seventy-two. During his term, the campus was enlarged, and the student body increased in size nearly four times.

Eggleston was the author of *The Work of the Rural School* (with R. W. Bruire, 1913). He wrote editorials for leading newspapers in Virginia, North Carolina, and Tennesee and contributed articles to professional publications. He served on the Virginia state board of education (1939–43). He was a member of professional associations and historical societies. He received honorary degrees from Hampden-Sydney College and Washington and Lee University.

REFERENCES: *LE* (III); *NCAB* (42:550); *WW* (XXVI); *WWAE* (XIV); *WWW* (III); Franklin Ross Jones, "The Curriculum Development in Educational Administration in Eight Selected Southern Institutions Preparing School Administrators" (Ed.D. diss., Duke University, 1960), pp. 258-68; Duncan Lyle Kinnear, *The First Hundred Years: A History of Virginia Polytechnic Institute and State University* (Blacksburg, Va.: VPI Educational Foundation, 1972), pp. 219-52; *Virginian Pilot* (Norfolk), March 14, 1953, p. 17.   *Franklin Ross Jones*

EISENHART, Luther Pfahler. B. January 13, 1876, York, Pennsylvania, to Charles Augustus and Emma Catherine (Pfahler) Eisenhart. M. August 17, 1908, to Anna Maria Dandridge Mitchell. M. June 1, 1918, to Katharine Riely Schmidt. Ch. three. D. October 28, 1965, Princeton, New Jersey.

Luther Pfahler Eisenhart, mathematician, was taught by his mother before he entered school and completed grade school in three years. He attended York (Pennsylvania) High School and was encouraged by the principal to withdraw and devote his time to independent study of Latin and Greek for early admission to Gettysburg (Pennsylvania) College. He enrolled in Gettysburg College, where he studied advanced mathematics through independent guided reading. He received the A.B. degree from Gettysburg in 1896. He began graduate study at Johns Hopkins University in Baltimore, Maryland, in 1897 and received the Ph.D. degree in 1900.

He taught at Gettysburg College's preparatory school (1896–97). Eisenhart taught mathematics at Princeton University (1900–45), serving as dean of the faculty (1925–33) and dean of the graduate school (1933–45). Because of his experience with independent study, Eisenhart proposed a four-course plan of study, which was adopted at Princeton in 1923, providing for independent study and writing of a thesis.

Eisenhart's mathematical research covered two fields within differential geometry. To about 1920, his studies were concerned with the theory of deformations of surfaces and systems of surfaces. Most of Eisenhart's work after 1921 was directed toward the generalization of Reimannian geometry.

Eisenhart was the author of books in mathematics, including *Differential Geometry of Curves and Surfaces* (1909), *Transformations of Surfaces* (1923), *Reimannian Geometry* (1926), *Non-Reimannian Geometry* (1927), *Continuous Groups of Transformations* (1933), *Coordinate Geometry* (1939), and *An Introduction to Differential Geometry* (1940). He also wrote *The Process of Education* (1945). He authored many papers and abstracts that appeared in major scholarly and scientific journals. He edited *Transactions of the American Mathematical Society* (1917–23).

He was a trustee of Pennsylvania College (1907–14), president of the Association of American Colleges (1930), and chairman of the Order Crown of Belgium (1937). He was a member of the American Mathematical Society (president, 1931–32), the American Philosophical Society (executive officer, 1942–59), the American Association for the Advancement of Science (vice-president and chairman of section A, 1916–17), and the National Academy of Sciences (vice-president, 1944–48). He received many honorary degrees. An archway at Princeton University was named in his honor.

REFERENCES: *DSB; LE* (III); *WWW* (IV); Gilbert Chinard, Harry Levy, and George W. Corner, "Luther Pfahler Eisenhart (1876–1965)," in *Year*

Book of the American Philosophical Society for 1966 (Philadelphia, 1967), pp. 127-134; Solomon Lefschetz, "Luther Pfahler Eisenhart," in *Biographical Memoirs. National Academy of Sciences* 40 (1969): 69-90; *NYT,* October 29, 1965, p. 43.   *Daniel S. Yates*

EISENHOWER, Milton Stover. B. September 15, 1899, Abilene, Kansas, to David Jacob and Ida (Stover) Eisenhower. M. October 12, 1927, to Helen Elsie Eakin. Ch. two.

Milton Stover Eisenhower was graduated from Abilene (Kansas) High School in 1917. He received the B.S. degree (1924) in industrial journalism from Kansas State College (later, University) and for a short time after graduation was an assistant professor of journalism. While a student, he worked on the *Abilene Daily Reflector,* part of the time as city editor. He served as American vice-consul in Edinburgh, Scotland (1924–26), and studied at the University of Edinburgh.

Returning to the United States in 1926, he became an assistant to William Jardine, secretary of agriculture (1926–28), was director of information in the United States Department of Agriculture (1928–40), edited the *Yearbook of Agriculture* (1929–36), and coordinated the land-use program (1937–42). President Franklin D. Roosevelt appointed Eisenhower director of the War Relocation Authority in 1942, and in 1943 he became associate director of the Office of War Information.

Eisenhower was president of Kansas State College (1943–50). The enrollment increased, and the curriculum was changed to include general courses in the liberal arts.From 1950 to 1956 he served as president of Pennsylvania State College (later, University). Students and faculty were given a voice in university affairs. He encouraged the development of closed circuit television for instructional purposes. He was president of Johns Hopkins University in Baltimore, Maryland (1956–67); while there he led a development campaign to raise needed funds.

Eisenhower was the coauthor of *The United States Department of Agriculture: Its Structure and Functions* (with A. P. Chew, 1931). He wrote *The Wine Is Bitter* (1963), *The President Is Calling* (1974), and many government bulletins. He was a vice-president of the Society for the Advancement of Management (1944–45) and was active in the Association of Land-Grant Colleges and State Universities (executive committee, 1944–47, 1950–53, and president, 1951–52). He was a fellow of the American Academy of Arts and Sciences. He was a director of the Freedoms Foundation and the Fund of Adult Education of the Ford Foundation (1953–61) and a member of the board of visitors of the United States Naval Academy (1958–61). In 1946 he was chosen permanent chairman of the United States Commission on Educational, Scientific and Cultural Cooperation and was a delegate to UNESCO conferences.

Eisenhower served on many governmental boards and commissions. In 1945 he assisted in the reorganization of the department of agriculture. He was on the Famine Emergency Relief Commission (1946), the President's Commission on Higher Education (1946), and the President's Advisory Committee of Government Organization (1953–60). He made fact-finding visits to Central and South America. In 1968 President Lyndon B. Johnson chose Eisenhower chairman of the President's Commission on Causes and Prevention of Violence.

Eisenhower received many awards, including the Horatio Alger Award of the American Schools and Colleges Association (1952), the Thomas E. Cunningham Award for promoting inter-American understanding (1954), and the American Farm Bureau distinguished service award (1953). He received awards from Colombia, Bolivia, Venezuela, Ecuador, and Korea and honorary degrees from over thirty American and foreign universities.

REFERENCES: *CB* (December 1946); *LE* (III); *NCAB* (I:332); *WW* (XXXVI); *WWAE* (XVI); Milton S. Eisenhower, *The President Is Calling* (New York: Doubleday, 1974); Bela Kornitzer, *The Great American Heritage: The Story of the Five Eisenhower Brothers* (New York: Farrar, Straus and Cudahy, 1955). *Shirley M. Ohles*

ELIOT, Charles William. B. March 20, 1834, Boston, Massachusetts, to Samuel Atkins and Mary (Lyman) Eliot. M. October 27, 1858, to Ellen Derby Peabody. M. October 30, 1877, to Grace Mellen Hopkinson. Ch. four. D. August 22, 1926, Northeast Harbor, Maine.

A Boston Latin School graduate, Charles William Eliot entered Harvard University at the age of fifteen and was graduated second in his class with the A.B. degree (1853) and received the A.M. degree in 1856.

Unique experiences in Josiah Cooke's *(q.v.)*laboratory interested Eliot in laboratory techniques in teaching chemistry. In 1854 he tutored in mathematics at Harvard and four years later became the first assistant professor of mathematics and chemistry. He practiced the laboratory method in his classroom and gave Harvard's first written examinations in place of the traditional oral tests. Failing to receive promotion in rank in 1863, Eliot went to Europe to visit and study foreign schools. Returning to the United States, he was appointed professor of chemistry at the Massachusetts Institute of Technology in 1865. He returned to Europe to study education again in 1867. Two of his articles entitled "The New Education: Its Organization" (1869), published in the February and March issues of *Atlantic Monthly* attracted wide attention and were credited with contributing to his election as the twenty-second president of Harvard University.

During Eliot's forty-year tenure as president (1869–1909), he organized Harvard's specialty schools under the collegiate system and turned the institution into a major university. Eliot's program of reform strengthened the schools of law and medicine; he established Radcliffe College, and introduced business administration as a graduate study. The theological program was broadened from training for the Unitarian ministry to serving many denominations. In the face of opposition, Eliot established the elective system at Harvard, a reform followed throughout American higher education. He was chairman of the National Educational Association's Committee of Ten. He wrote the committee report (1892) that set the curricular pattern for the American high school. As a result of the report, the study of foreign languages and mathematics was introduced in the seventh grade, a curricular change that was facilitated by the development of the junior high school.

Eliot's forty annual reports as Harvard president were landmark documents in the history of American education. He coauthored with Francis H. Storer *Manual of Qualitative Chemical Analysis* (1869) and *Manual of Inorganic Chemistry* (1867) and was the author of *The Happy Life* (1896), *Five American Contributions to Civilization* (1897), *Educational Reform, Essays and Addresses, 1869–1897* (1898), *More Money for the Public Schools* (1903), *University Administration* (1908), *The Religion of the Future* (1909), *The Durable Satisfactions of Life* (1910), *The Conflict Between Individualism and Collectivism in a Democracy* (1910), and *A Late Harvest* (1924). He edited the famous fifty-volume "five-foot bookshelf" of Harvard Classics and Junior Classics.

Recognition came to Eliot through the award of many honorary degrees and foreign honors, including the Legion of Honor of France, the Imperial Order of the Rising Sun of Japan, and the Order of the Crown of Belgium. He was president of the National Educational Association (1903) and the Massachusetts Society of Social Hygiene (1915–20). He was a fellow of the American Academy of Arts and Sciences and a member of the General Education Board (1908–17), the Rockefeller Foundation (1914–17), and the International Health Board (1913–17). He was a corresponding member of French and British academies and a member of many American associations. Eliot was awarded the first gold medal of the American Academy of Arts and Sciences in 1915 and the Roosevelt Medal for distinguished service in 1924.

REFERENCES: *DAB; EB; NCAB* (6:421); *NYT,* August 23, 1926, p. 1; *WWW* (I); Edward Howe Cotton, *The Life of Charles W. Eliot* (Boston: Small, Maynard & Co., 1926); Frederick Rudolph, *The American College and University: A History* (New York: Vintage Books, 1965).

Stephen J. Clarke

ELIOT, John. B. August 5, 1604, Widford, Hertfordshire, England, to Benjamin and Lettice (Apgar) Eliot. M. October 1632 to Ann Mumford. Ch. six. D. May 21, 1690, Roxbury, Massachusetts.

John Eliot was graduated from Jesus College at Cambridge, England, in 1622 with a reputation in the classics. He taught in the grammar school at Little Baddow, Essex, and came under the influence of Thomas Hooker. He became a preacher and emigrated with some Puritan friends to New England, arriving in Boston, Massachusetts, in November 1631.

He settled in Roxbury, Massachusetts, and was pastor there for nearly fifty years (1632–90). He became involved in missionary work with the Indians that inspired the organization of the Company for Propagating the Gospel in New England and Parts Adjacent in North America (1649).

Eliot began preaching in 1646 at Nonantun (later, Newton, Massachusetts), first in English and later in the Indian language. As Indians were converted to Christianity, they were gathered in small villages and followed the English life-style. Many Indian Christian villages were eradicated during King Philip's War (1675) but Eliot's missionary methods were the basic pattern followed for almost two hundred years. He trained Indian teachers, established native schools and wrote an Indian language grammar (1666).

Eliot produced a literature in the Algonkian language. He translated the *Catechism* (1653), the *New Testament* (1661), and *Old Testament* (1663). He wrote in English *The Christian Commonwealth* (1659) and *Harmony of the Gospels* (1678).

REFERENCES: *AC; DAB; EB; NCAB* (2:419); *TC; WWW* (H).

Michael R. Cioffi

ELLIOTT, Aaron Marshall. B. January 24, 1846, Wilmington, North Carolina, to Aaron and Rhoda (Mendenhall) Elliott. M. June 14, 1905, to Lily Tyson Manly. Ch. none. D. November 9, 1910, Baltimore, Maryland.

Aaron Marshall Elliott, renowned philologist, pioneered the scientific study of the modern languages and literature in the United States. After studying with tutors, his Quaker parents sent him from North Carolina through military lines in 1862 to fellow Quakers in the North. He was graduated from Haverford (Pennsylvania) College with the A.B. (1866) and A.M. (1878) degrees and received the A.B. degree from Harvard University (1868). He spent eight years abroad studying firsthand the languages and peoples of Europe. He studied at Collège de France, École de hautes études in Paris (1868–71), in Florence, Italy (1871–72), at the University of Madrid, Spain (1873), and at universities of Munich, Tübingen, and Berlin, Germany, and Vienna, Austria (1874–76). He supported himself in Europe by tutoring and writing accounts of his travels. In 1876 he returned to the United States and received the Ph.D. degree (1877) from the College of New Jersey (later, Princeton University).

He was an original member of the faculty at Johns Hopkins University in Baltimore, Maryland, as professor of Romance languages (1876–1910). His summers were spent abroad, and he expanded his command of languages to include Roumanian, Arabic, Russian, modern Greek, and Canadian French. Elliott was responsible for the development of the graduate school of Romance languages at Johns Hopkins University, which produced many leaders in the field.

Elliott was associated with numerous professional organizations. He established the Modern Language Association of America in 1883 and was secretary for nine years and then president (1894). He established *Modern Language Notes,* the first American technical journal of philology (1886). He contributed numerous linguistic and literary articles to the journal, employed his own typesetter, and for the first seventeen years printed it each month on his own press.

He was a delegate to the Paris Exposition (1900) and was awarded the French Legion of Honor (1907). He was awarded four honorary degrees.

REFERENCES: *DAB; NCAB* (14:229); *WWW* (I); *NYT,* November 10, 1910, p. 11.   *John P. Burgess*

ELLIOTT, Edward Charles. B. December 21, 1874, Chicago, Illinois, to Frederick and Susan (Petts) Elliott. M. June 15, 1907, to Elizabeth Nowland. Ch. four. D. June 16, 1960, Lafayette, Indiana.

Edward C. Elliott was graduated from the University of Nebraska with the B.S. (1895) and A.M. (1897) degrees. In the summer of 1904, he studied in Germany at the University of Jena, and he received the Ph.D. degree (1905) from Teachers College, Columbia University.

Elliott was a high school teacher (1897-98) and superintendent of schools (1898-1903) in Leadville, Colorado. He was professor of education at the University of Wisconsin (1905-16), chancellor of the University of Montana (1916-22), and president of Purdue University from 1922 until his retirement as president emeritus in 1945.

During his tenure, Purdue University gained recognition as one of the major technical and engineering schools in the nation. Elliot was credited with many administrative and academic accomplishments, including improving the administrative procedures, establishing four foundations to provide financial support for the university, and increasing the academic program by creating several new instructional departments.

He was the author of several books, including *City School Supervision* (1913), *State and County School Administration* (with Elwood P. Cubberly, *q.v.,* 1915-16), *Unit Costs of Higher Education* (with E. B. Stevens, 1925), *Charters and Basic Laws of Selected American Universities and Colleges* (with M. M. Chambers, *q.v.,* 1934), *The Government of Higher Education* (with M. M. Chambers and W. A. Ashbrook, 1935), and *The Colleges and the Courts* (with M. M. Chambers, 1936). He was editor of *The Rise of a University—Columbia* (1937).

Elliott assumed many civic and professional responsibilities; he was a member of President Herbert Hoover's National Advisory Committee (1929) and President Franklin D. Roosevelt's National Resources Committee (1937), chairman of the American Council on Education (1937), conciliator for the Indiana coal industry (1929-30), director of a nationwide survey for the American Pharmaceutical Association (1946-49), chief of the Division of Professional and Technical Training of the War Manpower Commission (1942-43), member of the board of trustees of the Carnegie Foundation for the Advancement of Teaching (1934-45, chairman, 1944-45), adviser to the regents of the University of the Philippines (1938), and recipient of an award for meritorious civilian service from the War Department (1955). He was the recipient of eleven honorary degrees.

REFERENCES: *LE* (III); *NCAB* (B:361, 48:14); *WWAE* (I); *WWW* (IV); *NYT*, June 17, 1960, p. 31. *David L. Jolliff*

ELLIS, Alston. B. January 26, 1847, Kenton County, Kentucky, to Absalom and Mary (Ellis) Ellis. M. July 23, 1867, to Katherine Anne Cox. Ch. none. D. November 14, 1920, Athens, Ohio.

Alston Ellis was graduated from Miami University (Ohio) with the B.S. (1865), A.B. (1867), and A.M. (1872) degrees.

Ellis was principal of a district school (1867-68) and the Cabot Street School in Newport, Kentucky (1868-71). He was superintendent of the Hamilton (Ohio) schools (1871-79 and 1887-92) and Sandusky (Ohio) schools (1880-87). He was the Ohio representative for a publishing company (1879-80). He was active as a lecturer at teachers' institutes in Ohio.

In 1892 Ellis was selected president of the State Agricultural College of Colorado (later, Colorado State University) at Fort Collins. During his administration the student body tripled in size and the physical plant was enlarged. He served as president of Ohio University in Athens, Ohio, from 1901 to his death in 1920. The student enrollment increased nearly ten times, and the faculty increased nearly four times. A number of buildings were constructed, and the state normal school and department of civil engineering were established.

Ellis was the author of *History of Ungraded Schools of Ohio* (1876). He served as a colonel on the staff of the governor of Colorado and was active in professional associations. He was president of the Ohio Superintendents' Association (1875), the Ohio Teachers' Association (1888), the Ohio College Association (1892-93), the Ohio Speech Association (1905-11), and the Ohio Association of College Presidents and Deans (1910-11). A life member of the Victoria Institute of Great Britain (from 1887), he served on the Ohio state board of school examiners (1875-79 and 1887-92). He was a member of the first board of trustees of Ohio State University (1878-83) and of the board of trustees of Oxford (Ohio) Female College (later, Western College for Women of Miami University) from 1874 to 1887. He was awarded two honorary degrees by Ohio State University and honorary degrees by Wooster and Miami universities.

REFERENCES: *NCAB* (26:352); *WWW* (I).   *John F. Ohles*

ELSON, Louis Charles. B. April 17, 1848, Boston, Massachusetts, to Julius and Rosalie (Schnell) Elson. M. 1873 to Bertha Lissner. Ch. one. D. February 14, 1920, Boston, Massachusetts.

Louis Charles Elson received his early education in the public schools of Boston, Massachusetts. His first instruction in music was under the direction of his mother, who began his piano lessons at the age of six. He continued his studies in Boston, where he studied piano with August Hamann, and in Leipzig, Germany, where he studied voice under August Kreissman, a prominent singer of German lieder, and composition with Carl Gloggner-Castelli. At the Conservatory of Leipzig, he first attempted to compose music under Gloggner-Castelli.

Elson began his career in 1876 as a reviewer on the staff of *Musician and Artist* in Boston. He became editor of *Vox Humana* in 1876 and music critic for the *Boston Courier*. In 1886 he joined the staff of the *Boston Advertiser*, a position he held until his death.

From 1880, Elson was a member of the faculty of the New England Conservatory of Music as instructor of theory and voice and was named head of the department of musical theory in 1882. Under his leadership, the department developed a full and thorough course equal to that of the best European conservatories. The curriculum included study of musical forms and analysis, which gave students broader experience in the appreciation of music. Lectures were divided into series on the instruments in the orchestra and the history of music and lives of great composers. Used for over forty years, Elson's course of study became known throughout the country.

Elson was in great demand as a lecturer and appeared throughout the United States and Canada, lecturing on national schools of music, folk songs, and an analysis of works performed at concerts. Most popular were the Boston municipal lectures, which were free and were presented at concerts of small orchestras and occasional soloists. He was president of the Music Teachers' National Association (1904).

Elson wrote music and librettos for operettas and a number of poems. He was the author of many books devoted to the study and history of music, including *Curiosities of Music* (1880), *German Songs and Song Writers* (1882), *The Theory of Music* (1890), *The Realm of Music* (1894), *Great Composers and Their Works* (1898), *The National Music of America* (1899), *Shakespeare in Music* (1901), *History of German Song* (1903), *Elson's Music Dictionary* (1905), *Mistakes and Disputed Points in Music and Music Teaching* (1910), *Women in Music* (1918), *Children in Music*

(1918), and his most important work, *The History of American Music* (1904). He edited or contributed to the *University Musical Encyclopedia* (1912), *The Musician's Guide* (1913), and a supplementary volume to *Famous Composers and Their Works* (1902). He wrote *European Reminiscences Musical and Otherwise* (1893), an account of his foreign vacations.

REFERENCES: *A C; DAB; NCAB* (8:449); *TC; WWW* (I).

Roger H. Jones

ELSON, William Harris. B. November 22, 1854, Carroll County, Ohio, to Thomas and Hannah (Alexander) Elson. M. June 20, 1874, to Minnie Trueblood. M. November 19, 1879, to Mattie Welch. Ch. two. D. February 2, 1935, Chicago, Illinois.

William Harris Elson, a noted administrator and author, was educated in local Indiana common schools and continued his studies at Indiana University, from which he received the A.B. degree (1895).

Elson began his educational career as a teacher in the rural schools of his home state. He was superintendent of schools for Parke County, Indiana (1881-91), acting superintendent at La Porte, Indiana (1892), school supervisor at Indianapolis, Indiana (1893), and superintendent of schools at Superior, Wisconsin (1895-1900), Grand Rapids, Michigan (1900-06), and Cleveland, Ohio (1906-12). He was a lecturer in education at Cornell University (1912-13). From 1913, he was a writer of school textbooks.

Elson provided leadership in the development of the technical high school. He is credited with establishing the first technical high school in the country in Cleveland, Ohio, in 1907.

Elson wrote the *Elson Grammar School Reader* (with Christine Kech and Laura E. Runkle), a series of nine readers published in 1909. They presented a new approach to developing reading skills and revolutionized the teaching of reading at that time, selling over fifty million copies. Revisions and additions to the series written with Laura E. Runkle include *Good English* (three volumes, 1916) and *Child-Library Readers* (nine volumes, 1923-24). *The Elson Basic Readers* (with William S. Gray) were published as nine volumes in 1931, and *Elson Junior Literature* (two volumes) appeared in 1932. It is estimated that in 1937 the *Elson Basic Readers* were used by children in thirty-four different countries throughout the world.

Elson was a fellow of the American Geographic Society and a member of the Department of Superintendency of the National Education Association (president, 1908-09) and the Wisconsin State Teachers' Association (president, 1900).

REFERENCES: *LE* (I); *NCAB* (26:367); *WWW* (I). *George Lucht*

ELY, Charles Wright. B. March 14, 1839, Madison, Connecticut, to Elias S. and Hester (Wright) Ely. M. 1867 to Mary G. Darling. Ch. four. D. October 1, 1912, Washington, D.C.

Charles Wright Ely stayed on the homestead until 1858 when he left for school. He received the A.B. (1862) and A.M. (1865) degrees from Yale College. He served in the Union army as a sergeant in the Twenty-seventh Connecticut (1862-63).

Ely moved to Columbus, Ohio, where he taught in the State Institute for the Deaf and Dumb (1863-70). In 1870 he became principal of the Maryland School for the Deaf and Dumb in Frederick. Founded in 1867 by the state general assembly and opened in September 1868, the school was the first institution of its kind in Maryland. Ely was its second principal and served in this position until his death in 1912. The school grew rapidly under his leadership and came to be recognized as one of the best of its type in the nation.

Ely wrote two brief histories of the institution in 1884 and 1893. He was president of the first board of health in Frederick, Maryland, and was a director of the Frederick College and Young Men's Christian Association.

REFERENCES: *NCAB* (15:117); *WWW* (I); C. W. Ely, *An Outline History of the Maryland School for the Deaf and Dumb* (Frederick: The School, 1884); C. W. Ely, *An Outline History of the Maryland State School for the Deaf* (Frederick: The School, 1893); Bernard C. Steiner, *An Outline History of the Maryland State School for the Deaf* (Frederick: The School, 1919).   *Richard J. Cox*

ELY, Richard Theodore. B. April 13, 1854, Ripley, New York, to Ezra and Harriet (Gardner) Ely. M. June 25, 1884, to Anna Morris Anderson. M. August 8, 1931, to Margaret Hahn. Ch. four. D. October 4, 1943, Old Lyme, Connecticut.

Richard T. Ely was graduated from Columbia College with the A.B. (1876) and A.M. (1879) degrees. He received an appointment to a fellowship in letters, which enabled him to pursue his studies in Europe. He earned the Ph.D. degree summa cum laude at the University of Heidelberg, Germany, in 1879. He studied under the noted German economist Karl Knies. While in Europe during these years, Ely studied in Switzerland at the University of Geneva and in Germany at Halle and Heidelberg and at the Royal Statistical Bureau in Berlin.

Ely returned to the United States in 1881 to become the first professor of political economy at Johns Hopkins University, where he gained his reputation as one of America's most consistent supporters of academic freedom. His belief in what he referred to as the "freedom of teaching" was continued at the University of Wisconsin, where he served as head of the department of political economy (1892-1925). He was professor of economics at Northwestern University in Evanston, Illinois (1925-33).

Ely trained a generation of economists and was one of the outstanding economics teachers of modern times. He was a critic of classical economics and big business and a defender of the labor movement. With other progressives of his era, Ely paved the way for the acceptance of the economic philosophy of the 1930s. He was an advocate of legal protection for women and children and asserted that workers were better off organized.

Through his prolific writings, Ely distinguished himself as a scholar in the field of political economy. His best-known publications include *French and German Socialism in Modern Times* (1883), *Taxation in American States and Cities* (with J. H. Finley, 1889), *Introduction to Political Economy* (1889), *Outlines of Economics* (with Ralph H. Hess, 1893) the most widely used principles text for many years, *Monopolies and Trusts* (1900), *Studies in the Evaluation of Industrial Society* (1903), *Foundations of National Prosperity* (1917), *Elements of Land Economics* (1926), *Hard Times–The Way In and the Way Out* (1931), *Ground under Our Feet* (1938), and *Land Economics* (1940). His interests in the study of religion and socialism were reflected in *Recent American Socialism* (1885), *Social Aspects of Christianity* (1889), and *Socialism and Social Reform* (1894). He was editor of Macmillan's Social Science Textbook Series, Macmillan's Land Economic Series, and Macmillan's Citizen's Library of Economics.

Ely was one of the founders of the American Economic Association (first secretary, 1885-92, president , 1899-1901). Ely was a member of the Baltimore Tax Commission (1885-86) and the Maryland Tax Commission (1886-88). He was the first president of the American Association for Labor Legislation (1907-08) and a member of the President's Conference on Home Building and Home Ownership (1931-32). He was founder, director, and president of the Institute for Economic Research and president of the School of Land Economics. Ely was a member of the International Statistical Institute and was elected an honorary associate in economics at Columbia University in 1937. He was the recipient of honorary degrees.

REFERENCES: *DAB* (supp. 3); *EB; LE* (II); *NCAB* (9:200, B: 204); *WWW* (II); *NYT,* October 4, 1943, p. 25.   *Jeffrey Sussman*

EMERSON, George Barrell. B. September 12, 1797, Wells, Maine, to Samuel and Sarah (Barrell) Emerson. M. June 11, 1823, to Olivia Buckminster. M. November 12, 1834, to Mary (Rotch) Fleming. Ch. four. D. March 4, 1881, Newton, Massachusetts.

George Barrell Emerson was graduated from Harvard University in 1817. He became principal of a school in Lancaster, Massachusetts, but ill health forced him to relinquish this position, and he became a tutor in mathematics at Harvard (1819–20). He was principal of the English Classical School for Boys in Boston (1821–23) and opened a school for girls in Boston in 1823, operating it until his retirement in the mid-1850s.

Emerson was influential in educational circles. Although he was personally involved with private education, he was a strong supporter of public schools and a frequent speaker on common school reform. During and after the Civil War, Emerson was active in efforts to educate freedmen in the South.

Emerson was a student of natural history. He wrote *Report on the Trees and Shrubs Growing Naturally in the Forests of Massachusetts* (1846), a publication based on nine summers of study. Emerson wrote part 2 of *The School and the Schoolmaster* (1842); part 1 was written by Alonzo Potter (*q.v.*). He was also the author of *Massachusetts Common School System* (1841), *The Classical Reader* (with F. W. P. Greenwood, 1843), *Manual of Agriculture* (with Charles L. Flint, 1862), and *Reminiscences of an Old Teacher* (1878).

Emerson was active in many educational and scholarly organizations. He was a founder of the Boston Mechanics Institute for instruction in sciences related to industry, founder and president of the American Institute of Instruction, president of the Boston Society of Natural History (1837–43), and chairman of a committee that conducted a zoological and botanical survey of Massachusetts. He was awarded an honorary degree by Harvard University.

REFERENCES: *AC; DAB; NCAB* (11:526); *TC; WWW* (H); George B. Emerson, *Reminiscences of an Old Teacher* (Boston: A. Mudge and Sons, 1878); *NYT,* March 6, 1881, p. 2.   *B. Edward McClellan*

EMERSON, Joseph. B. October 14, 1777, Hollis, New Hampshire, to Daniel and Ama (Fletcher) Emerson. M. October 1803 to Nancy Eaton. M. July 1805 to Eleanor Reed. M. January 16, 1810, to Rebecca Hasseltine. Ch. eleven. D. May 14, 1833, Wethersfield, Connecticut.

Joseph Emerson was a clergyman and educator recognized for his interest and work in the cause of education of women. He was graduated from Harvard University in 1798 and studied theology in Cambridge, Massachusetts. He received his license to preach in 1801.

He served as pastor of a Congregational church in Beverly, Massachusetts (1803–16). He taught a brief term at Framingham (Massachusetts) Academy, where his first wife was one of his pupils and he became interested in the education of women. After a visit to the South following his resignation from the Beverly church, he opened a seminary for women at Byfield, Massachusetts (1816). He moved the seminary to Saugus, Massachusetts, in 1821, where he also served as pastor. The seminary was relocated in Wethersfield, Connecticut, from 1824 to 1833. Emerson's seminary was recognized for the broad range of subjects in the curriculum.

Emerson revised Isaac Watts' *The Improvement of the Mind* for use in teaching young women. He wrote *The Evangelical Primer* (1809), *A Union Catechism* (1821), and *Poetic Reader* (1832). He edited and revised textbooks by Samuel Whelpley and Charles A. Goodrich.

Emerson was one of the original members of the American Institute of Instruction. Two of his pupils became the founders of institutions for women: Zilpah Grant *(q.v.)*, who founded Ipswich Academy, and Mary Lyon *(q.v.)*, the founder of Mount Holyoke Seminary.

REFERENCES: *AC; DAB; WWW* (H). *David E. Koontz*

ENGELHARDT, Fred. B. April 15, 1885, Naugatuck, Connecticut, to George John and Helena (Deubel) Engelhardt. M. June 19, 1911, to Ruth Strickland. M. September 19, 1929, to Marion E. Haskell. Ch. none. D. February 3, 1944, Durham, New Hampshire.

Fred Engelhardt was assisted by a scholarship to the Sheffield Scientific School of Yale University from which he was graduated in 1908 with the Ph.B. degree in physics. He was awarded the M.A. (1915) and Ph.D. (1924) degrees from Teachers College, Columbia University.

Upon graduation from Yale, Engelhardt stayed for a year as an assistant instructor. He was a teacher at the Alton (Illinois) Military Academy (1901–11), principal of a Malone (New York) school (1911–16), and head of the science department at William Penn Charter School in Philadelphia, Pennsylvania (1916–17). During World War I, he served as a major in the coast artillery and coauthored a military textbook on gunnery. In 1919 he was appointed elementary school inspector for the New York State Department of Education and in 1920 became director of the bureau of education for Pennsylvania. He was assistant dean of the college of liberal arts at the University of Pittsburgh (1922–24).

Engelhardt served as professor of educational administration at the University of Minnesota (1924–37), where he distinguished himself as a national expert in the fields of educational finance, organization, and administration. He conducted educational surveys of colleges and large city school systems and served on several key national committees that dealt with American educational policies. Some of his writings in the field of educational administration were used as textbooks in graduate education courses and as references for school administrators. He was the author of *Forecasting School Population* (1924), *Public School Organization and Administration* (1931), and *Syllabus for Public School Organization and Administration* (1930). He coauthored many books, including with his brother, Nickolaus L. Engelhardt *(q.v.)*, *Public School Business Administration* (1927), *Planning School Building Programs* (1930), and *Survey of Public Schools Business Administration* (1936). He assisted in the preparation of several mathematics textbooks for junior and senior high school, including *First Course in Algebra* (1927), *Second Course in*

Algebra (1929), and *Mathematics for Junior High Schools* (3 volumes, 1931).

In 1937 Englehardt took office as the ninth president of the University of New Hampshire. He held that position until he died in 1944. His presidency was characterized by decisive administrative leadership with finances secured for the construction, renovation, or expansion of a number of buildings. Engelhardt established a faculty retirement plan and a system of permanent tenure, and he encouraged the development of a faculty senate.

REFERENCES:*LE* (II); *NCAB* (33:323, F: 250); *WWW* (II); *Addresses at a Memorial Service in Honor of Fred Engelhardt* (Durham, N.H.: University of New Hampshire Printing Service, February 22, 1944); Donald C. Babcock, *History of the University of New Hampshire, 1866–1941* (Rochester, N.H.: Record Press, 1941); *NYT*, February 4, 1944, p. 15; Everett B. Sackett, *New Hampshire's University* (Somersworth, N.H.: N.H. Publishing Company, 1974).   *Gary C. Ensign*

ENGELHARDT, Nickolaus Louis. B. October 8, 1882, Naugatuck, Connecticut, to George John and Helena (Deubel) Engelhardt. M. June 14, 1905, to Bessie Edna Gardner. Ch. three. D. February 24, 1960, New York, New York.

Nickolaus Louis Engelhardt attended local schools and was graduated from Yale University with the A.B. degree (1903); he received the Ph.D. degree (1918) from Columbia University.

Engelhardt taught in private schools in Newport, Rhode Island, and Haverford, Pennsylvania (1903–06). He was a high school teacher at Auburn, New York, and a high school principal in Dunkirk, New York (1906–12). He was appointed superintendent of the Dunkirk public schools in 1912 and served to 1916, when he joined the faculty at Teachers College, Columbia University. Engelhardt served as associate director (1929–42) and director (1942) of the division of field studies and chairman of the executive committee of the department of advanced professional education (1939–42). He was on leave of absence from 1942 to 1947, when he was associate superintendent of the New York City schools in charge of housing and business administration. He retired from Teachers College in 1947. He was an educational consultant with his son Nickolaus L. Engelhardt, Jr., in the firm of Engelhardt, Engelhardt and Leggett (later, Engelhardt and Engelhardt) from 1947 to his death in 1960. He conducted many school surveys and educational studies.

Engelhardt was the author of *A School Building Program for Cities* (1918) and *School Building Programs in American Cities* (1928) and was coauthor with George D. Strayer *(q.v.)* of *The Classroom Teacher* (1919), *Problems in Educational Administration* (1925), *School Building Problems* (1927), and *Revised Standards for Elementary School Buildings* (1933). He coauthored with his brother Fred Engelhardt *(q.v.) Public School Business Administration* (1927) and *Planning School Building Programs* (1930). He also coauthored *Planning the Community School* (with his son, 1940), *School Finance and Business Management Problems* (with C. Alexander, 1929), and *Junior High School Building Standards* (with others, 1932). He was coauthor of the Engelhardt-Smith-Kline Arithmetic Series (1930). He was a contributing editor to *School Executive* and participated in the publication of yearbooks for the Department of Superintendence of the National Education Association (1933) and the National Society for the Study of Education.

A member of many professional associations, Engelhardt was president of the American Association of School Administrators (1944–45) and chairman of the Commission on Education of the Correctional Institutions in New York State (1933–42). He received the Nicholas Murray Butler Silver Medal from Columbia University (1937).

REFERENCES: *LE* (II); *NCAB* (52:431); *NYT,* February 25, 1960, p. 29; *WWAE* (VIII); *WWW* (III). *John F. Ohles*

ENGLISH, John Colin. B. July 3, 1895, Alva, Florida, to John Cornelius and Ida (Blont) English. M. May 1, 1920, to Ruth McWilliams. Ch. one.

Colin English attended local schools in Alva, Florida, and attended Emory University in Oxford (later, Atlanta), Georgia, graduating with the Ph.B. degree (1917). He received the A.M. (1934) and Ed.D. (1945) degrees from Columbia University. He attended the University of Edinburgh, Scotland (1918–19), following service with the American Expeditionary Force in World War I.

English spent his professional career in Florida as a teacher at Ocala High School (1920) and principal of White Springs (1921) and Fort Myers high schools (1922–24). He was Lee County superintendent of schools (1925–33) and supervising principal at Ocala (1935–37), and he was elected three times as Florida state superintendent of schools (1937–48). As state superintendent, English provided guidance for legislative action creating a unified system of education and establishing a basic state-funding law providing a county taxing plan to support the schools.

English resigned as state superintendent in 1948 and waged an unsuccessful campaign for the Democratic nomination as candidate for governor. After his retirement, he served as an educational consultant and citrus farmer. He was a member of many professional associations.

REFERENCES: *LE* (III); *WW* (XXVI). *Richard B. Morland*

ERSKINE, John. B. October 5, 1879, New York, New York, to James Morrison and Eliza Jane (Hollingsworth) Erskine. M. June 9, 1910, to

Pauline Ives. M. July 3, 1945, to Helen Worden. Ch. two. D. June 2, 1951, New York, New York.

John Erskine grew up in a wealthy and deeply religious family. He started piano lessons at five, becoming choir accompanist at thirteen and choir director at sixteen. In his middle teens he decided on a career in literature instead of music. First educated by governesses, he entered Columbia Grammar School and attended Columbia University, where he received the A.B. (1900), A.M. (1901), and Ph.D. (1903) degrees.

He taught English at Amherst (Massachusetts) College (1903–09). At Amherst he began a long career lecturing outside the classroom and started writing for publication. Erskine became adjunct professor of English at Columbia University in 1909 and remained there to his retirement in 1937. His academic years were crowded with participation in musical and literary groups. He organized and became the educational director of the American Expeditionary Force University in 1918. He placed American troops in French and British universities and organized a university in a deserted American army hospital at Beaune, France.

Erskine renewed his interest in music in 1920. After intense practice, he played with the New York Philharmonic Orchestra in 1924. His concert appearances, often with major symphonic groups, continued until 1935, when a hand injury limited him at the peak of his performance. While still on the Columbia faculty, he served as president of the Juilliard School (1928–37).

Erskine wrote eight volumes of poetry and essays before writing his first fiction, *The Private Life of Helen of Troy* (1925). He wrote many books using historical or legendary characters to expound his social ideas. Themes of intelligence, ideal beauty, and individual liberty dominated his work. Among Erskine's many books were *The Elizabethan Lyric* (1903), *Actaeon and Other Poems* (1907), *Leading American Novelists* (1910), *Written English* (with Helen Erskine, 1910), *Great American Writers* (with William P. Trent, 1912), *The Moral Obligation to Be Intelligent and Other Essays* (1915), *The Kinds of Poetry* (1920), *The Literary Discipline* (1923), *Galahad, Enough of His Life to Explain His Reputation* (1926), *Adam and Eve* (1927), *Prohibition and Christianity, and Other Paradoxes of the American Spirit* (1927), *The Delight of Great Books* (1928), *Cinderella's Daughter* (1930), *Bachelor of Arts* (1934), *Solomon, My Son!* (1935), *Influence of Women and Its Cure* (1936), *The Brief Hour of François Villon* (1937), *Casanova's Women* (1941), *The Complete Life* (1943), *What is Music?* (1944), *The Human Life of Jesus* (1945), *The Memory of Certain Persons* (1947), *My Life as a Teacher* (1948), and *My Life in Music* (1950). Among the books he edited were *Selections from Spenser's the Faerie Queene* (1905), *Selections from Tennyson's the Idylls of the King* (1912), *Contemporary War Poems* (1914), and Lafcadio Hearn's *Interpretations of Literature* (1915), *Appreciations of Poetry* (1916), *Life and Literature*

(1917), *Talks to Writers* (1920), and *Books and Habits* (1921). He was a joint editor of *Cambridge History of American Literature* (three volumes, 1917–19).

Erskine was secretary and treasurer of the American Council of Learned Societies (1921–24), on the board of the Juilliard School, and a trustee of the Juilliard Music Foundation. He was a director of the Metropolitan Opera Association and a trustee of the Protestant-Episcopal Schools of New York (1916–41, president, 1939–41). He was a member of the Municipal Art Committee (1935–37), the Poetry Society of America (president, 1922), the National Institute of Arts and Letters, and the American Academy of Arts and Sciences. He was chairman of the National Committee for Music Appreciation (1940–41). He received many honorary degrees from American and foreign universities and was awarded the French Legion of Honor and the American Distinguished Service Medal. He was made an honorary citizen of Beaune, France.

REFERENCES: *LE* (II); *NCAB* (E:105); *WWW* (III); John Erskine, *My Life as a Teacher* (Philadelphia: J. B. Lippincott Co., 1948); John Erskine, *My Life in Music* (New York: Morrow, 1950); *NYT*, June 3, 1951, p. 92.

M. Jane Dowd

ESPINOSA, Aurelio Macedonio. B. September 12, 1880, Carneo, Colorado, to Celso and Rafaela (Martinez) Espinosa. M. June 14, 1905, to Margarita Garcia. Ch. four. D. September 4, 1958, Stanford, California.

Aurelio Macedonio Espinosa was a student at the University of Colorado, from which he received the Ph.B. (1902) and M.A. (1904) degrees. He received the Ph.D. degree (1909) from the University of Chicago.

Espinosa was professor of modern languages at the University of New Mexico (1902–10), fellow and instructor of Spanish at the University of Chicago (1908–09), and professor of Spanish at Stanford (California) University (1910–47), where he also served as head of the department (1932–47).

The author of a dozen scholarly works and over thirty textbooks, Espinosa was a translator of books from Spanish to English and English to Spanish. His studies on the tar baby story were instrumental in demonstrating the origin of folk tales. Among his books were *Studies in New Mexican Spanish* (1909), *Elementary Spanish Grammar* (1915), *Elementary Spanish Reader* (1916), *Advanced Spanish Composition and Conversation* (1917), *Beginning Spanish* (with C. G. Allen, 1921), *Cuentos, Romances y Cantares* (1925), *Primer of Spanish Pronunciation* (with Tomas T. Tomas, 1926), *Leciones de Literature Española* (1927), *Easy Spanish Conversation* (1927), and *Romancero de Nuevo Mejico* (1953). He was first editor (1918–25) and then consulting editor from 1925 of *Hispania* and associate editor of the *Journal of American Folk-Lore*.

A member of many associations, Espinosa was president of the American Folk-Lore Society (1923–24), the American Association of Teachers of Spanish (1928), and the Pacific Coast branch of the American Philological Association (1929). He was an honorary member of the New Mexico Historical Society, the Mexican Society of Geography and Statistics, and the Chile Folk-Lore Society and a corresponding member of the Hispanic Society of America and foreign academies. He was decorated Knight Commander of the Royal Order of Isabella the Catholic and received honorary degrees from the University of San Francisco (1930) and the University of New Mexico (1934).

REFERENCES: *LE* (I); *WWW* (III); George E. McSpadden, "Aurelio M. Espinosa (1880–1958)," *Hispania* 42 (March 1959): 20-21; *Palo Alto* (California) *Times*, September 5, 1958, p. 1.   *John F. Ohles*

EURICH, Alvin Christian. B. June 14, 1902, Bay City, Michigan, to Christian Henry and Hulda (Steinke) Eurich. M. June 14, 1926, to Alice Albert. M. March 15, 1953, to Nell (Plopper) Hutchinson. Ch. two.

Alvin Christian Eurich received his early education in the public schools of Bay City, Michigan. He earned the B.A. degree (1924) from North Central College in Naperville, Illinois, the M.A. degree (1926) from the University of Maine, and the Ph.D. degree (1929) from the University of Minnesota. While at Maine (1924–26) he was a speech instructor.

He taught educational psychology at the University of Minnesota, was active in the bureau of educational research, and was assistant dean of the college of education and professor of educational psychology (1927–36). He was professor of education at Northwestern University (1937–38) and at Stanford (California) University (1938–44).

Following two years of military service with the United States Navy (1942–44), Eurich returned to Stanford where he was vice-president of the university (1944–48) and acting president throughout 1948. He organized the Stanford Research Institute, served as vice-chairman of its board of directors (1946–47), and was chairman (1948). In 1949 he was named the first president of the State University of New York. He continued in this post until 1951, when he became vice-president of the Ford Fund for the Advancement of Education. He remained with the fund until 1964, serving as a member of its board of directors (1952–57). He was executive director of the educational division of the Ford Foundation (1958–64). From 1963 he was president of the Academy for Educational Development, New York City.

Eurich wrote many books, including *The Reading Abilities of College Students* (1931), *Studies in College Examinations* (with others, 1934), *Educational Psychology* (with Herbert A. Carroll, 1935), *The General College Curriculum* (with others, 1937), *Guidance in Educational Institu-*

tions (1938), *Social Education* (with others, 1939), *The Improvement of College Instruction* (with others, 1940), *Modern Education: An Evaluation* (with others, 1942), *Campus 1980* (1968), and *High School 1980* (1970). He contributed articles to psychological and educational journals and general periodicals. He was education editor of Farrar and Rinehart (1940–44).

He was active in professional associations; he was a fellow in the American Association for the Advancement of Science (member of the council, 1941–45) and the American Psychological Association and president of the American Educational Research Association (1945). He was a member of the problems and policies committee of the American Council on Education (1945–49), the President's Commission on Higher Education, the Citizens Committee for the Hoover Commission, and the Committee on International Exchange of Persons. He directed surveys of public schools and state systems of higher education.

In 1951 the University of Minnesota awarded him its Distinguished Achievement Award. He received numerous additional awards, including more than thirteen honorary degrees.

REFERENCES: *CA* (17–18); *CB* (June 1949); *LE* (III); *NCAB* (L:449); *WW* (XXXVIII); *WWAE* (XXII). *Norman J. Bauer*

EVANS, Lawton Bryan. B. October 27, 1862, Lumpkin, Georgia, to Clement Anselm and Mary Allen (Walton) Evans. M. 1887 to Florence Eve Campbell. Ch. three. D. April 6, 1934, Augusta, Georgia.

Lawton Bryan Evans was the son of an officer of the Confederate army who was later a member of the state board of prisons and pardons. After completing work at Richmond Academy in Augusta, Georgia (1878), he entered the sophomore class at Emory College in Oxford, Georgia, and was graduated at the head of the class (1880). He received the M.A. degree from the University of Georgia (1881).

While studying law in Augusta, he was elected to fill a vacancy as principal of Richmond Academy (1881–82). A year later he became superintendent of schools for Augusta and Richmond County and held the post for over forty years, with the exception of two years (1892–94) when he was president of the State Normal School in Athens.

He wrote a *History of Georgia* (1900), which met with great approval from the Georgia press. Other books include *Elements of English Language* (1908), *Essential Facts of American History* (1923), *First Lessons in American History* (1924), and *Our Old World Beginnings* (1927). He also wrote books for juveniles: *Worth While Stories* (1916), *America First* (1919), *Old Time Tales* (1921), *Heroes of Israel* (1922), *Heroes of Troy* (1923), *The Trail Blazers* (1924), *The Pirate of Barataria* (1925), *With Whip and Spur* (1927), *With Wind and Tide* (1928), and *With Pack and Saddle* (1929).

Evans was a popular lecturer for a number of years before Chautauqua assemblies and metropolitan audiences. He was a trustee of the Carnegie Endowment for International Peace. He was awarded a medal for distinguished service by Columbia University (1933).

REFERENCES: *LE* (I); *NCAB* (B:326); *WWAE* (I); *WWW* (I); Dorothy Orr, *A History of Education in Georgia* (Chapel Hill: University of North Carolina Press, 1950).   *Betty Leslein*

EWELL, Benjamin Stoddert. B. June 10, 1810, Washington, D.C. to Thomas and Elizabeth (Stoddert) Ewell. M. April 17, 1839, to Julia McIlvain. Ch. one. D. June 19, 1894, James City, Virginia.

Benjamin Ewell was graduated third in his class from the United States Military Academy at West Point, New York (1832). He served as an assistant professor of mathematics and natural philosophy at West Point (1832–36). He resigned from the army and worked for three years as a railroad engineer (1836–39). He was professor of mathematics and natural philosophy at Hampden-Sydney (Virginia) College (1839–46). He was the first to be appointed Cincinnati Professor of Mathematics and Military Science at Washington College (later, Washington and Lee University) in Lexington, Virginia (1846–48). He was elected professor of mathematics and acting president of William and Mary College in Williamsburg, Virginia (1848), and became the institution's sixteenth president (1854–61 and 1865–81).

With the onset of the Civil War in 1861, the college suspended activities. Ewell and most of the professors and students entered the Confederate army. He served as chief of staff under General Joseph E. Johnston. He resigned in 1865 and returned to the presidency of William and Mary. He successfully opposed moving the college to Richmond. He restored buildings burned by federal troops in 1862, organized a faculty and reopened the college in 1869.

Congress indemnified the college for the war damage, but the cost of repairs and increased operating expenses forced the college to close in 1881. For seven years, Ewell spent his own money and maintained the buildings. In 1888 the legislature included the college in the state educational system; Ewell did not play an active role at the reopened college because of his age, but he was named president emeritus.

Ewell was credited with the publication of the *Historical Catalogue* of the college (1859), one of the first in the country.

REFERENCES: *AC; DAB; NCAB* (3:236); *TC.*   *Daniel S. Yates*

F

FAIRCHILD, Edward Thomson. B. October 30, 1854, Doylestown, Ohio, to Samuel and Eliza Jane (Huestis) Fairchild. M. October 10, 1883, to Frances L. Postlewait. Ch. four. D. January 23, 1917, Durham, New Hampshire.

Edward Thomson Fairchild was educated at Ohio Wesleyan in Delaware, Ohio, and Wooster (Ohio) universities. He taught in rural schools in Ohio in 1872, served on the teaching staff of Haysville (Ohio) Normal Academy (1874–78), and was school superintendent at Columbus Grove, Ohio (1878–83).

Fairchild moved to Ellsworth, Kansas, where he was superintendent of schools (1885–1903) and also served four years as superintendent of Ellsworth County schools, where he established the first consolidated school system west of Ohio. He was elected state superintendent of public instruction in Kansas in 1906, was reelected twice, and held the position to 1912. As state superintendent he upgraded rural education in Kansas, increased the school year to seven months, provided transportation for students, and introduced normal courses in the high schools. He was a regent of the State Agricultural College (later, Kansas State University) from 1889 to 1907.

Fairchild left Kansas in 1912 to assume the presidency of the New Hampshire College of Agriculture and Mechanic Arts (later, University of New Hampshire) at Durham and held that position until his death in 1917. During his presidency, the college doubled in student enrollment, new courses of study were offered, new facilities were constructed, and additional faculty were employed.

Fairchild was a life member of the National Education Association (chairman of the department of rural schools, 1911, and president, 1912) and was a member of the National Council of Education. He received honorary degrees from Kansas State Agricultural College and Baker University.

REFERENCES: *NCAB* (19:38); *WWW* (I); *NYT,* January 24, 1917, p. 9. *Robert H. Truman*

FAIRCHILD, George Thompson. B. October 6, 1838, Brownhelm, Ohio, to Grandison and Nancy (Harris) Fairchild. M. November 25, 1863, to Charlotte Pearl Halsted. Ch. five. D. March 16, 1901, Columbus, Ohio.

George Thompson Fairchild received the A.B. (1862) and A.M. (1865)

degrees from Oberlin (Ohio) College. He was an instructor at Michigan State Agricultural College (later, Michigan State University) from 1865 to 1879. While at Michigan, he was professor of English literature, taught moral philosophy and French, served as secretary of the college, and was acting president for one year. He was active in increasing the college library collection.

Fairchild moved to Kansas in 1879 as president of Kansas State Agricultural College (later, Kansas State University) and held that position until 1897 when he resigned with most of the faculty under pressure from the Populist movement in Kansas. Under his administration at Kansas State, general education subjects were strengthened, and much of the industrial work was organized as laboratory experiences. The graduate program was improved, and requirements were increased. The physical plant was enlarged, and there was a large increase in faculty and students.

Fairchild was professor of English and vice-president of Berea (Kentucky) College (1898–1901). He organized departments of agriculture and industry, which grew and expanded their activities so that many of the students were able to earn all or part of their college expenses while attending college.

Fairchild was active in educational and civic endeavors; he was a member of the National Teachers' Association (later, National Education Association) and a life director and president of the Industrial Section. An organizer of the Association of Agricultural Colleges and Experimental Stations, he served on various committees and was vice-president for several terms and president in 1897. He was the author of *Rural Wealth and Welfare* (1900) and many reports and papers on educational and agricultural subjects. He received an honorary degree from Oberlin College. Fairchild's brothers were also presidents of colleges: James Harris Fairchild *(q.v.)* of Oberlin College and Edward Henry Fairchild of Berea College.

REFERENCES: *DAB; NCAB* (25:265); *TC; WWW* (I).   *Claude A. Bell*

FAIRCHILD, James Harris. B. November 25, 1817, Stockbridge, Massachusetts, to Grandison and Nancy (Harris) Fairchild. M. 1841 to Mary Fletcher Kellogg. Ch. eight. D. March 19, 1902, Oberlin, Ohio.

James Harris Fairchild moved at the age of one to the western reserve of Ohio near Brownhelm in Lorain County. He went to a small school in that area and attended high school in Elyria, Ohio. In 1834, at the age of seventeen, Fairchild began his long association with Oberlin (Ohio) College, which had been founded in 1833 as the first coeducational college. He was graduated in 1838 and, after one year's absence from Oberlin, returned as a theological student and a tutor. He was ordained in 1841 and in 1842 became professor of Greek and Latin at the college.

In 1847 Fairchild was transferred to the chair of mathematics and later to the area of theology and moral philosophy (1858). At the age of thirty-one he became a member of the executive committee of the board of trustees. Fairchild was elected president of Oberlin in 1866 and served in that office for twenty-three years. During his term the college grew from a faculty of nine to twenty-three, and, at the end of his presidency, the college property was valued at $1 million.

Fairchild retired as president in 1889 and continued on the faculty for nine more years. He was a member of the board of trustees for the last five years of his life.

Fairchild published *Moral Philosophy or the Science of Obligation* (1869), *Oberlin: The Colony and the College* (1883), *Woman's Right to the Ballot* (1890), and *Elements of Theology, Natural and Revealed* (1892). He edited *Memoirs of Charles G. Finney* (1876) and *Finney's Systematic Theology* (1878). Some fifty of his historical and religious monographs, sermons, and reviews were published. He was a brother of George Thompson Fairchild *(q.v.)*.

REFERENCES: *AC; DAB; NCAB* (2:464); *TC; WWW* (I); *NYT,* March 20, 1902, p. 2. *Joan Duff Kise*

FAIRCHILD, Mary Salome Cutler. B. June 21, 1855, Dalton, Massachusetts, to Artemas Hubbard and Lydia (Wakefield) Cutler. M. July 1, 1897, to Edwin Milton Fairchild. Ch. none. D. December 20, 1921, Takoma Park, Maryland.

(Mary) Salome Cutler Fairchild was graduated from Mount Holyoke Seminary in South Hadley, Massachusetts, in 1875; she stayed there to teach until 1878.

With the founding of the American Library Association in 1876, Fairchild's interests turned toward librarianship. In 1884 she sought assistance in finding a position from Melvil Dewey *(q.v.)*, who invited her to serve as a cataloger in the Columbia College Library. She was promoted to the rank of instructor of cataloging in the newly formed library school at Columbia in 1887 and remained in this position for two years. She was caught in the argument between Dewey and the Columbia administration over employment of women in the library school. She resigned from the Columbia faculty and moved with Dewey to Albany in 1889. Dewey became the secretary of the New York Board of Regents and the state librarian and transferred the library school to Albany. Fairchild was vice-director of the school (1889–1905) and was librarian of the New York State Library for the Blind at Albany (1889–1905).

During her tenure in Albany, Fairchild built upon her work at Columbia in book selection, cataloging and libraries for the blind, and the development and implementation of standards for library training. In recognition for her achievements, she was awarded the B.L.S. degree from the University of the State of New York on behalf of the State Library School in 1891. As the chairman of an American Library Association committee she was asked to compile a catalog designed to guide librarians in book selection, which was published by the United States Bureau of Education in 1893.

Fairchild suffered a nervous breakdown and retired from her position as vice-director of the library school in 1905. She lectured and wrote about library work and served as director of the Drexel Institute Library School in Philadelphia for a few months in 1909.

She was the author of *Children's Home Catalog of A.L.A. Library* (1894) and *Function of the Library* (1901). She was active in the American Library Association (member of the council, 1892–98, and 1908–14, and vice-president, 1894–95 and 1900–01). She was a delegate to the British Library Association Conference (1903).

REFERENCES: *DAB; NAW; NCAB* (20:263); *TC; WWW* (I).

Anne Raymond-Savage

FAIRCLOUGH, Henry Rushton. B. July 15, 1862, near Barrie, Ontario, Canada, to James and Elizabeth (Erving) Fairclough. M. August 29, 1888, to Frederica Blanche Allen. M. September 24, 1930, to Mary Charlotte Holly. Ch. one. D. February 12, 1938, Palo Alto, California.

Henry Rushton Fairclough attended the Hamilton Collegiate Institute and received the A.B. (1883) and A.M. (1886) degrees from the University of Toronto, Canada. He earned the Ph.D. degree (1896) from Johns Hopkins University in Baltimore, Maryland.

He taught in Canada as a master in classics and English at the Brockville High School (1884) and was a fellow in classics (1883–84) and lecturer in Greek (1887–93) at the University College of the University of Toronto. He moved to Stanford (California) University in 1893, where he taught Greek, Latin, and classical literature to 1927, when he retired. He also taught at the American School of Classical Studies in Rome, Italy (1910–11), and was professor of New Testament literature at the Church Divinity School of the Pacific in San Francisco, California (1921–27).

Recognized as the major Virgil scholar, Fairclough was the author of books on the classics, including *The Attitude of the Greek Tragedians toward Nature* (1896), *The Andria of Terence* (1901), *The Classics and Our Twentieth Century Poets* (1927), *Love of Nature Among the Greeks and Romans* (1930), *Aspects of Horace* (1935), and *Some Aspects of Nature* (1935). He translated *Antigone of Sophocles* (1903), *Virgil's Aeneid* (with S. L. Brown, 1908), *The Phormio of Terence* (with L. J. Richardson, 1908), and *Trinummus of Plautus* (1909). He was editor of Students' Series Latin Classics and director and editor of *Art and Archaeology* (1925).

A participant in professional activities, Fairclough was a delegate to the centennial celebration of the University of Berlin, Germany (1910), the Toronto (Canada) University Centenary (1927), and the International Congress of Anthropological Sciences (1934). He served with the American Red Cross in Switzerland (1918–19) and Montenegro (1918–19). He was a fellow of the American Geographical Society and president of the Classical Association of the Pacific States (1918) and the American Philological Association (1926). He was vice-president of the Archaelogical Institute of America (1918). He was decorated by the governments of Serbia, Montenegro, and Belgium and received honorary degrees from the universities of Toronto (1922) and British Columbia (1938).

REFERENCES: *LE* (I); *NCAB* (C:59, 28:413); *NYT,* February 13, 1938, sec. 2, p. 6; *WWAE* (VIII); *WWW* (I). *John F. Ohles*

FANNING, Tolbert. B. May 10, 1810, Cannon County, Tennessee, to William and Nancy (Bromley) Fanning. M. to Sarah Shreeve. M. December 25, 1836, to Charlotte Fall. Ch. none. D. May 3, 1874, Davidson County, Tennessee.

Tolbert Fanning's family moved to Lauderdale County, Alabama, in 1816 during a period of land speculation. Fanning was graduated from the University of Nashville in 1835.

He engaged periodically in evangelistic work most of his life. He made extensive trips with Alexander Campbell and was a Disciples of Christ minister. He opened a boarding school for girls in Franklin, Tennessee, in 1837. In 1840 he moved to a farm outside of Nashville where he worked to improve the breeds of several farm animals. In 1843 Fanning opened an agriculture school, which became Franklin College in 1844. The college emphasized agriculture and manual training. Students entering the ministry were not charged tuition. The college became a major institution for the Disciples of Christ in the South. After the Civil War, the main college building was destroyed by fire and the college closed. The Fannings bought a nearby girls' school and renamed it Hope Institute. It was continued until Fanning's death in 1874 when his widow gave the Hope Institute to the trustees to establish the Fanning Orphan School.

Fanning was the author of the *Naturalist and Journal of Natural History, Agriculture, Education, and Literature* (aided by the Franklin College faculty, 1846) and *True Method of Searching the Scriptures* (1854). He founded and edited *Naturalist* (with Charles Foster, 1850–51, merged with *Southern Agriculturist* in 1851), *Christian Review* (from 1844; later, *Christian Magazine*), *Gospel Advocate* (with William Lipscomb and David Lipscomb, 1854–60 and 1866–68), and *Religious Historian* (1872–74).

REFERENCES: *DAB; WWW* (H); *Republican Banner* (Nashville, Tennessee), May 5, 1874. *Jerry C. McGee*

FARMER, Fannie Merritt. B. March 23, 1857, Boston, Massachusetts, to John Franklin and Mary (Watson) Farmer. M. no. D. January 15, 1915, Boston, Massachusetts.

Fanny Merritt Farmer attended the Medford (Massachusetts) High School. She suffered a paralytic stroke and slowly recovered her health. She was graduated from the Boston (Massachusetts) Cooking School in 1889.

Farmer was an assistant to Mrs. C. M. Dearborn, principal of the Boston Cooking School (1889), and became principal of the school on the death of Mrs. Dearborn in 1891. She resigned in 1902 to open Miss Farmer's School of Cookery, which she conducted to her death in 1915. The Boston Cooking School (which became affiliated with Simmons College in 1903), prepared home economics teachers, while Farmer's school sought to serve housewives. Farmer specialized in food for the sick and invalids. She lectured across the country and gained a national reputation. She suffered a second stroke and spent her last years confined to a wheelchair, from which she continued to lecture and conduct her school.

Farmer was the author of a number of cookbooks, including *Boston Cooking School Cook Book* (1896), *Chafing Dish Possibilities* (1898), *Food and Cookery for the Sick and Convalescent* (1904), *What to Have for Dinner* (1905), *Catering for Special Occasions* (1911), and *A New Book of Cookery* (1912). She was coauthor with her sister, Cora Dexter Farmer Perkins, of a cooking column in the *Woman's Home Companion* (1905–15).

REFERENCES: *DAB; NAW; NCAB* (22:206); *WWW* (I). *John F. Ohles*

FARNSWORTH, Charles Hubert. B. November 29, 1859, Cesarea, Turkey, to Wilson Amos and Caroline E. (Palmer) Farnsworth. M. 1890 to Charlotte Joy Allen. Ch. none. D. May 22, 1947, Hanover, New Hampshire.

Charles Hubert Farnsworth was born in Turkey, the son of American missionaries. He was educated at Thetford (Vermont) Academy and Robert College in Constantinople, Turkey. At the age of seventeen, he served on a vessel sailing around Cape Horn to Valparaiso, Chile. He lived in Worcester, Massachusetts, where he taught music and studied with Benjamin Dwight Allen (1876–87). Moving to Boulder, Colorado, in 1887, he became a music teacher and conductor of group singing at Boulder College (later, University of Colorado). With Edward Whiteman, father of Paul Whiteman, Farnsworth was one of the earliest organizers of high school orchestras. In 1901 he joined the staff of Teachers College, Columbia University, as head of the music and speech departments. He held this position for twenty-five years.

He was the author of many books on music, including *The Teaching of Elementary Music* (1904), *Education Through Music* (1909), *How to Pro-*

duce and Listen to Music (1920), *How to Study Music* (1920), *The Why and How of Music Study* (1927), and *Short Studies in Musical Psychology* (1929). He compiled *Songs for Schools* (1906), *Folk Songs* (with Cecil J. Sharp, 1909), *Grammar School Songs* (1916), and *Tonal Phrase Book* (with William J. Kraft, 1920). He was editor of *The World's Music* (1927), *Singing Youth* (1935), and *Our Songs* (1939).

Farnsworth conducted research preparing musical programs for recording firms, including the Edison Company. He worked for the National Broadcasting Company collaborating in the production of the *NBC Music Appreciation Hour Notebooks* and, with Walter Damrosch, the "Music Appreciation Hour." He was founder of a camp for girls and a trustee of the Thetford (Vermont) Academy. He was president (1912–15) of the Music Teachers' National Association.

REFERENCES: *LE* (II); *WWW* (II); F. Dunham, "Charles Hubert Farnsworth," *Music Educators Journal* 34 (November 1947): 27–28; K. W. Gehrkens *(q.v.)* "Charles Hubert Farnsworth," *Educational Music Magazine* 27 (November 1947): 8; *NYT*, May 23, 1947, p. 23; *School and Society* 65 (May 31, 1947): 396.   *Albert S. Weston*

FARNUM, Royal Bailey. B. June 11, 1884, Somerville, Massachusetts, to Daniel Stoddard and Flora L. (Bailey) Farnum. M. December 19, 1907, to Adeline Burnett. Ch. three. D. August 29, 1967, Plainfield, Connecticut.

Royal Bailey Farnum was graduated in 1906 from the Massachusetts Normal Art School (later, Massachusetts College of Art) in Boston. He also received the Master of Education in Art degree (1929) from the Cleveland (Ohio) School of Art. He studied summers in England, France, Italy, Germany, and Scandinavia.

Farnum was director of the normal department of the Cleveland School of Art (1906–10) and an instructor in the Cleveland public schools (1907–09). He was director of art education for the state of New York (1909–18). He was president of the Rochester Athenaeum and Mechanics Institute (1919–21). He was president of the Massachusetts College of Art and also director of art education for the state of Massachusetts (1921–29). He was the educational director (1929–37) and executive vice-president (1937–46) of the Rhode Island School of Design in Providence. For a number of years Farnum served on the editorial staff of the Practical Drawing Company. During World War II he was instrumental in the development of a color combination for military camouflage.

Farnum was the author of a number of articles and books, including *Present Status of Drawing and Art in the Elementary and Secondary Schools in the United States* (1914), *Decoration for Rural Schools* (1914), *The Manual Arts in New York State* (1916), *Manual Arts in New York State* (1917), *Gum, Hot Dogs, and Beauty* (1929), *Art Education in Los*

Angeles County (1936), *Learning More About Pictures* (1948), and *Industrial Design in Retrospect* (1949). He was the author of *Biennial Surveys* (1922–30), editor of *School Arts* magazine (1917–19), and associate art editor of *Education* (1931–49).

Active in the National Art Education Association, Farnum headed American delegations to many international arts congresses. He was president of the National Association for Art Education (1936–38), the National Association of Schools of Design, and the Federal Council on Art Education (1925–36). During his tenure on the Federal Council he served on the committee on high schools (1934–35) and was active in the production of the report, *Art Education in the High Schools.* Farnum served on the committee for the fortieth yearbook of the National Society for the Study of Education, *Art in American Life and Education* (1941).

In recognition of his lifetime devotion to art education, Farnum received the Michael Friedsam Medal (1942). He was the recipient of several honorary degrees.

REFERENCES: *LE (III); WW* (XXVIII); *WWAE* (VIII); Frederick M. Logan, *Growth of Art in American Schools* (New York: Harper & Brothers, 1955); *NYT,* August 30, 1967, p. 43.   *Roger H. Jones*

FARRAR, John. B. July 1, 1779, Lincoln, Massachusetts, to Samuel and Mary (Hoar) Farrar. M. to Lucy Maria Buckminster. M. 1828 to Eliza Ware Rotch. Ch. none. D. May 8, 1853, Cambridge, Massachusetts.

John Farrar was graduated from Harvard University in 1803 and studied at Andover (Massachusetts) Theological Seminary to train for the ministry. He terminated his stay there in 1805 and returned to Harvard to tutor Greek. In 1807 he was made Hollis Professor of Mathematics and Natural Philosophy, a position he held until 1836, when he resigned because of ill health.

Farrar modernized and reformed the science and mathematics curriculum at Harvard. He introduced the best materials on mathematics from France and other European countries. He was instrumental in shifting from the Newtonian fluxional notations to Leibniz's algorithm for calculus.

Although he wrote few scientific papers, his translations ensured good college texts that were kept abreast of the most recent advances. These translations were used at Harvard and many other colleges. He translated Arago's 1832 *Tract on Comets* and mathematics books from the French, including S. F. La Croix's *An Elementary Treatise on Arithmetic* (1825), *Elements of Algebra* (1831), and *An Elementary Treatise on Plane and Spherical Trigonometry* (1833), A. M. Legendre's *Elements of Geometry* (1825), and E. G. Fischer's *Elements of Natural Philosophy* (1827). He wrote textbooks, including *An Elementary Treatise on the Application of Trigonometry* (1822), *An Elementary Treatise on Mechanics* (1825), *An Elementary Treatise on Astronomy* (1826), *An Elementary Treatise on*

Optics (1826), and *Elements of Electricity, Magnetism and Electrodynamics* (1839). His work was described by his second wife in *Recollections of Seventy Years* (1866).

He was elected in 1808 a fellow of the American Academy of Arts and Sciences (recording secretary, 1811–23, member of the committee on publications, 1828–29, and vice-president, 1829–31). He received an honorary degree from Brown University in 1833.

REFERENCES: *AC; DAB; DSB; TC; WWW* (H);. *Saul Barron*

FAY, Edward Allen. B. November 22, 1843, Morristown, New Jersey, to Barnabus M. and Louise (Mills) Fay. M. July 6, 1871, to Mary Bradshaw. Ch. seven. D. July 14, 1923, Washington, D.C.

Edward Allen Fay, son of an educator of the deaf, was educated at the University of Michigan from which he received the A.B. (1862) and A.M. (1865) degrees. He received the Ph.D. degree (1881) from Johns Hopkins University.

Fay was appointed an instructor in the New York Institution for the Deaf (1862–66). He was the third professor appointed to the faculty of Gallaudet College in Washington, D.C. (1866). During his fifty-four years as a professor and from 1885 as vice-president at Gallaudet, Fay gained international eminence as an educator and author. He strongly advocated the use of sign language and was a master of manual communication.

He was commissioned by the Dante Society of Cambridge, Massachusetts, to write *Concordance of the Divina Commedia* (1888). His most enduring work was *Marriages of the Deaf in America* (1898), one of the earliest studies of the question of the inheritance of deafness. He directed and edited a compilation of *Histories of American Schools for the Deaf* (1893). He edited the *American Annals of the Deaf* (1870–1920). He was fluent in Latin and also had an excellent command of French, Italian, Spanish, and German.

Fay was a member of scholarly and professional associations. He was awarded honorary degrees by the University of Michigan (1912) and Gallaudet College (1916).

REFERENCES: *DAB; NCAB* (20:62); *WWW* (I); *American Annals of the Deaf* 68 (1923): 257–66. *Jerome D. Schein*

FEDER, Daniel Dunn. B. April 12, 1910, Philadelphia, Pennsylvania, to Jacob and Minnie (Orlovitz) Feder. M. September 2, 1934, to Florence Esther Malbin. Ch. one.

After his graduation from the University of Denver with the A.B. (1930) and A.M. (1931) degrees, Daniel Dunn Feder was awarded a fellowship in research in the department of psychology by the University of Iowa, from which he received the Ph.D. degree (1934).

Feder was research associate (1934–35) and associate in psychology and personnel (1935–38) at the University of Iowa and assistant director of the personnel bureau and assistant professor of psychology (1938–42) at the University of Illinois. Following Civil Service Commission administrative work (1942–46) with the state of Illinois and an intervening period (1942–45) when he served as lieutenant commander in the Bureau of Naval Personnel during World War II, he was appointed dean of students and professor of psychology at the University of Denver, Colorado (1946). Feder resigned his position fifteen years later to go to San Francisco (California) State University as chairman of the division of psychology (1961–63), dean of the school of humanities and sciences (1963–64), dean of academic planning (1964–73), and dean of faculty affairs (1973–75).

A nationally known specialist on college guidance and counseling for many years, Feder did extensive research in various phases of student personnel work and counseling and wrote more than two hundred articles for publication in psychological, educational, and technical journals, pamphlets, and books.

Feder served in several official roles, including presidencies of the American College Personnel Association (1945–47), the Council of Guidance and Personnel Associations (CGPA) during 1947–48, and the American Personnel and Guidance Association (APGA) during 1960–61. His presidential address to the CGPA group at their national convention in Chicago (1948) led to the creation of a special study commission, whose report led to the formation of APGA in 1951.

REFERENCES: *LE* (V); *WW* (XXXVIII); *WWAE* (XIV).

Vernon Lee Sheeley

FERNALD, Charles Henry. B. March 16, 1838, Mt. Desert, Maine, to Eben and Sophronia (Wasgatt) Fernald. M. August 24, 1862, to Maria Elizabeth Smith. Ch. one. D. February 22, 1921, Amherst, Massachusetts.

Charles Henry Fernald was a leader in the systematic instruction of entomology in American graduate schools. His Maine childhood on a farm and near the sea coast kindled an interest in all forms of natural history. He prepared for college at the Maine Wesleyan Seminary. He studied with Louis Agassiz *(q.v.)* at the seaside school on Penikese Island (Massachusetts). He was principal of Litchfield (Maine) Academy (1865) and Houlton (Maine) Academy (1866–71). He served as a professor at Maine State College (later, University of Maine) at Orono (1871–86), where he taught all branches of natural history, but gradually developed a special interest in insects.

In 1886 Fernald accepted a position as professor of zoology at the Massachusetts Agricultural College (later, University of Massachusetts) where he remained until his retirement in 1910. He was credited with being the first college-level teacher of economic entomology. Under his direction, Massachusetts Agricultural College became one of the centers for entomological study in America. The success of a master's degree program in entomology led to the establishment of a doctoral program, the first for the college. Fernald and his students supplemented courses with fieldwork at experimental stations and nurseries. Special concern was placed on commercial economic entomology. They fought insect pests, such as the asparagus and buffalo carpet beetles, the spruce gall louse, the white fly, and the cattle tick. He was aided in his efforts by his wife, and his work was continued at Massachusetts by his son Henry Torsey Fernald.

Fernald was well known to his peers in Europe and traveled there frequently. He was in Europe in the summer of 1889 when his wife in Amherst was given a caterpillar that was seriously damaging plants in Malden, Massachusetts. She identified it as the gypsy moth, and Charles Fernald was placed in charge of the scientific aspects of the fight that the state waged against the pest.

Fernald held numerous positions in state and professional organizations. He was Massachusetts state entomologist and president of the American Association of Economic Entomologists (1896). Among his publications were *Butterflies of Maine* (1884), *Grasses of Maine* (1885), *Sphingidae of New England* (1886), *Orthoptera of New England* (1888), and *The Pterophoridae of North America* (1898).

REFERENCES: *AC; DAB; NCAB* (9: 232); *TC; WWW* (I); Henry T. Fernald, *History of Entomology at the Massachusetts Agricultural College, 1867–1930* (Amherst, Mass.: Agricultural College, 1938); *NYT*, February 23, 1921, p. 13.   *William Kornegay*

FESS, Simeon Davidson. B. December 11, 1861, Harrod, Ohio, to Henry and Barbara (Herring) Fess. M. March 1890 to Eva Candas Thomas. Ch. three. D. December 23, 1936, Washington, D.C.

Simeon Davidson Fess attended a county school where his primary education was obtained under difficult circumstances. His family was destitute following the father's death, but Fess struggled to continue his education by reading every book he could borrow. He passed the schoolteachers' examination at the age of nineteen and began his teaching career.

Fess received the A.B. (1889) and A.M. (1891) degrees from Ohio Northern University in Ada, Ohio, and joined the faculty in 1889 as a professor of American history, a position he held until 1896. During these years he attended the university's law school and was awarded the LL.B. degree (1896). He was dean of the law school (1896–1900) and vice-president of the university (1900–02). A graduate student and lecturer in the extension department at the University of Chicago (1902–07), he served as president and professor of history of Antioch College in Yellow Springs, Ohio (1907–17), guiding the school through some of the most difficult years of its existence.

Fess was the author of many books, including *A Compendium of United States History* (1891), *A Compendium of Anatomy, Physiology and Hygiene* (1892), *Outline of United States History* (1897), *Outlines of Physiology* (1899), *History of Political Theory and Party Organization* (1907), *Civics in Ohio* (1910), *Problems of Neutrality When the World Is at War* (1917), and *Four Volume Reference Library* (history of Ohio, 1936).

During his years as student and administrator, Fess was active in Republican politics. He served on numerous committees and held various offices, including vice-president of the Ohio constitutional convention and chairman of the committee on education (1912). He was the author of the provision creating the department of state superintendent of public instruction. He served in the United States House of Representatives (1913–23) and the United States Senate (1923–35). He was chairman of the House of Representatives Committee on Education and was appointed by President Woodrow Wilson *(q.v.)* a member of the Vocational Education Commission, which drafted the Smith-Hughes Vocational Education Act of 1917. He was temporary chairman and keynote speaker of the Republican National Convention in 1920 and was chairman of the Republican National Committee (1930–31). He received honorary degrees from Ohio Northern and Wilberforce universities.

REFERENCES: *DAB* (supp. 2); *NCAB* (27:340, C:283); *TC; WWW* (I); *NYT,* December 24, 1936, p. 17.   *Gary C. Barlow*

FEW, William Preston. B. December 29, 1867, Greenville, South Carolina, to Benjamin Franklin and Rachael (Kendrick) Few. M. August 17, 1911, to Mary Reamey Thomas. Ch. five. D. October 16, 1940, Durham, North Carolina.

William Preston Few, first president of Duke University, received his preparatory education from private tutors and the Greer (South Carolina) public schools. He was graduated with the A.B. degree (1889) from Wofford College in Spartanburg, South Carolina. He received the A.M. (1893) and Ph.D. (1896) degrees from Harvard University.

Few taught at St. John's Academy in Darlington, South Carolina (1890–91), and was an English instructor at Wofford College (1891–92). He was professor of English literature at Trinity College, Durham, North Carolina, and manager of athletics (1896–1902). He became dean of the college (1902) and was elected president (1910). He was president of Trinity College until 1924, when it became part of Duke University. Few was first president of Duke from its founding in 1924 until his death in 1940.

Few was on intimate terms with the Duke family, the noted tobacco manufacturers, who had made large gifts to Trinity College. In 1924 James Duke established an endowment of $40 million for educational and charitable purposes, stipulating that a large part of this money should be used to fund a great educational center, with Trinity College as its nucleus. The result was Duke University. Under Few, Duke expanded to include ten separate schools with a total student enrollment of 3,673 and a faculty of 446 in 1940.

Few was editor of the *South Atlantic Quarterly* (1909–19), a member of the board of directors of the Southern Educational Foundation, and a trustee of the Jeanes Foundation. He was a life member of the North Carolina Education Association and a member of the North Carolina State Literary and Historical Association (president, 1913) and the Association of Colleges and Secondary Schools of the Southern states (president, 1932–33). He was active in the Methodist church. He was the recipient of many honorary degrees.

REFERENCES: *CB* (December 1940); *DAB* (supp. 2); *LE* (I); *NCAB* (29:17); *WWW* (I); *NYT,* October 17, 1940, p. 25; Robert H. Woody, *Papers and Addresses of William Preston Few* (Durham, N.C.: Duke University Press, 1951). *Linda C. Gardner*

FILLMORE, John Comfort. B. February 4, 1843, Franklin, Connecticut, to John L. and Mary Ann (Palmer) Fillmore. M. October 5, 1865, to Eliza Hill. Ch. three. D. August 14, 1898, Norwich, Connecticut.

John Comfort Fillmore entered Oberlin (Ohio) College in 1862 where he studied organ and piano under George W. Steele. He decided to pursue a musical career during his college course. After his graduation (1865), he went to Leipzig, Germany, where he studied under Moritz Hauptmann, Ernst Richter, and Benjamin Papperitz, eminent theorists as well as fine organists.

He was an instructor in instrumental music at Oberlin (1867–68). In 1868 he became professor of music at Ripon (Wisconsin) College and in 1878 accepted a position at the Milwaukee (Wisconsin) College for Women. He was the founder (1884) and director of the Milwaukee Music School (1884–95). In 1895 he accepted a position at Pomona College (Claremont, California), which he held until his death.

Fillmore was interested in adding music to the college curriculum. He was recognized as a theorist as early as 1883. He published *A History of Piano-forte Music with Critical Estimates of Its Greatest Masters and Sketches of Their Lives* (1885), *New Lessons in Harmony* (1887), *Lessons in Musical History* (1895), *A Study of Omaha Indian Music* (with Alice C. Fletcher and Francis La Flesche, 1893), and *On the Value of Certain Modern Theories* (n.d.), chiefly about the theories of von Ottingen and Hugo Riemann.

An authority on Indian music, he visited many tribes and recorded their tribal calls, rhythms, and ceremonial songs. He was a member of the American Folk-Lore Society and the American Association for the Advancement of Science.

REFERENCES: *DAB; NCAB* (23:152); *TC; WWW* (H); Nicholas Slonimsky, ed., *Baker's Biographical Dictionary of Musicians,* 5th ed. (New York: G. Schirmer, 1958); Frances Densmore, *The American Indians and Their Music* (New York: The Womans Press, 1936).   *Betty S. Harper*

FINEGAN, Thomas Edward. B. September 29, 1866, West Fulton, New York, to Michael and Ann (Welch) Finegan. M. December 10, 1894, to Grace Emma Browne. Ch. one. D. November 25, 1932, Rochester, New York.

Lawyer, educator, and author, Thomas E. Finegan served over twenty-five years as an administrator in state departments of education. He was graduated from the New York State College for Teachers (later, State University of New York at Albany) in 1889 and received the M.A. degree from Hamilton College in Clinton, New York (1894).

Finegan joined the New York State Department of Public Instruction as supervisor of examinations in 1892. In 1904 he became chief of the law division of the newly created state education department and served successively as assistant commissioner of elementary education from 1908 to 1915 and as deputy commissioner of education from 1915 to 1919. Finegan served under Andrew S. Draper *(q.v.)* from 1904 to 1913 and played a major role in implementing many of the reforms associated with Draper.

In 1919 Finegan accepted the position of state superintendent of public instruction in Pennsylvania where he reorganized both the state education department and the public school system. Declining reappointment in 1923, Finegan became active in the field of visual aids in teaching, an activity that brought him into contact with George Eastman who incorporated Eastman Teaching Films in 1928 with Finegan as president. Over two hundred educational films were produced, with a wide circulation in the United States and abroad.

Finegan wrote many studies published by the New York State Education Department, including *Textbook on New York School Law* (1914), *Judicial Decisions in Education* (1914), *Teacher Training Agencies* (1915), *Elementary Education* (1917), *Free Schools* (1921), and *The Township System* (1921).

He directed surveys of several major school systems and served on President Herbert Hoover's Advisory Committee on Education (1929–31). He strongly supported a federal department of education with cabinet rank. While opposing federal control of education, he saw the need for federal support and coordination of educational research. He was the recipient of many honorary degrees from American colleges and universities.

REFERENCES: *LE* (I); *NCAB* (23:268); *WWAE* (I); *WWW* (I); *National Education Association Journal* 22 (January 1933): 37; *School and Society* 37 (January 21, 1933): 89; *NYT,* November 26, 1932, p. 10. *Carey W. Brush*

FINLEY, John Huston. B. October 19, 1863, near Grand Ridge, Illinois, to James Gibson and Lydia Margaret (McCombs) Finley. M. June 29, 1892, to Margaret Ford Boyden. Ch. four. D. March 7, 1940, New York, New York.

John Huston Finley was graduated from Knox College in Galesburg, Illinois, with the A.B. (1887) and A.M. (1890) degrees. He moved east to Johns Hopkins University in Baltimore, Maryland, for graduate study to prepare for a career in journalism. He came under the tutelage of Richard T. Ely *(q.v.)*, whom he assisted in writing *Taxation in American States and Cities* (1889). After three years as secretary of the Charities Aid Association and editor of *Charities Review* in New York (1889–92), Finley returned to Knox College as president (1892–99).

He spent a year as editor of *Harper's Weekly* (1899) before he accepted a post at Princeton University as professor of politics (1900–03). In 1903 he took the advice of Nicholas M. Butler *(q.v.)* and accepted the presidency of the City College of New York (1903–13). Finley has been credited with making City College into an institution with a national and international reputation.

Finley took over the dual role of New York State commissioner of education and president of the University of the State of New York (1913–21). As commissioner he placed emphasis on improving rural schools, having better health and medical inspections in the schools, requiring more physical and industrial training, expanding continuation schools for working boys and girls who dropped out of regular school programs, and providing literacy education for adults. He stressed the upgrading of professional standards and better salaries for teachers.

Finley was made an associate editor (1921) and editor (1937) of the *New York Times,* retiring in 1938, although he continued to write editorials until his death in 1940.

Finley was the author of *The American Executive and Executive Methods* (with John F. Sanderson, 1908), *The French in the Heart of America* (1914), *Report of a Visit to Schools of France in War Time* (1917), *A Pilgrimage in Palestine* (1919), *The Debt Eternal* (1923), *The Mystery of the Mind's Desire* (1936), and *The Coming of the Scot* (1940), which was published posthumously. He was an editor of *Nelson's Encyclopedia.*

Finley was active in professional and civic organizations, serving as director of the Hall of Fame, New York University (1938–40) and trustee of the Sage Foundation, Knox College, Berea College, and the New York Public Library. He was chairman of the New York State Commission for the Blind (1913), president of the New York Association for the Blind, and a member of the New York State Constitutional Convention Commission (1914–15), the National Institute of Arts and Letters (vice-president), the American Academy of Arts and Letters, and the National Council of the Boy Scouts of America. He was an honorary vice-president of the Boy

Scouts of Scotland. He received a gold medal from the Geographic Society of Paris, France, for his book on the French in America. He was decorated by many foreign governments and was awarded thirty-two honorary degrees by American and foreign colleges and universities.

REFERENCES: *DAB* (supp. 2); *LE* (I); *NCAB* (30:90); *WWW* (I); Hubert Joseph Keenan, "A View from the Tower: An Investigation of the Writings of John Huston Finley on the School and Higher Education from 1921 to 1940" (Ph.D. diss., New York University, 1970); *NYT,* March 8, 1940, p. 1; S. Willis Rudy, *The College of the City of New York: A History, 1847–1947* (New York: City College Press, 1949).   *Hubert J. Keenan*

FINNEY, Charles Grandison. B. August 29, 1792, Warren, Connecticut, to Sylvester and Rebecca (Rice) Finney. M. October 1824 to Lydia Andrews. M. to Elizabeth Ford Atkinson. M. 1863 to Rebecca Allen Rayl. Ch. none. D. August 16, 1875, Oberlin, Ohio.

Charles Grandison Finney attended common schools and Hamilton Oneida Academy in Clinton, New York, for two years, where the master encouraged his musical ability and urged him to pursue a college education. He taught in a district school for several years and prepared for college in Warren, Connecticut. Rather than attend college he spent two years teaching and studying in New Jersey, entered a law office in Adams, New York (1818), and was admitted to the bar. After a religious conversion in 1821, he studied theology with two ministers of the St. Lawrence (New York) presbytery (1823). Although independent in his theological beliefs, Finney was licensed by the presbytery and ordained (1824).

Finney conducted revivals in the Northeast and became known around the country. His unorthodox beliefs and methods of preaching brought about a convention of Presbyterian and Congregational clergy in New Lebanon, New York (1827), to discuss the controversy he aroused. They decided in favor of Finney.

He was minister of the Second Free Presbyterian Church in New York City (1832) where his success in conversion resulted in the establishment of several churches. He organized the Broadway Tabernacle, which broke from the Presbyterian church in 1836 and united with the Congregational church. In New York he delivered a course of theological lectures. When a group of students left Lane Seminary in Cincinnati in 1835 over the issue of slavery, they invited Finney to establish a theological department in the newly founded Oberlin (Ohio) College. For two years he served both his New York pastorate and the school.

Finney was pastor of the First Congregational Church in Oberlin (1837–72). He served as professor of theology at Oberlin College and was president from 1851 to 1866. He spent part of each year in evangelistic work, including two visits to Great Britain (1849–50 and 1859–60). His theology continued to arouse opposition. His Oberlin theology was opposed by conservative Calvinists. He opposed popular amusements, alcohol, tobacco, coffee, and tea.

Many of Finney's lectures were published in the *New York Evangelist* and in book form as *Sermons on Important Subjects* (1835), *Lectures to Professing Christians* (1837), *Skeletons of a Course of Theological Lectures* (1840), *Lectures on Systematic Theology* (two volumes, 1846 and 1847), *England* (1851), and posthumously, *Sermons on Gospel Themes* (1876) and *Sermons on the Way of Salvation* (1891). He was an editor of the *Oberlin Quarterly Review* in the 1840s.

REFERENCES: *AC; DAB; EB; NCAB* (2:462); *TC; WWW* (H).

M. Jane Dowd

FISCHER, John Henry. B. July 16, 1910, Baltimore, Maryland, to Henry and Minnie (Muth) Fischer. M. November 28, 1934, to Norma Frederick. Ch. two.

John Henry Fischer was graduated from Maryland State Normal School (later, Towson State College) in 1930 and received the B.S. degree (1940) from Johns Hopkins University. He received the M.A. (1949) and Ed.D (1951) degrees from Teachers College, Columbia University.

Fischer served in the Baltimore public schools as an elementary school teacher (1930–33), as a junior high school teacher (1933–35), as assistant principal (1935–38), as junior high school principal (1938–42), and as director of special services (1942–45). He was assistant superintendent (1945–52), deputy superintendent (1952–53), and superintendent (1953–59) of the Baltimore public schools. He served as dean (1959–62) and president (1962–74) of Teachers College, Columbia University. From September 1974 to 1975, he served as professor of education and then retired as president emeritus.

Fischer served as a trustee of the New York Foundation, a director of Cowles Communications, and a trustee of the Educational Testing Service, the Johns Hopkins University Institute for Educational Development, and the Center for Urban Education.

He served on numerous government commissions related to educational purposes, nationally and internationally. He was chairman of the United States delegations to the International Conference on Public Education in Geneva, Switzerland (1963), and the United Nations Educational, Scientific, and Cultural Organization Conference on Youth in Grenoble, France (1965). He was a member and chairman of the Educational Policies Commission and a member of the National Commission on the Education of the Disadvantaged and the National Advisory Commission on Education of Disadvantaged Children (1965–69). He was chairman of the advisory committee on community tensions of the New York State Department of

Education. He was a member of the National Advisory Council for the Peace Corps, the President's Task Force on International Education, the President's Commission on School Finance, and the national executive board of the Boy Scouts of America. He served as president of the Maryland Teachers Association (1945) and New York City trustee for the Public Education Association.

Fischer was the recipient of several awards from the Boy Scouts of America and of honorary degrees from several American colleges and universities.

REFERENCES: *CB* (July 1960); *LE* (V); *WW* (XXXVII); *WWAE* (XVI); *Who's Who in the East* (Chicago: Marquis, 1969).

William Summerscales

FISHER, Ebenezer. B. February 6, 1815, near Charlotte, Maine, to Ebenezer and Sally (Johnson) Fisher. M. September 27, 1841, to Amy W. Leighton. Ch. three. D. February 21, 1879, Canton, New York.

Ebenezer Fisher was self-taught except for four months in Wesleyan Academy in Readville, Maine. At the age of sixteen he went to Massachusetts to spend three years in the furniture business. On returning to Maine, he taught school for four years (1835–39).

In 1839 he founded the Milltown (Maine) Universalist Society, served as pastor for six months, and joined the Maine Universalist Convention in 1840. He was elected to the Maine legislature in 1840 and was named to a committee that revised the state legal codes. He served as pastor of Universalist churches at Addison Point, New York (1841–47), Salem, Massachusetts (1847–53), and South Dedham, Massachusetts (1853–58).

St. Lawrence University in Canton was chartered by the state of New York in 1856 as the first Universalist theological school in the country. Fisher became first principal of the school on April 15, 1858, and continued to serve until his death (1879). In the early years, he was the only professor except for a part-time professor who lent occasional assistance in ancient languages. After the Civil War, Fisher built the endowment funds so that he could hire a full-time professor of biblical languages and literature.

Fisher temporarily served a pulpit in Potsdam, New York, for several years, introduced the graded school system in the Canton public schools, lectured on natural science, and spoke at temperance meetings and political conventions. His articles appeared in the *Universalist Quarterly* (1849–76) and his sermons in the *Trumpet* (1849–57). *The Christian Doctrine of Salvation,* discussions between Fisher and the Reverend J. H. Walden, was published in 1869. He received an honorary degree from Lombard University in 1872.

REFERENCES: *DAB; NCAB* (10:201); *TC; WWW* (H).   *M. Jane Dowd*

FISHER, Irving. B. February 27, 1867, Saugerties, New York, to George Whitefield and Ella (Wescott) Fisher. M. June 24, 1893, to Margaret Hazard. Ch. three. D. April 29, 1947, New Haven, Connecticut.

Irving Fisher received the A.B. degree in mathematics (1888) and the Ph.D. degree (1891) from Yale University. He studied in Berlin, Germany, and Paris, France (1893-94).

Fisher was appointed a tutor in mathematics at Yale in 1891 and became professor of political economy (1898), a position he held until his retirement in 1935. Ill from tuberculosis (1898-1901), he became interested in statistics on and the history of tuberculosis and how to reduce death through preventative medicine and hygiene. He invented two tents that made camping comfortable in all weather and won a prize from the *New York Medical Journal*. He wrote extensively on tuberculosis and conducted experiments at Yale on diet, which led to the invention of a food indicator for computing food constituents.

Fisher instituted a weekly commodity index number service and expanded this in 1926 to include four new stock indexes on the New York Stock Exchange with price, volume and value of sales, rate of return, and the purchasing power of the dollar. He organized the Index Number Institute to bring this information to a larger public. Fisher invented an overlapping card index for libraries. He organized a company to market his index (1913) and the Index Visible Company merged with Rand Kardex Bureau (1925), which merged with the Remington Rand Corporation in 1927 with Fisher as a director of the company.

Among Fisher's many publications were *Elements of Geometry* (with A. W. Phillips, 1896), *A Brief Introduction to Inferential Calculus* (1897), *Economics as a Science* (1906), *Are Savings Income?* (1908), *Humanizing Industry* (1909), *Why Is the Dollar Shrinking?* (1914), *Elementary Principles of Economics* (1910), *How to Live* (with E. L. Fisk, 1915), *Stabilizing the Dollar* (1920), *The Money Illusion* (1928), *The Theory of Interest* (1930), *The Stock Market Crash* (1930), *Stable Money: A History of the Movement* (1934), *Money* (1935), *Constructive Income Taxation* (1942), and *World Maps and Globes* (with O. M. Miller, 1944). He was an editor of the *Yale Review* (1896-1910).

Fisher was active in many projects and associations; he was vice-president for the United States of the Third International Commission on Eugenics, member of President Theodore Roosevelt's National Conservation Commission, and member of the Hygiene Reference Board of the Life Extension Institute (chairman from 1914). He was president of the American Association for Labor Legislation (1915-17), the National Institute of Social Sciences (1917), the American Economic Association (1918), the Eugenics Research Association (1920), the Econometric Society (1931-33), and the American Statistical Association (1932). He was a founder of the American Eugenics Society (president, 1915–17), the Vitality Records Office (1937), and the Stable Money Association. He was a fellow of the Royal Statistical Society (England) and the American Association for the Advancement of Science (chairman of a committee of one hundred to promote public health). He was a member of many foreign learned societies and was on the board of directors of several institutions and corporations. He was active in peace and temperance movements. He received honorary degrees from Rollins College in Winter Park, Florida, and the universities of Athens, Greece, and Lausanne, Switzerland.

REFERENCES: *DAB* (supp. 4); *LE* (II); *NCAB* (14:86, C:51); *WWAE* (IX); *WWW* (II); *NYT,* April 30, 1947, p. 25.   *Barbara Ruth Peltzman*

FISK, Wilbur. B. August 31, 1792, Brattleboro, Vermont, to Isaiah and Hannah (Bacon) Fisk. M. June 9, 1823, to Ruth Peck. Ch. one. D. February 22, 1839, Middletown, Connecticut.

Wilbur Fisk spent his childhood in Brattleboro, Vermont. His health was poor during his early years, and he had only two or three years of common schooling up to the age of sixteen. He attended Peacham (Vermont) Academy and entered the University of Vermont as a sophomore in July 1812. He transferred to Brown University in Providence, Rhode Island, in 1814, where he earned the A.B. (1815) and Ph.D. (1820) degrees.

After receiving the A.B. degree, he returned to Vermont and read law in the office of an attorney in the village of Lyndon. He served as a tutor in a family living near Baltimore, Maryland, and by March 1818 returned to Lyndon as a minister in the Methodist church. He was the first college-trained Methodist minister. He served churches in Craftsbury, Vermont, and Charlestown, Massachusetts (1819–25).

Fisk was principal of Wesleyan (later, Wilbraham) Academy in Wilbraham, Massachusetts (1825–30). In a report made to the Committee on Education of the Methodist Episcopal General Conference in 1828, Fisk advocated the establishment of academies for the instruction of youth.

He was influential in the founding of Wesleyan University in Middletown, Connecticut, and was its first president from 1831 to his death in 1839. Fisk was twice chosen a bishop in the Methodist church, in 1828 and in 1836, but refused the honor, preferring to remain in education.

His best-known published work was *Travels on the Continent of Europe* (1838). He also authored a number of religious works, including *Calvinistic Controversy* (1835). He was a member of the Connecticut Board of Education (1838).

REFERENCES: *DAB; EB; NCAB* (3:177); *TC; WWW* (H); Joseph Holdich, *The Life of Wilbur Fisk, D.D., First President of the Wesleyan University* (New York: Harper & Brothers, 1842); George Prentice, *Wilbur Fisk* (Boston: Houghton Mifflin, 1890).   *Richard G. Durnin*

FISKE, George Walter. B. June 3, 1872, Holliston, Massachusetts, to George Batchelder and Ada M. (Perry) Fiske. M. August 1, 1898, to Alice May Stewart. Ch. one. D. October 10, 1945, Framingham, Massachusetts.

George Walter Fiske was graduated with the B.A. (1895) and M.A. (1898) degrees from Amherst (Massachusetts) College, and he received the B.D. degree (1898) from the Hartford (Connecticut) Theological Seminary and the Ph.D. degree (1919) from Boston University.

He was ordained in the Congregational ministry in 1898 and served pastorates in Massachusetts at Huntington (1898–1900) and South Hadley Falls (1900–03), and at Auburn, Maine (1903–07). He joined the faculty of the Oberlin (Ohio) Graduate School of Theology as professor of practical theology and religious education.

While teaching at Oberlin, he also acted as junior dean (1908–21), acting dean (1928), and dean (1929). He was a frequent lecturer at conferences and summer sessions for educators, clergymen, and others. He retired in 1937 and was an exchange professor at the American University, Beirut, Lebanon, and the Near East School of Theology (1937–38).

Fiske wrote many books, including *Boy Life and Self Government* (1910), *The Challenge of the Country* (1912), *Finding the Comrade God* (1918), *Community Forces for Religious Education, Middle Adolescence* (1921), *Community Forces for Religious Education, Early Adolescence* (1922), *Jesus' Ideal of Living* (1922), *Purpose in Teaching Religion* (1927), *The Changing Family* (1928), *The Christian Family* (1929), *A Study of Jesus' Own Religion* (1932), *Studies in Spiritual Energy* (1933), and *Problems of Christian Family Life Today* (1934). He was a coauthor of *Education and Religion* (1929), *The Lesson Round Table* (1930), *Studies in Religious Education* (1931), *The Quest for God Through Worship* (1935), and *The Quest for God Through Understanding* (1937).

Fiske was active in the Federal Council of Churches of Christ in America and served as a member of several committees, including the committee on worship and the committee on marriage and the family. He was a member of various educational and fraternal societies. He received an honorary degree from Amherst College in 1925.

REFERENCES: *LE* (II); *NCAB* (35:241); *WWAE* (I); *WWW* (I); *NYT*, October 11, 1945, p. 23.   *Gloria Tribble*

FITTON, James. B. April 10, 1805, Boston, Massachusetts, to Abraham and Sarah (Williams) Fitton. M. no. D. September 15, 1881, East Boston, Massachusetts.

James Fitton received his early schooling in Boston (Massachusetts) public schools and Virgil Barber's Academy in Claremont, New Hampshire. He studied for the priesthood under Bishop Benjamin Fenwick of Boston and was ordained on December 23, 1827.

The first three years of his priesthood were spent primarily in mission assignments, including to the Passamaquoddy Indians in Maine (1828) and in Vermont (1829). In 1830 he went to Hartford, Connecticut, serving Catholics throughout New England. In 1836 he moved to Worcester, Massachusetts, to serve Irish immigrants attracted to the area by the jobs in canal and railroad building.

Seeing the need for preparing additional clergy to serve the growing Catholic population, he purchased sixty acres in the south part of Worcester and founded Mount St. James Seminary (1840). He transferred the land to Bishop Fenwick in 1842, and the educational program was entrusted to the Jesuits, who established the College of the Holy Cross in 1843. Fitton moved to Providence (1843) and Newport, Rhode Island, where he continued his parish work and church building (1846–55). In 1855 he finished his missionary work and returned to East Boston where he remained until his death. He was the first priest in New England to celebrate the fiftieth anniversary of his ordination (1877).

Fitton was the editor of the Hartford, Connecticut, *Catholic Press* and the author of *The Youth's Companion* (1833), *The Triumph of Religion* (1833), *Familiar Instructions* (n.d.), and *St. Joseph's Manual* (1877). His best-known work, *Sketches of the Establishment of the Church in New England,* appeared in 1872.

REFERENCES: *AC; DAB; WWW* (H); *New Catholic Encyclopedia* (New York: McGraw-Hill, 1967), L. P. McCarthy, *Sketch of the Life and Missionary Labors of Rev. James Fitton* (Boston: New England Catholic Historical Society, 1908).   *Anne E. Scheerer*

FITZ-GERALD, John Driscoll, II. B. May 2, 1873, Newark, New Jersey, to Aaron Ogden and Harriet Minerva (Haines) Fitz-Gerald. M. May 16, 1900, to Leora Almita Whitfield. Ch. three. D. June 8, 1946, Urbana, Illinois.

John Driscoll Fitz-Gerald was graduated with the A.B. degree (1895) from Columbia University, where he was a scholar and fellow in Romance languages (1895–96 and 1897–98). After further study of Romance philology at the universities of Leipzig, Berlin, Paris, and Madrid (1896–97 and 1900–02) Fitz-Gerald returned to Columbia, where he received the Ph.D. degree (1906).

At Columbia he taught Romance languages and literature (1902–07). In 1909, he was named assistant professor at the University of Illinois, where he also served as professor of Spanish (1915–25) and professor of Romance philology (1925–29). In 1929 he accepted a post at the University of Arizona as professor of Romance philology and head of the department of Spanish. He retired to half-time teaching in 1943 and relinquished his position as department chairman, but continued as professor of Romance philology until shortly before his death in 1946.

A prolific writer, Fitz-Gerald was consulting editor of *Hispania* and an associate editor of the *Romanic Review*. He also served as editor of the department of Hispanic subjects for the *New International Encyclopedia*. His books include *Versification of the Cuaderna Via as found in Berceo's "Vida de Santo Domingo de Silos"* (1905), *Rambles in Spain* (1910), *Apuntes Sobre Literatura Americana* (1924), and *Relaciones Hispano-Americanas* (1925). In addition, he authored many articles about Spanish-American literature, law, history, and language.

Fitz-Gerald was recognized for his influence in the development of cultural relations with Spain and the countries of Central and South America. He was a delegate to South America for the American Association for International Conciliation (1914) and assistant secretary of the second Pan-American Scientific Congress (1915–16). He served as president of the American Association of Teachers of Spanish (1921–23) and the National Federation of Modern Language Teachers (1924–26) and held membership in many other language associations.

He was the recipient of an honorary degree (1920) from Syracuse University and the University Medal for Excellence from Columbia University (1931) and was made Knight Commander, con placa, of the Royal Order of Isabella Católica by King Alfonso XIII of Spain.

REFERENCES: *LE* (II); *NCAB* (37:107); *WWW* (II); William Milwitzky, "In Memoriam: John Driscoll Fitz-Gerald," *Modern Language Journal* 30 (October 1946): 365–66; *NYT,* June 9, 1946, p. 40.   *Jerry L. Johns*

FITZPATRICK, Edward Augustus. B. August 29, 1884, New York, New York, to Thomas and Ellen (Radley) Fitzpatrick. M. July 15, 1913, to Lillian V. Taylor. Ch. five. D. September 13, 1960, Washington, D.C.

Perhaps the outstanding Catholic lay spokesman in education in the mid-twentieth century, Edward Fitzpatrick grew up in New York City, where he taught in the public schools (1903–08). He was graduated from the New York Training School for Teachers and received the B.A. (1906), M.A. (1907), and Ph.D. (1911) degrees from Columbia University.

He moved to Wisconsin where he was credited with drafting important educational legislation, including the first minimum wage for teachers in Wisconsin (1913). After serving as a major in the United States Army during World War I, Fitzpatrick was secretary of the Wisconsin State Board of Education (1919–23) and taught at the University of Wisconsin. From 1924 to 1939 he was dean of the graduate school of Marquette University in Milwaukee and was educational director of the College of Hospital Administration, the first of its kind in the country. In 1928 he was named president of Mount Mary College in Milwaukee and held the post until 1954.

Active as an editor and author, Fitzpatrick served as a bridge between public and Catholic education. His books include *Educational Views and Influence of De Witt Clinton* (1911), *Budget-Making in a Democracy* (1918), *Public Administration and the Public Welfare in the Freedman's America and the New Era* (1920), *The Scholarship of Teachers in Secondary Schools* (1927), *Wisconsin* (1927), *Industrial Citizenship* (1927), *Foundations of Christian Education* (1929), *A Curriculum in Religion* (1931), *Life of the Soul* (1931), *Highway to God* (1933), *St. Ignatius and Ratio Studiorum* (1933), *Readings in the Philosophy of Education* (1936), *I Believe in Education* (1938), *How to Educate Human Beings* (1950), *La Salle, Patron of All Teachers* (1951), and *Philosophy of Education* (1953). He edited *The College and the City* (1914), *Universities and Public Service* (1914), *Experts in City Government* (1919), and *The Autobiography of a College* (1939). He edited the Highway to Heaven Series and was editor of *Hospital Progress* (1924–27), *Catholic School Journal* (from 1929), *The Public Servant* (1916–17), *Wisconsin's Educational Horizon* (1919–23), and Marquette Monographs on Education.

Fitzpatrick was active in educational associations, including the Association of Presidents and Deans of Wisconsin Colleges (president, 1937). He was a fellow of the American Association for the Advancement of Science and a member of many other groups. He participated in hospital matters as chairman of several committees for the American Hospital Association and a member of the National Committee on Grading Schools of Nursing and the library committee of the Library and Service Bureau of the American Hospital Conference (1924–28). He received many awards for distinguished service and was awarded honorary degrees by nine Catholic colleges and universities.

REFERENCES: *LE* (III); *NCAB* (46:30); *NYT,* September 14, 1960, p. 43; *WWAE* (XVI); *WWW* (IV); *New Catholic Encyclopedia* (New York: McGraw-Hill, 1967).   *James M. Vosper*

FLEMING, Walter Lynwood. B. April 8, 1874, Pike County, Alabama, to William LeRoy and Mary Love (Edwards) Fleming. M. September 17, 1902, to Mary Wright Boyd. Ch. four. D. August 3, 1932, Nashville, Tennessee.

Walter Lynwood Fleming received the B.A. degree (1896) from Alabama Polytechnic Institute (later, Auburn University) and the M.A. (1901) and Ph.D. (1904) degrees from Columbia University.

Fleming was professor of history at West Virginia University (1903–07), Louisiana State University (1907–17), and Vanderbilt University in Nashville, Tennessee (1917–29). He was dean at Vanderbilt from 1923 to 1929, where he developed and expanded the graduate facilities and coordinated the social science departments. The Rockefeller Foundation granted

Vanderbilt funds for research development in the social sciences because of Fleming's authoritative work on the history of the Reconstruction era.

Fleming authored *Reconstruction of the Seceded States* (1905), *Civil War and Reconstruction in Alabama* (1905), *Life of Jefferson Davis* (1907–09), *William Tecumseh Sherman as College President* (1912), *The Sequel of Appomattox* (1919), and *The Freedman's Savings Bank* (1927). He edited *Lester and Wilson's History of the Ku Klux Klan* (1905) and *Documentary History of the Reconstruction* (two volumes, 1906–07). He was an associate editor of the *Historian's History of the World* and a member of the board of editors of the *Mississippi Valley Historical Review*. He was a member of many historical and professional associations and was a veteran of theSpanish-American War.

REFERENCES: *DAB* (supp. 1); *LE* (I); *NCAB* (46:567); *WWW* (I).

Kenneth Sipser

FLEXNER, Abraham. B. November 13, 1866, Louisville, Kentucky, to Morris and Esther (Abraham) Flexner. M. June 23, 1898, to Anne Laziere Crawford. Ch. two. D. September 21, 1959, Falls Church, Virginia.

Abraham Flexner attended Louisville (Kentucky) High School (1880–84). After two years of concentrated study of the classics at the recently established Johns Hopkins University in Baltimore, Maryland, he received the B.A. degree (1886).

He returned to Louisville High School as a teacher of Latin and Greek (1886–90). He engaged in self-study, reading the educational works of Rousseau, Pestalozzi, Herbart, and other European pedagogical writers and biographies of many distinguished European scholars in various fields. In 1890, on the basis of his practical experience and study, he opened a secondary school to prepare pupils for college. In "Mr. Flexner's School" he relied on enthusiasm, good humor, and initiative as motivation toward the achievement of a high level of scholarship; he was not concerned with rules, records, reports, and examinations.

After fifteen years of successfully operating this school, he studied at the graduate school of Harvard University, receiving the A.M. degree (1906). He also studied the anatomy of the brain in relation to psychology at the Rockefeller Institute for Medical Research in New York City. He studied psychology and philosophy at the University of Berlin (1906–07) where he was influenced by Friedrich Paulsen. Flexner was associated with the Carnegie Foundation for the Advancement of Teaching in New York City (1908–28). He was director of the Institute for Advanced Study at Princeton, New Jersey (1930–39), which he had founded and organized.

Flexner distinguished himself as a critic, innovator, and writer in education. Through *The American College* (1908), he came to the attention of President Henry S. Pritchett *(q.v.)* of the Carnegie Foundation for the

Advancement of Teaching, who commissioned Flexner to make a study of American medical schools. The subsequent report, *Medical Education in the United States and Canada* (1910), was a devastating analysis of 154 medical schools, which brought about a fundamental transformation of medical education. Flexner also wrote *Medical Education in Europe* (1912) and *Prostitution in Europe* (1914), the latter under the auspices of the Rockefeller Foundation.

As secretary of the General Education Board (1912–28), Flexner prepared studies, including *Public Education in Maryland* (1916), *A Modern School* (1916), *The Gary Schools* (1918), and *A Modern College* (1923). He also wrote *Do Americans Really Value Education?* (1927), *Universities: American, English, German* (1930), *I Remember* (1940), which was his autobiography, *Henry S. Pritchett: A Biography* (1943), *Daniel Coit Gilman, Creator of the American Type of University* (1946), *Funds and Foundations* (1952), and *Abraham Flexner: An Autobiography* (1960), a revision of *I Remember*.

Flexner was the recipient of several honorary degrees and of the French Legion of Honor.

REFERENCES: *CB* (June 1941); *EB; LE* (III); *NCAB* (D:61, 52:320); *WWW* (III); *NYT,* September 22, 1959, p. 1; Abraham Flexner, *Abraham Flexner: An Autobiography* (New York: Simon and Schuster, 1960).

William W. Brickman

FLINT, Austin. B. October 20, 1812, Petersham, Massachusetts, to Joseph Henshaw Flint and n.a. M. 1835 to Anne Skillings. Ch. one. D. March 13, 1886, New York, New York.

After three years of undergraduate study at Amherst (Massachusetts) College and in Cambridge, Massachusetts, Austin Flint began his study of medicine at Harvard University. In addition to the traditional course of medical study he was exposed through his teachers to the principles of statistics and case recording emphasized by French physicians. He was graduated with the M.D. degree (1833).

The fourth generation of his family to practice medicine, Flint practiced briefly in Massachusetts at Northampton and Boston and moved to Buffalo, New York, in 1836. He moved to Chicago, Illinois, where he was professor of medical theory and practice at Rush Medical College (1844–45). He returned to Buffalo and founded the *Buffalo Medical Journal,* for which he was editor and a major contributor (1846–56). With F. H. Hamilton and J. P. White, he founded the Buffalo Medical College in 1847 and was professor of principles and practice of medicine and of clinical medicine (1847–52). He had become well known through his publications, and his teaching skills had become respected throughout the United States.

In 1852 Flint accepted a position teaching theory and practice of medicine at the University of Louisville, Kentucky, but returned to Buffalo in 1856 and resumed his relations with both the medical college and the *Journal*. From 1858 to 1861 he spent the winters in New Orleans, where he was professor of clinical medicine at New Orleans Medical College and visiting physician to the local charity hospital. In 1859 he moved his permanent residence to New York City, established a medical practice, and was appointed chairman of pathology and practical medicine at Long Island College Hospital. He was a founder of Bellevue Medical College and served as its first chairman of internal medicine.

Flint wrote *A Treatise on the Principles and Practice of Medicine,* first published in 1866. It was a popular American medical textbook and a standard reference volume. Among his many other works were *Clinical Reports on Continued Fever* (1852), *Clinical Report on Chronic Pleurisy* (1852), *Physical Exploration and Diagnosis of Diseases Affecting Respiratory Organs* (1856), *Essays on Conservative Medicine and Kindred Topics* (1874), and *Medical Ethics and Etiquette* (1882). Other of his publications include articles and monographs on fever, dysentery, chest diseases, and physical diagnosis.

Flint was considered an authority on chest pathology, a pioneer in the field of heart research, and a leader in the field of physical diagnosis. He was active in professional associations as a member of many American and foreign medical societies. He was president of the New York Academy of Medicine (1872) and the American Medical Association (1883–84). He was a delegate to the International Medical Congress at London, England (1881), and was elected to preside over the International Medical Congress in Washington, D.C., held in 1887 after his death. He received an honorary degree from Yale University in 1881.

REFERENCES: *AC; DAB; EB; NCAB* (8:311); *NYT,* March 14, 1886, p. 2; *TC; WWW* (H).   *C. Michael Powell*

FOLLEN, Karl (Charles) Theodore Christian. B. September 4, 1796, Ranrod, Hesse-Darmstadt, Germany, to Christoph Follenius and his wife (n.a.). M. September 15, 1828, to Eliza Lee Cabot. Ch. one. D. January 13, 1840, at sea.

Charles Follen, German-American author and educator, received his education at a classical secondary school and the University of Giessen, Germany. He joined the army when the German war of liberation broke out in 1813. He resumed his study of jurisprudence at Giessen in 1814 and received his doctor's diploma in civil and ecclesiastical law (1817).

Follen returned from the war with ideas of social and moral reform and began to lecture at the University of Jena in 1818. Because of his activity in movements for German national unity and civic freedom, he was forced to leave Jena. He returned to Giessen but had to go into exile (1820), first in

France and then in Switzerland, where he taught at the University of Basel (1821–24).

To avoid being extradited to Prussia on charges of radicalism, Follen emigrated to the United States in 1824 where he was the first instructor in German at Harvard University (1825–30). Follen introduced F. L. Jahn's system of gymnastics and was instrumental in opening the first college gymnasium in the United States at Harvard and the first public gymnasium in Boston (1826).

By 1830 interest in Jahn's system of gymnastics had waned, but Follen was a naturalized citizen and received a five-year appointment as professor of German literature at Harvard (1830–35). He became a leader in the Anti-Slavery Society, and, as a consequence, his professorship was not renewed.

Follen was ordained as a minister in the Unitarian church in 1836 and took a church in East Lexington, Massachusetts. He was a private teacher and lecturer until his death in 1840.

Follen's wife published his songs, lectures, and sermons in five volumes, *The Works of Charles Follen, with a Memoir of His Life* (1841–42).

REFERENCES: *AC; DAB; EB; NCAB* (7:289); *TC; WWW* (H).

Adelaide M. Cole

FOLWELL, William Watts. B. February 14, 1833, Romulus, New York, to Thomas J. and Joan F. (Bainbridge) Folwell. M. March 13, 1863, to Sarah Hubbard Heywood. Ch. one. D. September 18, 1929, Minneapolis, Minnesota.

William Watts Folwell was graduated from Hobart College in Geneva, New York, with the B.A. (1857) and M.A. (1860) degrees.

After one year of teaching languages at Ovid (New York) Academy (1857–58), he returned to Hobart College as a professor of mathematics (1858–60). He studied in Berlin, Germany (1860–61), and served in the Union army with the Fiftieth New York Engineers (1862–65), advancing in military rank from first lieutenant to brevet colonel. Following the war, he was in private business in Ohio (1865–69) and returned to education as a mathematics professor at Kenyon College in Gambier, Ohio (1869).

Folwell accepted an appointment as the first president of the University of Minnesota in 1869. He served as president until 1884 and as professor of political science (1875–1907). He was the university librarian for many years.

Folwell was the author of *Minnesota, the North Star State* (1908), *University Addresses* (1909), *Economic Addresses* (1918), and *History of Minnesota* (four volumes, 1921–30).

Folwell was a member of state and local community organizations and professional associations, including the Minneapolis Board of Park Commissioners (1889–1907, president, 1894–1900), and the State Board of Charities and Corrections (chairman, 1895–1901), the Minnesota Centennial Commission (1876), the Minnesota Society of Fine Arts (1882–92), the Minnesota Improvement League (president, 1902–05), the Minnesota Historical Society (president, 1924–27), and the American Economic Association (acting president, 1892). He received honorary degrees from Hobart College and the University of Minnesota.

REFERENCES: *AC; DAB; NCAB* (13:328); *TC; WWW* (I); Solon J. Buck, ed., *William Watts Folwell: The Autobiography and Letters of a Pioneer of Culture* (Minneapolis: University of Minnesota Press, 1933).

Robert V. Krejci

FORBES, John Franklin. B. June 13, 1853, Middlesex, New York, to Merrill and Maria Jane (Palmer) Forbes. M. June 25, 1879, to Ida Idella Higbie. Ch. three. D. March 30, 1926, Rochester, New York.

John Franklin Forbes attended the Middlebury Academy in Wyoming, New York, and the University of Rochester, New York, for a year (1871–72). With his twin brother, he spent a year of travel in Europe, studying in Berlin and Leipzig, Germany, and Paris, France. They returned to the United States, where they both graduated from the University of Rochester with A.B. degrees (1878); John Forbes was later awarded the A.M. degree.

Forbes was professor of Latin and Greek at the State Normal School (later, State University of New York College) at Brockport, New York (1878–85). He founded the DeLand (Florida) Academy in 1885. The academy attracted the attention of John B. Stetson, wealthy hat manufacturer of Philadelphia, Pennsylvania, who donated $1 million to develop the academy into a university in 1886 and endowed the Forbes Chair with fifty thousand dollars. In 1895 an agreement was reached with William R. Harper *(q.v.)* of the University of Chicago, which permitted students with health problems or whose parents spent the winter in the South to attend John B. Stetson University, with credit accepted by Chicago.

In 1903 Forbes resigned from Stetson and returned to the University of Rochester. He entered into a partnership in conducting the Rochester Business Institute, serving as president from 1910 to his death in 1926. He was the first to lecture on psychology and ethics in a private commercial school.

Forbes was associated with his son in the American Drafting Furniture Company. He was active in local affairs as treasurer and director of the Social Welfare League and director of the Public Health Nursing Association. He was awarded an honorary degree by the University of Rochester.

REFERENCES: *NCAB* (22:360); *TC; WWW* (IV); *NYT,* March 31, 1926, p. 23.

John F. Ohles

FORD, Jeremiah Denis Matthias. B. July 2, 1873, Cambridge, Massachusetts, to Jeremiah Denis and Mary Agnes (Collins) Ford. M. January 1, 1902, to Anna Winifred Fearns. Ch. four. D. November 13, 1958, Cambridge, Massachusetts.

Jeremiah D. M. Ford received his preliminary education at public schools in Cambridge, Massachusetts, and preparatory schools in Ireland and England. He received the A.B. (1894), A.M. (1895), and Ph.D. (1897) degrees from Harvard University. During 1897–98, he was Harris Fellow at Harvard in residence in Paris. He continued his studies at the University of Paris, the Sorbonne, École des chartes, and Collège de France.

In 1895 he began his teaching career at Harvard as an instructor in French and Italian. He was Smith Professor of French and Spanish Languages at Harvard and Radcliffe College (1907) and chairman of the department of Romance languages and literature from 1911 until his retirement in 1943.

Among Ford's books were *The Old Spanish Sibilants* (1900), *Exercises in Spanish Composition* (1901), *Spanish Grammar* (with E. C. Hills, *q.v.,* 1904), *First Spanish Course* (1917), *Main Current of Spanish Literature* (1919), *Portuguese Grammar* (1925), *Spanish Grammar for Colleges* (1928), and *Old French Grammar* (1937). He edited Goldoni's *Curioso Accidente* (1899), Martin's *Si de las Niñas* (1899), Alarcon's *Capitan Veneno* (1900), *A Spanish Anthology* (1904), *Old Spanish Readings* (1906), *Selections from Don Quixote* (1908), and many others. Ford served as Italian and Spanish editor of the *New International Encyclopedia* (1901–04), general editor of Henry Holt and Company's Spanish series (1907), and editor-in-chief of *Speculum* (1927–37). He wrote many articles for philological publications.

He served as chief examiner for Spanish under the College Entrance Examination Board (1908–24). He was exchange professor of Harvard to the University of Paris and to Spanish universities (1921–22) and visiting professor to French and Spanish universities while acting director of the American University Union for the Continent of Europe (1925–26).

Ford received honorary degrees from American and European universities and many awards, including the Laetare Medal from the University of Notre Dame (1937), officer of the French Legion of Honor (1927), and knight of the Roumanian Royal Order of Cultural Merit (1930). He was active in learned societies as a fellow of the American Academy of Arts and Sciences (president, 1931–33), the Medieval Academy of America (president, 1939–40), corresponding member of the Spanish Academy of Belles-Lettres and Académie des inscriptions et belles-lettres (Paris), member of the Dante Society (president, 1932–40), and the American Catholic Historical Association (president, 1935).

REFERENCES: *LE* (II); *NCAB* (44:80); *WWW* (III); Alfred Coestler, "A

Tribute," *Hispania* (October 1942): 261–62; H. G. Doyle, "J. D. M. Ford Receives Laetare Medal," *Modern Languages Journal* 21 (May 1937): 619–22; *NYT,* November 14, 1958, p. 27.   *Edward B. Goellner*

FOSHAY, Arthur Wellesley. B. July 23, 1912, Oakland, California, to Arthur Wellesley and Amelia Gertrude (Brazill) Foshay. M. August 26, 1938, to Irene Finette Partridge. Ch. two.

Arthur W. Foshay was graduated with the A.B. degree (1934) from the University of California at Berkeley. He received the Ed.D. degree (1949) from Teachers College, Columbia University.

He began his teaching career in the Oakland (California) public schools where he taught English, social studies, science, and French (1936–40). He became a guidance counselor and elementary school principal in the Oakland schools (1940–46).

While at Columbia University, he served as assistant principal to the Horace Mann-Lincoln Schools (1946–48) and was assistant and associate professor of education and research associate for the Horace Mann-Lincoln Institute (1948–52). He accepted a position as director of the Bureau of Educational Research at the Ohio State University (1952–57). In 1957 he was asked to return to the Horace Mann-Lincoln Institute as the director. He served as associate dean of research and field studies at Teachers College from 1964 until his appointment as professor of education, curriculum, and teaching in 1968.

Foshay's interests in elementary education and curriculum are shown in his writings, including *Education in the Elementary School* (with Hollis Caswell, *q.v.,* 1950), *Children's Social Values, An Action Research Study* (with K. D. Wann and associates, 1954), *Handbook of Education* (1963), *The Professional as Educator* (1970), *Curriculum for the 70's, An Agenda for Invention* (1970), and editor of *Research for Curriculum Improvement* (1954).

Foshay was elected president of the Association for Supervision and Curriculum Development (1960–61) and was a consultant with the United States Office of Education (1950), the Ford Foundation (1960–61), United Nations Educational, Scientific, and Cultural Organization Institute of Education Study (1962), and a member of the International Association of Evaluation of Educational Attainment (1970–72). He was a member of many other professional associations.

REFERENCES: *LE* (IV); *WW* (XXXVIII).   *Marcella L. Kysilka*

FOSTER, Thomas Jefferson. B. January 1, 1843, Pottsville, Pennsylvania, to Thomas and Amanda (Ruch) Foster. M. 1869 to Fanny C. Millet. M. to Blandina Harrington. Ch. six. D. October 14, 1936, Scranton, Pennsylvania.

Thomas J. Foster, founder of the International Correspondence Schools, received his early schooling in Pottsville, Pennsylvania. He attended the Eastman Business College in Poughkeepsie, New York (1864–65). At the age of eighteen he enlisted in the Civil War. After the war he sold advertising novelties.

In 1870 he moved to Shenandoah, Pennsylvania, a mining community. There he founded with Henry C. Boyer the *Weekly Herald* (1870) and later the *Evening Herald* (1875). He became interested in mining and, particularly, mine safety, devoting columns in his newspaper, the *Mining Herald,* to questions and answers about mine safety. He printed pamphlets on accident prevention and played an active role in a campaign for laws regulating safety provisions in coal mines. He was influential in the passage of mine safety laws by the Pennsylvania state legislature in 1885.

He moved his paper to Scranton, Pennsylvania, in 1888 and changed its name to the *Colliery Engineer.* There was widespread interest in his "Question and Answer Column," and Foster prepared pamphlets dealing with questions asked by the state examining board in qualifying mine foremen and inspectors and about more advanced mining problems. The pamphlets met with much success, and Foster decided to prepare a course concerned with important technical information concerning mining. This original course (1891) proved popular, and other courses were requested. Foster incorporated his courses of study in 1891 as the Colliery Engineering School of Mines; it later became the International Correspondence Schools, which grew to offer over 214 courses.

Foster had built a holding company that controlled his correspondence schools and other interests. The financial structure collapsed, and local banks refinanced the operation on the condition that Foster not be involved in the firm's financial operations. He chose to resign in 1916 and wrote salesmanship and personality development courses for industrial firms (1916–26) and organized correspondence schools in various cities.

REFERENCES: *DAB* (supp. 2); *WWW* (IV); Richard B. Kennan, *The Private Correspondence School Enrollee* (New York: Bureau of Publications, Teachers College, Columbia University, 1940); Ossian MacKenzie et al., *Correspondence Instruction in the United States* (New York: McGraw-Hill, 1969); *NYT,* October 15, 1936, p. 27.*Ralph E. Ackerman*

FOSTER, William Trufant. B. January 18, 1879, Boston, Massachusetts, to William Henry and Sarah Jane (Trufant) Foster. M. December 25, 1905, to Bessie Lucile Russell. Ch. four. D. October 8, 1950, Jaffrey, New Hampshire.

William Trufant Foster worked his way through Boston's Roxbury High School and Harvard University, from which he was graduated with the A.B. (1901) and A.M. (1904) degrees. He received the Ph.D. degree (1911) from Teachers College, Columbia University.

Foster taught English at Bates College in Lewiston, Maine (1901–03), and was professor of English and argumentation at Bowdoin College in Brunswick, Maine (1905–10).

In 1910 Foster was elected the first president of Reed College in Portland, Oregon, and he served in the post until 1919. Given a free hand to build an ideal college, he rejected competitive intercollegiate sports and fraternities in favor of a demanding and purely academic education. He introduced a graduate approach to undergraduate studies with comprehensive examinations, senior seminars, theses, and final oral examinations. Reed developed into one of the great small liberal arts colleges in the United States.

After resigning from Reed College, Foster became director (1920–50) of the Pollak Foundation of Economic Research in Newton, Massachusetts, an institution founded by Waddell Catchings to study economic problems. Foster and Catchings collaborated in writing *Money* (1923), *Profits* (1925), *Business without a Buyer* (1927), *The Road to Plenty* (1928), and *Progress and Plenty* (1930). Foster was also the author of *Argumentation and Debating* (1908), *Administration of the College Curriculum* (1910), *Essentials of Exposition and Argument* (1911), *Social Hygiene and Morals* (1913), *Should Students Study?* (1917), *Basic Principles of Speech* (1936), and *Speech* (1942). He was editor of *The Problem of Business Forecasting* (with Warren M. Persons, 1924) and *Modern Speeches on Basic Issues* (1939).

Foster served on a number of committees, including the consumers' advisory board of the National Recovery Administration (1933–35), the Public Affairs Committee of New York, and the State Planning Board of Massachusetts, and he was economic adviser to the International Labor Conference in Geneva, Switzerland (1938). He was a fellow of the American Association for the Advancement of Science, a member of the American Academy of Arts and Sciences and an elector of the New York University Hall of Fame. He was a trustee of Rollins College and was the recipient of five honorary degrees.

REFERENCES: *LE* (III); *DAB* (supp. 4); *NCAB* (15:300); *WWAE* (I); *WWW* (III); *NYT,* October 9, 1950, p. 25.   *Robert H. Truman*

FOUST, Julius Isaac. B. November 23, 1865, Graham, North Carolina, to Thomas Corbey and Mary E. (Robbins) Foust. M. November 22, 1893, to Sarah Price. M. August 25, 1932, to Clara McNeill. Ch. two. D. February 15, 1946, Lakeland, Florida.

Julius Isaac Foust attended local schools in North Carolina and was graduated from the University of North Carolina with the Ph.B. degree (1890).

He was superintendent of the Goldsboro, North Carolina (1890–91 and 1894–1902), and Wilson, North Carolina (1891–94), schools. He was professor of pedagogy (1902–07) and president (1907–34) of the State Normal and Industrial College in Greensboro, North Carolina (later, Woman's College of the University of North Carolina). During the twenty-seven years that he headed the institution, the enrollment and faculty nearly quadrupled. Land was purchased for future expansion and thirty buildings were constructed.

He was the author of *Geography of North Carolina* (1903) and *A Spelling Book* (with others, 1906). Foust was president of a number of professional organizations, including the North Carolina Association of City School Superintendents (1902), the North Carolina Teachers Assembly (1904), and the North Carolina Association of Colleges. He served on the committee of supervisors of state normal schools for Negroes and was a trustee and chairman of the board of the Agricultural and Technical College for Negroes of Greensboro (later, Agricultural and Technical College of North Carolina). He conducted teachers' institutes throughout the state and was a member of the first textbook commission of North Carolina. He received an honorary degree from the University of North Carolina.

REFERENCES: *LE* (II); *NCAB* (35:249); *WWAE* (VIII); *WWW* (II); *NYT,* February 16, 1946, p. 13.   *Robert Emans*

FOWLE, William Bentley. B. October 17, 1795, Boston, Massachusetts, to Henry and Elizabeth (Bentley) Fowle. M. September 28, 1818, to Antoinette Moulton. M. November 26, 1860, to Mary Baxter Adams. Ch. one. D. February 6, 1865, Medfield, Massachusetts.

William Bentley Fowle was an educator, author, and member of the state legislature. Fowle aroused the animosity of conservative teachers when he introduced the Lancastrian, or monitorial system, into a school for about two hundred children, whom the primary school committee of Boston considered too old for primary schools and too ignorant for grammar schools. Fowle had become interested in educational reforms through conversations with teachers he had met while serving an apprenticeship in Caleb Bingham's *(q.v.)* bookstore. In 1821 he was appointed to the primary school committee where he had an opportunity to put into practice some of his ideas.

Fowle introduced innovative teaching methods in the new school he established: the blackboard, the drawing of maps, written spelling lessons, and no corporal punishment. The most novel change was the monitorial system in which advanced pupils helped to teach the others. The school was successful; it won commendation from the mayor of Boston and drew attention to Fowle's ideas and methods.

When Caleb Bingham died in 1817, heirs entrusted the bookstore to Fowle. His successful educational venture led a number of wealthy individuals to build and equip a French monitorial school in Boston. The school was the forerunner of public lyceums of the state and the normal school system. Fowle gave up his book business in 1823 to take charge of the school, which was one of the first in the nation to have adequate scientific apparatus to illustrate the subjects taught. Fowle supervised the construction of most of the equipment. The school offered instruction in vocal and instrumental music, calisthenics, and needlework, the first time most of these areas were included in a school curriculum.

Fowle was the author of more than fifty textbooks and numerous published lectures. Among his books were *Catechism of English Grammar* (1823), *The Child's Arithmetick* (1823), *Manual of Mutual Instruction* (1826), which promoted the monitorial system of instruction, *The French First Class Book* (1832), *English Grammar* (1833), *The Common School Grammar* (1842), *The Common School Speller* (1842), *The Common School Geography* (1843), *The Common School Speaker* (1844), *The Eye and Hand: A Series of Practical Lessons in Drawing* (1847), *The Teachers Institute* (1847), a teaching methods book, *The Bible, the Rod, and Religion in Common Schools* (1847), and *An Elementary Geography* (1849). He was editor of *Boyer's French Dictionary* (1830). Fowle was also the publisher of many of his books.

In 1824 Fowle became publisher of the *Common School Journal*, which had been introduced by Horace Mann *(q.v.)* four years earlier; he was also the editor from 1848 to 1852. His last public activity was establishment of a monitorial school in Boston, which he headed until 1860.

REFERENCES: *AC; DAB; NCAB* (10:220); *WWW* (H); Elliot Eisner and David W. Ecker, *Readings in Art Education* (Waltham, Mass.: Blaisdell Publishing Co., 1966).   *Roger H. Jones*

FRANK, Michael. B. December 12, 1804, Virgil, New York, to John Michael and Catherine (Oak) Frank. M. to Caroline J. Carpenter. Ch. at least one. D. December 26, 1894, Kenosha, Wisconsin.

Michael Frank was the son of a German immigrant and veteran of the Revolutionary War. He was the Father of Wisconsin Public Schools.

During his lifetime, Frank was a reformer, politician and newspaperman. As a boy, he developed a keen interest in social reform. He moved to Preble, New York, in 1836 and was a pioneer settler in Southport (Kenosha), Wisconsin, in 1839. In partnership with C. L. Sholes, he published the *Southport Telegraph* (1839), the first newspaper in Kenosha County. He served as editor or publisher intermittently until 1892. Under Sholes and Frank the paper was an advocate of temperance, anti-slavery, and free-soil sentiments.

Frank was the first village president of Southport (1840). He assisted in the founding of the first literary magazine in Wisconsin, *Garland of the West* (1843). He experimented for a time with Fourierist socialism and in

1844 was president of the local abolitionist society.

Frank served in the Wisconsin territorial upper house (1843–46), where he succeeded in passing a bill (1845) to establish a free school in Southport. He persuaded his fellow townsmen to ratify the measure, but it was not until 1849 that funds were secured to build and operate a completely tax-supported school. Meanwhile, other Wisconsin leaders joined Frank in spreading the free school idea, and the provision was incorporated in the state constitution of 1848. He was selected to revise and codify the state school laws in 1848.

Frank remained active in politics, served as mayor of Kenosha (1850), and joined the Republican party. He was state assemblyman (1861), a University of Wisconsin regent (1861–66), and postmaster of Kenosha (1861–66). He was coeditor of the *Beloit Journal* (1869–70) and from 1870 to 1882 lived in Washington, D.C., where he held a position in the United States Treasury Department. On leaving Washington, he returned to Kenosha and to the newspaper business. In 1889 (at the age of eighty-five), he retired from public life and died at the age of ninety.

REFERENCES: Clay J. Daggett, *Education in Wisconsin* (Whitewater, Wis.: The Whitewater Press, 1936); *Dictionary of Wisconsin Biography* (Madison: State Historical Society, 1960), p. 134; Fred L. Holmes, *Badger Saints and Sinners* (Milwaukee: E. M. Hale and Co., 1939); pp. 79-92; *Kenosha Union,* January 3, 1895; Conrad E. Patzer, *Public Education in Wisconsin* (Madison: State Department of Education, 1924).

Lawrence S. Master

FRANKLIN, Benjamin. B. January 17, 1706, Boston, Massachusetts, to Josiah and Abiah (Folger) Franklin. M. September 1, 1730, to Deborah Read. Ch. three. D. April 17, 1790, Philadelphia, Pennsylvania.

A tallowmaker's son, Benjamin Franklin completed his formal education by the age of ten. He was apprenticed to his brother, a printer. At the age of seventeen, Franklin ran away to Philadelphia, where he settled in 1726. After a voyage to England (1724–26) Franklin started his own print shop in Philadelphia, where he published the *Pennsylvania Gazette* (1730–50). He started the Junto (1727), a society where members met to debate the issues of the day. Franklin organized the Library Company of Philadelphia (1731), established the first lending library in that city, and founded the Philosophical Society in 1743. The society was founded for the discussion and research of natural history and all aspects of science.

In 1751 Franklin founded the Academy of Philadelphia. The academy taught penmanship, grammar, astronomy, natural history, geography, morality, logic, and oratory. Franklin's academy represented a profound break with educational tradition and evolved into the academy movement and the public high school movement that provided a broad educational experience for the American citizenry. This academy became the University of Pennsylvania in 1799.

Franklin was a noted scientist and was particularly interested in electricity. After the invention of Leyden jars (1746), he performed experiments, eventually proving that lightning is an electrical phenomenon. He contributed to knowledge in other areas, such as meteorology and was a student of many aspects of the natural sciences.

Active in politics, Franklin served as clerk of the Public Assembly of Pennsylvania (1736–51) and as a member from Philadelphia (1751–64). He was Pennsylvania's agent in England (1757–62 and 1764–75) and helped to get Pennsylvania's royal charter converted to a constitution (1764).

Franklin took charge of the mails in the northern colonies in 1753 and was postmaster of Philadelphia (1737–53). He proposed the Albany plan of union that was adopted by the Albany Congress of 1754. He was a member of the Second Continental Congress (1775) and served on committees that organized a postal system and drafted the Declaration of Independence, which Franklin signed. Appointed first postmaster general by the Continental Congress (1775–76) he is credited with establishing the postal service.

Franklin was a delegate to France (1776), a signer of the treaty with France (1778), and minister to France (1778–85). He was appointed a commissioner to negotiate peace with Great Britain (1781).

Returning to Philadelphia in 1785, he was president of the Pennsylvania Executive Council (1785–87). He presided over the Constitutional Convention in Philadelphia (1787).

Franklin was the author of *A Dissertation on Liberty and Necessity, Pleasures, and Pain* (1725), *Modest Enquiry into the Nature and Necessity of a Paper Currency* (1729), *Plain Truth* (1747), *Proposals Relating to the Education of Youth in Pennsylvania* (1749), *Experiments and Observations on Electricity* (1751), *In the Interest of Great Britain Considered* (1760), *Observations on the Increase of Mankind* (1775), and *Autobiography* (published posthumously). He was editor of *Poor Richard's Almanack* (1732–57) and owner and publisher of the *Pennsylvania Gazette* (1730–50).

Franklin was active in many scholarly and civic organizations in the United States and abroad and was a founder of the Philadelphia City Hospital (1751) and the Society for Political Enquiries (first president, 1787). He received many awards and was the recipient of honorary degrees from Harvard, Yale, and William and Mary colleges and the universities of Edinburgh, Scotland, and Oxford, England.

REFERENCES: *AC; DAB; EB; NCAB* (1:328); *TC; WWW* (H); Thomas Fleming, *Benjamin Franklin; A Biography in His Own Words* (New York: Newsweek, 1972); Paul Ford, *The Many-Sided Franklin* (New York: The

Century Co., 1899); Benjamin Franklin, *Autobiography and Other Pieces* (New York: Oxford University Press, 1970); Nathan G. Goodman, *Benjamin Franklin Reader* (New York: Thomas Y. Crowell Co., 1945); Leonard W. Labaree et al., *The Autobiography of Benjamin Franklin* (New Haven, Conn.: Yale University Press, 1964); Carl Van Doren, *Benjamin Franklin* (New York: Viking Press, 1938).   *Mark Fravel, Jr.*

FRASER, John. B. March 22, 1827, Cromarty, Scotland, to n.a. M. December 19, 1872, to Fannie Saunders. Ch. none. D. June 4, 1878, Pittsburgh, Pennsylvania.

John Fraser is remembered as a militant educator and activist. He attended the universities of Edinburgh and Aberdeen, Scotland, graduating from the latter in 1844, and was winner of the Huttonian Prize in mathematics. He traveled to Bermuda and taught at the Hamilton Institute but left because of the climate. He started a school in New York City, served as a private tutor to two boys, and opened an academy in Connellsville, Pennsylvania, in 1850. He became a professor of mathematics and astronomy at Jefferson College in Canonsburg, Pennsylvania (1855–62).

When Abraham Lincoln called for volunteers in 1862 after a series of Union army defeats, Fraser announced that he would give up his chair and recruit a company to fight. The Canonsburg Brown Infantry, with Fraser as captain, joined the Union army. He engaged in major battles, was wounded, and was taken prisoner. He spent eight months in various Confederate prisons. Released from prison after the war, he was discharged from the army with the rank of brevet brigadier general.

He was professor of mathematics and lecturer on tactics in 1865 at the Agricultural College at Bellefonte, Pennsylvania (later, Pennsylvania State University at State College), and later was appointed president. He resigned after two years to become chancellor of the University of Kansas on June 12, 1868. During Fraser's chancellorship, the University of Kansas doubled its faculty, tripled course offerings and enrollment, built a model general-purpose building, and reorganized the constitution and bylaws.

Fraser was superintendent of public instruction in Kansas (1875–77). He became professor at the Western University of Pennsylvania in Pittsburgh (later, University of Pittsburgh), Pennsylvania.

REFERENCES: *NCAB* (9:493); Wayland F. Dunaway, *History of the Pennsylvania State College* (State College: Pennsylvania State College, 1946), pp. 65-70; Clifford S. Griffen, *The University of Kansas: A History* (Lawrence: University of Kansas, 1974), pp. 42-71; Hannah Oliver, "Chancellor Fraser as His Students Knew Him," *Graduate Magazine of the University of Kansas* 6 (May 1908): 285; S. A. Riggs, "Recollections of John Fraser," *Graduate Magazine of the University of Kansas* 4 (January 1906): 117-23.   *William F. Marquardt*

FRAZIER, Edward Franklin. B. September 24, 1894, Baltimore, Maryland, to James Edward and Mary (Clark) Frazier. M. September 14, 1922, to Marie Ellen Brown. Ch. none. D. May 17, 1962, Washington, D.C.

E. Franklin Frazier was graduated from the Baltimore (Maryland) High School (1912) and attended Howard University in Washington, D.C., where he received the A.B. degree (1916). He was awarded the A.M. degree (1920) from Clark University in Worcester, Massachusetts, and the Ph.D. degree (1931) from the University of Chicago. He was a research fellow at the New York School of Social Work in New York City (1920–21) and, as the first black Fellow of the American Scandinavian Foundation, studied folk high schools in Denmark (1921–22).

Frazier taught mathematics at Tuskegee (Alabama) Institute (1916–17), Fort Valley (Georgia) High and Industrial School (later, Fort Valley State College) (summer 1917), St. Paul's Normal and Industrial School (later, St. Paul's College) in Lawrenceville, Virginia (1917–18), and Baltimore High School (1918–19). He was director of the summer school at Livingstone College in Salisbury, North Carolina (1922), and was instructor of sociology at Morehouse College in Atlanta, Georgia (1922–24), and director of the Atlanta School of Social Work (1922–27). After two years at the University of Chicago as a research assistant (1927–29), he was a special lecturer in sociology (1929–31) and research professor (1931–34) at Fisk University in Nashville, Tennessee.

In 1934 Frazier joined the faculty of Howard University, where he was professor and head of the department of sociology to his retirement in 1959; he continued to teach and conduct research at Howard to his death.

Frazier was the author of important studies of black Americans, including *The Free Negro Family* (1932), *The Negro Family in Chicago* (1932), *The Negro Family in the United States* (1939), *Negro Youth at the Crossroads* (1940), prepared for the American Youth Commission, *Inequality of Opportunity in Higher Education* (with David S. Berkowitz, 1948), *The Negro in the United States* (1949), *Bourgeoisie Noire* (1955), *Black Bourgeoisie* (1957), *Race and Culture Contacts in the Modern World* (1957), and *The Negro Church in America* (1964).

Active in professional associations, Frazier was a fellow of the American Association for the Advancement of Science and a member of the American Sociological Society (president, 1948) and Eastern Sociological Society (president). He was a founder of the African Studies Association (vice-president, 1962). He received the first MacIver Lectureship Award of the American Sociological Society in 1956 and was awarded honorary degrees by Morgan State College (1955) and the University of Edinburgh, Scotland (1960).

REFERENCES: *CB* (July 1940); *NYT,* May 22, 1962, p. 37; *WWW* (IV); Arthur P. Davis, "E. Franklin Frazier (1894–1962): A Profile," *The Jour-*

nal of Negro Education 31 (Fall 1962): 429–35; *Who's Who in Colored America,* 7th ed. (Yonkers, N.Y.: Burckel & Associates, 1950).

John F. Ohles

FREEMAN, Frank Nugent. B. April 17, 1880, Rockwood, Ontario, Canada, to John Weldon and Amanda T. (Nugent) Freeman. M. June 18, 1908, to Bertha Longley Wright. M. December 24, 1937, to Flora M. Dunn. Ch. five. D. October 17, 1961, El Cerrito, California.

Frank Nugent Freeman received the B.A. degree (1904) from Wesleyan University in Middletown, Connecticut, and studied at Yale University, where he received the M.A. (1906) and Ph.D. (1908) degrees under C. H. Judd *(q.v.).*

He became an instructor in educational psychology at the University of Chicago in 1909, where Judd was appointed director of the school of education. Freeman continued at Chicago until 1939 when he was named dean of the school of education at the University of California, Berkeley, a position he held until his retirement in 1948.

Freeman was one of the nation's most distinguished educational psychologists in the period between the world wars. His major work was a textbook, *Mental Tests: Their History, Principles, and Applications* (1926), one of the first major attempts to go beyond cataloging and description of tests to a historical, systematic, and critical account of the fundamentals, principles, and limitations of achievement, intelligence, aptitude, and personality tests.

Freeman's major publications dealt with several themes. The psychology and pedagogy of handwriting was the topic of *The Teaching of Handwriting* (1914), *The Handwriting Movement* (1918), and *How to Teach Handwriting* (with M. L. Dougherty, 1923). The experimental psychology of school learning was the subject of *The Psychology of the Common Branches* (1916), *Experimental Education* (1916), *How Children Learn* (1917), and *The Bases of Learning* (1932). Comparative evaluation of new instructional media and technology was discussed in *Visual Education* (1924), *Motion Pictures in the Classroom* (with B. D. Wood, 1929), and *An Experimental Study of the Educational Influences of the Typewriter in the Elementary School Classroom* (with B. D. Wood, 1932). What mental tests reveal about intellectual development and heredity and environment is central to *Growth in Intellectual Ability as Measured by Repeated Tests* (with C. D. Flory, 1937), and *Twins* (with H. H. Newman and K. J. Holzinger, *q.v.,* 1937). He also wrote *Education and the Creed of the Free World* (1952).

Freeman was active in professional organizations; he was a fellow of the American Association for the Advancement of Science (secretary of the section on psychology, 1919–28) and a member of the American

Psychológical Association (council, 1937–41), the National Society for the Study of Education (chairman of the board, 1937–39), the American Educational Research Association (secretary, 1922–23, and chairman of the editorial board, 1930–37), the Society for Research in Child Development (chairman, 1938–40), and the American Association of Colleges and Departments of Education (president, 1947–48). He was a member of the United States Educational Mission to Japan and received the Christian X Medal of Liberation from Denmark (1946).

REFERENCES: *LE* (III); *WWAE* (VIII); *WWW* (IV); L. J. Cronbach, " 'Mental Tests' by Frank N. Freeman," *School Review* 75 (Spring 1967): 67–75. *Ronald D. Szoke*

FRELINGHUYSEN, Theodore. B. March 28, 1787, Millstone, New Jersey, to Frederick and Gertrude (Schench) Frelinghuysen. M. 1809 to Charlotte Mercer. M. October 14, 1857, to Harriet Pumpelly. Ch. one. d. April 12, 1861, New Brunswick, New Jersey.

Theodore Frelinghuysen was educated in a grammar school affiliated with Queen's (later, Rutgers) College in New Brunswick, New Jersey. He left school for farming, but his stepmother intervened and sent him to Dr. Finley's Academy in Basking Ridge, New Jersey. He studied at the College of New Jersey (later, Princeton University) and was graduated second in his class in 1804. He studied law with Richard Stockton and was admitted to the bar in 1808. He became a counselor at law in 1811 and sergeant at law in 1817.

He began to practice law in Newark, New Jersey, in 1809 and was elected attorney general of New Jersey (1817–27). He served in the United States Senate (1829–35). He was elected mayor of Newark (1836–39). He resigned from the office and from his law practice in 1839 to accept the chancellorship of the University of the City of New York (later, New York University). Frelinghuysen resigned as chancellor in 1850 to accept the position of president of Rutgers College, where he served to 1862. The college prospered under his leadership, growing in enrollment and endowment and with an increase in the number and variety of the courses of study.

Frelinghuysen was also very active in various organizations. He served sixteen years as president of the American Board of Commissioners for Foreign Missions and was president of the American Bible Society (1846–62), president of the American Tract Society (1842–48), and for fifty years an officer of the American Sunday School Union. For many years he was an officer of both the American Temperance Union and the American Colonization Society.

REFERENCES: *AC; DAB; NCAB* (3:401); *TC; WWW* (H). *William J. Parente*

FRETWELL, Elbert Kirtley. B. September 27, 1878, Williamstown, Missouri, to James Leonard and Hettie (Tompkins) Fretwell. M. August 27, 1919, to Jean Hosford. Ch. two. D. August 22, 1962, Norwalk, Connecticut.

Elbert Kirtley Fretwell, leader in school extracurricular activities, was educated in local rural schools and received the B.A. degree (1899) from La Grange (Missouri) College, the M.A. degree (1904) from Brown University in Providence, Rhode Island, and the Ph.D. degree (1917) from Columbia University. He also studied at the University of Chicago (1905–06) and the University of Dijon, France (1907), and was a student of music in Germany at Berlin and Bayreuth (1911).

Fretwell was a high school principal at Canton, Missouri (1899–1903), and also was commissioner of schools for Lewis County (1901–04). He was professor of English at La Grange College (1903–05), vice-president of the Peddie Institute in Hightstown, New Jersey (1906–07), and English teacher at the Polytechnic Preparatory School in Brooklyn, New York (1907–13). He joined the faculty of Teachers College, Columbia University, in 1918, became professor of education (1930), and retired in 1943. Particularly interested in extracurricular activities, he organized and directed one of the first courses to train camp leaders (1920–38) and established and directed the country's first courses to train Boy Scout leaders. He began voluntary work with the Boy Scouts of America in 1921 and became national chief scout executive after his retirement (1943–48). He was made honorary chief scout in 1949.

Fretwell was the author of *A Study in Educational Prognosis* (1919) and *Extra Curricular Activities in Secondary Schools* (1931). He contributed to books and wrote many articles on games and extracurricular activities and was associate editor of *School Activities* (1934–62) and *Clearing House*. He organized a physical education and recreation program for United States reconstruction hospitals for wounded soldiers of World War I (1918), He was chairman of the camping section of the White House Conference on Child Health and Protection (1930) and adviser of the high school section of the National Safety Council. He served on survey staffs of several American city school systems. He was a member of many professional associations. He received the Silver Buffalo Award from the Boy Scouts and foreign awards for scouting. He received honorary degrees from Culver-Stockton College and Illinois Wesleyan University.

REFERENCES: *LE* (III); *NCAB* (49:370); *NYT,* August 23, 1962, p. 29; *WWAE* (XIV); *WWW* (IV); *School Activities* 34 (September 1962): 11.

John F. Ohles

FRIEZE, Henry Simmons. B. September 15, 1817, Boston, Massachusetts, to Jacob and Betsey (Slade) Frieze. M. 1847 to Anna Brownell Roffee. Ch. none. D. December 7, 1889, Ann Arbor, Michigan.

Henry Simmons Frieze completed preparatory school in Newport, Rhode Island, where he supported himself by playing the organ and teaching music. In 1837 he entered Brown University at Providence, where he was graduated in 1841.

He was a tutor at Brown (1841–44), primarily of Latin. In 1844 he and a colleague founded the University Grammar School in Providence, where Frieze was associate principal (1844–54).

Frieze accepted a position in 1854 teaching Latin and Latin literature at the University of Michigan. Upon the resignation of Erastus Otis Haven as president of the university in 1869, Frieze served as acting president until 1871. Although he was offered the presidency, he declined and was succeeded by James B. Angell *(q.v.)*. While Frieze was acting president, graduates of certain accredited preparatory schools were permitted to enter the university without admission examination, and women were admitted (1870). Frieze served as acting president during the absences of President Angell (June 1880 to February 1882 and October 1887 to January 1888). Throughout his life, Frieze gave public organ performances. He was one of those responsible for establishing the University of Michigan School of Music and served as professor of music in the school.

Frieze edited a popular school edition of Virgil's *Aeneid* (1860). He was also the author of *The Tenth and Twelfth Books of the Institutes of Quintilian* (1865), *Ancient and Modern Education* (1867), *Life and Works of Henry Philip Tappan* (1867), *Giovanni Dupre, The Story of a Florentine Sculptor* (1886), *The Bocolics, Georgics and the First Six Books of the Aeneid of Virgil* (1883), *P. Vergili Maronis Opera* (1883), *The Relations of the State University to Religion* (1888), and *Art Museums and Their Connection with Public Libraries* (1876).

Frieze was a member of a number of scholarly and professional associations and was the recipient of three honorary degrees.

REFERENCES: *DAB; NCAB* (1:250); *TC; WWW* (H).

Gerald G. Szymanski

FRISSELL, Hollis Burke. B. July 14, 1851, South Amenia, New York, to Amasca C. and Lavinia (Barker) Frissell. M. November 8, 1883, to Julia Frame. Ch. one. D. August 5, 1917, Whitefield, New Hampshire.

Hollis Burke Frissell, son of a minister, worked his way through Phillips Academy in Andover, Massachusetts, and Yale University, where he received the A.B. degree (1874). He attended Union Theological Seminary in New York City, graduating in 1879. He was ordained in the Presbyterian church in 1880.

Before he entered the seminary, Frissell taught for two years at the De Garmo Institute in Rhinebeck, New York. He served as assistant pastor of the Madison Avenue Presbyterian Church in New York City (1880) and became chaplain at Hampton (Virginia) Institute (1880–93). He was principal of Hampton from 1893 to his death in 1917.

Frissell played a leading role in organizing an educational conference held at Capon Springs, West Virginia, in 1898. The conference was held to create a favorable climate in the South for better educational facilities for underprivileged blacks and whites, an idea that expanded to improvement of public education in general. He believed that better education for southern whites was a necessary preliminary to the education of blacks.

He was a member of the General Education Board, the Negro Rural Fund, and the Anna T. Jeanes Foundation and an organizer of the Southern Education Board. He was chairman of the board of trustees of Calhoun Colored School, trustee of the Virginia Manual Labor School of the Negro Reformatory Association of Virginia, and president of the New York State Colonization Society (1914). He received honorary degrees from four universities.

REFERENCES: *DAB; NCAB* (18:387); *TC; WWW* (I); *NYT,* August 7, 1917, p. 9.   *S. S. Britt, Jr.*

FROST, John. B. January 26, 1800, Kennebunk, Maine, to Nathaniel and Abigail (Kimball) Frost. M. May 4, 1830, to Sarah Ann White. Ch. none. D. December 28, 1859, Philadelphia, Pennsylvania.

John Frost was graduated from Harvard University in 1822. He was principal of the Mayhew School in Boston, Massachusetts (1822–27). He moved to Philadelphia where he conducted a school for girls from 1827 through 1838. He was professor of English literature at Central High School in Philadelphia (1838–45).

Frost resigned his teaching position in 1845 to devote himself to researching and writing histories and biographies. Assisted by a corps of writers, he edited and published over three hundred works.

His publications were widely used; among them were *Elements of English Grammar* (1829), *The Youth's Book of Seasons* (1835), *The Class Book of Nature* (1836), *Book of the Navy* (1842), *Indian Wars of the United States* (1843), *Pictorial History of the United States* (two volumes, 1844), *Book of the Army* (1845), *Heroes and Battles of the American Revolution* (1845), *Life of Major-General Zachary Taylor* (1847), *Pictorial Life of Andrew Jackson* (1847), *Pictorial Life of George Washington* (1848), *Pictorial History of the World* (three volumes, 1848), *The American Generals* (1848), *The American Speaker* (1851), *The Book of the Colonies* (1852), *Great Cities of the World* (1853), and *The Presidents of the United States* (1855).

Frost was the recipient of several honorary degrees.

REFERENCES: *AC; TC.*   *Gorman L. Miller*

FROST, William Goodell. B. July 2, 1854, LeRoy, New York, to Lewis Phidelo and Maria (Goodell) Frost. M. August 10, 1876, to Louise Rainey.

M. July 5, 1891, to Eleanor Marsh. Ch. five. D. September 12, 1938, Berea, Kentucky.

William Goodell Frost, the son of an independent Congregational minister, began his higher education at Wilson (Wisconsin) College and received the A.B. (1876) and A.M. (1879) degrees from Oberlin (Ohio) College. He did postgraduate study at the University of Wooster (Ohio), Harvard University, and the University of Göttingen in Germany, and received the Ph.D. degree (1891) from the University of Wooster (later, College of Wooster).

He taught Greek language and literature at Oberlin College (1877–92), where he promoted religious work and secured gifts for new college buildings. Following travels in Germany, England, Greece, and Palestine in 1891, he became president of Berea (Kentucky) College (1892–1920). Founded by anti-slavery southerners in a region almost lacking in funds, Berea College had offended some southern feelings by admitting Negro students. Frost sought to make the school attractive to northern students in an effort to overcome prejudice against blacks. He adapted the industrial departments to meet regional needs. He organized a foundation school for those who had not attended school in their early years, supported by financial assistance he received from across the nation. The Kentucky legislature passed a law in 1904 prohibiting white and Negro students from attending the same school, and Frost got financial support from Andrew Carnegie and Mrs. Russell Sage to develop a separate school for black students, the Lincoln Institute of Kentucky (1909). Berea College (later, Berea College and Allied Schools) grew steadily under Frost. All Berea students earned part of their expenses by working on the college farms and gardens or in its shop. Frost adapted educational methods to conditions in the southern mountains.

Frost was the author of *Greek Primer* (1887), *Inductive Studies in Oratory* (1890), the autobiographical *For the Mountains* (1937) and various pamphlets, including *German Ideas for American Schools*. He was the recipient of five honorary degrees.

REFERENCES: *LE* (I); *NCAB* (30:355); *TC; WWAE* (I); *WWW* (I); *NYT,* September 13, 1938, p. 23; William Goodell Frost, *For the Mountains* (New York: Fleming H. Revell Co., 1937).

Bruce D. Mattson

FRYE, Alexis Everett. B. November 2, 1859, North Haven, Maine, to Erastus Stevenson and Jane (King) Frye. M. January 1, 1901, to Maria Teresa Belén Arruebarrena y Perez. Ch. five. D. July 1, 1936, Loma Linda, California.

Alexis Everett Frye was educated in public schools in Boston, Massachusetts, attended a teacher-training class in Boston (1878), and was graduated with the LL.B. (1890) and M.A. (1897) degrees from Harvard

University. He made relief maps in Hyde Park, Massachusetts, with his brother (1880–83) and taught in the Cook County Normal School (later, Chicago State University) in Chicago, Illinois (1883–86). He returned to Boston in 1886, lecturing to teachers about methods of teaching geography. In 1890 he was admitted to the Massachusetts bar but did not practice law.

Frye was superintendent of schools in San Bernardino County, California (1891–93). He wrote school books for Ginn & Company of Boston, Massachusetts. Frye was superintendent of schools in Cuba (1899–1901), wrote the first Cuban national school law, and organized and conducted the first Cuban public school system. He arranged for over a thousand Cuban schoolteachers to visit Harvard University in 1900, where they received free instruction in pedagogy conducted in Spanish at the Harvard summer school.

From 1901 Frye wrote and revised geography books and grew oranges in the San Bernardino Valley of California. Among Frye's books were *Child and Nature* (1888), *Brooks and Basins* (1891), *Primary Geography* (1894), *Complete Geography* (1895), *Home and School Atlas* (1896), *Elements of Geography* (1898), *Advanced Geography* (1899), *Introductory Geography* (1899), *Geografia Elemental* (1899), *Grammar School Geography* (1902), *Easy Steps in Geography* (1906), *First Book in Geography* (1906), *Home Geography* (1911), *Leading Facts of Geography* (1911), *New Geography: Book One* (1917), and *The Brooklet's Story* (1927). He wrote *Geography* (1903) for use in the Philippines.

Frye was honorary president of the National Teachers of Cuba (1904–06), a life fellow of the American Geographical Society, and honorary member of La Asociación Pedagogíca Universitaria de la Habana, and a member of many other associations. He received an honorary degree from the University of Redlands in California (1929) and was awarded the medal of the Legion of Honor of Cuba (1900) and the medal of the Louisiana Purchase Exposition for textbooks written for use in the Philippine Islands (1903).

REFERENCES: *AC; NCAB* (40:518); *TC; WWW* (I).

Lawrence S. Master

FUERTES, Estevan Antonio. B. May 10, 1838, San Juan, Puerto Rico, to Estevan and Demetria (Charbonnier) Fuertes. M. December 21, 1860, to Mary Stone Perry. Ch. five, including Louis Agassiz Fuertes, artist-naturalist, and James Hillhouse Fuertes, engineer. D. January 16, 1903, Ithaca, New York.

Estevan Antonio Fuertes, the son of a distinguished Puerto Rican official, was educated in the best local San Juan schools and attended the University of Salamanca, Spain, where he received the Ph.D. degree. He received the civil engineering degree (1861) from Rensselaer Polytechnic Institute in Troy, New York.

Fuertes was an assistant engineer in the Puerto Rican public-works department (1861–62) and director of the western district (1862–63). He was an engineer for the Croton Aqueduct Board in New York (1863–69) and served as engineer-in-chief with a United States ship canal expedition to Tehuantepec, Mexico, and Nicaragua (1870–71). He was a consulting engineer in New York City (1871–73).

In 1873 Fuertes was appointed dean of the department of civil engineering at Cornell University in Ithaca, New York. For a time, Fuertes taught all subjects in the department, except mathematics. He built up a program of instruction, organized laboratories, and set up a balance between practice and theory.

REFERENCES: *DAB; NCAB* (4:483); *WWW* (I)   *John F. Ohles*

FULLER, Sarah. B. February 15, 1836, Weston, Massachusetts, to Harvey and Celynda (Fiske) Fuller. M. no. D. August 1, 1927, Newton, Massachusetts.

Sarah Fuller attended local schools and the West Newton (Massachusetts) English and Classical School, where she became acquainted with Cyrus Peirce *(q.v.)* who encouraged her to go into teaching.

Fuller taught in Newton and Boston schools (1855–69). The Reverend Dexter S. King, a member of the Boston School Committee, had organized the founding of a school for the deaf based on the Clarke School for the Deaf in Northampton, Massachusetts, that had opened in 1867. Fuller was selected to teach at the school and spent three months at Northampton under the tutelage of Harriet B. Rogers *(q.v.)*.

The Boston School for Deaf-Mutes opened on November 10, 1869, and was renamed the Horace Mann School for the Deaf (1877) with Fuller as principal (1869–1910). Alexander Graham Bell *(q.v.)* instructed the Horace Mann staff in the "visible speech" techniques of his father, Alexander Melville Bell. In 1890 Fuller gave the first speech lessons to a little deaf and blind girl, Helen Keller. Fuller's particular contribution to education for the deaf was her pioneering work on oral instruction instead of sign language, establishment of the first day school for deaf children in place of the general practice of residential schooling, and the promotion of education of the deaf at the earliest age possible.

Fuller was the author of *An Illustrated Primer* (1888), which served to aid instructors to teach language to the deaf. She also prepared charts of speech exercises. She founded, with Alexander Graham Bell and Caroline Yale *(q.v.)*, the American Association to Promote the Teaching of Speech to the Deaf (1890). A home and school for teaching young deaf children was named the Sarah Fuller Home for Little Children Who Cannot Hear (1888–1925) and was succeeded by the Sarah Fuller Foundation for Little Deaf Children.

REFERENCES: *NAW; NYT,* August 2, 1927, p. 21. *Dorothy J. Sievers*